Networking Essentials Companion Guide Version 3: Cisco Certified Support Technician (CCST) Networking 100-150

T0293322

Cisco Press

Networking Essentials Companion Guide Version 3: Cisco Certified Support Technician (CCST) Networking 100-150

Published by:
Cisco Press

Hoboken, New Jersey

2 2024

Library of Congress Control Number: 2023948264

ISBN-13: 978-0-13-832133-8

ISBN-10: 0-13-832133-7

Warning and Disclaimer

This book is designed to provide information about the Cisco Networking Academy Networking Essentials course. Every effort has been made to make this book as complete and as accurate as possible, but no warranty or fitness is implied.

The information is provided on an "as is" basis. The authors, Cisco Press, and Cisco Systems, Inc. shall have neither liability nor responsibility to any person or entity with respect to any loss or damages arising from the information contained in this book or from the use of the discs or programs that may accompany it.

The opinions expressed in this book belong to the author and are not necessarily those of Cisco Systems, Inc.

This book is part of the Cisco Networking Academy® series from Cisco Press. The products in this series support and complement the Cisco Networking Academy curriculum. If you are using this book outside the Networking Academy, then you are not preparing with a Cisco trained and authorized Networking Academy provider.

For more information on the Cisco Networking Academy or to locate a Networking Academy, Please visit www.netacad.com

Vice President, IT Professional
Mark Taub

Alliances Manager, Cisco Press
Caroline Antonio

Director, ITP Product Management
Brett Bartow

Executive Editor
James Manly

Managing Editor
Sandra Schroeder

Development Editor
Eleanor Bru

Senior Project Editor
Tonya Simpson

Copy Editor
Bill McManus

Technical Editor
Dave Holzinger

Editorial Assistant
Cindy Teeters

Cover Designer
Chuti Prasertsith

Composition
codeMantra

Indexer
Timothy Wright

Proofreader
Donna E. Mulder

Trademark Acknowledgments

All terms mentioned in this book that are known to be trademarks or service marks have been appropriately capitalized. Cisco Press or Cisco Systems, Inc., cannot attest to the accuracy of this information. Use of a term in this book should not be regarded as affecting the validity of any trademark or service mark.

Special Sales

For information about buying this title in bulk quantities, or for special sales opportunities (which may include electronic versions; custom cover designs; and content particular to your business, training goals, marketing focus, or branding interests), please contact our corporate sales department at corpsales@pearsoned.com or (800) 382-3419.

For government sales inquiries, please contact governmentsales@pearsoned.com.

For questions about sales outside the U.S., please contact intlcs@pearson.com.

Feedback Information

At Cisco Press, our goal is to create in-depth technical books of the highest quality and value. Each book is crafted with care and precision, undergoing rigorous development that involves the unique expertise of members from the professional technical community.

Readers' feedback is a natural continuation of this process. If you have any comments regarding how we could improve the quality of this book, or otherwise alter it to better suit your needs, you can contact us through email at feedback@ciscopress.com. Please make sure to include the book title and ISBN in your message.

We greatly appreciate your assistance.

Please contact us with concerns about any potential bias at www.pearson.com/report-bias.html.

CISCO

Americas Headquarters
Cisco Systems, Inc.
San Jose, CA

Asia Pacific Headquarters
Cisco Systems (USA) Pte. Ltd.
Singapore

Europe Headquarters
Cisco Systems International BV Amsterdam,
The Netherlands

Cisco has more than 200 offices worldwide. Addresses, phone numbers, and fax numbers are listed on the Cisco Website at **www.cisco.com/go/offices.**

About the Contributing Authors

Rick Graziani teaches computer science and computer networking at Cabrillo College and the University of California, Santa Cruz. Rick is best known for authoring the Cisco Press book *IPv6 Fundamentals*. Prior to teaching, Rick worked in the information technology field for Santa Cruz Operation, Tandem Computers, and Lockheed Missiles and Space Company, and served in the U.S. Coast Guard. He holds an MA in Computer Science and Systems Theory from California State University, Monterey Bay. Rick also works as a curriculum developer for the Cisco Networking Academy Curriculum Engineering team. When Rick is not working, he is most likely surfing at one of his favorite Santa Cruz surf breaks.

Allan Johnson entered the academic world in 1999 after 10 years as a business owner/operator to dedicate his efforts to his passion for teaching. He holds both an MBA and an MEd in training and development. He taught CCNA courses at the high school level for seven years and has taught both CCNA and CCNP courses at Del Mar College in Corpus Christi, Texas. In 2003, Allan began to commit much of his time and energy to the CCNA Instructional Support Team providing services to Networking Academy instructors worldwide and creating training materials. He now splits his time between working as a Curriculum Lead for Cisco Networking Academy and as Account Lead for Unicon (unicon.net) supporting Cisco's educational efforts.

Contents at a Glance

Online Element

Contents

Command Syntax Conventions

The conventions used to present command syntax in this book are the same conventions used in the IOS Command Reference. The Command Reference describes these conventions as follows:

- **Boldface** indicates commands and keywords that are entered literally as shown. In actual configuration examples and output (not general command syntax), boldface indicates commands that are manually input by the user (such as a **show** command).
- *Italic* indicates arguments for which you supply actual values.
- Vertical bars (|) separate alternative, mutually exclusive elements.
- Square brackets ([ ]) indicate an optional element.
- Braces ({ }) indicate a required choice.
- Braces within brackets ([{ }]) indicate a required choice within an optional element.

Introduction

Networking Essentials Companion Guide Version 3: Cisco Certified Support Technician (CCST) Networking 100-150 is the official supplemental textbook for the Cisco Network Academy Networking Essentials version 3 course. Cisco Networking Academy is a comprehensive program that delivers information technology skills to students around the world. The curriculum emphasizes real-world practical application while providing opportunities for you to gain the skills and hands-on experience needed to design, install, operate, and maintain networks in small- to medium-sized businesses as well as enterprise and service provider environments.

As a textbook, this book provides a ready reference to explain the same networking concepts, technologies, protocols, and devices as the online curriculum. This book emphasizes key topics, terms, and activities and provides some alternate explanations and examples as compared with the course. You can use the online curriculum as directed by your instructor and then use this Companion Guide's study tools to help solidify your understanding of all the topics.

This book is a reflection of the Cisco Network Academy Networking Essentials version 3 online course. The format, content, and sequence of topics within this book are meant to mirror the online content for those who want an alternative version to the online course. The online course includes videos, animations, and activities not included in this book. It is recommended that you use this book along with the online course to get the full benefit from the course material.

Who Should Read This Book?

The book, as well as the course, is designed to provide learners with a broad foundational understanding of networking. It is suitable for anyone interested in a career in Information and Communication Technology (ICT), or a related career pathway. Networking Essentials is instructor-led. In this course you will learn how networks operate, including the devices, media, and protocols that enable network communication. You will also develop key skills so you can perform basic troubleshooting, using effective methodologies and help desk best practices.

There is a self-paced version of this course called the Network Technician Career Path. This is a collection of four courses that prepares you for the Cisco Certified Support Technician (CCST) Networking certification. This Career Path includes activities that expand on the course material presented. Upon completion of the online course, the end-of-course survey, and the end-of-course assessment, you will receive a Certificate of Completion. You will also receive a digital badge if the course is taken with an instructor in an instructor-led class.

For those who may wish a more traditional and thorough approach to networking, you may be interested in the Cisco Press CCNAv7 Companion Guide series: Introduction to Networks (ITN), Switching, Routing, and Wireless Essentials (SWRE), and Enterprise Networking, Security, and Automation (ENSA).

Online Course Enrollment

If you are interested in completing this Networking Essentials curriculum through one of our academies (e.g., instructor-led), please visit https://www.netacad.com/portal/netacad_academy_search to find a location near you.

The Network Technician Career Path is the online, self-paced version of this curriculum. You can enroll for free by visiting https://skillsforall.com/career-path/network-technician.

Book Features

The educational features of this book focus on supporting topic coverage, readability, and practice of the course material to facilitate your full understanding of the course material.

Topic Coverage

The following features give you a thorough overview of the topics covered in each chapter so that you can make constructive use of your study time:

- **Objectives:** Listed at the beginning of each chapter, the objectives reference the core concepts covered in the chapter. The objectives match the objectives stated in the corresponding chapters of the online curriculum; however, the question format in the *Companion Guide* encourages you to think about finding the answers as you read the chapter.
- **Notes:** These are short sidebars that point out interesting facts, timesaving methods, and important safety issues.
- **Chapter summaries:** At the end of each chapter is a summary of the chapter's key concepts. It provides a synopsis of the chapter and serves as a study aid.
- **Practice:** At the end of the chapter there is a full list of all the labs, class activities, and Packet Tracer activities to refer back to for study time.

Readability

The following features assist your understanding of the networking vocabulary:

- **Key terms:** Each chapter begins with a list of key terms, along with a page-number reference from inside the chapter. The terms are listed in alphabetical order. This handy reference allows you to find a term, flip to the page where the term appears, and see the term used in context. The Glossary defines all the key terms.
- **Glossary:** This book contains an all-new Glossary with more than 328 terms.

Practice

Practice makes perfect. This *Companion Guide* offers you ample opportunities to put what you learn into practice. You will find the following features valuable and effective in reinforcing the instruction that you receive:

Interactive Graphic

- **Check Your Understanding questions and answer key:** Review questions are presented at the end of each chapter as a self-assessment tool. These questions match the style of questions that you see in the online course. Appendix A, "Answers to the 'Check Your Understanding' Questions," provides an answer key to all the questions and includes an explanation of each answer.
- **Labs and activities:** Throughout each chapter, you will be directed back to the online course to take advantage of the activities created to reinforce concepts. In addition, at the end of each chapter, there is a "Practice" section that collects a list of all the labs and activities to provide practice with the topics introduced in this chapter.

Video

- **Page references to online course:** After headings, you will see, for example, (1.1.2). This number refers to the page number in the online course so that you can easily jump to that spot online to view a video, practice an activity, perform a lab, or review a topic.

About Packet Tracer Software and Activities

Packet Tracer Activity

Interspersed throughout the chapters you'll find a few Cisco Packet Tracer activities. Packet Tracer allows you to create networks, visualize how packets flow in the network, and use basic testing tools to determine whether the network would work. When you see this icon, you can use Packet Tracer with the listed file to perform a task suggested in this book. The activity files are available in the course. For self-enrolled courses on SkillsForAll.com, Packet Tracer software is available through a link in your course after you enroll. For instructor-led courses on the Cisco Networking Academy website (netacad.com), Packet Tracer software is available from the Resources menu.

How This Book Is Organized

This book corresponds closely to the Cisco Networking Academy Switching, Routing, and Wireless Essentials course and is divided into 39 chapters, one appendix, and a glossary of key terms:

- **Chapter 1, "Communications in a Connected World":** This chapter explains important concepts in network communication including the concept of a network, network data, and network transmission speeds and capacity.
- **Chapter 2, "Network Components, Types, and Connections":** This chapter explains the role of clients, servers, and networking devices. It also covers the different ISP connectivity options.
- **Chapter 3, "Wireless and Mobile Networks":** This chapter provides a brief overview of the networks used by mobile devices and how you configure basic connectivity in iOS and Android devices.
- **Chapter 4, "Build a Home Network":** This chapter covers how to configure an integrated wireless router and wireless client to connect securely to the Internet including a description of the components required to build a home network, and the wired and wireless network technologies used.
- **Chapter 5, "Communication Principles":** This chapter underscores the importance of standards and protocols in network communications, explains the role of network communication protocols in regulating data exchange, outlines network communication standards for consistent implementation, and compares the OSI and TCP/IP models as frameworks for understanding network layers and protocols.
- **Chapter 6, "Network Media":** This chapter covers the various common types of network cables used for data transmission.
- **Chapter 7, "The Access Layer":** This chapter covers the communication process on Ethernet networks, including the explanation of encapsulation and Ethernet framing, along with insights into how to improve network communication at the access layer.
- **Chapter 8, "The Internet Protocol":** This chapter covers the features of an IP address, the purpose of an IPv4 address, and how IPv4 addresses and subnets are used together for network communication.
- **Chapter 9, "IPv4 and Network Segmentation":** This chapter covers the utilization and segmentation of IPv4 addresses in network communication, including a comparison of unicast, broadcast, and multicast addresses, as well as an explanation of public, private, and reserved IPv4 addresses, and how subnetting enhances network communication through segmentation.

- **Chapter 10, "IPv6 Addressing Formats and Rules":** This chapter discusses the features of IPv6 addressing, the necessity for its implementation, and the methods for representing IPv6 addresses.
- **Chapter 11, "Dynamic Addressing with DHCP":** This chapter explores the comparison between static and dynamic IPv4 addressing, and demonstrates the configuration of a DHCPv4 server for the dynamic assignment of IPv4 addresses.
- **Chapter 12, "Gateways to Other Networks":** This chapter introduces network boundaries and discusses the purpose of Network Address Translation in small networks.
- **Chapter 13, "The ARP Process":** This chapter compares the roles of MAC and IP addresses, discusses the significance of containing broadcasts within a network, and covers how ARP facilitates network communication.
- **Chapter 14, "Routing Between Networks":** This chapter discusses the necessity of routing, explains how routers use routing tables, and demonstrates how to configure a fully connected network.
- **Chapter 15, "TCP and UDP":** This chapter discusses the comparison of TCP and UDP, explains the use of port numbers, and details how clients access Internet services.
- **Chapter 16, "Application Layer Services":** This chapter covers the functions of common application layer services that typically use client/server interactions. It describes various network applications including DNS, HTTP, HTML, FTP, Telnet, SSH, and email protocols.
- **Chapter 17, "Network Testing Utilities":** This chapter describes the use of various tools to test and troubleshoot network connectivity.
- **Chapter 18, "Network Design":** This chapter outlines the four fundamental prerequisites for a dependable network and delves into the operational role of each layer within a three-layer hierarchical network design.
- **Chapter 19, "Cloud and Virtualization":** This chapter covers the characteristics of clouds and cloud services, as well as the purpose and attributes of virtualization.
- **Chapter 20, "Number Systems":** This chapter covers converting numbers between decimal, binary, and hexadecimal systems.
- **Chapter 21, "Ethernet Switching":** This chapter details Ethernet operations within a switched network, covering OSI model Layer 1 and Layer 2 functions, the relationship between Ethernet sublayers and frame fields, various types of Ethernet MAC addresses, and the process by which a switch constructs its MAC address table and forwards frames.

- **Chapter 22, "Network Layer":** This chapter describes how routers use network layer protocols and services to facilitate end-to-end connectivity, including the use of IP protocols for dependable communication, and the significance of key header fields within both IPv4 and IPv6 packets.
- **Chapter 23, "IPv4 Address Structure":** This chapter describes the structure of an IPv4 address, its network portion, host portion, and subnet mask. It then details how to calculate an efficient IPv4 subnetting scheme for network segmentation.
- **Chapter 24, "Address Resolution":** This chapter highlights the purpose of ARP in establishing efficient data transmission. It discusses how ARP facilitates communication within a local area network by resolving IP addresses to MAC addresses.
- **Chapter 25, "IP Addressing Services":** This chapter explains how DNS and DHCP services operate.
- **Chapter 26, "Transport Layer":** This chapter provides an overview of the transport layer's role in end-to-end communications, detailing TCP and UDP characteristics, their use of port numbers, the reliability facilitated by TCP's session establishment and termination, the transmission and acknowledgment of TCP protocol data units for assured delivery, and the UDP client processes involved in establishing communication with a server.
- **Chapter 27, "The Cisco IOS Command Line":** This chapter covers the use of Cisco IOS, including the correct command usage for navigating its modes, guidance on configuring network devices, and the use of **show** commands for monitoring device operations.
- **Chapter 28, "Build a Small Cisco Network":** This chapter covers the process of building a basic computer network using Cisco devices, including initial Cisco switch and router configuration, secure remote management configuration, and default gateway configuration.
- **Chapter 29, "ICMP":** This chapter explains how ICMP works and explores using ICMP diagnostic tools, ping and traceroute, to test network connectivity.
- **Chapter 30, "Physical Layer":** This chapter explores how physical layer protocols, services, and network media facilitate communication within data networks, including topics such as the role and functions of the physical layer, characteristics of copper cabling, the utilization of UTP cable in Ethernet networks, and the distinct advantages of fiber-optic cabling in comparison to other communication media.
- **Chapter 31, "Data Link Layer":** This chapter covers how media access control in the data link layer facilitates communication across physical and logical networks, including a comparison of the attributes of physical and logical topologies, and an explanation of how devices access a LAN to transmit frames.

- **Chapter 32, "Routing at the Network Layer":** This chapter describes the use of routing tables by network devices to effectively route packets to their intended destination networks. It further explains the significance and role of the various fields within a router's routing table.
- **Chapter 33, "IPv6 Addressing":** This chapter covers the implementation of an IPv6 addressing scheme, including a comparison of different types of IPv6 network addresses, explanations of configuring static global unicast and link-local IPv6 addresses, dynamic configuration of global unicast addresses, configuring link-local addresses dynamically, and the identification of IPv6 addresses.
- **Chapter 34, "IPv6 Neighbor Discovery":** This chapter describes how IPv6 neighbor discovery facilitates network communication by explaining its discovery mechanisms and operations.
- **Chapter 35, "Cisco Switches and Routers":** This chapter provides an overview of Cisco routers and switches, including Cisco LAN switches, switch forwarding methods, port settings on Layer 2 switch ports, the Cisco LAN switch boot process, Cisco small business routers, and the Cisco router boot process.
- **Chapter 36, "Troubleshoot Common Network Problems":** This chapter covers troubleshooting basic network connectivity issues, including approaches for network troubleshooting, detecting physical layer problems, addressing wireless network problems, explaining common Internet connectivity issues, and using external sources and Internet resources for effective troubleshooting.
- **Chapter 37, "Network Support":** This chapter covers effective troubleshooting methodologies and help desk best practices, including creating network documentation, explaining help desk best practices, verifying network connectivity on various operating systems, troubleshooting network issues, and explaining remote connectivity troubleshooting.
- **Chapter 38, "Cybersecurity Threats, Vulnerabilities, and Attacks":** This chapter provides an overview of common threats, vulnerabilities, and attacks on endpoints that occur in various domains, the deception methods used by attackers, as well as prevalent types of network, wireless, mobile device, and application attacks.
- **Chapter 39, "Network Security":** This chapter covers foundational security concepts, access control configuration, cybersecurity processes, malware mitigation methods, endpoint security operation, and how to configure basic wireless security on a home router using WPAx.
- **Appendix, "Answers to the 'Check Your Understanding' Questions":** This appendix lists the answers to the "Check Your Understanding" review questions that are included at the end of each chapter.
- **Glossary:** The Glossary provides you with definitions for all the key terms identified in each chapter.

CHAPTER 1

Communications in a Connected World

Objectives

Upon completion of this chapter, you will be able to answer the following questions:

- What is the concept of a network?
- What is network data?
- What is network transmission speed and capacity?

Key Terms

This chapter uses the following key terms. You can find the definitions in the Glossary.

bandwidth *Page 17*

Internet *Page 2*

latency *Page 18*

small office/home office (SOHO) *Page 3*

throughput *Page 18*

Introduction (1.0)

Welcome to Communications in a Connected World! Hi, I'm Webster! I'll be accompanying you as you move through this course. Let me introduce you to my friend, Kishori! Kishori has been a nurse in a hospital in Karnataka, India, for about 20 years. When Kishori went to nursing school, she had no idea how much networking technology she would be using daily as a practicing nurse. At home, she only has a laptop, a smartphone, and a tablet. At work she uses a laptop, a desktop, a printer, and network-connected hospital equipment. Sometimes these devices do not communicate properly. When equipment does not work properly in a hospital, lives can be at risk! Kishori would like to better understand how it all works. Would you?

Network Types (1.1)

Networks are all around us. They provide us with a way to communicate and share information and resources with individuals in the same location or around the world. Everyone and everything are becoming connected to the network and the Internet.

Video

Video—Welcome to the World of Networking (1.1.1)

Refer to the online course to view this video.

Everything Is Online (1.1.2)

"Hey Shad, are you online?" "Of course, I am!" How many of us still think about whether or not we are "online"? We expect our devices, cell phones, tablets, laptops, and desktop computers to always be connected to the global Internet. We use this network to interact with our friends, shop, share pictures and experiences, and learn. The Internet has become such a part of everyday life that we almost take it for granted.

Normally, when people use the term *Internet*, they are not referring to the physical connections in the real world. Rather, they tend to think of it as a formless collection of connections. It is the "place" people go to find or share information.

Who Owns "The Internet"? (1.1.3)

The Internet is not owned by any individual or group. The *Internet* is a worldwide collection of interconnected networks (internetwork or Internet for short), cooperating with each other to exchange information using common standards. Through telephone wires, fiber-optic cables, wireless transmissions, and satellite links, Internet users can exchange information in a variety of forms, as shown in Figure 1-1.

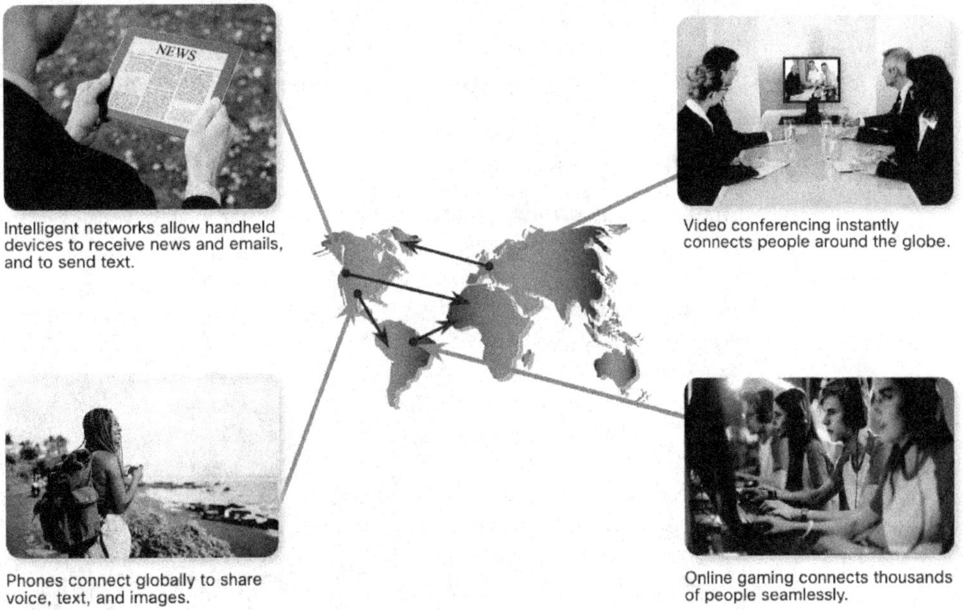

Figure 1-1 Online Interactions

Everything that you access online is located somewhere on the global Internet. Social media sites, multiplayer games, messaging centers that provide email, online courses—all of these Internet destinations are connected to local networks that send and receive information through the Internet.

Think about all of your daily interactions that require you to be online. Some examples are shown in Figure 1-1.

Local Networks (1.1.4)

Local networks come in all sizes. They can range from simple networks consisting of two computers to networks connecting hundreds of thousands of devices. A network installed in a small office or a home office (or a home generally) is referred to as a *small office/home office (SOHO)* network. A SOHO network enables a few local users to share resources such as printers, documents, pictures, and music.

In business, large networks can be used to advertise and sell products, order supplies, and communicate with customers. Communication over a network is usually more efficient and less expensive than traditional forms of communication, such as regular mail or long-distance phone calls. Networks allow for rapid communication, such as email and instant messaging, and provide consolidation and access to information stored on network servers.

Business and SOHO networks usually provide a shared connection to the Internet. The Internet is considered a "network of networks" because it is literally made up of thousands of local networks that are connected to each other.

Small Home Networks

Small home networks connect a few computers to each other and to the Internet (see Figure 1-2).

Figure 1-2 Example of a Small Home Network

Small Office and Home Office Networks

A SOHO network (see Figure 1-3) allows computers in a home office or a remote office to connect to a corporate network or access centralized, shared resources.

Medium to Large Networks

Medium to large networks, such as those used by corporations and schools (see Figure 1-4), can have many locations with hundreds or thousands of interconnected hosts.

Figure 1-3 Example of a SOHO Network

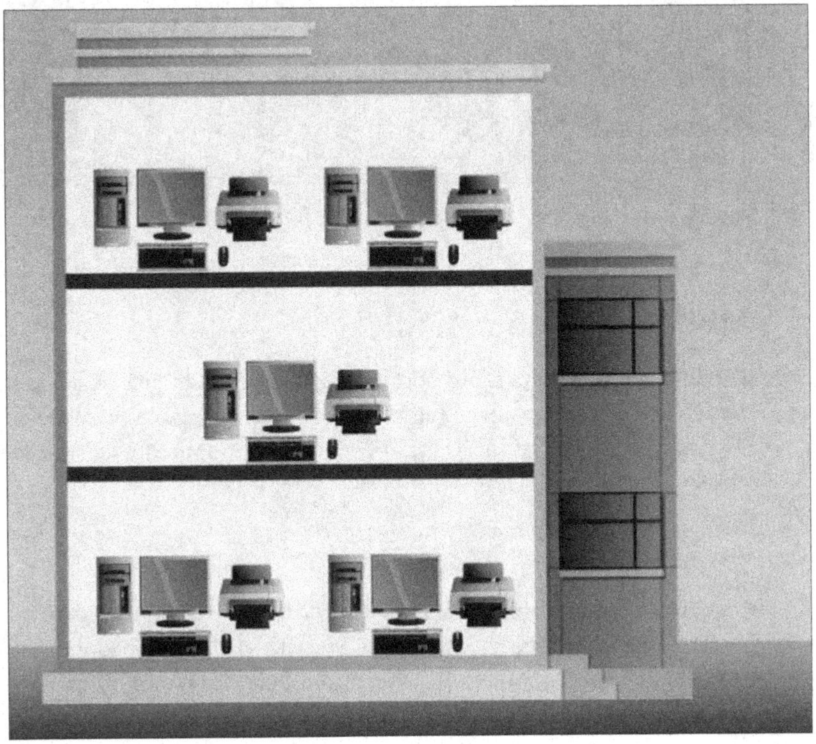

Figure 1-4 Example of a Medium to Large Network

Worldwide Networks

The Internet is a network of networks that connects hundreds of millions of computers worldwide, as shown in Figure 1-5.

Figure 1-5 Example of a Worldwide Network

Mobile Devices (1.1.5)

The Internet connects more computing devices than just desktop and laptop computers. There are devices all around that you may interact with on a daily basis that are also connected to the Internet. These include mobile devices, home devices, and a variety of other connected devices.

Smartphone

Smartphones (see Figure 1-6) are able to connect to the Internet from almost anywhere. Smartphones combine the functions of many different products, such as a telephone, camera, GPS receiver, media player, and touchscreen computer.

Figure 1-6 Example of a Smartphone

Tablet

Tablets (see Figure 1-7), like smartphones, also have the functionality of multiple devices. With the additional screen size, tablets are ideal for watching videos and reading magazines or books. With on-screen keyboards, users are able to do many of the things they can do on their laptop computers, such as composing emails or browsing the web.

Figure 1-7 Example of a Tablet

Smartwatch

A smartwatch (see Figure 1-8) can connect to a smartphone to provide the user with alerts and messages. Additional functions, such as heart rate monitoring and counting steps, like a pedometer, can help people who are wearing the device to track their health.

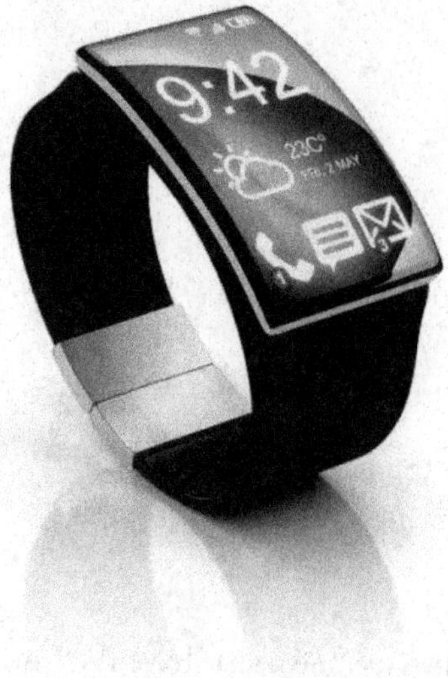

Figure 1-8 Example of a Smartwatch

Smart Glasses

A wearable computer in the form of glasses, such as the original Google Glass, contains a tiny screen that displays information to the wearer in a similar fashion to the head-up display (HUD) of a fighter pilot. A small touchpad on the side allows the user to navigate menus while still being able to see through the smart glasses (see Figure 1-9).

Connected Home Devices (1.1.6)

Many of the things in your home can also be connected to the Internet so that they can be monitored and configured remotely.

Security System

Many of the items in a home, such as security systems, lighting, and climate controls, can be monitored and configured remotely using a mobile device, as shown in Figure 1-10.

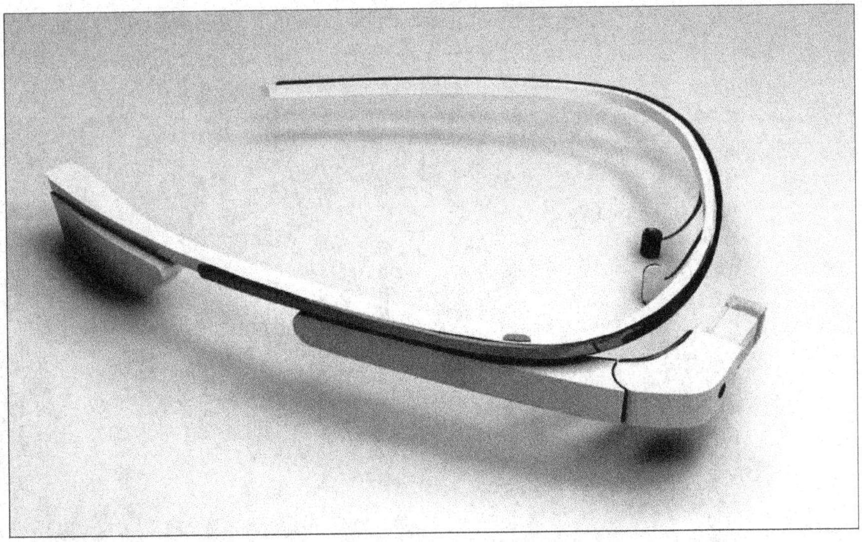

Figure 1-9 Example of Smart Glasses

Figure 1-10 Using a Mobile Device to Manage Home Security

Appliances

Household appliances such as refrigerators, ovens, and dishwashers can be connected to the Internet, as shown in Figure 1-11. This allows the homeowner to power them

on or off, monitor the status of the appliance, and also be alerted to preset conditions, such as when the temperature in the refrigerator rises above an acceptable level.

Figure 1-11 Examples of Smart Appliances

Smart TV

A smart TV (see Figure 1-12) can be connected to the Internet to access content without the need for TV service provider equipment. Also, a smart TV can allow a user to browse the web, compose email, or display video, audio, or photos stored on a computer.

Figure 1-12 Example of a Smart TV

Gaming Console

Gaming consoles (see Figure 1-13) can connect to the Internet to download games and to play games with friends online.

Figure 1-13 Example of a Gaming Console

Other Connected Devices (1.1.7)

There are also many connected devices in the world outside your home that provide convenience and useful, or even vital, information.

Smart Cars

Many modern cars can connect to the Internet to access maps, audio and video content, or information about a destination. They can even send a text message or email to the car owner if there is an attempted theft or call emergency services for assistance in case of an accident. These cars can also connect to smartphones and tablets, as shown in Figure 1-14, to display information about the different engine systems, provide maintenance alerts, or display the status of the security system.

Figure 1-14 Using a Tablet to Connect to a Smart Car

RFID Tags

Radio frequency identification (RFID) tags, shown in Figure 1-15, can be placed in or on objects to track them or monitor sensors for many conditions.

Figure 1-15 Example of RFID Tags

Sensors and Actuators

Connected sensors can provide temperature, humidity, wind speed, barometric pressure, and soil moisture data. Actuators can then be automatically triggered based on current conditions. For example, a smart sensor can periodically send soil moisture data to a monitoring station (see Figure 1-16). The monitoring station can then send a signal to an actuator to begin watering. The sensor will continue to send soil moisture data so that the monitoring station can determine when to deactivate the actuator.

Figure 1-16 Using a Tablet to Monitor Sensors and Actuators

Medical Devices

Medical devices such as pacemakers, insulin pumps, and hospital monitors provide users or medical professionals with direct feedback or alerts when vital signs are at specific levels. A tablet, shown in Figure 1-17, is often used to connect to these devices for monitoring purposes.

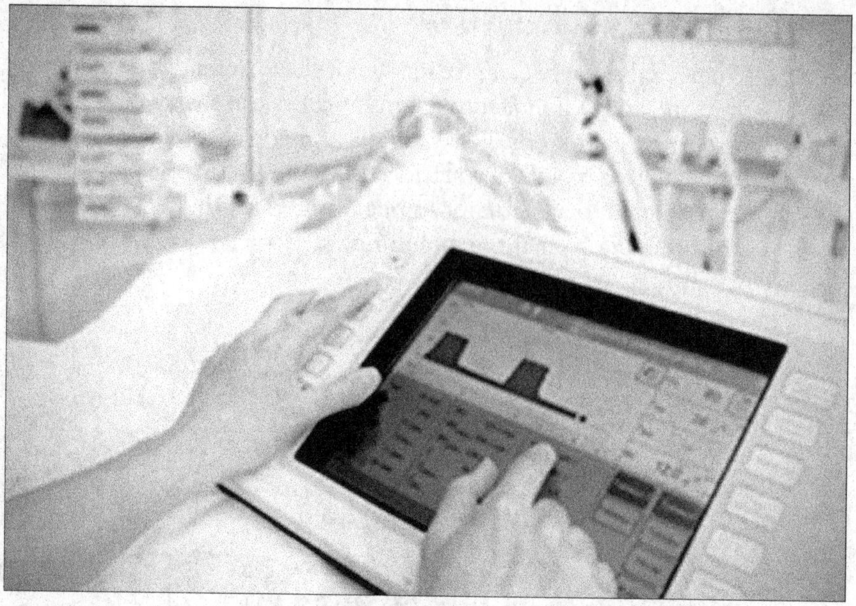

Figure 1-17 Using a Tablet to Monitor Medical Devices

Interactive Graphic

Check Your Understanding—Network Types (1.1.8)

Refer to the online course to complete this activity.

Data Transmission (1.2)

Computer networks transmit data from the original source to a final destination. This section introduces you to the different types of data and how the data is physically transmitted.

Video

Video—Types of Personal Data (1.2.1)

Refer to the online course to view this video.

The Bit (1.2.2)

Did you know that computers and networks work only with binary digits, zeros and ones? It can be difficult to imagine that all of our data is stored and transmitted as a series of bits. Each bit can have only one of two possible values, 0 or 1. The term *bit* is an abbreviation of *binary digit* and represents the smallest piece of data. Humans interpret words and pictures; computers interpret only patterns of bits.

A bit is stored and transmitted as one of two possible discrete states. This can include two directions of magnetization, two distinct voltage or current levels, two distinct levels of light intensity, or any other physical system of two discrete states. For example, a light switch can be either on or off; in binary representation, these states would correspond to 1 and 0, respectively.

Every input device (mouse, keyboard, voice-activated receiver) translates human interaction into binary code for the CPU to process and store. Every output device (printer, speakers, monitors, etc.) takes binary data and translates it back into human-recognizable form. Within the computer itself, all data is processed and stored as binary.

Computers use binary codes to represent and interpret letters, numbers, and special characters with bits. A commonly used code is the American Standard Code for Information Interchange (ASCII). With ASCII, each character is represented by eight bits. For example:

- **Capital letter**—A = 01000001
- **Number**—9 = 00111001
- **Special character**—# = 00100011

Each group of eight bits, such as the representations of letters and numbers, is known as a *byte*.

Codes can be used to represent almost any type of information digitally, including computer data, graphics, photos, voice, video, and music.

Interactive Graphic

Check Your Understanding—Convert Characters to ASCII Bits

Refer to the online course to complete this activity.

Common Methods of Data Transmission (1.2.3)

After the data is transformed into a series of bits, it must be converted into signals that can be sent across the network media to its destination. *Media* refers to the physical medium on which the signals are transmitted. Examples of media are copper wire, fiber-optic cable, and electromagnetic waves through the air. A *signal* consists of electrical or optical patterns that are transmitted from one connected device to another. These patterns represent the digital bits (that is, the data) and travel across the media from source to destination as a series of either pulses of electricity, pulses of light, or radio waves. Signals may be converted many times before ultimately reaching the destination, as corresponding media changes between source and destination.

Three common methods of signal transmission are used in networks, as shown in Figure 1-18:

- **Electrical signals**—Transmission is achieved by representing data as electrical pulses on copper wire.
- **Optical signals**—Transmission is achieved by converting the electrical signals into light pulses.
- **Wireless signals**—Transmission is achieved by using infrared, microwave, or radio waves through the air.

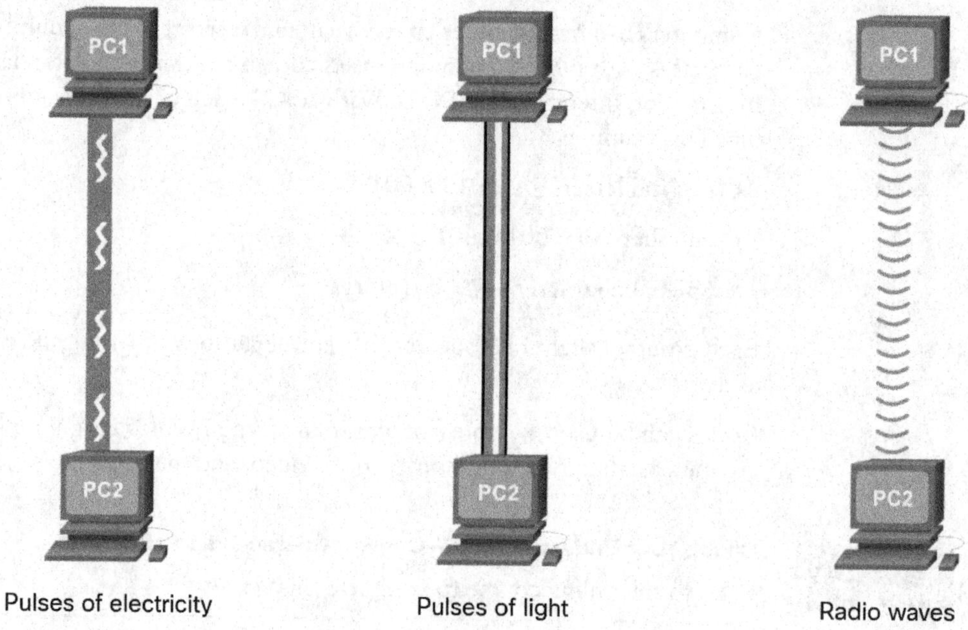

Figure 1-18 Three Types of Signal Transmissions

In most homes and small businesses, network signals are transmitted across copper wires (cables) or Wi-Fi–enabled wireless connections. Larger networks employ fiber-optic cables to reliably carry signals for longer distances.

Interactive Graphic

Check Your Understanding—Data Transmission (1.2.4)

Refer to the online course to complete this activity.

Bandwidth and Throughput (1.3)

Network performance at times is measured by the speed at which users are sending or receiving information. Bandwidth and throughput are two ways of measuring how much data is transferred from source to destination.

Bandwidth (1.3.1)

Streaming a movie or playing a multiplayer game requires reliable, fast connections. To support these "high bandwidth" applications, networks have to be capable of transmitting and receiving bits at a very high rate.

Different physical media support the transfer of bits at different speeds. The rate of data transfer is usually discussed in terms of bandwidth and throughput.

Bandwidth is the capacity of a medium to carry data. Digital bandwidth measures the amount of data that can flow from one place to another in a given amount of time. Bandwidth is typically measured in the number of bits that (theoretically) can be sent across the media in a second. Common bandwidth measurements are as follows:

- Thousands of bits per second (Kbps or Kb/s)
- Millions of bits per second (Mbps or Mb/s)
- Billions of bits per second (Gbps or Gb/s)

Physical media properties, current technologies, and the laws of physics all play a role in determining available bandwidth.

Table 1-1 shows the commonly used units of measure for bandwidth.

Table 1-1 Units of Bandwidth

Unit of Bandwidth	Abbreviation	Equivalence
Bits per second	bps or b/s	1 bps = fundamental unit of bandwidth
Kilobits per second	Kbps or Kb/s	1 Kbps = 1,000 bps = 10^3 bps
Megabits per second	Mbps or Mb/s	1 Mbps = 1,000,000 bps = 10^6 bps
Gigabits per second	Gbps or Gb/s	1 Gbps = 1,000,000,000 bps = 10^9 bps
Terabits per second	Tbps or Tb/s	1 Tbps = 1,000,000,000,000 bps = 10^{12} bps

Throughput (1.3.2)

Like bandwidth, *throughput* is the measure of the transfer of bits across the media over a given period of time. However, due to a number of factors, throughput does not usually match the specified bandwidth. Many factors influence throughput, including

- The amount of data being sent and received over the connection
- The types of data being transmitted
- The latency created by the number of network devices encountered between source and destination

Latency refers to the amount of time, including delays, for data to travel from one given point to another.

Throughput measurements do not take into account the validity or usefulness of the bits being transmitted and received. Many messages received through the network are not destined for specific user applications. An example would be network control messages that regulate traffic and correct errors.

In an internetwork or network with multiple segments, throughput cannot be faster than the slowest link of the path from the sending device to the receiving device. Even if all or most of the segments have high bandwidth, it will only take one segment in the path with lower bandwidth to create a slowdown of the throughput of the entire network.

There are many online speed tests that can reveal the throughput of an Internet connection.

Video

Video—Throughput (1.3.3)

Refer to the online course to view this video.

Interactive Graphic

Check Your Understanding—Bandwidth and Throughput (1.3.4)

Refer to the online course to complete this activity.

Communications in a Connected World Summary (1.4)

The following is a summary of each topic in the chapter and some questions for your reflection.

What Did I Learn in This Chapter? (1.4.1)

- **Network Types**—The Internet is not owned by any individual or group. The Internet is a worldwide collection of interconnected networks (internetwork or Internet for short), cooperating with each other to exchange information using common standards. Through telephone wires, fiber-optic cables, wireless transmissions, and satellite links, Internet users can exchange information in a variety of forms.

  Small home networks connect a few computers to each other and to the Internet. The SOHO network allows computers in a home office or a remote office to connect to a corporate network or access centralized, shared resources. Medium to large networks, such as those used by corporations and schools, can have many locations with hundreds or thousands of interconnected hosts. The Internet is a network of networks that connects hundreds of millions of computers worldwide.

  There are devices all around that you may interact with on a daily basis that are also connected to the Internet. These include mobile devices such as smartphones, tablets, smartwatches, and smart glasses. Things in your home can be connected to the Internet, too, such as a security system, appliances, your smart TV, and your gaming console. Outside your home there are smart cars, RFID tags, sensors and actuators, and even medical devices that can be connected.

- **Data Transmission**—The following categories are used to classify types of personal data:

  - **Volunteered data**—This is created and explicitly shared by individuals, such as social network profiles. This type of data might include video files, pictures, text, or audio files.
  - **Observed data**—This is captured by recording the actions of individuals, such as location data when using cell phones.
  - **Inferred data**—This is data such as a credit score, which is based on analysis of volunteered or observed data.

  The term *bit* is an abbreviation of *binary digit* and represents the smallest piece of data. Each bit can have only one of two possible values, 0 or 1.

  Three common methods of signal transmission are used in networks:

  - **Electrical signals**—Transmission is achieved by representing data as electrical pulses on copper wire.
  - **Optical signals**—Transmission is achieved by converting the electrical signals into light pulses.
  - **Wireless signals**—Transmission is achieved by using infrared, microwave, or radio waves through the air.

- **Bandwidth and Throughput**—Bandwidth is the capacity of a medium to carry data. Digital bandwidth measures the amount of data that can flow from one place to another in a given amount of time. Bandwidth is typically measured in the number of bits that (theoretically) can be sent across the media in a second. Common bandwidth measurements are as follows:
  - Thousands of bits per second (Kbps or Kb/s)
  - Millions of bits per second (Mbps or Mb/s)
  - Billions of bits per second (Gbps or Gb/s)

  Throughput does not usually match the specified bandwidth. Many factors influence throughput, including
  - The amount of data being sent and received over the connection
  - The types of data being transmitted
  - The latency created by the number of network devices encountered between source and destination

  Latency refers to the amount of time, including delays, for data to travel from one given point to another.

Reflection Questions (1.4.2)

Maybe you don't work in a hospital, as does Kishori, but because you are reading this book, you likely also use computers and want to know more about networks. Did you know that the Internet is a massive network of networks that are connected, either directly or indirectly, to each other? It's kind of like this web that I live in. One part can be broken, but my web doesn't fall apart; I can fix it, and even make it stronger. Would you like to be able to do that for your network?

Practice

There are no labs or Packet Tracer activities in this chapter.

Check Your Understanding Questions

Complete all the review questions listed here to test your understanding of the topics and concepts in this chapter. Appendix A, "Answers to 'Check Your Understanding' Questions," lists the answers.

1. Which of the following correctly explains a network characteristic?
   a. Availability indicates how easily the network can accommodate more users and data transmission requirements.
   b. Reliability is often measured as a probability of failure or as the mean time between failures (MTBF).
   c. Scalability is the likelihood that the network is available for use when it is required.
   d. Usability is how effectively end users can use the network.

2. What is the Internet?
   a. The type of physical media used by computers to access the World Wide Web
   b. A network of networks
   c. An application used to access the World Wide Web
   d. A small isolated internal network of a company

3. What is an example of a binary value from everyday life?
   a. Room temperature
   b. A simple light switch
   c. Speed of a traveling car
   d. Brightness of a light bulb

4. Which category of network components includes wires and cables used in a wired network?
   a. Media
   b. Devices
   c. Peripherals
   d. Hosts

5. What type of device is able to create physical movement?
   a. Actuator
   b. Sensor
   c. RFID tag
   d. Console
6. What are three options for signal transmission on a network? (Choose three.)
   a. Radio waves
   b. Vibration pulses
   c. Sound waves
   d. Electrical pulses
   e. Light pulses
7. Who owns the Internet?
   a. Bill Gates
   b. Cisco
   c. The government
   d. No one person or group
8. Which type of connected device is placed on objects to track and monitor them?
   a. RFID tags
   b. Sensors
   c. Actuators
   d. Consoles
9. A byte consists of how many bits?
   a. 2
   b. 4
   c. 8
   d. 16
10. Which two numbers are possible values of a bit? (Choose two.)
    a. 0
    b. 1
    c. 2
    d. 8
    e. 16

11. What measurement is used to indicate thousands of bits per second?

    a. Kbps
    b. Mbps
    c. Tbps
    d. Gbps

12. What type of network must a home user access to do online shopping?

    a. A SOHO network
    b. The Internet
    c. A local area network

CHAPTER 2

Network Components, Types, and Connections

Objectives

Upon completion of this chapter, you will be able to answer the following questions:

- What are the roles of clients and servers in a network?
- What are the roles of network infrastructure devices?
- What are ISP connectivity options?

Key Terms

This chapter uses the following key terms. You can find the definitions in the Glossary.

cable Page 35

cellular Page 36

client Page 27

dial-up Page 36

DSL—Digital Subscriber Line Page 35

end devices Page 31

intermediary devices Page 31

Internet service provider (ISP) Page 33

peer-to-peer (P2P) Page 27

satellite Page 36

server Page 27

Introduction (2.0)

Kishori does not yet understand network infrastructure device roles in the network, including end devices, intermediary devices, and network media. When she first started her nursing career, she was writing patient medical notes in a paper notebook! At home, Kishori only has a laptop, a smartphone, and a tablet. This makes her most familiar with end devices, or hosts. She understands that those devices are connected to the Internet somehow through that box in the corner of her living room. At work she uses a laptop, a desktop, a printer, and other network-connected hospital equipment. She wants to learn more about network components and how they all connect.

Kishori leaves her patient's room, sets down her laptop, and continues her work on the desktop computer at the nursing station. She wonders how the electronic notes she just took on the laptop appear on the patient's record on the desktop computer. How are they connected? How does the computer reach the Internet in the first place? Kishori has a lot to learn, and you might too! Read this chapter to learn more.

Clients and Servers (2.1)

In the client/server network model, one computer acts as a client and another computer acts as a server. The client computer requests the services or information from a server and the server responds with the requested content.

Video

Video—Clients and Servers (2.1.1)

Refer to the online course to view this video.

Client and Server Roles (2.1.2)

All computers connected to a network that participate directly in network communication are classified as *hosts*. Hosts can send and receive messages on the network. In modern networks, computer hosts can act as a client, a server, or both, as shown in Figure 2-1. The software installed on the computer determines which role the computer plays.

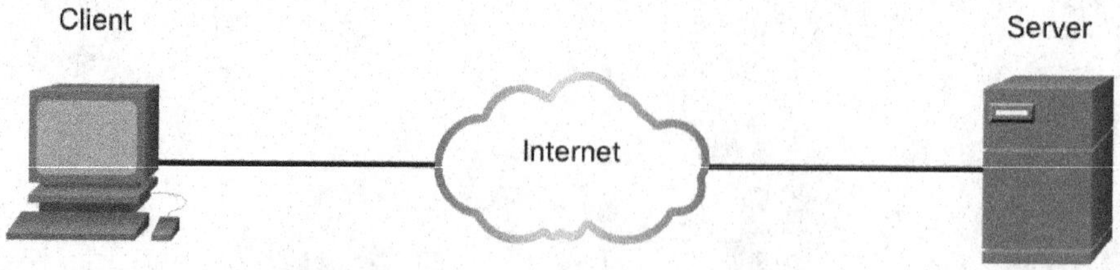

Figure 2-1 Client and Server

Servers are computer hosts that have software installed that enables them to provide information, like email or web pages, to other hosts on the network. Each service requires separate server software. For example, a host requires web server software in order to provide web services to the network. Every destination that you visit online is provided to you by a server located somewhere on a network that is connected to the global Internet.

Clients are computer hosts that have software installed that enables them to request and display the information obtained from the server. An example of client software is a web browser, such as Microsoft Edge, Safari, Mozilla Firefox, or Google Chrome.

Table 2-1 describes three of the most common types of client and server software.

Table 2-1 Examples of Client/Server Software

Type	Description
Email	The email server runs email server software. Clients use mail client software, such as Microsoft Outlook, to access email on the server.
Web	The web server runs web server software. Clients use browser software, such as Microsoft Edge, to access web pages on the server.
File	The file server stores corporate and user files in a central location. The client devices access these files with client software such as the Windows File Explorer.

Peer-to-Peer Networks (2.1.3)

Client software and server software usually run on separate computers, but it is also possible for one computer to run both client and server software at the same time. In small businesses and homes, many computers function as both the servers and clients on the network. This type of network is called a *peer-to-peer (P2P)* network.

The simplest P2P network consists of two directly connected computers using either a wired connection or a wireless connection. Both computers are then able to use this simple network to exchange data and services with each other, acting as either a client or a server as necessary.

Multiple PCs can also be connected to create a larger P2P network, but this requires a network device, such as a switch, to interconnect the computers.

The main disadvantage of a P2P environment is that the performance of a host can be slowed down if it is acting as both a client and a server at the same time. Figure 2-2 lists some of the advantages and disadvantages of peer-to-peer networks.

In larger businesses, because of the potential for high amounts of network traffic, it is often necessary to have dedicated servers to support the number of service requests.

The advantages and disadvantages of P2P networking are summarized in Figure 2-2.

Figure 2-2 Peer-to-Peer Network

The following are the advantages of peer-to-peer networking:

- Easy to set up
- Less complex
- Lower cost because network devices and dedicated servers may not be required
- Can be used for simple tasks such as transferring files and sharing printers

These are the disadvantages of peer-to-peer networking:

- No centralized administration
- Not as secure
- Not scalable
- All devices may act as both clients and servers, which can slow their performance

Peer-to-Peer Applications (2.1.4)

A P2P application allows a device to act as both a client and a server within the same communication, as shown in Figure 2-3. In this model, every client is a server and every server is a client. P2P applications require that each end device provide a user interface and run a background service.

Some P2P applications use a hybrid system where resource sharing is decentralized, but the indexes that point to resource locations are stored in a centralized directory. In a hybrid system, each peer accesses an index server to get the location of a resource stored on another peer. Both clients can simultaneously send and receive messages.

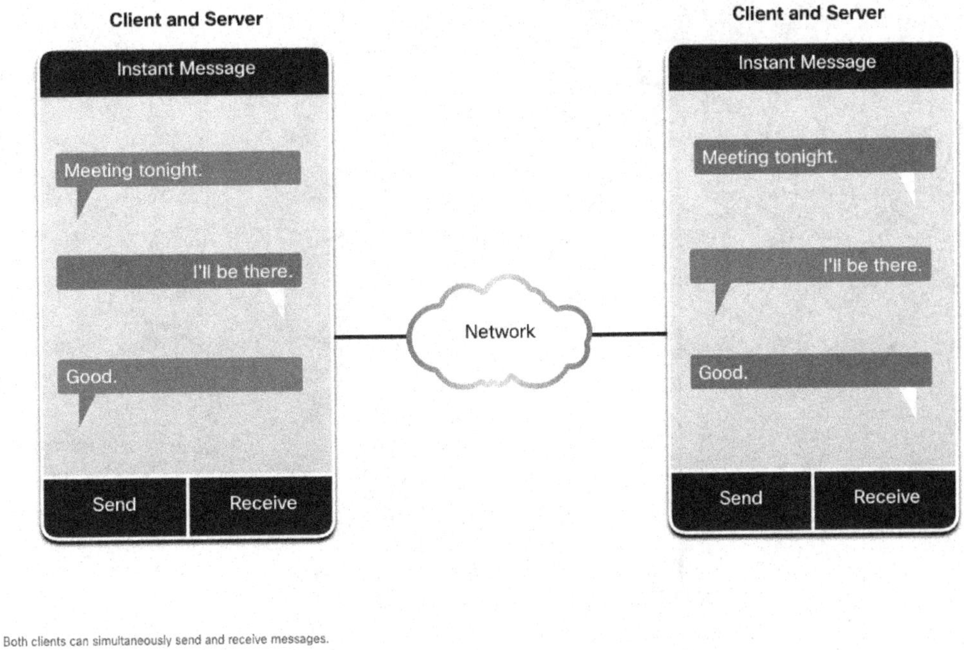

Figure 2-3 Texting Is a P2P Application

Multiple Roles in the Network (2.1.5)

A computer with server software can provide services simultaneously to one or many clients, as shown in Figure 2-4.

Additionally, a single computer can run multiple types of server software. In a home or small business, it may be necessary for one computer to act as a file server, a web server, and an email server.

A single computer can also run multiple types of client software. There must be client software for every service required. With multiple clients installed, a host can connect to multiple servers at the same time. For example, a user can check email and view a web page while instant messaging and listening to Internet radio.

Interactive Graphic

Check Your Understanding—Clients and Servers (2.1.6)

Refer to the online course to complete this activity.

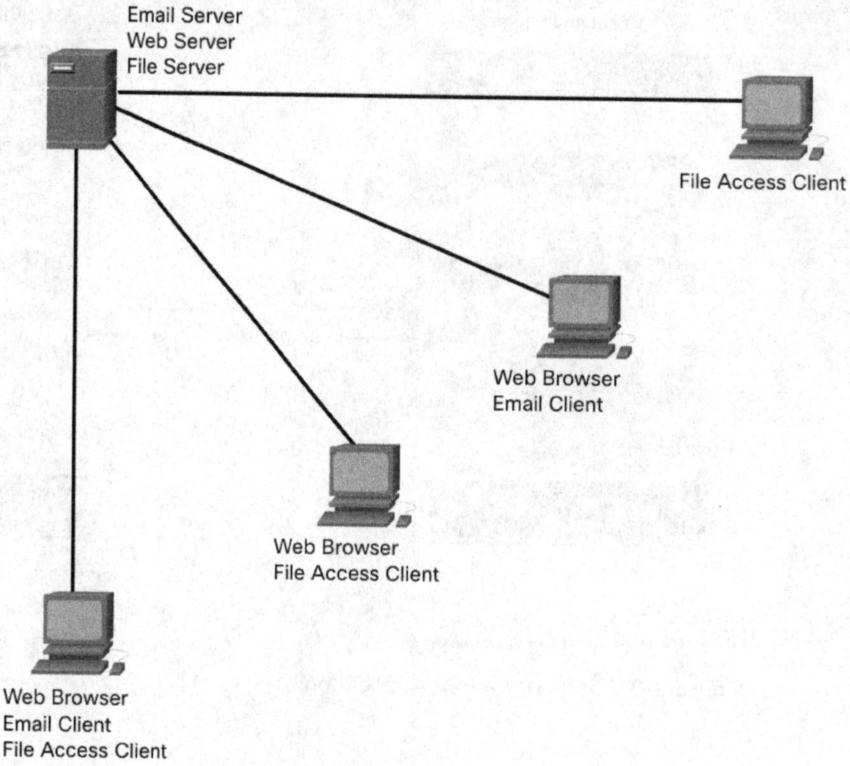

Figure 2-4 Clients Accessing Services on the Server

Network Components (2.2)

Network components include end devices, such as laptop computers and mobile phones, and network infrastructure devices, such as Ethernet switches and routers.

Video

Video—Network Infrastructure Symbols (2.2.1)

Refer to the online course to view this video.

Network Infrastructure (2.2.2)

The path that a message takes from its source to destination can be as simple as a single cable connecting one computer to another, or as complex as a network that literally spans the globe. This network infrastructure is the platform that supports the network. It provides the stable and reliable channel over which communications can occur.

The network infrastructure contains three categories of hardware components, as shown in Figure 2-5:

- *End devices*
- *Intermediary devices*
- Network media

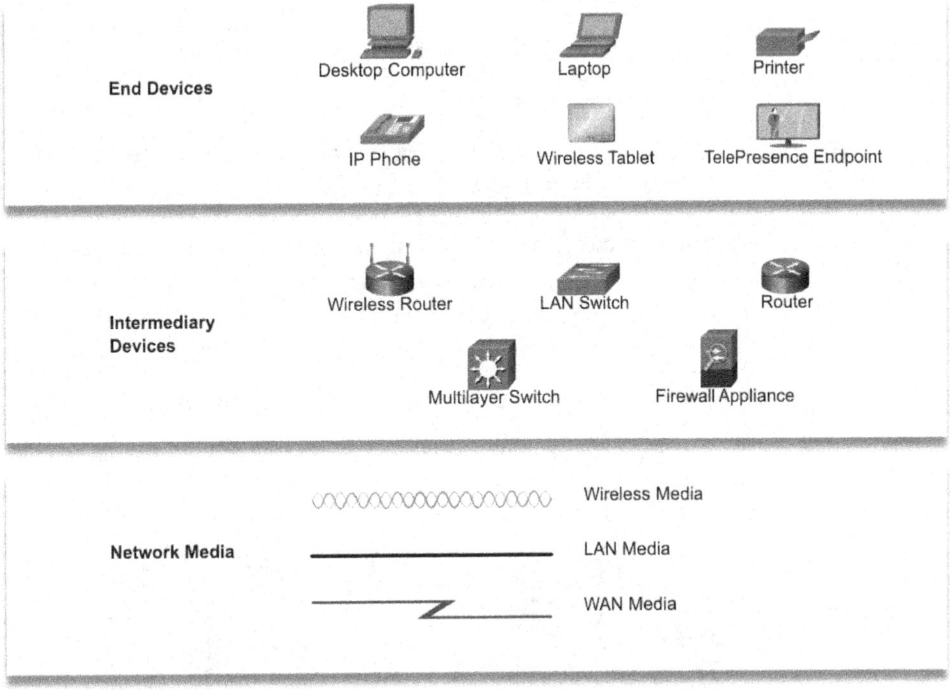

Figure 2-5 End Devices, Intermediary Devices, and Network Media

Devices and media are the physical elements, or hardware, of the network. Hardware is often the visible components of the network platform, such as a laptop, PC, switch, router, wireless access point (AP), or the cabling used to connect the devices. Occasionally, some components may not be so visible. In the case of wireless media, messages are transmitted through the air using invisible radio frequencies or infrared waves.

Make a list of the network infrastructure components installed in your home network. Include the cables or wireless access points that provide your network connections.

End Devices (2.2.3)

The network devices that people are most familiar with are called *end devices*, or *hosts*. These devices form the interface between users and the underlying communication network.

Some examples of end devices are as follows:

- Computers (workstations, laptops, file servers, web servers)
- Network printers
- Telephones and teleconferencing equipment
- Security cameras
- Mobile devices (such as smartphones, tablets, PDAs, and wireless debit/credit card readers and barcode scanners)

An end device (or host) is either the source or destination of a message transmitted over the network, as shown in Figure 2-6. Addresses are used to uniquely identify hosts. When a host initiates communication, it uses the address of the destination host to specify where the message should be sent.

Figure 2-6 shows an example of data flowing through a network.

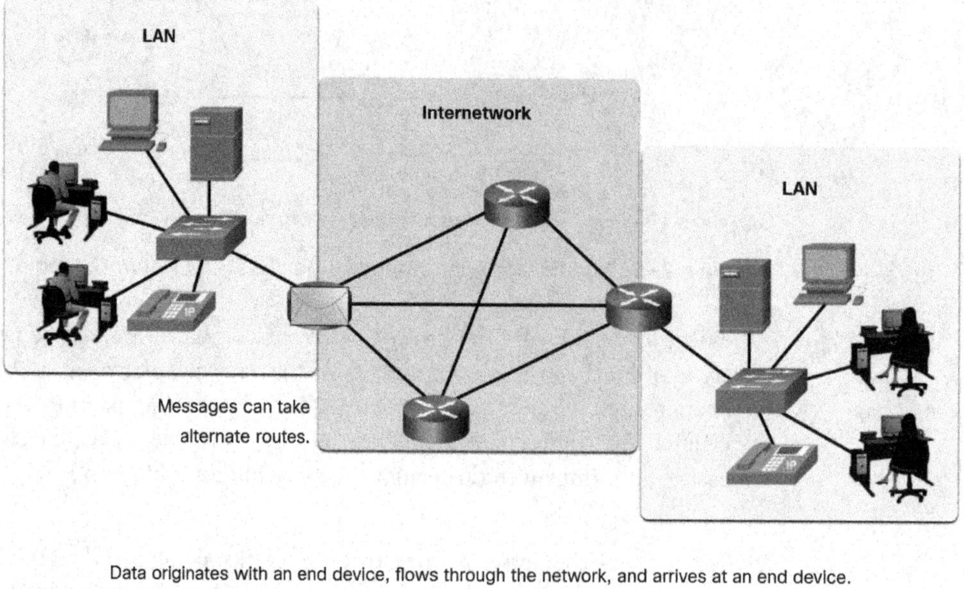

Figure 2-6 Data Flow in a Network

Interactive Graphic

Check Your Understanding—Network Components (2.2.4)

Refer to the online course to complete this activity.

ISP Connectivity Options (2.3)

An *Internet service provider (ISP)* provides the link between a home network and the Internet. An ISP can be the local cable provider, a landline telephone service provider, the cellular network that provides your smartphone service, or an independent provider that leases bandwidth on the physical network infrastructure of another company.

ISP Services (2.3.1)

Many ISPs also offer additional services to their contract subscribers, examples of which are shown in Figure 2-7. These services can include email accounts, network storage, website hosting, and automated backup or security services.

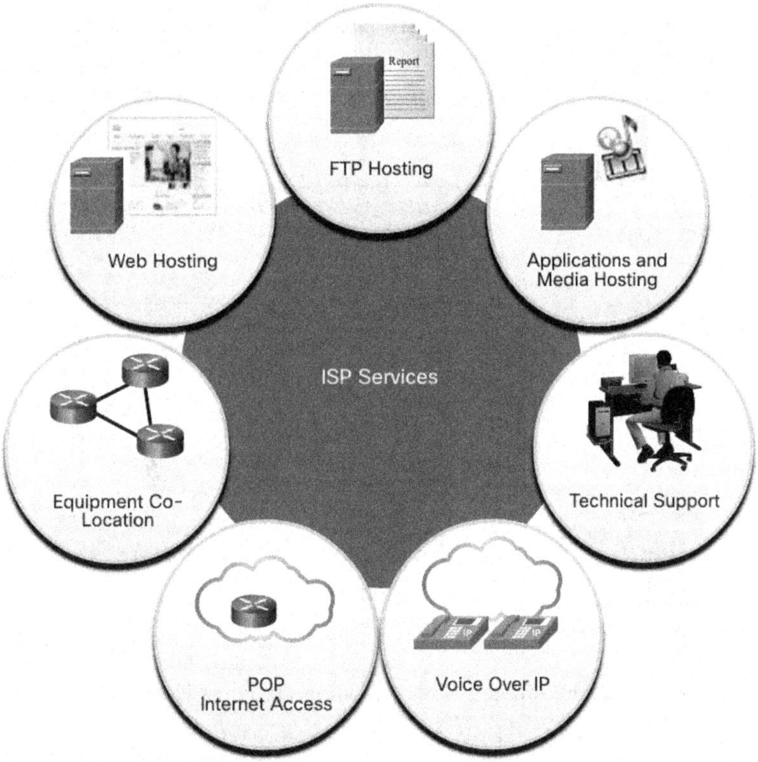

Figure 2-7 Examples of ISP Services

ISPs are critical to communications across the global Internet. Each ISP connects to other ISPs to form a network of links that interconnect users all over the world. ISPs are connected in a hierarchical manner that ensures that Internet traffic generally takes the shortest path from the source to the destination.

The Internet backbone is like an information superhighway that provides high-speed data links to connect the various service provider networks in major metropolitan areas around the world. The primary medium that connects the Internet backbone is fiber-optic cable. This cable is typically installed underground to connect cities within continents. Fiber-optic cables also run under the sea to connect continents, countries, and cities.

ISP Connections (2.3.2)

The interconnection of ISPs that forms the backbone of the Internet is a complex web of fiber-optic cables with expensive networking switches and routers that direct the flow of information between source and destination hosts. Average home users are not aware of the infrastructure outside of their network. For a home user, connecting to the ISP is a fairly uncomplicated process.

The top portion of Figure 2-8 displays the simplest ISP connection option. It consists of a modem that provides a direct connection between a computer and the ISP. This option should not be used though, because your computer is not protected on the Internet.

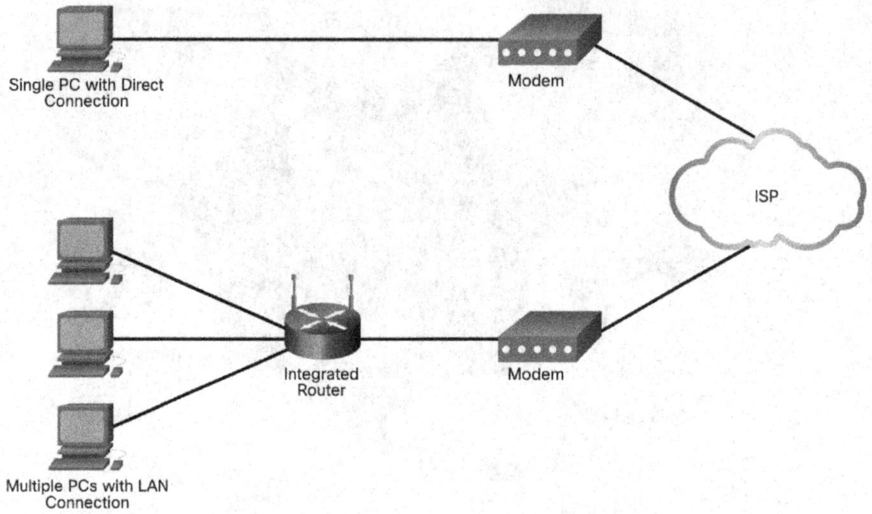

Figure 2-8 Connecting a Single User and Multiple Users to the Internet

As shown in the bottom portion of Figure 2-8, a router is required to securely connect a computer to an ISP. This is the most common connection option. It consists of using a wireless integrated router to connect to the ISP. The router includes both a

switch to connect wired hosts and a wireless AP to connect wireless hosts. The router also provides client IP addressing information and security for inside hosts.

Cable and DSL Connections (2.3.3)

Most home network users do not connect to their Internet service providers with fiber-optic cables. Figure 2-9 illustrates common connection options for small office and home users. The two most common methods are as follows:

- *Cable*—Typically offered by cable television service providers, the Internet data signal is carried on the same coaxial cable that delivers cable television. It provides a high-bandwidth, always-on connection to the Internet. A special cable modem separates the Internet data signal from the other signals carried on the cable and provides an Ethernet connection to a host computer or LAN.
- *DSL—Digital Subscriber Line*—It provides a high-bandwidth, always-on connection to the Internet. It requires a special high-speed modem that separates the DSL signal from the telephone signal and provides an Ethernet connection to a host computer or LAN. DSL runs over a telephone line, with the line split into three channels. One channel is used for voice telephone calls. This channel allows an individual to receive phone calls without disconnecting from the Internet. A second channel is a faster download channel, used to receive information from the Internet. The third channel is used for sending or uploading information. This channel is usually slightly slower than the download channel. The quality and speed of the DSL connection depend mainly on the quality of the phone line and the distance from the central office of your phone company. The farther you are from the central office, the slower the connection.

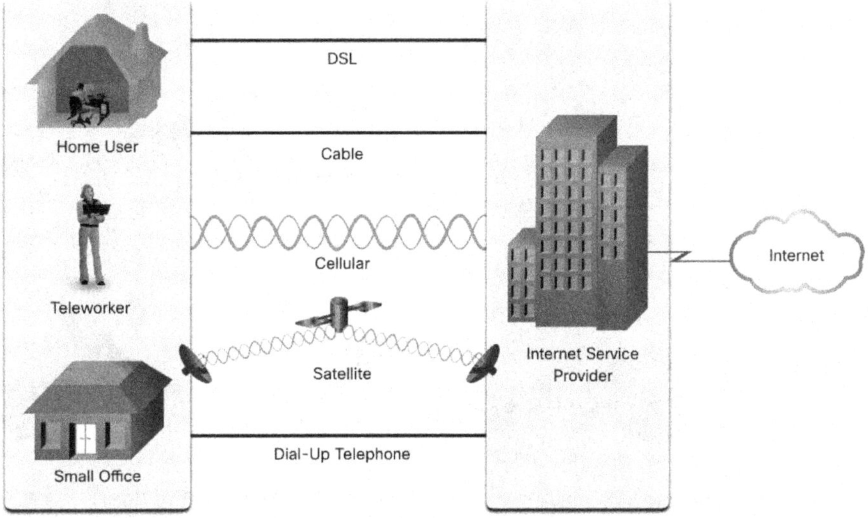

Figure 2-9 Internet Connection Options for Individuals, Homes, and Small Businesses

Additional Connectivity Options (2.3.4)

Other ISP connection options for home users include the following:

- *Cellular*—Cellular Internet access uses a cell phone network to connect. Wherever you can get a cellular signal, you can get cellular Internet access. Performance will be limited by the capabilities of the phone and the cell tower to which it is connected. The availability of cellular Internet access is a real benefit for people in areas that would otherwise have no Internet connectivity at all, and for people who are constantly on the move. The downside of cellular connectivity is that the carrier usually meters the bandwidth usage of the connection and may charge extra for bandwidth that exceeds the contract data plan.
- *Satellite*—Satellite service is a good option for homes or offices that do not have access to DSL or cable. Satellite dishes require a clear line of sight to the satellite (see Figure 2-10) and so might be difficult to set up in heavily wooded areas or places with other overhead obstructions. Speeds will vary depending on the contract, though they are generally good. Equipment and installation costs can be high (but providers sometimes offer special deals), with a moderate monthly fee thereafter. Like cellular access, the availability of satellite Internet access is a real benefit in areas that would otherwise have no Internet connectivity at all.
- *Dial-up*—Dial-up telephone is an inexpensive option that uses any phone line and a modem. To connect to the ISP, a user calls the ISP access phone number. The low bandwidth provided by a dial-up modem connection is usually not sufficient for large data transfer, although it is useful for mobile access while traveling. A modem dial-up connection should be considered only when higher-speed connection options are not available.

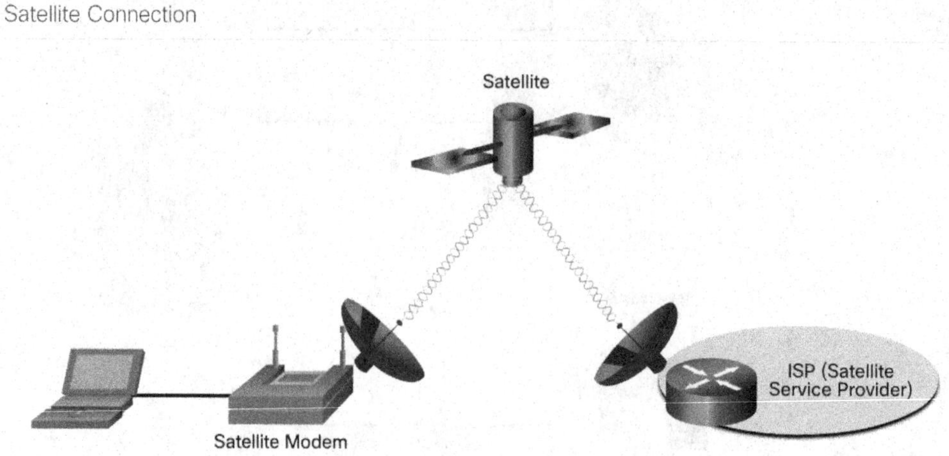

Figure 2-10 Example of Satellite Internet Service Provider

In metropolitan areas, many apartments and small offices are being connected directly with fiber-optic cables. This enables an ISP to provide higher bandwidth speeds and support more services such as Internet, phone, and TV.

The choice of connection varies depending on geographical location and ISP availability.

Interactive Graphic

Check Your Understanding—ISP Connectivity Options (2.3.5)

Refer to the online course to complete this activity.

Network Components, Types, and Connections Summary (2.4)

The following is a summary of each topic in the chapter and some questions for your reflection.

What Did I Learn in This Chapter? (2.4.1)

- **Clients and Servers**—All computers connected to a network that participate directly in network communication are classified as hosts. Hosts can send and receive messages on the network. In modern networks, computer hosts can act as a client, a server, or both. The software installed on the computer determines which role the computer plays.

  Client software and server software usually run on separate computers, but it is also possible for one computer to run both client and server software at the same time. In small businesses and homes, many computers function as both the servers and clients on the network. This type of network is called a peer-to-peer (P2P) network. In larger businesses, because of the potential for high amounts of network traffic, it is often necessary to have dedicated servers to support the number of service requests. P2P networks are easy to set up, less complex, lower in cost, and can be used for simple tasks such as transferring files and sharing printers. However, there is no centralized administration. They have less security, are not scalable, and can have slower performance.

- **Network Components**—There are symbols that represent various types of networking equipment. The network infrastructure is the platform that supports the network. It provides the stable and reliable channel over which communications can occur. The network infrastructure contains three categories of hardware components: end devices, intermediary devices, and network media. Hardware is often the visible components of the network platform such as a laptop, PC,

switch, router, wireless access point, or the cabling used to connect the devices. Components that are not visible include wireless media.

End devices, or hosts, form the interface between users and the underlying communication network. Some examples of end devices include

- Computers (workstations, laptops, file servers, web servers)
- Network printers
- Telephones and teleconferencing equipment
- Security cameras
- Mobile devices (such as smartphones, tablets, PDAs, and wireless debit/credit card readers and barcode scanners)

- **ISP Connectivity Options**—An ISP provides the link between a home network and the Internet. An ISP can be the local cable provider, a landline telephone service provider, the cellular network that provides your smartphone service, or an independent provider that leases bandwidth on the physical network infrastructure of another company. Each ISP connects to other ISPs to form a network of links that interconnect users all over the world. ISPs are connected in a hierarchical manner that ensures that Internet traffic generally takes the shortest path from the source to the destination.

  The interconnection of ISPs that forms the backbone of the Internet is a complex web of fiber-optic cables with expensive networking switches and routers that direct the flow of information between source and destination hosts.

  For a home user, connecting to the ISP is a fairly uncomplicated process. This is the most common connection option. It consists of using a wireless integrated router to connect to the ISP. The router includes both a switch to connect wired hosts and a wireless access point to connect wireless hosts. The router also provides client IP addressing information and security for inside hosts. The two most common IPS connection methods are cable and DSL. Other options include cellular, satellite, and dial-up telephone.

Reflection Questions (2.4.2)

As you may have experienced, if you order a piece of furniture that you have to assemble yourself, the box has all the pieces and parts that you need along with the assembly instructions. It helps to look at all these items while you read through the instructions. Think of your network. Did you know what all the different devices and connection types were before you read this chapter? Do you look at these pieces and parts differently now?

Practice

There are no labs or Packet Tracer activities in this chapter.

Check Your Understanding Questions

Complete all the review questions listed here to test your understanding of the topics and concepts in this chapter. Appendix A, "Answers to 'Check Your Understanding' Questions," lists the answers.

1. What type of network is defined by two computers that can both send and receive requests for resources?
   a. Client/server
   b. Peer-to-peer
   c. Enterprise
   d. Campus

2. What are two functions of end devices on a network? (Choose two.)
   a. They originate the data that flows through the network.
   b. They direct data over alternate paths in the event of link failures.
   c. They filter the flow of data to enhance security.
   d. They are the interface between humans and the communication network.
   e. They provide the channel over which the network message travels.

3. A home user is looking for an ISP connection that provides high-speed digital transmission over regular phone lines. What ISP connection type should the home user choose?
   a. DSL
   b. Dial-up
   c. Satellite
   d. Cell modem
   e. Cable modem

4. What type of Internet connection would be best for a residence in a remote area without mobile phone coverage or wired connectivity?
   a. Dial-up
   b. Cellular
   c. Satellite
   d. DSL

5. Which term correctly describes the function of an ISP?
   a. Responsible for managing local networks
   b. Responsible for the maintenance of SOHO networks
   c. Responsible for providing the link between a private network and the Internet
   d. Responsible for providing security on private networks

6. Which device is an intermediary device?
   a. Firewall
   b. PC
   c. Server
   d. Smart device

7. Which scenario describes a peer-to-peer network?
   a. Users access shared files from a file server.
   b. A user visits a web page on the company website.
   c. A user shares a printer attached to the workstation.
   d. Users print documents from a network printer that has a built-in NIC.

8. Which term is used to describe a network device with the primary function of providing information to other devices?
   a. Workstation
   b. Console
   c. Server
   d. Client

9. What is an advantage of the peer-to-peer network model?
   a. Scalability
   b. High level of security
   c. Ease of setup
   d. Centralized administration

10. What is a characteristic of a peer-to-peer application?
    a. Each device using the application provides a user interface and runs a background service.
    b. Each device can act both as a client and a server, but not simultaneously.
    c. The resources required for the application are centralized.
    d. One device is designated a server and one device is designated a client for all communications and services.

CHAPTER 3

Wireless and Mobile Networks

Objectives

Upon completion of this chapter, you will be able to answer the following questions:

- What are the different types of networks used by cell phones and mobile devices?
- How do you configure mobile devices for wireless connectivity?

Key Terms

This chapter uses the following key terms. You can find the definitions in the Glossary.

Bluetooth *Page 43*

Global Positioning System (GPS) *Page 43*

Near Field Communication (NFC) *Page 43*

SSID (Service Set Identifier) *Page 46*

Wi-Fi *Page 43*

Introduction (3.0)

Kishori has just ended her 10-hour shift at the hospital. As she is walking to her car, her mobile phone rings. It is her son, Shridhar, calling to remind her to pick up the dinner he ordered. While they are verifying their plans, Kishori gets into her car and starts the engine. Her conversation then transfers from her mobile phone to her speakers in her car. She confirms that she will pick up the food and that she will see him in an hour. Before she drives away, she does an Internet search for the restaurant and clicks the directions link. She listens to the directions coming through her speakers. "Your destination is on the left." She purchases the food and drives home. While Kishori and Shridhar enjoy their dinner, Kishori tells Shridhar how she is starting to think about all of this technology at home and at work. She knows how to use it but she does not understand how it works. She gives him the example of her mobile phone. Today she answered calls, texted, did an Internet search, and used it for driving directions. How does a mobile phone do all of this? How does the phone connect to all of these things? Shridhar is familiar with the different types of networks used by mobile devices. Shridhar explains the 4G/5G mobile network, GPS, Bluetooth, NFC, and Wi-Fi.

If you do not have a friend or family member like Shridhar to explain this to you, do not worry! In this chapter, you will learn about the various ways mobile devices communicate. Ready to learn more?

Wireless Networks (3.1)

Wireless networks provide mobility and access to network resources where a wired connection may not be available. Wireless networks are also used in communications such as with mobile phones.

Video

Video—Types of Wireless Networks (3.1.1)

Refer to the online course to view this video.

Video

Video—Cell Phone Interactions with Different Networks (3.1.2)

Refer to the online course to view this video.

Other Wireless Networks (3.1.3)

In addition to the GSM and 4G/5G transmitters and receivers, smartphones make connections in a variety of ways.

Global Positioning System

The *Global Positioning System (GPS)* uses satellites to transmit signals that cover the globe. A smartphone can receive these signals and calculate the phone's location to an accuracy of within 10 meters.

Wi-Fi

Wi-Fi transmitters and receivers located within the smartphone enable the phone to connect to local networks and the Internet. To receive and send data on a Wi-Fi network, the phone needs to be within the range of the signal from a wireless network access point. *Wi-Fi* networks are usually privately owned but often provide guest or public access hotspots. A *hotspot* is an area where Wi-Fi signals are available. Wi-Fi network connections on the phone are similar to the network connections on a laptop computer.

Bluetooth

Bluetooth is a low-power, short-range wireless technology that is intended to replace wired connectivity for accessories such as speakers, headphones, and microphones. Bluetooth can also be used to connect a smartwatch to a smartphone. Because Bluetooth technology can be used to transmit both data and voice, it can be used to create small local networks. Bluetooth is wireless technology that allows devices to communicate over short distances. Multiple devices can be connected at the same time with Bluetooth.

NFC

Near Field Communication (NFC) is a wireless communication technology that enables data to be exchanged by devices that are in very close proximity to each other, usually less than a few centimeters. For example, NFC can be used to connect a smartphone and a payment system. NFC uses electromagnetic fields to transmit data.

Interactive Graphic

Check Your Understanding—Wireless Networks (3.1.4)

Refer to the online course to complete this activity.

Mobile Device Connectivity (3.2)

Mobile devices give us the freedom to work, learn, play, and communicate wherever we want. People using mobile devices do not need to be tied to a physical location to send and receive voice, video, and data communications.

Mobile Devices and Wi-Fi (3.2.1)

Wireless facilities, such as Internet cafes, are available in many countries. College campuses use wireless networks to allow students to sign up for classes, watch lectures, and submit assignments in areas where physical connections to the network are unavailable. With mobile devices becoming more powerful, many tasks that needed to be performed on large computers connected to physical networks can now be completed using mobile devices on wireless networks.

Almost all mobile devices are capable of connecting to Wi-Fi networks. It is advisable to connect to Wi-Fi networks when possible because data used over Wi-Fi does not count against the cellular data plan. Also, because Wi-Fi radios use less power than cellular radios, connecting to Wi-Fi networks conserves battery power.

As with other Wi-Fi–enabled devices, it is important to use security when connecting mobile devices to Wi-Fi networks. Take these precautions to protect Wi-Fi communications on mobile devices:

- Never send login or password information using unencrypted text (plaintext).
- Use a virtual private network (VPN) connection when possible if you are sending sensitive data.
- Enable security on home networks.
- Use WPA2 or higher encryption for security.

Wi-Fi Settings (3.2.2)

The two most popular operating systems for mobile devices are Android and Apple iOS. Each operating system has settings that enable you to configure your device to connect to wireless networks. Figures 3-1 and 3-2 show examples of where to turn Wi-Fi on and off on Android devices and iOS devices, respectively.

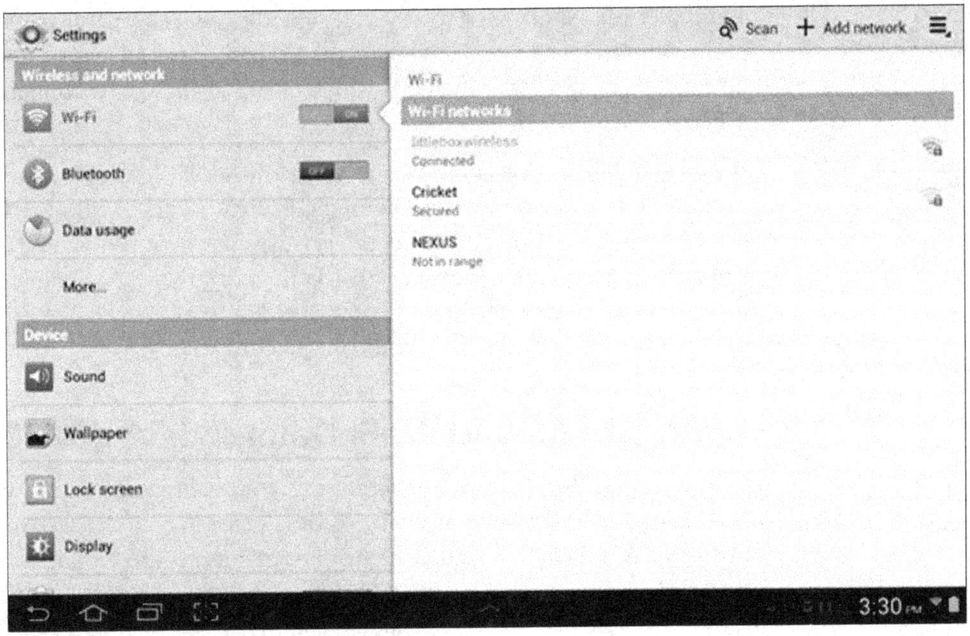

Figure 3-1 Android Wi-Fi Switch

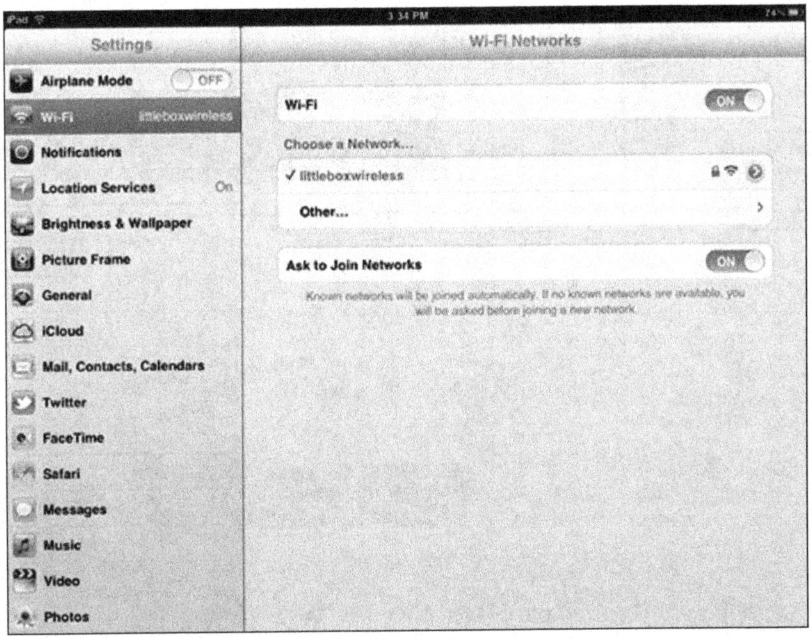

Figure 3-2 iOS Wi-Fi Switch

To connect an Android or iOS device when it is within the coverage range of a Wi-Fi network, turn on Wi-Fi. The device then searches for all available Wi-Fi networks and displays them in a list. Touch a Wi-Fi network in the list to connect. Enter a password if needed.

When a mobile device is out of the range of the Wi-Fi network, it attempts to connect to another Wi-Fi network in range. If no Wi-Fi networks are in range, the mobile device connects to the cellular data network. When Wi-Fi is on, the mobile device will automatically connect to any Wi-Fi network that it has connected to previously. If the network is new, the mobile device either displays a list of available networks that can be used or asks if it should connect to it.

Configure Mobile Wi-Fi Connectivity (3.2.3)

If your mobile device does not prompt to connect to a Wi-Fi network, the network SSID broadcast may be turned off, or the device may not be set to connect automatically. Manually configure the Wi-Fi settings on the mobile device. Remember that SSIDs and passphrases must be typed exactly as entered on the wireless router setup or the device will not connect properly, as shown in Figure 3-3. *SSID (Service Set Identifier)* is the name assigned to a wireless network. *Passphrase* is simply the wireless password.

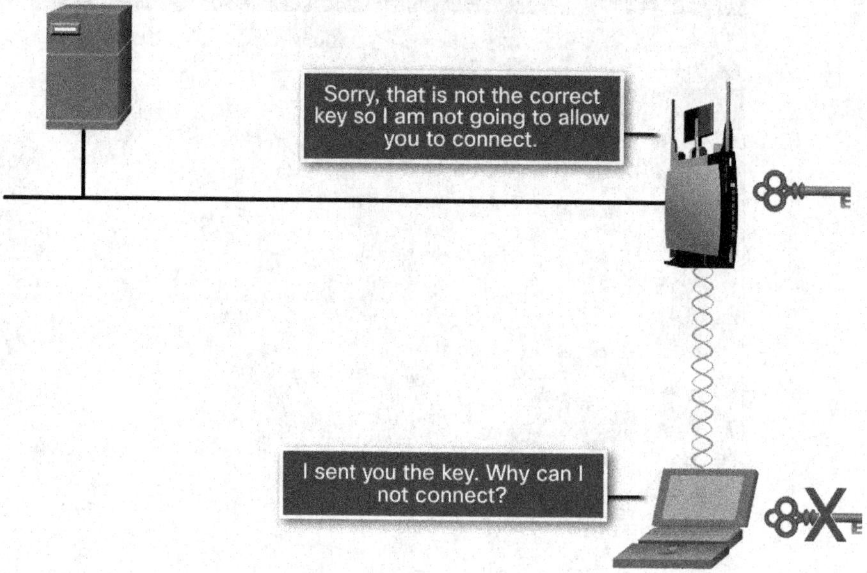

Figure 3-3 Example of Misconfigured Wireless Key

To connect to a Wi-Fi network manually on an Android device, follow these steps (or similar):

Step 1. Select **Settings > Add Network.**

Step 2. Enter the network SSID.

Step 3. Touch **Security** and select a security type.

Step 4. Touch **Password** and enter the password.

Step 5. Touch **Save.**

Operating systems for mobile devices are updated frequently and may be customized by the device manufacturer. The options listed here and in the following sections may not be exactly the same on your device. If not, check your device manufacturer's website for an online manual or simply do a web search for device-specific instructions.

To connect to a Wi-Fi network manually on an iOS device, follow these steps:

Step 1. Select **Settings > Wi-Fi > Other.**

Step 2. Enter the network SSID.

Step 3. Touch **Security** and select a security type.

Step 4. Touch **Other Network.**

Step 5. Touch **Password** and enter the password.

Step 6. Touch **Join.**

Configure Cellular Data Settings (3.2.4)

Most cell phone carriers offer cellular data plans, but the bandwidth limitations and charges for usage vary widely by carrier and by plan within carriers. As a result, many mobile device users use their cellular data plans only when Wi-Fi service is not available.

The following are examples of how to turn cellular data on and off on Android and iOS devices.

Android Cellular Data

To turn on or off cellular data on an Android device, as shown in Figure 3-4, use the following steps:

Step 1. Select **Settings.**

Step 2. Under Wireless and Networks, touch **More.**

Step 3. Touch **Mobile Networks.**

Step 4. Touch **Data Enabled.**

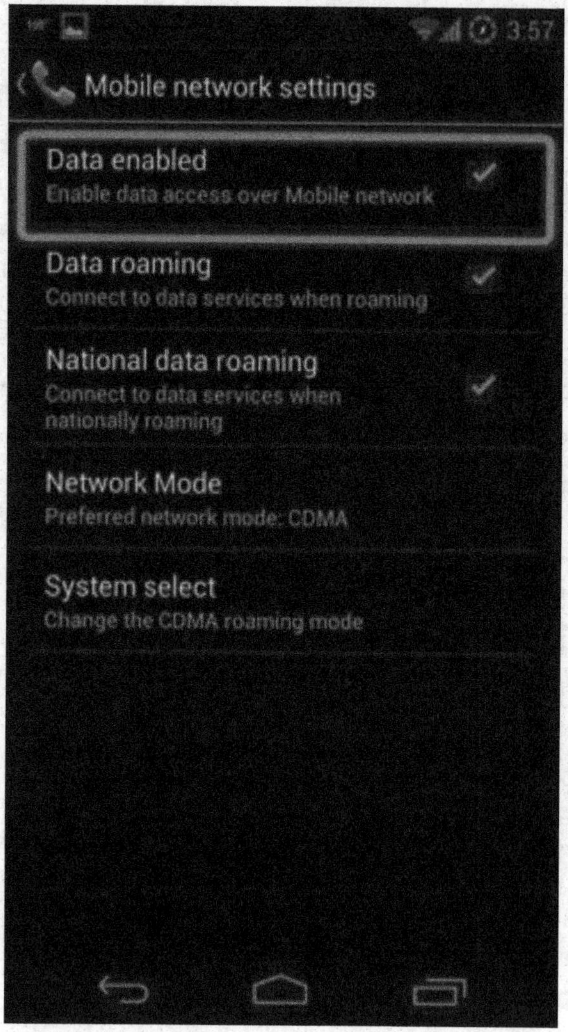

Figure 3-4 Android Cellular Data Setting

iOS Cellular Data

To turn on or off cellular data on an iOS device, simply select **Settings > Cellular Data** and slide the Cellular Data setting to **On** or **Off**, as shown in Figure 3-5.

Figure 3-5 iOS Cellular Data Setting

Mobile devices are preprogrammed to use a Wi-Fi network for Internet access if one is available and the device can connect to the access point and receive an IP address. If no Wi-Fi network is available, the device uses the cellular data capability if it is configured. Most of the time, transitions from one network to another are not obvious to the user. For example, as a mobile device moves from an area of 4G coverage to 3G coverage, the 4G radio shuts off and turns on the 3G radio. Connections are not lost during this transition.

Video

Video—Bluetooth Configuration on a Windows Laptop (3.2.5)

Refer to the online course to view this video.

Simple Connectivity with Bluetooth (3.2.6)

Mobile devices connect using many different methods. Cellular and Wi-Fi can be difficult to configure and require extra equipment such as towers and access points.

Cable connections are not always practical when connecting headsets or speakers. Bluetooth technology provides a simple way for mobile devices to connect to each other and to wireless accessories. Bluetooth is wireless, automatic, and uses very little power, which helps conserve battery life. Up to eight Bluetooth devices can be connected together at any one time.

These are some examples of how devices use Bluetooth:

- **Hands-free headset**—A small earpiece with a microphone can be used for making and receiving calls.
- **Keyboard or mouse**—A keyboard or mouse can be connected to a mobile device to make input easier.
- **Stereo control**—A mobile device can connect to a home or car stereo to play music.
- **Car speakerphone**—A device that contains a speaker and a microphone can be used for making and receiving calls.
- **Tethering**—A mobile device can connect to another mobile device or computer to share a network connection. (Tethering can also be performed with a Wi-Fi connection or a cable connection such as USB.)
- **Mobile speaker**—Portable speakers can connect to mobile devices to provide high-quality audio without a stereo system.

Bluetooth Pairing (3.2.7)

Bluetooth pairing occurs when two Bluetooth devices establish a connection to share resources. In order for the devices to pair, the Bluetooth radios are turned on, and one device begins searching for other devices. Other devices must be set to discoverable mode, also called visible, so that they can be detected. When a Bluetooth device is in discoverable mode, it transmits the following information when another Bluetooth device requests it:

- Name
- Bluetooth class
- Services that the device can use
- Technical information, such as the features or the Bluetooth specification that it supports

During the pairing process, a personal identification number (PIN) may be requested to authenticate the pairing process. The PIN is often a number but can also be a numeric code or passkey. The PIN is stored using pairing services, so it does not have to be entered the next time the device tries to connect. This is convenient when using

a headset with a smartphone, because they are paired automatically when the headset is turned on and within range.

To pair a Bluetooth device with an Android device, follow these steps:

Step 1. Follow the instructions for your device to place it in discoverable mode.

Step 2. Check the instructions for your device to find the connection PIN.

Step 3. Select **Settings > Wireless and Networks.**

Step 4. Touch **Bluetooth** to turn it on.

Step 5. Touch the **Bluetooth** tab.

Step 6. Touch **Scan for Devices.**

Step 7. Touch the discovered device to select it.

Step 8. Type the PIN.

Step 9. Touch the device name again to connect to it.

To pair a Bluetooth device with an iOS device, follow these steps:

Step 1. Follow the instructions for your device to place it in discoverable mode.

Step 2. Check the instructions for your device to find the connection PIN.

Step 3. Select **Settings > Bluetooth.**

Step 4. Touch **Bluetooth** to turn it on.

Step 5. Touch the discovered device to select it.

Step 6. Type the PIN.

Remember that mobile device operating systems are updated frequently. Always refer to the documentation from the manufacturer for your specific model device for the latest command reference.

Explore Your Network Settings on Your Mobile Device (3.2.8)

Now that you have reviewed the steps to configure and verify your Wi-Fi, cellular, and Bluetooth access, explore these settings on your own phone. If you have access to a Bluetooth device, like headphones or a speaker, connect it to your phone. Notice that you can be using all three of these wireless services simultaneously, each serving a different role. You could be listening to music (Bluetooth), researching on the Internet (Wi-Fi), and receiving text messages (cellular).

Wireless and Mobile Networks Summary (3.3)

The following is a summary of each topic in the chapter and some questions for your reflection.

What Did I Learn in This Chapter? (3.3.1)

- **Wireless Networks**—Mobile phones use radio waves to transmit voice signals to antennas mounted on towers located in specific geographic areas. When a telephone call is made, the voice signal is relayed from one tower to another tower until it is delivered to its destination. This type of network is used when you make a phone call to another mobile phone or to a wired telephone. It is also used to send text messages directly from the phone. The most common type of cellular telephone network is called a GSM network. The abbreviations 3G, 4G, 4G-LTE, and 5G are used to describe enhanced cell phone networks that are optimized for the fast transmission of data. Currently, 4G still dominates as the current mobile network used by most phones.

  In addition to the GSM and 4G/5G transmitters and receivers, smartphones make connections in a variety of ways.

  Wi-Fi transmitters and receivers located within the smartphone enable the phone to connect to local networks and the Internet. Wi-Fi networks are usually privately owned but often provide guest or public access hotspots. A hotspot is an area where Wi-Fi signals are available.

  Bluetooth is wireless technology that allows devices to communicate over short distances. Multiple devices can be connected at the same time with Bluetooth.

  NFC is a wireless communication technology that enables data to be exchanged by devices that are in very close proximity to each other, usually less than a few centimeters.

- **Mobile Device Connectivity**—Almost all mobile devices are capable of connecting to Wi-Fi networks. Take these precautions to protect Wi-Fi communications on mobile devices:
  - Never send login or password information using unencrypted text (plaintext).
  - Use a VPN connection when possible if you are sending sensitive data.
  - Enable security on home networks.
  - Use WPA2 or higher encryption for security.

The two most popular operating systems for mobile devices are Android and Apple iOS. Mobile devices are preprogrammed to use a Wi-Fi network for Internet access if one is available, and the device can connect to the access point and receive an IP address. If no Wi-Fi network is available, the device uses the cellular data capability if it is configured.

Bluetooth technology provides a simple way for mobile devices to connect to each other and to wireless accessories. Bluetooth is wireless, automatic, and uses very little power, which helps conserve battery life. Some examples of devices that use Bluetooth include hands-free headsets, keyboards, a mouse, stereo controls, car speakerphones, and mobile speakers.

Bluetooth pairing occurs when two Bluetooth devices establish a connection to share resources. In order for the devices to pair, the Bluetooth radios are turned on, and one device begins searching for other devices. Other devices must be set to discoverable mode, also called visible, so that they can be detected.

When a Bluetooth device is in discoverable mode, it transmits the following information when another Bluetooth device requests it:

- Name
- Bluetooth class
- Services that the device can use
- Technical information, such as the features or the Bluetooth specification that it supports

During the pairing process, a PIN may be requested to authenticate the pairing process.

Reflection Questions (3.3.2)

I find it fascinating that you can send and receive data without plugging one device into another using a cable. I am going to get a tablet so I can take this course while I am at the beach! How many ways does your tablet or smartphone communicate when you are away from your home network?

Practice

There are no labs or Packet Tracer activities in this chapter.

Check Your Understanding Questions

Complete all the review questions listed here to test your understanding of the topics and concepts in this chapter. Appendix A, "Answers to 'Check Your Understanding' Questions," lists the answers.

1. What term is used to describe connecting a mobile device to another mobile device or computer to share a network connection?
   a. Joining
   b. Syncing
   c. Pairing
   d. Tethering

2. Which wireless technology uses a device-pairing process to communicate and operates over short distances of 100 meters?
   a. Wireless wide area network
   b. Wi-Fi
   c. Bluetooth
   d. GPS

3. What technology enables a cell phone to be used as a hands-free device?
   a. Wi-Fi
   b. Bluetooth
   c. 4G
   d. NFC

4. A student purchased a new Wi-Fi–enabled tablet computer. What is required to connect this device to the Internet?
   a. A 3G or 4G network
   b. A telephone company
   c. A wireless LAN
   d. A mobile phone service provider

5. Which technology allows a mobile device to establish wireless communication with another mobile device by touching them together?

   a. Bluetooth
   b. NFC
   c. GPS
   d. 4G

6. Which technology will allow a mobile device to share an Internet connection with other devices via tethering?

   a. GPS
   b. Bluetooth
   c. Near Field Communication
   d. Wi-Fi

7. What are two methods typically used on a mobile device to provide Internet connectivity? (Choose two.)

   a. Cellular
   b. Bluetooth
   c. Wi-Fi
   d. NFC
   e. GPS

8. Which wireless technology allows a customer to connect to a payment system with a smartphone?

   a. NFC
   b. Wi-Fi
   c. GPS
   d. Bluetooth

9. A salesperson is using a smartphone map application to locate a business. What wireless technology enables the smartphone to receive satellite geolocation information for the map application?

   a. GPS
   b. NFC
   c. Wi-Fi
   d. Bluetooth

10. What two pieces of information are required when manually connecting either an iOS device or an Android device to a secured wireless network? (Choose two.)

    a. IP address
    b. SSID
    c. Username
    d. Password

11. Which wireless technology can be used to connect wireless headphones to a computer?

    a. NFC
    b. Bluetooth
    c. Wi-Fi
    d. 4G

CHAPTER 4

Build a Home Network

Objectives

Upon completion of this chapter, you will be able to answer the following questions:

- What are the components required to build a home network?
- What are wired and wireless network technologies?
- What is Wi-Fi?
- How do you configure wireless devices for secure communications?

Key Terms

This chapter uses the following key terms. You can find the definitions in the Glossary.

coaxial cable   *Page 62*

fiber-optic cable   *Page 63*

wireless LAN (WLAN)   *Page 61*

Introduction (4.0)

Kishori and Shridhar are washing the dishes after dinner. Kishori is watching a favorite movie on her tablet while putting the dishes away. She asks Shridhar if her tablet works exactly as her mobile phone does. He explains that there are some tablets that do use a mobile network, but that her tablet works on the Wi-Fi network in her house. She tells him that she knows the Internet service must come in from that box in the corner of the living room. That is all she knows!

Shridhar explains that the box in the corner is a home router. The router is connected to the Internet. Home routers typically have two primary types of ports: Ethernet ports and Internet ports. In addition to the wired ports, many home routers include a radio antenna and a built-in wireless access point. Kishori mostly uses wireless at home. Now Shridhar is worried about his mother's wireless security. Since she did not know what the router was, she probably did not change her default password on the router! Shridhar logs into the router and makes some changes to keep Kishori's network and devices safer.

Have you ever set up a router? Have you thought about the need to have secure communications over wireless devices? This chapter will give you the knowledge to build a home network and configure wireless devices for secure communication.

Home Network Basics (4.1)

Not long ago, home networks consisted of a desktop PC, a modem for Internet service, and perhaps a printer. In the homes of today, there are dozens of devices that rely on network connectivity. We can watch our security cameras from apps on our smartphones, make a telephone call from our PCs, and stream live video content from anywhere in the world.

Video

Video—Typical Home Network Setup (4.1.1)

Refer to the online course to view this video.

Components of a Home Network (4.1.2)

In addition to an integrated router, many different types of devices might be connected to a home network, as shown in Figure 4-1. Here are a few examples:

- Desktop and laptop computers
- Gaming systems

- Smart TV systems
- Printers
- Scanners
- Security cameras
- Telephones
- Climate control devices

As the new technologies come on the market, more and more household functions will rely on the network to provide connectivity and control.

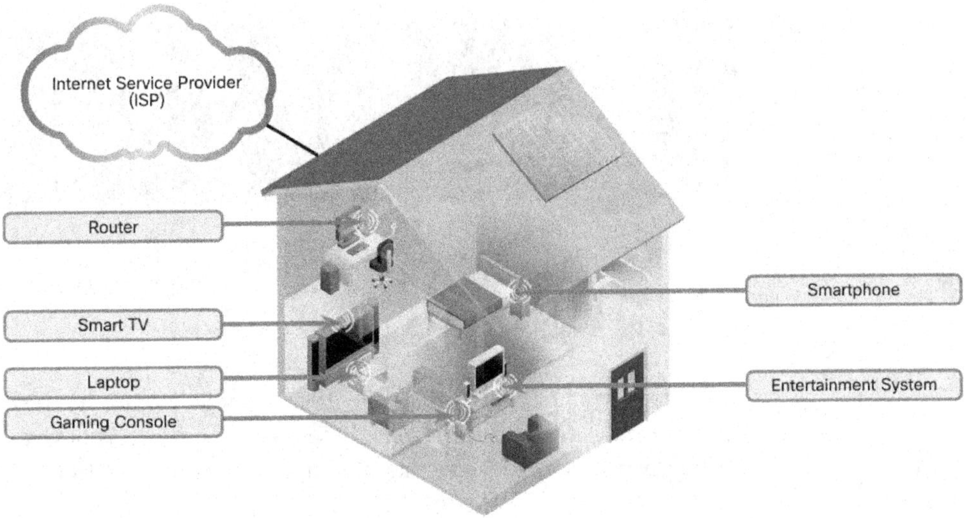

Figure 4-1 Home Wireless Local Area Network (WLAN)

Typical Home Network Routers (4.1.3)

Small business and home routers typically have two primary types of ports:

- **Ethernet ports**—These ports connect to the internal switch portion of the router. These ports are usually labeled Ethernet or LAN, as shown in Figure 4-2. All devices connected to the switch ports are on the same local network.
- **Internet port**—This port is used to connect the device to another network. The Internet port connects the router to a different network than the Ethernet ports. This port is often used to connect to the cable or DSL modem in order to access the Internet.

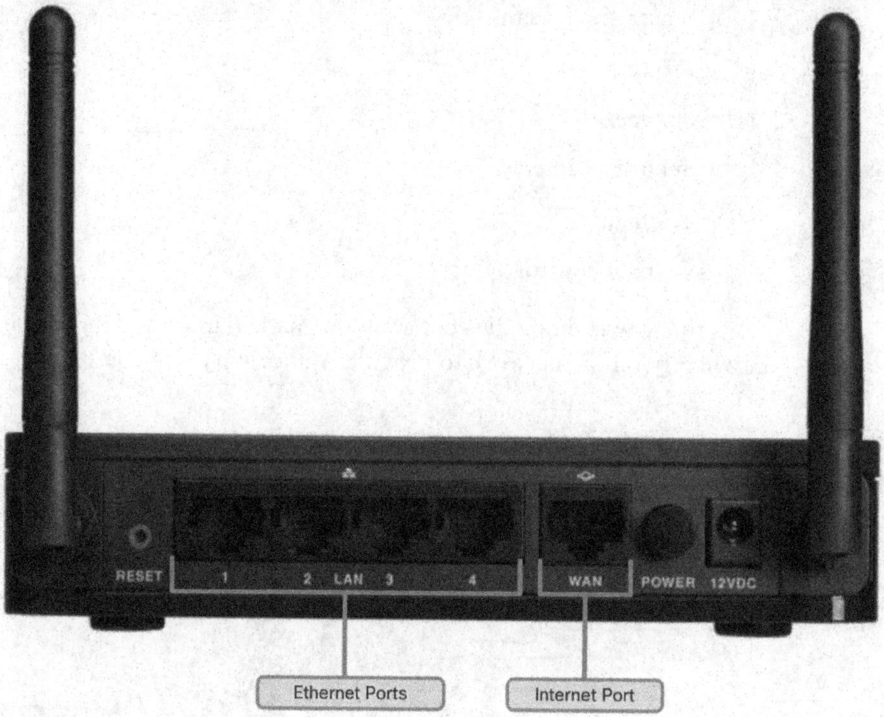

Figure 4-2 Back Panel of a Home Wireless Router

In addition to the wired ports, many home routers include a radio antenna and a built-in wireless access point (AP). By default, the wireless devices are on the same local network as the devices that are physically plugged into the LAN switch ports. The Internet port or WAN port is the only port that is on a different network in the default configuration.

Interactive Graphic

Check Your Understanding—Home Network Basics (4.1.4)

Refer to the online course to complete this activity.

Network Technologies in the Home (4.2)

What would we do without wireless? Because of the ever-increasing number of things that have the capability of connecting to the Internet using wireless technologies, most home networks include some type of wireless network functionality.

LAN Wireless Frequencies (4.2.1)

The wireless technologies most frequently used in home networks are in the unlicensed 2.4 GHz and 5 GHz frequency ranges.

Bluetooth is a technology that makes use of the 2.4 GHz band. It is limited to low-speed, short-range communications but can communicate with many devices at the same time. This one-to-many communication has made Bluetooth technology the preferred method for connecting computer peripherals such as wireless mice, keyboards, and printers. Bluetooth also is a good method for transmitting audio to speakers or headphones.

Other technologies that use the 2.4 GHz and 5 GHz bands are the modern *wireless LAN (WLAN)* technologies that conform to the various IEEE 802.11 standards. Unlike Bluetooth technology, 802.11 devices transmit at a much higher power level, giving them a greater range and improved throughput. Certain areas of the electromagnetic spectrum can be used without a permit.

Figure 4-3 shows where wireless technologies exist on the electromagnetic spectrum.

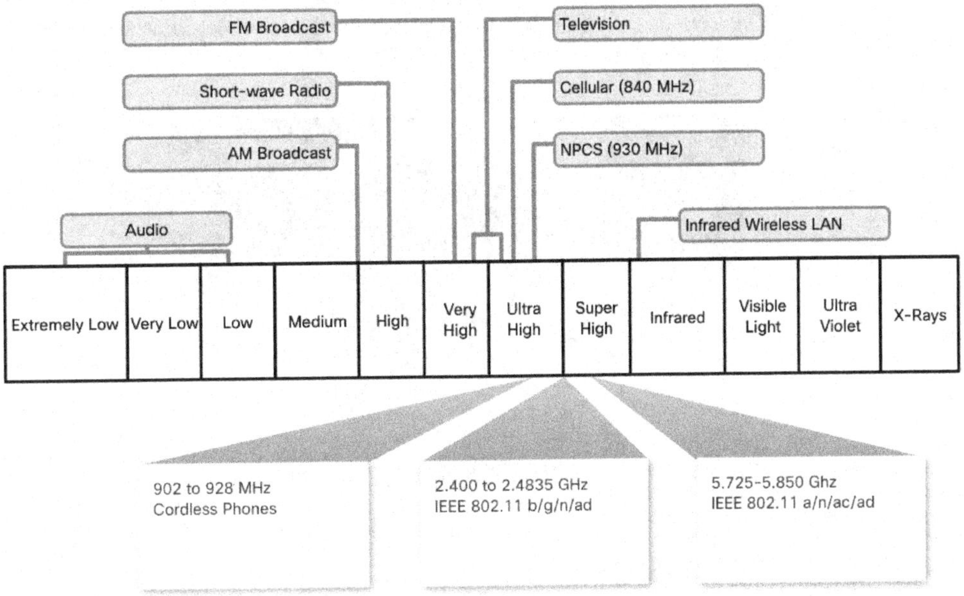

Figure 4-3 Electromagnetic Spectrum

Wired Network Technologies (4.2.2)

Although many home network devices support wireless communications, there are still a few applications where devices benefit from a wired switch connection that is not shared with other users on the network.

The most commonly implemented wired protocol is the Ethernet protocol. Ethernet uses a suite of protocols that allows network devices to communicate over a wired LAN connection. An Ethernet LAN can connect devices using many different types of wiring media.

Directly connected devices use an Ethernet patch cable, usually unshielded twisted-pair (UTP). These cables come in various lengths and can be purchased with the RJ-45 connectors already installed. Recently constructed homes may have Ethernet jacks already wired in the walls of the home. For those homes that do not have UTP wiring, there are other technologies, such as powerline, that can distribute wired connectivity throughout the premises.

Category 5e Cable

Category 5e cable (see Figure 4-4) is the most common type of wiring used in a LAN. The cable is made up of four pairs of wires that are twisted to reduce electrical interference.

Figure 4-4 Example of Category 5e Cable

Coaxial Cable

Coaxial cable (see Figure 4-5) has an inner wire surrounded by a tubular insulating layer, which in turn is surrounded by a tubular conducting shield. Most coax cables also have an external insulating sheath or jacket.

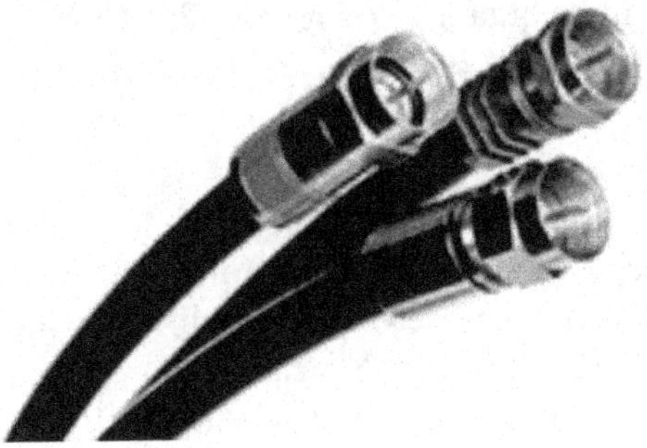

Figure 4-5 Example of a Coaxial Cable

Fiber-Optic Cable

Fiber-optic cable (see Figure 4-6) can be either glass or plastic with a diameter about the same as a human hair, and it can carry digital information at very high speeds over long distances. Fiber-optic cables have a very high bandwidth, which enables them to carry very large amounts of data.

Figure 4-6 Example of a Fiber-Optic Cable

Interactive Graphic

Check Your Understanding—Network Technologies in the Home (4.2.3)

Refer to the online course to complete this activity.

Wireless Standards (4.3)

A number of standards have been developed to ensure that wireless devices can communicate. They specify the RF spectrum used, data rates, how the information is

transmitted, and more. The main organization responsible for the creation of wireless technical standards is the Institute of Electrical and Electronics Engineers (IEEE).

Wi-Fi Networks (4.3.1)

The IEEE 802.11 standard governs the WLAN environment. Various amendments to the IEEE 802.11 standard describe characteristics for different standards of wireless communications. Wireless standards for LANs use the 2.4 GHz and 5 GHz frequency bands. Collectively these technologies are referred to as Wi-Fi.

Another organization, known as the Wi-Fi Alliance, is responsible for testing wireless LAN devices from different manufacturers. The Wi-Fi logo on a device means that this equipment meets standards and should operate with other devices that use the same standards.

Wireless standards are constantly improving the connectivity and speed of Wi-Fi networks. It is important to be aware of new standards as they are introduced because manufacturers of wireless devices will implement these standards quickly in their new products.

Do you have a wireless network in your home? Do you know what standards are supported by your wireless router?

Wireless Settings (4.3.2)

The Packet Tracer Basic Wireless Settings interface is shown in Figure 4-7. Wireless routers using the 802.11 standards have multiple settings that have to be configured. These settings include the following:

- **Network Mode**—Determines the type of technology that must be supported; for example, 802.11b, 802.11g, 802.11n, or Mixed Mode.
- **Network Name (SSID)**—Used to identify the WLAN. All devices that wish to participate in the WLAN must have the same SSID.
- **Standard Channel**—Specifies the channel over which communication will occur. By default, this is set to Auto to allow the AP to determine the optimum channel to use.
- **SSID Broadcast**—Determines if the SSID will be broadcast to all devices within range. By default, this is set to Enabled.

Note

SSID stands for Service Set Identifier.

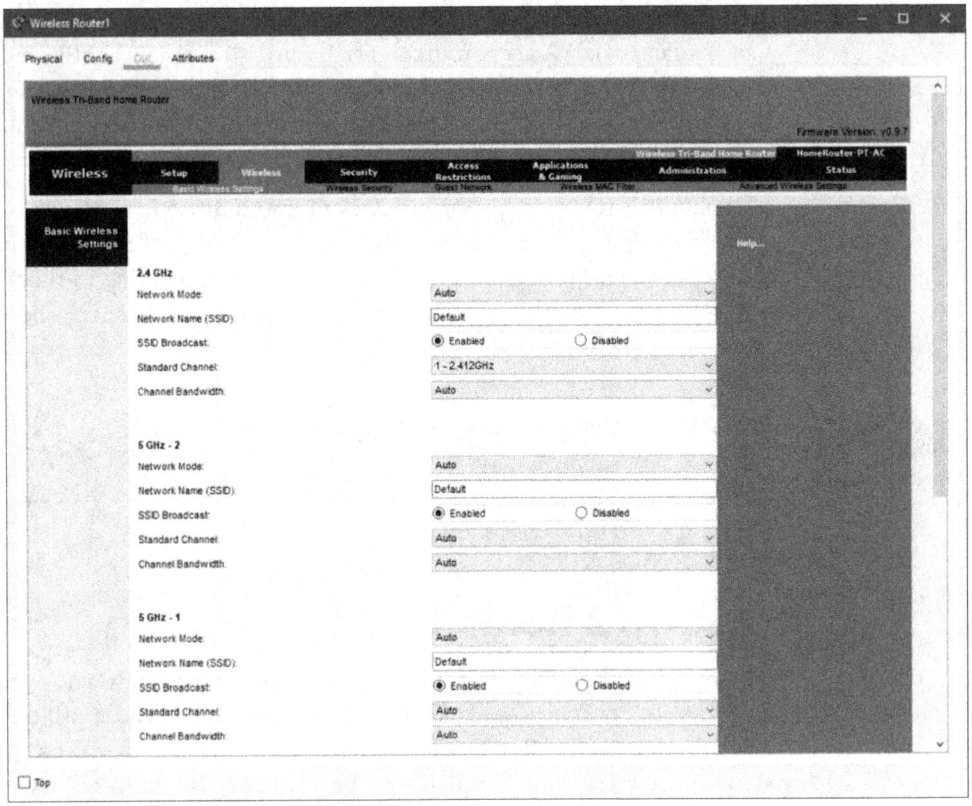

Figure 4-7 Packet Tracer Basic Wireless Settings Interface

Network Mode

The 802.11 protocol can provide increased throughput based on the wireless network environment. If all wireless devices connect with the same 802.11 standard, maximum speeds can be obtained for that standard. If the access point is configured to accept only one 802.11 standard, devices that do not use that standard cannot connect to the access point.

A mixed mode wireless network environment can include devices that use any of the existing Wi-Fi standards. This environment provides easy access for older devices that need a wireless connection but do not support the latest standards.

When building a wireless network, make sure that the wireless components connect to the appropriate WLAN. This is done using the SSID.

The SSID is a case-sensitive, alphanumeric string that contains up to 32 characters. It is sent in the header of all frames transmitted over the WLAN. The SSID is used to tell wireless devices, called wireless stations (STAs), which WLAN they belong to and with which other devices they can communicate.

The SSID is used to identify a specific wireless network. It is essentially the name of the network. Wireless routers usually broadcast their configured SSIDs by default. The SSID broadcast allows other devices and wireless clients to automatically discover the name of the wireless network. When the SSID broadcast is disabled, you must manually enter the SSID on wireless devices.

Disabling SSID broadcasting can make it more difficult for legitimate clients to find the wireless network. However, simply turning off the SSID broadcast is not sufficient to prevent unauthorized clients from connecting to the wireless network. All wireless networks should use the strongest available encryption to restrict unauthorized access.

Interactive Graphic

Check Your Understanding—Wireless Standards (4.3.3)

Refer to the online course to complete this activity.

Set Up a Home Router (4.4)

Many wireless routers designed for home use have an automatic setup utility that can be used to configure the basic settings on the router. These utilities usually require a PC or laptop to be connected to a wired port on the router. If no device is available that has a wired connection, it may be necessary to configure the wireless client software on the laptop or tablet first.

First Time Setup (4.4.1)

To connect to the router using a wired connection, plug an Ethernet patch cable into the network port on the computer. Plug the other end into a LAN/Ethernet port on the router. Do not plug the cable into the port or interface that is labeled Internet (or WAN). The Internet port connects to the DSL or cable modem. Some home routers may have a built-in modem for Internet connections. If this is the case, verify that the type of connection is correct for your Internet service. A cable modem connection has a coaxial terminal to accept a BNC-type connector. A DSL connection will have a port for a telephone-type cable, usually an RJ-11 connector.

After you confirm that the computer is connected to the network router and the link lights on the NIC indicate a working connection, the computer needs an IP address. Most network routers are set up so that the computer receives an IP address automatically from a local Dynamic Host Configuration Protocol (DHCP) server that is

automatically configured on the wireless router. If the computer does not have an IP address, check the router documentation and configure the PC or tablet with a unique IP address, subnet mask, default gateway, and Domain Name System (DNS) information.

Design Considerations (4.4.2)

Before entering the configuration utility or manually configuring the router through a web browser, you should consider the following questions regarding your network and how it will be used. You do not want to configure the router and have that configuration limit what you are able to do on the network, nor do you want to leave your network unprotected.

- **What should I name my network?**—If SSID broadcasting is enabled, the SSID name will be seen by all wireless clients within your signal range. Many times the SSID gives away too much information about the network to unknown client devices. You should not include the device model or brand name as part of the SSID. Wireless devices have default settings that are easy to find on the Internet, as well as known security weaknesses.
- **What types of devices will attach to my network?**—Wireless devices contain radio transmitter/receivers that function within a specific frequency range. If a device has the necessary radio only for 802.11 b/g, it will not connect if the wireless router or AP is configured to accept only 802.11n or 802.11ac standards. If all devices support the same standard, the network will work at its optimum speed. If you have devices that do not support the 802.11n or 802.11ac standards, then you will have to enable legacy mode (see Figure 4-8). A legacy mode wireless network environment varies among router models but can include a combination of 802.11a, 802.11b, 802.11g, 802.11n, and 802.11ac. This environment provides easy access for legacy devices that need a wireless connection.
- **How do I add new devices?**—The decision regarding who can access your home network should be determined by how you plan to use the network. On some wireless routers, it is possible to set up guest access. This is a special SSID coverage area that allows open access but restricts that access to using the Internet only.

Note

Some wireless routers may label legacy mode as mixed mode.

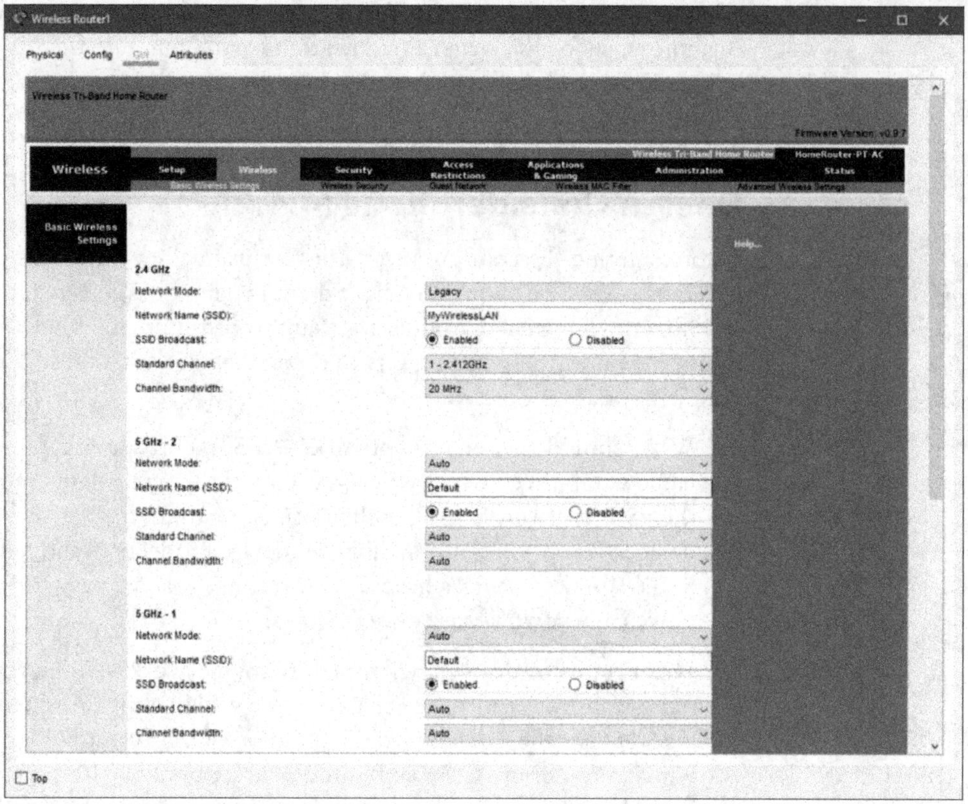

Figure 4-8 Packet Tracer WLAN Configuration Example

Video

Video—Wireless Router and Client Configuration (4.4.3)

Refer to the online course to view this video.

Packet Tracer Activity

Packet Tracer—Configure a Wireless Router and Client (4.4.4)

In this Packet Tracer activity, you will complete the following objectives:

- Part 1: Connect the Devices
- Part 2: Configure the Wireless Router
- Part 3: Configure IP Addressing and Test Connectivity

Refer to the online course to complete this activity.

Build a Home Network Summary (4.5)

The following is a summary of each topic in the chapter and some questions for your reflection.

What Did I Learn in This Chapter? (4.5.1)

- **Home Network Basics**—Most home networks consist of at least two separate networks. The public network comes in from the service provider. The router is connected to the Internet. Most likely, the home router is equipped with both wired and wireless capabilities. A home network is a small LAN with devices that usually connect to an integrated router and to each other to exchange information.

  Wireless technology is fairly easy and inexpensive to install. Advantages of wireless LAN technology include mobility, scalability, flexibility, cost savings, reduced installation time, and reliability in harsh environments.

  In addition to an integrated router, many different types of devices might be connected to a home network. Examples include desktop and laptop computers, gaming systems, smart TV systems, printers, scanners, security cameras, and climate control devices.

  Small business and home routers typically have two primary types of ports: Ethernet/LAN ports and Internet/WAN ports. In addition to the wired ports, many home routers include a radio antenna and a built-in wireless access point.

- **Network Technologies in the Home**—Wireless technologies use electromagnetic waves to carry information between devices. The electromagnetic spectrum includes radio and television broadcast bands, visible light, X-rays, and gamma-rays. Some types of electromagnetic waves are not suitable for carrying data. Other parts of the spectrum are regulated by governments and licensed to various organizations for specific applications.

  Certain unlicensed sections of the spectrum are incorporated into consumer products, including the Wi-Fi routers found in most homes. The wireless technologies most frequently used in home networks are in the unlicensed 2.4 GHz and 5 GHz frequency ranges. Bluetooth uses the 2.4 GHz band. Other technologies that use the 2.4 GHz and 5 GHz bands are the modern wireless LAN (WLAN) technologies that conform to the various IEEE 802.11 standards. Unlike Bluetooth technology, 802.11 devices transmit at a much higher power level, giving them a greater range and improved throughput.

  Although many home network devices support wireless communications, there are still a few applications where devices benefit from a wired switch connection.

Ethernet is the most commonly implemented wired protocol. Directly connected devices use an Ethernet patch cable, usually unshielded twisted-pair. Category 5e cable is the most common type of wiring used in a LAN. The cable is made up of four pairs of wires that are twisted to reduce electrical interference. For homes that do not have UTP wiring, other technologies, such as powerline, can distribute wired connectivity throughout the premises.

- **Wireless Standards**—The IEEE 802.11 standard governs the WLAN environment. Wireless standards for LANs use the 2.4 GHz and 5 GHz frequency bands. Collectively, these technologies are referred to as Wi-Fi. The Wi-Fi Alliance is responsible for testing wireless LAN devices from different manufacturers.

  Wireless routers using the 802.11 standards have multiple settings that have to be configured, including the following:

  - **Network Mode**—Determines the type of technology that must be supported, such as 802.11b, 802.11g, 802.11n, or Mixed Mode.
  - **Network Name (SSID)**—Used to identify the WLAN. All devices that wish to participate in the WLAN must have the same SSID.
  - **Standard Channel**—Specifies the channel over which communication will occur; set to Auto by default to allow the AP to determine the optimum channel to use.
  - **SSID Broadcast**—Determines if the SSID will be broadcast to all devices within range; set to Enabled by default.

  The 802.11 protocol can provide increased throughput based on the wireless network environment. If all wireless devices connect with the same 802.11 standard, maximum speeds can be obtained for that standard. If the AP is configured to accept only one 802.11 standard, devices that do not use that standard cannot connect to the AP. A mixed mode wireless network environment can include devices that use any of the existing Wi-Fi standards.

  When building a wireless network, make sure that the wireless components connect to the appropriate WLAN. The SSID is used to tell wireless devices, called STAs, which WLAN they belong to and with which other devices they can communicate. The SSID broadcast allows other devices and wireless clients to automatically discover the name of the wireless network. When the SSID broadcast is disabled, you must manually enter the SSID on wireless devices.

- **Set Up a Home Router**—Many wireless routers designed for home use have an automatic setup utility that can be used to configure the basic settings on the router. To connect to the router using a wired connection, plug an Ethernet patch cable into the network port on the computer. Plug the other end into a LAN port on the router.

After the computer is connected to the network router and the link lights on the NIC indicate a working connection, the computer needs an IP address. Most network routers are set up so that the computer receives an IP address automatically from a local DHCP server that is automatically configured on the wireless router.

Before entering the configuration utility or manually configuring the router through a web browser, you should consider how your network will be used. Consider what you will call your network and what devices should connect to your network. It is not a good practice to include the device model or brand name as part of the SSID since Internet searches can expose security weaknesses.

You should decide who can access your home network based on how you plan to use the network. Many routers support MAC address filtering. This enables you to specifically identify who is allowed on the wireless network. This makes the wireless network more secure, but it is also less flexible when connecting new devices. On some wireless routers, it is possible to set up guest access. This is a special SSID coverage area that allows open access but restricts that access to using the Internet only.

Reflection Questions (4.5.2)

I had such a good time reading this chapter at the beach that I think I'm going to set up a wireless network at home. That way, I can keep up with this course anywhere in my home. Building your home network to be a wireless network just makes sense. I can work in the west side of my web and catch the sun setting, then move back to the east side in the morning. It's so much nicer than being stuck at my desk all day! Have you set up your own home network? If not, could you do it if you had to?

Practice

The following Packet Tracer activity provides practice with the topics introduced in this chapter.

Packet Tracer Activity

Packet Tracer Activities

Packet Tracer—Configure a Wireless Router and Client (4.4.4)

Check Your Understanding Questions

Complete all the review questions listed here to test your understanding of the topics and concepts in this chapter. Appendix A, "Answers to 'Check Your Understanding' Questions," lists the answers.

1. Which type of wireless communication is based on 802.11 standards?
   a. Wi-Fi
   b. Cellular WAN
   c. Bluetooth
   d. Infrared
2. What wireless router configuration would stop outsiders from using your home network?
   a. IP address
   b. Encryption
   c. Router location
   d. Network name
3. What type of device is commonly connected to the Ethernet switch ports on a home wireless router?
   a. DSL modem
   b. Cable modem
   c. Wireless antenna
   d. LAN device

4. Which type of network technology is used for low-speed communication between peripheral devices?

    a. Bluetooth
    b. Ethernet
    c. 802.11
    d. Channels

5. What can be used to allow visitors' mobile devices to connect to a wireless network and restrict access of those devices to only the Internet?

    a. MAC address filtering
    b. Guest SSID
    c. Encryption
    d. Authentication

6. What purpose would a home user have for implementing Wi-Fi?

    a. To hear various radio stations
    b. To connect a keyboard to a PC
    c. To connect wireless headphones to a mobile device
    d. To create a wireless network usable by other devices

7. What is another term for the Internet port of a wireless router?

    a. WAN port
    b. LAN port
    c. Local port
    d. Switch port

8. Which type of network cable consists of four pairs of twisted wires?

    a. Category 5e
    b. Coaxial
    c. Ethernet over powerline
    d. Fiber optic

9. What is the default SSID Broadcast setting on a wireless router?

    a. Enabled
    b. Disabled
    c. Auto
    d. Off

10. Which is a characteristic of the network SSID?

    a. It is case sensitive.

    b. It contains exactly 16 characters.

    c. It is encrypted by default.

    d. It is required only for guest access.

CHAPTER 5

Communication Principles

Objectives

Upon completion of this chapter, you will be able to answer the following questions:

- What are network communication protocols?
- What are network communication standards?
- What is the difference between the OSI and TCP/IP models?

Key Terms

This chapter uses the following key terms. You can find the definitions in the Glossary.

International Organization for Standardization (ISO)   *Page 83*

Internet Engineering Task Force (IETF)   *Page 80*

Open Systems Interconnection (OSI)   *Page 83*

protocol   *Page 79*

protocol suite   *Page 82*

reference model   *Page 82*

Request for Comments (RFC)   *Page 80*

Introduction (5.0)

The next day at the hospital, Kishori has a new patient, Srinivas, who has just been admitted to a room. He is from Narayanpet and speaks Telugu. Kishori speaks Marathi. These two Indian languages are very different. Kishori and Srinivas do not speak each other's native language. However, they do both speak English. Therefore, they decide to communicate using English.

Before beginning to communicate with each other, we establish rules or agreements to govern the conversation. Just like Kishori and Srinivas, we decide what method of communication we should use, and what language we should use. We may also need to confirm that our messages are received. For example, Kishori may have Srinivas sign a document verifying that he has understood Kishori's care instructions.

Networks also need rules, or protocols, to ensure successful communication. This chapter will cover the communication principles for networks. Let's get started!

Networking Protocols (5.1)

Before communicating with one another, individuals must use established rules or agreements to govern the conversation. Rules are also required for devices on a network to communicate.

Communication Protocols (5.1.1)

Communication in our daily lives takes many forms and occurs in many environments. We have different expectations depending on whether we are chatting via the Internet or participating in a job interview. Each situation has its corresponding expected behaviors and styles.

Before beginning to communicate with each other, we establish rules or agreements to govern the conversation. These agreements include the following:

- **Method**—What method of communication should we use? (See Figure 5-1.)
- **Language**—What language should we use? (See Figure 5-2.)
- **Confirmation**—Do we need to confirm that our messages are received? (See Figure 5-3.)

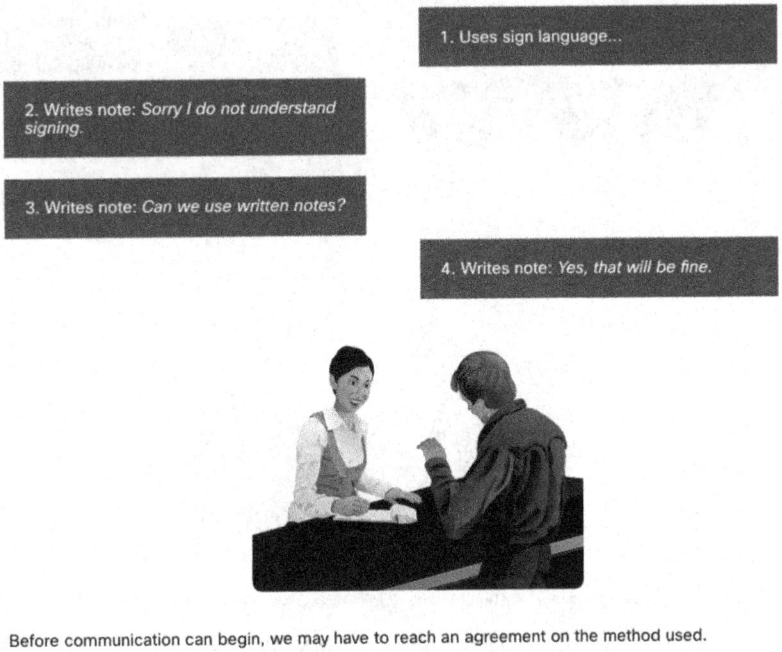

Figure 5-1 Choosing a Method of Communication

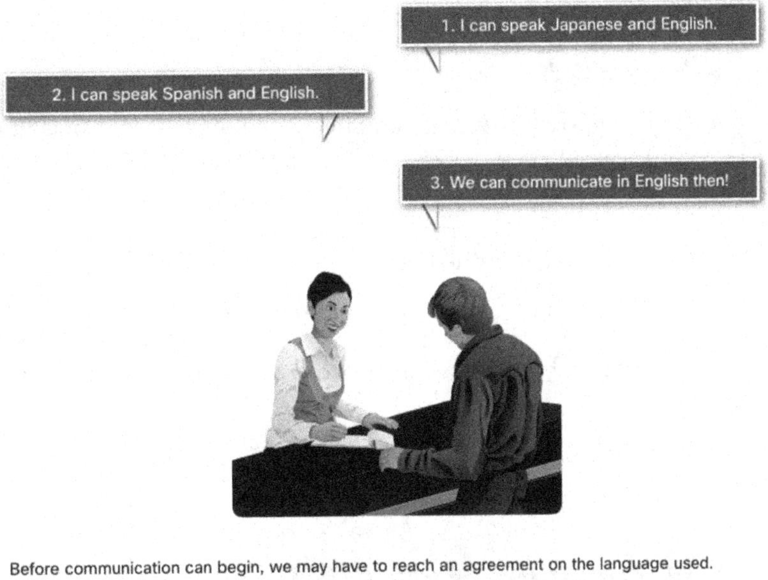

Figure 5-2 Choosing a Language for Communication

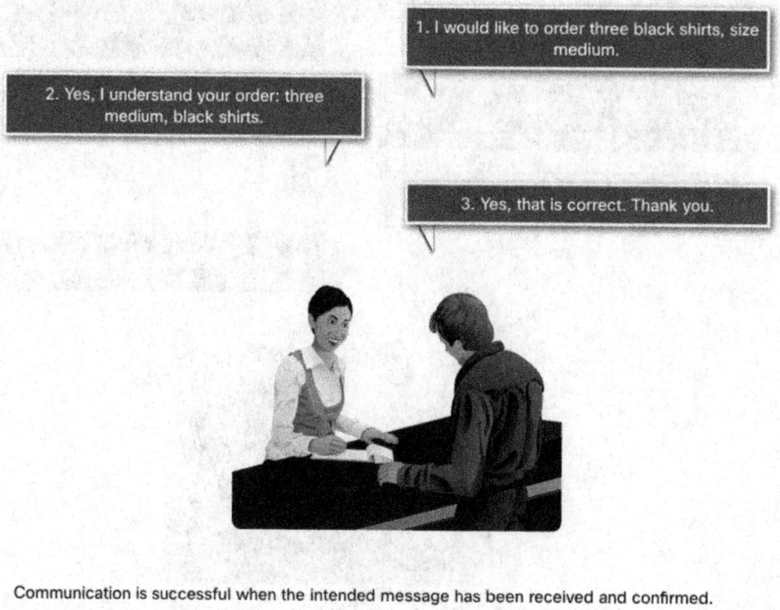

Figure 5-3 Verifying That Communication Was Successful

These rules, or *protocols*, must be followed for the message to be successfully delivered and understood. Among the protocols that govern successful human communication are these:

- An identified sender and receiver
- Agreed-upon method of communicating (face-to-face, telephone, letter, photograph)
- Common language and grammar
- Speed and timing of delivery
- Confirmation or acknowledgment requirements

The techniques that are used in network communications share these fundamentals with human conversations.

Think about the commonly accepted protocols for sending text messages to your friends.

Why Protocols Matter (5.1.2)

Just like humans, computers use rules, or protocols, to communicate. Protocols are required for computers to properly communicate across the network. In both a wired

and wireless environment, a local network is defined as an area where all hosts must "speak the same language," which in computer terms means they must "share a common protocol."

If everyone in the same room spoke a different language, they would not be able to communicate. Likewise, if devices in a local network did not use the same protocols, they would not be able to communicate.

Networking *protocols* define many aspects of communication over the local network. As shown in Table 5-1, these include message format, message size, timing, encoding, encapsulation, and message pattern.

Table 5-1 Protocol Characteristics

Protocol Characteristic	Description
Message format	When a message is sent, it must use a specific format or structure. Message formats depend on the type of message and the channel that is used to deliver the message.
Message size	The rules that govern the size of the pieces communicated across the network are very strict. They can also be different, depending on the channel used. When a long message is sent from one host to another over a network, it may be necessary to break the message into smaller pieces to ensure that the message can be delivered reliably.
Timing	Many network communication functions are dependent on timing. Timing determines the speed at which the bits are transmitted across the network. It also affects when an individual host can send data and the total amount of data that can be sent in any one transmission.
Encoding	Messages sent across the network are first converted into bits by the sending host. Each bit is encoded into a pattern of sounds, light waves, or electrical pulses depending on the network media over which the bits are transmitted. The destination host receives and decodes the signals to interpret the message.
Encapsulation	Each message transmitted on a network must include a header that contains addressing information that identifies the source and destination hosts; otherwise, it cannot be delivered. Encapsulation is the process of adding this information to the pieces of data that make up the message. In addition to addressing, there may be other information in the header that ensures that the message is delivered to the correct application on the destination host.
Message pattern	Some messages require an acknowledgment before the next message can be sent. This type of request/response pattern is a common aspect of many networking protocols. However, there are other types of messages that may be simply streamed across the network, without concern as to whether they reach their destination.

Communication Standards (5.2)

Communication standards are required in all aspects of human communications. For example, when addressing an envelope, there is a standard regarding the placement of the sender's address, the destination address, and the stamp. Network communication also requires standards to ensure that all the devices in the network are using the same rules to send and receive information.

Video

Video—Devices in a Bubble (5.2.1)

Refer to the online course to view this video.

The Internet and Standards (5.2.2)

With the increasing number of new devices and technologies coming online, how is it possible to manage all the changes and still reliably deliver services such as email? The answer is Internet standards.

A *standard* is a set of rules that determines how something must be done. Networking and Internet standards ensure that all devices connecting to the network implement the same set of rules or protocols in the same manner. Using standards enables different types of devices to send information to each other over the Internet. For example, the way in which an email is formatted, forwarded, and received by all devices is done according to a standard. If one person sends an email via a personal computer, another person can use a mobile phone to receive and read the email as long as the mobile phone uses the same standards as the personal computer.

Network Standards Organizations (5.2.3)

An Internet standard is the end result of a comprehensive cycle of discussion, problem solving, and testing. These different standards are developed, published, and maintained by a variety of organizations. When a new standard is proposed, each stage of the development and approval process is recorded in a numbered *Request for Comments (RFC)* document so that the evolution of the standard is tracked. RFCs for Internet standards are published and managed by the *Internet Engineering Task Force (IETF)*.

The logos of IETF and other standards organizations that support the Internet are shown in Figure 5-4.

Figure 5-4 Internet Standards Organizations

Network Communication Models (5.3)

Network communication models help us understand the various components and protocols used in network communications. These models help us see the function of each protocol and their relationship to other protocols.

Video

Video—Network Protocols (5.3.1)

Refer to the online course to view this video.

Video

Video—The Protocol Stack (5.3.2)

Refer to the online course to view this video.

The TCP/IP Model (5.3.3)

Layered models help us visualize how the various protocols work together to enable network communications. A layered model depicts the operation of the protocols

occurring within each layer, as well as the interaction with the layers above and below it. The layered model has many benefits:

- Assists in protocol design, because protocols that operate at a specific layer have defined information that they act upon and a defined interface to the layers above and below.
- Fosters competition because products from different vendors can work together.
- Enables technology changes to occur at one level without affecting the other levels.
- Provides a common language to describe networking functions and capabilities.

The first layered model for internetwork communications was created in the early 1970s and is referred to as the Internet model. It defines four categories of functions that must occur for communications to be successful. The suite of TCP/IP protocols that are used for Internet communications follows the structure of this model, as shown in Table 5-2. Because of this, the Internet model is commonly referred to as the TCP/IP model.

Table 5-2 The Layers of the TCP/IP Model

TCP/IP Model Layer	Description
Application	Represents data to the user, plus encoding and dialog control.
Transport	Supports communication between various devices across diverse networks.
Internet	Determines the best path through the network.
Network Access	Controls the hardware devices and media that make up the network.

The OSI Reference Model (5.3.4)

Two basic types of models are used to describe the functions that must occur for network communications to be successful:

- **Protocol model**—This type of model closely matches the structure of a particular protocol suite. A *protocol suite* includes the set of related protocols that typically provide all the functionality required for people to communicate with the data network. The TCP/IP model is a protocol model because it describes the functions that occur at each layer of protocols within the TCP/IP suite.
- *Reference model*—This type of model describes the functions that must be completed at a particular layer but does not specify exactly how a function should be accomplished. A reference model is not intended to provide a sufficient

level of detail to define precisely how each protocol should work at each layer. The primary purpose of a reference model is to aid in clearer understanding of the functions and processes necessary for network communications.

The most widely known internetwork reference model was created by the *Open Systems Interconnection (OSI)* project at the *International Organization for Standardization (ISO)*. It is used for data network design, operation specifications, and troubleshooting. This model is commonly referred to as the OSI model. The OSI layers are described in Table 5-3.

Table 5-3 The Layers of the OSI Model

OSI Model Layer	Description
7—Application	The application layer contains protocols used for process-to-process communications.
6—Presentation	The presentation layer provides for common representation of the data transferred between application layer services.
5—Session	The session layer provides services to the presentation layer to organize its dialogue and to manage data exchange.
4—Transport	The transport layer defines services to segment, transfer, and reassemble the data for individual communications between the end devices.
3—Network	The network layer provides services to exchange the individual pieces of data over the network between identified end devices.
2—Data link	The data link layer protocols describe methods for exchanging data frames between devices over a common media.
1—Physical	The physical layer protocols describe the mechanical, electrical, functional, and procedural means to activate, maintain, and de-activate physical connections for a bit transmission to and from a network device.

OSI Model and TCP/IP Model Comparison (5.3.5)

Because TCP/IP is the protocol suite in use for Internet communications, why do you need to learn the OSI model as well?

The TCP/IP model is a method of visualizing the interactions of the various protocols that make up the TCP/IP protocol suite. It does not describe general functions that are necessary for all networking communications. It describes the networking functions specific to those protocols in use in the TCP/IP protocol suite. For example, at the network access layer, the TCP/IP protocol suite does not specify which protocols to use when transmitting over a physical medium, nor the method of encoding the

signals for transmission. OSI Layers 1 and 2 discuss the necessary procedures to access the media and the physical means to send data over a network.

The protocols that make up the TCP/IP protocol suite can be described in terms of the OSI reference model. The functions that occur at the Internet layer in the TCP/IP model are contained in the network layer of the OSI model, as shown in Figure 5-5. The transport layer functionality is the same between both models. However, the network access layer and the application layer of the TCP/IP model are further divided in the OSI model to describe discrete functions that must occur at these layers.

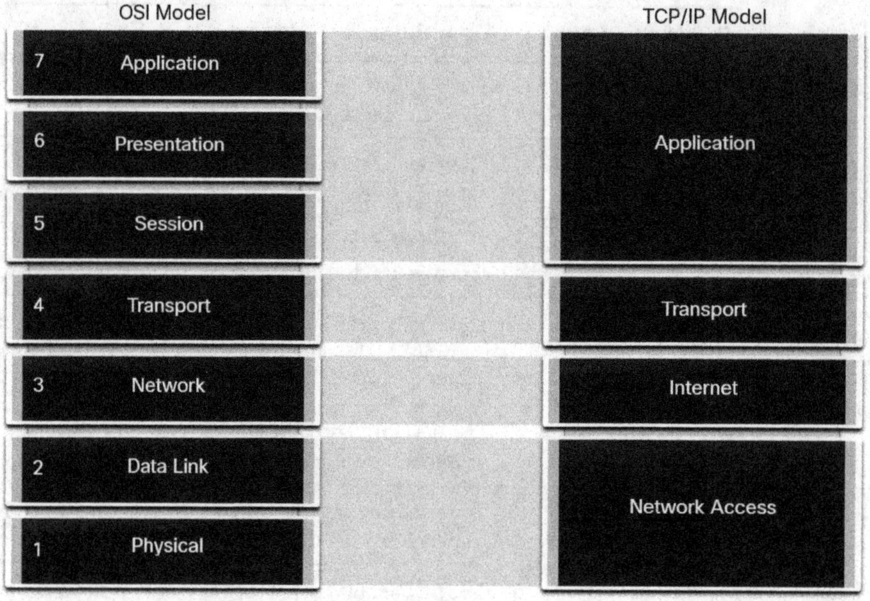

Figure 5-5 The OSI and TCP/IP Models

The key similarities are in the transport and network layers; however, the two models differ in how they relate to the layers above and below each layer:

- OSI Layer 3, the network layer, maps directly to the TCP/IP Internet layer. This layer is used to describe protocols that address and route messages through an internetwork.
- OSI Layer 4, the transport layer, maps directly to the TCP/IP transport layer. This layer describes general services and functions that provide ordered and reliable delivery of data between source and destination hosts.
- The TCP/IP application layer includes several protocols that provide specific functionality to a variety of end-user applications. The OSI model Layers 5, 6,

and 7 are used as references for application software developers and vendors to produce applications that operate on networks.

- Both the TCP/IP and OSI models are commonly used when referring to protocols at various layers. Because the OSI model separates the data link layer from the physical layer, it is commonly used when referring to these lower layers.

Communication Principles Summary (5.4)

The following is a summary of each topic in the chapter and some questions for your reflection.

What Did I Learn in This Chapter? (5.4.1)

- **Communication Protocol**—Protocols are required for computers to properly communicate across the network. Protocols define the following aspects of communication over the local network:
  - **Message format**—When a message is sent, it must use a specific format or structure.
  - **Message size**—The rules that govern the size of the pieces communicated across the network are very strict. They can also be different, depending on the channel used.
  - **Timing**—Timing determines the speed at which the bits are transmitted across the network. It also affects when an individual host can send data and the total amount of data that can be sent in any one transmission.
  - **Encoding**—Messages sent across the network are first converted into bits by the sending host. Each bit is encoded into a pattern of sounds, light waves, or electrical pulses depending on the network media over which the bits are transmitted.
  - **Encapsulation**—Each message transmitted on a network must include a header that contains addressing information that identifies the source and destination hosts. Encapsulation is the process of adding this information to the pieces of data that make up the message.
  - **Message pattern**—Some messages require an acknowledgment before the next message can be sent. This type of request/response pattern is a common aspect of many networking protocols. However, other types of messages may be simply streamed across the network, without concern as to whether they reach their destination.

- **Communication Standards**—Topologies allow us to see the networking using representation of end devices and intermediary devices. How does a device see a network? Think of a device in a bubble. The only thing a device sees is its own addressing information. How does the device know it is on the same network as another device? The answer is network protocols. Most network communications are broken up into smaller data units, or packets.

  A standard is a set of rules that determines how something must be done. Networking and Internet standards ensure that all devices connecting to the network implement the same set of rules or protocols in the same manner. Using standards enables different types of devices to send information to each other over the Internet.

  An Internet standard is the end result of a comprehensive cycle of discussion, problem solving, and testing. Internet standards are developed, published, and maintained by a variety of organizations. When a new standard is proposed, each stage of the development and approval process is recorded in a numbered RFC document so that the evolution of the standard is tracked. RFCs for Internet standards are published and managed by the IETF.

- **Network Communication Models**—Protocols are the rules that govern communications. Successful communication between hosts requires interaction between a number of protocols. Protocols include HTTP, TCP, IP, and Ethernet. These protocols are implemented in software and hardware that are installed on each host and networking device.

  The interaction between the different protocols on a device can be illustrated as a protocol stack. A stack illustrates the protocols as a layered hierarchy, with each higher-level protocol depending on the services of the protocols shown in the lower levels. The separation of functions enables each layer in the stack to operate independently of others.

  The suite of TCP/IP protocols that are used for Internet communications follows the structure of this model:

  - **Application**—Represents data to the user, plus encoding and dialog control
  - **Transport**—Supports communication between various devices across diverse networks
  - **Internet**—Determines the best path through the network
  - **Network Access**—Controls the hardware devices and media that make up the network

  A reference model describes the functions that must be completed at a particular layer but does not specify exactly how a function should be accomplished. The

primary purpose of a reference model is to aid in clearer understanding of the functions and processes necessary for network communications.

The most widely known internetwork reference model was created by the OSI project at the ISO. It is used for data network design, operation specifications, and troubleshooting. This model is commonly referred to as the OSI model.

The layers in the OSI model are as follows:

- **7—Application**—Contains protocols used for process-to-process communications
- **6—Presentation**—Provides for common representation of the data transferred between application layer services
- **5—Session**—Provides services to the presentation layer to organize its dialogue and to manage data exchange
- **4—Transport**—Defines services to segment, transfer, and reassemble the data for individual communications between the end devices
- **3—Network**—Provides services to exchange the individual pieces of data over the network between identified end devices
- **2—Data link**—Includes protocols that describe methods for exchanging data frames between devices over a common media
- **1—Physical**—Includes protocols that describe the mechanical, electrical, functional, and procedural means to activate, maintain, and de-activate physical connections for a bit transmission to and from a network device

Reflection Questions (5.4.2)

Recall that Kishori and Srinivas had to determine a common language. Do you have any friends or relatives whose first language is different than yours? Do you know anyone who uses sign language? How would you communicate with them if you did not know sign language? Did you realize before reading this chapter that you were using a protocol (using a shared language or communicating in writing) to interact with family and friends?

Practice

There are no labs or Packet Tracer activities in this chapter.

Check Your Understanding Questions

Complete all the review questions listed here to test your understanding of the topics and concepts in this chapter. Appendix A, "Answers to 'Check Your Understanding' Questions," lists the answers.

1. What is the purpose of the OSI physical layer?
    a. To control access to media
    b. To transmit bits across the local media
    c. To perform error detection on received frames
    d. To exchange frames between nodes over physical network media
2. Which statement is correct about network protocols?
    a. They define the type of hardware that is used and how it is mounted in racks.
    b. They define how messages are exchanged between the source and the destination.
    c. They all function in the network access layer of TCP/IP.
    d. They are required only for exchange of messages between devices on remote networks.
3. What networking term describes a particular set of rules at one layer that governs communication at that layer?
    a. Duplex
    b. Encapsulation
    c. Error checking
    d. Protocol
4. Which layer of the OSI model defines services to segment and reassemble data for individual communications between end devices?
    a. Application
    b. Presentation
    c. Session
    d. Transport
    e. Network

5. What is the purpose of protocols in data communications?

   a. To specify the bandwidth of the channel or medium for each type of communication

   b. To specify the device operating systems that will support the communication

   c. To provide the rules required for a specific type of communication to occur

   d. To dictate the content of the message sent during communication

6. Which term refers to a formalized protocol, usually approved by an accepted authority or organization, which can then be implemented by different vendors?

   a. Standard

   b. Protocol

   c. Model

   d. Domain

7. Which three layers of the OSI model make up the application layer of the TCP/IP model? (Choose three.)

   a. Data link

   b. Network

   c. Transport

   d. Session

   e. Presentation

   f. Application

8. Which organization publishes and manages the Request for Comments (RFC) documents?

   a. IEEE

   b. ISO

   c. IETF

   d. TIA/EIA

9. Which two OSI model layers have the same functionality as a single layer of the TCP/IP model? (Choose two.)

   a. Data link

   b. Network

   c. Physical

   d. Session

   e. Transport

CHAPTER 6

Network Media

Objectives

Upon completion of this chapter, you will be able to answer the following question:

- What are the common types of network cables?

Key Terms

This chapter uses the following key terms. You can find the definitions in the Glossary.

coaxial cable Page 94

fiber-optic cable Page 95

Introduction (6.0)

Kishori knows that the 15 to 20 devices in a patient's room wirelessly connect to the network. She also uses a wireless tablet. While working at the nurses' station, she noticed that the wireless network on her desktop computer was disabled. However, she still has access to patient records. How is the desktop connected?

How does communication transmit across a network? The answer is network media. Media provides a channel over which the message travels from source to destination. In modern networks, there are primarily three types of media used. Do you know what they are? Read this chapter to learn about media.

Network Media Types (6.1)

Network media refers to the communication channels used to interconnect devices on a network. The communication channels can be wired or wireless.

Video

Video—Network Media Types (6.1.1)

Refer to the online course to view this video.

Three Media Types (6.1.2)

Data is transmitted across a network on media. The media provides the channel over which the message travels from source to destination.

Modern networks primarily use three types of media to interconnect devices, as shown in Figure 6-1:

- **Metal wires within cables**—Data is encoded into electrical pulses.
- **Glass or plastic fibers within cables (fiber-optic cable)**—Data is encoded into pulses of light.
- **Wireless transmission**—Data is encoded via modulation of specific frequencies of electromagnetic waves.

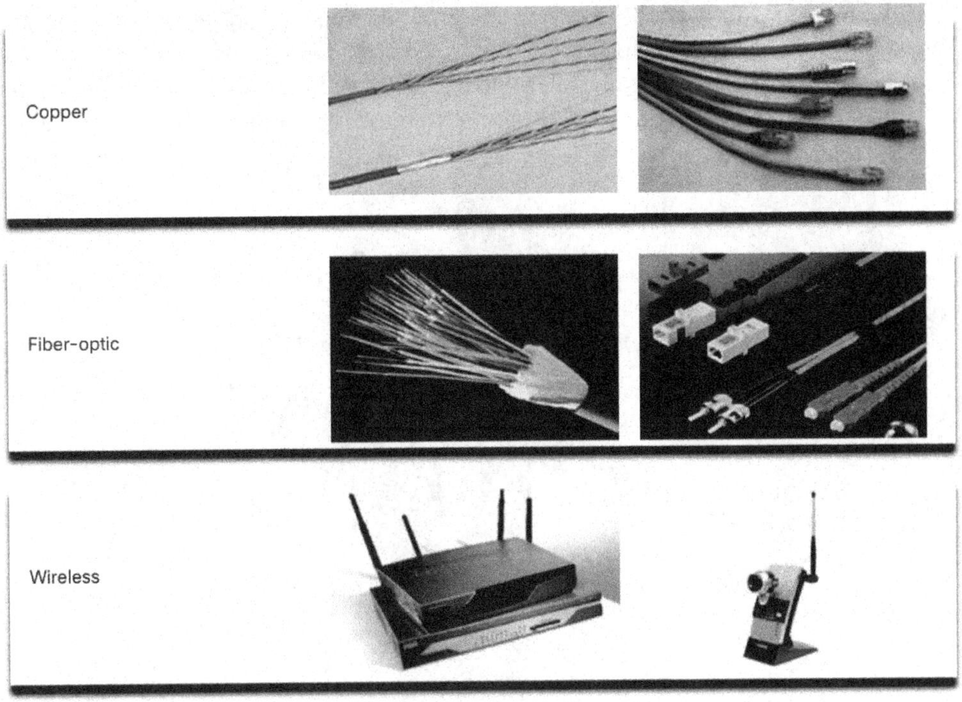

Figure 6-1 Three Network Media Types

The four main criteria for choosing network media are these:

- What is the maximum distance that the media can successfully carry a signal?
- What is the environment in which the media will be installed?
- What is the amount of data and at what speed must it be transmitted?
- What is the cost of the media and installation?

Common Network Cables (6.1.3)

The three most common network cables are twisted-pair, coaxial cable, and fiber-optic cable.

Twisted-Pair Cable

Ethernet technology generally uses twisted-pair cables to interconnect devices. Because Ethernet is the foundation for most local networks, twisted-pair is the most commonly encountered type of network cabling.

In twisted-pair, wires are grouped in pairs and twisted together to reduce interference. The pairs of wires are colored so that you can identify the same wire at each end. Typically, in each pair, one of the wires is a solid color and its partner is the same color striped onto a white background, as shown in Figure 6-2.

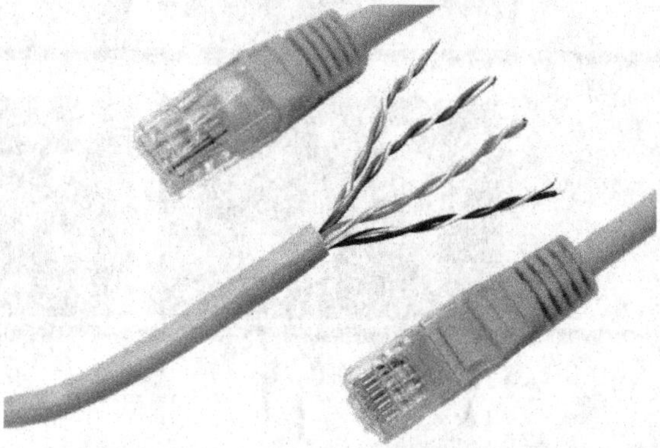

Figure 6-2 Example of a Twisted-Pair Cable

Coaxial Cable

Coaxial cable, one of the earliest types of network cabling developed, is the kind of copper cable used by cable TV companies. It is also used for connecting the various components that make up satellite communication systems. Coaxial cable has a single rigid copper core that conducts the signal, as shown in Figure 6-3. This core is typically surrounded by a layer of insulation, braided metal shielding, and a protective jacket. It is used as a high-frequency transmission line to carry high-frequency or broadband signals.

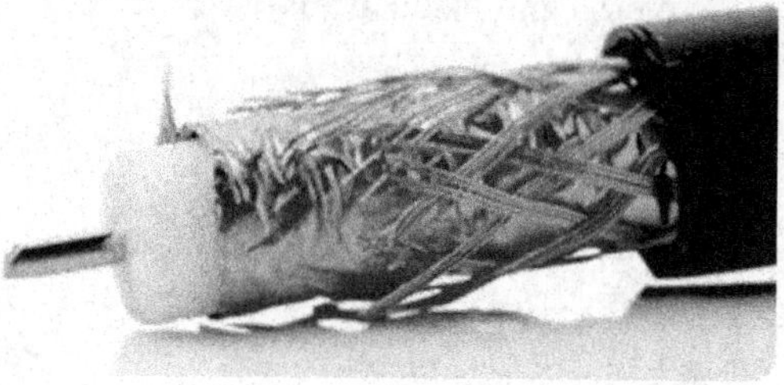

Figure 6-3 Example of a Coaxial Cable

Fiber-Optic Cable

Fiber-optic cable can be either glass or plastic with a diameter about the same as a human hair, and it can carry digital information at very high speeds over long distances. Because light is used instead of electricity, electrical interference does not affect the signal. Fiber-optic cables, shown in Figure 6-4, have many uses in addition to communications. They are also used in medical imaging, medical treatment, and mechanical engineering inspection.

Figure 6-4 Example of Fiber-Optic Cable

Fiber-optic cables have a very high bandwidth, which enables them to carry very large amounts of data. Fiber is used in backbone networks, large enterprise environments, and large data centers. It is also used extensively by telephone companies.

Network Media Summary (6.2)

The following is a summary of each topic in the chapter and some questions for your reflection.

What Did I Learn in This Chapter? (6.2.1)

Communication transmits across a network on media. The media provides the channel over which the message travels from source to destination.

Modern networks primarily use three types of media to interconnect devices:

- **Metal wires within cables**—Data is encoded into electrical pulses.
- **Glass or plastic fibers within cables (fiber-optic cable)**—Data is encoded into pulses of light.

- **Wireless transmission**—Data is encoded via modulation of specific frequencies of electromagnetic waves.

The four main criteria for choosing media are the following:

- What is the maximum distance that the media can successfully carry a signal?
- What is the environment in which the media will be installed?
- What is the amount of data and at what speed must it be transmitted?
- What is the cost of the media and installation?

The three most common types of network cables are twisted-pair cable, coaxial cable, and fiber-optic cable. Ethernet technology generally uses twisted-pair cables to interconnect devices. Coaxial cable is the kind of copper cable used by cable TV companies. It is also used for connecting the various components that make up satellite communication systems. Fiber-optic cable can be either glass or plastic with a diameter about the same as a human hair and it can carry digital information at very high speeds over long distances. Because light is used instead of electricity, electrical interference does not affect the signal.

Reflection Questions (6.2.2)

I had no idea that a network needed to have different cables for different uses, did you? I thought all the cables were the same and that they all carried the same type of signal. And electrical interference? Now I get why my smartphone connection sometimes drops if I stand too close to my microwave! Do you know about all the cables that are used in your school or office network?

Practice

There are no labs or Packet Tracer activities in this chapter.

Check Your Understanding Questions

Complete all the review questions listed here to test your understanding of the topics and concepts in this chapter. Appendix A, "Answers to 'Check Your Understanding' Questions," lists the answers.

1. A network technician is extending the network from the main office building over several hundred meters to a new security station. The security station needs a high-speed connection to support video surveillance of the main building. What type of cable is best suited to connect the security station to the rest of the main office network?

    a. Coax

    b. Fiber-optic

    c. Shielded twisted-pair

    d. Unshielded twisted-pair

2. What are two common types of media used in networks? (Choose two.)

    a. Copper

    b. Water

    c. Nylon

    d. Fiber

    e. Wood

3. Which type of network cable is commonly used to connect office computers to the local network?

    a. Coaxial cable

    b. Twisted-pair cable

    c. Glass fiber-optic cable

    d. Plastic fiber-optic cable

4. Which three factors should be considered when choosing the appropriate network media? (Choose three.)

    a. The speed of the CPU and amount of memory in servers

    b. The environment in which the media is installed

c. The data security and fault tolerance requirement
d. The amount of data and the data transfer rate desired
e. The distance between hosts that the media will connect
f. The operating systems used on network devices in the network

5. Refer to the graphic. What type of cabling is shown?

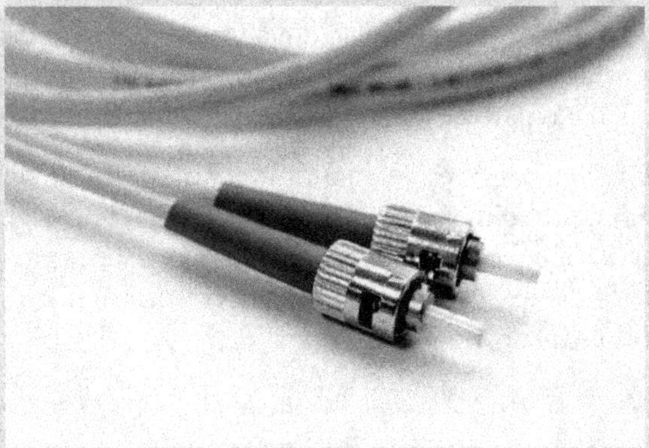

a. STP
b. UTP
c. Coax
d. Fiber

6. What makes fiber-optic cabling preferable to copper cabling for interconnecting buildings? (Choose three.)

a. Greater distances per cable run
b. Lower installation cost
c. Unaffected by electrical interference
d. Durable connections
e. Greater bandwidth potential
f. Easily terminated

7. Which type of network media carries data encoded into electrical pulses?

a. Copper cable
b. Wireless media
c. Fiber-optic cable
d. Cellular communication media

8. Which two types of network media carry data encoded into electrical pulses? (Choose two.)

   a. Coaxial cable
   b. Wireless media
   c. Twisted-pair cable
   d. Glass fiber-optic cable
   e. Plastic fiber-optic cable

9. Which type of network media carries data encoded into pulses of light?

   a. Coaxial cable
   b. Wireless media
   c. Fiber-optic cable
   d. Twisted-pair cable

10. A network administrator in a small office is upgrading the local network within the building. The administrator needs new network cables to connect office computers and networking devices. Which network media should the administrator use?

    a. Coaxial cable
    b. Wireless solution
    c. Fiber-optic cable
    d. Twisted-pair cable

11. What is the purpose of using twisted pairs of wires in an Ethernet cable?

    a. To reduce interference
    b. To provide higher bandwidth
    c. To identify paths of data flow
    d. To ensure that the transmission of electrical signals is extended over a longer distance

CHAPTER 7

The Access Layer

Objectives

Upon completion of this chapter, you will be able to answer the following questions:

- What is the process of encapsulation and Ethernet framing?
- How can network communication be improved at the access layer?

Key Terms

This chapter uses the following key terms. You can find the definitions in the Glossary.

de-encapsulation Page 103

encapsulation Page 103

protocol data unit (PDU) Page 105

Introduction (7.0)

During a lunch break, Kishori sees her friend, Rina, and they decide to eat together. Rina works as an IT support technician at the hospital. Kishori thinks this might be a good opportunity to ask Rina a question she's been pondering. Kishori now knows that her desktop computer in the nurses' station connects to the network using a twisted-pair cable. Most other devices she uses connect to the network wirelessly. She wonders if there is any difference in the way wired devices and wireless devices communicate on the network. Rina knows that Kishori has relatives in the United States. She explains that the differences between wired and wireless network communication are similar to the differences in addressing formats used for mailing packages to different countries. The contents inside might be exactly the same, but the addressing and possibly packaging could be very different.

How does a message get delivered? When you write a letter and place it in the envelope, you need to make sure it has the correct address information to be delivered to the recipient. In your network, the process of placing one message format (the letter) inside another message format (the envelope) is called encapsulation. Ready to learn more? Read this chapter!

Encapsulation and the Ethernet Frame (7.1)

Ethernet is a protocol used to deliver information from one Ethernet network interface card (NIC) to another Ethernet NIC on the same network. This section explains the process known as encapsulation and how the fields of an Ethernet frame are used to transmit the embedded information.

Ethernet is technology commonly used in local area networks. Devices access the Ethernet LAN using an Ethernet NIC. Each Ethernet NIC has a unique address permanently embedded on the card known as a Media Access Control (MAC) address. The MAC address for both the source and destination are fields in an Ethernet frame.

Video

Video—The Fields of the Ethernet Frame (7.1.1)

Refer to the online course to view this video.

Encapsulation (7.1.2)

When sending a letter, the letter writer uses an accepted format to ensure that the letter is delivered and understood by the recipient. In the same way, a message that is sent over a computer network follows specific format rules in order for it to be delivered and processed.

Encapsulation is the process of placing one message format (the letter) inside another message format (the envelope). *De-encapsulation* occurs when the process is reversed by the recipient and the letter is removed from the envelope. Just as a letter is encapsulated in an envelope for delivery, so computer messages are encapsulated.

Each computer message is encapsulated in a specific format, called a *frame*, before it is sent over the network. A frame acts like an envelope; it provides the address of the intended destination and the address of the source host. The format and contents of a frame are determined by the type of message being sent and the channel over which it is communicated. Messages that are not correctly formatted are not successfully delivered to or processed by the destination host.

A common example of requiring the correct format in human communications is when sending a letter, as shown in Figure 7-1. An envelope has the address of the sender and receiver, each located at the proper place on the envelope. If the destination address and formatting are not correct, the letter is not delivered.

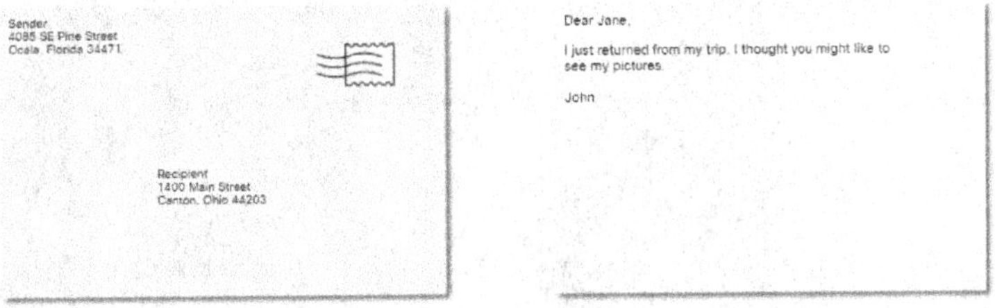

Recipient (destination) Location address	Sender (source) Location address	Salutation (start of message indicator)	Recipient (destination) identifier	Content of Letter (encapsulated data)	Sender (source) identifier	End of Frame (End of message indicator)
Envelope Addressing		Encapsulated Letter				
1400 Main Street Canton, Ohio 44203	4085 SE Pine Street Ocala, Florida 34471	Dear	Jane	I just returned from my trip. I thought you might like to see my pictures.	John	

Figure 7-1 Format for Sending a Letter

Similar to sending a letter, a message that is sent over a computer network follows specific format rules for it to be delivered and processed.

Internet Protocol (IP) is a protocol with a similar function to the envelope example. In Figure 7-2, the fields of the Internet Protocol version 6 (IPv6) packet identify the source of the packet and its destination. IP is responsible for sending a message from the message source to destination over one or more networks.

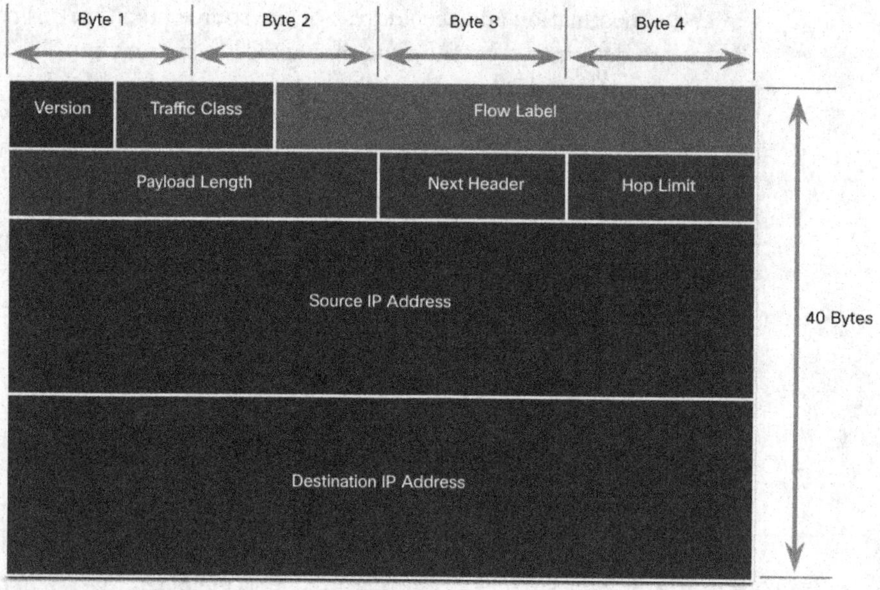

Figure 7-2 Fields in an IPv6 Header

Note

The fields of the IPv6 packet are discussed in detail in Chapter 33.

The Access Layer (7.2)

The access layer describes the network components used to provide an end device access to the network and the LAN.

Ethernet Frame (7.2.1)

The Ethernet protocol standards define many aspects of network communication including frame format, frame size, timing, and encoding.

When messages are sent between hosts on an Ethernet network, the hosts format the messages into the frame layout that is specified by the standards. Frames are also referred to as Layer 2 *protocol data units (PDUs)* because the protocols that provide the rules for the creation and format of the frame perform the functions that are specified at the data link layer (Layer 2) of the OSI model.

The format, shown in Figure 7-3, for Ethernet frames specifies the location of the destination and source MAC addresses and the following additional information:

- Preamble for sequencing and timing
- Start of frame delimiter
- Length and type of frame
- Frame check sequence to detect transmission errors

Ethernet Frame Fields

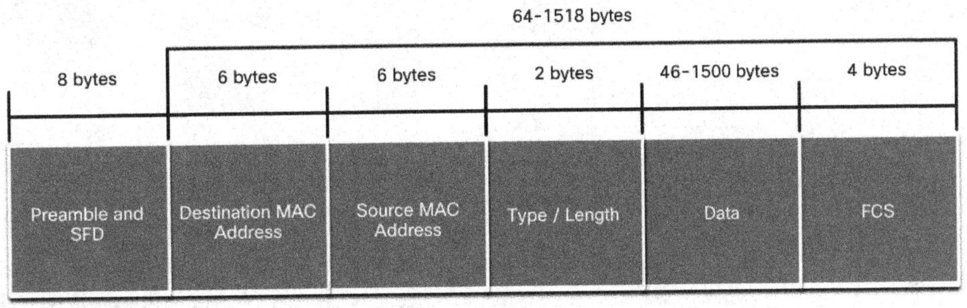

Figure 7-3 Ethernet Frame Structure and Field Size

The size of Ethernet frames is normally limited to a maximum of 1518 bytes and a minimum size of 64 bytes from the Destination MAC Address field through the Frame Check Sequence (FCS). The preamble and the Start of Frame Delimiter (SFD) are used to indicate the beginning of the frame. They are not used in the calculation of the frame size. Frames that do not match these limits are not processed by the receiving hosts. In addition to the frame formats, sizes, and timing, Ethernet standards define how the bits making up the frames are encoded onto the channel. Bits are transmitted as either electrical pulses over copper cable or as light pulses over fiber-optic cable.

Access Layer Devices (7.2.2)

The access layer is the basic level of the network. It is the part of the network in which people gain access to other hosts and to shared files and printers. The access layer provides the first line of networking devices that connect hosts to the wired Ethernet network.

Networking devices enable us to connect many hosts with each other and also provide those hosts access to services offered over the network. Unlike the simple network consisting of two hosts connected by a single cable, in the access layer, each host is connected to a networking device. This type of connectivity is shown in Figure 7-4.

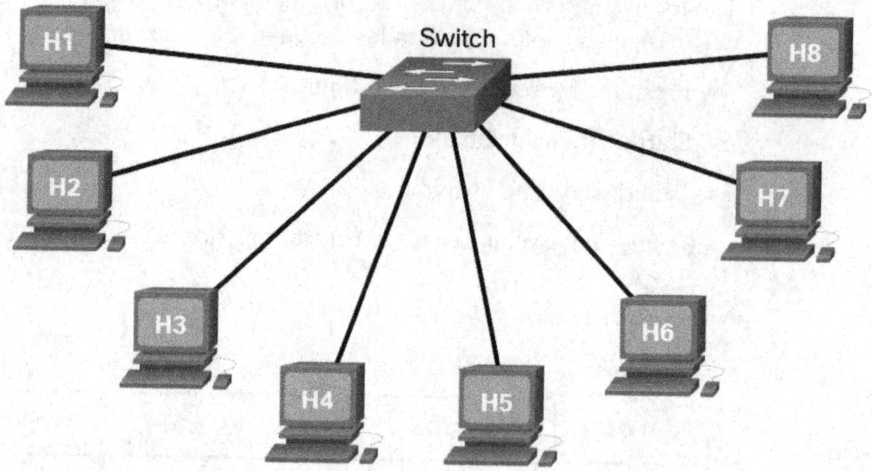

Figure 7-4 Multiple Hosts Connected to a Networking Device

Within an Ethernet network, each host is able to connect directly to an access layer networking device using an Ethernet cable. These cables are manufactured to meet specific Ethernet standards. Each cable is plugged into a host NIC and then into a port on the networking device. There are several types of networking devices that can be used to connect hosts at the access layer, including Ethernet switches.

Ethernet Hubs (7.2.3)

The original Ethernet networks connected all hosts with a single cable, similar to how cable TV cables are connected in your home. All users on the network shared the bandwidth available on the cable. As Ethernet networks became more popular, connecting everyone on a single cable was no longer practical, nor even possible. Engineers developed a different type of network technology that made it easier to connect and reconnect multiple devices to the network. The first of these types of networking devices were Ethernet hubs.

Hubs contain multiple ports that are used to connect hosts to the network. Hubs are simple devices that do not have the necessary electronics to decode the messages sent between hosts on the network. Hubs cannot determine which host should get any particular message. A hub simply accepts electronic signals from one port

and regenerates (or repeats) the same message out all of the other ports. All hosts attached to the hub share the bandwidth and receive the message. Hosts ignore the messages that are not addressed to them. Only the host specified in the destination address of the message processes the message and responds to the sender.

Only one message can be sent through an Ethernet hub at a time. If two or more hosts connected to a hub attempt to send a message at the same time, the electronic signals that make up the messages collide with each other at the hub. This is known as a *collision*. The message is unreadable by hosts and must be retransmitted. The area of the network where a host can receive a garbled message resulting from a collision is known as a *collision domain*.

Because excessive retransmissions can clog up the network and slow down network traffic, hubs are now considered obsolete and have been replaced by Ethernet switches.

Figure 7-5 shows how a hub delivers messages.

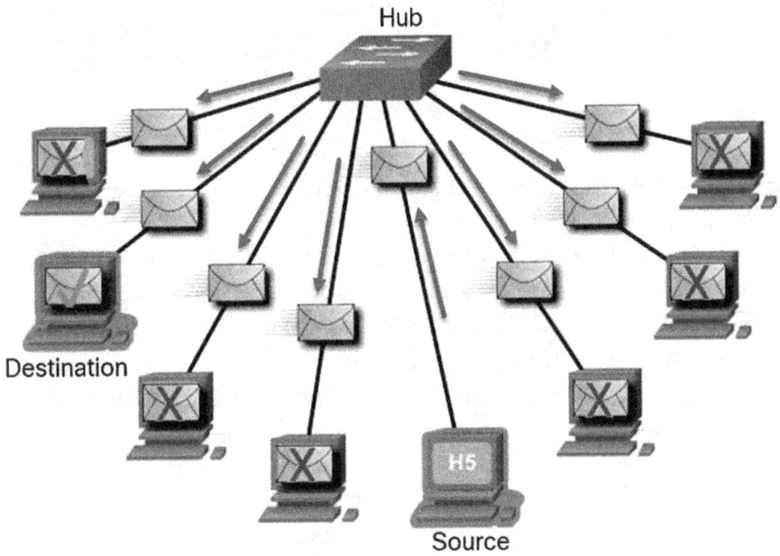

Figure 7-5 Example of Hub Operation

Ethernet Switches (7.2.4)

An Ethernet switch is a device that is used at the access layer. When a host sends a message to another host connected to the same switched network, the switch accepts and decodes the frames to read the physical (MAC) address portion of the message, and then sends the message to the destination, as shown in Figure 7-6.

MAC Table

fa0/1	fa0/2	fa0/3	fa0/4
206d.8c01.0000	206d.8c01.1111	206d.8c01.2222	206d.8c01.3333
fa0/5	fa0/6	fa0/7	fa0/8
206d.8c01.4444	206d.8c01.5555	206d.8c01.6666	206d.8c01.7777

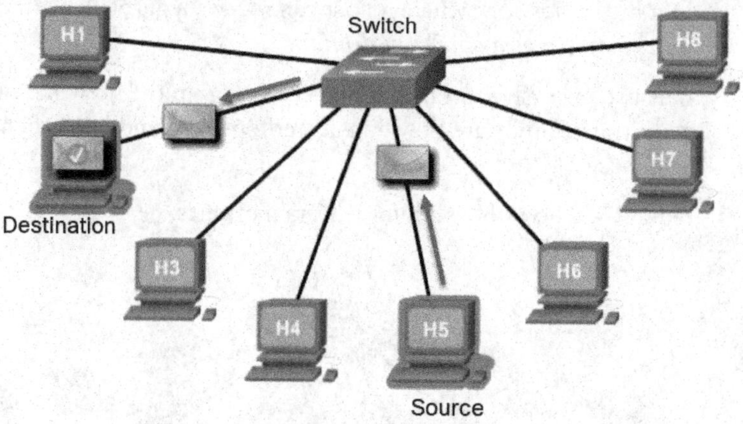

Figure 7-6 Example of Switch Operation

A table on the switch, called a *MAC address table*, contains a list of all the active ports and the host MAC addresses that are attached to them. When a message is sent between hosts, the switch checks whether the destination MAC address is in the table. If it is, the switch builds a temporary connection, called a *circuit*, between the source and destination ports. This new circuit provides a dedicated channel over which the two hosts can communicate. Other hosts attached to the switch do not share bandwidth on this channel and do not receive messages that are not addressed to them. A new circuit is built for every new conversation between hosts. These separate circuits allow many conversations to take place at the same time, without collisions occurring. Ethernet switches also allow for the sending and receiving of frames over the same Ethernet cable simultaneously. This improves the performance of the network by eliminating collisions.

Video

Video—Ethernet Switches (7.2.1)

Refer to the online course to view this video.

The MAC Address Table (7.2.5)

What happens when the switch receives a frame addressed to a new host that is not yet in the MAC address table? If the destination MAC address is not in the table, the switch does not have the necessary information to create an individual circuit. When the switch cannot determine where the destination host is located, it uses a process called *flooding* to forward the message out to all attached hosts except the sending host. Each host compares the destination MAC address in the message to its own MAC address, but only the host with the correct destination address processes the message and responds to the sender.

How does the MAC address of a new host get into the MAC address table? A switch builds the MAC address table by examining the source MAC address of each frame that is sent between hosts. When a new host sends a message or responds to a flooded message, the switch immediately learns its MAC address and the port to which it is connected. The table is dynamically updated each time a new source MAC address is read by the switch. In this way, a switch quickly learns the MAC addresses of all attached hosts. Figures 7-7 through 7-10 demonstrate this operation.

In Figure 7-7, Source PC H3 is sending data to Destination PC H7. The switch does not yet have a MAC address for H7.

MAC Table			
fa0/1	fa0/2	fa0/3	fa0/4
260d.8c01.0000	260d.8c01.1111	**260d.8c01.2222**	260d.8c01.3333
fa0/5	fa0/6	fa0/7	fa0/8
260d.8c01.4444	260d.8c01.5555	?	260d.8c01.7777

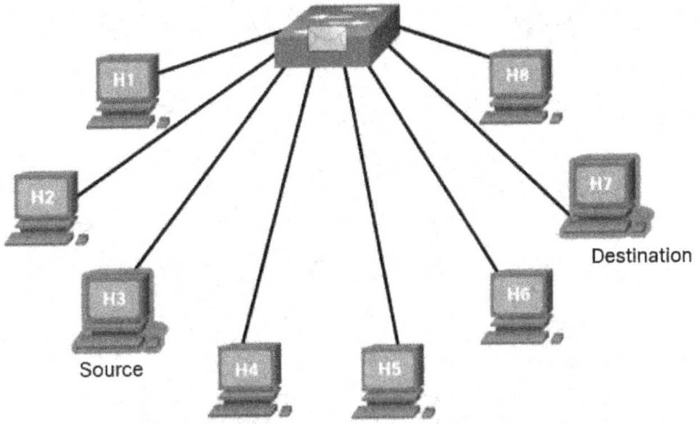

Figure 7-7 Source Sends a Message to the Destination

In Figure 7-8, the switch floods the frame received from H3 out every other port.

MAC Table			
fa0/1	fa0/2	fa0/3	fa0/4
260d.8c01.0000	260d.8c01.1111	260d.8c01.2222	260d.8c01.3333
fa0/5	fa0/6	fa0/7	fa0/8
260d.8c01.4444	260d.8c01.5555	?	260d.8c01.7777

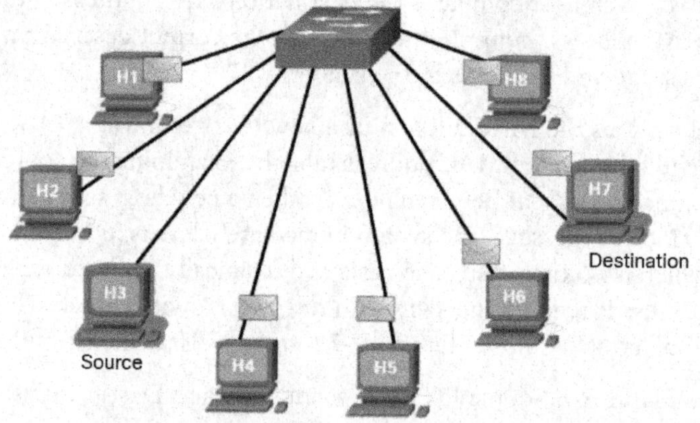

Figure 7-8 Switch Floods the Message

In Figure 7-9, after H7 receives the frame, the IP address of the encapsulated packet matches H7's IP address. Therefore, H7 replies to H3.

MAC Table			
fa0/1	fa0/2	fa0/3	fa0/4
260d.8c01.0000	260d.8c01.1111	260d.8c01.2222	260d.8c01.3333
fa0/5	fa0/6	fa0/7	fa0/8
260d.8c01.4444	260d.8c01.5555	?	260d.8c01.7777

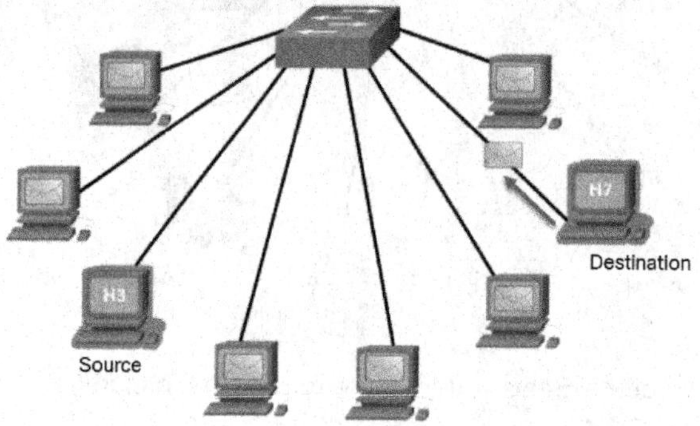

Figure 7-9 The Destination Replies to the Message

In Figure 7-10, the switch updates its table with the MAC address for H7 to map the MAC address to the port.

MAC Table			
fa0/1	fa0/2	fa0/3	fa0/4
260d.8c01.0000	260d.8c01.1111	260d.8c01.2222	260d.8c01.3333
fa0/5	fa0/6	fa0/7	fa0/8
260d.8c01.4444	260d.8c01.5555	260d.8c01.6666	260d.8c01.7777

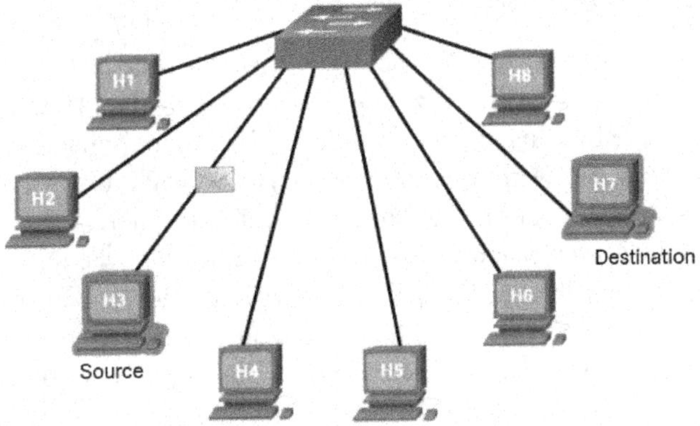

Figure 7-10 The Switch Records the MAC Address for the Destination

Video

Video—MAC Address Tables (7.2.2)

Refer to the online course to view this video.

Interactive Graphic

Check Your Understanding—The Access Layer (7.2.3)

Refer to the online course to complete this activity.

The Access Layer Summary (7.3)

The following is a summary of each topic in the chapter and some questions for your reflection.

What Did I Learn in This Chapter? (7.3.1)

- Encapsulation and the Ethernet Frame—Encapsulation is the process of placing one message format inside another message format. De-encapsulation occurs

when the process is reversed by the recipient and the letter is removed from the envelope. Just as a letter is encapsulated in an envelope for delivery, so computer messages are encapsulated. A message that is sent over a computer network follows specific format rules for it to be delivered and processed.

The Ethernet protocol standards define many aspects of network communication including frame format, frame size, timing, and encoding. The format for Ethernet frames specifies the location of the destination and source MAC addresses, and additional information including a preamble for sequencing and timing, start of frame delimiter, length and type of frame, and frame check sequence to detect transmission errors.

- **The Access Layer**—The access layer is the part of the network in which people gain access to other hosts and to shared files and printers. The access layer provides the first line of networking devices that connect hosts to the wired Ethernet network. Within an Ethernet network, each host can connect directly to an access layer networking device using an Ethernet cable. Ethernet hubs contain multiple ports that are used to connect hosts to the network. Only one message can be sent through an Ethernet hub at a time. Two or more messages sent at the same time will cause a collision. Because excessive retransmissions can clog up the network and slow down network traffic, hubs are now considered obsolete and have been replaced by Ethernet switches.

  An Ethernet switch is a device that is used at Layer 2. When a host sends a message to another host connected to the same switched network, the switch accepts and decodes the frames to read the MAC address portion of the message. A MAC address table on the switch contains a list of all the active ports and the host MAC addresses that are attached to them. When a message is sent between hosts, the switch checks if the destination MAC address is in the table. If it is, the switch builds a temporary connection, called a circuit, between the source and destination ports. Ethernet switches also allow for sending and receiving frames over the same Ethernet cable simultaneously. This improves the performance of the network by eliminating collisions.

  A switch builds the MAC address table by examining the source MAC address of each frame that is sent between hosts. When a new host sends a message or responds to a flooded message, the switch immediately learns its MAC address and the port to which it is connected. The table is dynamically updated each time a new source MAC address is read by the switch.

Reflection Questions (7.3.2)

There is a lot going on behind the scenes when I send an email to a friend. Way more than I knew about! Data gets encapsulated when I send an email and then it's de-encapsulated when my friend opens that email. The access layer of the OSI model is where all of this happens. Now that you know about encapsulation and the access layer, what else do you do on your computer, tablet, or smartphone that requires encapsulation and the protocols used at the access layer?

Practice

There are no labs or Packet Tracer activities in this chapter.

Check Your Understanding Questions

Complete all the review questions listed here to test your understanding of the topics and concepts in this chapter. The appendix "Answers to 'Check Your Understanding' Questions," lists the answers.

1. What does a Layer 2 switch do when the destination MAC address of a received frame is not in the MAC table?
   a. It initiates an ARP request.
   b. It broadcasts the frame out all ports on the switch.
   c. It notifies the sending host that the frame cannot be delivered.
   d. It forwards the frame out all ports except the port at which the frame was received.

2. Which network device has the primary function to send data to a specific destination based on the information found in the MAC address table?
   a. Hub
   b. Router
   c. Switch
   d. Modem

3. What addressing information is recorded by a switch to build its MAC address table?
   a. The destination Layer 3 address of incoming packets
   b. The destination Layer 2 address of outgoing frames
   c. The source Layer 3 address of outgoing packets
   d. The source Layer 2 address of incoming frames

4. What is the purpose of the FCS field in a frame?
   a. To obtain the MAC address of the sending node
   b. To verify the logical address of the sending node
   c. To compute the CRC header for the data field
   d. To determine whether errors occurred in the transmission and reception

5. What is one function of a Layer 2 switch?

   a. Forwards data based on logical addressing
   b. Duplicates the electrical signal of each frame to every port
   c. Learns the port assigned to a host by examining the destination MAC address
   d. Determines which interface is used to forward a frame based on the destination MAC address

6. Which information does a switch use to keep the MAC address table information current?

   a. The destination MAC address and the incoming port
   b. The destination MAC address and the outgoing port
   c. The source and destination MAC addresses and the incoming port
   d. The source and destination MAC addresses and the outgoing port
   e. The source MAC address and the incoming port

7. What process is used to place one message inside another message for transfer from the source to the destination?

   a. Access control
   b. Decoding
   c. Encapsulation
   d. Flow control
   e. The source MAC address and the incoming port

8. Refer to the exhibit. The exhibit shows a small switched network and the contents of the MAC address table of the switch. PC1 has sent a frame addressed to PC3. What will the switch do with the frame?

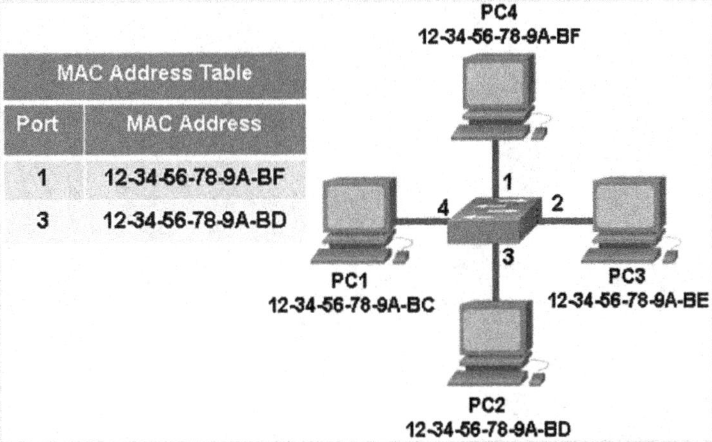

a. The switch will discard the frame.
b. The switch will forward the frame only to port 2.
c. The switch will forward the frame to all ports except port 4.
d. The switch will forward the frame to all ports.
e. The switch will forward the frame only to ports 1 and 3.

9. Which three fields are found in an 802.3 Ethernet frame? (Choose three.)

a. Source physical address
b. Source logical address
c. Media type identifier
d. Frame check sequence
e. Destination physical address
f. Destination logical address

10. What will a host on an Ethernet network do if it receives a frame with a unicast destination MAC address that does not match its own MAC address?

a. It will discard the frame.
b. It will forward the frame to the next host.
c. It will remove the frame from the media.
d. It will strip off the data-link frame to check the destination IP address.

11. Which statement is correct about Ethernet switch frame forwarding decisions?

a. Frame forwarding decisions are based on MAC address and port mappings in the MAC address table.
b. Frames addressed to unknown MAC addresses are dropped.
c. Switches build up their MAC address tables based on the destination MAC address of incoming frames.
d. Unicast frames are always forwarded regardless of the destination MAC address.

CHAPTER 8

The Internet Protocol

Objectives

Upon completion of this chapter, you will be able to answer the following questions:

- What is the purpose of an IPv4 address?
- How are IPv4 addresses and subnets used together?

Introduction (8.0)

Kishori is learning a lot from Rina! She understands that when she sends or receives a package in the mail, there is a unique address involved. A postal code is critical in the address to route the package to the correct post office. She asks Rina if computers use something like a postal code to route the message to the correct place. Rina goes into more detail about the process and explains that much like Kishori's home address identifies where she lives, an IPv4 address identifies a host on the network. A host needs an IPv4 address to participate on the Internet and almost all LANs today. Every packet sent across the Internet has a source and destination IPv4 address. This information is required by networking devices to ensure that the information gets to the destination and any replies are returned to the source.

My friend Kishori never thought she would be so interested in all of this tech information, but she really wants to learn more! Do you? Read this chapter to learn about the Internet Protocol and the structure of IPv4 addresses!

Purpose of an IPv4 Address (8.1)

Devices on the same network or different networks use IPv4 addresses to communicate. Messages are sent from the IPv4 address of the source to the IPv4 address of the destination.

The IPv4 Address (8.1.1)

A host needs an IPv4 address to participate on the Internet and almost all LANs today. The IPv4 address is a logical network address that identifies a particular host. It must be properly configured and unique within the LAN, for local communication. It must also be properly configured and unique in the world, for remote communication. This is how a host is able to communicate with other devices on the Internet.

An IPv4 address is assigned to the network interface connection for a host. This connection is usually a network interface card (NIC) installed in the device. Examples of end-user devices with network interfaces include workstations, servers, network printers, and IP phones. Some servers can have more than one NIC, each of which has its own IPv4 address. Router interfaces that provide connections to an IP network also have an IPv4 address.

Every packet sent across the Internet has a source and destination IPv4 address. This information is required by networking devices to ensure the information gets to the destination and any replies are returned to the source.

Octets and Dotted-Decimal Notation (8.1.2)

IPv4 addresses are 32 bits in length. Here is an IPv4 address in binary:

```
11010001101001011100100000000001
```

Notice how difficult this address is to read. Imagine having to configure devices with a series of 32 bits! For this reason, the 32 bits are grouped into four 8-bit bytes called *octets*, like this:

```
11010001.10100101.11001000.00000001
```

That's better, but it's still difficult to read. That's why we convert each octet into its decimal value, separated by a decimal point or period. The preceding binary IPv4 address becomes this dotted-decimal representation:

```
209.165.200.1
```

Packet Tracer Activity

Packet Tracer—Connect to a Web Server (8.1.3)

In this activity, you will observe how packets are sent across the Internet using IP addresses.

Refer to the online course to complete this activity.

The IPv4 Address Structure (8.2)

IPv4 addresses have a structure that makes the address unique and identifies the network the address belongs to.

Video

Video—The IPv4 Address Structure (8.2.1)

Refer to the online course to view this video.

Networks and Hosts (8.2.2)

The logical 32-bit IPv4 address is hierarchical and is made up of two parts: the network and the host. Both parts are required in an IPv4 address. Both networks have the subnet mask 255.255.255.0. The subnet mask is used to identify the network on which the host is connected.

For example, Figure 8-1 points to the network number and host number of a host that has the IPv4 address 192.168.5.11 with a subnet mask of 255.255.255.0. The first three octets, (192.168.5), identify the network portion of the address, and the last

octet, (11), identifies the host. This is known as *hierarchical addressing* because the network portion indicates the network on which each unique host address is located. Routers need to know only how to reach each network, not the location of each individual host.

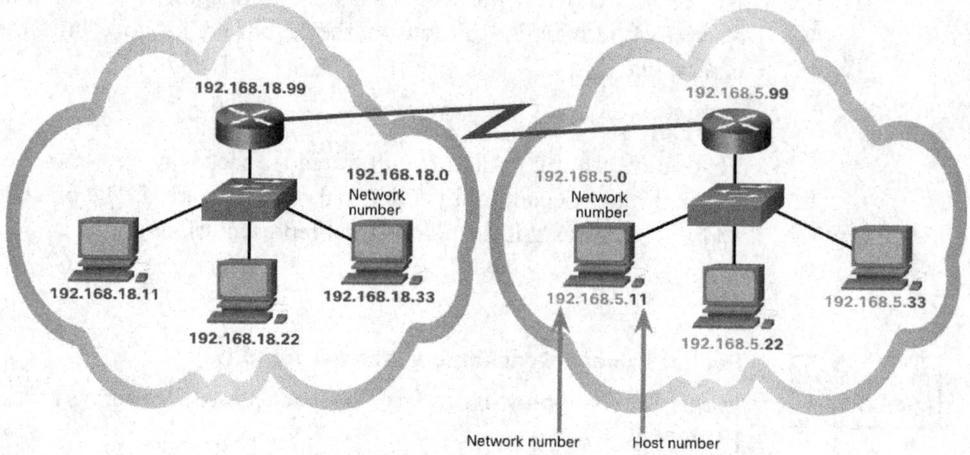

Figure 8-1 Example of Network Number and Host Number

With IPv4 addressing, multiple logical networks can exist on one physical network if the network portion of the logical network host addresses is different. For example, in Figure 8-1, three hosts on a single, physical local network have the same network portion of their IPv4 address (192.168.18), and three other hosts have different network portions of their IPv4 address (192.168.5). The three hosts with the same network number in their IPv4 addresses will be able to communicate with each other but will not be able to communicate with the other three hosts without the use of routing. In this example, there is one physical network and two logical IPv4 networks.

Another example of a hierarchical network is the telephone system. With a telephone number, the country code, area code, and exchange represent the network address and the remaining digits represent a local phone number.

Interactive Graphic

Check Your Understanding—IPv4 Address Structure (8.2.3)

Refer to the online course to complete this activity.

Summary (8.3)

The following is a summary of each topic in the chapter and some questions for your reflection.

What Did I Learn in This Chapter? (8.3.1)

- **Purpose of the IPv4 Address**—The IPv4 address is a logical network address that identifies a particular host. For local communication, the IPv4 address must be properly configured and unique within the LAN. For remote communication, it must also be properly configured and unique in the world.

  An IPv4 address is assigned to the network interface connection for a host. This connection is usually a NIC installed in the device. Every packet sent across the Internet has a source and destination IPv4 address. This information is required by networking devices to ensure that the information gets to the destination and any replies are returned to the source.

- **The IPv4 Address Structure**—The logical 32-bit IPv4 address is hierarchical and is made up of two parts, the network and the host. As an example, there is a host with an IPv4 address 192.168.5.11 with a subnet mask of 255.255.255.0. The first three octets, (192.168.5), identify the network portion of the address, and the last octet, (11), identifies the host. This is known as hierarchical addressing because the network portion indicates the network on which each unique host address is located.

  Routers need to know only how to reach each network, not the location of each individual host. With IPv4 addressing, multiple logical networks can exist on one physical network if the network portion of the logical network host addresses is different.

Reflection Questions (8.3.2)

It makes sense that every device on the network has an IP address, and routers use these addresses to send packets from the source to the destination. When I send a letter through the mail, I put my address and the address of the recipient on the envelope. But now I see the other connection to how networks operate. The postal code and city of my recipient is a little bit like the network portion of the IP address, and the street address is like the host portion of the IP address. Can you think of any other analogies to network operations and IP addresses?

Practice

The following Packet Tracer activity provides practice with the topics introduced in this chapter.

Packet Tracer Activity

Packet Tracer Activities

Packet Tracer—Connect to a Web Server (8.1.3)

Check Your Understanding Questions

Complete all the review questions listed here to test your understanding of the topics and concepts in this chapter. Appendix A, "Answers to 'Check Your Understanding' Questions," lists the answers.

1. What criterion must be followed in the design of an IPv4 addressing scheme for end devices?
   a. Each IPv4 address must match the address that is assigned to the host by DNS.
   b. Each IPv4 address must be unique within the local network.
   c. Each IPv4 address must be compatible with the MAC address.
   d. Each local host must be assigned an IPv4 address with a unique network component.

2. How many octets exist in an IPv4 address?
   a. 4
   b. 8
   c. 16
   d. 32

3. Which two parts are components of an IPv4 address? (Choose two.)
   a. Subnet portion
   b. Network portion
   c. Logical portion
   d. Host portion
   e. Physical portion
   f. Broadcast portion

4. What is the purpose of the subnet mask in conjunction with an IP address?

    a. To uniquely identify a host on a network
    b. To identify whether the address is public or private
    c. To determine the network (or subnet) to which the host belongs
    d. To mask the IP address to outsiders

5. A technician is setting up equipment on a network. Which three devices will need IP addresses? (Choose three.)

    a. A printer with an integrated NIC
    b. A web camera that is attached directly to a host
    c. A server with two NICs
    d. An IP phone
    e. A wireless mouse

6. Which statement describes the relationship of a physical network and logical IPv4 addressed networks?

    a. A local physical network supports one IPv4 logical network.
    b. A physical network can connect multiple devices of different IPv4 logical networks.
    c. All devices connected to a physical network need to belong to the same IPv4 logical network.
    d. End devices on different IPv4 logical networks can communicate with each other if they all connect to the same switch.

7. How large are IPv4 addresses?

    a. 8 bits
    b. 16 bits
    c. 32 bits
    d. 64 bits
    e. 128 bits

8. What is the network number for an IPv4 address 172.16.34.10 with the subnet mask of 255.255.255.0?

    a. 10
    b. 34.10
    c. 172.16.0.0
    d. 172.16.34.0

9. What are two features of IPv4 addresses? (Choose two.)

   a. An IPv4 address contains eight octets.
   b. IPv4 is a logical addressing scheme.
   c. An IPv4 addressing scheme is hierarchical.
   d. IPv4 addresses are used only for communications on the Internet.
   e. An IPv4 address is bound to a network interface card to make it unique.

10. Consider the following group of five IPv4 addresses, each with the subnet mask of 255.255.255.0. Which two IPv4 addresses belong to the same local network? (Choose two.)

    a. 192.168.10.2
    b. 193.168.10.16
    c. 192.168.10.56
    d. 192.167.10.74
    e. 192.168.100.62

11. The IT group needs to design and deploy IPv4 network connectivity in a new high school computer lab. The network design requires multiple logical networks to be deployed on one physical network. Which technology is required to enable computers on different logical networks to communicate with each other?

    a. Routing
    b. Hosting
    c. Mapping
    d. Switching

CHAPTER 9

IPv4 and Network Segmentation

Objectives

Upon completion of this chapter, you will be able to answer the following questions:

- What are the characteristics and uses of the unicast, broadcast, and multicast IPv4 addresses?
- What are public, private, and reserved IPv4 addresses?
- How does subnetting segment a network to enable better communication?

Key Terms

This chapter uses the following key terms. You can find the definitions in the Glossary.

broadcast transmission Page 127

Internet Assigned Numbers Authority (IANA) Page 134

link-local address Page 133

loopback address Page 132

multicast transmission Page 129

Network Address Translation (NAT) Page 131

private IPv4 address Page 130

public IPv4 address Page 130

Regional Internet Registry (RIR) Page 134

unicast transmission Page 126

Introduction (9.0)

Kishori has a new patient, Divya, who was admitted to the hospital today. Like her previous patient, Srinivas, Divya speaks Telugu, which Kishori doesn't understand, but unlike Srinivas, Diya understands only limited English, so Kishori can't communicate with her in English as she did with Srinivas. Kishori wants to send an email to all the nurses on the next shift to determine whether any of them speak Telugu. Kishori can send a multicast email message, which is a single email message sent to specific multiple recipients. You know about the structure of IPv4 addresses. Now it is time to learn more about them. Have you heard of unicast, broadcast, and multicast IPv4 addresses? What are public, private, and reserved IPv4 addresses? Dive into this chapter to get a deeper understanding of IPv4 addresses!

IPv4 Unicast, Broadcast, and Multicast (9.1)

There are three types of destination IPv4 addresses: unicast, broadcast, and multicast. The type of address determines if the packet is intended for a single device or multiple devices.

Video

Video—IPv4 Unicast (9.1.1)

Refer to the online course to view this video.

Unicast (9.1.2)

In Chapter 8 you learned about the structure of an IPv4 address and that each address has a network portion and a host portion. There are different ways to send a packet from a source device, and these different types of transmission affect the destination IPv4 addresses.

Unicast transmission refers to one device sending a message to one other device in one-to-one communications, as shown in Figure 9-1.

A unicast packet has a destination IP address that is a unicast address which goes to a single recipient. A source IP address can only be a unicast address, because the packet can only originate from a single source. This applies regardless of whether the destination IP address is a unicast, broadcast, or multicast address.

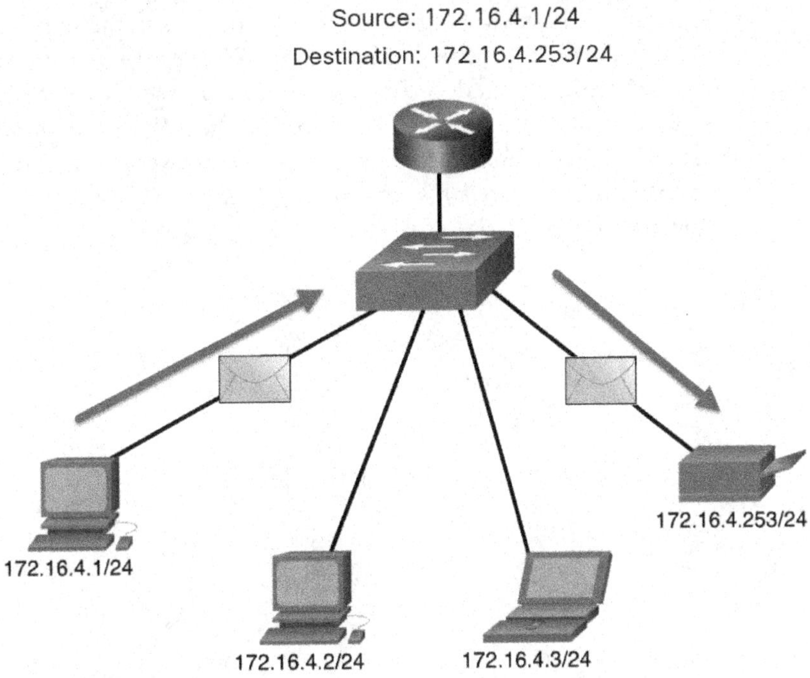

Figure 9-1 Unicast Transmission

Note

In this course, all communication between devices is unicast unless otherwise noted.

IPv4 unicast host addresses are in the address range of 1.1.1.1 to 223.255.255.255. However, within this range are many addresses that are reserved for special purposes. These special-purpose addresses will be discussed later in this chapter.

Video

Video—IPv4 Broadcast (9.1.3)

Refer to the online course to view this video.

Broadcast (9.1.4)

Broadcast transmission refers to a device sending a message to all the devices on a network in one-to-all communications. A broadcast packet has a destination IP address with all ones (1s) in the host portion, or 32 one (1) bits.

Note

IPv4 uses broadcast packets. However, there are no broadcast packets with IPv6.

A broadcast packet must be processed by all devices in the same broadcast domain. A broadcast domain identifies all hosts on the same network segment. A broadcast may be directed or limited. A *directed broadcast* is sent to all hosts on a specific network. For example, in Figure 9-2 a host on the 172.16.4.0/24 network sends a packet to 172.16.4.255. Directed broadcasts are not very common in today's networks. A *limited broadcast* is sent to 255.255.255.255. By default, routers do not forward broadcasts.

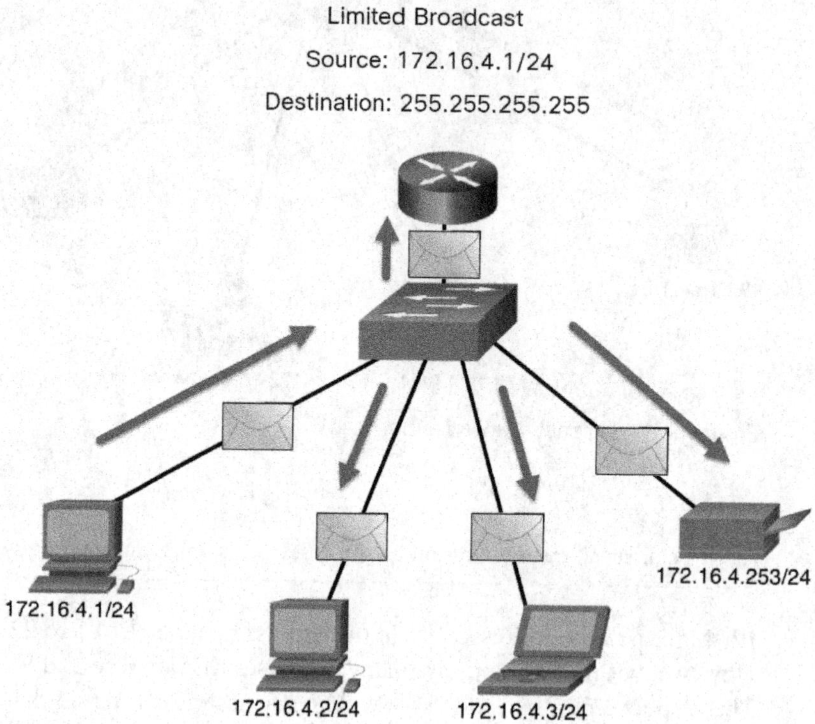

Figure 9-2 Broadcast Transmission

Broadcast packets use resources on the network and make every receiving host on the network process the packet. Therefore, broadcast traffic should be limited so that it does not adversely affect the performance of the network or devices. Because routers separate broadcast domains, subdividing networks can improve network performance by eliminating excessive broadcast traffic.

Video

Video—IPv4 Multicast (9.1.5)

Refer to the online course to view this video.

Multicast (9.1.6)

Multicast transmission reduces traffic by allowing a host to send a single packet to a selected set of hosts that subscribes to a multicast group.

A multicast packet is a packet with a destination IP address that is a multicast address. IPv4 has reserved the 224.0.0.0 to 239.255.255.255 addresses as a multicast range.

Hosts that receive particular multicast packets are called *multicast clients*. The multicast clients use services requested by a client program to subscribe to the multicast group.

Each multicast group is represented by a single IPv4 multicast destination address. When an IPv4 host subscribes to a multicast group, the host processes both packets addressed to this multicast address and packets addressed to its uniquely allocated unicast address.

Routing protocols such as Open Shortest Path First (OSPF) use multicast transmissions, as shown in Figure 9-3. For example, routers enabled with OSPF communicate with each other using the reserved OSPF multicast address 224.0.0.5. Only devices enabled with OSPF will process these packets with 224.0.0.5 as the destination IPv4 address. All other devices will ignore these packets.

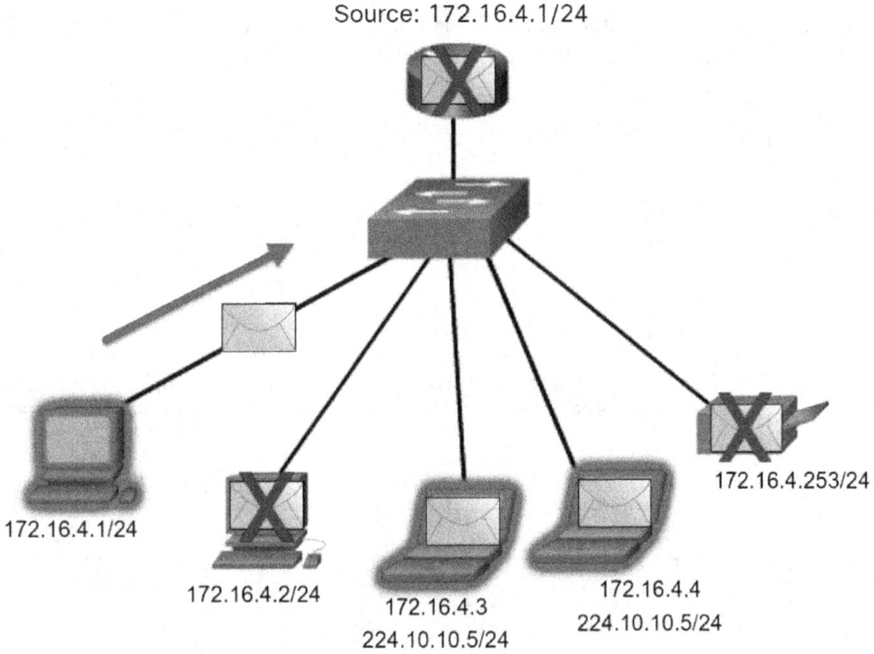

Figure 9-3 Multicast Transmission

Interactive Graphic

Activity—Unicast, Broadcast, or Multicast (9.1.7)

Refer to the online course to complete this activity.

Types of IPv4 Addresses (9.2)

This section discusses the different types of IPv4 addresses including public, private, and legacy classful addressing.

Public and Private IPv4 Addresses (9.2.1)

Just as there are different ways to transmit an IPv4 packet, there are also different types of IPv4 addresses. Some IPv4 addresses cannot be used to go out to the Internet, and others are specifically allocated for routing to the Internet. Some are used to verify a connection and others are self-assigned. As a network administrator, you will eventually become very familiar with the types of IPv4 addresses, but for now, you should at least know what they are and when to use them.

Public IPv4 addresses are addresses that are globally routed between Internet service provider (ISP) routers. However, not all available IPv4 addresses can be used on the Internet. There are blocks of addresses called private addresses that are used by most organizations to assign IPv4 addresses to internal hosts.

In the mid-1990s, with the introduction of the World Wide Web (WWW), the private IPv4 addresses shown in Table 9-1 were introduced because of the depletion of IPv4 address space. *Private IPv4 addresses* are not unique and can be used internally within any network.

Note

IPv6 is the long-term solution to IPv4 address depletion.

Table 9-1 The Private Address Blocks

Network Address and Prefix	RFC 1918 Private Address Range
10.0.0.0/8	10.0.0.0–10.255.255.255
172.16.0.0/12	172.16.0.0–172.31.255.255
192.168.0.0/16	192.168.0.0–192.168.255.255

Note

Private addresses are defined in RFC 1918 and sometimes referred to as RFC 1918 address space.

Routing to the Internet (9.2.2)

Most internal networks, from large enterprise networks to home networks, use private IPv4 addresses for addressing all internal devices (intranet), including hosts and routers. However, private addresses are not globally routable.

In Figure 9-4, customer networks 1, 2, and 3 are sending packets to destinations outside their internal networks. These packets have a source IPv4 address that is a private address and a destination IPv4 address that is public (globally routable). Packets with a private address must be filtered (discarded) or translated to a public address before forwarding the packet to an ISP.

Private IPv4 Addresses and Network Address Translation (NAT)

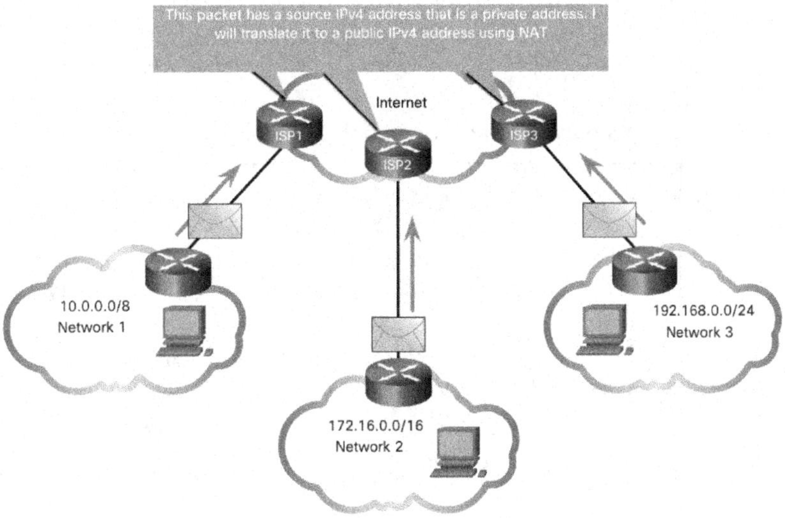

Figure 9-4 Private IPv4 Addresses Translated to Public IPv4 Addresses

Before the ISP can forward this packet, it must translate the source IPv4 address, which is a private address, to a public IPv4 address using *Network Address Translation (NAT)*. NAT is used to translate between private IPv4 addresses and public IPv4 addresses. This is usually done on the router that connects the internal network to the ISP network. Private IPv4 addresses in the organization's intranet will be translated to public IPv4 addresses before routing to the Internet.

Interactive Graphic

Activity—Pass or Block IPv4 Addresses (9.2.3)

Refer to the online course to complete this activity.

Special-Use IPv4 Addresses (9.2.4)

There are certain addresses, such as the network address and broadcast address, that cannot be assigned to hosts. There are also special addresses that can be assigned to hosts, but with restrictions on how those hosts can interact within the network.

Loopback Addresses

Loopback addresses (127.0.0.0 /8 or 127.0.0.1 to 127.255.255.254) are more commonly identified as only 127.0.0.1. These are special addresses used by a host to direct traffic to itself. For example, the **ping** command is commonly used to test connections to other hosts. But you can also use the **ping** command to test the IP configuration on your own device, as shown in Example 9-1.

Note

You will learn more about the **ping** command later in this course.

Example 9-1 Pinging the Loopback Interface

```
C:\Users\NetAcad> ping 127.0.0.1
Pinging 127.0.0.1 with 32 bytes of data:
Reply from 127.0.0.1: bytes=32 time<1ms TTL=128
Reply from 127.0.0.1: bytes=32 time<1ms TTL=128
Reply from 127.0.0.1: bytes=32 time<1ms TTL=128
Reply from 127.0.0.1: bytes=32 time<1ms TTL=128
Ping statistics for 127.0.0.1:
    Packets: Sent = 4, Received = 4, Lost = 0 (0% loss),
Approximate round trip times in milli-seconds:
    Minimum = 0ms, Maximum = 0ms, Average = 0ms
C:\Users\NetAcad> ping 127.1.1.1
Pinging 127.1.1.1 with 32 bytes of data:
Reply from 127.1.1.1: bytes=32 time<1ms TTL=128
Reply from 127.1.1.1: bytes=32 time<1ms TTL=128
Reply from 127.1.1.1: bytes=32 time<1ms TTL=128
Reply from 127.1.1.1: bytes=32 time<1ms TTL=128
Ping statistics for 127.1.1.1:
    Packets: Sent = 4, Received = 4, Lost = 0 (0% loss),
Approximate round trip times in milli-seconds:
    Minimum = 0ms, Maximum = 0ms, Average = 0ms
C:\Users\NetAcad>
```

Link-Local addresses

Link-local addresses (169.254.0.0 /16 or 169.254.0.1 to 169.254.255.254) are more commonly known as the Automatic Private IP Addressing (APIPA) addresses or self-assigned addresses. They are used by a Windows client to self-configure in the event that the client cannot obtain an IP addressing through other methods. Link-local addresses can be used in a peer-to-peer connection but are not commonly used for this purpose.

Legacy Classful Addressing (9.2.5)

In 1981, IPv4 addresses were assigned using classful addressing as defined in RFC 790, "Assigned Numbers" (https://tools.ietf.org/html/rfc790). Customers were allocated a network address based on one of three classes, A, B, or C. RFC 790 divided the unicast ranges into specific classes as follows:

- **Class A (0.0.0.0/8–127.0.0.0/8)**—Designed to support extremely large networks with more than 16 million host addresses. Class A used a fixed /8 prefix with the first octet to indicate the network address, and used the remaining three octets for host addresses (more than 16 million host addresses per network).
- **Class B (128.0.0.0 /16–191.255.0.0 /16)**—Designed to support the needs of moderate to large size networks with up to approximately 65,000 host addresses. Class B used a fixed /16 prefix with the two high-order octets to indicate the network address and the remaining two octets for host addresses (more than 65,000 host addresses per network).
- **Class C (192.0.0.0 /24–223.255.255.0 /24)**—Designed to support small networks with a maximum of 254 hosts. Class C used a fixed /24 prefix with the first three octets to indicate the network and used the remaining octet for the host addresses (only 254 host addresses per network).

Note

There is also a Class D multicast block consisting of 224.0.0.0 to 239.0.0.0 and a Class E experimental address block consisting of 240.0.0.0–255.0.0.0.

At the time, with a limited number of computers using the Internet, classful addressing was an effective means to allocate addresses. As shown in Figure 9-5, Class A and B networks have a very large number of host addresses and Class C has very few. Class A networks accounted for 50 percent of the IPv4 networks. This caused most of the available IPv4 addresses to go unused.

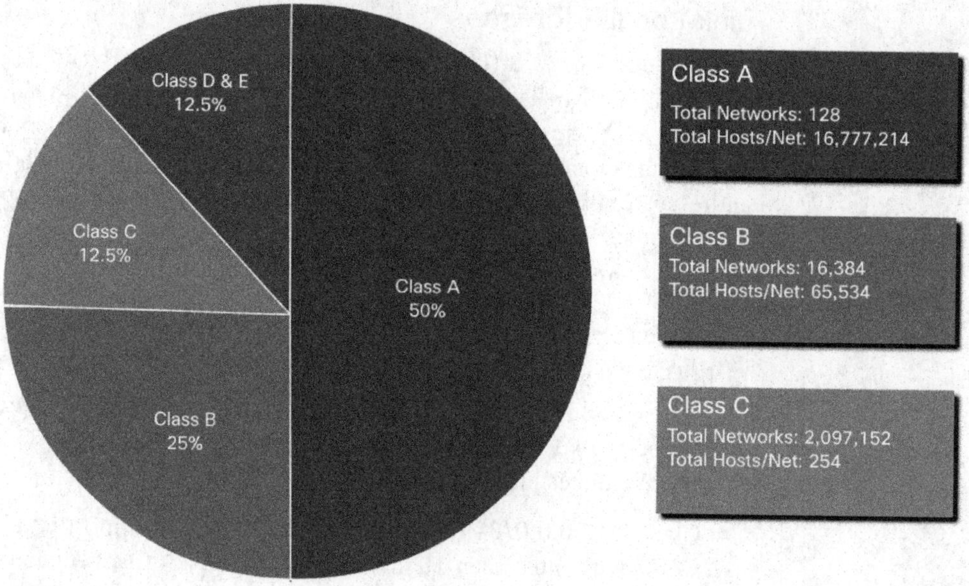

Figure 9-5 Classful Addressing

In the mid-1990s, with the introduction of the Web, classful addressing was deprecated to more efficiently allocate the limited IPv4 address space. Classful address allocation was replaced with classless addressing, which is used today. Classless addressing ignores the rules of classes (A, B, C). Public IPv4 network addresses (network addresses and subnet masks) are allocated based on the number of addresses that can be justified.

Assignment of IP Addresses (9.2.6)

As previously introduced, public IPv4 addresses are addresses that are globally routed over the Internet and must be unique.

Both IPv4 and IPv6 addresses are managed by the *Internet Assigned Numbers Authority (IANA)*. The IANA allocates blocks of IP addresses to five *Regional Internet Registries (RIRs)*. The RIRs are responsible for allocating IP addresses to ISPs that provide IPv4 address blocks to organizations and smaller ISPs. Organizations can also get their addresses directly from an RIR (subject to the policies of that RIR).

The geographical regions of the five RIRs are shown in Figure 9-6 and described here:

- AfriNIC (African Network Information Centre)—Africa Region
- APNIC (Asia Pacific Network Information Centre)—Asia/Pacific Region

- ARIN (American Registry for Internet Numbers)—North America Region
- LACNIC (Regional Latin-American and Caribbean IP Address Registry)—Latin America and some Caribbean Islands
- RIPE NCC (Réseaux IP Européens Network Coordination Centre)—Europe, the Middle East, and Central Asia

Figure 9-6 Five Regional Internet Registries

Interactive Graphic

Activity—Public or Private IPv4 Address (9.2.7)

Refer to the online course to complete this activity.

Interactive Graphic

Check Your Understanding—Types of IPv4 Addresses (9.2.8)

Refer to the online course to complete this activity.

Network Segmentation (9.3)

This section discusses network segmentation and the reasons to divide larger networks into smaller networks, known as subnets.

Video

Video—Network Segmentation (9.3.1)

Refer to the online course to view this video.

Broadcast Domains and Segmentation (9.3.2)

Have you ever received an email that was addressed to every person at your organization or school? If you have, then you've received a broadcast email. Hopefully, it contained information that you and each of the other recipients needed to know. But often a broadcast is not really pertinent to everyone in the mailing list. Sometimes, only a segment of the recipient population needs to read that information.

In an Ethernet LAN, devices use broadcasts and the Address Resolution Protocol (ARP) to locate other devices. ARP sends Layer 2 broadcasts to a known IPv4 address on the local network to discover the associated MAC address. Devices on Ethernet LANs also locate other devices using services. A host typically acquires its IPv4 address configuration using the Dynamic Host Configuration Protocol (DHCP), which sends broadcasts on the local network to locate a DHCP server.

Switches propagate broadcasts out all interfaces except the interface on which it was received. For example, if one of the four switches in the broadcast domain shown in Figure 9-7 were to receive a broadcast, it would forward it to the other switches and other users connected in the network.

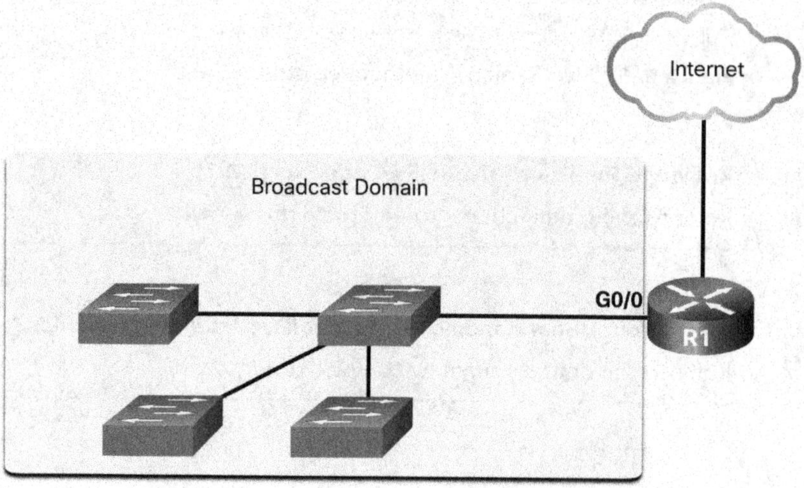

Figure 9-7 Broadcast Domain with Four Switches

Routers do not propagate broadcasts. When a router receives a broadcast, it does not forward it out other interfaces. For instance, when R1 in Figure 9-7 receives a broadcast on its Gigabit Ethernet 0/0 interface, it does not forward it out another interface.

Therefore, each router interface connects to a broadcast domain and broadcasts are propagated only within that specific broadcast domain.

Problems with Large Broadcast Domains (9.3.3)

A large broadcast domain is a network that connects many hosts. A problem with a large broadcast domain is that these hosts can generate excessive broadcasts and negatively affect the network. In Figure 9-8, LAN 1 connects 400 users that could generate an excessive amount of broadcast traffic. This results in slow network operations due to the significant amount of traffic it can cause and slow device operations because a device must accept and process each broadcast packet.

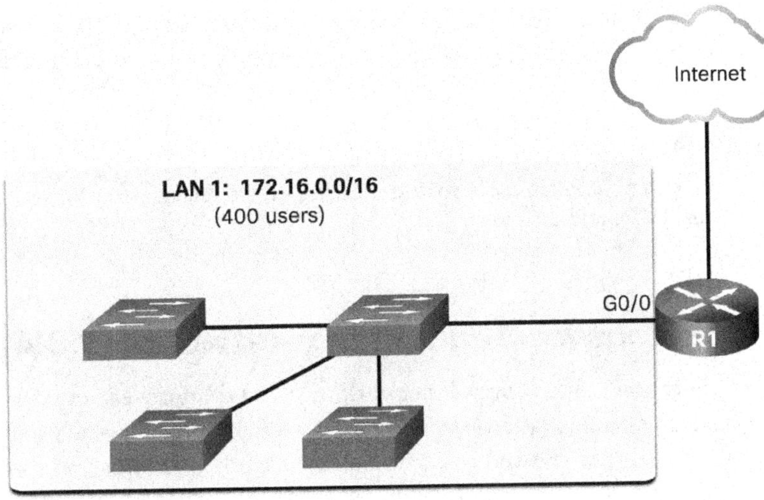

Figure 9-8 Large Broadcast Domain

The solution is to reduce the size of the network to create smaller broadcast domains in a process called *subnetting*. These smaller network spaces are called *subnets*.

In Figure 9-9, the 400 users in LAN 1 with network address 172.16.0.0 /16, depicted in Figure 9-8, have been divided into two subnets of 200 users each: 172.16.0.0 /24 and 172.16.1.0 /24. Broadcasts are propagated only within the smaller broadcast domains. Therefore, a broadcast in LAN 1 would not propagate to LAN 2.

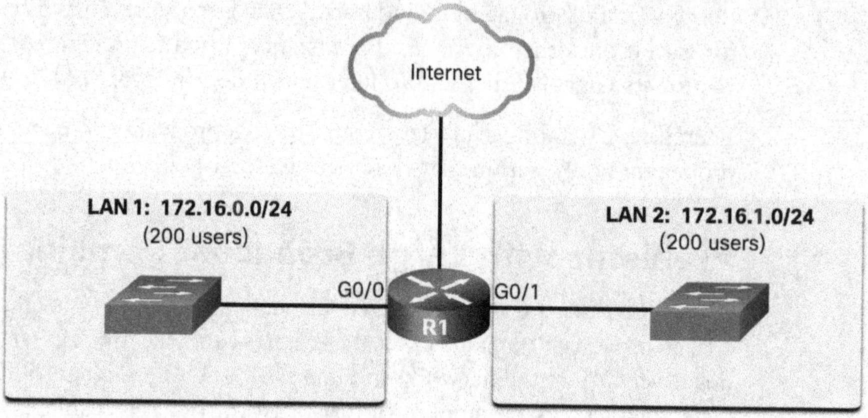

Figure 9-9 Segmenting a Large Broadcast Domain

Notice how the prefix length has changed from a single /16 network to two /24 networks. This is the basis of subnetting: using host bits to create additional subnets.

Note

The terms *subnet* and *network* are often used interchangeably. Most networks are a subnet of some larger address block.

Reasons for Segmenting Networks (9.3.4)

Subnetting reduces overall network traffic and improves network performance. It also enables an administrator to implement security policies, such as which subnets are allowed or not allowed to communicate together. Another reason for segmenting networks is that it reduces the number of devices affected by abnormal broadcast traffic resulting from misconfigurations, hardware/software problems, or malicious intent.

There are various ways of using subnets to help manage network devices, as shown in Figures 9-10 through 9-12.

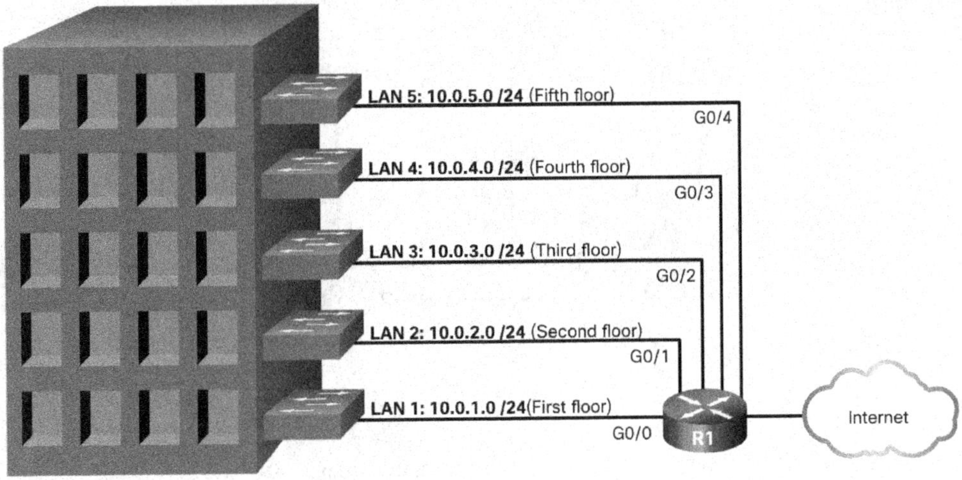

Figure 9-10 Subnetting by Location

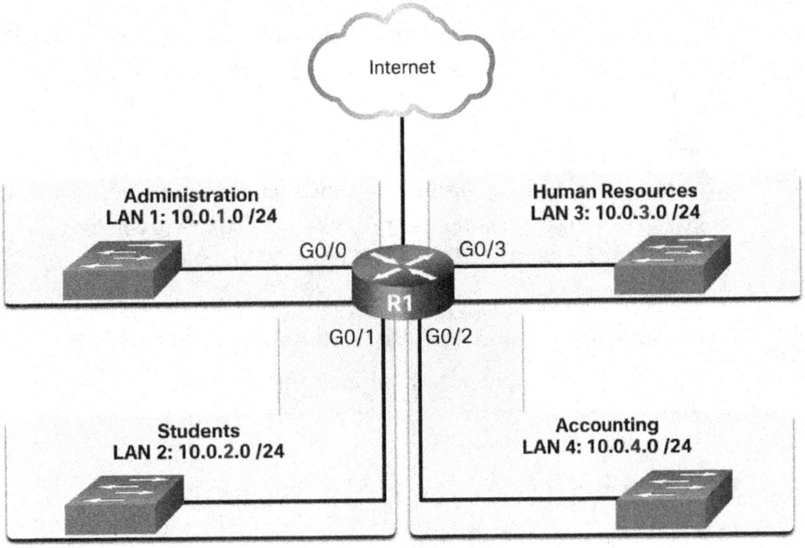

Figure 9-11 Subnetting by Group or Function

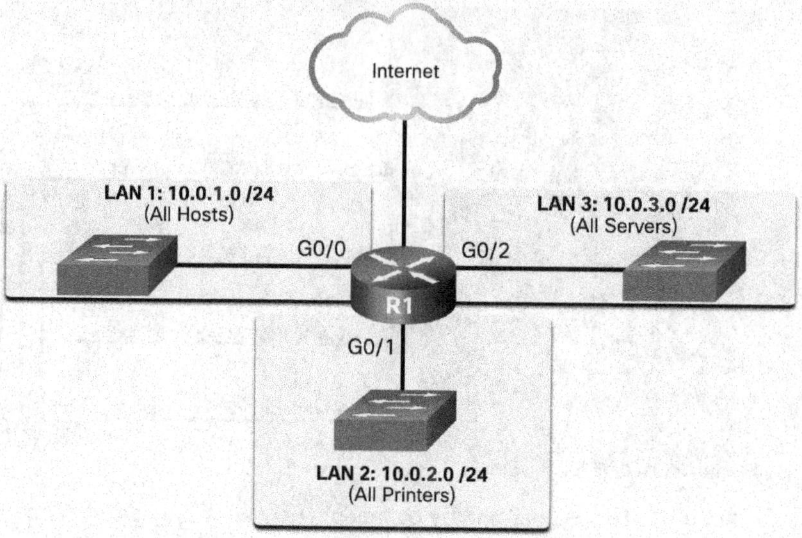

Figure 9-12 Subnetting by Device Type

Network administrators can create subnets using any other division that makes sense for the network. Notice in each figure that the subnets use longer prefix lengths to identify networks.

Understanding how to subnet networks is a fundamental skill that all network administrators must develop. Various methods have been created to help understand this process. Although learning the process is a little overwhelming at first, pay close attention to the detail and, with practice, subnetting will become easier.

Interactive Graphic

Check Your Understanding—Network Segmentation (9.3.4)

Refer to the online course to complete this activity.

IPv4 and Network Segmentation Summary (9.4)

The following is a summary of each topic in the chapter and some questions for your reflection.

What Did I Learn in This Chapter? (9.4.1)

- **IPv4 Unicast, Broadcast, and Multicast**—Unicast transmission refers to one device sending a message to one other device in one-to-one communications. A

unicast packet has a destination IP address that is a unicast address which goes to a single recipient. A source IP address can only be a unicast address because the packet can only originate from a single source. This applies regardless of whether the destination IP address is a unicast, broadcast, or multicast. IPv4 unicast host addresses are in the address range of 1.1.1.1 to 223.255.255.255.

Broadcast transmission refers to a device sending a message to all the devices on a network in one-to-all communications. A broadcast packet has a destination IP address with all ones (1s) in the host portion, or 32 one (1) bits. A broadcast packet must be processed by all devices in the same broadcast domain. A broadcast may be directed or limited. A directed broadcast is sent to all hosts on a specific network. A limited broadcast is sent to 255.255.255.255. By default, routers do not forward broadcasts.

Multicast transmission reduces traffic by allowing a host to send a single packet to a selected set of hosts that subscribes to a multicast group. A multicast packet is a packet with a destination IP address that is a multicast address. IPv4 has reserved the 224.0.0.0 to 239.255.255.255 addresses as a multicast range. Each multicast group is represented by a single IPv4 multicast destination address. When an IPv4 host subscribes to a multicast group, the host processes both packets addressed to this multicast address and packets addressed to its uniquely allocated unicast address.

- **Types of IPv4 Addresses**—Public IPv4 addresses are addresses that are globally routed between ISP routers. However, not all available IPv4 addresses can be used on the Internet. There are blocks of addresses called private addresses that are used by most organizations to assign IPv4 addresses to internal hosts. Most internal networks, from large enterprises to home networks, use private IPv4 addresses for addressing all internal devices (intranet), including hosts and routers. However, private addresses are not globally routable. Before the ISP can forward this packet, it must translate the source IPv4 address, which is a private address, to a public IPv4 address using NAT.

  Loopback addresses (127.0.0.0 /8 or 127.0.0.1 to 127.255.255.254) are more commonly identified as only 127.0.0.1. These are special addresses used by a host to direct traffic to itself. Link-local addresses (169.254.0.0 /16 or 169.254.0.1 to 169.254.255.254) are more commonly known as the Automatic Private IP Addressing (APIPA) addresses or self-assigned addresses. They are used by a Windows DHCP client to self-configure in the event that there are no DHCP servers available.

  In 1981, IPv4 addresses were assigned using classful addressing as defined in RFC 790, "Assigned Numbers." Customers were allocated a network address

based on one of three classes, A, B, or C. RFC 790 divided the unicast ranges into specific classes as follows:

- **Class A (0.0.0.0/8–127.0.0.0/8)**—Designed to support extremely large networks with more than 16 million host addresses.
- **Class B (128.0.0.0 /16–191.255.0.0 /16)**—Designed to support the needs of moderate to large size networks with up to approximately 65,000 host addresses.
- **Class C (192.0.0.0 /24–223.255.255.0 /24)**—Designed to support small networks with a maximum of 254 hosts.

There is also a Class D multicast block consisting of 224.0.0.0 to 239.0.0.0 and a Class E experimental address block consisting of 240.0.0.0–255.0.0.0.

Public IPv4 addresses are addresses that are globally routed over the Internet. Public IPv4 addresses must be unique. Both IPv4 and IPv6 addresses are managed by the IANA. The IANA allocates blocks of IP addresses to the five RIRs. RIRs are responsible for allocating IP addresses to ISPs that provide IPv4 address blocks to organizations and smaller ISPs. Organizations can also get their addresses directly from an RIR.

- **Network Segmentation**—In an Ethernet LAN, devices use broadcasts and ARP to locate other devices. ARP sends Layer 2 broadcasts to a known IPv4 address on the local network to discover the associated MAC address. Devices on Ethernet LANs also locate other devices using services. A host typically acquires its IPv4 address configuration using DHCP, which sends broadcasts on the local network to locate a DHCP server. Switches propagate broadcasts out all interfaces except the interface on which it was received.

  A large broadcast domain is a network that connects many hosts. A problem with a large broadcast domain is that these hosts can generate excessive broadcasts and negatively affect the network. The solution is to reduce the size of the network to create smaller broadcast domains in a process called subnetting. These smaller network spaces are called subnets. The basis of subnetting is to use host bits to create additional subnets. Subnetting reduces overall network traffic and improves network performance. It helps administrators to implement security policies, such as which subnets are allowed or not allowed to communicate together. Subnetting also reduces the number of devices affected by abnormal broadcast traffic caused by misconfigurations, hardware/software problems, or malicious intent.

Reflection Questions (9.4.2)

I just sent party invitations to several of my friends and family. The invitations went to different addresses, but the card inside is the same for everyone. This is like a multicast email, isn't it? I didn't know you could do that, and I also didn't know you could send a broadcast email to every person on your network! Can you think of a good reason to send a broadcast email to everyone in your network? Can you think of a reason why you should be careful before you send a broadcast email?

Practice

There are no labs or Packet Tracer activities in this chapter.

Check Your Understanding Questions

Complete all the review questions listed here to test your understanding of the topics and concepts in this chapter. Appendix A, "Answers to 'Check Your Understanding' Questions," lists the answers.

1. Which statement describes one purpose of the subnet mask setting for a host?
   a. It is used to describe the type of the subnet.
   b. It is used to identify the default gateway.
   c. It is used to determine to which network the host is connected.
   d. It is used to determine the maximum number of bits within one packet that can be placed on a particular network.

2. What is one reason for subnetting an IP network?
   a. To reduce the scope of broadcast flooding
   b. To increase the number of available host addresses on the network
   c. To remove the need for network services that rely on broadcasts, such as DHCP
   d. To ensure that all devices can communicate with each other without requiring a router

3. A message is sent to all hosts on a remote network. Which type of message is it?
   a. Limited broadcast
   b. Multicast
   c. Directed broadcast
   d. Unicast

4. A user is unable to access the company server from a computer. The user issues the **ipconfig** command and finds that the IP address of the computer is displayed as 169.254.0.2. What type of address is this?
   a. Private
   b. Link-local
   c. Loopback
   d. Experimental

5. Which three IP addresses are private? (Choose three.)

   a. 10.1.1.1
   b. 172.32.5.2
   c. 192.167.10.10
   d. 172.16.4.4
   e. 192.168.5.5
   f. 224.6.6.6

6. Match each description with an appropriate IP address.

   198.133.219.2

   169.254.1.5

   127.0.0.1

   240.2.6.255

   a. Link-local address
   b. Loopback address
   c. Public address
   d. Experimental address

7. Which network device can serve as a boundary to divide a Layer 2 broadcast domain?

   a. Router
   b. Ethernet bridge
   c. Ethernet hub
   d. Access point

8. What is the role of IANA?

   a. To maintain standards related to electrical wiring and connectors
   b. To document developments for new protocols and update existing protocols
   c. To manage the allocation of IP addresses and domain names
   d. To promote the development and evolution of the Internet around the world

9. Which address prefix range is reserved for IPv4 multicast?

   a. 240.0.0.0–254.255.255.255
   b. 224.0.0.0–239.255.255.255
   c. 169.254.0.0–169.254.255.255
   d. 127.0.0.0–127.255.255.255

10. A high school in New York (school A) is using videoconferencing technology to establish student interactions with a high school (school B) in Poland. The video-conferencing is conducted between two end devices through the Internet. The network administrator of school A configures the end device with the IP address 209.165.201.10. The administrator sends a request for the IP address of the end device in school B, and the response is 192.168.25.10. Neither school is using a VPN. The administrator knows immediately that this IP address will not work. Why?

    a. This is a loopback address.
    b. This is a link-local address.
    c. This is a private IP address.
    d. There is an IP address conflict.

11. A host is transmitting a broadcast. Which host or hosts will receive it?

    a. All hosts on the same network
    b. A specially defined group of hosts
    c. The closest neighbor on the same network
    d. All hosts on the Internet

CHAPTER 10

IPv6 Addressing Formats and Rules

Objectives

Upon completion of this chapter, you will be able to answer the following questions:

- Why is IPv6 addressing needed?
- How are IPv6 addresses represented?

Key Terms

This chapter uses the following key terms. You can find the definitions in the Glossary.

dual stack *Page 150*

Network Address Translation 64 (NAT64) *Page 151*

tunneling *Page 150*

Introduction (10.0)

Kishori meets Rina for lunch again. Kishori is excited to tell Rina all that she has learned about IPv4 addresses. Rina congratulates her and asks her if she has heard about IPv6. IPv6? Kishori has no idea what IPv6 is! Do you? Let me help you out with that. Let's get started with this chapter!

IPv4 Issues (10.1)

This section examines the reasons for the migration to IPv6.

The Need for IPv6 (10.1.1)

You already know from Chapter 9 that IPv4 is running out of addresses. That is why you need to learn about IPv6.

IPv6 is designed to be the successor to IPv4 and its 32-bit address space. IPv6 has a larger, 128-bit address space, providing a theoretical maximum of 340 undecillion (340 followed by 36 zeroes) possible addresses, whereas IPv4 has a theoretical maximum of 4.3 billion addresses. However, IPv6 is more than just a larger address space.

When the IETF began its development of a successor to IPv4, it used this opportunity to fix the limitations of IPv4 and include enhancements. One example of an enhancement is Internet Control Message Protocol version 6 (ICMPv6), which includes address resolution and address autoconfiguration not found in ICMP for IPv4 (ICMPv4).

The depletion of IPv4 address space has been the motivating factor for moving to IPv6. As Africa, Asia, and other areas of the world become more connected to the Internet, there are not enough IPv4 addresses to accommodate this growth. As shown in Figure 10-1, all five RIRs have run out of IPv4 addresses.

Private addresses in combination with Network Address Translation (NAT) have been instrumental in slowing the depletion of IPv4 address space. However, NAT is problematic for many applications, creates latency, and has limitations that severely impede peer-to-peer communications.

With the ever-increasing number of mobile devices, mobile providers have been leading the way with the transition to IPv6. The top two mobile providers in the United States report that over 90% of their traffic is over IPv6.

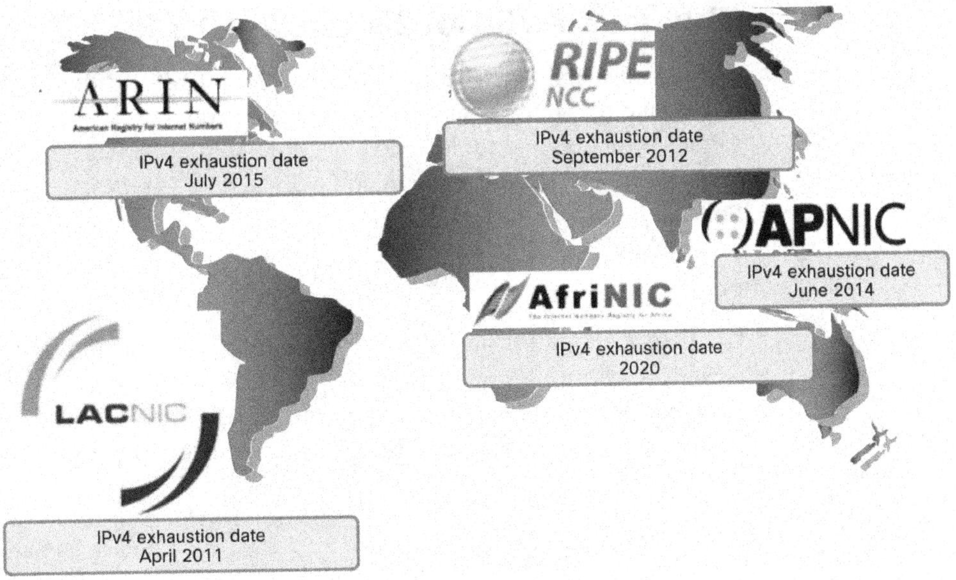

Figure 10-1 RIR IPv4 Exhaustion Dates

Most top ISPs and content providers such as YouTube, Facebook, and Netflix have also made the transition. Many companies like Microsoft, Facebook, and LinkedIn are transitioning to IPv6-only internally. In 2022, broadband ISP Comcast reported an IPv6 deployment of over 80% and British Sky Broadcasting reported an IPv6 deployment of over 90%.

Internet of Things

The Internet of today is significantly different than the Internet of past decades. The Internet of today is more than email, web pages, and file transfers between computers. The evolving Internet is becoming an *Internet of Things (IoT)*. No longer will the only devices accessing the Internet be computers, tablets, and smartphones. The sensor-equipped, Internet-ready devices of tomorrow will include everything from automobiles and biomedical devices to household appliances and natural ecosystems.

With an increasing Internet population, a limited IPv4 address space, issues with NAT, and the burgeoning IoT, the time has come to begin the transition to IPv6.

IPv4 and IPv6 Coexistence (10.1.2)

There is no specific date to move to IPv6. Both IPv4 and IPv6 will coexist in the near future, and the transition to IPv6 will take several more years. The IETF has created various protocols and tools to help network administrators migrate their networks to IPv6. The migration techniques can be divided into three categories: dual stack, tunneling, and translation.

Dual Stack

Dual stack allows IPv4 and IPv6 to coexist on the same network segment. Dual stack devices run both IPv4 and IPv6 protocol stacks simultaneously (see Figure 10-2). Known as *native IPv6*, this means the customer network has an IPv6 connection to its ISP and is able to access content found on the Internet over IPv6.

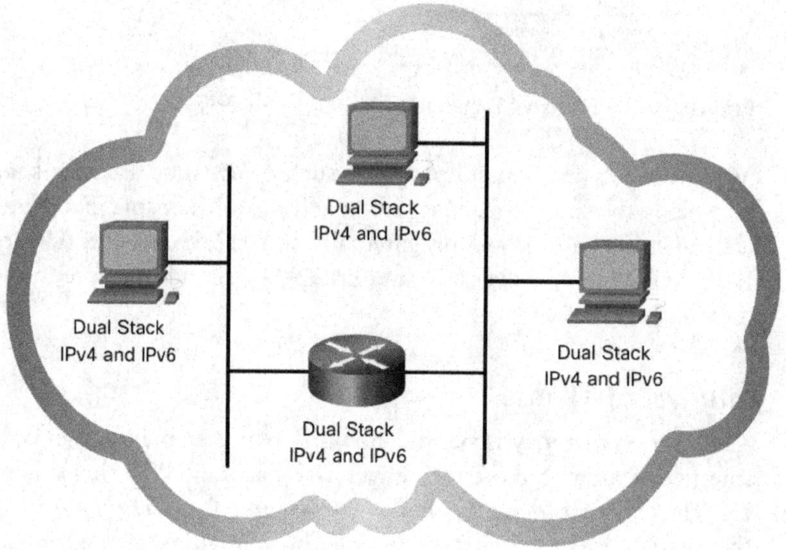

Figure 10-2 Dual Stack Topology

Tunneling

Tunneling is a method of transporting an IPv6 packet over an IPv4 network (see Figure 10-3). The IPv6 packet is encapsulated in an IPv4 packet, similar to other types of data.

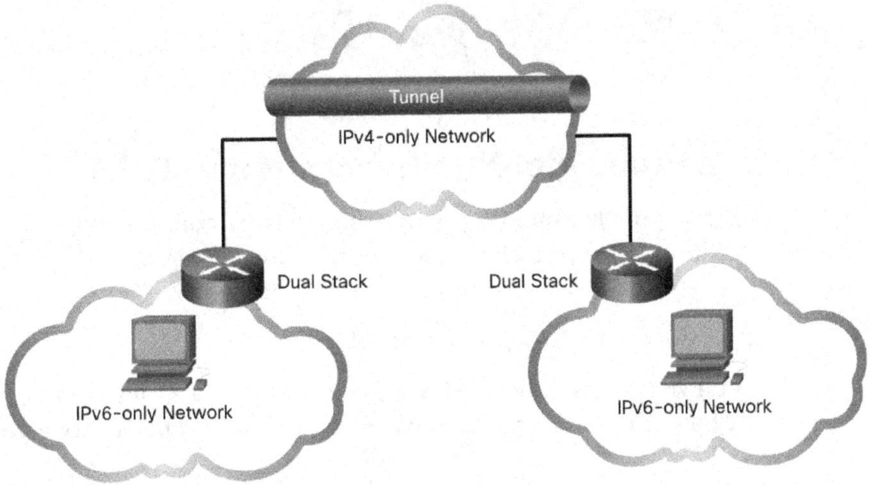

Figure 10-3 Tunneling Topology

Translation

Network Address Translation 64 (NAT64) allows IPv6-enabled devices to communicate with IPv4-enabled devices using a translation technique similar to NAT for IPv4. An IPv6 packet is translated to an IPv4 packet, and an IPv4 packet is translated to an IPv6 packet (see Figure 10-4).

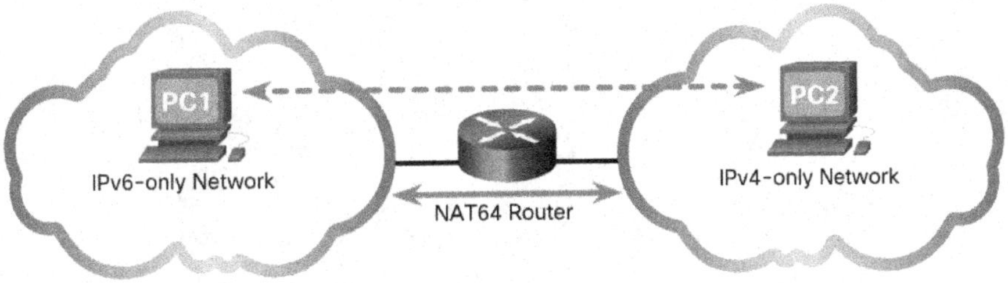

Figure 10-4 NAT64 Topology

Note

The tunneling and translation migration techniques should be used only to help transition from IPv4 to IPv6. The goal should be native IPv6 communications from source to destination.

Interactive Graphic

Check Your Understanding—IPv4 Issues (10.1.3)

Refer to the online course to complete this activity.

IPv6 Addressing (10.2)

This section discusses the representation of IPv6 addresses.

Hexadecimal Number System (10.2.1)

Before you dive into IPv6 addressing, it's important that you know that IPv6 addresses are represented using hexadecimal numbers. This base-16 number system uses the digits 0 to 9 and the letters A to F:

0 1 2 3 4 5 6 7 8 9 A B C D E F

In IPv6 addresses, these 16 digits are represented as hextets (discussed next), which allows us to represent these massive addresses in a much more readable format.

IPv6 Addressing Formats (10.2.2)

The first step to learning about the use of IPv6 in networks is to understand the way an IPv6 address is written and formatted. The IPv6 address space is much larger than the IPv4 address space, which is why the world is unlikely to run out of IPv6 addresses.

IPv6 addresses are 128 bits in length and written as a string of hexadecimal values. Every 4 bits is represented by a single hexadecimal digit, for a total of 32 hexadecimal values, as shown in Figure 10-5. IPv6 addresses are not case-sensitive and can be written in either lowercase or uppercase.

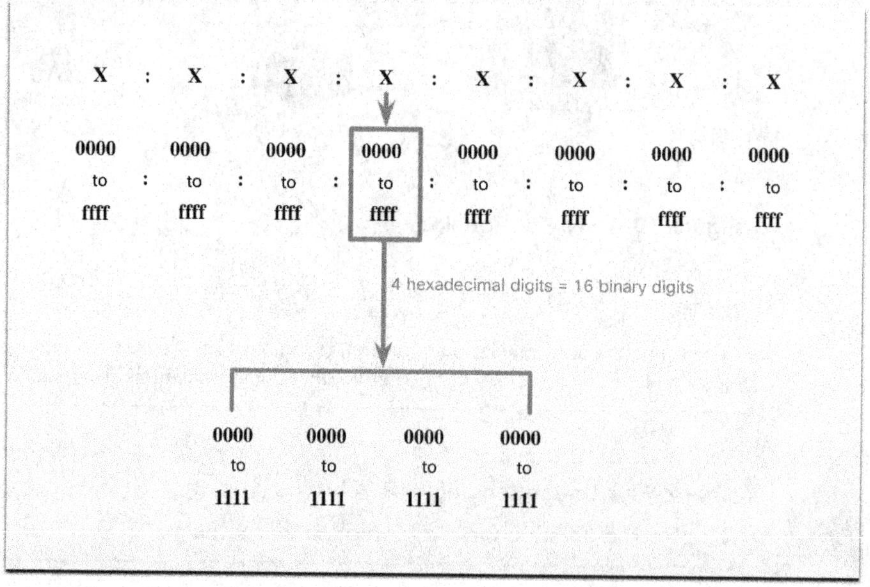

Figure 10-5 16-bit Segments or Hextets

Preferred Format

Figure 10-5 also shows that the preferred format for writing an IPv6 address is x:x:x:x:x:x:x:x, with each x consisting of four hexadecimal values. The term *octet* refers to the 8 bits of an IPv4 address. In IPv6, *hextet* is the unofficial term used to refer to a segment of 16 bits, or four hexadecimal values. Each x is a single hextet, which is 16 bits or four hexadecimal digits.

"Preferred format" means that you write an IPv6 address using all 32 hexadecimal digits. It does not necessarily mean that it is the ideal method for representing the IPv6 address. Two rules that help to reduce the number of digits needed to represent an IPv6 address are explained in the following sections.

Several IPv6 addresses in the preferred format are shown in Example 10-1.

Example 10-1 IPv6 Address Preferred Format

```
2001 : 0db8 : 0000 : 1111 : 0000 : 0000 : 0000: 0200
2001 : 0db8 : 0000 : 00a3 : abcd : 0000 : 0000: 1234
2001 : 0db8 : 000a : 0001 : c012 : 9aff : fe9a: 19ac
2001 : 0db8 : aaaa : 0001 : 0000 : 0000 : 0000: 0000
fe80 : 0000 : 0000 : 0000 : 0123 : 4567 : 89ab: cdef
fe80 : 0000 : 0000 : 0000 : 0000 : 0000 : 0000: 0001
fe80 : 0000 : 0000 : 0000 : c012 : 9aff : fe9a: 19ac
fe80 : 0000 : 0000 : 0000 : 0123 : 4567 : 89ab: cdef
0000 : 0000 : 0000 : 0000 : 0000 : 0000 : 0000: 0001
0000 : 0000 : 0000 : 0000 : 0000 : 0000 : 0000: 0000
```

Video

Video—IPv6 Formatting Rules (10.2.3)

Refer to the online course to view this video.

Rule 1—Omit Leading Zeros (10.2.4)

The first rule to help reduce the notation of IPv6 addresses is to omit any leading zeros in any hextet. Here are four examples of ways to omit leading zeros:

- 01ab can be represented as 1ab.
- 09f0 can be represented as 9f0.
- 0a00 can be represented as a00.
- 00ab can be represented as ab.

This rule applies only to leading zeros, *not* to trailing zeros, because otherwise the address would be ambiguous. For example, if the rule were to apply to trailing zeros, the hextet abc could be either 0abc or abc0, but these do not represent the same value. Table 10-1 shows full examples of omitting leading zeros.

Table 10-1 Omitting Leading 0s

Type	Format
Preferred	2001 : 0db8 : 0000 : 1111 : 0000 : 0000 : 0000 : 0200
No leading zeros	2001 : db8 : 0 : 1111 : 0 : 0 : 0 : 200
Preferred	2001 : 0db8 : 0000 : 00a3 : ab00 : 0ab0 : 00ab : 1234
No leading zeros	2001 : db8 : 0 : a3 : ab00 : ab0 : ab : 1234
Preferred	2001 : 0db8 : 000a : 0001 : c012 : 90ff : fe90 : 0001
No leading zeros	2001 : db8 : a : 1 : c012 : 90ff : fe90 : 1
Preferred	2001 : 0db8 : aaaa : 0001 : 0000 : 0000 : 0000 : 0000
No leading zeros	2001 : db8 : aaaa : 1 : 0 : 0 : 0 : 0
Preferred	fe80 : 0000 : 0000 : 0000 : 0123 : 4567 : 89ab : cdef
No leading zeros	fe80 : 0 : 0 : 0 : 123 : 4567 : 89ab : cdef
Preferred	fe80 : 0000 : 0000 : 0000 : 0000 : 0000 : 0000 : 0001
No leading zeros	fe80 : 0 : 0 : 0 : 0 : 0 : 0 : 1
Preferred	0000 : 0000 : 0000 : 0000 : 0000 : 0000 : 0000 : 0001
No leading zeros	0 : 0 : 0 : 0 : 0 : 0 : 0 : 1
Preferred	0000 : 0000 : 0000 : 0000 : 0000 : 0000 : 0000 : 0000
No leading zeros	0 : 0 : 0 : 0 : 0 : 0 : 0 : 0

Rule 2—Double Colon (10.2.5)

The second rule to help reduce the notation of IPv6 addresses is that a double colon (::) can replace any single, contiguous string of one or more 16-bit hextets consisting of all zeros. For example, 2001:db8:cafe:1:0:0:0:1 (leading zeros omitted) could be represented as 2001:db8:cafe:1::1. The double colon is used in place of the three all-zero hextets (0:0:0).

The double colon can be used only once within an address; otherwise, there would be more than one possible resulting address. Using this technique along with the technique of omitting leading zeros can often greatly reduce the notation of IPv6 addresses. This is commonly known as the *compressed format*.

Here is an example of the incorrect use of the double colon:

2001:db8::abcd::1234

The double colon is used twice in this example. Here are the possible expansions of this incorrect compressed format address:

- 2001:db8::abcd:0000:0000:1234
- 2001:db8::abcd:0000:0000:0000:1234
- 2001:db8:0000:abcd::1234
- 2001:db8:0000:0000:abcd::1234

If an address has more than one contiguous string of all-zero hextets, best practice is to use the double colon on the longest string. If the strings are equal, use the double colon on the first string.

Table 10-2 shows examples of omitting leading zeros and all-zero segments.

Table 10-2 Omitting Leading Zeros and All-Zero Segments

Type	Format
Preferred	2001 : **0**db8 : **0000** : 1111 : **0000** : **0000** : **0000** : 0200
Compressed/spaces	2001 : db8 : 0 : 1111 : : 200
Compressed	2001:db8:0:1111::200
Preferred	2001 : **0**db8 : **0000** : **0000** : ab00 : **0000** : **0000** : **0000**
Compressed/spaces	2001 : db8 : 0 : 0 : ab00 ::
Compressed	2001:db8:0:0:ab00::

Type	Format
Preferred	2001 : 0db8 : aaaa : **0001 : 0000 : 0000 : 0000 : 0000**
Compressed/spaces	2001 : db8 : aaaa : 1 ::
Compressed	2001:db8:aaaa:1::
Preferred	fe80 : **0000 : 0000 : 0000** : 0123 : 4567 : 89ab : cdef
Compressed/spaces	fe80 : : 123 : 4567 : 89ab : cdef
Compressed	fe80::123:4567:89ab:cdef
Preferred	fe80 : **0000 : 0000 : 0000 : 0000 : 0000 : 0000** : 0001
Compressed/spaces	fe80 : : 1
Compressed	fe80::0
Preferred	**0000 : 0000 : 0000 : 0000 : 0000 : 0000 : 0000 : 0001**
Compressed/spaces	:: 1
Compressed	::1
Preferred	**0000 : 0000 : 0000 : 0000 : 0000 : 0000 : 0000 : 0000**
Compressed/spaces	::
Compressed	::

Interactive Graphic

Activity—IPv6 Address Representations (10.2.6)

Refer to the online course to complete this activity.

IPv6 Addressing Formats and Rules Summary (10.3)

The following is a summary of each topic in the chapter and some questions for your reflection.

What Did I Learn in This Chapter? (10.3.1)

- **IPv4 Issues**—The depletion of IPv4 address space has been the motivating factor for moving to IPv6. IPv6 has a larger, 128-bit address space, providing 340 undecillion possible addresses. When the IETF began its development of a successor to IPv4, it used this opportunity to fix the limitations of IPv4 and include enhancements, such as ICMPv6, which includes address resolution and address autoconfiguration not found in ICMPv4.

  IPv4 and IPv6 currently coexist and the transition to only IPv6 will take several more years. The IETF has created various protocols and tools to help network administrators migrate their networks to IPv6. The migration techniques can be divided into three categories: dual stack, tunneling, and translation. Dual stack devices run both IPv4 and IPv6 protocol stacks simultaneously. Tunneling is a method of transporting an IPv6 packet over an IPv4 network. The IPv6 packet is encapsulated in an IPv4 packet, similar to other types of data. NAT64 allows IPv6-enabled devices to communicate with IPv4-enabled devices using a translation technique similar to NAT for IPv4. An IPv6 packet is translated to an IPv4 packet, and an IPv4 packet is translated to an IPv6 packet.

- **IPv6 Addressing**—IPv6 addresses are 128 bits in length and written as a string of hexadecimal values. Every 4 bits is represented by a single hexadecimal digit, for a total of 32 hexadecimal values. IPv6 addresses are not case-sensitive and can be written in either lowercase or uppercase. In IPv6, a hextet refers to a segment of 16 bits, or four hexadecimal values. Each x is a single hextet, which is 16 bits or four hexadecimal digits. "Preferred format" means that you write an IPv6 address using all 32 hexadecimal digits. Here is one example—fe80:0000:0000:0000:0123:4567:89ab:cdef.

  Two rules help to reduce the number of digits needed to represent an IPv6 address.

  Rule 1—Omit leading zeros. You can omit only leading zeros, not trailing zeros.

  - 01ab can be represented as 1ab.
  - 09f0 can be represented as 9f0.
  - 0a00 can be represented as a00.
  - 00ab can be represented as ab.

  Rule 2—Double colon. A double colon (::) can replace any single, contiguous string of one or more 16-bit hextets consisting of all zeros. For example, 2001:db8:cafe:1:0:0:0:1 (leading zeros omitted) could be represented as 2001:db8:cafe:1::1. The double colon is used in place of the three all-zero hextets (0:0:0). The double colon can be used only once within an address; otherwise,

there would be more than one possible resulting address. If an address has more than one contiguous string of all-zero hextets, best practice is to use the double colon on the longest string. If the strings are equal, use the double colon on the first string.

Reflection Questions (10.3.2)

Just when I was starting to get the hang of IPv4 addresses, I learned about IPv6 addresses! But since it looks like most networks use both types of addresses, I'm glad that I know a bit about each type. I guess it's like cars on the road. Some are old but they still run. Newer cars have many more features and options than the older cars. And both older and newer cars are all driving on the same road. What is one obvious advantage to using IPv6 addresses instead of using IPv4 addresses?

Practice

There are no labs or Packet Tracer activities in this chapter.

Check Your Understanding Questions

Complete all the review questions listed here to test your understanding of the topics and concepts in this chapter. Appendix A, "Answers to 'Check Your Understanding' Questions," lists the answers.

1. What is an advantage of using IPv6 over IPv4?
   a. More addresses for networks and hosts
   b. Faster connectivity
   c. Higher bandwidth
   d. More frequencies

2. What was the reason for the creation and implementation of IPv6?
   a. To make reading a 32-bit address easier
   b. To relieve IPv4 address depletion
   c. To provide more address space in the Internet Names Registry
   d. To allow NAT support for private addressing

3. Which letter represents the hexadecimal value of the decimal number 15?
   a. f
   b. g
   c. h
   d. b

4. A PC is configured with both an IPv4 address and an IPv6 address on the same network adapter. What IPv4 and IPv6 coexistence strategy is implemented on the PC?
   a. Dual stack
   b. NAT64
   c. Tunneling
   d. NAT

5. What are two methods that can be used to shorten the IPv6 address notation? (Choose two.)

   a. Use of a double colon to represent a string of all-zero hextets
   b. Omit all leading zeros from all hextets in the address
   c. Remove all trailing zeros contained in the IPv6 address
   d. Use of a double colon to represent a string of the same non-zero value

6. Which network migration technique encapsulates IPv6 packets in IPv4 packets to carry them over IPv4 network infrastructures?

   a. Encapsulation
   b. Translation
   c. Dual stack
   d. Tunneling

7. What does a double colon represent in IPv6 address notation?

   a. A continuous string of one or more hextets that contain only zeros
   b. At least eight occurrences of the same non-zero value
   c. The boundary between the network portion and the host portion of the address
   d. The beginning of the MAC address assigned to the IPv6 device

8. IPv6 increases the IP address size from 32 bits to how many bits?

   a. 64
   b. 96
   c. 128
   d. 192
   e. 256

9. Which technology enables devices in an IPv6-only network to communicate with devices in an IPv4-only network?

   a. NAT64
   b. Tunneling
   c. DHCP
   d. Link-local addressing

10. Which IPv6 address notation is valid?

    a. 2001:0db8::abcd::1234
    b. abcd:160d::4gab:ffab
    c. 2001:db8:0:1111::200
    d. 2001::abcd::

11. Which two statements are correct about IPv4 and IPv6 addresses? (Choose two.)

    a. IPv6 addresses are represented by hexadecimal numbers.
    b. IPv4 addresses are represented by hexadecimal numbers.
    c. IPv6 addresses are 32 bits in length.
    d. IPv4 addresses are 32 bits in length.
    e. IPv4 addresses are 128 bits in length.
    f. IPv6 addresses are 64 bits in length.

CHAPTER 11

Dynamic Addressing with DHCP

Objectives

Upon completion of this chapter, you will be able to answer the following questions:

- What is the difference between static and dynamic IPv4 addressing?
- Configure a DHCPv4 server to dynamically assign IPv4 addresses.

Key Term

This chapter uses the following key term. You can find the definition in the Glossary.

Dynamic Host Configuration Protocol (DHCP) *Page 165*

Introduction (11.0)

Kishori's nursing station just received a new laptop from the IT department. The IT specialist, Madhav, is setting it up on the desk and trying to connect to the network. He asks Kishori to log in to the computer. She enters her username and password and attempts to access a patient file. She explains that there must be a connection error. Madhav takes a seat to further investigate. Madhav checks the cable and it is connected. On his tablet, he pulls up the list of IPv4 addresses for all of the computers on this floor on this network. He found the issue! There is an error in the IPv4 address. Madhav explains that the intern in their department may have manually configured the network information on this host instead of using DHCP. Kishori has not heard about DHCP. She is going to do some reading on this topic.

Are you ready to learn about DHCP? I am here to help! Let's get started with this chapter!

Static and Dynamic Addressing (11.1)

It is important that devices have the correct IPv4 addressing information. This includes the IPv4 address, subnet mask, default gateway address, and DNS server address.

Static IPv4 Address Assignment (11.1.1)

IPv4 addresses can be assigned either statically or dynamically.

With a static assignment, the network administrator must manually configure the network information for a host. At a minimum, as shown in Figure 11-1, this includes the following:

- **IP address**—Identifies the host on the network
- **Subnet mask**—Identifies the network on which the host is connected
- **Default gateway**—Identifies the networking device that the host uses to access the Internet or another remote network

Static addresses have some advantages. For instance, they are useful for printers, servers, and other networking devices that need to be accessible to clients on the network. If hosts normally access a server at a particular IPv4 address, a change of that address would cause problems.

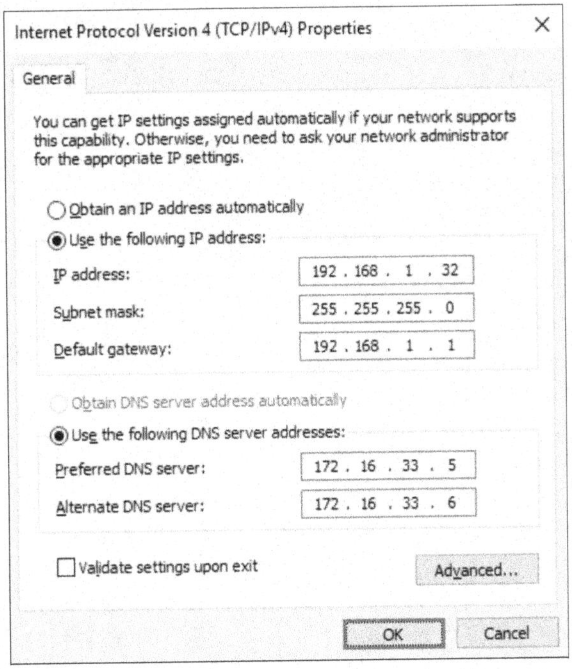

Figure 11-1 Static IPv4 Addressing on a Windows PC

Static assignment of addressing information can provide increased control of network resources, but manually entering the information on each host can be time consuming. Also, when IPv4 addresses are entered statically, the host performs only basic error checks on the IPv4 addresses, so errors are more likely to occur.

When using static IPv4 addressing, it is important to maintain an accurate list of which IPv4 addresses are assigned to which devices. Additionally, these are permanent addresses and are not normally reused.

Dynamic IPv4 Address Assignment (11.1.2)

On local networks, the user population tends to changes frequently. New users arrive with laptops and need a connection. Other users receive new workstations that need to be connected. An easier alternative to having the network administrator manually assign IPv4 addresses for each workstation is to have IPv4 addresses assigned automatically. This is done using a protocol known as *Dynamic Host Configuration Protocol (DHCP)*.

DHCP automatically assigns addressing information such as IPv4 address, subnet mask, default gateway, and other configuration information, as shown in Figure 11-2.

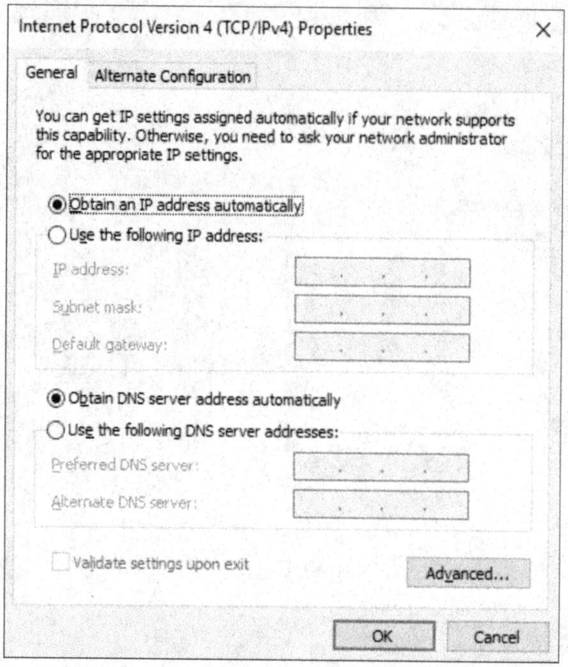

Figure 11-2 Dynamic IPv4 Addressing on a Windows PC

DHCP is generally the preferred method of assigning IPv4 addresses to hosts on large networks because it reduces the burden on network support staff and virtually eliminates entry errors.

Another benefit of DHCP is that an address is not permanently assigned to a host but is only leased for a period of time. If the host is powered down or taken off the network, the address is returned to the pool for reuse. This is especially helpful with mobile users that come and go on a network.

DHCP Servers (11.1.3)

If you enter an airport or coffee shop that has a wireless hotspot, DHCP enables you to access the Internet. As you enter the area, your laptop DHCP client contacts the local DHCP server via a wireless connection. The DHCP server assigns an IPv4 address to your laptop.

Various types of devices can be DHCP servers as long as they are running DHCP service software. With most medium to large networks, the DHCP server is usually a local dedicated PC-based server.

With home networks, the DHCP server may be located at the ISP, in which case a host on the home network receives its IPv4 configuration directly from the ISP, as shown in Figure 11-3.

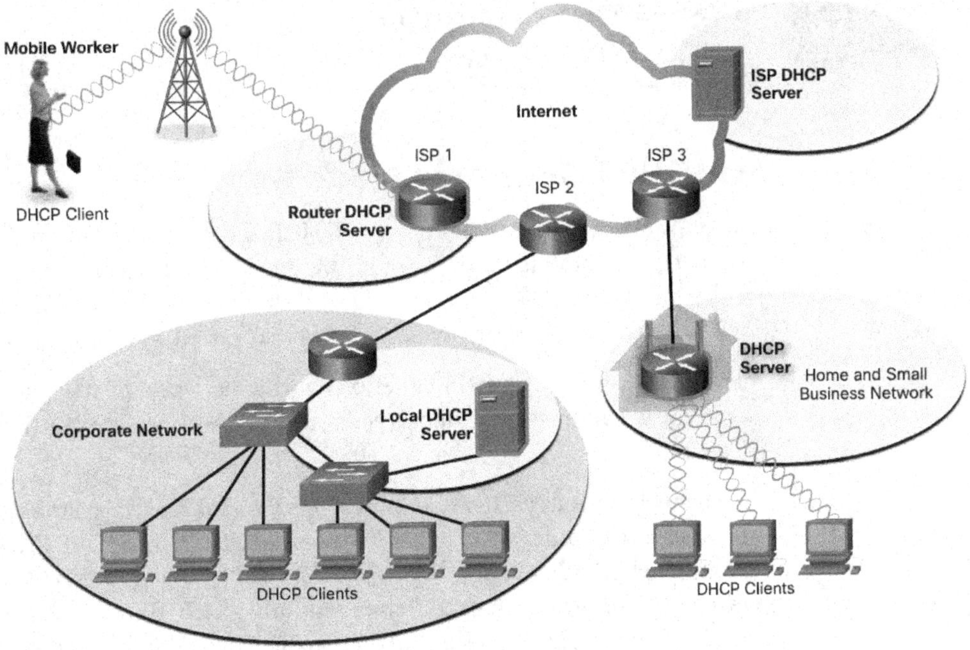

Figure 11-3 Examples of DHCP Servers and Clients

Many home networks and small businesses use a wireless router and modem. In this case, the wireless router is both a DHCP client and a server. The wireless router acts as a client to receive its IPv4 configuration from the ISP and then acts as a DHCP server for internal hosts on the local network. The router receives the public IPv4 address from the ISP, and in its role as a DHCP server, it distributes private addresses to internal hosts.

In addition to PC-based servers and wireless routers, other types of networking devices such as dedicated routers can provide DHCP services to clients, although this is not as common.

Interactive Graphic

Check Your Understanding—Static and Dynamic Addressing (11.1.4)

Refer to the online course to complete this activity.

DHCPv4 Configuration (11.2)

A device can receive its IPv4 addressing information dynamically from a DHCPv4 server. Most client computers, including desktop computers, laptops, smartphones, and tablets, receive their IPv4 addressing using DHCPv4.

Video

Video—DHCPv4 Operation (11.2.1)

Refer to the online course to view this video.

DHCPv4 Operation (11.2.1)

When a host is first configured as a DHCP client, it does not have an IPv4 address, subnet mask, or default gateway. It obtains this information from a DHCP server, either on the local network or one located at the ISP. The DHCP server is configured with a range, or pool, of IPv4 addresses that can be assigned to DHCP clients.

The DHCP server may be located on another network. DHCP clients are still able to obtain IPv4 addresses as long as the routers in between are configured to forward DHCP requests.

A client that needs an IPv4 address sends a DHCP Discover message, which is a broadcast with a destination IPv4 address of 255.255.255.255 (32 ones) and a destination MAC address of FF-FF-FF-FF-FF-FF (48 ones). All hosts on the network receive this broadcast DHCP frame, but only a DHCP server will reply. The server responds with a DHCP Offer, suggesting an IPv4 address for the client. The host then sends a DHCP Request asking to use the suggested IPv4 address. The server responds with a DHCP Acknowledgment. The exchange is shown in Figure 11-4.

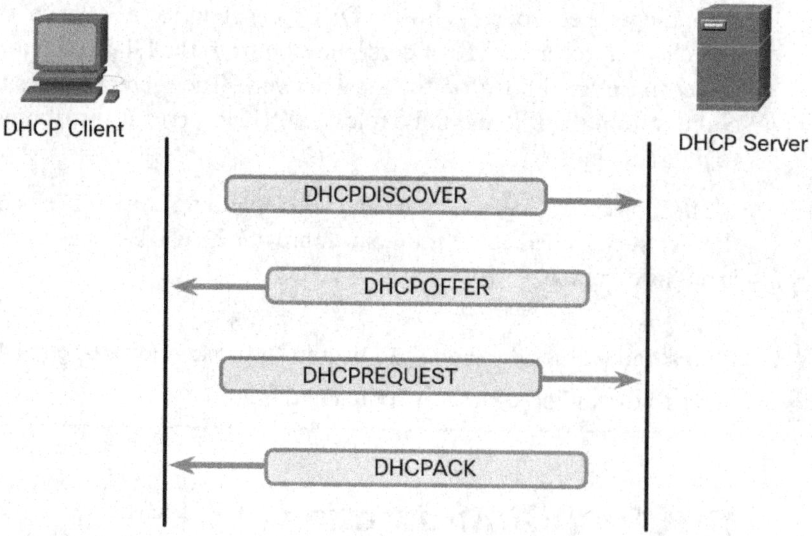

Figure 11-4 DHCPv4 Messages

DHCP Service Configuration (11.2.3)

For most home and small business networks, a wireless router provides DHCP services to the local network clients. To configure a home wireless router, you first need to access its graphical web interface by opening the browser and entering the router default IPv4 address 192.168.0.1 in the IP Address field, as shown in Figure 11-5 for a Packet Tracer wireless router. Home routers typically have a similar interface.

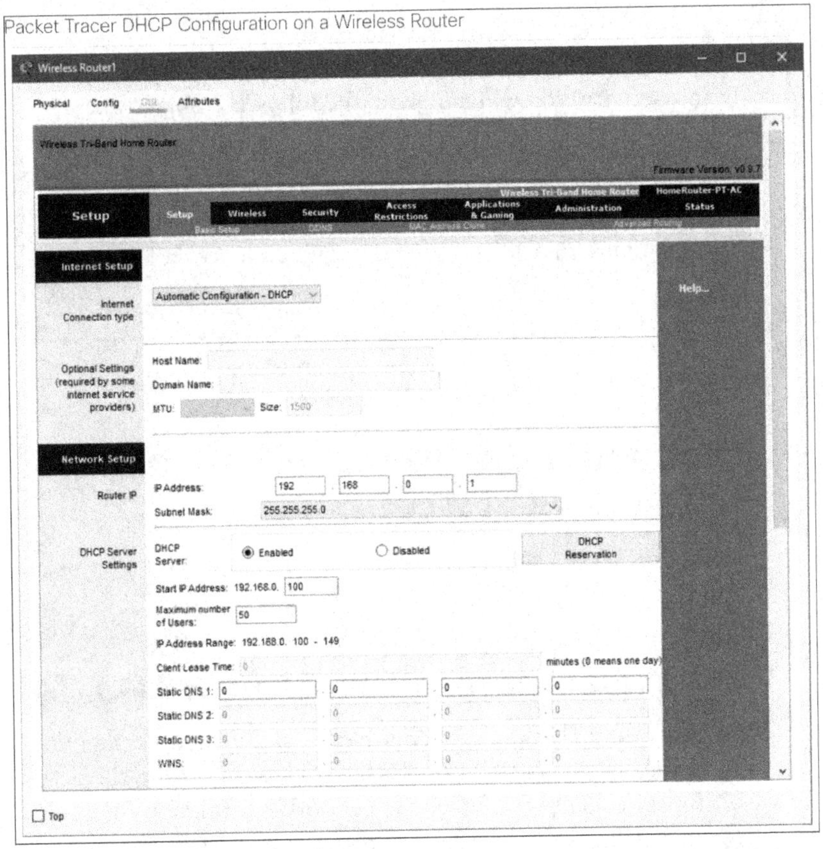

Figure 11-5 Packet Tracer DHCP Configuration on a Wireless Router

The IPv4 address of 192.168.0.1 and subnet mask of 255.255.255.0 are the defaults for the internal router interface. This is the default gateway for all hosts on the local network and also the internal DHCP server IPv4 address. Most home wireless routers have the DHCP Server option set to Enabled by default.

On the DHCP configuration screen, a default DHCP range is available. You can also specify a starting address for the DHCP range (do not use 192.168.0.1, because the router is assigned this address) and the number of addresses to be assigned. The lease

time can also be modified (the default in Figure 11-5 is 24 hours). The DHCP configuration feature on most routers gives information about connected hosts and IPv4 addresses, their associated MAC address, and lease times.

Video

Video—DHCP Service Configuration (11.2.2)

Refer to the online course to view this video.

Packet Tracer Activity

Packet Tracer—Configure DHCP on a Wireless Router (11.2.3)

In this activity, you will complete the following objectives:

- Connect three PCs to a wireless router.
- Change the DHCP setting to a specific network range.
- Configure the clients to obtain their address via DHCP.

Refer to the online course to complete this Packet Tracer.

Dynamic Addressing with DHCP Summary (11.3)

The following is a summary of each topic in the chapter and some questions for your reflection.

What Did I Learn in This Chapter? (11.3.1)

- **Static and Dynamic Addressing**—An IPv4 address can be assigned either statically or dynamically. With a static assignment, the network administrator must manually configure the network information for a host. At a minimum, this includes the host IPv4 address, subnet mask, and default gateway. Static assignment of addressing information can provide increased control of network resources, but manually entering the information on each host can be time consuming and prone to error. When using static IPv4 addressing, it is important to maintain an accurate list of which IPv4 addresses are assigned to which devices.

  IPv4 addresses can be assigned automatically using the Dynamic Host Configuration Protocol. DHCP is generally the preferred method of assigning IPv4 addresses to hosts on large networks because it reduces the burden on network

support staff and virtually eliminates entry errors. Another benefit of DHCP is that an address is not permanently assigned to a host but is only leased for a period of time. If the host is powered down or taken off the network, the address is returned to the pool for reuse.

As you enter an area with a wireless hotspot, your laptop DHCP client contacts the local DHCP server via a wireless connection. The DHCP server assigns an IPv4 address to your laptop. With home networks, the DHCP server may be located at the ISP, in which case a host on the home network receives its IPv4 configuration directly from the ISP. Many home networks and small businesses use a wireless router and modem. In this case, the wireless router is both a DHCP client and a server.

- **DHCPv4 Configuration**—The DHCP server is configured with a range, or pool, of IPv4 addresses that can be assigned to DHCP clients. A client that needs an IPv4 address sends a DHCP Discover message, which is a broadcast with a destination IPv4 address of 255.255.255.255 (32 ones) and a destination MAC address of FF-FF-FF-FF-FF-FF (48 ones). All hosts on the network receive this broadcast DHCP frame, but only a DHCP server will reply. The server responds with a DHCP Offer, suggesting an IPv4 address for the client. The host then sends a DHCP Request asking to use the suggested IPv4 address. The server responds with a DHCP Acknowledgment.

  For most home and small business networks, a wireless router provides DHCP services to the local network clients. To configure a home wireless router, access its graphical web interface by opening the browser and entering the router default IPv4 address. The IPv4 address 192.168.0.1 and the subnet mask 255.255.255.0 are the defaults for the internal router interface. This is the default gateway for all hosts on the local network and also the internal DHCP server IPv4 address. Most home wireless routers have the DHCP Server option set to Enabled by default.

Reflection Questions (11.3.2)

Have you manually entered an IPv4 address for all the devices on your home network? These are called static addresses. I did this for my home network, and I made a mistake when entering the address for my tablet. I had to redo it. Can you imagine having to do this for a huge corporate network with hundreds or even thousands of devices? What other advantages are there to using DHCP for device addressing?

Practice

The following Packet Tracer activity provides practice with the topics introduced in this chapter.

Packet Tracer
Activity

Packet Tracer Activities

Packet Tracer—Configure DHCP on a Wireless Router (11.2.3)

Check Your Understanding Questions

Complete all the review questions listed here to test your understanding of the topics and concepts in this chapter. Appendix A, "Answers to 'Check Your Understanding' Questions," lists the answers.

1. Match each description with an appropriate type of DHCP message.

   DHCP Messages:

   DHCPDISCOVER

   DHCPOFFER

   DHCPREQUEST

   DHCPACK

   a. The client accepting the IP address provided by the DHCP server
   b. The DHCP server confirming to the client that the address and lease have been accepted
   c. A client initiating a message to find a DHCP server
   d. A DHCP server responding to the initial request by a client

2. Which two reasons generally make DHCP the preferred method of assigning IP addresses to hosts on large networks? (Choose two.)

   a. It eliminates most address configuration errors.
   b. It ensures that addresses are applied only to devices that require a permanent address.
   c. It guarantees that every device that needs an address gets one.
   d. It provides an address only to devices that are authorized to be connected to the network.
   e. It reduces the burden on network support staff.

3. Which message does an IPv4 host use to reply after it receives a DHCPOFFER message from a DHCP server?
   a. DHCPACK
   b. DHCPDISCOVER
   c. DHCPOFFER
   d. DHCPREQUEST
4. Which destination IPv4 address does a DHCPv4 client use to send the initial DHCP Discover packet when the client is looking for a DHCP server?
   a. 127.0.0.1
   b. 224.0.0.1
   c. 255.255.255.255
   d. The IP address of the default gateway
5. Which type of packet is sent by a DHCP server after receiving a DHCP Discover message?
   a. DHCP ACK
   b. DHCP Discover
   c. DHCP Offer
   d. DHCP Request
6. What is one advantage of using DHCP to assign addresses to mobile devices?
   a. Address leases are temporary and are returned to the pool when the device is turned off.
   b. Addresses are permanently assigned to the mobile device and are valid on any network.
   c. Using DHCP creates many more registered IPv4 addresses.
   d. DHCP enables multiple internal IPv4 addresses to use a single registered global address.
7. A home wireless router is configured to act as a DHCP server. The IP address range is configured to be 192.168.0.100–149. What IP address will be assigned automatically to the first device that connects to the wireless router?
   a. 192.168.0.1
   b. 192.168.0.50
   c. 192.168.0.100
   d. 192.168.0.149

8. PC1 is configured to obtain a dynamic IP address 192.168.1.130 from the DHCP server. PC1 has been shut down for two weeks. When PC1 boots and tries to request an available IP address, which destination IP address will PC1 place in the IP header?

   a. 192.168.1.1
   b. 192.168.1.8
   c. 192.168.1.255
   d. 255.255.255.255

9. Which type of server dynamically assigns an IP address to a host?

   a. ARP
   b. DHCP
   c. DNS
   d. FTP

10. Which three statements describe a DHCP Discover message? (Choose three.)

   a. The source MAC address is 48 ones (FF-FF-FF-FF-FF-FF).
   b. The destination IP address is 255.255.255.255.
   c. The message comes from a server offering an IP address.
   d. The message comes from a client seeking an IP address.
   e. All hosts receive the message, but only a DHCP server replies.
   f. Only the DHCP server receives the message.

11. A host PC is attempting to lease an address through DHCP. What message is sent by the server to let the client know it is confirming that this client is allocated the IP address?

   a. DHCPDISCOVER
   b. DHCPOFFER
   c. DHCPREQUEST
   d. DHCPACK

CHAPTER 12

Gateways to Other Networks

Objectives

Upon completion of this chapter, you will be able to answer the following questions:

- What are network boundaries?
- What is the purpose of Network Address Translation in small networks?

Key Term

This chapter uses the following key term. You can find the definition in the Glossary.

Network Address Translation (NAT) *Page 178*

Introduction (12.0)

Kishori receives an email from Rina asking if they can meet in the cafeteria for lunch. Kishori meets Rina and is eager to ask her a few more networking questions. Rina is always happy to share her knowledge. When Kishori was speaking with Madhav, she learned that her department is part of a LAN. Each department within the hospital has its own LAN. Kishori asks Rina how she is able to send and receive emails that are outside of her network. Rina explains that gateways and Network Address Translation (NAT) make all of this seamless communication possible. Rina is impressed with Kishori's new knowledge and interest in networking! She mentions that there are several nurses in the hospital that have this knowledge and are paid more because they are able to troubleshoot the devices in patient rooms. She recommends that Kishori take some courses so that she could eventually apply for this promotion. Wow! Who knew that nurses could get promoted by learning technology!

This chapter will help Kishori understand gateways and NAT. Are you ready to learn more? Let's go!

Network Boundaries (12.1)

A router connects one network to another network. Only devices on separate networks need to forward their packets to a router in order to communicate.

Video

Video—Gateways to Other Networks (12.1.1)

Refer to the online course to view this video.

Routers as Gateways (12.1.2)

A router provides a gateway through which hosts on one network can communicate with hosts on different networks. Each interface on a router is connected to a separate network. The IPv4 address assigned to the interface identifies which local network is connected directly to it.

Every host on a network must use the router as a gateway to other networks. Therefore, each host must know the IPv4 address of the router interface connected to the network where the host is attached. This address is known as the *default gateway address*. It can be either statically configured on the host or received dynamically by DHCP.

When a wireless router is configured to be a DHCP server for the local network, it automatically sends the correct interface IPv4 address to the hosts as the default gateway address. In this manner, all hosts on the network can use that IPv4 address

to forward messages to hosts located at the ISP and get access to hosts on the Internet. Wireless routers are usually set to be DHCP servers by default.

The IPv4 address of that local router interface becomes the default gateway address for the host configuration. The default gateway is provided, either statically or by DHCP.

When a wireless router is configured as a DHCP server, it provides its own internal IPv4 address as the default gateway to DHCP clients. It also provides them with their respective IPv4 address and subnet mask, as shown in Figure 12-1.

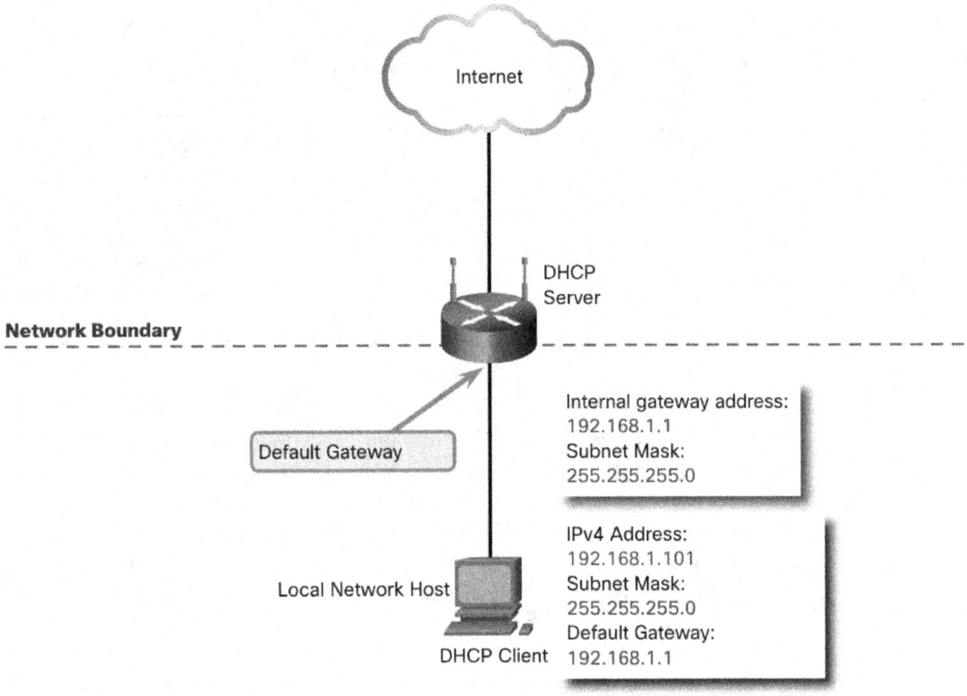

Figure 12-1 Example of a Router Serving as a Default Gateway

Routers as Boundaries Between Networks (12.1.3)

The wireless router acts as a DHCP server for all local hosts attached to it, either by Ethernet cable or wirelessly. These local hosts are referred to as being located on an *internal*, or *inside*, network. Most DHCP servers are configured to assign to the hosts on the internal network private addresses rather than Internet-routable public addresses. This configuration ensures that, by default, the internal network is not directly accessible from the Internet.

The default IPv4 address configured on the local wireless router interface is usually the first host address on that network. Internal hosts must be assigned addresses

within the same network as the wireless router, either statically configured or through DHCP. When configured as a DHCP server, the wireless router provides addresses in this range. It also provides the subnet mask information and its own interface IPv4 address as the default gateway, as shown in Figure 12-2.

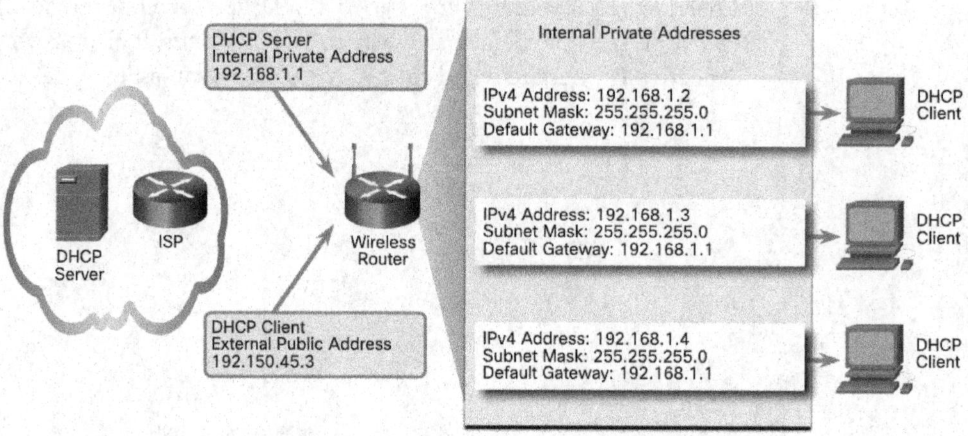

Figure 12-2 Default Router as Both a DHCP Server and a DHCP Client

Many ISPs also use DHCP servers to provide IPv4 addresses to the Internet side of the wireless router installed at their customer sites. The network assigned to the Internet side of the wireless router is referred to as the *external*, or *outside*, network.

When a wireless router is connected to the ISP, it acts like a DHCP client to receive the correct external network IPv4 address for the Internet interface. ISPs usually provide an Internet-routable address, which enables hosts connected to the wireless router to have access to the Internet.

The wireless router serves as the boundary between the local internal network and the external Internet.

Interactive Graphic

Check Your Understanding—Network Boundaries (12.1.4)

Refer to the online course to complete this activity.

Network Address Translation (12.2)

The number of public IPv4 addresses is severely limited, which was one of the primary reasons for RFC 1918 private IPv4 addresses. *Network Address Translation (NAT)* for IPv4 provides for the translation between private and public IPv4 addresses.

NAT Operation (12.2.1)

A wireless router receives a public address from the ISP, which allows the router to send and receive packets on the Internet. The wireless router, in turn, provides private addresses to local network clients. Because private addresses are not allowed on the Internet, a process is needed for translating private addresses into unique public addresses to allow local clients to communicate on the Internet.

The process used to convert private addresses to Internet-routable addresses is called Network Address Translation (NAT). With NAT, a private (local) source IPv4 address is translated to a public (global) address. The process is reversed for incoming packets. The wireless router is able to translate many internal IPv4 addresses to the same public address by using NAT.

Only packets destined for other networks need to be translated. These packets must pass through the gateway, where the wireless router replaces the private IPv4 address of the source host with its own public IPv4 address.

Although each host on the internal network has a unique private IPv4 address assigned to it, the hosts must share the single Internet-routable address assigned to the wireless router.

In Figures 12-3 and 12-4, a home router translates packets using NAT.

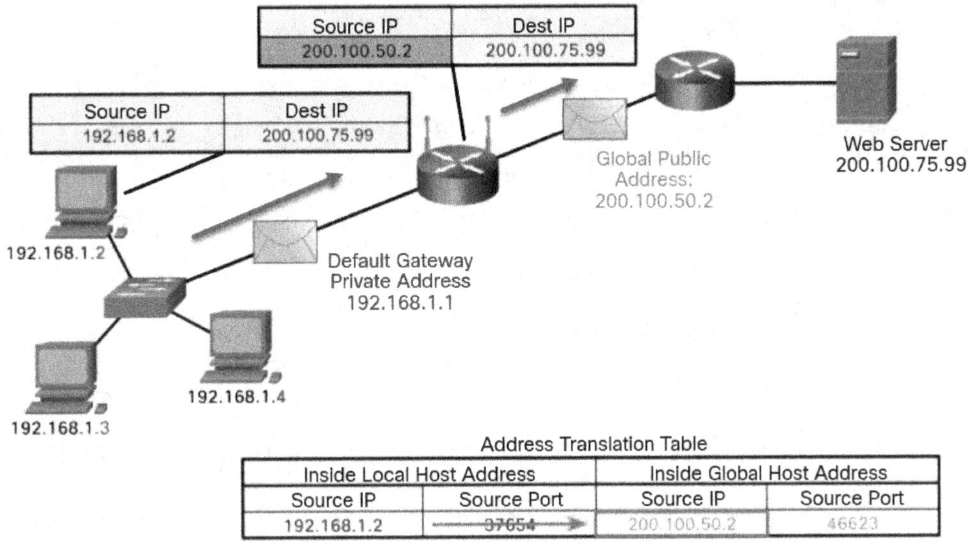

Figure 12-3 Wireless Router Using NAT to Translate Outbound Traffic

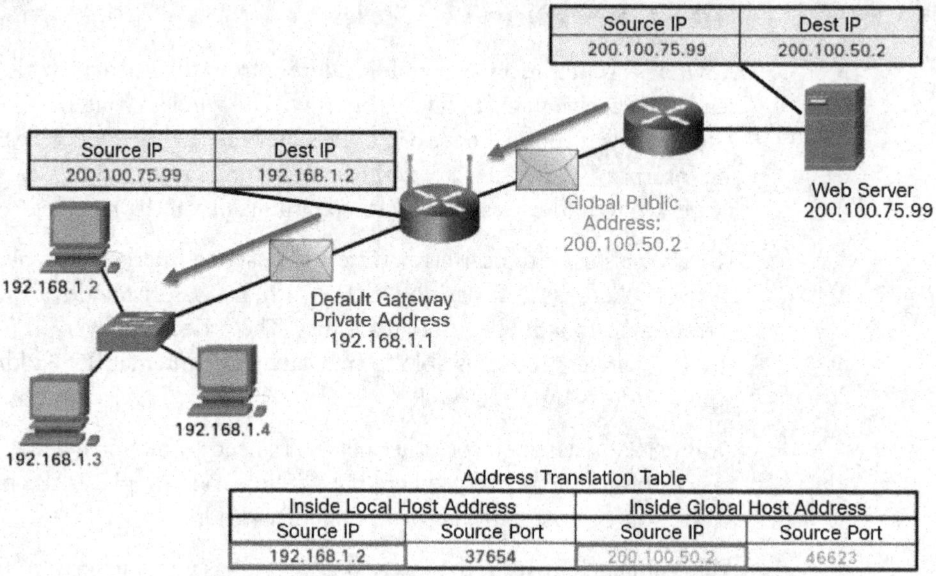

Figure 12-4 Wireless Router Using NAT to Translate Inbound Traffic

Video

Video—Introduction to NAT (12.2.1)

Refer to the online course to view this video.

Packet Tracer Activity

Packet Tracer—Examine NAT on a Wireless Router (12.2.2)

In this activity, you will complete the following objectives:

- Examine NAT configuration on a wireless router.
- Set up four PCs to connect to a wireless router using DHCP.
- Examine traffic that crosses the network using NAT.

Refer to the online course to complete this Packet Tracer.

Gateways to Other Networks Summary (12.3)

The following is a summary of each topic in the chapter and some questions for your reflection.

What Did I Learn in This Chapter? (12.3.1)

- **Network Boundaries**—Every host on a network must use the router as a gateway to other networks. Therefore, each host must know the IPv4 address of

the router interface connected to the network where the host is attached. This address is known as the default gateway address. It can be either statically configured on the host or received dynamically by DHCP.

The wireless router acts as a DHCP server for all local hosts attached to it, either by Ethernet cable or wirelessly. These local hosts are located on an internal, or inside, network. When a wireless router is connected to the ISP, it acts like a DHCP client to receive the correct external network IPv4 address for the Internet interface. ISPs usually provide an Internet-routable address, which enables hosts connected to the wireless router to have access to the Internet. The wireless router serves as the boundary between the local internal network and the external Internet.

- **NAT Operation**—A wireless router receives a public address from the ISP, which allows the router to send and receive packets on the Internet. The router, in turn, provides private addresses to local network clients.

  Network Address Translation (NAT) is the process used to convert private addresses to Internet-routable addresses. With NAT, a private (local) source IPv4 address is translated to a public (global) address. The process is reversed for incoming packets. The wireless router is able to translate many internal IPv4 addresses to the same public address by using NAT.

  Only packets destined for other networks need to be translated. These packets must pass through the gateway, where the wireless router replaces the private IPv4 address of the source host with its own public IPv4 address.

Reflection Questions (12.3.2)

It turns out that the IPv4 addresses on the devices in my home network are private addresses that are used only in my LAN. But if I need to venture out beyond my home network, perhaps to go to the Internet or send an email to someone outside of my network, my device needs to be assigned a public address. How does your router know if you are trying to get access to a device or a website that is outside of your LAN? How do you know that your private address has been translated into a public address?

Practice

The following Packet Tracer activity provides practice with the topics introduced in this chapter.

Packet Tracer Activity

Packet Tracer Activities

Packet Tracer—Examine NAT on a Wireless Router (12.2.2)

Check Your Understanding Questions

Complete all the review questions listed here to test your understanding of the topics and concepts in this chapter. Appendix A, "Answers to 'Check Your Understanding' Questions," lists the answers.

1. A computer has to send a packet to a destination host in the same LAN. How will the packet be sent?
   a. The packet will be sent to the default gateway first, and then, depending on the response from the gateway, it may be sent to the destination host.
   b. The packet will be sent directly to the destination host.
   c. The packet will first be sent to the default gateway, and then from the default gateway it will be sent directly to the destination host.
   d. The packet will be sent only to the default gateway.

2. Typically, which network device would be used to perform NAT for a corporate environment?
   a. DHCP server
   b. Host device
   c. Router
   d. Server
   e. Switch

3. Which characteristic describes the default gateway of a host computer?
   a. The logical address of the router interface on the same network as the host computer
   b. The physical address of the switch interface connected to the host computer
   c. The physical address of the router interface on the same network as the host computer
   d. The logical address assigned to the switch interface connected to the router

4. What is the purpose of configuring a default gateway address on a host?

   a. To provide a permanent address to a computer
   b. To identify the network to which a computer is connected
   c. To identify the logical address of a networked computer and uniquely identify it to the rest of the network
   d. To identify the device that allows local network computers to communicate with devices on other networks

5. If the default gateway is configured incorrectly on a host, what is the impact on communications?

   a. The host is unable to communicate on the local network.
   b. The host is unable to communicate with hosts on remote networks.
   c. The host is unable to communicate with hosts on both the local and remote networks.
   d. The host cannot get an IP address from the DHCP server.

6. Which three IPv4 network addresses are private IP addresses? (Choose three.)

   a. 10.0.0.0
   b. 172.32.0.0
   c. 192.157.0.0
   d. 172.16.0.0
   e. 192.168.0.0
   f. 224.6.0.0

7. What is the purpose of NAT?

   a. To allow hosts configured with registered public IP addresses to access the Internet
   b. To translate private IP addresses to a public registered IP address
   c. To route private IP addresses over the public Internet
   d. To assign a private IP address to a host for Internet access

8. What is the primary advantage of using NAT?

   a. It allows a large group of users to share one or more public IP addresses.
   b. It allows a large group of users to share the same private IP address within a LAN.
   c. It allows static mapping of public inside addresses to private outside addresses.
   d. It allows dynamic mapping of registered inside addresses to private outside addresses.

9. Which three settings must be configured on a PC for it to communicate with devices located across the Internet? (Choose three.)

    a. IP address
    b. Subnet mask
    c. Default gateway address
    d. DHCP server address
    e. Hostname

10. The default configuration on a home wireless router provides which type of addresses to devices using DHCP?

    a. Private IP addresses
    b. Public registered IPv4 addresses
    c. Public registered IPv6 addresses
    d. Vendor-specific MAC addresses

11. Which type of intermediary device acts as a boundary between a home wireless network and the Internet?

    a. Layer 2 switch
    b. Access point
    c. DNS server
    d. Wireless router

CHAPTER 13

The ARP Process

Objectives

Upon completion of this chapter, you will be able to answer the following questions:

- What is the difference between the roles of the MAC address and the IP address?
- Why is it important to contain broadcasts within a network?

Key Term

This chapter uses the following key term. You can find the definition in the Glossary.

ARP (Address Resolution Protocol) *Page 192*

Introduction (13.0)

Kishori was looking at her phone and noticed that her phone actually has its own IP address. When she went home, she noticed that the IP address had changed to a value that is different from the address that she had at the hospital. She remembered from reading about DHCP that it provides addresses to devices automatically, so she thinks that she gets IP addresses from different places depending on where she is. This makes sense to her because she knows that IP addresses permit devices to join different networks. Kishori also noticed that her phone has a MAC address and that it is always the same, no matter which network she is attached to. It makes sense to Kishori, that her IP address changes when she is connected to different networks in different locations, but her MAC address is always the same, because her phone is her phone no matter where she is.

Kishori realizes that both the IP address and MAC address must be required for the phone to receive data. The IP address tells the sender of data where she is, and once the data gets to her location, the MAC address of her phone permits the device to receive data that is meant just for her. Thinking further, Kishori wonders how MAC addresses can be known to the network. DHCP provides the correct IP addresses for the network, but each device has its own, unique MAC address.

Kishori is ready to learn more! Are you? Keep reading!

MAC and IP (13.1)

This section discusses the differences between Layer 2 data link addresses, such as Ethernet MAC addresses, and Layer 3 network addresses—IP addresses.

Destination on Same Network (13.1.1)

Sometimes a host must send a message but only knows the IP address of the destination device. The host needs to know the MAC address of that device, but how can it be discovered? That is where address resolution becomes critical.

Two primary addresses are assigned to a device on an Ethernet LAN:

- **Physical address (the MAC address)**—Used for NIC-to-NIC communications on the same Ethernet network.
- **Logical address (the IP address)**—Used to send the packet from the source device to the destination device. The destination IP address may be on the same IP network as the source, or it may be on a remote network.

Layer 2 physical addresses (that is, Ethernet MAC addresses) are used to deliver the data link frame with the encapsulated IP packet from one NIC to another NIC that is on the same network. If the destination IP address is on the same network, the destination MAC address will be that of the destination device.

In Figure 13-1, PC1 wants to send a packet to PC2. The figure displays the Layer 2 destination and source MAC addresses and the Layer 3 IPv4 addressing that would be included in the packet sent from PC1.

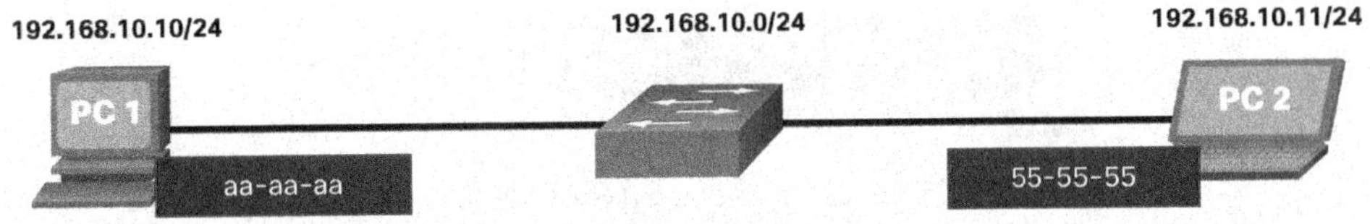

Destination MAC	Source MAC	Source IPv4	Destination IPv4
55-55-55	aa-aa-aa	192.168.10.10	192.168.10.11

Figure 13-1 Destination on Same Network Example

The Layer 2 Ethernet frame contains the following:

- **Destination MAC address**—This is the simplified MAC address of PC2, 55-55-55.
- **Source MAC address**—This is the simplified MAC address of the Ethernet NIC on PC1, aa-aa-aa.

The Layer 3 IP packet contains the following:

- **Source IPv4 address**—This is the IPv4 address of PC1, 192.168.10.10.
- **Destination IPv4 address**—This is the IPv4 address of PC2, 192.168.10.11.

Destination on Remote Network (13.1.2)

When the destination IP address (IPv4 or IPv6) is on a remote network, the destination MAC address is the address of the host default gateway (that is, the router interface).

In Figure 13-2, PC1 wants to send a packet to PC2. PC2 is located on a remote network. Because the destination IPv4 address is not on the same local network as PC1, the destination MAC address is that of the local default gateway on the router.

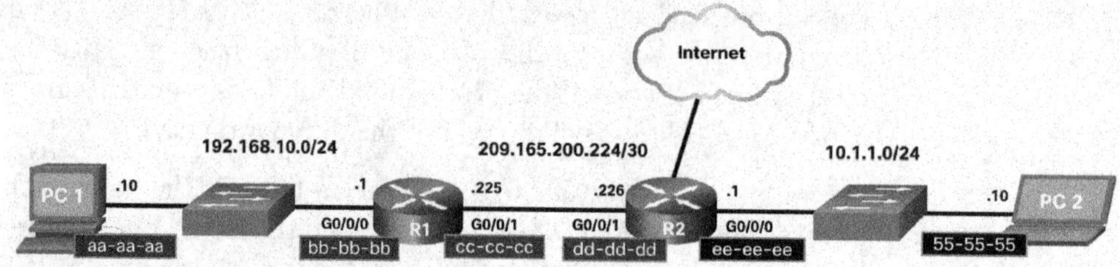

Destination MAC	Source MAC	Source IPv4	Destination IPv4
bb-bb-bb	aa-aa-aa	192.168.10.10	10.1.1.10

Figure 13-2 Destination on Remote Network Example—PC1 to R1

Routers examine the destination IPv4 address to determine the best path to forward the IPv4 packet. When a router receives the Ethernet frame, it de-encapsulates the Layer 2 information. Using the destination IPv4 address, the router determines the next-hop device and then encapsulates the IPv4 packet in a new data link frame for the outgoing interface.

In the example introduced in Figure 13-2, R1 would now encapsulate the packet with new Layer 2 address information, as shown in Figure 13-3.

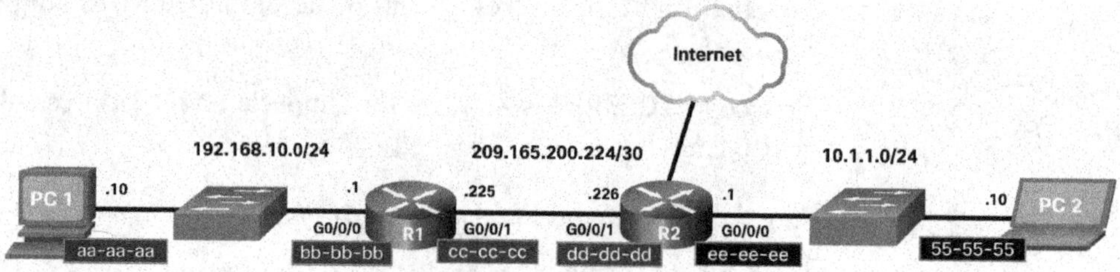

Destination MAC	Source MAC	Source IPv4	Destination IPv4
dd-dd-dd	cc-cc-cc	192.168.10.10	10.1.1.10

Figure 13-3 Destination on Remote Network Example—R1 to R2

The new destination MAC address would be that of the R2 G0/0/1 interface, and the new source MAC address would be that of the R1 G0/0/1 interface.

Along each link in a path, an IP packet is encapsulated in a frame. The frame is specific to the data link technology that is associated with that link, such as Ethernet.

If the next-hop device is the final destination, the destination MAC address is that of the device's Ethernet NIC, as shown in Figure 13-4.

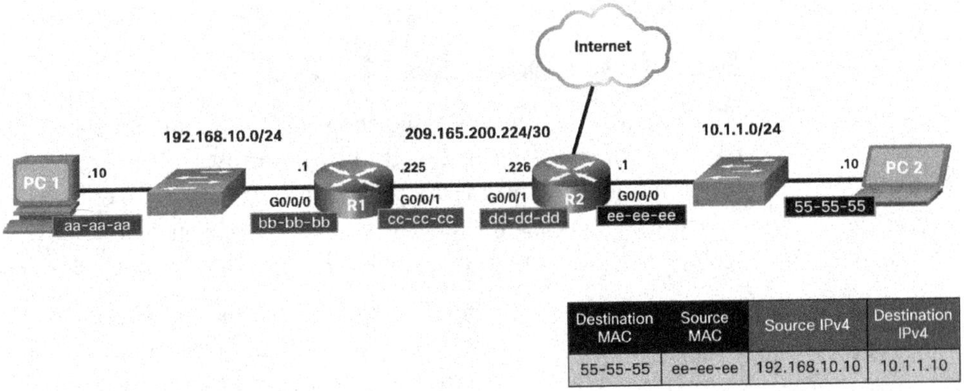

Figure 13-4 Destination on Remote Network Example—R2 to PC2

How are the IP addresses of the IP packets in a data flow associated with the MAC addresses on each link along the path to the destination? For IPv4 packets, this is done through a process called Address Resolution Protocol (ARP). For IPv6 packets, the process is ICMPv6 Neighbor Discovery (ND).

Packet Tracer
☐ Activity

Packet Tracer—Identify MAC and IP Addresses (13.1.3)

In this Packet Tracer activity, you will complete the following objectives:

- Gather PDU Information for Local Network Communication
- Gather PDU Information for Remote Network Communication

This activity is optimized for viewing PDUs. The devices are already configured. You will gather PDU information in simulation mode and answer a series of questions about the data you collect.

Refer to the online course to complete this Packet Tracer.

Broadcast Containment (13.2)

At times an end device may need to send an Ethernet frame to all devices on the same Ethernet LAN. Although these Ethernet broadcasts are common, it is important that they are kept to a minimum so that they do not affect the overall performance of the network.

Video

Video—The Ethernet Broadcast (13.2.1)

Refer to the online course to view this video.

Broadcast Domains (13.2.2)

When a host receives a message addressed to the broadcast address, it accepts and processes the message as though the message was addressed directly to it. When a host sends a broadcast message, switches forward the message to every connected host within the same local network. For this reason, a local area network, a network with one or more Ethernet switches, is also referred to as a *broadcast domain*.

If too many hosts are connected to the same broadcast domain, broadcast traffic can become excessive. The number of hosts and the amount of network traffic that can be supported on the local network are limited by the capabilities of the switches used to connect them. As the network grows and more hosts are added, network traffic, including broadcast traffic, increases. To improve performance, it is often necessary to divide one local network into multiple networks, or broadcast domains, as shown in Figure 13-5. Routers are used to divide the network into multiple broadcast domains.

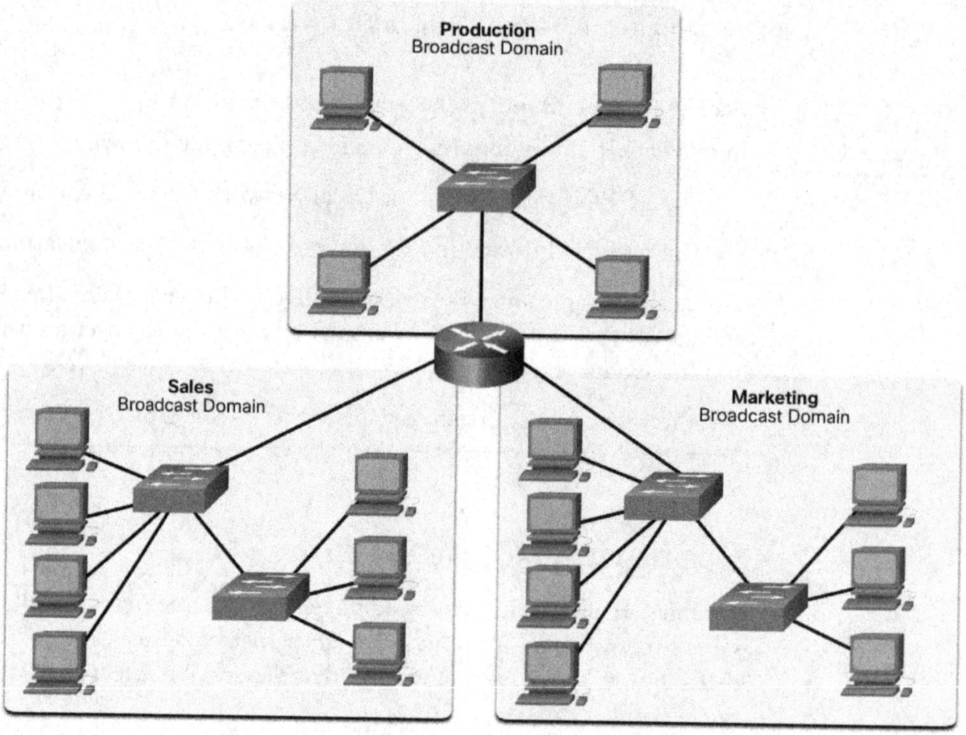

Figure 13-5 Example of Broadcast Domains Segmented by a Router

Access Layer Communication (13.2.3)

On a local Ethernet network, a NIC accepts a frame only if the destination address either is the broadcast MAC address or the MAC address of the NIC.

Most network applications, however, rely on the logical destination IP address to identify the location of the servers and clients. Figure 13-6 illustrates the problem that arises if a sending host only has the logical IP address of the destination host. How does the sending host determine what destination MAC address to place within the frame?

The sending host can use an IPv4 protocol called Address Resolution Protocol (ARP) to discover the MAC address of any host on the same local network. IPv6 uses a similar method known as Neighbor Discovery.

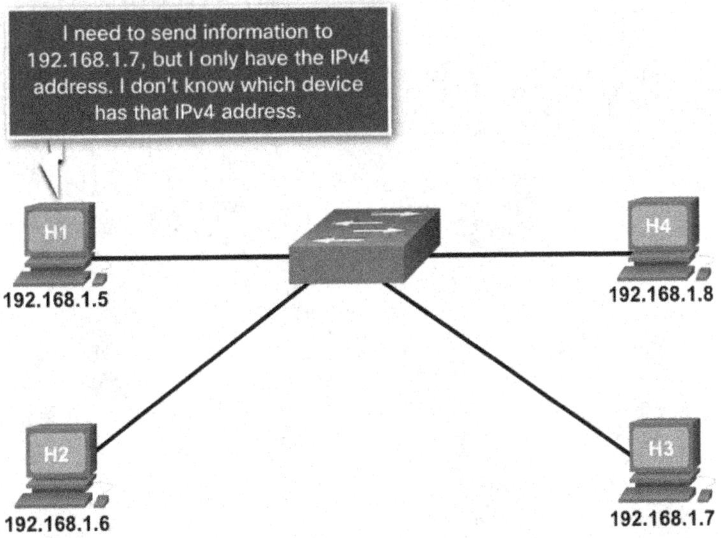

Figure 13-6 A Host Needs the IPv4 Address of the Destination

Video

Video—Address Resolution Protocol (13.2.4)

Refer to the online course to view this video.

ARP (13.2.5)

ARP (Address Resolution Protocol) uses a three-step process, as shown in Figure 13-7, to discover and store the MAC address of a host on the local network when only the IPv4 address of the host is known:

1. The sending host creates and sends a frame addressed to a broadcast MAC address. The frame contains a message with the IPv4 address of the intended destination host.
2. Each host on the network receives the broadcast frame and compares the IPv4 address in the message with its configured IPv4 address.
3. The host with the matching IPv4 address sends its MAC address back to the original sending host. The sending host receives the message and stores the MAC address and IPv4 address information in a table called an ARP table.

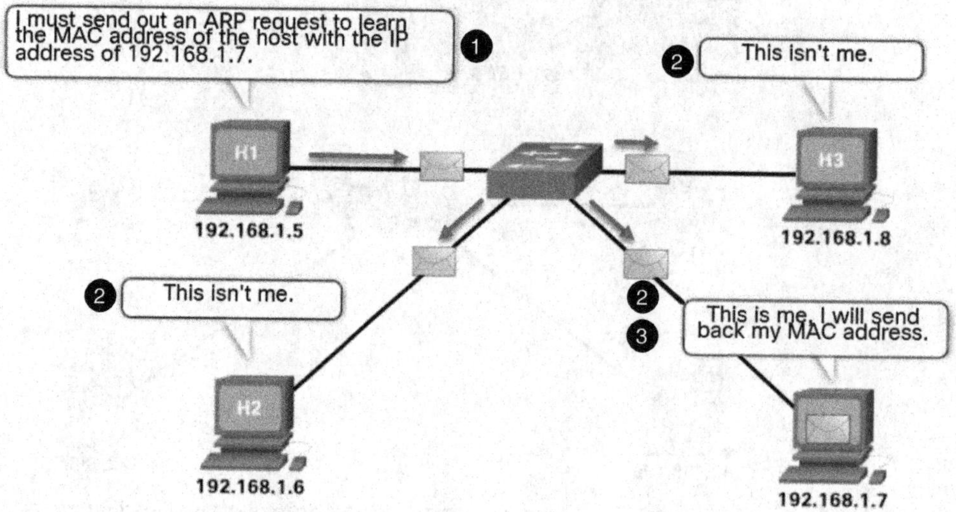

Figure 13-7 Example of a Host Using ARP to Determine the IPv4 Address

When the sending host has the MAC address of the destination host in its ARP table, it can send frames directly to the destination host without doing an ARP request. Because ARP messages rely on broadcast frames to deliver the requests, all hosts in the local IPv4 network must be in the same broadcast domain.

Interactive Graphic

Check Your Understanding—Broadcast Containment (13.2.6)

Refer to the online course to complete this activity.

The ARP Process Summary (13.3)

The following is a summary of each topic in the chapter and some questions for your reflection.

What Did I Learn in This Chapter? (13.3.1)

- **MAC and IP**—Sometimes a host must send a message but only knows the IP address of the destination device. The host needs to know the MAC address of that device. The MAC address can be discovered using address resolution. There are two primary addresses assigned to a device on an Ethernet LAN:
    - **Physical address (the MAC address)**—Used for NIC-to-NIC communications on the same Ethernet network.
    - **Logical address (the IP address)**—Used to send the packet from the source device to the destination device. The destination IP address may be on the same IP network as the source, or it may be on a remote network.

  When the destination IP address (IPv4 or IPv6) is on a remote network, the destination MAC address is the address of the host default gateway (that is, the router interface). Routers examine the destination IPv4 address to determine the best path to forward the IPv4 packet. When the router receives the Ethernet frame, it de-encapsulates the Layer 2 information. Using the destination IPv4 address, it determines the next-hop device and then encapsulates the IPv4 packet in a new data link frame for the outgoing interface. Along each link in a path, an IP packet is encapsulated in a frame. The frame is specific to the data link technology that is associated with that link, such as Ethernet. If the next-hop device is the final destination, the destination MAC address is that of the device Ethernet NIC.

- **Broadcast Containment**—A message can contain only one destination MAC address. Address resolution lets a host send a broadcast message to a unique MAC address that is recognized by all hosts. The broadcast MAC address is a 48-bit address made up of all ones. MAC addresses are usually represented in hexadecimal notation. The broadcast MAC address in hexadecimal notation is FFFF.FFFF.FFFF. Each F in the hexadecimal notation represents four ones in the binary address.

  When a host sends a broadcast message, switches forward the message to every connected host within the same local network. For this reason, a local area network, a network with one or more Ethernet switches, is also referred to as a broadcast domain.

If too many hosts are connected to the same broadcast domain, broadcast traffic can become excessive. The number of hosts and the amount of network traffic that can be supported on the local network is limited by the capabilities of the switches used to connect them. To improve performance, it is often necessary to divide one local network into multiple networks, or broadcast domains. Routers are used to divide the network into multiple broadcast domains.

On a local Ethernet network, a NIC accepts a frame only if the destination address is either the broadcast MAC address, or else corresponds to the MAC address of the NIC. Most network applications rely on the logical destination IP address to identify the location of the servers and clients. How does the sending host determine what destination MAC address to place within the frame? The sending host can use ARP to discover the MAC address of any host on the same local network.

ARP uses a three-step process to discover and store the MAC address of a host on the local network when only the IPv4 address of the host is known:

1. The sending host creates and sends a frame addressed to a broadcast MAC address. The frame contains a message with the IPv4 address of the intended destination host.

2. Each host on the network receives the broadcast frame and compares the IPv4 address in the message with its configured IPv4 address.

3. The host with the matching IPv4 address sends its MAC address back to the original sending host. The sending host receives the message and stores the MAC address and IPv4 address information in an ARP table.

IPv6 uses a similar method known as Neighbor Discovery.

Reflection Questions (13.3.2)

All of my devices (and all of your devices) have an IP address and a MAC address. When someone wants to send a message to my phone, my IP address tells their router where my device is located. My MAC address is how my phone knows to let me see the message. That router also needs to know my MAC address and uses ARP to find it. Do you know how to look up the MAC address of each of your connected devices?

Practice

The following Packet Tracer activity provides practice with the topics introduced in this chapter.

Packet Tracer
Activity

Packet Tracer Activities

Packet Tracer—Identify MAC and IP Addresses (13.1.3)

Check Your Understanding Questions

Complete all the review questions listed here to test your understanding of the topics and concepts in this chapter. Appendix A, "Answers to 'Check Your Understanding' Questions," lists the answers.

1. What is one function of the ARP protocol?
   a. Obtaining an IPv4 address automatically
   b. Mapping a domain name to its IP address
   c. Resolving an IPv4 address to a MAC address
   d. Maintaining a table of domain names with their resolved IP addresses
2. Which destination address is used in an ARP request frame?
   a. 0.0.0.0
   b. 255.255.255.255
   c. FFFF.FFFF.FFFF
   d. 127.0.0.1
   e. 01-00-5E-00-AA-23
3. Which statement describes the treatment of ARP requests on the local link?
   a. They must be forwarded by all routers on the local network.
   b. They are received and processed by every device on the local network.
   c. They are dropped by all switches on the local network.
   d. They are received and processed only by the target device.
4. What important information in the Ethernet frame header does a Layer 2 switch examine in order to forward the data onward?
   a. Source MAC address
   b. Source IP address

c. Destination MAC address
d. Ethernet type
e. Destination IP address

5. What are two functions of MAC addresses in a LAN? (Choose two.)

a. To allow the transfer of frames from source to destination
b. To determine which host has priority to transfer data
c. To indicate the best path between separate networks
d. To associate with a specific network IP address
e. To uniquely identify a node on a network

6. PC1 and PC2 have IPv4 addresses on the same network. PC1 issues an ARP request because it needs to send a packet to PC2. In this scenario, what will happen next?

a. PC2 will send an ARP reply with the PC2 MAC address.
b. RT1 will send an ARP reply with the RT1 Fa0/0 MAC address.
c. RT1 will send an ARP reply with the PC2 MAC address.
d. SW1 will send an ARP reply with the PC2 MAC address.
e. SW1 will send an ARP reply with the SW1 Fa0/1 MAC address.

7. What addresses are mapped by ARP?

a. IPv4 address to a destination MAC address
b. Destination IPv4 address to the source MAC address
c. Destination IPv4 address to the destination host name
d. Destination MAC address to the source IPv4 address

8. Switches Sw1 and Sw2 are interconnected. Hosts H1 and H2 are both connected to switch Sw1. Hosts H3 and H4 are both connected to switch Sw1. If host H1 sends a frame with destination address FFFF.FFFF.FFFF, what will be the result?

a. Sw1 will discard the frame.
b. Sw1 will flood the frame out all ports except the inbound port. The frame will be discarded by Sw2 but processed by host H2.
c. Sw1 will flood the frame out all ports except the inbound port. The frame will be flooded by Sw2 but discarded by hosts H2, H3, and H4.
d. Sw1 will flood the frame out all ports except the inbound port. The frame will be flooded by Sw2 and processed by hosts H2, H3, and H4.

9. Refer to the figure below. Host A needs to send data to the server but does not know its MAC address. When host A sends out an ARP request, what response will be in the ARP reply?

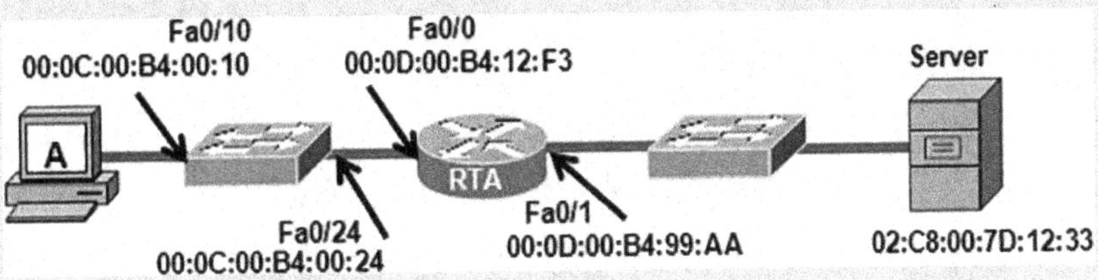

a. 00:0C:00:B4:00:10
b. 00:0C:00:B4:00:24
c. 00:0D:00:B4:12:F3
d. 00:0D:00:B4:99:AA
e. 02:C8:00:7D:12:33

10. What statement describes a characteristic of MAC addresses?

a. They are the physical address of the NIC or interface.
b. They are routable only within the private network.
c. They are added as part of a Layer 3 PDU.
d. They have a 32-bit binary value.

11. Which two characteristics describe MAC addresses? (Choose two.)

a. Physical address assigned to the NIC
b. Identifies source and destination in Layer 2 header
c. Logical address assigned by DHCP
d. Used by routers to select the best path to a destination

CHAPTER 14

Routing Between Networks

Objectives

Upon completion of this chapter, you will be able to answer the following questions:

- What is the need for routing?
- How do routers use tables?
- How do you build a fully connected network?

Key Terms

This chapter uses the following key terms. You can find the definitions in the Glossary.

default gateway *Page 203*

routing *Page 200*

Introduction (14.0)

Kishori leaves work for the day and begins her drive home. A friend called her earlier to warn her that there is a lot of traffic congestion on her usual route home, so she is using a GPS app on her phone to reroute to a less congested road. Kishori wonders if networks can get congested. Do they find a faster route?

Great question, Kishori! A network can also have this issue of congestion slowing down its performance. In a network, the router can determine the best path. How does a network become congested? What can you do to limit that congestion? You and Kishori will find out in this chapter!

The Need for Routing (14.1)

Most network communication involves sending packets over multiple networks. Routing is the process of forwarding IP packets from one network to another network.

Video

Video—Dividing the Local Network (14.1.1)

Refer to the online course to view this video.

Now We Need Routing (14.1.2)

In most situations we want our devices to be able to connect beyond our local network: out to other homes, businesses, and the Internet. Devices that are beyond the local network segment are known as *remote hosts*. When a source device sends a packet to a remote destination device, the help of routers and routing is needed. *Routing* is the process of identifying the best path to a destination.

A *router* is a networking device that connects multiple Layer 3 IP networks. Routers, like switches, are able to decode and read the messages that are sent to them. Unlike switches, which make their forwarding decision based on the Layer 2 MAC address, routers make their forwarding decision based on the Layer 3 IP address, as shown in Figure 14-1.

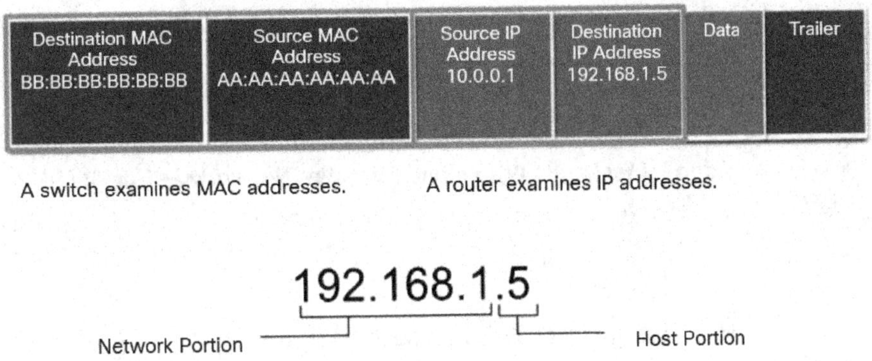

Figure 14-1 IP Packet Encapsulated in an Ethernet Frame

The packet format contains the IP addresses of the destination and source hosts, as well as the message data being sent between them. The router reads the network portion of the destination IP address and uses it to find which one of the attached networks is the best way to forward the message to the destination.

Any time the network portion of the IP addresses of the source and destination hosts do not match, a router must be used to forward the message. For example, if a host located on network 1.1.1.0 needs to send a message to a host on network 5.5.5.0, the host forwards the message to the router. The router receives the message, de-encapsulates the Ethernet frame, and then reads the destination IP address in the IP packet. It then determines where to forward the message. It re-encapsulates the packet into a new frame and forwards the frame on to its destination.

Interactive Graphic

Check Your Understanding—The Need for Routing (14.1.3)

Refer to the online course to complete this activity.

The Routing Table (14.2)

A router is a Layer 3 intermediary device that performs the packet forwarding or routing. Routers have routing tables that contain the information the router needs to forward the packet.

Video

Video—Router Packet Forwarding (14.2.1)

Refer to the online course to view this video.

Video

Video—Messages Within and Between Networks—Part 1 (14.2.2)

Refer to the online course to view this video.

Video

Video—Messages Within and Between Networks—Part 2 (14.2.3)

Refer to the online course to view this video.

Routing Table Entries (14.2.4)

Routers move information between local and remote networks. To do this, routers use routing tables to store information. Routing tables are not concerned with the addresses of individual hosts. Routing tables contain the addresses of networks and the best path to reach those networks. Entries can be made to the routing table in two ways: dynamically updated by information received from other routers in the network, or manually entered by a network administrator. Routers use the routing tables to determine which interface to use to forward a message to its intended destination. In Figure 14-2 and Table 14-1, the router has a routing table with two entries to directly connected networks: 10.0.0.0/8 and 172.16.0.0/16.

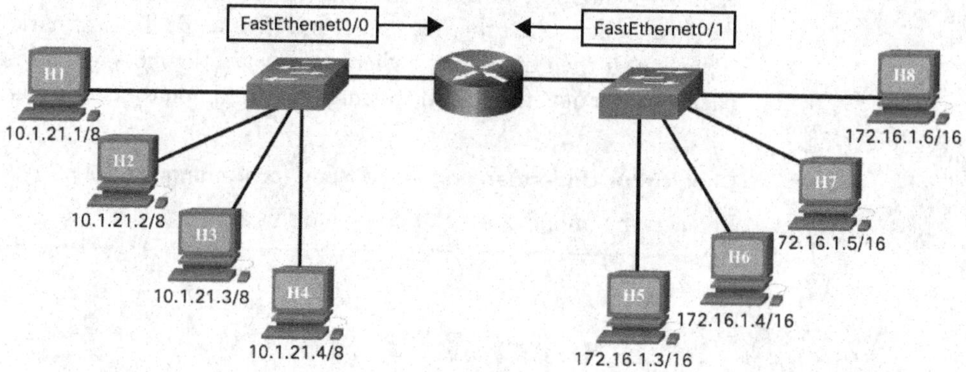

Figure 14-2 Example of a Router's Directly Connected Networks

Table 14-1 Routing Table with Directly Connected Routes

Type	Network	Port
C	10.0.0.0/8	FastEthernet0/0
C	172.16.0.0/16	FastEthernet0/1

- **Type**—The connection type. C stands for directly connected.
- **Network**—The network address.
- **Port**—The interface used to forward packets to the network.

If the router cannot determine where to forward a message, it drops it. Network administrators configure a static default route that is placed into the routing table so that a packet will not be dropped due to the destination network not being in the routing table. A default route is the interface through which the router forwards a packet containing an unknown destination IP network address. This default route usually connects to another router that can forward the packet toward its final destination network.

The Default Gateway (14.2.5)

The method that a host uses to send messages to a destination on a remote network differs from the way a host sends messages on the same local network. When a host needs to send a message to another host located on the same network, it forwards the message directly. A host uses ARP to discover the MAC address of the destination host. The IPv4 packet contains the destination IPv4 address and encapsulates the packet into a frame containing the MAC address of the destination and forwards it out.

When a host needs to send a message to a remote network, it must use the router. The host includes the IP address of the destination host within the packet just like before. However, when it encapsulates the packet into a frame, it uses the MAC address of the router as the destination for the frame. In this way, the router will receive and accept the frame based on the MAC address.

How does the source host determine the MAC address of the router? A host is given the IPv4 address of the router through the default gateway address configured in its TCP/IP settings. The *default gateway* address is the address of the router interface connected to the same local network as the source host. All hosts on the local network use the default gateway address to send messages to the router. When the host knows the default gateway IPv4 address, it can use ARP to determine the MAC address. The MAC address of the router is then placed in the frame, destined for another network.

It is important that the correct default gateway be configured on each host on the local network, as shown in Figure 14-3 and Table 14-2. If no default gateway is configured in the host TCP/IP settings, or if the wrong default gateway is specified, messages addressed to hosts on remote networks cannot be delivered.

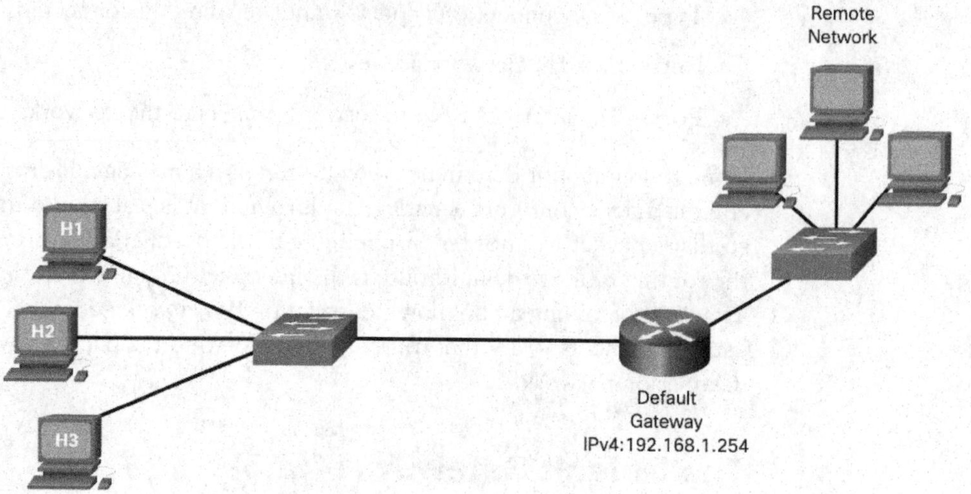

Figure 14-3 A Router as the Default Gateway

Table 14-2 Addressing Table for Hosts Including Default Gateway

PC	IPv4 Address	Subnet Mask	Default Gateway
H1	192.168.1.1	255.255.255.0	192.168.1.254
H2	192.168.1.2	255.255.255.0	192.168.1.254
H3	192.168.1.3	255.255.255.0	192.168.1.254

Interactive Graphic

Check Your Understanding—Select the Default Gateway (14.2.6)

Refer to the online course to complete this activity.

Interactive Graphic

Check Your Understanding—The Routing Table (14.2.7)

Refer to the online course to complete this activity.

Create a LAN (14.3)

End devices, both clients and servers, are connected to LANs. The LAN is how users access their network and reach other networks.

Local Area Networks (14.3.1)

The term *local area network (LAN)* refers either to a single local network or, as shown in Figure 14-4, to a group of interconnected local networks that are under the same administrative control. In the early days of networking, the definition of LAN was limited to a small network that exists in a single physical location, such as in a home or small office. Today, the definition of LAN has evolved and expanded to also include interconnected local networks consisting of many hundreds of hosts, installed in multiple buildings and locations.

The important thing to remember is that all the local networks within a LAN are under one administrative control. Other common characteristics of LANs are that they typically use Ethernet or wireless protocols, and they support high data rates.

The term *intranet* is often used to refer to a private LAN that belongs to an organization and is designed to be accessible only by the members of the organization, employees, or others with authorization.

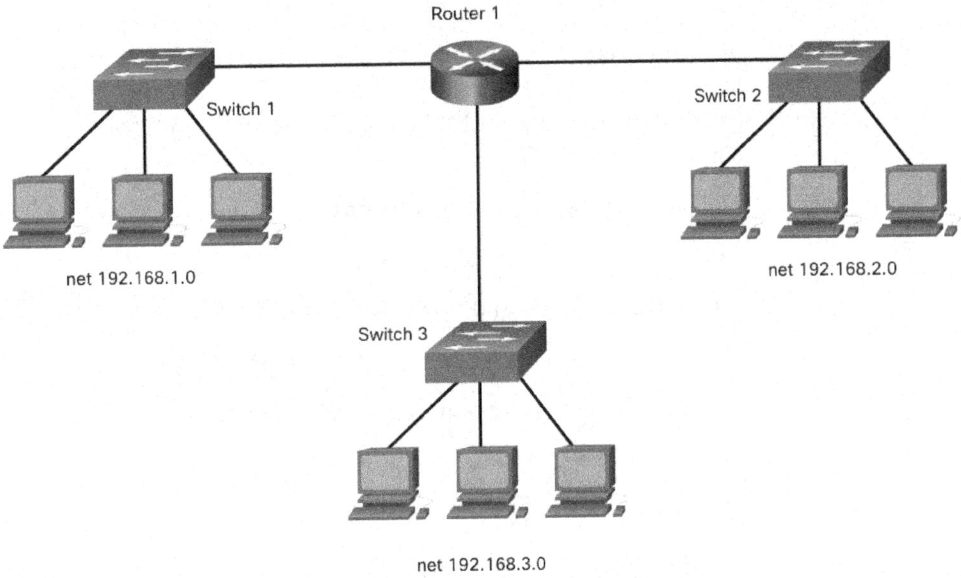

Figure 14-4 Collection of Local Networks Under the Same Administrative Control

Local and Remote Network Segments (14.3.2)

Within a LAN, it is possible to place all hosts on a single local network or to divide them between multiple networks connected by a distribution layer device. How this placement is determined depends on the desired results.

All Hosts in One Local Segment

Placing all hosts on a single local network allows them to be seen by all other hosts, as shown in Figure 14-5, because there is one broadcast domain and hosts use ARP to find each other.

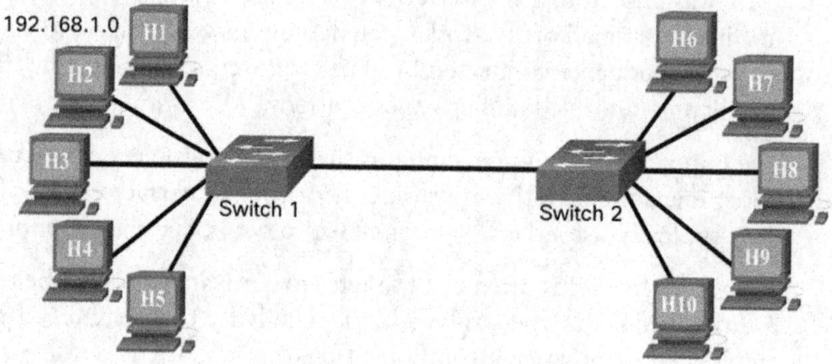

Figure 14-5 Example of a Local Segment

In a simple network design, it may be beneficial to keep all hosts within a single local network. However, as a network grows in size, increased traffic decreases network performance and speed. In this case, it may be beneficial to move some hosts onto a remote network.

Advantages of a single local segment:

- Appropriate for simpler networks
- Less complexity and lower network cost
- Allows devices to be "seen" by other devices
- Faster data transfer—more direct communication
- Ease of device access

Disadvantages of a single local segment:

- Slower network performance, because keeping all hosts in one broadcast domain causes more traffic on the segment
- Harder to implement QoS
- Harder to implement security

Hosts on a Remote Segment

Placing additional hosts on a remote network decreases the impact of traffic demands, as shown in Figure 14-6. However, hosts on one network cannot

communicate with hosts on the other without the use of routing. Routers increase the complexity of the network configuration and can introduce latency, or time delay, on packets sent from one local network to the other.

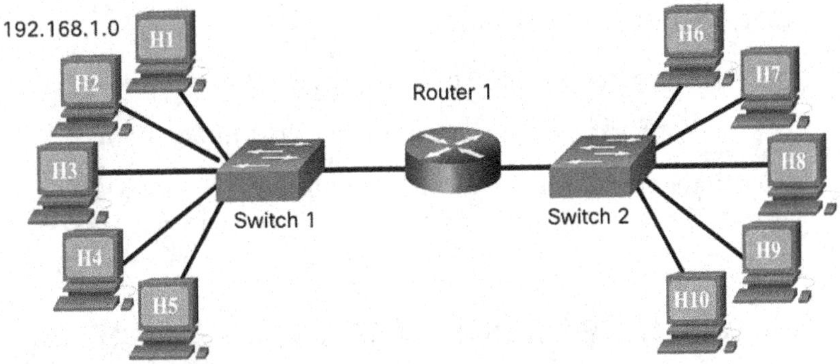

Figure 14-6 Example of Router Segmenting the Local Network

Advantages of network segmentation:

- More appropriate for larger, more complex networks
- Splits up broadcast domains and decreases traffic
- Can improve performance on each segment
- Makes the machines invisible to those on other local network segments
- Can provide increased security
- Can improve network organization

Disadvantages of network segmentation:

- Requires the use of routing (distribution layer)
- Router can slow traffic between segments
- More complexity and expense (requires a router)

Packet Tracer
☐ Activity

Packet Tracer—Observe Traffic Flow in a Routed Network (14.3.3)

In this Packet Tracer activity, you will complete the following objectives:

- Part 1: Observe Traffic Flow in an Unrouted LAN
- Part 2: Reconfigure the Network to Route Between LANs
- Part 3: Observe Traffic Flow in the Routed Network

Refer to the online course to complete this Packet Tracer.

Packet Tracer
☐ Activity

Packet Tracer—Create a LAN (14.3.4)

In this Packet Tracer activity, you will complete the following objectives:

- Connect Network Devices and Hosts
- Configure Devices with IPv4 Addressing
- Verify the End Device Configuration and Connectivity
- Use Networking Commands to View Host Information

Refer to the online course to complete this Packet Tracer.

Routing Between Networks Summary (14.4)

The following is a summary of each topic in the chapter and some questions for your reflection.

What Did I Learn in This Chapter? (14.4.1)

- **The Need for Routing**—As networks grow, it is often necessary to divide one access layer network into multiple access layer networks. There are many ways to divide networks based on different criteria:
  - **Broadcast containment**—Routers in the distribution layer can limit broadcasts to the local network where they need to be heard.
  - **Security requirements**—Routers in the distribution layer can separate and protect certain groups of computers where confidential information resides.
  - **Physical locations**—Routers in the distribution layer can be used to interconnect local networks at various locations of an organization that are geographically separated.
  - **Logical grouping**—Routers in the distribution layer can be used to logically group users, such as departments within a company, who have common needs or for access to resources.

  The distribution layer connects these independent local networks and controls the traffic flowing between them. It is responsible for ensuring that traffic between hosts on the local network stays local.

  A router is a networking device that connects multiple Layer 3 IP networks. At the distribution layer of the network, routers direct traffic and perform other functions critical to efficient network operation. Routers, like switches, are able to decode and read the messages that are sent to them. Unlike switches, which

make their forwarding decision based on the Layer 2 MAC address, routers make their forwarding decision based on the Layer 3 IP address.

Any time the network portions of the IP addresses of the source and destination hosts do not match, a router must be used to forward the message.

- **The Routing Table**—Each port, or interface, on a router connects to a different local network. Every router contains a table of all locally connected networks and the interfaces that connect to them.

  When a router receives a frame, it decodes the frame to get to the packet containing the destination IP address. It matches the network portion of the destination IP address to the networks that are listed in the routing table. If the destination network address is in the table, the router encapsulates the packet in a new frame and forwards the new frame out of the interface associated with the path to the destination network. The process of forwarding the packets toward their destination network is called routing.

  A router forwards a packet to one of two places: a directly connected network containing the actual destination host, or to another router on the path to reach the destination host. When a router encapsulates the frame to forward it out a routed interface, it must include a destination MAC address. If the router must forward the packet to another router through a routed interface, it will use the MAC address of the connected router. Routers obtain these MAC addresses from ARP tables.

  A host is given the IPv4 address of the router through the default gateway address configured in its TCP/IP settings. The default gateway address is the address of the router interface connected to the same local network as the source host. All hosts on the local network use the default gateway address to send messages to the router.

  Routing tables contain the addresses of networks and the best paths to reach those networks. Entries can be made to the routing table in two ways: dynamically updated by information received from other routers in the network, or manually entered by a network administrator.

- **Create a LAN**—The term LAN refers either to a local network or to a group of interconnected local networks that are under the same administrative control. All the local networks within a LAN are under one administrative control. Other common characteristics of LANs are that they typically use Ethernet or wireless protocols, and they support high data rates.

  Within a LAN, it is possible to place all hosts on a single local network or divide them up between multiple networks connected by a distribution layer device.

Placing all hosts on a single local network allows them to be seen by all other hosts, because there is one broadcast domain and hosts use ARP to find each other.

Placing additional hosts on a remote network will decrease the impact of traffic demands. However, hosts on one network will not be able to communicate with hosts on the other network without the use of routing. Routers increase the complexity of the network configuration and can introduce latency, or time delay, on packets sent from one local network to the other.

Reflection Questions (14.4.2)

On my home network (LAN), I do not usually have enough network traffic to experience congestion, although it can happen when all my children are streaming different movies and I am trying to upload a document to my work. Can you think of a way that I could divide my LAN into multiple networks?

Practice

The following Packet Tracer activities provide practice with the topics introduced in this chapter.

Packet Tracer
Activity

Packet Tracer Activities

Packet Tracer—Observe Traffic Flow in a Routed Network (14.3.3)

Packet Tracer—Create a LAN (14.3.4)

Check Your Understanding Questions

Complete all the review questions listed here to test your understanding of the topics and concepts in this chapter. Appendix A, "Answers to 'Check Your Understanding' Questions," lists the answers.

1. Which information is used by routers to forward a data packet toward its destination?

   a. Source IP address

   b. Destination IP address

   c. Source data-link address

   d. Destination data-link address

2. If the default gateway is configured incorrectly on the host, what is the impact on communications?

   a. The host is unable to communicate on the local network.

   b. The host can communicate with other hosts on the local network but is unable to communicate with hosts on remote networks.

   c. The host can communicate with other hosts on remote networks but is unable to communicate with hosts on the local network.

   d. There is no impact on communications.

3. What role does a router play on a network?

   a. Forwarding Layer 2 broadcasts

   b. Forwarding frames based on a MAC address

c. Selecting the path to destination networks and forwarding packets to those networks

d. Connecting smaller networks into a single broadcast domain

4. Which address should be configured as the default gateway address of a client device?

a. The Layer 2 address of the switch management interface

b. The Layer 2 address of the switch port that is connected to the workstation

c. The IPv4 address of the router interface that is connected to the same LAN

d. The IPv4 address of the router interface that is connected to the Internet

5. Which device is used to transfer data from one IP local network to a remote network?

a. NIC card

b. Switch

c. Router

d. Server

6. To allow IP communication between the two separate IP networks, what type of device is required?

a. Server

b. Router

c. Switch

d. Access point

7. What is a benefit of adding a router within an IP network?

a. Increases the size of the local network

b. Keeps broadcasts contained within a local network

c. Reduces the number of hosts that can connect to the network

d. Controls host-to-host traffic within a single local network

8. Refer to the following figure. Host H7 sends a packet with the destination IP address of 255.255.255.255. What does router R1 do when it receives the packet from host H7?

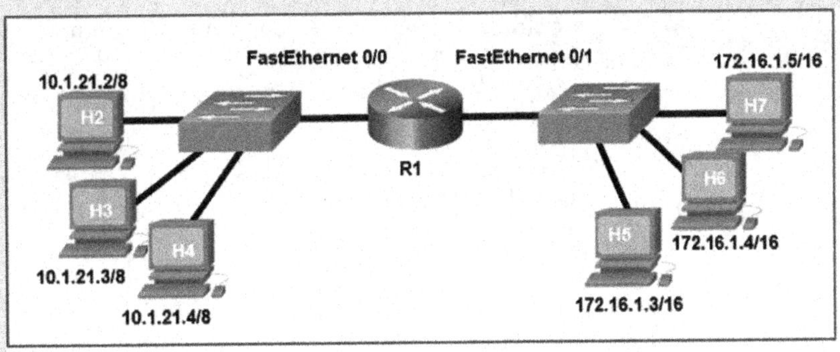

R1 – Routing Table

Type	Network	Port
C	10.0.0.0/8	FastEthernet0/0
C	172.16.0.0/16	FastEthernet0/1

a. Examines the packet received on interface FastEthernet0/1 and does not forward the packet

b. Changes the Layer 2 header information and forwards the packet out all connected interfaces

c. Checks the routing table and forwards the packet out interface FastEthernet0/0

d. Changes the destination IP address and forwards the packet out interface FastEthernet0/0

9. What action does a router take when it receives a frame with a broadcast MAC address?

a. It does not forward the frame to another network.

b. It forwards the frame back to the sending host.

c. It forwards the frame out of all connected interfaces.

d. It forwards the frame back out the receiving interface.

10. What are two reasons to install routers to segment a network? (Choose two.)

a. To limit the number of devices that can connect to the network

b. To expand the network to a different geographic location

c. To create smaller broadcast domains within the network

d. To reduce the number of switches needed to connect devices

11. Which table does a router use to determine which interface to use to send packets to the destination network?

    a. ARP table

    b. Routing table

    c. Network table

    d. Forwarding table

12. What action does the router take when it does not find a route to the destination network in its routing table?

    a. It drops the packet.

    b. It sends the packet as a broadcast.

    c. It returns the packet to the sender.

    d. It sends the packet out all connected interfaces.

CHAPTER 15

TCP and UDP

Objectives

Upon completion of this chapter, you will be able to answer the following questions:

- What is the difference between TCP and UDP transport layer functions?
- How do TCP and UDP use port numbers?

Key Terms

This chapter uses the following key terms. You can find the definitions in the Glossary.

socket Page 222

Transmission Control Protocol (TCP) Page 218

User Datagram Protocol (UDP) Page 218

Introduction (15.0)

Kishori arrives at work early to get on a video conference call on the desktop computer at her nursing station. She logs into the session about mask protocol at the hospital. As she intently listens to the presenter, she notices a few dropped words. She wonders if the problem is similar to her tablet losing its wireless connection for a moment. But then she remembers that she is using a computer that is hardwired to the network.

Immediately after the call, Kishori sends an email to Madhav in the IT department requesting his troubleshooting help. Madhav comes to check out Kishori's computer at the nursing station. Kishori tells him she is confused because all of the devices do seem to be connected. Madhav explains that UDP and TCP are transport layer protocols that operate a little differently. He tells her that UDP is a "best effort" delivery system that does not require acknowledgment of receipt. UDP is preferable with applications such as streaming audio and VoIP. UDP is used for video conference calls.

Kishori had not heard of this before. Have you? In this chapter you will compare these protocols. Keep reading!

TCP and UDP (15.1)

The transport layer includes two protocols: TCP and UDP. TCP is used to deliver messages reliably, whereas UDP is only concerned about getting the messages to the destination as quickly as possible.

Protocol Operations (15.1.1)

A web server and a web client use specific protocols and standards in the process of exchanging information to ensure that the messages are received and understood. The various protocols necessary to deliver a web page function at the four different levels of the TCP/IP model as follows:

- **Application layer protocol**—Hypertext Transfer Protocol (HTTP) governs the way that a web server and a web client interact. HTTP defines the format of the requests and responses exchanged between the client and server. HTTP relies on other protocols to govern how the messages are transported between client and server.
- **Transport layer protocol**—Transmission Control Protocol (TCP) ensures that IP packets are sent reliably and that any missing packets are resent. TCP provides proper ordering of packets received out of order.

- **Internet layer protocol**—The most common internetwork protocol is Internet Protocol (IP). IP is responsible for taking the formatted segments from TCP, assigning the logical addressing, and encapsulating them into packets for routing to the destination host.
- **Network access layer**—The specific protocol at the network access layer, such as Ethernet, depends on the type of media and transmission methods used in the physical network.

TCP and UDP (15.1.2)

Each service available over the network has its own application protocols that are implemented in the server and client software. In addition to the application protocols, all of the common Internet services use Internet Protocol (IP) to address and route messages between source and destination hosts, as shown in Figure 15-1.

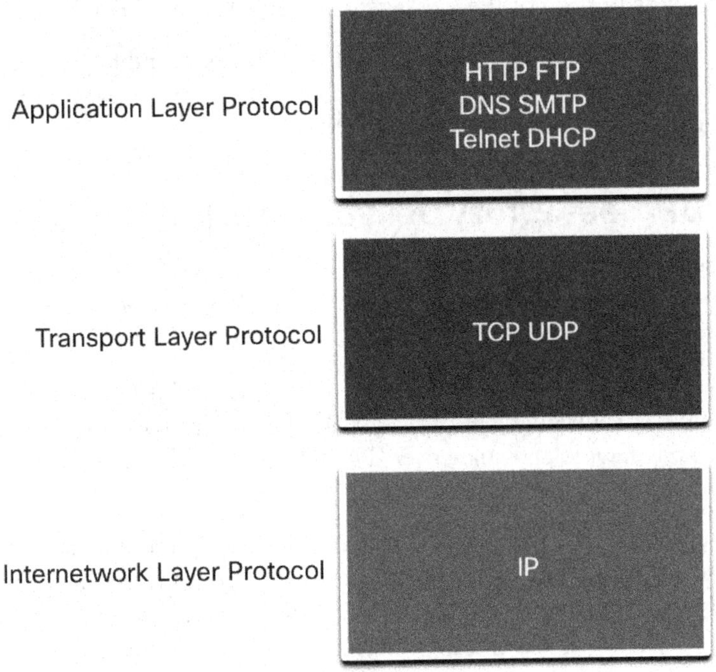

Figure 15-1 Common Protocols Used Between Source and Destination Hosts

IP is concerned only with the structure, addressing, and routing of packets. IP does not specify how the delivery or transportation of the packets takes place. The application decides which transport protocol to use. Transport protocols specify how to manage the transfer of messages between hosts. The two transport protocols are Transmission

Control Protocol (TCP) and User Datagram Protocol (UDP). The IP protocol uses these transport protocols to enable hosts to communicate and transfer data.

TCP Reliability (15.1.3)

With all of the millions and millions of web pages being transmitted at any time over the Internet, how can a server be certain that the page it sent is received by the client that requested it? One of the mechanisms that helps ensure reliable delivery is the *Transmission Control Protocol (TCP)*.

When an application requires acknowledgment that a message is delivered, it uses TCP. TCP breaks up a message into small pieces known as *segments*. The segments are numbered in sequence and passed to the IP process for assembly into packets. TCP keeps track of the number of segments that have been sent to a specific host from a specific application. If the sender does not receive an acknowledgment within a certain period of time, it assumes that the segments were lost and retransmits them. Only the portion of the message that is lost is resent, not the entire message.

On the receiving host, TCP is responsible for reassembling the message segments and passing them to the application. FTP and HTTP are examples of applications that use TCP to ensure delivery of data.

UDP Best Effort Delivery (15.1.4)

In some cases, the TCP acknowledgment protocol is not required and actually slows down information transfer. In those cases, UDP may be a more appropriate transport protocol.

UDP (User Datagram Protocol) is a "best effort" delivery system that does not require acknowledgment of receipt. UDP is preferable with applications such as streaming audio and voice over IP (VoIP). Acknowledgments would slow down delivery, and retransmissions are undesirable.

An example of an application that uses UDP is Internet radio. If some of the message is lost during its journey over the network, it is not retransmitted. If a few packets are missed, the listener might hear a slight break in the sound. If TCP were used and the lost packets were resent, the transmission would pause to receive them, and the disruption would be more noticeable.

To illustrate how UDP is used, consider how a host resolves domain names to IP addresses using DNS. DNS does not require the services of TCP because most DNS queries are resolved in one packet. DNS will use UDP to resolve a name. The example in Figure 15-2 illustrates this. The client does not know the IP address of www.cisco.com so it sends a DNS request to the DNS server using UDP. The server responds with the IP address of cisco.com in one packet.

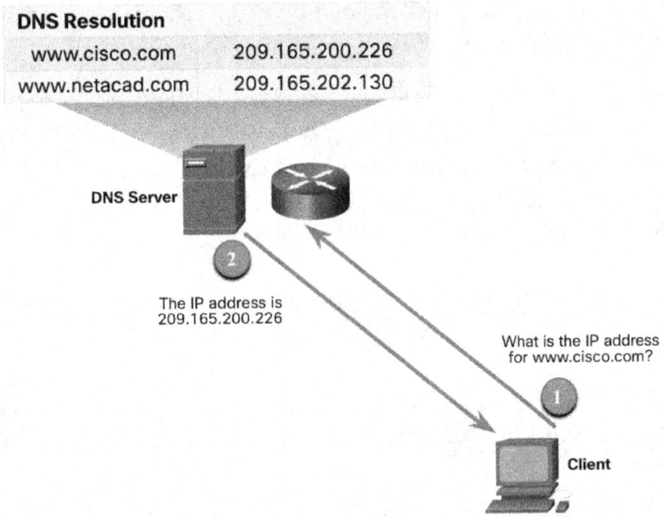

Figure 15-2 Example of DNS Resolution

Video

Video—TCP and UDP Operation (15.1.1)

Refer to the online course to view this video.

Interactive Graphic

Check Your Understanding—TCP and UDP (15.1.2)

Refer to the online course to complete this activity.

Port Numbers (15.2)

TCP and UDP use port numbers. Port numbers indicate a network process or service from the perspective of both the source of the message and the destination.

Video

Video—Transport Layer Port Numbers (15.2.1)

Refer to the online course to view this video.

TCP and UDP Port Numbers (15.2.1)

Many services are accessed through the Internet daily. DNS, web, email, FTP, IM, and VoIP are just some of the services provided by client/server systems around the

world. These services may be provided by a single server or by several servers, which may exist in a small office network or in large data centers.

When a message is delivered using either TCP or UDP, the protocols and services requested are identified by a port number, as shown Figure 15-3. A port is a numeric identifier within each segment that is used to keep track of specific conversations between a client and server. Every message that a host sends contains both a source port and a destination port.

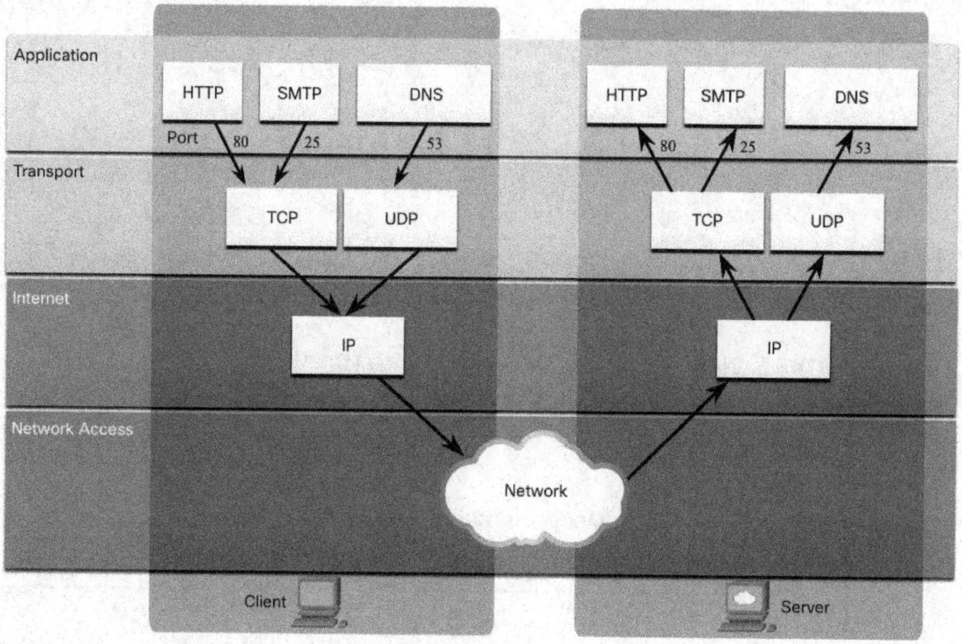

Figure 15-3 Port Numbers Identify the Application in Use

When a server receives a message, the server needs to be able to determine which service the client is requesting. Clients are preconfigured to use a destination port that is registered on the Internet for each service. For example, web browser clients are preconfigured to send requests to web servers using port 80, the well-known port for HTTP web services.

Ports are assigned and managed by an organization known as the Internet Corporation for Assigned Names and Numbers (ICANN). Ports are broken into three categories and range in number from 1 to 65535:

- **Well-known ports**—Destination ports that are associated with common network applications are identified as well-known ports. These ports are in the range of 1 to 1023.

- **Registered ports**—Ports 1024 through 49151 can be used as either source or destination ports. These can be used by organizations to register specific applications such as IM applications.
- **Private ports**—Ports 49152 through 65535 are often used as source ports. These ports can be used by any application.

Table 15-1 displays some common well-known port numbers and their associated applications.

Table 15-1 Well-Known Port Numbers and Applications

Port Number	Transport	Application Protocol
20	TCP	File Transfer Protocol (FTP)—Data
21	TCP	File Transfer Protocol (FTP)—Control
22	TCP	Secure Shell (SSH)
23	TCP	Telnet
25	TCP	Simple Mail Transfer Protocol (SMTP)
53	UDP, TCP	Domain Name Service (DNS)
67	UDP	Dynamic Host Configuration Protocol (DHCP)—Server
68	UDP	Dynamic Host Configuration Protocol—Client
69	UDP	Trivial File Transfer Protocol (TFTP)
80	TCP	Hypertext Transfer Protocol (HTTP)
110	TCP	Post Office Protocol version 3 (POP3)
143	TCP	Internet Message Access Protocol (IMAP)
161	UDP	Simple Network Management Protocol (SNMP)
443	TCP	Hypertext Transfer Protocol Secure (HTTPS)

Some applications may use both TCP and UDP. For example, DNS uses UDP when clients send requests to a DNS server. However, communication between two DNS servers always uses TCP.

Search the IANA website for port registry to view the full list of port numbers and associated applications.

Socket Pairs (15.2.2)

The source and destination ports are placed within the segment. The segments are then encapsulated within an IP packet. The IP packet contains the IP addresses of the source and destination. The combination of the source IP address and source port number, or the destination IP address and destination port number, is known as a *socket*.

In the example shown in Figure 15-4, the PC is simultaneously requesting FTP and web services from the destination server.

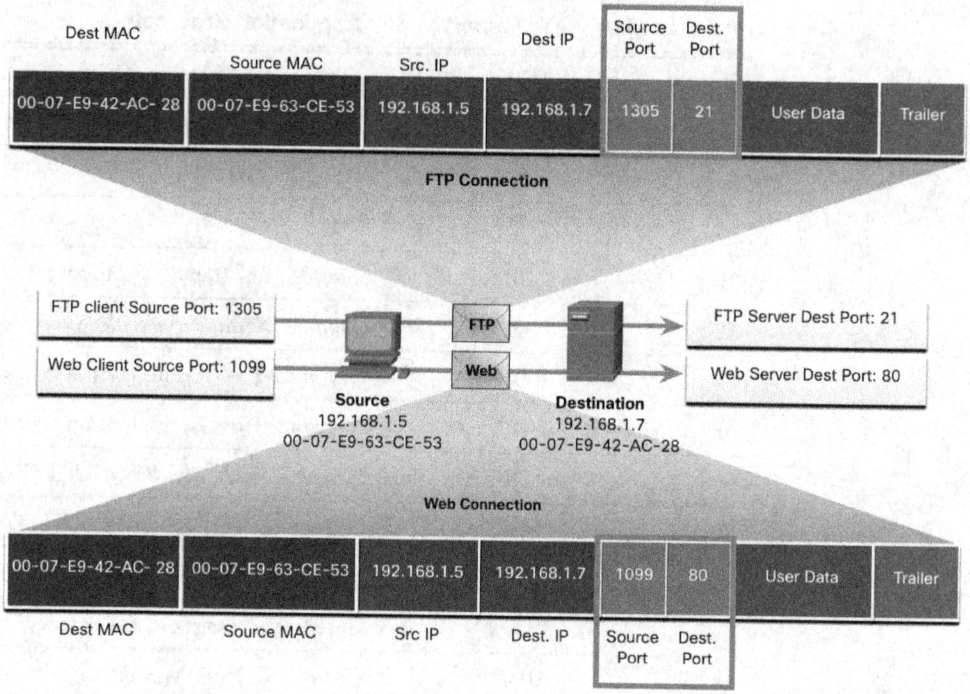

Figure 15-4 A Client and Server Use Port Numbers to Simultaneously Track FTP and Web Traffic

In Figure 15-4, the FTP request generated by the PC includes the Layer 2 MAC addresses and the Layer 3 IP addresses. The request also identifies the source port number 1305 (dynamically generated by the host) and destination port, identifying the FTP services on port 21. The host also has requested a web page from the server using the same Layer 2 and Layer 3 addresses. However, it is using the source port number 1099 (dynamically generated by the host) and destination port identifying the web service on port 80.

The socket is used to identify the server and service being requested by the client. A client socket might look like this, with 1099 representing the source port number: 192.168.1.5:1099.

The socket on a web server might be 192.168.1.7:80.

Together, these two sockets combine to form a socket pair: 192.168.1.5:1099, 192.168.1.7:80.

Sockets enable multiple processes, running on a client, to distinguish themselves from each other, and enable multiple connections to a server process to be distinguished from each other.

The source port number acts as a return address for the requesting application. The transport layer keeps track of this port and the application that initiated the request so that when a response is returned, it can be forwarded to the correct application.

The netstat Command (15.2.3)

Unexplained TCP connections can pose a major security threat. They can indicate that something or someone is connected to the local host. Sometimes it is necessary to know which active TCP connections are open and running on a networked host. Netstat is an important network utility that can be used to verify those connections. As shown in Example 15-1, enter the command **netstat** to list the protocols in use, the local address and port numbers, the foreign address and port numbers, and the connection state.

Example 15-1 Using the **netstat** Command to List Protocols in Use

```
C:\> netstat

Active Connections

  Proto  Local Address          Foreign Address            State
  TCP    192.168.1.124:3126     192.168.0.2:netbios-ssn    ESTABLISHED
  TCP    192.168.1.124:3158     207.138.126.152:http       ESTABLISHED
  TCP    192.168.1.124:3159     207.138.126.169:http       ESTABLISHED
  TCP    192.168.1.124:3160     207.138.126.169:http       ESTABLISHED
  TCP    192.168.1.124:3161     sc.msn.com:http            ESTABLISHED
  TCP    192.168.1.124:3166     www.cisco.com:http         ESTABLISHED
(output omitted)
C:\>
```

By default, the **netstat** command attempts to resolve IP addresses to domain names and port numbers to well-known applications. Adding the **-n** option displays IP addresses and port numbers in their numerical form.

Interactive Graphic

Check Your Understanding—Port Numbers (15.2.5)

Refer to the online course to complete this activity.

TCP and UDP Summary (15.3)

The following is a summary of each topic in the chapter and some questions for your reflection.

What Did I Learn in This Chapter? (15.3.1)

- **TCP and UDP**—UDP is a "best effort" delivery system that does not require acknowledgment of receipt. UDP is preferable with applications such as streaming audio and VoIP. Acknowledgments would slow down delivery, and retransmissions are undesirable. Packets take a path from the source to a destination. A few packets may be lost but it is usually not noticeable.

  TCP packets take a path from the source to the destination. However, each of the packets has a sequence number. TCP breaks up a message into segments. The segments are numbered in sequence and passed to the IP process for assembly into packets. TCP keeps track of the number of segments that have been sent to a specific host from a specific application. If the sender does not receive an acknowledgment within a certain period of time, it assumes that the segments were lost and retransmits them. Only the portion of the message that is lost is resent, not the entire message.

- **Port Numbers**—When a message is delivered using either TCP or UDP, the protocols and services requested are identified by a port number. A port is a numeric identifier within each segment that is used to keep track of specific conversations between a client and server. Every message that a host sends contains both a source and destination port.

  When a message is received by a server, it is necessary for the server to be able to determine which service is being requested by the client. Clients are preconfigured to use a destination port that is registered on the Internet for each service.

Ports are assigned and managed by ICANN. Ports are broken into three categories and range in number from 1 to 65535:

- **Well-known ports**—Destination ports that are associated with common network applications are identified as well-known ports. These ports are in the range of 1 to 1023.
- **Registered ports**—Ports 1024 through 49151 can be used as either source or destination ports. These can be used by organizations to register specific applications such as IM applications.
- **Private ports**—Ports 49152 through 65535 are often used as source ports. These ports can be used by any application.

The source port number is dynamically generated by the sending device to identify a conversation between two devices. This process allows multiple conversations to occur simultaneously. It is common for a device to send multiple HTTP service requests to a web server at the same time. Each separate HTTP conversation is tracked based on the source ports.

The client places a destination port number in the segment to tell the destination server what service is being requested. A server can offer more than one service simultaneously, such as web services on port 80 at the same time that it offers FTP connection establishment on port 21.

Unexplained TCP connections can pose a major security threat. They can indicate that something or someone is connected to the local host. Sometimes it is necessary to know which active TCP connections are open and running on a networked host. Netstat is an important network utility that can be used to verify those connections. The command **netstat** is used to list the protocols in use, the local address and port numbers, the foreign address and port numbers, and the connection state.

Reflection Questions (15.3.2)

I once ordered some furniture from one of those online stores. It was sent to me in three different boxes, over the span of two weeks. I was not worried that anything was missing because I received email updates that detailed the location of each box along its route from the store to my home. That example is like TCP. All along the route, there are built-in checks to ensure that what needs to be delivered gets delivered, and in the right order.

There is still a need for UDP in networking. I would not enjoy streaming a movie where it stops for minutes at a time waiting for the network to send the next scene. Can you think of a good analogy for UDP?

Practice

There are no labs or Packet Tracer activities in this chapter.

Check Your Understanding Questions

Complete all the review questions listed here to test your understanding of the topics and concepts in this chapter. Appendix A, "Answers to 'Check Your Understanding' Questions," lists the answers.

1. Which protocol operates at the application layer of the TCP/IP model?
   a. IP
   b. TCP
   c. HTTP
   d. ICMP
2. What is a characteristic of UDP?
   a. It establishes sessions with a three-way handshake.
   b. It uses sequence numbers to reassemble segments.
   c. It adds 20 bytes of overhead to application layer data.
   d. It provides unreliable delivery of segments.
3. Which type of applications are best suited to use UDP as the transport layer protocol?
   a. Applications that require flow control
   b. Applications that require data to be reassembled in a specific order
   c. Applications that require minimal transmission delay
   d. Applications that require stateful sessions
4. A student is sending files from a phone to a computer across a network. Which layer of the TCP/IP model is responsible for reassembling these messages as they are received on the computer?
   a. Application
   b. Transport
   c. Internet
   d. Network access

5. At which layer of the TCP/IP model does TCP operate?

   a. Transport
   b. Application
   c. Internetwork
   d. Network access

6. What protocol header information is used at the transport layer to identify a target application?

   a. Port number
   b. IP address
   c. Sequence number
   d. MAC address

7. What type of port number is assigned by IANA to commonly used services and applications?

   a. Well-known port
   b. Registered port
   c. Dynamic port
   d. Private port

8. What is the purpose of using a source port number in a TCP communication?

   a. To notify the remote device that the conversation is over
   b. To assemble the segments that arrived out of order
   c. To keep track of multiple conversations between devices
   d. To inquire about a non-received segment

9. What is an advantage of UDP over TCP?

   a. UDP communication requires less overhead.
   b. UDP communication is more reliable.
   c. UDP reorders segments that are received out of order.
   d. UDP acknowledges received data.

10. When is UDP preferred over TCP?

    a. When a client sends a segment to a server
    b. When all the data must be fully received before any part of it is considered useful

c. When an application can tolerate some loss of data during transmission

d. When segments must arrive in a very specific sequence to be processed successfully

11. Which statement correctly describes data transmission at the transport layer?

a. Retransmission of lost packets is provided by both TCP and UDP.

b. Segmentation is provided by the window size field when the TCP protocol is used.

c. A single datagram can include both a TCP header and a UDP header.

d. Both UDP and TCP use port numbers.

e. Segmentation is provided by sequence numbers when UDP is used.

CHAPTER 16

Application Layer Services

Objectives

Upon completion of this chapter, you will be able to answer the following questions:

- How do clients and servers interact?
- What are common network applications?
- How does DNS operate?
- How do HTTP and HTML operate?
- How does FTP operate?
- How do Telnet and SSH operate?
- How do email protocols operate?

Key Terms

This chapter uses the following key terms. You can find the definitions in the Glossary.

Domain Name System (DNS) Page 234

Dynamic Host Configuration Protocol (DHCP) Page 234

File Transfer Protocol (FTP) Page 234

Hypertext Markup Language (HTML) Page 237

Hypertext Transfer Protocol (HTTP) Page 234

Internet Message Access Protocol (IMAP) Page 234

Post Office Protocol (POP) Page 234

Secure Shell (SSH) Page 234

Simple Mail Transfer Protocol (SMTP) Page 234

Introduction (16.0)

Kishori needs to get access to a patient file. She has done this many times, but it is only now that she is wondering how this process actually happens in a network. Where does this electronic document come from? How is she able to access the hospital's intranet? How is she able to access the Internet at all? All of this is possible because of application layer services. Kishori realizes that she has more to learn before she applies for that promotion Rina mentioned other nurses have received for their advanced IT knowledge.

Many services work at the application layer, including some you're already familiar with, such as FTP, DHCP, and DNS. Just about any time you want to retrieve something that is not already located on your computer, you will be the client requesting that the appropriate server send you that item. And, of course, by now you know that there will be protocols involved. Read on!

The Client-Server Relationship (16.1)

Most network communications involves a client-server relationship. This includes many of the network services we use today, such as browsing the web, reading email, watching videos, and much more. Many internal and service provider infrastructures are based on this architecture.

Client and Server Interaction (16.1.1)

Every day, we use the services available over networks and the Internet to communicate with others and to perform routine tasks. We rarely think of the servers, clients, and networking devices that are necessary to receive an email, update our status on social media, or shop for the best bargains in an online store. Most of the commonly used Internet applications rely on complicated interactions between various servers and clients. Figure 16-1 shows a simple example of a client and server connected over the Internet.

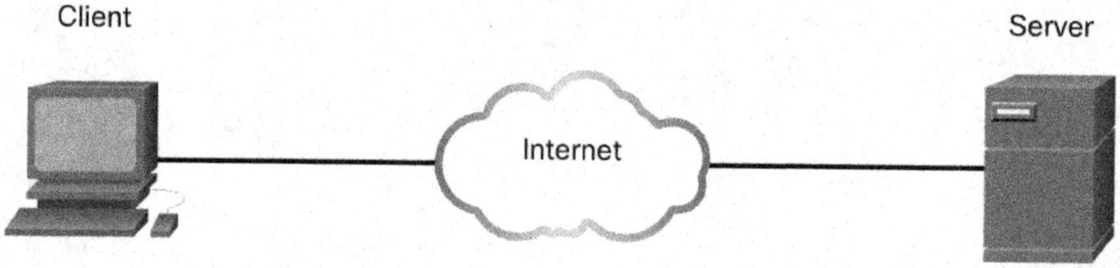

Figure 16-1 Example of a Client and Server Connection

The term *server* refers to a host running a software application that provides information or services to other hosts that are connected to the network. A well-known example of a server is a host running web server software. There are millions of servers connected to the Internet, providing services such as websites, email, financial transactions, and music downloads, among many others. A crucial factor to enable these complex interactions to function is that they all use agreed-upon standards and protocols.

An example of client software is a web browser, like Chrome or Firefox. A single computer can run multiple types of client software. For example, a user can check email and view a web page while instant messaging and listening to an audio stream. Table 16-1 lists three common types of server software.

Table 16-1 Common Types of Server Software

Type	Description
Email	The email server runs email server software. Clients use mail client software, such as Microsoft Outlook, to access email on the server.
Web	The web server runs web server software. Clients use browser software, such as Microsoft Edge, to access web pages on the server.
File	The file server stores corporate and user files in a central location. The client devices access these files with client software such as Windows File Explorer.

Client Requests a Web Page (16.1.2)

Much of the information that we receive over the Internet is provided in the form of web page documents. To request and view a web page, we use a device that is running web client software such as a web browser.

The key characteristic of client/server systems is that the client sends a request to a server, and the server responds by carrying out a function, such as sending the requested document back to the client. The combination of a web browser and a web server is perhaps the most commonly used instance of a client/server system. A web server is usually in a part of the network with other servers called a *server farm*, or within a data center.

A *data center* is a facility used to house computer systems and associated components. A data center can occupy one room of a building, one or more floors, or an entire building. Data centers are typically very expensive to build and maintain. For this reason, only large organizations use privately built data centers to house their data and provide services to users. Smaller organizations that cannot afford to maintain their own private data center can reduce the overall cost of ownership by leasing server and storage services from a larger data center organization in the cloud.

Video

Video—Web Server and Client IP Interactions (16.1.2)

Refer to the online course to view this video.

URI, URN, and URL (16.1.3)

Web resources and web services such as RESTful APIs are identified using a Uniform Resource Identifier (URI). A URI is a string of characters that identifies a specific network resource. As shown in Figure 16-2, a URI has two specializations:

- **Uniform Resource Name (URN)**—This identifies only the namespace of the resource (web page, document, image, etc.) without reference to the protocol.
- **Uniform Resource Locator (URL)**—This defines the network location of a specific resource on the network. HTTP or HTTPS URLs are typically used with web browsers. Other protocols such as FTP, SFTP, SSH, and others can use a URL. A URL using SFTP might look like sftp://sftp.example.com.

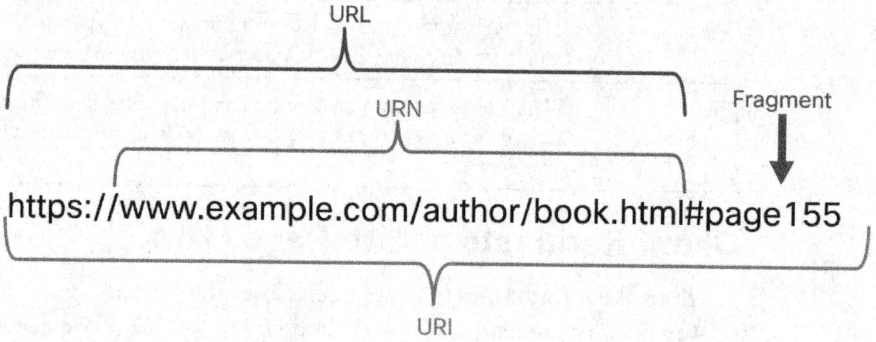

Figure 16-2 Parts of a URI

These are the parts of a URI, as shown in Figure 16-2:

- **Protocol/scheme**—HTTPS or other protocols such as FTP, SFTP, mailto, and NNTP
- **Hostname**—www.example.com
- **Path and file name**—/author/book.html
- **Fragment**—#page155

Video

Video—Web Traffic in Packet Tracer (16.1.4)

Refer to the online course to view this video.

Packet Tracer
☐ Activity

Packet Tracer—The Client Interaction (16.1.5)

In this activity, you will observe the client interaction between the server and PC.

Refer to the online course to complete this Packet Tracer.

Network Application Services (16.2)

Network application services allow users to use domain names instead of IP addresses, receive information from web servers, access email, and perform file transfers. These are the services in which users interact with networks and the Internet.

Common Network Application Services (16.2.1)

What are the most common Internet services that you use on a regular basis? For most people, the list includes services such as Internet searches, social media sites, video and audio streaming, online shopping sites, email, and messaging. Figure 16-3 shows some of the most common servers that provide these services. Each of these services relies on protocols from the TCP/IP protocol suite to reliably communicate the information between the clients and the servers, as described in Table 16-2.

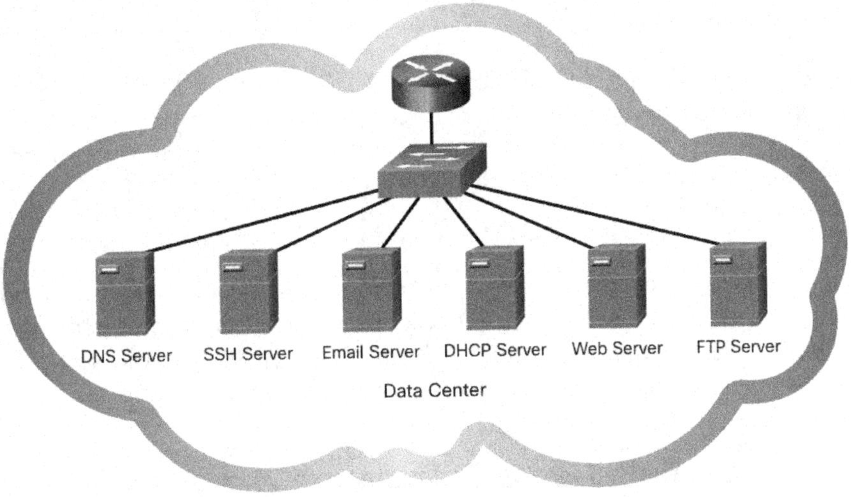

Figure 16-3 Example of Services in a Data Center

Table 16-2 Common Server Protocols

Protocol	Description
Domain Name System (DNS)	Used to resolve Internet names to IP addresses.
Secure Shell (SSH)	Used to provide remote access to servers and networking devices.
Simple Mail Transfer Protocol (SMTP)	Used to send email messages and attachments from clients to servers and from servers to other email servers.
Post Office Protocol (POP)	Used by email clients to retrieve email and attachments from a remote server.
Internet Message Access Protocol (IMAP)	Used by email clients to retrieve email and attachments from a remote server.
Dynamic Host Configuration Protocol (DHCP)	Used to automatically configure devices with IP addressing and other necessary information to enable them to communicate over the Internet.
Hypertext Transfer Protocol (HTTP)	Used by web browsers to request web pages and by web servers to transfer the files that make up web pages.
File Transfer Protocol (FTP)	Used for interactive file transfer between systems.

Interactive Graphic

Check Your Understanding—Common Network Applications (16.2.2)

Refer to the online course to complete this activity.

Domain Name System (16.3)

IP packets require source and destination IP addresses. Although IP addresses are ideal for network communications, humans communicate better with names rather than numbers. The Domain Name System (DNS) allows users to specify a destination or service using words instead of IP addresses.

Domain Name Translation (16.3.1)

Thousands of servers, installed in many different locations, provide the services that we use daily over the Internet. Each of these servers is assigned a unique IP address that identifies it on the local network where it is connected.

It would be impossible to remember all of the IP addresses for all of the servers hosting services on the Internet. Instead, there is an easier way to locate servers by associating a name with an IP address.

DNS provides a way for hosts to use this name to request the IP address of a specific server, as shown Figure 16-4. DNS names are registered and organized on the Internet within specific high-level groups, or domains. Some of the most common high-level domains on the Internet are .com, .edu, and .net.

Figure 16-4 DNS Server Responding to a Client

DNS Servers (16.3.2)

A DNS server contains a table that associates hostnames in a domain with corresponding IP addresses. When a client has the name of a server, such as a web server, but needs to find the IP address, it sends a request to the DNS server on port 53. The client uses the IP address of the DNS server configured in the DNS settings of the host IP configuration.

When the DNS server receives the request, it checks its table to determine the IP address associated with that web server. If the local DNS server does not have an entry for the requested name, it queries another DNS server within the domain. When the DNS server learns the IP address, it sends that information back to the client. If the DNS server cannot determine the IP address, the request will time out and the client will not be able to communicate with the web server.

Figure 16-4 shows a DNS server responding to a client's request for the IP address associated with the domain name www.cisco.com.

Video

Video—DNS Servers (16.3.1)

Refer to the online course to view this video.

A Note About Syntax Checker Activities (16.3.3)

When you are learning how to modify device configurations, you might want to start in a safe, nonproduction environment before trying it on real equipment. There are different simulation tools to help build your configuration and troubleshooting skills. Because these are simulation tools, they typically do not have all the functionality of real equipment. One such tool is the Syntax Checker. In each Syntax Checker, you are given a set of instructions to enter a specific set of commands. You cannot progress in Syntax Checker unless the exact and full command is entered as specified. More advanced simulation tools, such as Packet Tracer, let you enter abbreviated commands, much as you would do on real equipment.

Interactive Graphic

Syntax Checker—The nslookup Command (16.3.3)

When you manually configure a device for network connectivity, recall that you also include a DNS server address. For home networks, this configuration is typically handled by DHCP running on the home router. Your ISP provides the DNS server address to your home router, and then your home router uses DHCP to send the configuration to all the devices connected to its network. When you type the name for a website, such as www.cisco.com, the DNS client running on your device first asks the DNS server for the IP address, such as 172.230.155.162, before sending out your HTTP request.

You can use the command **nslookup** to discover the IP addresses for any domain name. In this Syntax Checker activity, practice entering the **nslookup** command in both Windows and Linux.

Refer to the online course to complete this activity.

Web Clients and Servers (16.4)

One of the earliest and most common network application services is the World Wide Web (www), or simply the web. The web uses a combination of the HTTP protocol and HTML markup (or coding) language to allow clients to request web pages and other web objects from a web server.

Video

Video—HTTP and HTML (16.4.1)

Refer to the online course to view this video.

HTTP and HTML (16.4.2)

When a web client receives the IP address of a web server, the client browser uses that IP address and port 80 to request web services. This request is sent to the server using the Hypertext Transfer Protocol (HTTP).

When the server receives a port 80 request, the server responds to the client request and sends the web page to the client. The information content of a web page is encoded using specialized markup languages. The *Hypertext Markup Language (HTML)* coding tells the browser how to format the web page and what graphics and fonts to use. HTML is the most commonly used markup language.

Figure 16-5 shows a client requesting a web page.

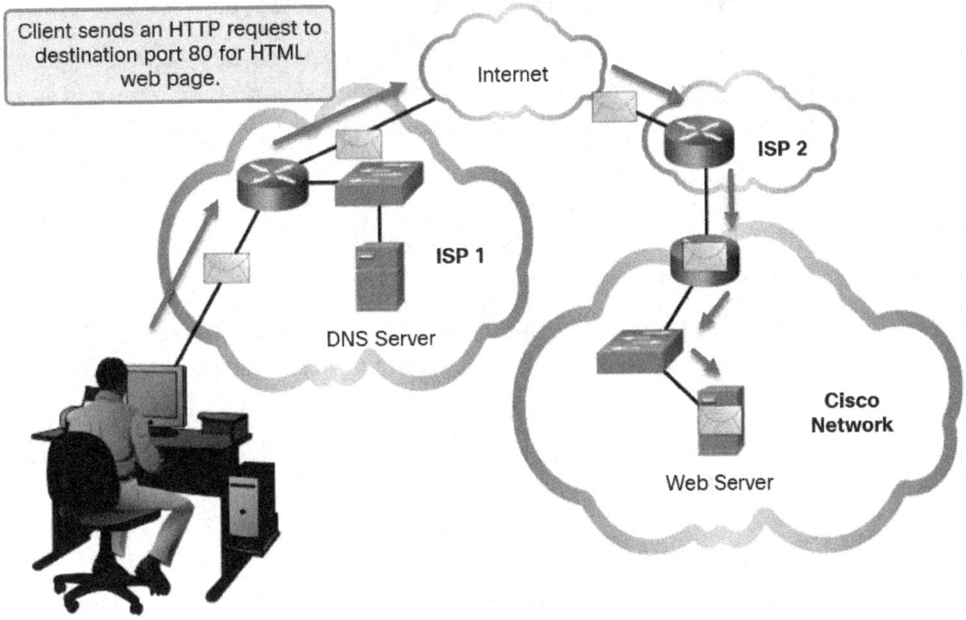

Figure 16-5 Client Requesting a Web Page

HTTP is not a secure protocol; information could easily be intercepted by other users as data is sent over the network. To provide security for the data, HTTP can be used with secure transport protocols. Requests for secure HTTP are sent to port 443. These requests use *https* instead of *http* in the website address in the browser.

Many different web servers and web clients are available. The HTTP and HTML standards make it possible for these servers and clients from many different vendors to work together seamlessly.

Packet Tracer
☐ Activity

Packet Tracer—Observe Web Requests (16.4.3)

In this activity, you will observe web requests when a client browser requests web pages from a server.

Refer to the online course to complete this Packet Tracer.

FTP Clients and Servers (16.5)

In addition to web services, another common service used across the Internet is one that allows users to transfer files.

File Transfer Protocol (16.5.1)

The File Transfer Protocol (FTP) provides an easy method to transfer files from one computer to another. A host running FTP client software can access an FTP server to perform various file management functions such as file uploads and downloads.

The FTP server enables a client to exchange files between devices. It also enables clients to manage files remotely by sending file management commands such as delete or rename. To accomplish this, the FTP service uses two different ports to communicate between client and server.

The example in Figure 16-6 illustrates how FTP operates. To begin an FTP session, control connection requests are sent to the server using destination TCP port 21. When the session is opened, the server uses TCP port 20 to transfer the data files.

FTP client software is built into computer operating systems and into most web browsers. Standalone FTP clients offer many options in an easy-to-use GUI-based interface.

Based on commands sent across the control connection, data can be downloaded from the server or uploaded from the client.

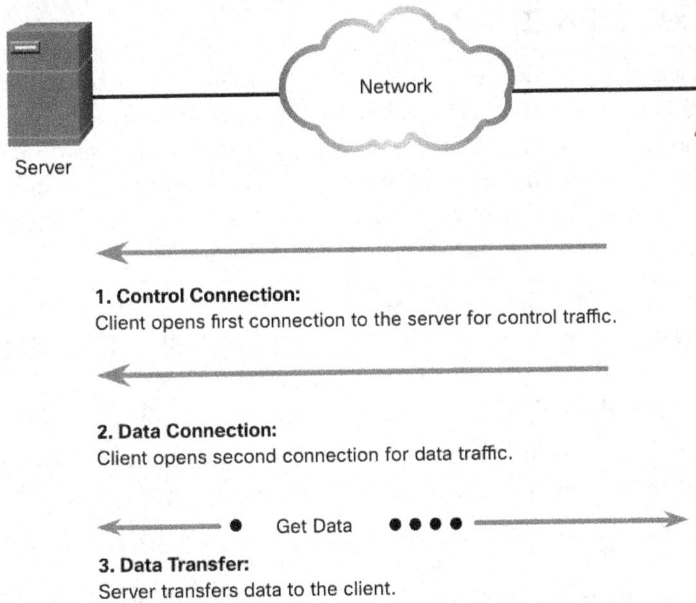

Figure 16-6 FTP Operation

Video

Video—FTP Client Software (16.5.2)

Refer to the online course to view this video.

Packet Tracer Activity

Packet Tracer—Use FTP Services (16.5.3)

In this activity, you will put a file on an FTP server and get a file from an FTP server.

Refer to the online course to complete this Packet Tracer.

Virtual Terminals (16.6)

Long before desktop computers with sophisticated graphical interfaces existed, people used text-based systems that were often just display terminals physically attached to a central computer. After networks became available, people needed a way to remotely access the computer systems in the same manner that they did with the directly attached terminals.

Video

Video—Remote Access with Telnet or SSH (16.6.1)

Refer to the online course to view this video.

Telnet (16.6.2)

Telnet was developed to provide a way to remotely access computer systems. Telnet dates back to the early 1970s and is among the oldest of the application layer protocols and services in the TCP/IP suite. Telnet provides a standard method of emulating text-based terminal devices over the data network. Both the protocol itself and the client software that implements the protocol are commonly referred to as Telnet. Telnet servers listen for client requests on TCP port 23.

Appropriately enough, a connection using Telnet is called a virtual terminal (vty) session, or connection. Rather than using a physical device to connect to the server, Telnet uses software to create a virtual device that provides the same features of a terminal session with access to the server's command-line interface (CLI).

In Figure 16-7, the client has remotely connected to the server via Telnet. The client is now able to execute commands as if it were locally connected to the server.

Note

Telnet is not considered to be a secure protocol. SSH should be used in most environments instead of Telnet. Telnet is used in several examples in this course for simplicity of configuration.

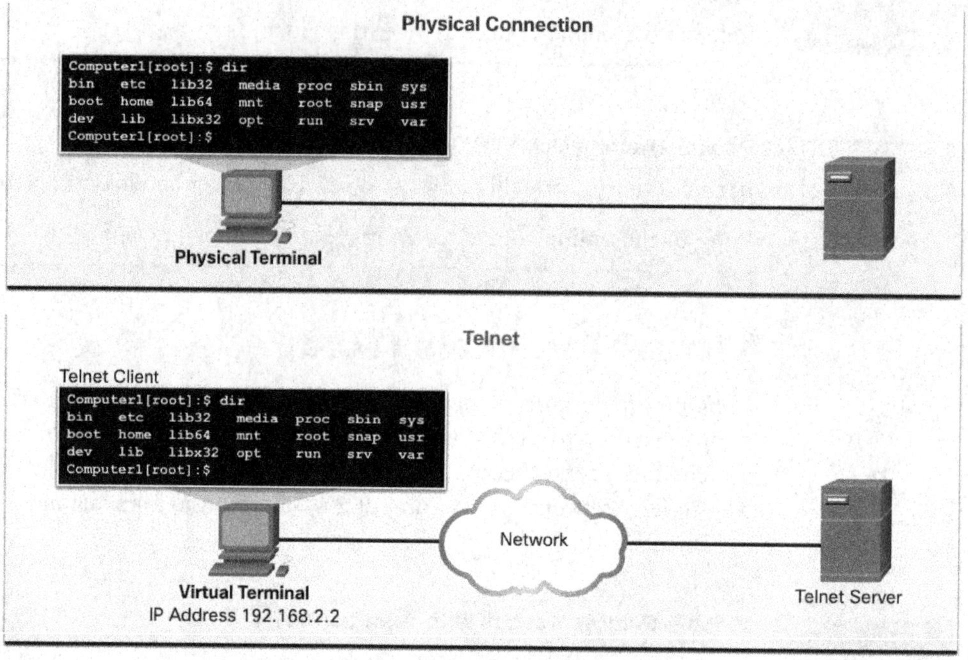

Figure 16-7 Client Remotely Accessing a Server

Security Issues with Telnet (16.6.3)

After a Telnet connection is established, users can perform any authorized function on the server, just as if they were using a command-line session on the server itself. If authorized, they can start and stop processes, configure the device, and even shut down the system.

Although the Telnet protocol can require a user to log in, it does not support transporting encrypted data. All data exchanged during Telnet sessions is transported as plaintext across the network. This means that the data can be easily intercepted and understood.

The Secure Shell (SSH) protocol offers an alternate and secure method for server access. SSH provides the structure for secure remote login and other secure network services. It also provides stronger authentication than Telnet and supports transporting session data using encryption. As a best practice, network professionals should always use SSH in place of Telnet, whenever possible.

Figure 16-8 illustrates how SSH is more secure than Telnet. Notice how the data captured by the hacker when Telnet is used is clearly readable, whereas the data captured when SSH is used is encrypted and therefore more secure.

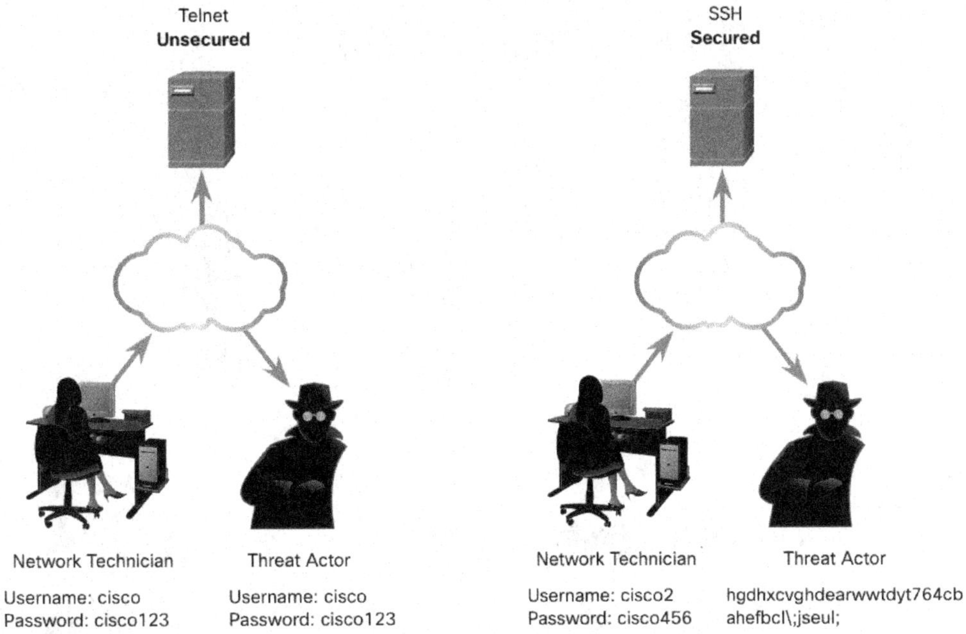

Figure 16-8 Telnet and SSH Comparison

Packet Tracer
☐ Activity

Packet Tracer—Use Telnet and SSH (16.6.4)

In this activity, you will establish remote sessions to a router using Telnet and SSH.

Refer to the online course to complete this Packet Tracer.

Email and Messaging (16.7)

Email is one of the most popular client/server applications on the Internet. Email servers run server software that enables them to interact with clients and with other email servers over the network.

Email Clients and Servers (16.7.1)

Each mail server receives and stores mail for users who have mailboxes configured on the mail server. Each user with a mailbox must then use an email client to access the mail server and read the messages in their mailbox. Many Internet messaging systems use a web-based client to access email. Examples of this type of client include Microsoft 365, Yahoo!, and Gmail.

Mailboxes are identified by the format *user@company.domain*.

Email Protocols (16.7.2)

Various application protocols used in processing email include SMTP, POP3, and IMAP4, as shown in Figure 16-9.

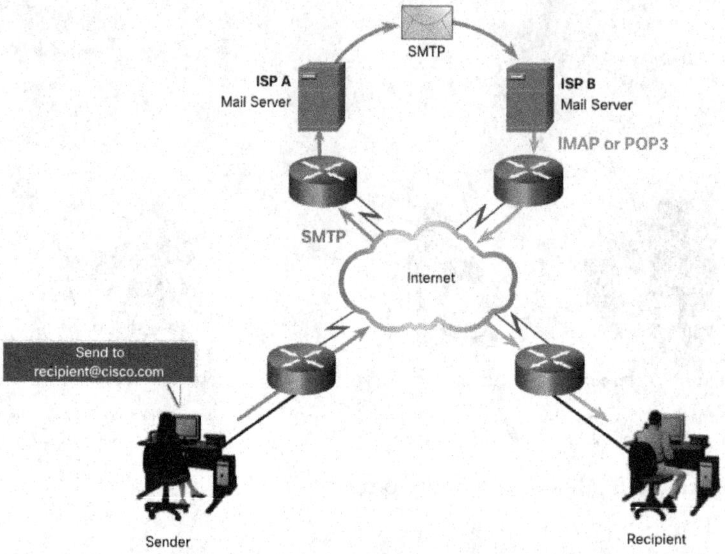

Figure 16-9 SMTP, POP3, and IMAP4 Mail Protocols in Operation

Simple Mail Transfer Protocol (SMTP)

SMTP is used by an email client to send messages to its local email server. The local server then determines whether the message is destined for a local mailbox or is addressed to a mailbox on another server.

If the server has to send the message to a different server, SMTP is used between those two servers as well. SMTP requests are sent to port 25. Figure 16-10 shows how SMTP is used to send email.

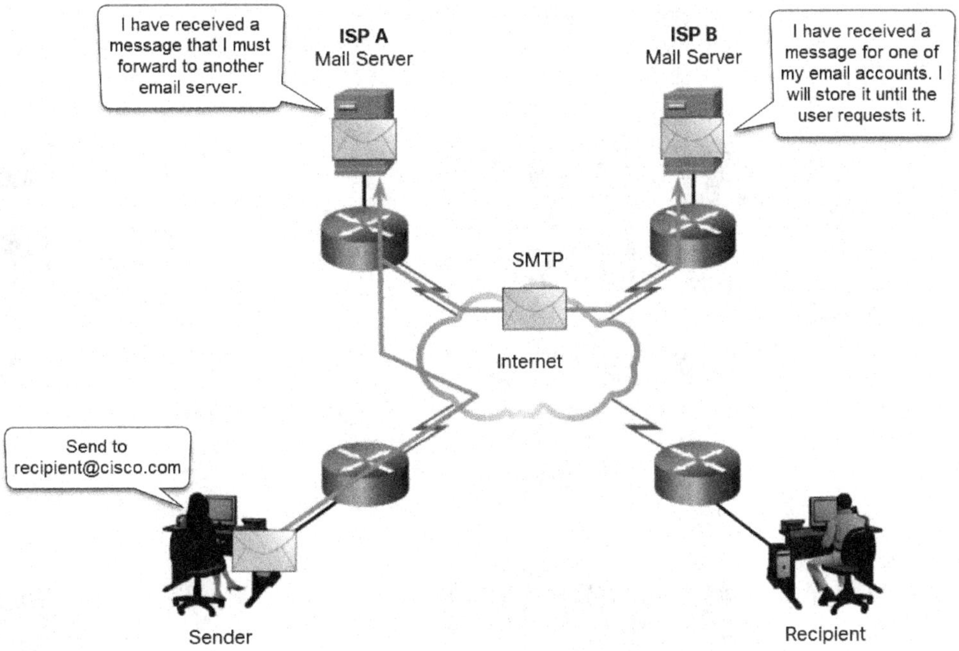

Figure 16-10 SMTP Operation

Post Office Protocol (POP3)

A server that supports POP clients receives and stores messages addressed to its users. When the client connects to the email server, the messages are downloaded to the client. By default, messages are not kept on the server after they have been accessed by the client. Clients contact POP3 servers on port 110.

Internet Message Access Protocol (IMAP4)

A server that supports IMAP clients also receives and stores messages addressed to its users. However, unlike POP, IMAP keeps the messages in the mailboxes on

the server, unless they are deleted by the user. The most current version of IMAP is IMAP4, which listens for client requests on port 143.

Many different email servers exist for the various network operating system platforms.

Text Messaging (16.7.3)

Text messaging, shown in Figure 16-11, is one of the most popular communication tools in use today. In addition, text messaging software is built into many online applications, smartphone apps, and social media sites.

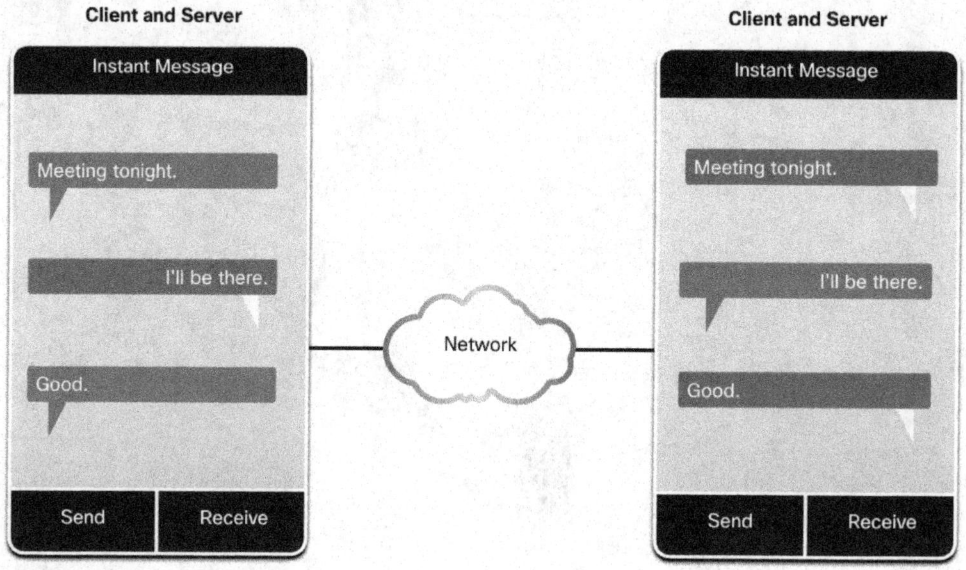

Figure 16-11 Text Messaging

Both clients can simultaneously send and receive messages.

Text messages may also be called instant messages, direct messages, private messages, and chat messages. Text messaging enables users to communicate or chat over the Internet in real time. Text messaging services on a computer are usually accessed through a web-based client that is integrated into a social media or information sharing site. These clients usually connect only to other users of the same site.

There are also a number of standalone text message clients such as Cisco Webex Teams, Microsoft Teams, WhatsApp, Facebook Messenger, and many others. These applications are available for a wide variety of operating systems and devices. A mobile version is typically offered. In addition to text messages, these clients support the transfer of documents, video, music, and audio files.

Internet Phone Calls (16.7.4)

Making telephone calls over the Internet is becoming increasingly popular. An Internet telephony client uses peer-to-peer technology similar to that used by instant messaging, as shown in Figure 16-12. IP telephony makes use of voice over IP (VoIP) technology, which converts analog voice signals into digital data. The voice data is encapsulated into IP packets that carry the phone call through the network.

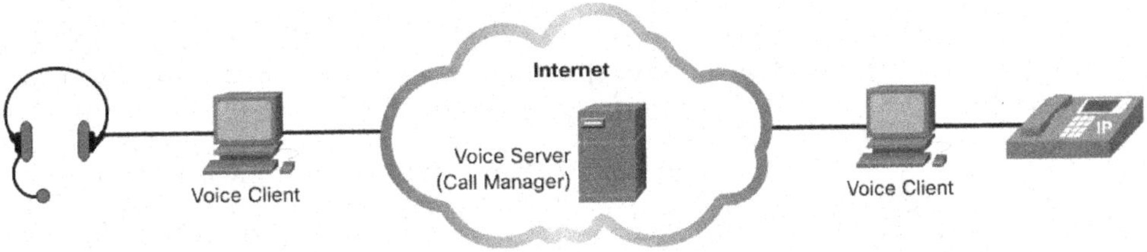

Figure 16-12 VoIP Phone Call Example

After the IP phone software has been installed, the user selects a unique name so that calls can be received from other users. Speakers and a microphone, built-in or separate, are required. A headset is frequently plugged into the computer to serve as a phone.

Calls are made to other users of the same service on the Internet by selecting the username from a list. A call to a regular telephone (landline or cell phone) requires using a gateway to access the public switched telephone network (PSTN). Depending on the service, this type of call may have associated charges. The protocols and destination ports used by Internet telephony applications can vary based on the software.

Interactive Graphic

Check Your Understanding—Email and Messaging (16.7.5)

Refer to the online course to complete this activity.

Application Layer Services Summary (16.8)

The following is a summary of each topic in the chapter and some questions for your reflection.

What Did I Learn in This Chapter? (16.8.1)

- **The Client-Server Relationship**—A server is a host running a software application that provides information or services to other hosts that are connected to the network, such as a web server. An example of client software is a web

browser, like Chrome or Firefox. A single computer can also run multiple types of client software. A crucial factor to enable these complex interactions to function is that they all use agreed-upon standards and protocols.

The key characteristic of client/server systems is that the client sends a request to a server, and the server responds by carrying out a function, such as sending the requested document back to the client. The combination of a web browser and a web server is perhaps the most commonly used instance of a client/server system.

A URI is a string of characters that identifies a specific network resource. The parts of a URI are protocol/scheme, hostname, path and file name, and fragment. A URI has two specializations:

- **Uniform Resource Name (URN)**—This identifies only the namespace of the resource (web page, document, image, etc.) without reference to the protocol.
- **Uniform Resource Locator (URL)**—This defines the network location of a specific resource on the network. HTTP or HTTPS URLs are typically used with web browsers. Other protocols such as FTP, SFTP, SSH, and others can use a URL. A URL using SFTP might look like sftp://sftp.example.com.

- **Network Application Services**—For most people, the most common Internet services that they use include Internet searches, social media sites, video and audio streaming, online shopping sites, email, and messaging. Each of these services relies on protocols from the TCP/IP protocol suite to reliably communicate the information between the clients and the servers. Common services include DNS, SSH, SMTP, POP, IMAP, DHCP, HTTP, and FTP.
- **Domain Name System**—DNS provides a way for hosts to request the IP address of a specific server. DNS names are registered and organized on the Internet within specific high-level groups, or domains. Some of the most common high-level domains on the Internet are .com, .edu, and .net.

  When the DNS server receives the request from a host, it checks its table to determine the IP address associated with that web server. If the local DNS server does not have an entry for the requested name, it queries another DNS server within the domain. When the DNS server learns the IP address, that information is sent back to the host.
- **Web Clients and Servers**—When a web client receives the IP address of a web server, the client browser uses that IP address and port 80 to request web services. This request is sent to the server using HTTP. HTTP is not a secure protocol; information could easily be intercepted by other users as data is sent over the network. To provide security for the data, HTTP can be used with secure transport protocols. Requests for secure HTTP are sent to port 443. These requests use *https* instead of *http* in the site address in the browser.

When the server receives a port 80 request, the server responds to the client request and sends the web page to the client. The information content of a web page is encoded using HTML. HTML coding tells the browser how to format the web page and what graphics and fonts to use.

Many different web servers and web clients are available. The HTTP protocol and HTML standards make it possible for these servers and clients from many different vendors to work together seamlessly.

- **FTP Clients and Servers**—FTP provides an easy method to transfer files from one computer to another. A host running FTP client software can access an FTP server to perform various file management functions such as file uploads and downloads. The FTP server enables a client to exchange files between devices. It also enables clients to manage files remotely by sending file management commands such as delete or rename. To accomplish this, the FTP service uses two different ports to communicate between client and server. To begin an FTP session, control connection requests are sent to the server using destination TCP port 21. When the session is opened, the server uses TCP port 20 to transfer the data files.

  Most client operating systems such as Windows, macOS, and Linux include a command-line interface for FTP. There is also GUI-based FTP client software that provides a simple drag-and-drop interface for FTP.

- **Virtual Terminals**—Telnet provides a standard method of emulating text-based terminal devices over the data network. Both the protocol itself and the client software that implements the protocol are commonly referred to as Telnet. Telnet servers listen for client requests on TCP port 23. A connection using Telnet is called a virtual terminal (vty) session, or connection. Rather than using a physical device to connect to the server, Telnet uses software to create a virtual device that provides the same features of a terminal session with access to the server's CLI.

  Telnet is not considered to be a secure protocol. Although the Telnet protocol can require a user to log in, it does not support transporting encrypted data. All data exchanged during Telnet sessions is transported as plaintext across the network. This means that the data can be easily intercepted and understood.

  SSH provides the structure for secure remote login and other secure network services. It also provides stronger authentication than Telnet and supports transporting session data using encryption. Network professionals should always use SSH in place of Telnet, whenever possible.

- **Email and Messaging**—Each mail server receives and stores mail for users who have mailboxes configured on the mail server. Each user with a mailbox must then use an email client to access the mail server and read the messages in their

mailbox. Many Internet messaging systems use a web-based client to access email, including Microsoft 365, Yahoo!, and Gmail. Application protocols used in processing email include SMTP, POP3, and IMAP4.

SMTP is used by an email client to send messages to its local email server. The local server then determines whether the message is destined for a local mailbox or is addressed to a mailbox on another server. If the server must send the message to a different server, SMTP is used between those two servers. SMTP requests are sent to port 25.

A server that supports POP clients receives and stores messages addressed to its users. When the client connects to the email server, the messages are downloaded to the client. By default, messages are not kept on the server after they have been accessed by the client. Clients contact POP3 servers on port 110.

A server that supports IMAP clients also receives and stores messages addressed to its users. However, unlike POP, IMAP keeps the messages in the mailboxes on the server, unless they are deleted by the user. The most current version of IMAP is IMAP4, which listens for client requests on port 143.

Text messages may be called instant messages, direct messages, private messages, and chat messages. Text messaging enables users to chat over the Internet in real time. Text messaging services on a computer are usually accessed through a web-based client that is integrated into a social media or information sharing site. These clients usually connect only to other users of the same site.

An Internet telephony client uses peer-to-peer technology similar to that used by instant messaging. IP telephony uses VoIP, which converts analog voice signals into digital data. The voice data is encapsulated into IP packets that carry the phone call through the network.

Reflection Questions (16.8.2)

As you now know, when you want to access a file or a website that is not located on your computer, your computer becomes the "client" sending a request to a "server." Maybe you are only looking at the file. What if you need to download a copy of it to your computer? Perhaps you are just visiting a website. All of this occurs at the application layer of the network. What else can you do online because of the protocols and services located in the application layer?

Practice

The following Packet Tracer activities provide practice with the topics introduced in this chapter.

Packet Tracer Activity

Packet Tracer Activities

Packet Tracer—The Client Interaction (16.1.5)

Packet Tracer—Observe Web Requests (16.4.3)

Packet Tracer—Use FTP Services (16.5.3)

Packet Tracer—Use Telnet and SSH (16.6.4)

Check Your Understanding Questions

Complete all the review questions listed here to test your understanding of the topics and concepts in this chapter. Appendix A, "Answers to 'Check Your Understanding' Questions," lists the answers.

1. What two characteristics describe an FTP connection? (Choose two.)
   a. Only a large file over 1 GB requires more than two connections between the client and the server to successfully download it.
   b. The server establishes the first connection with the client to control traffic that consists of server commands and client replies.
   c. Files can be downloaded from or uploaded to the server.
   d. The client needs to run a daemon program to establish an FTP connection with a server.
   e. The first connection established is for traffic control and the second connection is created to transfer a file.

2. Which statement is correct about network protocols?
   a. They define the type of hardware that is used and how it is mounted in racks.
   b. They define how messages are exchanged between the source and the destination.
   c. They all function in the network access layer of TCP/IP.
   d. They are required only for exchange of messages between devices on remote networks.

3. Which protocol is used by web servers to serve up a web page?
   a. FTP
   b. HTTP
   c. IMAP
   d. POP

4. Match the protocol with the function. (Not all options are used.)
   - Provides remote access to servers
   - Retrieves email messages by clients
   - Automatically configures hosts with IP addresses
   - Resolves Internet names to IP addresses

   a. DHCP
   b. SSH
   c. DNS

5. Which two protocols are used in the process of sending and receiving emails? (Choose two.)
   a. HTTP
   b. IMAP
   c. SSH
   d. SMTP
   e. FTP

6. Which two applications provide virtual terminal access to remote servers? (Choose two.)
   a. SSH
   b. DNS
   c. DHCP
   d. SMTP
   e. Telnet

7. What is the advantage of using SSH over Telnet?
   a. SSH is easier to use.
   b. SSH operates faster than Telnet.
   c. SSH provides secure communications to access hosts.
   d. SSH supports authentication for a connection request.

8. Which protocol allows a user to type www.cisco.com into a web browser instead of an IP address to access the web server?

   a. DNS
   b. FTP
   c. HTML
   d. HTTP
   e. SNMP

9. Which protocol is used to transfer web pages from a server to a client device?

   a. HTML
   b. SMTP
   c. HTTP
   d. SSH
   e. POP

10. Which two application layer protocols manage the exchange of messages between a client with a web browser and a remote web server? (Choose two.)

    a. DNS
    b. HTTP
    c. HTML
    d. DHCP
    e. HTTPS

11. Match the port number to the email protocol.

    - IMAP4
    - POP3
    - SMTP

    a. Port number 110
    b. Port number 25
    c. Port number 143

CHAPTER 17

Network Testing Utilities

Objectives

Upon completion of this chapter, you will be able to answer the following question:

- What network utilities can you use to troubleshoot networks?

Key Terms

There are no key terms for this chapter.

Introduction (17.0)

Kishori tries to reach a website using her desktop computer at her nursing station. She gets an error message when trying to reach the site. She checks the wired connection, and it is fine. She uses her laptop to try to reach that same website, with no success. On the desktop, she goes to the command prompt and pings a different website on the Internet. Now she realizes she has no connection. She calls the IT department. Madhav comes to the station to further investigate the issue. Madhav pings a website. Kishori explains that she tried that already. Then he pings the default gateway and receives a reply. The router is working. It is the ISP that is down. Madhav is impressed that Kishori has learned so much over the past few months. He tells her that she should apply for that promotion and that she can use him as a reference!

Are you ready to learn some troubleshooting commands? Keep reading!

Troubleshooting Commands (17.1)

Several software utility programs are available that can help you to identify network problems.

Overview of Troubleshooting Commands (17.1.1)

Most of the software utility programs are provided by the operating system as command-line interface (CLI) commands. The syntax for the commands may vary between operating systems.

Some of the available utilities include

- **ipconfig**—Displays IP configuration information
- **ping**—Tests connections to other IP hosts
- **netstat**—Displays network connections
- **tracert**—Displays the route taken to the destination
- **nslookup**—Directly queries the name server for information on a destination domain

The ipconfig Command (17.1.2)

When a device does not get an IP address, or has an incorrect IP configuration, it cannot communicate on the network or access the Internet. On Windows devices, you can view the IP configuration information with the **ipconfig** command at the

command prompt. The **ipconfig** command has several options that are helpful including **/all**, **/release**, and **/renew**.

The **ipconfig** command is used to display the current IP configuration information for a host. Issuing **ipconfig** from the command prompt displays basic configuration information including IP address, subnet mask, and default gateway, as shown in Example 17-1.

Example 17-1 The **ipconfig** Command

```
C:\> ipconfig

Windows IP Configuration


Ethernet adapter Ethernet:

   Media State . . . . . . . . . . . : Media disconnected
   Connection-specific DNS Suffix  . :

Wireless LAN adapter Wi-Fi:

   Connection-specific DNS Suffix  . : lan
   Link-local IPv6 Address . . . . . : fe80::a1cc:4239:d3ab:2675%6
   IPv4 Address. . . . . . . . . . . : 10.10.10.130
   Subnet Mask . . . . . . . . . . . : 255.255.255.0
   Default Gateway . . . . . . . . . : 10.10.10.1

C:\>
```

The command **ipconfig /all** displays additional information including the MAC address, IP addresses of the default gateway, and the DNS servers, as shown in Example 17-2. It also indicates if DHCP is enabled, the DHCP server address, and lease information.

How can this utility assist in the troubleshooting process? Without an appropriate IP configuration, a host cannot participate in communications on a network. If the host does not know the location of the DNS servers, it cannot translate names into IP addresses.

Example 17-2 The **ipconfig /all** Command

```
C:\> ipconfig /all

Windows IP Configuration
```

```
   Host Name . . . . . . . . . . . . : your-a9270112e3
   Primary Dns Suffix  . . . . . . . :
   Node Type . . . . . . . . . . . . : Hybrid
   IP Routing Enabled. . . . . . . . : No
   WINS Proxy Enabled. . . . . . . . : No
   DNS Suffix Search List. . . . . . : lan

Ethernet adapter Ethernet:

   Media State . . . . . . . . . . . : Media disconnected
   Connection-specific DNS Suffix  . :
   Description . . . . . . . . . . . : Realtek PCIe GBE Family Controller
   Physical Address. . . . . . . . . : 00-16-D4-02-5A-EC
   DHCP Enabled. . . . . . . . . . . : Yes
   Autoconfiguration Enabled . . . . : Yes

Wireless LAN adapter Wi-Fi:

   Connection-specific DNS Suffix  . : lan
   Description . . . . . . . . . . . : Intel(R) Dual Band Wireless-AC 3165
   Physical Address. . . . . . . . . : 00-13-02-47-8C-6A
   DHCP Enabled. . . . . . . . . . . : Yes
   Autoconfiguration Enabled . . . . : Yes
   Link-local IPv6 Address . . . . . : fe80::a1cc:4239:d3ab:2675%6(Preferred)
   IPv4 Address. . . . . . . . . . . : 10.10.10.130(Preferred)
   Subnet Mask . . . . . . . . . . . : 255.255.255.0
   Lease Obtained. . . . . . . . . . : Wednesday, September 2, 2020 10:03:43 PM
   Lease Expires . . . . . . . . . . : Friday, September 11, 2020 10:23:36 AM
   Default Gateway . . . . . . . . . : 10.10.10.1
   DHCP Server . . . . . . . . . . . : 10.10.10.1
   DHCPv6 IAID . . . . . . . . . . . : 98604135
   DHCPv6 Client DUID. . . . . . . . : 00-01-00-01-1E-21-A5-84-44-A8-42-FC-0D-6F
   DNS Servers . . . . . . . . . . . : 10.10.10.1
   NetBIOS over Tcpip. . . . . . . . : Enabled

C:\>
```

If IP addressing information is assigned dynamically, the command **ipconfig /release** releases the current DHCP bindings. The command **ipconfig /renew** requests fresh configuration information from the DHCP server. Both commands are demonstrated in Example 17-3. A host may contain faulty or outdated IP configuration information, and a simple renewal of this information is all that is required to regain connectivity.

If, after releasing the IP configuration, the host is unable to obtain fresh information from the DHCP server, the problem could be that there is no network connectivity. Verify that the NIC has an illuminated link light, indicating that it has a physical connection to the network. If this does not solve the problem, the issue may be with the DHCP server or network connections to the DHCP server.

Example 17-3 The **ipconfig /release** and **ipconfig /renew** Commands

```
C:\> ipconfig /release

Windows IP Configuration

No operation can be performed on Ethernet while it has its media disconnected.

Ethernet adapter Ethernet:

   Media State . . . . . . . . . . . : Media disconnected
   Connection-specific DNS Suffix  . :

Wireless LAN adapter Wi-Fi:

   Connection-specific DNS Suffix  . :
   Link-local IPv6 Address . . . . . : fe80::a1cc:4239:d3ab:2675%6
   Default Gateway . . . . . . . . . :

C:\> ipconfig /renew

Windows IP Configuration

No operation can be performed on Ethernet while it has its media disconnected.

Ethernet adapter Ethernet:

   Media State . . . . . . . . . . . : Media disconnected
   Connection-specific DNS Suffix  . :

Wireless LAN adapter Wi-Fi:

   Connection-specific DNS Suffix  . : lan
   Link-local IPv6 Address . . . . . : fe80::a1cc:4239:d3ab:2675%6
   IPv4 Address. . . . . . . . . . . : 10.10.10.130
   Subnet Mask . . . . . . . . . . . : 255.255.255.0
   Default Gateway . . . . . . . . . : 10.10.10.1

C:\>
```

Packet Tracer
Activity

Packet Tracer—Use the ipconfig Command (17.1.3)

In this activity, you will use the **ipconfig** command to identify incorrect configuration on a PC.

Refer to the online course to complete this Packet Tracer.

The ping Command (17.1.4)

Probably the most commonly used network utility is **ping**. Most IP-enabled devices support some form of the **ping** command to test whether network devices can be reached through the IP network.

If the IP configuration appears to be correctly configured on the local host, the next step is to test network connectivity by using **ping**. The **ping** command can be followed by either an IP address or the name of a destination host. In Example 17-4, the user pings the default gateway at 10.10.10.1 and then pings www.cisco.com.

Example 17-4 The **ping** Command

```
C:\> ping 10.10.10.1

Pinging 10.10.10.1 with 32 bytes of data:
Reply from 10.10.10.1: bytes=32 time=1ms TTL=64
Reply from 10.10.10.1: bytes=32 time=1ms TTL=64
Reply from 10.10.10.1: bytes=32 time=1ms TTL=64
Reply from 10.10.10.1: bytes=32 time=1ms TTL=64

Ping statistics for 10.10.10.1:
    Packets: Sent = 4, Received = 4, Lost = 0 (0% loss),
Approximate round trip times in milli-seconds:
    Minimum = 1ms, Maximum = 1ms, Average = 1ms

C:\> ping www.cisco.com

Pinging e2867.dsca.akamaiedge.net [104.112.72.241] with 32 bytes of data:
Reply from 104.112.72.241: bytes=32 time=25ms TTL=53
Reply from 104.112.72.241: bytes=32 time=25ms TTL=53
Reply from 104.112.72.241: bytes=32 time=27ms TTL=53
Reply from 104.112.72.241: bytes=32 time=24ms TTL=53

Ping statistics for 104.112.72.241:
    Packets: Sent = 4, Received = 4, Lost = 0 (0% loss),
Approximate round trip times in milli-seconds:
    Minimum = 24ms, Maximum = 27ms, Average = 25ms

C:\>
```

When a ping is sent to an IP address, a packet known as an echo request is sent across the network to the IP address specified. If the destination host receives the echo request, it responds with a packet known as an echo reply. If the source receives the echo reply, connectivity is verified by the reply from the specific IP address. The ping is not successful if a message such as request timed out or general failure appears.

If a **ping** command is sent to a name, such as www.cisco.com, a packet is first sent to a DNS server to resolve the name to an IP address. After the IP address is obtained, the echo request is forwarded to the IP address and the process proceeds. If a ping to the IP address succeeds but a ping to the name does not, there is most likely a problem with DNS.

Ping Results (17.1.5)

If **ping** commands to both the name and IP address are successful but the user is still unable to access the application, then the problem most likely resides in the application on the destination host. For example, the requested service might not be running.

If neither ping is successful, then network connectivity along the path to the destination is most likely the problem. If this occurs, it is common practice to ping the default gateway. If the ping to the default gateway is successful, the problem is not local. If the ping to the default gateway fails, the problem resides on the local network.

In some cases, the ping fails but network connectivity is not the problem. A ping may fail due to the firewall on the sending or receiving device, or a router along the path that is blocking the pings.

The basic **ping** command usually issues four echoes and waits for the replies to each one. It can, however, be modified to increase its usefulness. The options listed in Example 17-5 display additional features available.

Example 17-5 Options for the **ping** Command

```
C:\> ping

Usage: ping [-t] [-a] [-n count] [-l size] [-f] [-i TTL] [-v TOS]
            [-r count] [-s count] [[-j host-list] | [-k host-list]]
            [-w timeout] [-R] [-S srcaddr] [-c compartment] [-p]
            [-4] [-6] target_name

Options:
    -t             Ping the specified host until stopped.
                   To see statistics and continue - type Control-Break;
```

```
                        To stop - type Control-C.
    -a                  Resolve addresses to hostnames.
    -n count            Number of echo requests to send.
    -l size             Send buffer size.
    -f                  Set Don't Fragment flag in packet (IPv4-only).
    -i TTL              Time To Live.
    -v TOS              Type Of Service (IPv4-only. This setting has been deprecated
                        and has no effect on the type of service field in the IP
                        Header).
    -r count            Record route for count hops (IPv4-only).
    -s count            Timestamp for count hops (IPv4-only).
    -j host-list        Loose source route along host-list (IPv4-only).
    -k host-list        Strict source route along host-list (IPv4-only).
    -w timeout          Timeout in milliseconds to wait for each reply.
    -R                  Use routing header to test reverse route also (IPv6-only).
                        Per RFC 5095 the use of this routing header has been
                        deprecated. Some systems may drop echo requests if
                        deprecated.
    -S srcaddr          Source address to use.
    -c compartment Routing compartment identifier.
    -p                  Ping a Hyper-V Network Virtualization provider address.
    -4                  Force using IPv4.
    -6                  Force using IPv6.


C:\>
```

Packet Tracer Activity

Packet Tracer—Use the ping Command (17.1.6)

In this activity, you will use the **ping** command to identify an incorrect configuration on a PC.

Refer to the online course to complete this Packet Tracer.

Network Testing Utilities Summary (17.2)

The following is a summary of each topic in the chapter and some questions for your reflection.

What Did I Learn in This Chapter? (17.2.1)

Several software utility programs are available that can help you to identify network problems. Most of these utilities are provided by the operating system as CLI commands.

Some of the available utilities include

- **ipconfig**—Displays IP configuration information
- **ping**—Tests connections to other IP hosts
- **netstat**—Displays network connections
- **tracert**—Displays the route taken to the destination
- **nslookup**—Directly queries the name server for information on a destination domain

The **ipconfig** command is used to display the current IP configuration information for a host. Issuing **ipconfig** from the command prompt displays basic configuration information including IP address, subnet mask, and default gateway.

The command **ipconfig /all** displays additional information including the MAC address, IP addresses of the default gateway, and the DNS servers. It also indicates if DHCP is enabled, the DHCP server address, and lease information.

If IP addressing information is assigned dynamically, the command **ipconfig /release** releases the current DHCP bindings. The command **ipconfig /renew** requests fresh configuration information from the DHCP server. A host may contain faulty or outdated IP configuration information, and a simple renewal of this information is all that is required to regain connectivity.

Probably the most commonly used network utility is **ping**. Most IP-enabled devices support some form of the **ping** command to test whether network devices can be reached through the IP network. When a ping is sent to an IP address, a packet known as an echo request is sent across the network to the IP address specified. If the destination host receives the echo request, it responds with an echo reply. If the source receives the echo reply, connectivity is verified by the reply from the specific IP address.

Reflection Questions (17.2.2)

Congratulations! You've made it all the way through the first part of this course! Way back in the first chapter of this course, I mentioned that I can troubleshoot and fix my web. In fact, I can even make it stronger and more secure. Being able to do that is very satisfying. You have learned about the many commands that you can use to troubleshoot and fix your own network. You can use these commands to investigate your network, even if it is performing as it should. Which command(s) would you start with?

Practice

The following Packet Tracer activities provide practice with the topics introduced in this chapter.

Packet Tracer
Activity

Packet Tracer Activities

Packet Tracer—Use the ipconfig Command (17.1.3)

Packet Tracer—Use the ping Command (17.1.6)

Check Your Understanding Questions

Complete all the review questions listed here to test your understanding of the topics and concepts in this chapter. Appendix A, "Answers to 'Check Your Understanding' Questions," lists the answers.

1. What is a user trying to determine by issuing a **ping 10.1.1.1** command on a PC?
   a. If the TCP/IP stack is functioning on the PC, without putting traffic on the wire
   b. If there is connectivity with the destination device
   c. The path that traffic will take to reach the destination
   d. What type of device is at the destination
2. A user who is unable to connect to the file server contacts the help desk. The help desk technician asks the user to ping the IP address of the default gateway that is configured on the workstation. What is the purpose of running this **ping** command?
   a. To obtain a dynamic IP address from the server
   b. To request that the gateway forward the connection request to the file server
   c. To test that the host has the capability to reach hosts on other networks
   d. To resolve the domain name of the file server to its IP address
3. Which three pieces of information are revealed by the **ipconfig** command (without the **/all** switch)? (Choose three.)
   a. IP address
   b. DHCP server

c. Subnet mask
d. Default gateway
e. DNS server
f. MAC address

4. Which command is used to test network connectivity and provide a response to each packet received by the remote host?

a. **connect**
b. **ping**
c. **text**
d. **tracert**

5. Which command-line utility is used to display active network connections on a PC?

a. **nslookup**
b. **netstat**
c. **ipconfig**
d. **ipconfig /all**

6. A user needs to find the MAC address on the host PC. Which command-line utility can be used to display this information?

a. **nslookup**
b. **ipconfig /all**
c. **ping**
d. **tracert**

7. A user is able to ping www.cisco.com by its IP address but cannot browse to www.cisco.com in a browser. What is the possible cause?

a. The IP address of the source PC is wrong.
b. The IP address of the gateway is wrong.
c. The DHCP server is not configured correctly.
d. The DNS server is not working.

8. A technician troubleshooting a network problem has used CLI commands to determine that a PC has not been allocated correct IP addressing information from the DHCP server. After resolving the problem, which command can the technician use for the device to receive new IP addressing information from the DHCP server?

   a. **ping**
   b. **ipconfig /release**
   c. **tracert**
   d. **ipconfig /renew**

9. Which command-line utility is used to test connectivity to other IP hosts?

   a. **ping**
   b. **tracert**
   c. **ipconfig**
   d. **nslookup**

10. Match the command-line utility with its function.

   - **tracert**
   - **netstat**
   - **ipconfig**
   - **nslookup**
   - **ping**

   a. Displays IP configuration information.
   b. Tests connections to other IP hosts.
   c. Displays network connections.
   d. Displays the route taken to the destination.
   e. Directly queries the name server for information on a destination domain.

CHAPTER 18

Network Design

Objectives

Upon completion of this chapter, you will be able to answer the following questions:

- What are the four basic requirements of a reliable network?
- What is the function at each layer of the three-layer network design model?

Key Terms

This chapter uses the following key terms. You can find the definitions in the Glossary.

availability *Page 270*

confidentiality *Page 270*

fault-tolerant network *Page 267*

integrity *Page 270*

quality of service (QoS) *Page 269*

scalable network *Page 267*

Introduction (18.0)

Let me introduce you to my friend, Bob! Bob works in the IT field in Vancouver, Canada, and has some networking experience. He is consulting for his friends, Marcy and Vincent, who have purchased a furniture store. They want to expand their brick-and-mortar operations and establish an online store as well. Currently the store's internal network handles in-store transactions and inventory. Marcy and Vincent want to add security cameras and VoIP phones, and also expand it to include ecommerce and shipping. Bob explains that this will be more expensive than his friends had anticipated. He is thinking about designing the future network for the furniture store. He explains that he must consider fault tolerance, scalability, QoS, and security. Also, their network is currently flat, not hierarchical. Hierarchical networks scale well and will better accommodate this growing business.

Wow! That is a lot for Marcy and Vincent to understand. They are not familiar with these networking issues. Are you? Read this chapter to learn more about reliable networks and hierarchical network design!

Reliable Networks (18.1)

A network is a platform for distributing a wide range of services to end users in a reliable, efficient, and secure manner.

Network Architecture (18.1.1)

Have you ever been busy working online only to have "the Internet go down"? As you know by now, the Internet did not go down, you just lost your connection to it. It is very frustrating. With so many people in the world relying on network access to work and learn, network reliability is imperative. In this context, *reliability* means more than your connection to the Internet. This section focuses on the four aspects of network reliability.

The role of the network has changed from a data-only network to a system that enables connections between people, devices, and information in a media-rich, converged network environment. For a network to function efficiently and grow in this type of environment, the network must be built upon a standard network architecture.

Networks also support a wide range of applications and services. They must operate over the many different types of cables and devices that make up the physical infrastructure. The term *network architecture*, in this context, refers to the technologies that support the infrastructure and the programmed services and rules, or protocols, that move data across the network.

As networks evolve, we have learned that there are four basic characteristics that network architects must address to meet user expectations:

- Fault tolerance
- Scalability
- Quality of service (QoS)
- Security

Video

Video—Fault Tolerance (18.1.2)

Refer to the online course to view this video.

Fault Tolerance (18.1.3)

A *fault-tolerant network* is a network that limits the number of devices that are affected by a failure. It is built to allow quick recovery when such a failure occurs. Fault-tolerant networks depend on multiple paths between the source and destination of a message. If one path fails, the message is instantly sent over a different link. Having multiple paths to a destination is known as *redundancy*.

Implementing a packet-switched network is one way to provide redundancy. Packet switching splits traffic into packets that are routed over a shared network. A single message, such as an email or a video stream, is broken into multiple message blocks, called *packets*. Each packet has the necessary addressing information of the source and destination of the message. The routers within the network switch the packets based on the condition of the network at that moment. This means that all the packets in a single message could take very different paths to the same destination. In Figure 18-1, the user is unaware and unaffected by the router that is dynamically changing the route when a link fails.

Scalability (18.1.4)

A *scalable network* expands quickly to support new users and applications. It does this without degrading the performance of services that are being accessed by existing users. Figure 18-2 shows how a new network is easily added to an existing network. These networks are scalable because the designers have followed accepted standards and protocols. These standards and protocols enable software and hardware vendors to focus on improving products and services without having to design a new set of rules for operating within the network.

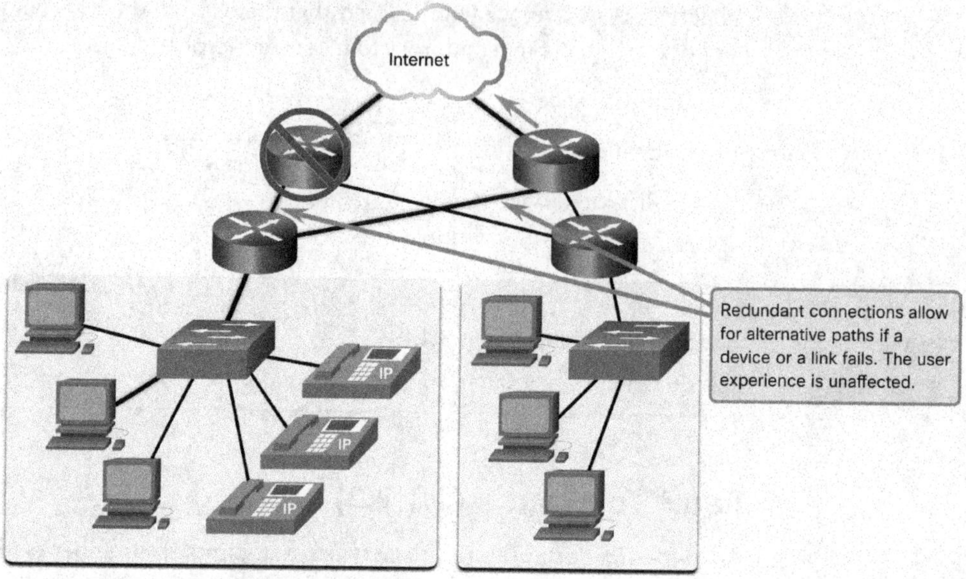

Figure 18-1 Fault-Tolerant Design

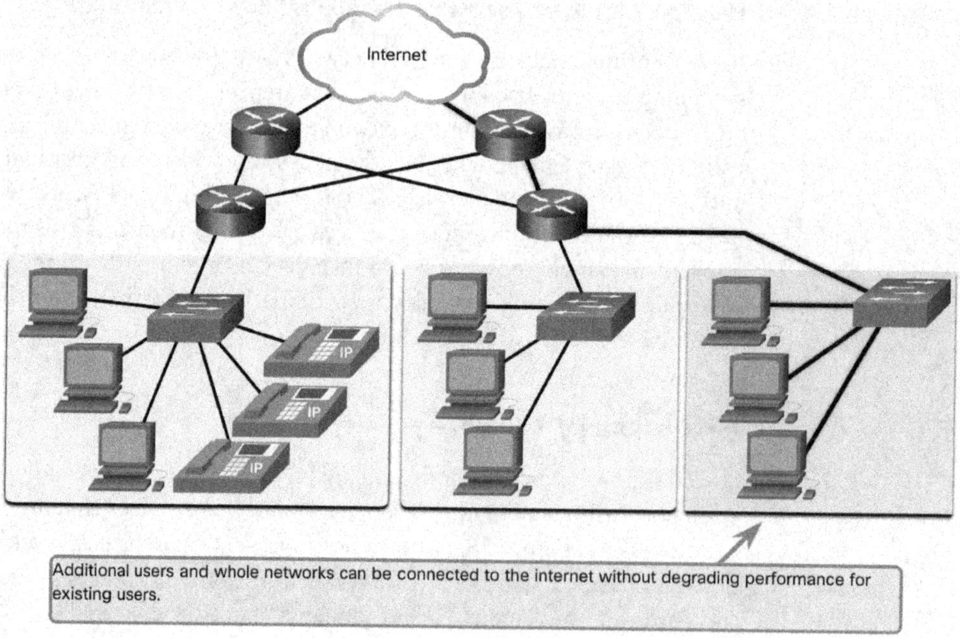

Figure 18-2 Scalable Design

Quality of Service (18.1.5)

Quality of service (QoS) is an increasing requirement in networks today. New applications available to users over networks, such as voice and live video transmissions, create higher expectations for the quality of the delivered services. Have you ever tried to watch a video online only to encounter constant breaks and pauses? As data, voice, and video content continue to converge onto the same network, QoS becomes a primary mechanism for managing congestion and ensuring reliable delivery of content to all users.

Congestion occurs when the demand for bandwidth exceeds the amount available. Network bandwidth is measured in the number of bits that can be transmitted in a single second, or *bits per second (bps)*. When simultaneous communications are attempted across the network, the demand for network bandwidth can exceed its availability, creating network congestion.

When the volume of traffic is greater than what can be transported across the network, devices hold the packets in memory until resources become available to transmit them. In Figure 18-3, one user is requesting a web page, and another user is on a phone call. With a QoS policy in place, the router can manage the flow of data and voice traffic, giving priority to voice communications if the network experiences congestion. The focus of QoS is to prioritize time-sensitive traffic. The type of traffic, not the content of the traffic, is what is important.

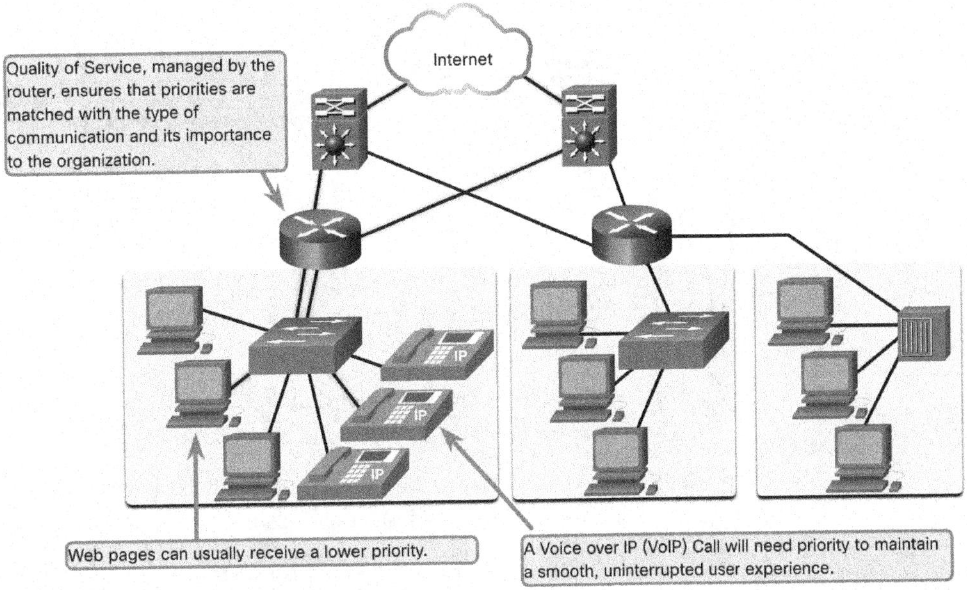

Figure 18-3 QoS Design

Network Security (18.1.6)

The network infrastructure, services, and the data contained on network-attached devices are crucial personal and business assets. Network administrators must address two types of network security concerns: network infrastructure security and information security.

Securing the network infrastructure includes physically securing devices that provide network connectivity and preventing unauthorized access to the management software that resides on them, as shown in Figure 18-4.

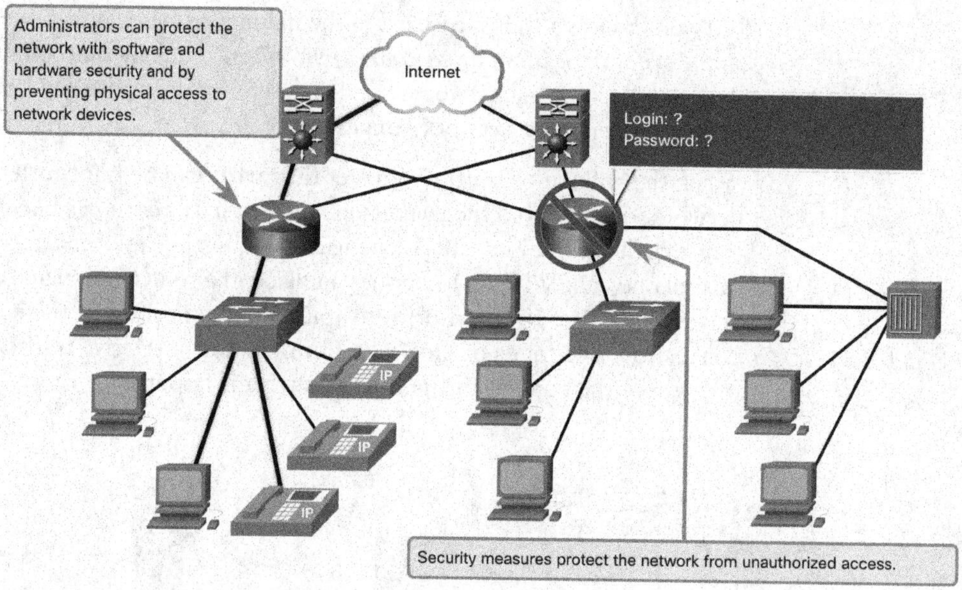

Figure 18-4 Security Design

Network administrators must also protect the information contained within the packets being transmitted over the network and the information stored on network-attached devices. To achieve the goals of network security, there are three primary requirements:

- *Confidentiality*—Data confidentiality means that only the intended and authorized recipients can access and read data.
- *Integrity*—Data integrity assures users that the information has not been altered in transmission, from origin to destination.
- *Availability*—Data availability assures users of timely and reliable access to data services for authorized users.

Interactive Graphic

Check Your Understanding—Reliable Networks (18.1.7)

Refer to the online course to complete this activity.

Hierarchical Network Design (18.2)

This section explores the two different types of addresses: logical addresses and physical addresses. Both types have a specific function in ensuring a message can be sent between two devices on the same network or between two devices on different networks.

Physical and Logical Addresses (18.2.1)

A person's name usually does not change. A person's address, on the other hand, relates to where the person lives and can change. On a host, the MAC address does not change; it is physically assigned to the host NIC and is known as the *physical address*. Like a person's name, the physical address remains the same regardless of where the host is placed on the network.

The IP address is similar to the address of a person. It is known as a *logical address* because it is assigned logically based on where the host is located. The IP address, or network address, is assigned to each host by a network administrator based on the local network.

IP addresses contain two parts. The first part identifies the network portion and is the same for all hosts connected to the same local network. The second part of the IP address identifies the individual host on that network. Within the same local network, the host portion of the IP address is unique to each host, as shown in Figure 18-5.

Both the physical MAC and logical IP addresses are required for a computer to communicate on a hierarchical network, just like both the name and address of a person are required to send a letter.

Video

Video—View Network Information on My Device (18.2.2)

Refer to the online course to view this video.

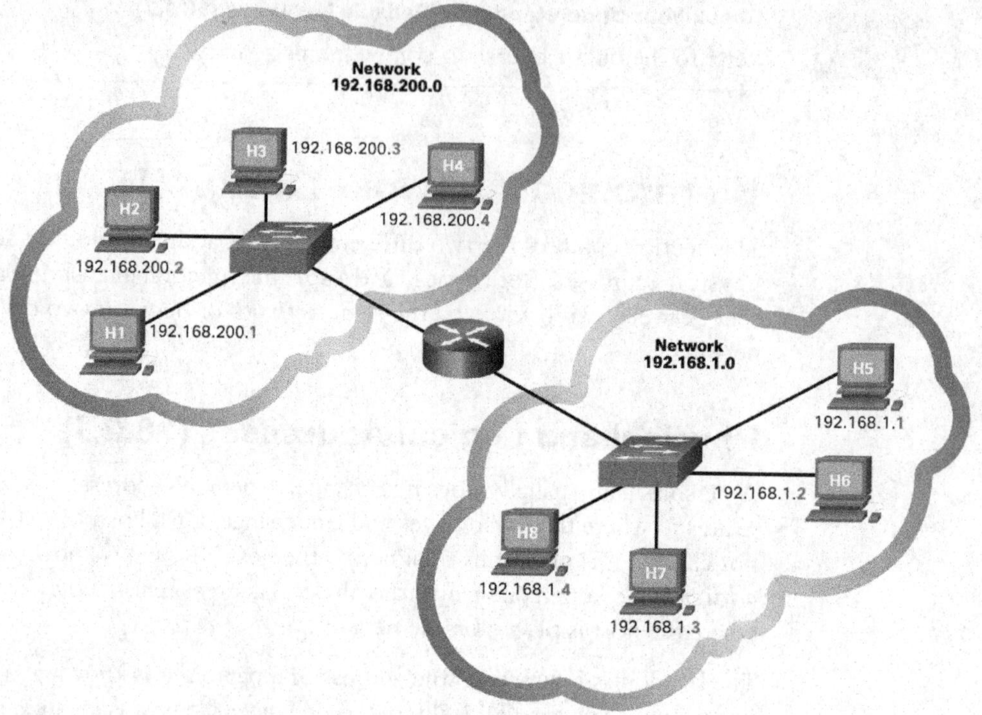

Figure 18-5 Network and Host Portion of the IPv4 Address

Lab—View Wireless and Wired NIC Information (18.2.3)

In this lab, you will complete the following objectives:

- Identify and work with PC NICs.
- Identify and use the System Tray network icons.

Refer to the online course to complete this lab.

Hierarchical Analogy (18.2.4)

Imagine how difficult communication would be if the only way to send a message to someone was to use the person's name. If there were no street addresses, cities, towns, or country boundaries, delivering a message to a specific person across the world would be nearly impossible.

On an Ethernet network, the host MAC address is similar to a person's name. A MAC address indicates the individual identity of a specific host, but it does not indicate where on the network the host is located. If all hosts on the Internet (millions and millions of them) were each identified by their unique MAC address only, imagine how difficult it would be to locate a single one.

Additionally, Ethernet technology generates a large amount of broadcast traffic for hosts to communicate. Broadcasts are sent to all hosts within a single network. Broadcasts consume bandwidth and slow network performance. What would happen if the millions of hosts attached to the Internet were all in one Ethernet network and were using broadcasts?

For these two reasons, large Ethernet networks consisting of many hosts are not efficient. It is better to divide larger networks into smaller, more manageable pieces. One way to divide larger networks is to use a hierarchical design model.

Video

Video—Benefits of a Hierarchical Network Design (18.2.5)

Refer to the online course to view this video.

Access, Distribution, and Core (18.2.6)

IP traffic is managed based on the characteristics and devices associated with each of the three layers of the hierarchical network design model: access, distribution, and core.

Access Layer

The access layer provides a connection point for end-user devices to the network and allows multiple hosts to connect to other hosts through a network device, usually a switch, such as the Cisco Catalyst 2960-XR series switch shown in Figure 18-6, or a wireless access point. Typically, all devices within a single access layer have the same network portion of the IP address.

Figure 18-6 Cisco 2960-XR

If a message is destined for a local host, based on the network portion of the IP address, the message remains local. If it is destined for a different network, it is passed up to the distribution layer. Switches provide the connection to the distribution layer devices, usually a Layer 3 device such as a router or Layer 3 switch.

Distribution Layer

The distribution layer provides a connection point for separate networks and controls the flow of information between the networks. It typically contains more powerful switches, such as the Cisco Catalyst 9300 series switch shown in Figure 18-7, than the access layer, as well as routers for routing between networks. Distribution layer devices control the type and amount of traffic that flows from the access layer to the core layer.

Figure 18-7 Cisco C9300 Series

Core Layer

The core layer is a high-speed backbone layer with redundant (backup) connections. It is responsible for transporting large amounts of data between multiple end networks. Core layer devices typically include very powerful, high-speed switches and routers, such as the Cisco Catalyst 9600 series switch shown in Figure 18-8. The main goal of the core layer is to transport data quickly.

Figure 18-8 Cisco Catalyst 9600

Network Design Summary (18.3)

The following is a summary of each topic in the chapter and some questions for your reflection.

What Did I Learn in This Chapter? (18.3.1)

- **Reliable Networks**—As networks evolve, we have learned that there are four basic characteristics that network architects must address to meet user expectations: fault tolerance, scalability, QoS, and security.

  A fault-tolerant network limits the number of devices that are affected by a failure. It allows quick recovery when such a failure occurs. These networks depend on multiple, redundant paths between the source and destination of a message. If one path fails, the message is instantly sent over a different link.

  A scalable network expands quickly to support new users and applications. It does this without degrading the performance of services that are being accessed by existing users. Networks are scalable if the designers have followed accepted standards and protocols.

  QoS is an increasing requirement in networks today. As data, voice, and video content continue to converge onto the same network, QoS becomes a primary mechanism for managing congestion and ensuring reliable delivery of content to all users. When simultaneous communications are attempted across the network, the demand for network bandwidth (measured in bps) can exceed its availability, creating network congestion. The focus of QoS is to prioritize time-sensitive traffic. The type of traffic, not the content of the traffic, is what is important.

  Network administrators must address two types of network security concerns: network infrastructure security and information security. Network administrators must also protect the information contained within the packets being transmitted over the network and the information stored on network-attached devices. The three primary requirements to achieve the goals of network security are confidentiality, integrity, and availability.

- **Hierarchical Network Design**—IP addresses contain two parts. The first part identifies the network portion and is the same for all hosts connected to the same local network. The second part of the IP address identifies the individual host on that network. Both the physical MAC and logical IP addresses are required for a computer to communicate on a hierarchical network.

  The Network and Sharing Center on a PC shows your basic network information and setup connections, including your active networks and whether you are connected wired or wirelessly to the Internet and within your LAN. You can view the properties of your connections here.

On an Ethernet network, the host MAC address is similar to a person's name. A MAC address indicates the individual identity of a specific host, but it does not indicate where on the network the host is located. If all hosts on the Internet (many millions) were each identified by their unique MAC address only, imagine how difficult it would be to locate a single one. It is better to divide larger networks into smaller, more manageable pieces. One way to divide larger networks is to use a hierarchical design model.

Hierarchical networks scale well. The access layer provides a connection point for end-user devices to the network and allows multiple hosts to connect to other hosts through a network device, usually a switch or a wireless access point. Typically, all devices within a single access layer have the same network portion of the IP address. The distribution layer provides a connection point for separate networks and controls the flow of information between the networks. Distribution layer devices control the type and amount of traffic that flows from the access layer to the core layer. The core layer is a high-speed backbone layer with redundant connections. It is responsible for transporting large amounts of data between multiple end networks. The main goal of the core layer is to transport data quickly.

Reflection Questions (18.3.2)

Marcy and Vincent are lucky to have Bob consult with them about the network at their store. Many small businesses have networks that grow over time, but they are not designed to scale reliably or securely. Marcy and Vincent understand that if they take the time and spend some money now, they will save themselves a lot of trouble as their network continues to grow. Knowing what you know now about reliable and scalable networks, is there anything you would like to do to update your own network at home, school, or work?

Practice

The following lab activity provides practice with the topics introduced in this chapter.

Labs

Lab—View Wireless and Wired NIC Information (18.2.3)

Check Your Understanding Questions

Complete all the review questions listed here to test your understanding of the topics and concepts in this chapter. Appendix A, "Answers to 'Check Your Understanding' Questions," lists the answers.

1. Which two devices would commonly be found at the access layer of the hierarchical enterprise LAN design model? (Choose two.)

    a. Access point
    b. Firewall
    c. Layer 2 switch
    d. Layer 3 device
    e. Modular switch

2. What characteristic of a network enables it to quickly grow to support new users and applications without impacting the performance of the services being delivered to existing users?

    a. Reliability
    b. Scalability
    c. Quality of service
    d. Accessibility

3. Match the definition to the security goal.

    ○ Ensuring confidentiality

    ○ Maintaining integrity

    ○ Ensuring availability

    a. Only the intended recipients can access and read the data
    b. The assurance that the information has not been altered during transmission
    c. The assurance of timely and reliable access to data

4. A student is streaming a movie to his computer but the movie keeps stopping. What service would give streaming traffic higher priority and avoid the movie stopping?

   a. HTTPS
   b. Security
   c. Fault tolerance
   d. Quality of service (QoS)

5. The impact of the failure of an important network device can be limited by a feature called fault tolerance. True or false?

   a. True
   b. False

6. Which type of address never changes on a device and is similar to a person's name?

   a. MAC address
   b. IP address
   c. Network address
   d. Logical address

7. What are the three layers of the switch hierarchical design model? (Choose three.)

   a. Access
   b. Data link
   c. Core
   d. Network access
   e. Enterprise
   f. Distribution

8. Which network feature uses redundancy as a means to limit the number of users that are affected in the event of a failure?

   a. Fault tolerance
   b. Scalability
   c. Quality of service
   d. Security

9. What characteristic of a network allows video traffic to have priority over traffic from an email application?

   a. Quality of service
   b. Fault tolerance
   c. Scalability
   d. Reliability

10. What is the responsibility of the distribution layer in a hierarchical network design?

    a. It controls the traffic flows between the other layers.
    b. It provides access to the network for end users.
    c. It provides a high-speed backbone for traffic flows.
    d. It controls which devices are allowed to connect to the network.

11. Which network design model improves efficiency by dividing the network into smaller pieces?

    a. Hierarchical
    b. Redundant
    c. Fault-tolerant
    d. Reliable

12. Match the feature with the description.

    - Scalability
    - Quality of service
    - Fault tolerance

    a. Provides reliability
    b. Allows the network to grow
    c. Prioritizes traffic

CHAPTER 19

Cloud and Virtualization

Objectives

Upon completion of this chapter, you will be able to answer the following questions:

- What are the characteristics of clouds and cloud services?
- What are the purpose and characteristics of virtualization?

Key Terms

This chapter uses the following key terms. You can find the definitions in the Glossary.

cloud computing Page 282

community cloud Page 283

hybrid cloud Page 283

hypervisor Page 286

Infrastructure as a Service (IaaS) Page 283

Platform as a Service (PaaS) Page 283

private cloud Page 283

public cloud Page 282

Software as a Service (SaaS) Page 283

virtualization Page 284

Introduction (19.0)

In planning the future network of Marcy and Vincent's furniture business, Bob concludes they should take advantage of cloud services and virtualization. Bob explains to Marcy and Vincent that they can lease services from a cloud provider. Marcy and Vincent want to know why they should consider this. Bob explains that using cloud services uses less energy, requires less equipment, and takes up less space. He also points out that it can help with disaster recovery, comparing it to Marcy and Vincent having pictures on their mobile phones backed up to a cloud. Even if the mobile phone gets damaged, the photos can still be retrieved.

Can you think of how you use the cloud? How much do you know about the cloud and virtualization? Let me help you out with learning more. Read this chapter!

Cloud and Cloud Services (19.1)

Cloud computing is one of the ways that we access and store data. Cloud computing allows us to store personal files, or even back up an entire drive, on servers over the Internet. It also allows us to access applications, such as word processing and photo editing applications, as cloud services. Cloud computing is possible because of data centers, which house the servers, storage devices, and other network infrastructure equipment that deliver cloud services.

Video

Video—Cloud and Virtualization (19.1.1)

The video describes the following cloud services:

- SaaS—Software as a Service
- PaaS—Platform as a Service
- IaaS—Infrastructure as a Service

Refer to the online course to view this video.

Types of Clouds (19.1.2)

There are four primary cloud models:

- *Public cloud*—Cloud-based applications and services offered in a public cloud are made available to the general population. Services may be free or may be offered on a pay-per-use model, such as paying for online storage. The public cloud uses the Internet to provide services.

- *Private cloud*—Cloud-based applications and services offered in a private cloud are intended for a specific organization or entity, such as a government agency. A private cloud can be set up using the private network of an organization, though this can be expensive to build and maintain. A private cloud can also be managed by an outside organization with strict access security.
- *Hybrid cloud*—A hybrid cloud is made up of two or more cloud types (for example, part private, part public), where each part remains a separate object, but both are connected using a single architecture. Individual users of a hybrid cloud have degrees of access to various services based on user access rights.
- *Community cloud*—A community cloud is created for exclusive use by a specific community. The differences between public clouds and community clouds are the functional needs that have been customized for the community. For example, healthcare organizations must remain compliant with policies and laws (such as HIPAA in the United States) that require any networks storing or processing patient data to maintain specific levels of authentication and confidentiality.

Cloud Services (19.1.3)

Cloud services are available in a variety of options, tailored to meet customer requirements. The three main cloud computing services or service models defined by the National Institute of Standards and Technology (NIST) in their Special Publication 800-145 are as follows:

- *Software as a Service (SaaS)*—The cloud provider is responsible for access to applications and services, such as email, communication, and Office 365, that are delivered over the Internet. The user does not manage any aspect of the cloud services except for limited user-specific application settings. The user only needs to provide their data.
- *Platform as a Service (PaaS)*—The cloud provider is responsible for providing users access to the development tools and services used to deliver the applications. PaaS users are typically programmers and may be given control over the configuration settings of the application hosting environment of the cloud provider.
- *Infrastructure as a Service (IaaS)*—The cloud provider is responsible for giving IT managers access to the network equipment, virtualized network services, and supporting network infrastructure. Using IaaS allows IT managers to deploy and run software code, which can include operating systems and applications.

Cloud service providers have extended this model to also provide IT support (ITaaS) for each of the cloud computing services. For businesses, ITaaS can extend the capability of the network without requiring investment in new infrastructure, training new personnel, or licensing new software. These services are available on demand and

delivered economically to any device anywhere in the world without compromising security or function.

Cloud Computing and Virtualization (19.1.4)

The terms *cloud computing* and *virtualization* are often used interchangeably; however, they mean different things. Virtualization is the foundation of cloud computing. Without it, cloud computing, as it is most widely implemented, would not be possible.

Introduced in 1999, VMware developed a virtualization technology that enabled a host OS to support one or more client OSs. Most virtualization technologies are now based on this technology. The transformation of dedicated servers to virtualized servers has been embraced and is widely implemented in data center and enterprise networks.

Virtualization means creating a virtual rather than physical version of something, such as a computer. An example would be running a "Linux computer" on your Windows PC, which you will do later in the lab.

To fully appreciate virtualization, you first need to understand some of the history of server technology. Historically, enterprise servers consisted of a server OS, such as Windows Server or Linux Server, installed on specific hardware, as shown in Figure 19-1. All server RAM, processing power, and hard drive space were dedicated to the service provided (for example, web, email services, etc.).

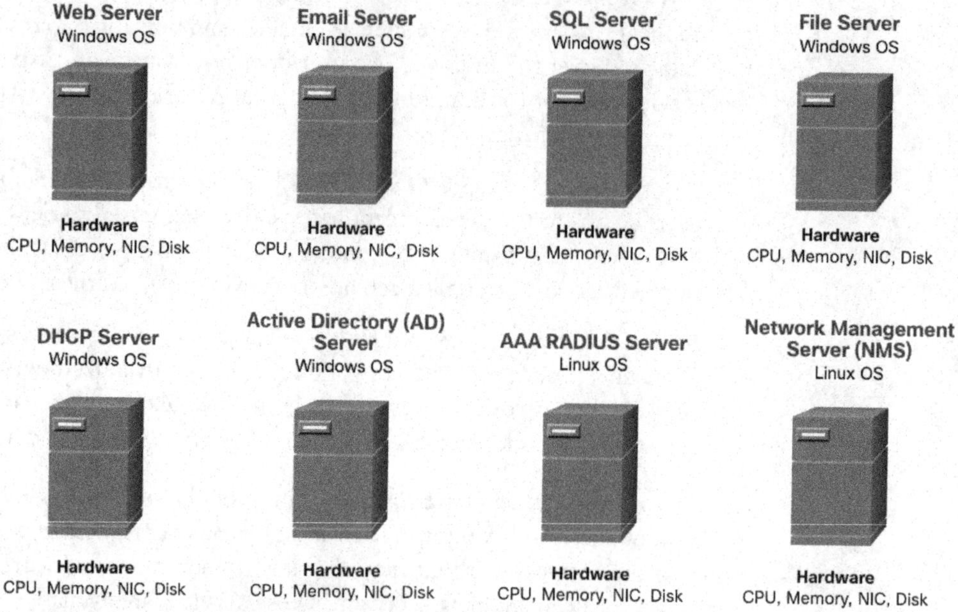

Figure 19-1 Examples of Dedicated Servers

The major problem with this configuration was that when a server failed, the service provided by this server became unavailable, known as a *single point of failure*. Another problem was that dedicated servers were underused. Dedicated servers often sat idle for long periods of time, waiting until there was a need to deliver the specific service they provided. These servers wasted energy and took up more space than was warranted by the amount of service provided, known as *server sprawl*.

Interactive Graphic

Check Your Understanding—Cloud and Cloud Services (19.1.4)

Refer to the online course to complete this activity.

Virtualization (19.2)

Network virtualization combines both hardware and software network resources. Network virtualization comes in many forms, and new types of virtualization are being developed.

Advantages of Virtualization (19.2.1)

One major advantage of virtualization is overall reduced cost:

- **Less equipment is required**—Virtualization enables server consolidation, which requires fewer physical devices and lowers maintenance costs.
- **Less energy is consumed**—Consolidating servers lowers the monthly power and cooling costs.
- **Less space is required**—Server consolidation reduces the amount of required floor space.

These are additional benefits of virtualization:

- **Easier prototyping**—Self-contained labs, operating on isolated networks, can be rapidly created for testing and prototyping network deployments.
- **Faster server provisioning**—Creating a virtual server is far faster than provisioning a physical server.
- **Increased server uptime**—Most server virtualization platforms now offer advanced redundant fault-tolerance features.
- **Improved disaster recovery**—Most enterprise server virtualization platforms have software that can help test and automate failover before a disaster happens.
- **Legacy support**—Virtualization can extend the life of OSs and applications, providing more time for organizations to migrate to newer solutions.

Hypervisors (19.2.2)

A *hypervisor* is a program, firmware, or hardware that adds an abstraction layer on top of the physical hardware. The abstraction layer is used to create virtual machines (VMs) that have access to all the hardware of the physical machine such as CPUs, memory, disk controllers, and NICs. Each of these VMs runs a complete and separate operating system. With virtualization, it is not uncommon for 100 physical servers to be consolidated as VMs on top of 10 physical servers that are using hypervisors.

Type 1 Hypervisor—"Bare Metal" Approach

Type 1 hypervisors are also called the "bare metal" approach because the hypervisor is installed directly on the server or networking hardware. Type 1 hypervisors are usually used on enterprise servers and data center networking devices.

After a Type 1 hypervisor is installed on the server or networking hardware, instances of an OS are installed on the hypervisor, as shown in Figure 19-2. Type 1 hypervisors have direct access to the hardware resources; therefore, they are more efficient than hosted architectures. Type 1 hypervisors improve scalability, performance, and robustness.

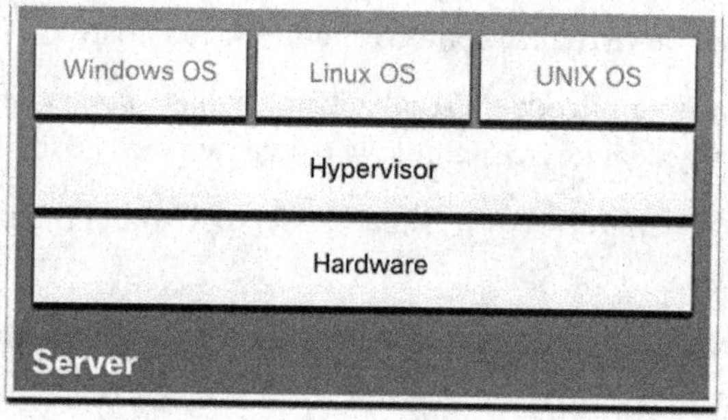

Figure 19-2 Type 1 Hypervisor

Type 2 Hypervisor—"Hosted" Approach

A Type 2 hypervisor is software that creates and runs VM instances. The computer on which a hypervisor is supporting one or more VMs is a host machine. Type 2 hypervisors are also called *hosted hypervisors* because they are installed on top of the existing OS, such as macOS, Windows, or Linux. Then, one or more additional OS instances are installed on top of the hypervisor, as shown in Figure 19-3. A big advantage of Type 2 hypervisors is that management console software is not required. Oracle VirtualBox and VMware Workstation are two examples of Type 2 hypervisor software.

Note

It is important to make sure that the host machine has enough CPU processing, RAM memory, and disk storage to install and run the VMs so that it does not run out of resources.

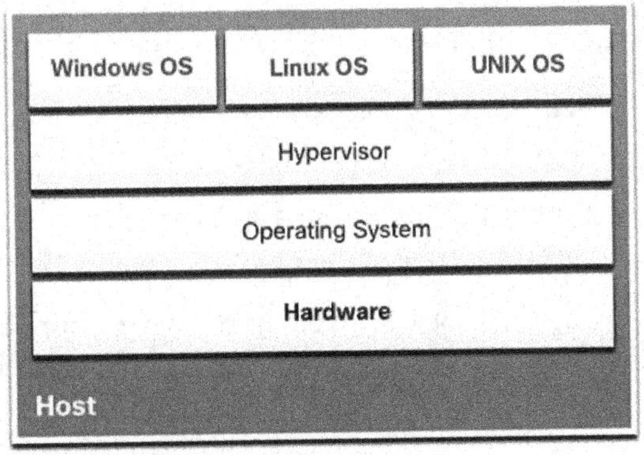

Figure 19-3 Type 2 Hypervisor

Lab—Install Linux in a Virtual Machine and Explore the GUI (19.2.3)

In this lab, you will install a Linux OS in a virtual machine using a desktop virtualization application, such as VirtualBox. After completing the installation, you will explore the GUI.

Refer to the online course to complete this lab.

Cloud and Virtualization Summary (19.3)

The following is a summary of each topic in the chapter and some questions for your reflection.

What Did I Learn in This Chapter? (19.3.1)

- Cloud and Cloud Services—In general, when talking about the cloud, we are talking about data centers, cloud computing, and virtualization. Data centers are usually large facilities that provide massive amounts of power, cooling, and bandwidth. Only very large companies can afford their own data centers. Most smaller organizations lease the services from a cloud provider.

Cloud services include the following:

- **SaaS**—Software as a Service
- **PaaS**—Platform as a Service
- **IaaS**—Infrastructure as a Service

There are four primary cloud models:

- **Public cloud**—Cloud-based applications and services offered in a public cloud are made available to the general population.
- **Private cloud**—Cloud-based applications and services offered in a private cloud are intended for a specific organization or entity, such as the government.
- **Hybrid cloud**—A hybrid cloud is made up of two or more cloud types, where each part remains a separate object, but both are connected using a single architecture.
- **Community cloud**—A community cloud is created for exclusive use by a specific community. The differences between public clouds and community clouds are the functional needs that have been customized for the community.

Virtualization is the foundation of cloud computing. Without it, cloud computing, as it is most widely implemented, would not be possible. Virtualization means creating a virtual rather than physical version of something, such as a computer. An example would be running a "Linux computer" on your Windows PC.

- **Virtualization**—One major advantage of virtualization is overall reduced cost:
  - **Less equipment is required**—Virtualization enables server consolidation, which requires fewer physical devices and lowers maintenance costs.
  - **Less energy is consumed**—Consolidating servers lowers the monthly power and cooling costs.
  - **Less space is required**—Server consolidation reduces the amount of required floor space.

  These are additional benefits of virtualization:

  - **Easier prototyping**—Self-contained labs, operating on isolated networks, can be rapidly created for testing and prototyping network deployments.
  - **Faster server provisioning**—Creating a virtual server is far faster than provisioning a physical server.
  - **Increased server uptime**—Most server virtualization platforms now offer advanced redundant fault-tolerance features.

- **Improved disaster recovery**—Most enterprise server virtualization platforms have software that can help test and automate failover before a disaster happens.
- **Legacy support**—Virtualization can extend the life of OSs and applications, providing more time for organizations to migrate to newer solutions.

A hypervisor is a program, firmware, or hardware that adds an abstraction layer on top of the physical hardware. The abstraction layer is used to create virtual machines that have access to all the hardware of the physical machine such as CPUs, memory, disk controllers, and NICs. Each of these VMs runs a complete and separate operating system.

Type 1 ("bare metal") hypervisors are installed directly on the hardware. Type 1 hypervisors are usually used on enterprise servers and data center networking devices.

A Type 2 hypervisor is software that creates and runs VM instances. The computer on which a hypervisor is supporting one or more VMs is a host machine. Type 2 hypervisors are also called hosted hypervisors because they are installed on top of the existing OS, such as macOS, Windows, or Linux. Then, one or more additional OS instances are installed on top of the hypervisor. A big advantage of Type 2 hypervisors is that management console software is not required.

Reflection Questions (19.3.2)

For now, Bob is suggesting that Marcy and Vincent use the cloud for data storage. They understand that it is a subscription service, but it will allow them to maintain their data more securely and it will be less expensive than buying their own data storage and server. As you now know, there are many other services provided by the cloud. Marcy and Vincent may eventually desire some of these services as well.

Have you ever had your hard drive go down and not be able to recover all your files? What if this happened to a computer or even a server at your school or work? Does your school or work network use other cloud services? If so, do you know what they are and why they were selected? If you were in Marcy and Vincent's situation, which cloud services would you consider using in addition to data storage?

Practice

The following lab activity provides practice with the topics introduced in this chapter.

Labs

Lab—Install Linux in a Virtual Machine and Explore the GUI (19.2.3)

Check Your Understanding Questions

Complete all the review questions listed here to test your understanding of the topics and concepts in this chapter. Appendix A, "Answers to 'Check Your Understanding' Questions," lists the answers.

1. Which term is associated with cloud computing?
   a. Teleworkers
   b. Wireless
   c. Tall servers
   d. Virtualization

2. Which three features represent benefits of virtualization? (Choose three.)
   a. Less power consumption
   b. Less employee technical training
   c. Less device monitoring
   d. Less equipment
   e. Improved disaster recovery
   f. Fewer security requirements

3. Which term describes the type of cloud computing service that provides applications over the web?
   a. IaaS
   b. ITaaS
   c. PaaS
   d. SaaS

4. Saving your photos to a storage location maintained by a cloud provider is an example of _______.

   a. virtualization
   b. big data
   c. cloud computing

5. Which cloud model provides services for a specific organization or entity?

   a. Hybrid cloud
   b. Community cloud
   c. Public cloud
   d. Private cloud

6. A company uses cloud services and is setting up the company's DNS server supplied by the cloud provider. Which cloud model is the company using?

   a. DaaS
   b. IaaS
   c. PaaS
   d. SaaS

7. What term is used to define the software process that creates VMs and performs hardware abstraction to support VMs?

   a. Hypervisor
   b. Container
   c. Element manager
   d. Virtualized Infrastructure Manager (VIM)

8. What type of software is installed on a host system with an existing OS, such as macOS, to support virtual machines?

   a. Type 2 hypervisor software
   b. Bare metal software
   c. Type 1 hypervisor software
   d. Edge computing software

9. Which piece of software is responsible for creating virtual machines and providing them access to resources on a physical machine?

   a. Hypervisor
   b. Supervisor

c. Host operating system
d. Hosted operating system

10. Which cloud type consists of two or more cloud types that are connected through a single architecture?

a. Hybrid
b. Private
c. Public
d. Community

11. Which two of the following are Type 2 hypervisors? (Choose two.)

a. VirtualBox
b. VMware ESXi
c. Xen
d. VMware Workstation
e. KVM

12. What is a characteristic of a public cloud?

a. It is available to everyone.
b. It is intended for a specific organization.
c. It is made up of two or more cloud types.
d. It is customized to meet specific functional needs of organizations.

CHAPTER 20

Number Systems

Objectives

Upon completion of this chapter, you will be able to answer the following questions:

- How do you calculate numbers between decimal and binary systems?
- How do you calculate numbers between decimal and hexadecimal systems?

Key Terms

This chapter uses the following key terms. You can find the definitions in the Glossary.

binary Page 294

hexadecimal Page 294

Introduction (20.0)

Webster here again! Bob is good at this networking stuff. When he was learning networking, he had to understand number systems, and so do you! You already use the base 10 decimal system, which uses integers 0 through 9. Do you know other number systems, too? I've seen base 12, base 60, and others. Do you know about the binary system computers use? The *binary* system uses just two integers, 0 and 1. Hosts, servers, and network devices use binary addressing. Another system is the *hexadecimal* number system, which is used in networking to represent IP version 6 (IPv6) addresses and Ethernet MAC addresses.

Read this chapter to learn more about these number systems and how to convert between them!

Binary Number System (20.1)

IPv4 addresses are 32-bit addresses expressed in decimal notation. This section discusses the binary number system along with the conversion between the binary and decimal number systems.

Binary and IPv4 Addresses (20.1.1)

IPv4 addresses begin as binary, a series of only 1s and 0s, called *bits*. These addresses are difficult to manage, so network administrators must convert them to decimal. This topic shows you a few ways to do this.

Binary is a numbering system that consists of the digits 0 and 1 called bits. In contrast, the decimal number system consists of 10 digits that include 0 through 9.

Network administrators need to understand binary because hosts, servers, and network devices use binary addressing. Specifically, they use binary IPv4 addresses, as shown in Figure 20-1, to identify each other.

Each address consists of a string of 32 bits, divided into four sections called *octets*. Each octet contains 8 bits (or 1 byte), and the octets are separated with a dot. For example, PC1 in Figure 20-1 is assigned IPv4 address 11000000.10101000.000010 10.00001010. Its default gateway address would be that of the R1 Gigabit Ethernet interface (G0/0/0): 11000000.10101000.00001010.00000001.

Binary works well with hosts and network devices, but it is very challenging for humans to work with. For ease of use by people, IPv4 addresses are commonly expressed in dotted decimal notation. Figure 20-2 shows the same network as Figure 20-1, but PC1 now is assigned the IPv4 address 192.168.10.10, and its default gateway address is 192.168.10.1.

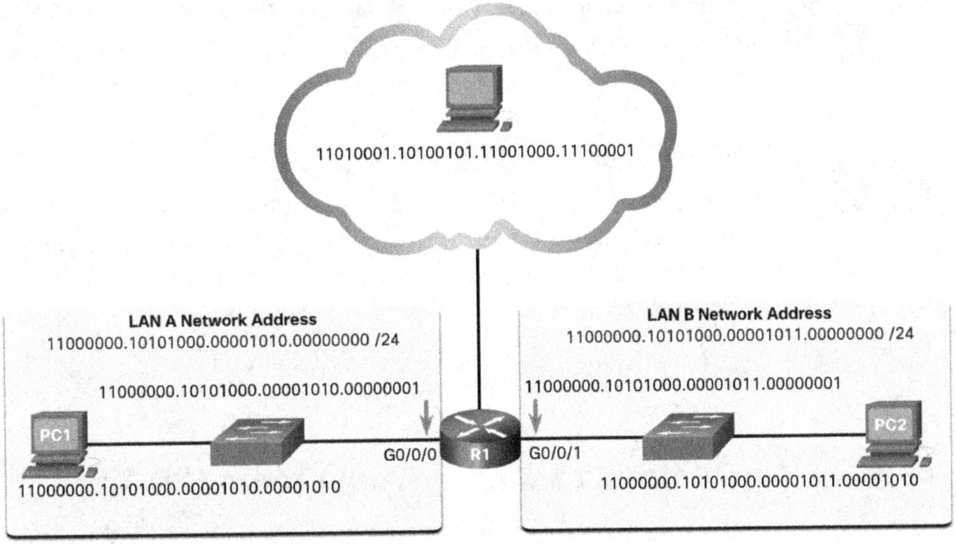

Figure 20-1 IPv4 Addresses in Binary Format

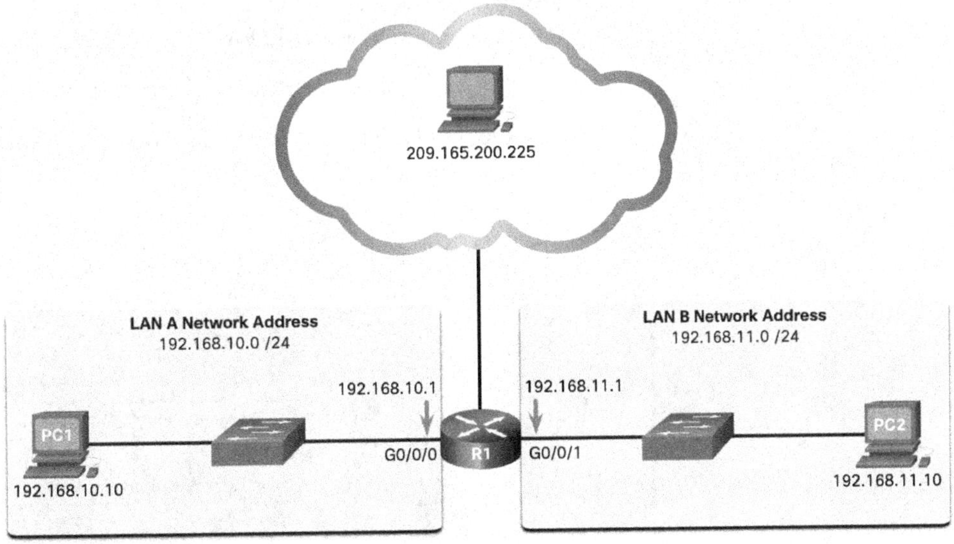

Figure 20-2 IPv4 Addresses in Dotted Decimal Format

For a solid understanding of network addressing, it is necessary to know binary addressing and gain practical skills converting between binary and dotted decimal IPv4 addresses. The following sections cover how to convert between base 2 (binary) and base 10 (decimal) number systems.

Video

Video—Converting Between Binary and Decimal Numbering Systems (20.1.2)

Refer to the online course to view this video.

Interactive Graphic

Activity—Binary to Decimal Conversions (20.1.4)

This activity allows you to practice 8-bit binary to decimal conversion as much as necessary. We recommend that you work with this tool until you are able to do the conversion without error. Convert the binary number shown in the octet to its decimal value.

Refer to the online course to complete this activity.

Decimal to Binary Conversion (20.1.5)

It is also necessary to understand how to convert a dotted decimal IPv4 address to binary. A useful tool is the binary positional value table, as demonstrated in Figures 20-3 through 20-10.

Step 1. In Figure 20-3, is the decimal number of the octet (*n*) equal to or greater than the most significant bit (128)?

- If no, then enter binary **0** in the **128** positional value.
- If yes, then add a binary **1** in the **128** positional value and subtract **128** from the decimal number.

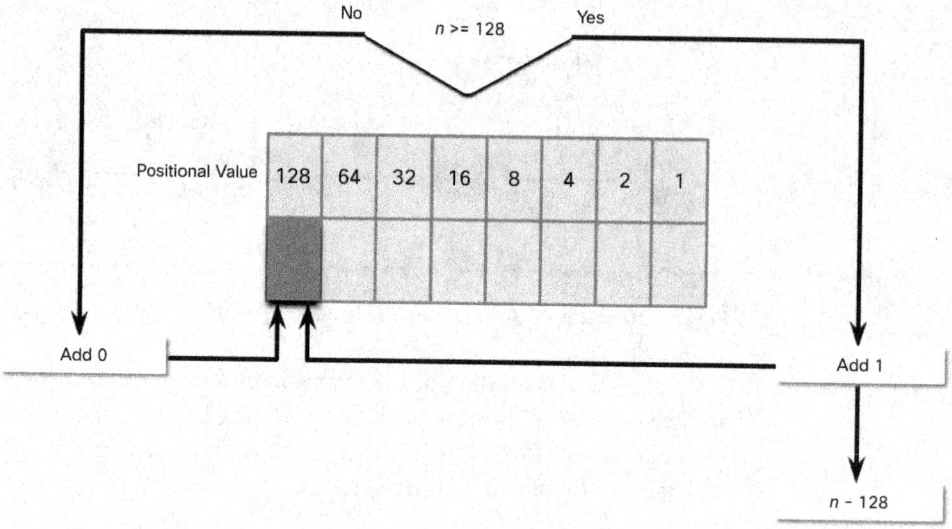

Figure 20-3 128 Positional Value

Step 2. In Figure 20-4, is the decimal number of the octet (*n*) equal to or greater than the next most significant bit (**64**)?

- If no, then enter binary **0** in the **64** positional value.
- If yes, then add a binary **1** in the **64** positional value and subtract **64** from the decimal number.

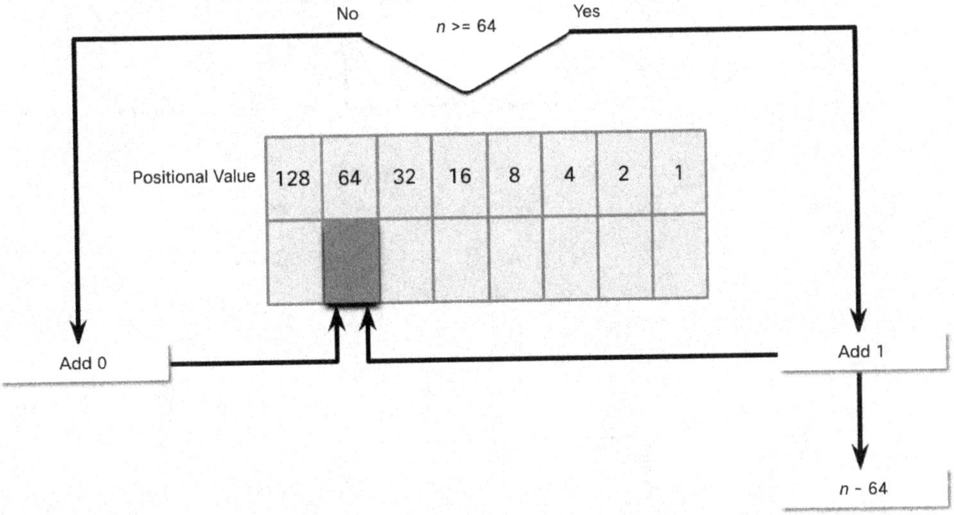

Figure 20-4 64 Positional Value

Step 3. In Figure 20-5, is the decimal number of the octet (*n*) equal to or greater than the next most significant bit (**32**)?

- If no, then enter binary **0** in the **32** positional value.
- If yes, then add a binary **1** in the **32** positional value and subtract **32** from the decimal number.

Step 4. In Figure 20-6, is the decimal number of the octet (*n*) equal to or greater than the next most significant bit (**16**)?

- If no, then enter binary **0** in the **16** positional value.
- If yes, then add a binary **1** in the **16** positional value and subtract **16** from the decimal number.

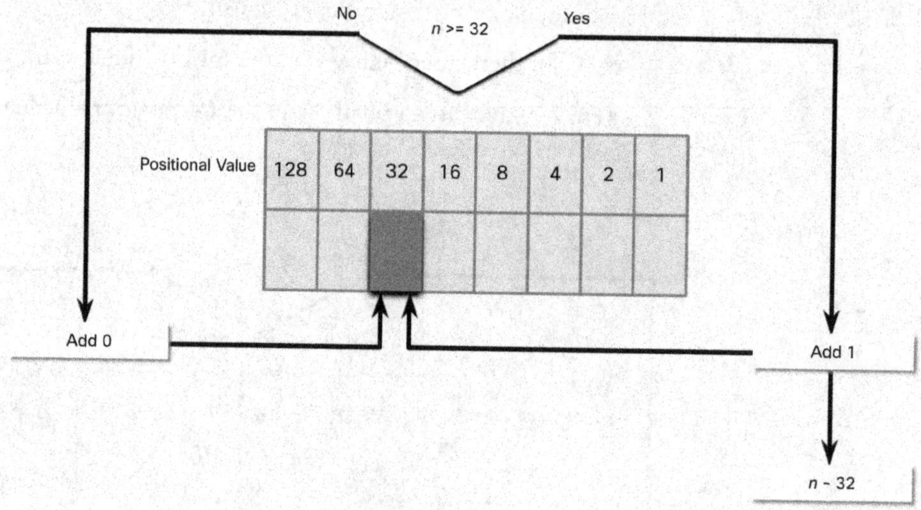

Figure 20-5 32 Positional Value

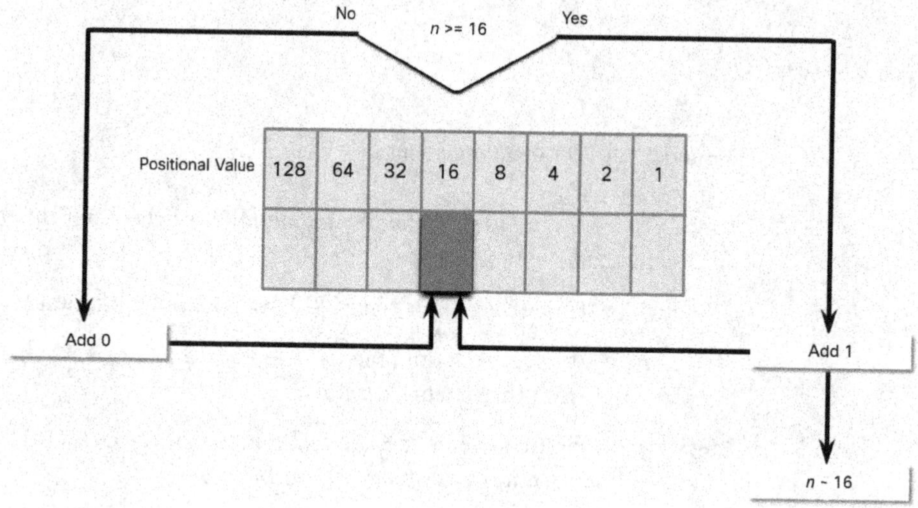

Figure 20-6 16 Positional Value

Step 5. In Figure 20-7, is the decimal number of the octet (*n*) equal to or greater than the next most significant bit (8)?

- If no, then enter binary **0** in the **8** positional value.
- If yes, then add a binary **1** in the **8** positional value and subtract **8** from the decimal number.

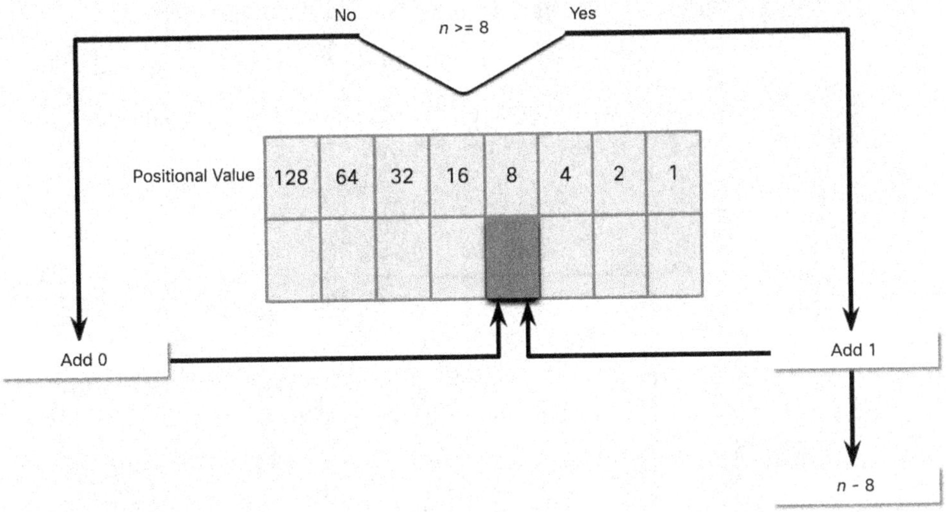

Figure 20-7 8 Positional Value

Step 6. In Figure 20-8, is the decimal number of the octet (*n*) equal to or greater than the next most significant bit (**4**)?

- If no, then enter binary **0** in the **4** positional value.
- If yes, then add a binary **1** in the **4** positional value and subtract **4** from the decimal number.

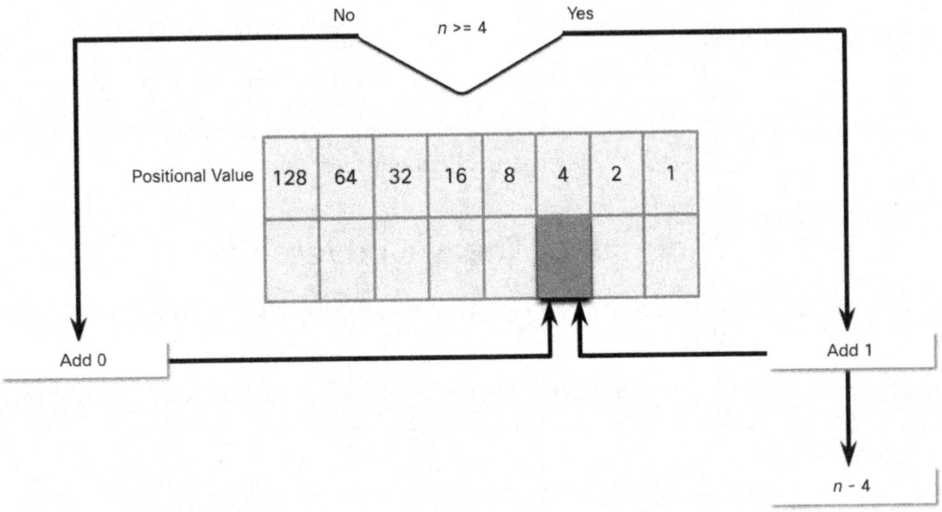

Figure 20-8 4 Positional Value

Step 7. In Figure 20-9, is the decimal number of the octet (*n*) equal to or greater than the next most significant bit (2)?

- If no, then enter binary **0** in the **2** positional value.
- If yes, then add a binary **1** in the **2** positional value and subtract **2** from the decimal number.

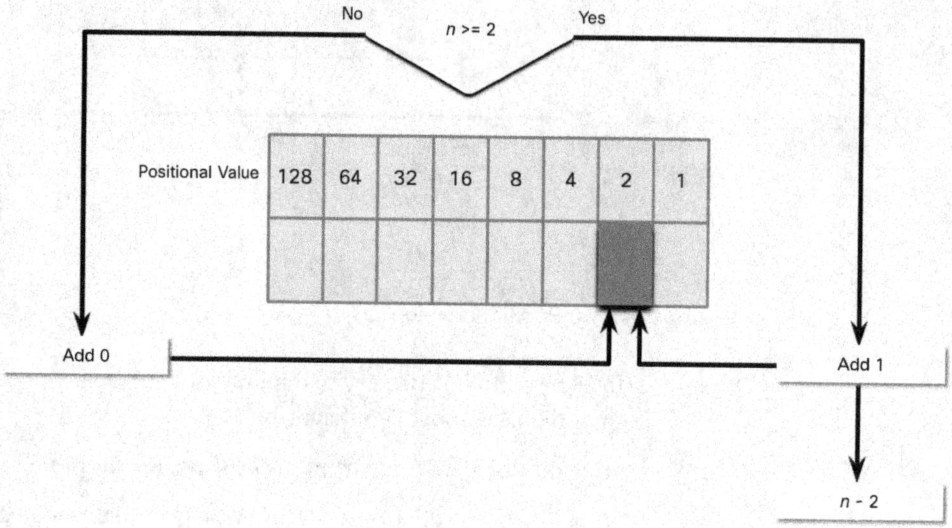

Figure 20-9 2 Positional Value

Step 8. In Figure 20-10, is the decimal number of the octet (*n*) equal to or greater than the last most significant bit (1)?

- If no, then enter binary **0** in the **1** positional value.
- If yes, then add a binary **1** in the **1** positional value and subtract **1** from the last decimal number.

Decimal to Binary Conversion Example (20.1.6)

To help understand the process of converting from decimal to binary, consider the IP address 192.168.11.10.

The first octet number 192 is converted to binary using the previously explained positional notation process.

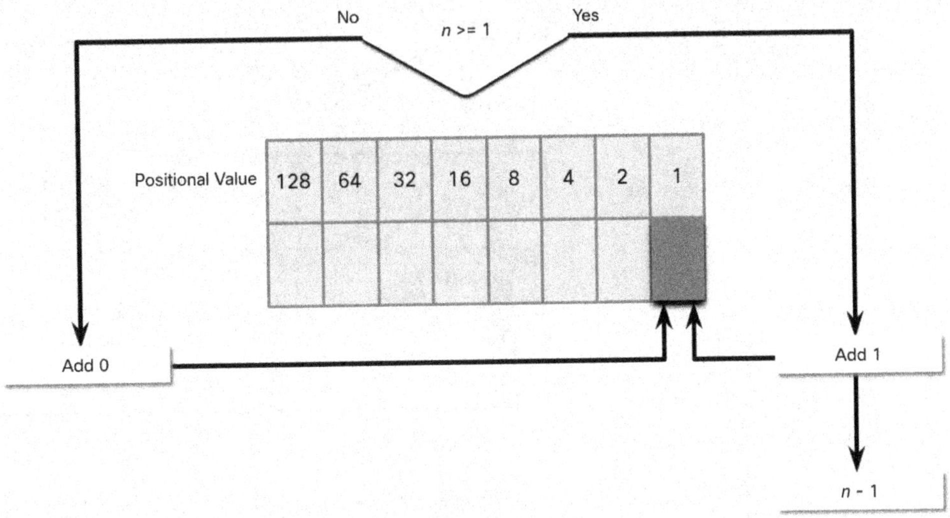

Figure 20-10 1 Positional Value

It is possible to bypass the process of subtraction with easier or smaller decimal numbers. For instance, notice that it is fairly easy to calculate the third octet converted to a binary number without actually going through the subtraction process (8 + 2 = 10). The binary value of the third octet is 00001010.

The fourth octet is 11 (8 + 2 + 1). The binary value of the fourth octet is 00001011.

Converting between binary and decimal may seem challenging at first, but with practice it should become easier over time.

Figures 20-11 through 20-21 illustrate the steps to convert the IP address 192.168.10.11 into binary.

Step 1. In Figure 20-11, is the first octet number **192** equal to or greater than the high-order bit **128**?

- Yes it is, so add a **1** to the high-order positional value to represent **128**.
- Subtract **128** from **192** to produce a remainder of **64**.

Step 2. In Figure 20-12, is the remainder **64** equal to or greater than the next high-order bit **64**?

- It is equal, so add a **1** to the next high-order positional value.

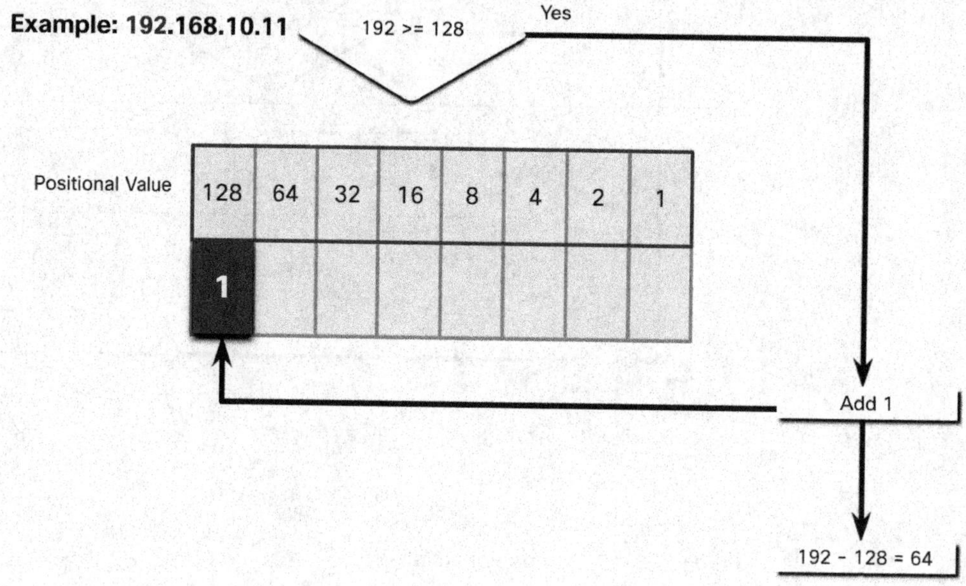

Figure 20-11 Step 1

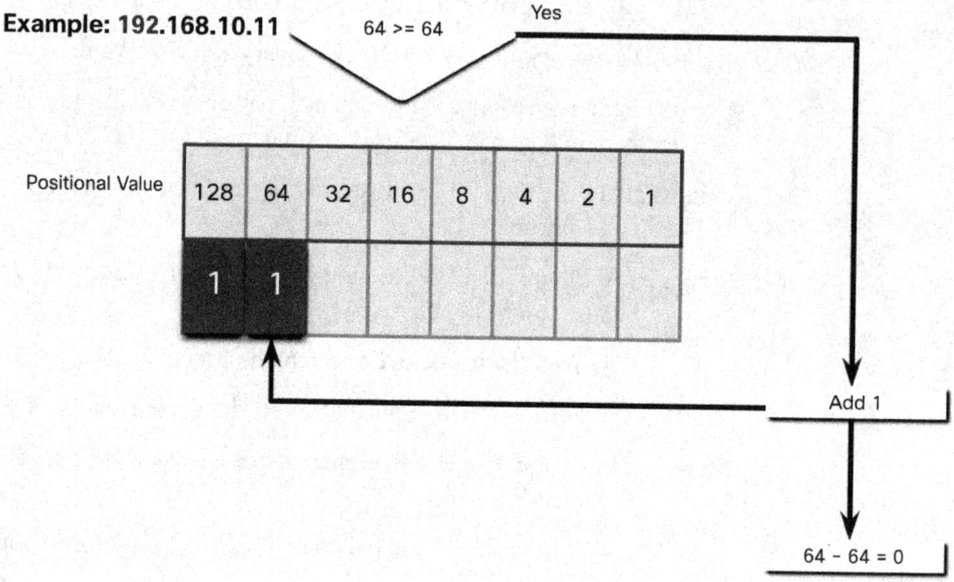

Figure 20-12 Step 2

Step 3. In Figure 20-13, since there is no remainder, enter binary **0** in the remaining positional values.

- The binary value of the first octet is **11000000**.

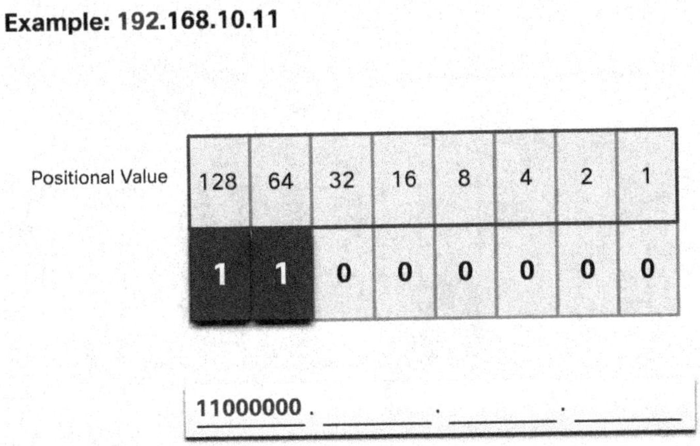

Figure 20-13 Step 3

Step 4. In Figure 20-14, is the second octet number **168** equal to or greater than the high-order bit **128**?

- Yes it is, so add a **1** to the high-order positional value to represent **128**.
- Subtract **128** from **168** to produce a remainder of **40**.

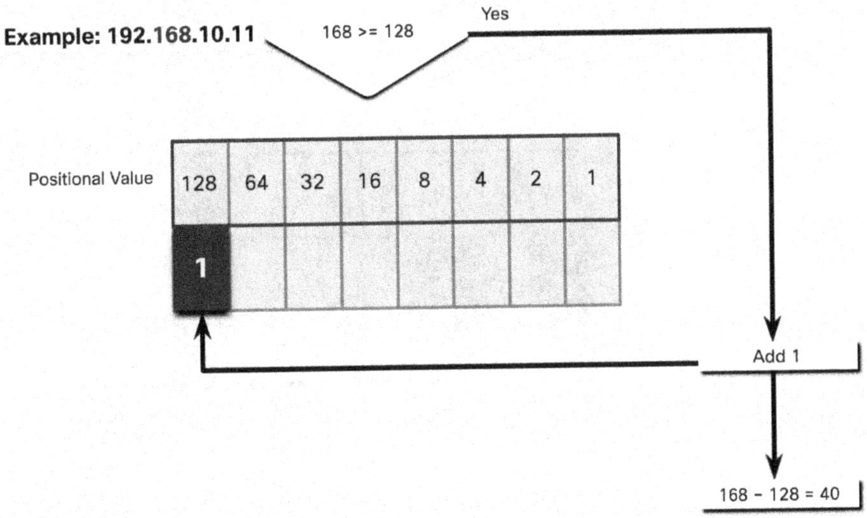

Figure 20-14 Step 4

Step 5. In Figure 20-15, is the remainder **40** equal to or greater than the next high-order bit **64**?

- No it is not, so enter a binary **0** in the positional value.

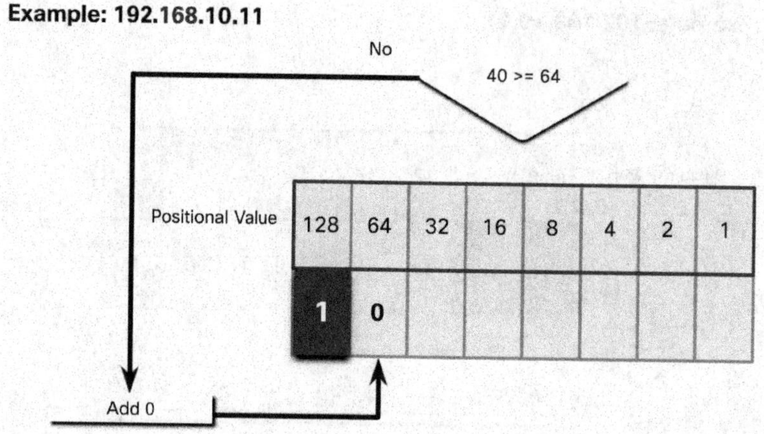

Figure 20-15 Step 5

Step 6. In Figure 20-16, is the remainder **40** equal to or greater than the next high-order bit **32**?

- Yes it is, so add a **1** to the high-order positional value to represent **32**.
- Subtract **32** from **40** to produce a remainder of **8**.

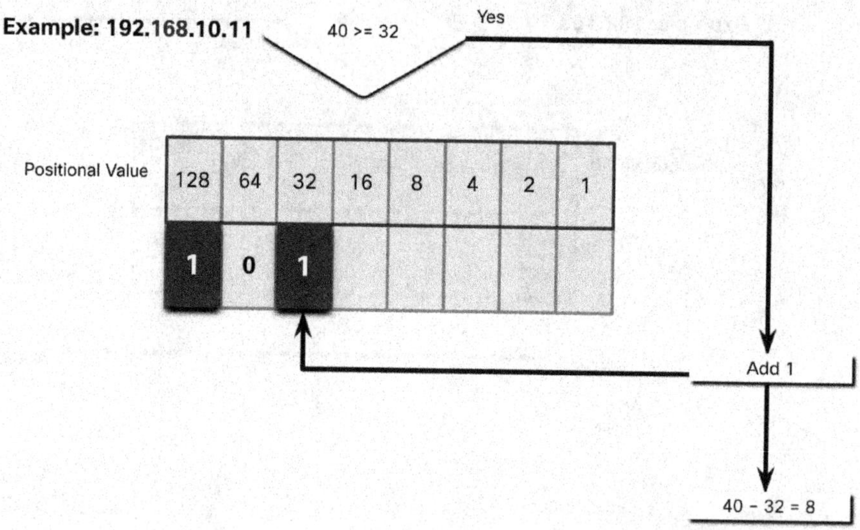

Figure 20-16 Step 6

Step 7. In Figure 20-17, is the remainder **8** equal to or greater than the next high-order bit **16**?

- No it is not, so enter a binary **0** in the positional value.

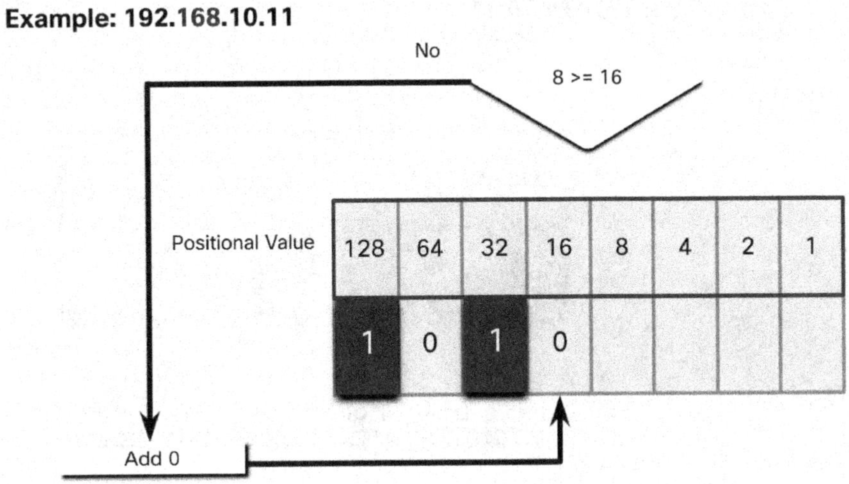

Figure 20-17 Step 7

Step 8. In Figure 20-18, is the remainder **8** equal to or greater than the next high-order bit **8**?

- It is equal, so add a **1** to the next high-order positional value.

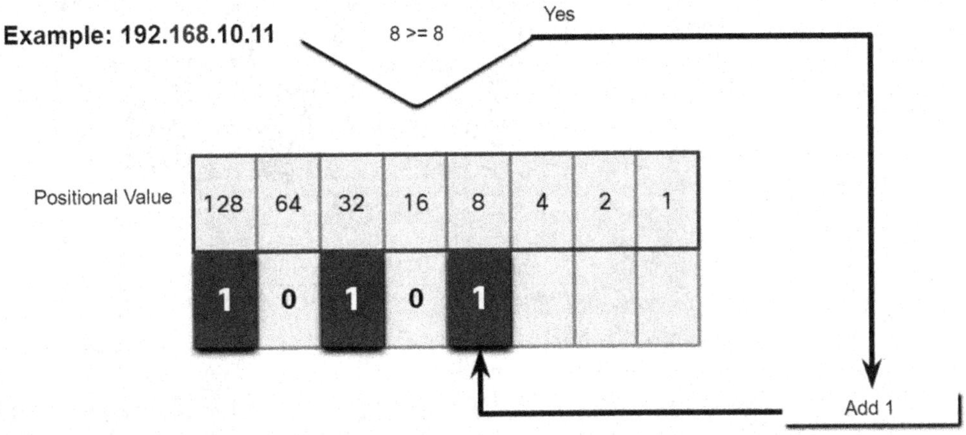

Figure 20-18 Step 8

Step 9. In Figure 20-19, since there is no remainder, enter binary **0** in the remaining positional values.

- The binary value of the second octet is **10101000**.

Example: 192.168.10.11

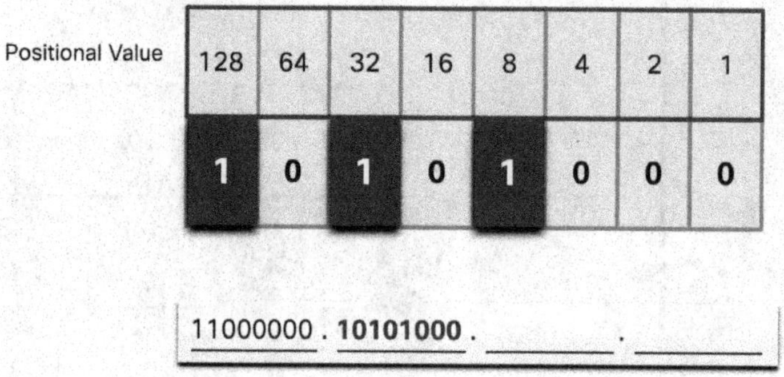

Figure 20-19 Step 9

Step 10. In Figure 20-20, the binary value of the third octet is **00001010**.

Example: 192.168.10.11

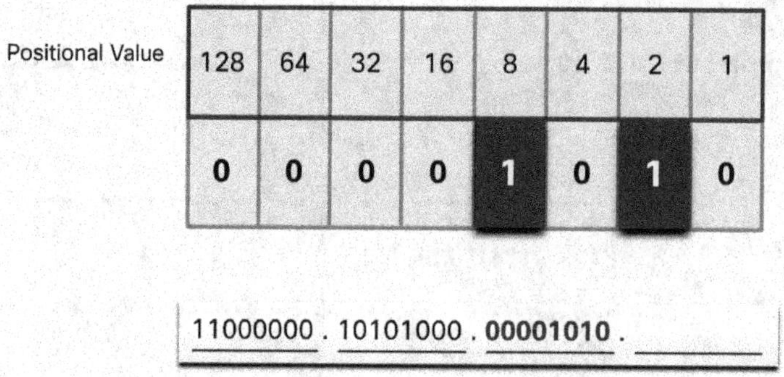

Figure 20-20 Step 10

Step 11. In Figure 20-21, the binary value of the fourth octet is **00001011**.

Example: 192.168.10.11

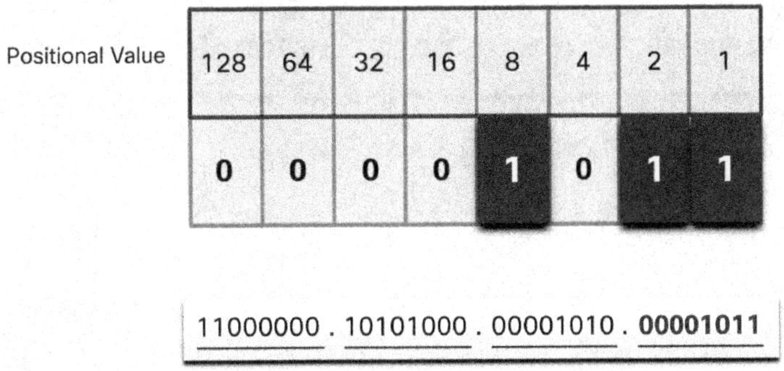

Figure 20-21 Step 11

Interactive Graphic

Activity—Decimal to Binary Conversions (20.1.7)

This activity allows you to practice decimal conversions to 8-bit binary values. We recommend that you work with this tool until you are able to do the conversion without error. Convert the decimal number shown in the Decimal Value row to its binary bits.

Refer to the online course to complete this activity.

Interactive Graphic

Activity—Binary Game (20.1.8)

This is a fun way to learn binary numbers for networking.

Game Link: https://learningcontent.cisco.com/games/binary/index.html

There are also a variety of free mobile binary games. Search for "Binary Game" in your app store.

Refer to the online course to complete this activity.

IPv4 Addresses (20.1.9)

As mentioned previously, hosts, servers, and network devices understand only binary, while humans work in decimal. To reiterate, it is important for you to gain a thorough understanding of these two number systems and how they are used in networking.

192.168.10.10 is an IP address that is assigned to a computer, as shown in Figure 20-22.

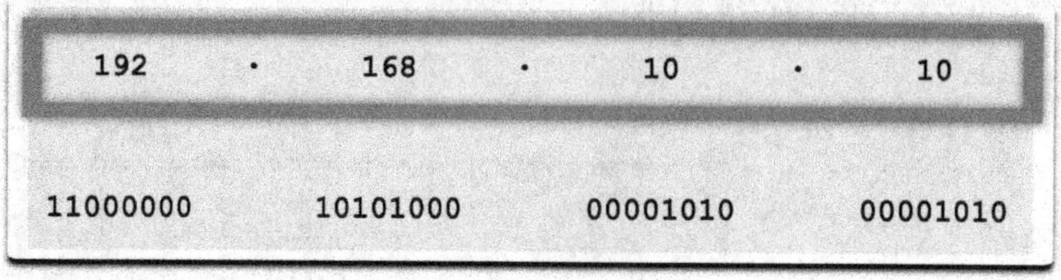

Figure 20-22 Dotted Decimal Address

This address is made up of four different octets, as shown in Figure 20-23.

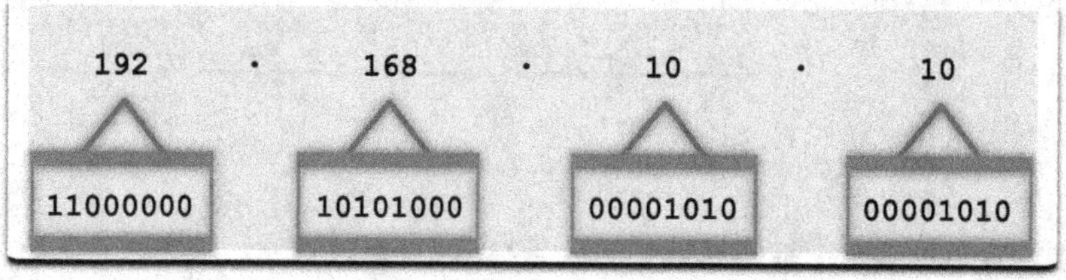

Figure 20-23 Octets

The computer stores the address as the entire 32-bit data stream, as shown in Figure 20-24.

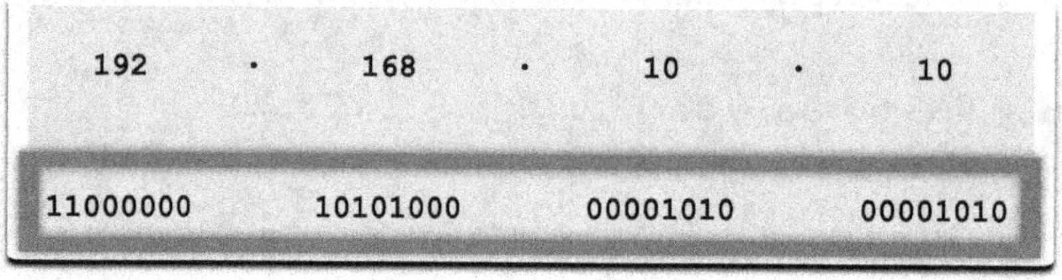

Figure 20-24 32-bit Address

Hexadecimal Number System (20.2)

IPv6 addresses are 128-bit addresses expressed in hexadecimal notation. This topic will discuss the hexadecimal number system along with the conversion between the hexadecimal and decimal number systems.

Hexadecimal and IPv6 Addresses (20.2.1)

Now you know how to convert binary to decimal and decimal to binary. You need that skill to understand IPv4 addressing in your network. But you are just as likely to

be using IPv6 addresses in your network. To understand IPv6 addresses, you must be able to convert hexadecimal to decimal and vice versa.

Just as decimal is a base 10 number system, hexadecimal is a base 16 system. The base 16 number system uses the digits 0 to 9 and the letters A to F. Figure 20-25 shows the equivalent decimal and hexadecimal values for binary 0000 to 1111.

Decimal	Binary	Hexadecimal
0	0000	0
1	0001	1
2	0010	2
3	0011	3
4	0100	4
5	0101	5
6	0110	6
7	0111	7
8	1000	8
9	1001	9
10	1010	A
11	1011	B
12	1100	C
13	1101	D
14	1110	E
15	1111	F

Figure 20-25 Comparing Decimal, Binary, and Hexadecimal Number Systems

Binary and hexadecimal work well together because it is easier to express a value as a single hexadecimal digit than as 4 binary bits.

The hexadecimal number system is used in networking to represent IPv6 addresses and Ethernet MAC addresses. IPv6 addresses are 128 bits in length, and every 4 bits is represented by a single hexadecimal digit, for a total of 32 hexadecimal values. IPv6 addresses are not case-sensitive and can be written in either lowercase or uppercase.

As shown in Figure 20-26, the preferred format for writing an IPv6 address is x:x:x:x:x:x:x:x, with each x consisting of four hexadecimal values. Whereas the term *octet* refers to 8 bits of an IPv4 address, in IPv6, a *hextet* is the unofficial term used to refer to a segment of 16 bits, or four hexadecimal values. Each x is a single hextet, 16 bits, or four hexadecimal digits.

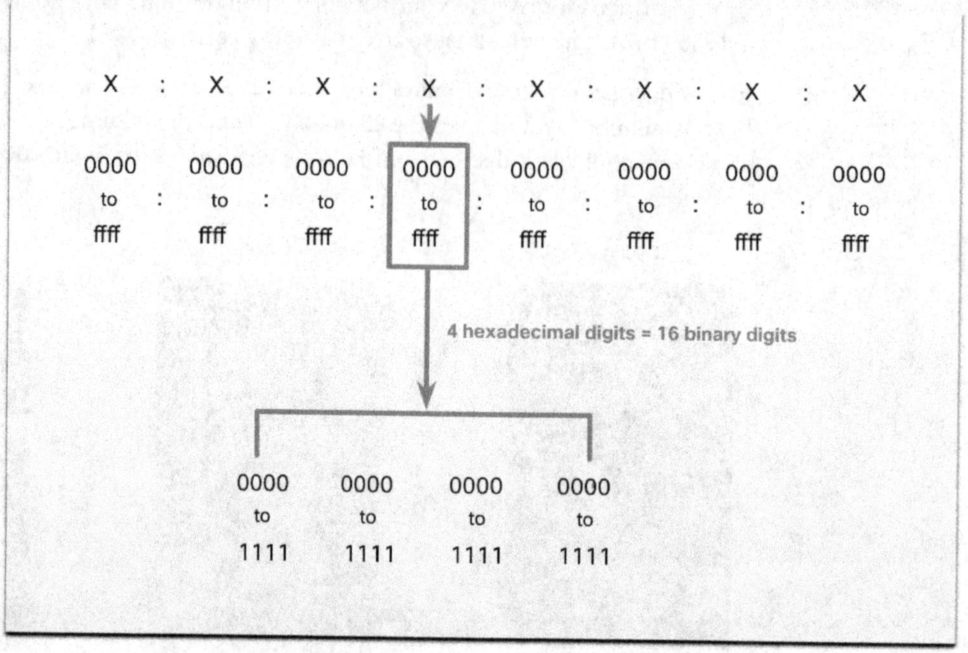

Figure 20-26 Hextets of an IPv6 Address

The sample topology in Figure 20-27 displays IPv6 hexadecimal addresses.

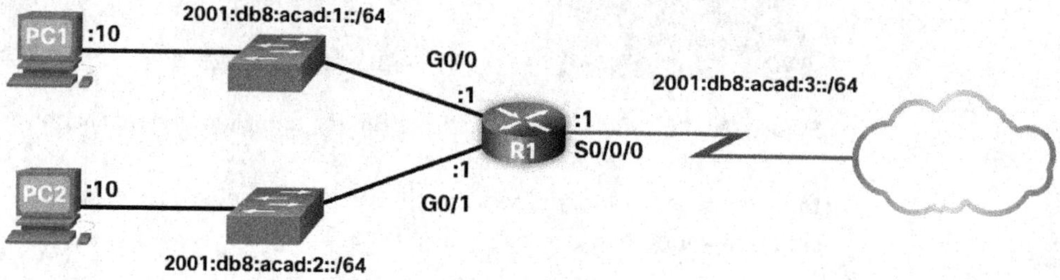

Figure 20-27 Topology with IPv6 Addresses

Video

Video—Converting Between Hexadecimal and Decimal Number Systems (20.2.2)

Refer to the online course to view this video.

Interactive Graphic

Check Your Understanding—Convert Between Decimal to Hexadecimal Number Systems (20.2.3)

Refer to the online course to complete this activity.

Number Systems Summary (20.3)

The following is a summary of each topic in the chapter and some questions for your reflection.

What Did I Learn in This Chapter? (20.3.1)

- **Binary Number System**—Binary is a number system that consists of the digits 0 and 1, called bits. In contrast, the decimal number system consists of the digits 0 through 9. Hosts, servers, and network devices use binary addressing. Specifically, they use binary IPv4 addresses. For ease of use by people, IPv4 addresses are commonly expressed in dotted decimal notation.

  The dotted decimal system uses base 10. For example, the number 2146 has a 2 in the thousands place, or 2000; a 1 in the hundreds place, or 100; a 4 in the tens place, or 40; and a 6 in the ones place, or 6.

  The binary system is a base 2 number system. Each place value can have a 0 or a 1. A useful tool is the binary positional value table. It is common to use a table with eight placeholders; 8 bits equal 1 byte.

- **Hexadecimal Number System**—The hexadecimal number system is used in networking to represent IPv6 addresses and Ethernet MAC addresses. This base 16 number system uses the digits 0 to 9 and the letters A to F. Binary and hexadecimal work well together because it is easier to express a value as a single hexadecimal digit than as 4 binary bits.

  IPv6 addresses are 128 bits in length, and every 4 bits is represented by a single hexadecimal digit, for a total of 32 hexadecimal values. IPv6 addresses are not case-sensitive and can be written in either lowercase or uppercase.

Reflection Questions (20.3.2)

I wasn't expecting to do math in the middle of my networking course, but I was surprised by how much fun it is to convert decimal numbers into their binary and hexadecimal equivalents. I have a better understanding of why IP addresses are represented the way that we see them. Before you read this chapter, what did you know about binary and hexadecimal number systems? Take a look at the MAC address on your computer's NIC. What do you recognize about this address that you may not have before?

Practice

There are no labs or Packet Tracer activities in this chapter.

Check Your Understanding Questions

Complete all the review questions listed here to test your understanding of the topics and concepts in this chapter. Appendix A, "Answers to 'Check Your Understanding' Questions," lists the answers.

1. What is the binary representation for the decimal number 173?
   a. 10100111
   b. 10100101
   c. 10101101
   d. 10110101
2. How many bits make up an octet in an IPv4 address?
   a. 4
   b. 8
   c. 16
   d. 32
3. What is the decimal equivalent of 0xC9?
   a. 185
   b. 200
   c. 201
   d. 199
4. What is the binary representation of 0xCA?
   a. 10111010
   b. 11010101
   c. 11001010
   d. 11011010
5. What is the range of hexadecimal values that can be used in a hextet?
   a. 0000 to 1111
   b. 0000 to ffff

c. 1111 to aaaa

d. 0000 to 9999

6. What is the hexadecimal equivalent of the binary number 10011101?

a. 85

b. 9D

c. A1

d. D9

7. How many bits are in an IPv4 address?

a. 32

b. 64

c. 128

d. 256

8. A network engineer wants to represent confidential data in binary format. What are the two possible values that the engineer can use? (Choose two.)

a. 0

b. 1

c. 2

d. A

e. F

9. What is the hexadecimal equivalent of the decimal number 139?

a. 8B

b. 92

c. A1

d. D7

10. Which is a valid hexadecimal value?

a. f

b. g

c. h

d. j

11. What is the binary equivalent of the decimal number 232?

   a. 11101000
   b. 11000110
   c. 10011000
   d. 11110010

12. Given the binary address of 11101100 00010001 00001100 00001010, which address does this represent in dotted decimal format?

   a. 234.17.10.9
   b. 234.16.12.10
   c. 236.17.12.6
   d. 236.17.12.10

CHAPTER 21

Ethernet Switching

Objectives

Upon completion of this chapter, you will be able to answer the following questions:

- How do the OSI model Layer 1 and Layer 2 function in an Ethernet network?
- How are the Ethernet sublayers related to the frame fields?
- What is the Ethernet MAC address?
- How does a switch build its MAC address table and forward frames?

Key Terms

This chapter uses the following key terms. You can find the definitions in the Glossary.

Ethernet Page 317

Institute of Electrical and Electronic Engineers (IEEE) Page 317

contention-based access method Page 321

collision fragment Page 322

runt frame Page 322

jumbo frame Page 322

baby giant frame Page 322

cyclic redundancy check (CRC) Page 323

Introduction (21.0)

Hey, it's Webster again! Marcy and Vincent are beginning to see the value of Bob's advice regarding the design of their furniture store's future network. However, they can't afford a lot of downtime, and they need to operate with the existing network until Bob can make the upgrades. They will not add the VoIP phones, security cameras, or online ordering system until then. Bob needs to evaluate their existing network prior to the upgrade to better understand what will need to be done.

The furniture store's network is an Ethernet network. Ethernet protocols define how data is formatted and how it is transmitted over the wired network and specifies protocols that operate at Layer 1 and Layer 2 of the OSI model.

Are you familiar with Ethernet? Why are the hexadecimal and binary number systems important in an Ethernet network? Read this chapter to learn more about Ethernet, Ethernet frames, and Ethernet MAC addresses. Let's get started!

Ethernet (21.1)

When you are connecting to a network using a wired interface, you are using the Ethernet protocol. Even most wireless networks ultimately connect to a wired Ethernet network. Ethernet is an important data link layer protocol used in local area networks (LANs) and most wide area networks (WANs).

The Rise of Ethernet (21.1.1)

In the early days of networking, each vendor used its own proprietary methods of interconnecting network devices and networking protocols. If you bought equipment from different vendors, there was no guarantee that the equipment would work together. Equipment from one vendor might not communicate with equipment from another.

As networks became more widespread, standards were developed that defined rules by which network equipment from different vendors operated. Standards are beneficial to networking in many ways, including the following:

- Facilitate design
- Simplify product development
- Promote competition
- Provide consistent interconnections

- Facilitate training
- Provide more vendor choices for customers

There is no official local area networking standard protocol, but over time, one technology, Ethernet, has become more common than the others. *Ethernet* protocols define how data is formatted and how it is transmitted over the wired network. The Ethernet standards specify protocols that operate at Layer 1 and Layer 2 of the OSI model. Ethernet has become a de facto standard, which means that it is the technology used by almost all wired LANs, as shown in Figure 21-1.

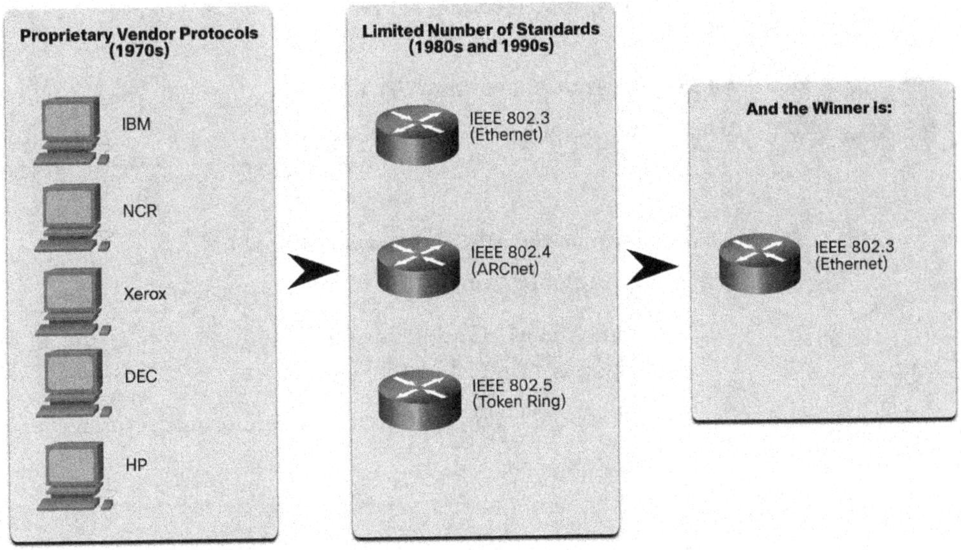

Figure 21-1 The Evolution from Proprietary LAN Protocols to Ethernet

Ethernet Evolution (21.1.2)

The *Institute of Electrical and Electronic Engineers*, or *IEEE* (pronounced "eye-triple-e"), maintains the networking standards, including Ethernet and wireless standards. IEEE committees are responsible for approving and maintaining the standards for connections, media requirements, and communications protocols. Each technology standard is assigned a number that refers to the committee that is responsible for approving and maintaining the standard. The committee responsible for the Ethernet standards is 802.3.

Since the creation of Ethernet in 1973, standards have evolved for specifying faster and more flexible versions of the technology. This adaptability of Ethernet to be improved over time is one of the main reasons that it has become so popular. Each

version of Ethernet has an associated standard. For example, 802.3 100BASE-T represents the 100 Mbps Ethernet using twisted-pair cable standards. The standard notation translates as follows:

- *100* is the speed in Mbps
- *BASE* stands for baseband transmission
- *T* stands for the type of cable, which is twisted-pair in this case

Early versions of Ethernet were relatively slow, at 10 Mbps. The latest versions of Ethernet operate at 10 Gbps and more. Imagine how much faster these new versions are than the original Ethernet networks.

Video

Video—Ethernet Addressing (21.1.3)

Refer to the online course to view this video.

Lab—Determine the MAC Address of a Host (21.1.4)

In this lab, you will complete the following objectives:

- Determine the MAC address of a Windows computer on an Ethernet network using the **ipconfig /all** command.
- Analyze a MAC address to determine the manufacturer.

Refer to the online course to complete this lab.

Ethernet Frames (21.2)

Ethernet operates in the data link layer and the physical layer. It is a family of networking technologies defined in the IEEE 802.2 and 802.3 standards.

Ethernet Encapsulation (21.2.1)

This chapter starts with a discussion of Ethernet technology including an explanation of the MAC sublayer and the Ethernet frame fields.

Ethernet is one of two LAN technologies used today, with the other being wireless LANs (WLANs). Ethernet uses wired communications, including twisted-pair cable, fiber-optic links, and coaxial cables.

Ethernet operates in the data link layer and the physical layer. It is a family of networking technologies defined in the IEEE 802.2 and 802.3 standards. Ethernet supports data bandwidths of the following:

- 10 Mbps
- 100 Mbps
- 1000 Mbps (1 Gbps)
- 10,000 Mbps (10 Gbps)
- 40,000 Mbps (40 Gbps)
- 100,000 Mbps (100 Gbps)

As shown in Figure 21-2, Ethernet standards define both the Layer 2 protocols and the Layer 1 technologies.

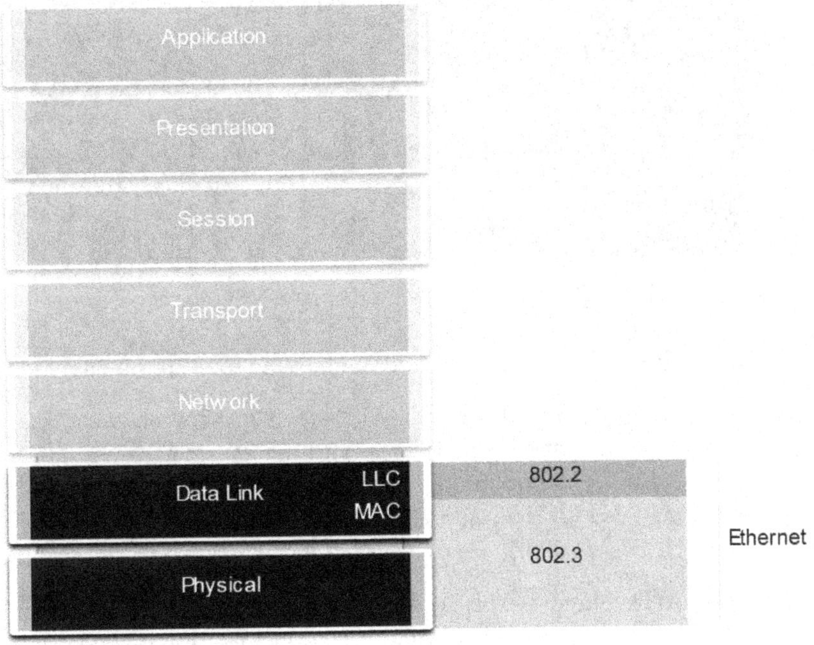

Figure 21-2 Ethernet in the OSI Model

Data Link Sublayers (21.2.2)

IEEE 802 LAN/MAN protocols, including Ethernet, use the two sublayers of the data link layer to operate (see Figure 21-3): Logical Link Control (LLC) and Media Access Control (MAC).

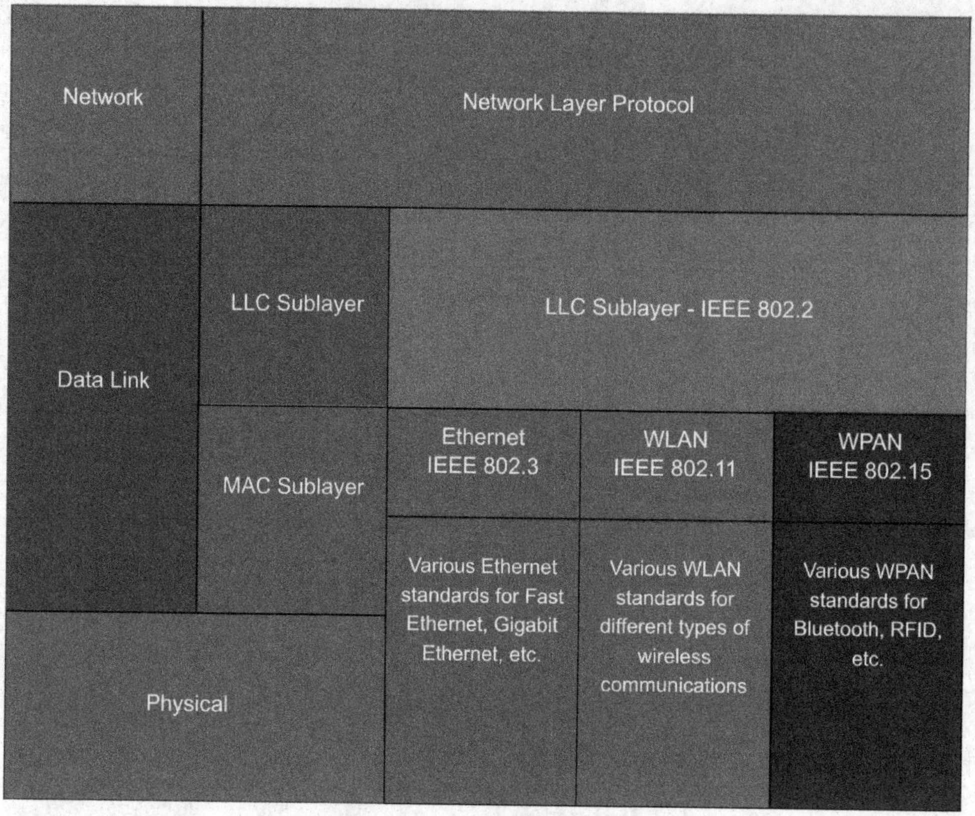

Figure 21-3 IEEE Ethernet Standards in the OSI Model

Recall that LLC and MAC have the following roles in the data link layer:

- **LLC sublayer**—This IEEE 802.2 sublayer communicates between the networking software at the upper layers and the device hardware at the lower layers. It places information in the frame that identifies which network layer protocol is being used for the frame. This information allows multiple Layer 3 protocols, such as IPv4 and IPv6, to use the same network interface and media.
- **MAC sublayer**—This sublayer (IEEE 802.3, 802.11, or 802.15, for example) is implemented in hardware and is responsible for data encapsulation and media access control. It provides data link layer addressing and is integrated with various physical layer technologies.

MAC Sublayer (21.2.3)

The MAC sublayer is responsible for data encapsulation and accessing the media.

Data Encapsulation

IEEE 802.3 data encapsulation includes the following:

- **Ethernet frame**—This is the internal structure of the Ethernet frame.
- **Ethernet addressing**—The Ethernet frame includes both source and destination MAC addresses to deliver the Ethernet frame from Ethernet NIC to Ethernet NIC on the same LAN.
- **Ethernet error detection**—The Ethernet frame includes a frame check sequence (FCS) trailer used for error detection.

Accessing the Media

As shown in Figure 21-4, the IEEE 802.3 MAC sublayer includes the specifications for different Ethernet communications standards over various types of media, including copper and fiber.

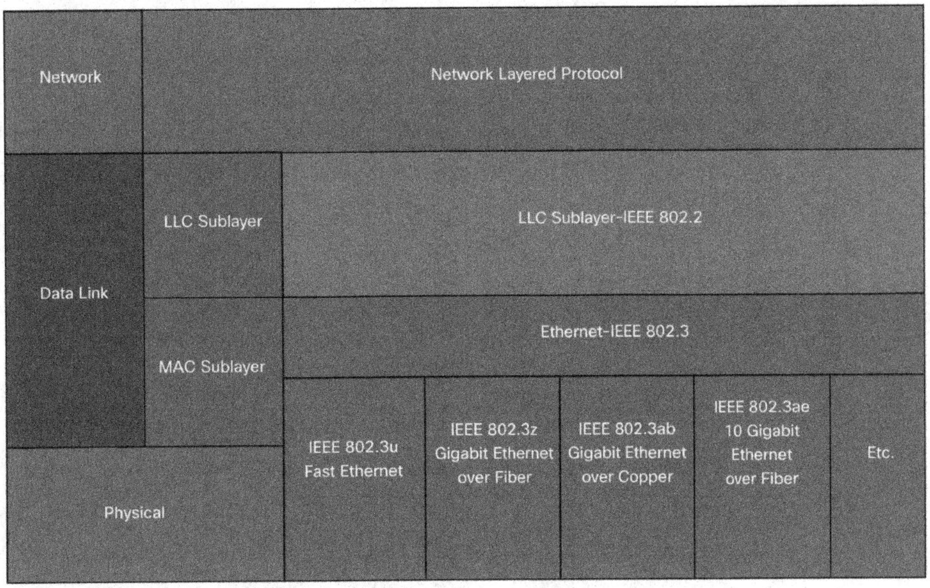

Figure 21-4 Ethernet Standards in the MAC Sublayer

Recall that legacy Ethernet using a bus topology or hubs is a shared, half-duplex medium. Ethernet over a half-duplex medium uses a *contention-based access method*, Carrier Sense Multiple Access/Collision Detection (CSMA/CD), to ensure that only one device is transmitting at a time. CSMA/CD allows multiple devices to share the same half-duplex medium and detects a collision when more than one device attempts to transmit simultaneously. It also provides a back-off algorithm for retransmission.

Ethernet LANs of today use switches that operate in full-duplex. Full-duplex communications with Ethernet switches do not require access control through CSMA/CD.

Ethernet Frame Fields (21.2.4)

The minimum Ethernet frame size is 64 bytes, and the expected maximum is 1518 bytes. This includes all bytes from the Destination MAC Address field through the Frame Check Sequence (FCS) field. The Preamble field is not included when describing the size of the frame.

Note

The frame size may be larger if additional requirements are included, such as VLAN tagging. VLAN tagging is beyond the scope of this course.

Any frame less than 64 bytes in length is considered a *collision fragment* or *runt frame* and is automatically discarded by receiving stations. A frame with more than 1500 bytes of data is considered a *jumbo frame* or *baby giant frame*.

If the size of a transmitted frame is less than the minimum or greater than the maximum, the receiving device drops the frame. Dropped frames are likely to result from collisions or unwanted signals. They are considered invalid. Jumbo frames are usually supported by most Fast Ethernet and Gigabit Ethernet switches and NICs.

Figure 21-5 shows each field in the Ethernet frame.

Ethernet Frame Fields

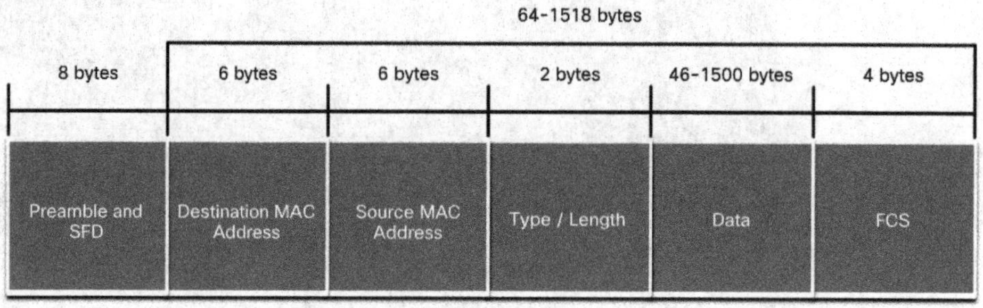

Figure 21-5 Ethernet Frame Structure and Field Size

Table 21-1 provides more information about the function of each field.

Table 21-1 Ethernet Frame Fields Detail

Field	Description
Preamble and Start Frame Delimiter fields	The Preamble (7 bytes) and Start Frame Delimiter (SFD), also called the Start of Frame (1 byte), fields are used for synchronization between the sending and receiving devices. These first 8 bytes of the frame are used to get the attention of the receiving nodes. Essentially, the first few bytes tell the receivers to get ready to receive a new frame.
Destination MAC Address field	This 6-byte field is the identifier for the intended recipient. Layer 2 uses this address to assist devices in determining if a frame is addressed to them. The address in the frame is compared to the MAC address in the device. If there is a match, the device accepts the frame. It can be a unicast, multicast, or broadcast address.
Source MAC Address field	This 6-byte field identifies the originating NIC or interface of the frame.
Type/Length field	This 2-byte field identifies the upper-layer protocol encapsulated in the Ethernet frame. Common values are, in hexadecimal, 0x800 for IPv4, 0x86DD for IPv6, and 0x806 for ARP. Note: You may also see this field referred to as EtherType, Type, or Length.
Data field	This field (46–1500 bytes) contains the encapsulated data from a higher layer, which is a generic Layer 3 PDU or, more commonly, an IPv4 packet. All frames must be at least 64 bytes long. If a small packet is encapsulated, additional bits (called a *pad*) are used to increase the size of the frame to this minimum size.
Frame Check Sequence field	The Frame Check Sequence (FCS) field (4 bytes) is used to detect errors in a frame. It uses a *cyclic redundancy check (CRC)*. The sending device includes the results of a CRC in the FCS field of the frame. The receiving device receives the frame and generates a CRC to look for errors. If the calculations match, no error occurred. Calculations that do not match are an indication that the data has changed, in which case the frame is dropped. A change in the data could be the result of a disruption of the electrical signals that represent the bits.

Interactive Graphic

Check Your Understanding—Ethernet Frame (21.2.5)

Refer to the online course to complete this activity.

Lab—View Captured Traffic in Wireshark (21.2.6)

In this lab, you will complete the following objectives:

- Download and install Wireshark.
- Capture and analyze ARP data in Wireshark.
- View the ARP cache entries on the PC.

Refer to the online course to complete this lab.

Lab—Use Wireshark to Examine Ethernet Frames (21.2.7)

In this lab, you will complete the following objectives:

- Part 1: Examine the Header Fields in an Ethernet II Frame
- Part 2: Use Wireshark to Capture and Analyze Ethernet Frames

Refer to the online course to complete this lab.

Ethernet MAC Address (21.3)

Ethernet technology relies on MAC addresses to function. MAC addresses are used to identify the frame source and destination.

MAC Address and Hexadecimal (21.3.1)

In networking, IPv4 addresses are represented using the decimal (base 10) number system and the binary (base 2) number system. IPv6 addresses and Ethernet addresses are represented using the hexadecimal (base 16) number system. To understand hexadecimal, you must first be very familiar with binary and decimal.

The hexadecimal number system uses the numbers 0 to 9 and the letters A to F.

An Ethernet MAC address consists of a 48-bit binary value. Hexadecimal is used to identify an Ethernet address because a single hexadecimal digit represents 4 binary bits. Therefore, a 48-bit Ethernet MAC address can be expressed using only 12 hexadecimal values.

Figure 21-6 compares the equivalent decimal and hexadecimal values for binary 0000 to 1111.

Given that 8 bits (1 byte) is a common binary grouping, binary 00000000 to 11111111 can be represented in hexadecimal as the range 00 to FF, as shown in the Figure 21-7.

Decimal	Binary	Hexadecimal
0	0000	0
1	0001	1
2	0010	2
3	0011	3
4	0100	4
5	0101	5
6	0110	6
7	0111	7
8	1000	8
9	1001	9
10	1010	A
11	1011	B
12	1100	C
13	1101	D
14	1110	E
15	1111	F

Figure 21-6 Decimal to Binary to Hexadecimal Conversion

Decimal	Binary	Hexadecimal
0	0000 0000	00
1	0000 0001	01
2	0000 0010	02
3	0000 0011	03
4	0000 0100	04
5	0000 0101	05
6	0000 0110	06
7	0000 0111	07
8	0000 1000	08
10	0000 1010	0A
15	0000 1111	0F
16	0001 0000	10
32	0010 0000	20
64	0100 0000	40
128	1000 0000	80
192	1100 0000	C0
202	1100 1010	CA
240	1111 0000	F0
255	1111 1111	FF

Figure 21-7 Selected Examples of Decimal to Binary to Hexadecimal Conversions

When using hexadecimal, leading zeros are always displayed to complete the 8-bit representation. For example, in Figure 21-7, the binary value 0000 1010 is shown in hexadecimal as 0A.

Hexadecimal numbers are often represented by the value preceded by 0x (for example, 0x73) to distinguish between decimal and hexadecimal values in documentation. Hexadecimal may also be represented by using a subscript 16 or by using the hex number followed by an H (for example, 73H).

If you ever have to convert between decimal and hexadecimal values, first convert the decimal or hexadecimal value to binary and then convert the binary value to either decimal or hexadecimal as appropriate.

Unicast MAC Address (21.3.2)

In Ethernet, different MAC addresses are used for Layer 2 unicast, broadcast, and multicast communications.

A unicast MAC address is the unique address that is used when a frame is sent from a single transmitting device to a single destination device.

In Figure 21-8, the destination MAC address and the destination IP address are both unicast.

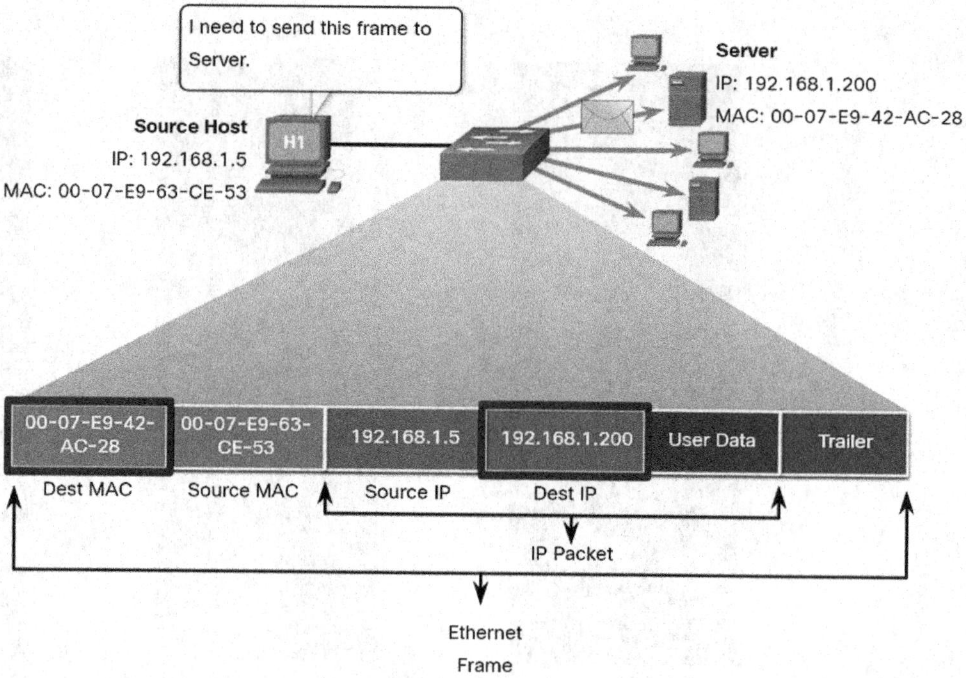

Figure 21-8 Unicast Frame Transmission

In the example shown in Figure 21-8, a host with IPv4 address 192.168.1.5 (source) requests a web page from the server at IPv4 unicast address 192.168.1.200. For a unicast packet to be sent and received, a destination IP address must be in the IP packet header. A corresponding destination MAC address must also be present in the Ethernet frame header. The IP address and MAC address combine to deliver data to one specific destination host.

The process that a source host uses to determine the destination MAC address associated with an IPv4 address is known as Address Resolution Protocol (ARP). The process that a source host uses to determine the destination MAC address associated with an IPv6 address is known as Neighbor Discovery (ND).

Note

The source MAC address must always be a unicast.

Broadcast MAC Address (21.3.3)

An Ethernet broadcast frame is received and processed by every device on the Ethernet LAN. The features of an Ethernet broadcast are as follows:

- It has a destination MAC address of FF-FF-FF-FF-FF-FF in hexadecimal (48 1s in binary).
- It is flooded out all Ethernet switch ports except the incoming port.
- It is not forwarded by a router.

If the encapsulated data is an IPv4 broadcast packet, this means the packet contains a destination IPv4 address that has all 1s in the host portion. This numbering in the address means that all hosts on that local network (broadcast domain) receive and process the packet.

In Figure 21-9, the destination MAC address and destination IP address are both broadcasts.

As shown in Figure 21-9, the source host sends an IPv4 broadcast packet to all devices on its network. The IPv4 destination address is a broadcast address, 192.168.1.255. When the IPv4 broadcast packet is encapsulated in the Ethernet frame, the destination MAC address is the broadcast MAC address of FF-FF-FF-FF-FF-FF in hexadecimal (48 1s in binary).

DHCP for IPv4 is an example of a protocol that uses Ethernet and IPv4 broadcast addresses.

However, not all Ethernet broadcasts carry an IPv4 broadcast packet. For example, ARP requests do not use IPv4, but the ARP message is sent as an Ethernet broadcast.

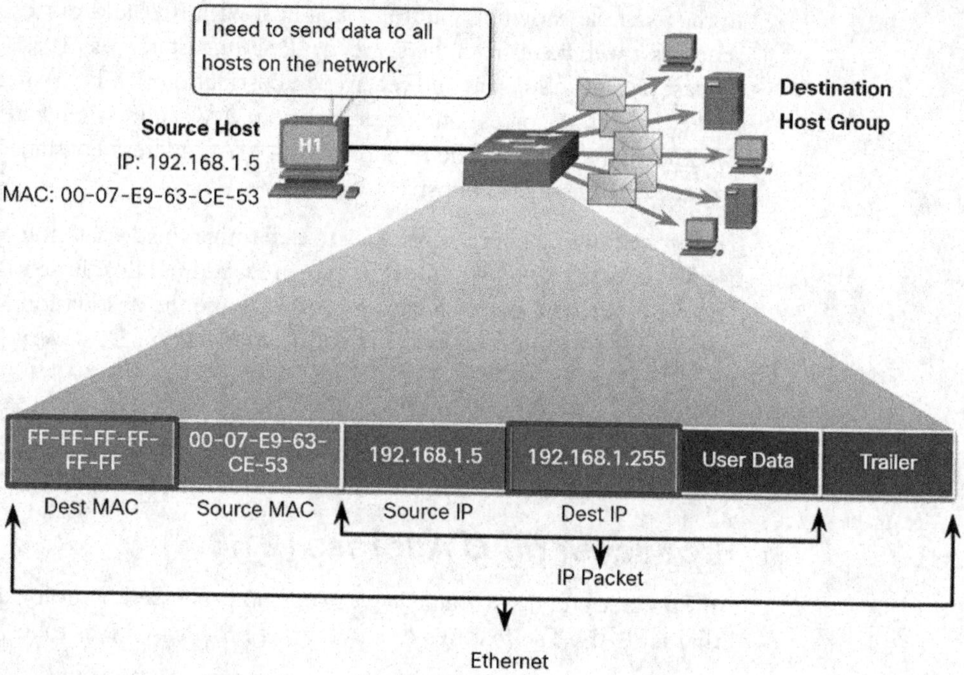

Figure 21-9 Broadcast Frame Transmission

Multicast MAC Address (21.3.4)

An Ethernet multicast frame is received and processed by a group of devices on the Ethernet LAN that belong to the same multicast group. The features of an Ethernet multicast are as follows:

- Its destination MAC address is 01-00-5E when the encapsulated data is an IPv4 multicast packet and is 33-33 when the encapsulated data is an IPv6 multicast packet.
- There are other reserved multicast destination MAC addresses for when the encapsulated data is not IP, such as Spanning Tree Protocol (STP) and Link Layer Discovery Protocol (LLDP).
- It is flooded out all Ethernet switch ports except the incoming port, unless the switch is configured for multicast snooping.
- It is not forwarded by a router unless the router is configured to route multicast packets.

If the encapsulated data is an IP multicast packet, the devices that belong to a multicast group are assigned a multicast group IP address. The range of IPv4 multicast addresses is 224.0.0.0 to 239.255.255.255. The range of IPv6 multicast addresses begins with ff00::/8. Because a multicast address represents a group of addresses (sometimes called a host group), it can be used only as the destination of a packet. The source is always a unicast address.

As with the unicast and broadcast addresses, a multicast IP address requires a corresponding multicast MAC address to deliver frames on a local network. The multicast MAC address is associated with, and uses addressing information from, the IPv4 or IPv6 multicast address.

In Figure 21-10, the destination MAC address and destination IP address are both multicasts.

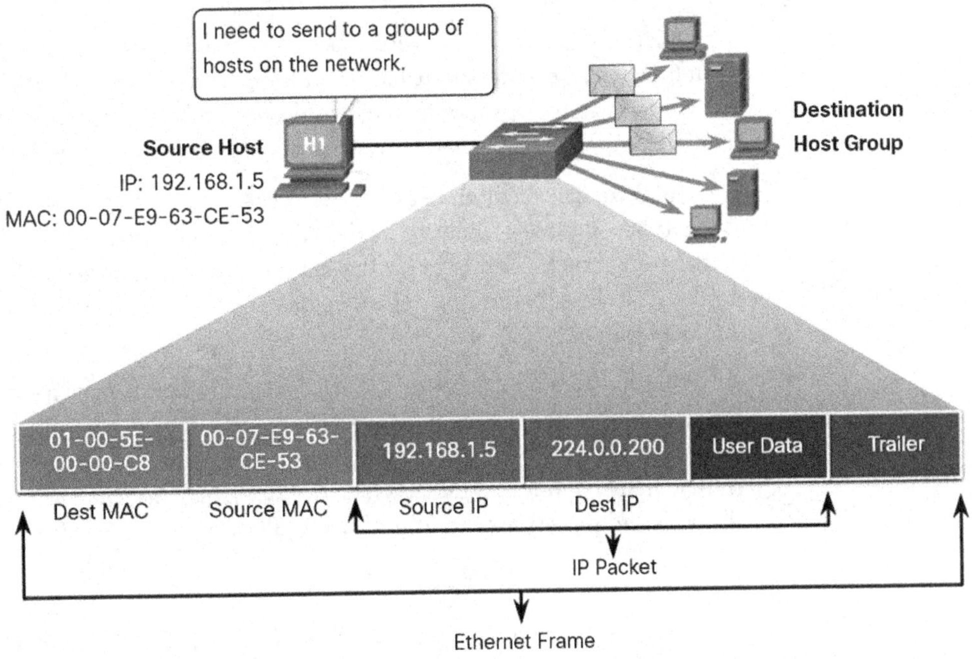

Figure 21-10 Multicast Frame Transmission

Routing protocols and other network protocols use multicast addressing. Applications such as video and imaging software may also use multicast addressing, although multicast applications are not as common.

Interactive Graphic

Check Your Understanding—Ethernet MAC Address (21.3.5)

Refer to the online course to complete this activity.

The MAC Address Table (21.4)

Compared to legacy Ethernet hubs, Ethernet switches improve efficiency and overall network performance. Although traditionally most LAN switches operate at Layer 2 of the OSI model, an increasing number of Layer 3 switches are now being implemented. This section focuses on Layer 2 switches. Layer 3 switches are beyond the scope of this book.

Switch Fundamentals (21.4.1)

Now that you know all about Ethernet MAC addresses, it is time to talk about how a switch uses these addresses to forward (or discard) frames to other devices on a network. If a switch just forwarded every frame it received out all ports, your network would be so congested that it would probably come to a complete halt.

A Layer 2 Ethernet switch uses Layer 2 MAC addresses to make forwarding decisions. It is completely unaware of the data (protocol) being carried in the data portion of the frame, such as an IPv4 packet, an ARP message, or an IPv6 ND packet. The switch makes its forwarding decisions based solely on the Layer 2 Ethernet MAC addresses.

An Ethernet switch examines its MAC address table to make a forwarding decision for each frame, unlike legacy Ethernet hubs that repeat bits out all ports except the incoming port. In Figure 21-11, the four-port switch was just powered on. The table shows the MAC address table, which is empty because the switch has not yet learned the MAC addresses for the four attached PCs.

Note

MAC addresses are shortened throughout this topic for demonstration purposes.

The switch MAC address table is empty.

Note

The MAC address table is sometimes referred to as a *content-addressable memory (CAM) table*. While the term *CAM table* is fairly common, for the purposes of this course, we will refer to it as a MAC address table.

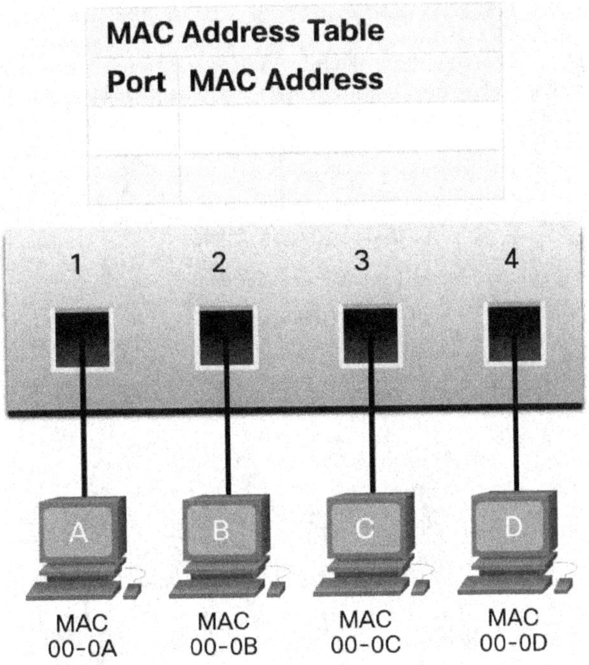

Figure 21-11 Switch Powers Up with an Empty MAC Address Table

Switch Learning and Forwarding (21.4.2)

A switch dynamically builds its MAC address table by examining the source MAC addresses of the frames received on a port. The switch forwards frames by searching for a match between the destination MAC address in the frame and an entry in the MAC address table.

Examine the Source MAC Address

A switch checks every frame that enters it for new information to learn. It does this by examining the source MAC address of the frame and the number of the port through which the frame entered the switch. If the source MAC address does not exist, the switch adds it to the table along with the incoming port number. If the source MAC address does exist, the switch updates the refresh timer for that entry in the table. By default, most Ethernet switches keep an entry in the table for 5 minutes.

In Figure 21-12, for example, PC-A is sending an Ethernet frame to PC-D. The MAC address table shows that the switch adds the incoming port number and MAC address for PC-A to the MAC address table.

Note

If the source MAC address exists in the table but on a different port, the switch treats this as a new entry. It replaces the entry using the same MAC address but with the more current port number.

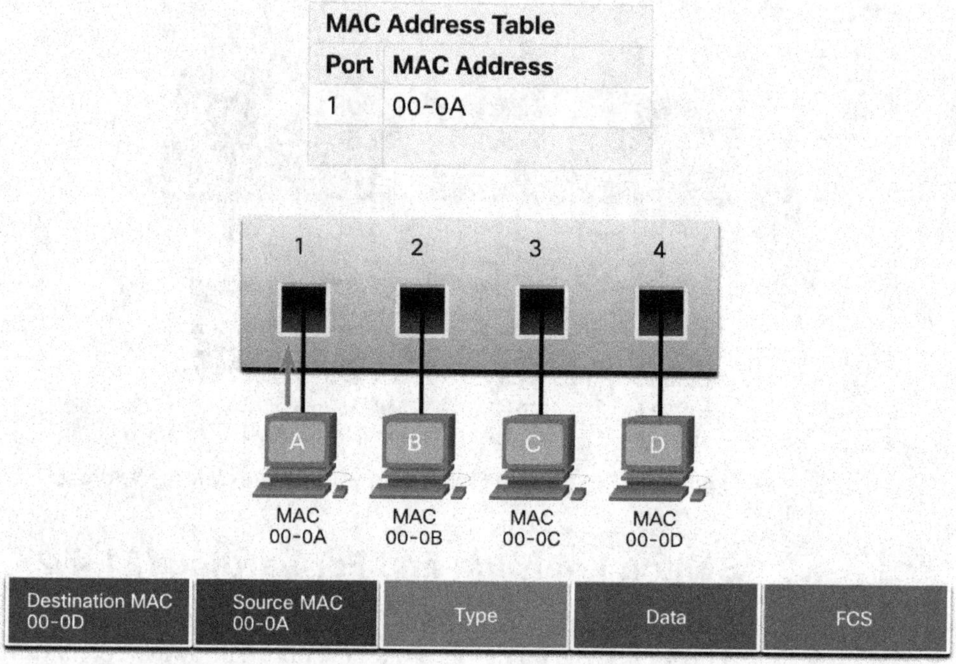

Figure 21-12 Switch Learns the MAC Address for PC-A

1. PC-A sends an Ethernet frame.
2. The switch adds the port number and MAC address for PC-A to the MAC address table.

Find the Destination MAC Address

If the destination MAC address is a unicast address, the switch looks for a match between the destination MAC address of the frame and an entry in its MAC address table. If the destination MAC address is in the table, the switch forwards the frame out the specified port. If the destination MAC address is not in the table, the switch forwards the frame out all ports except the incoming port. This is called an *unknown unicast*.

As shown in Figure 21-13, the switch does not have the destination MAC address in its table for PC-D, so it sends the frame out all ports except port 1.

Note

If the destination MAC address is a broadcast or a multicast, the frame is also flooded out all ports except the incoming port.

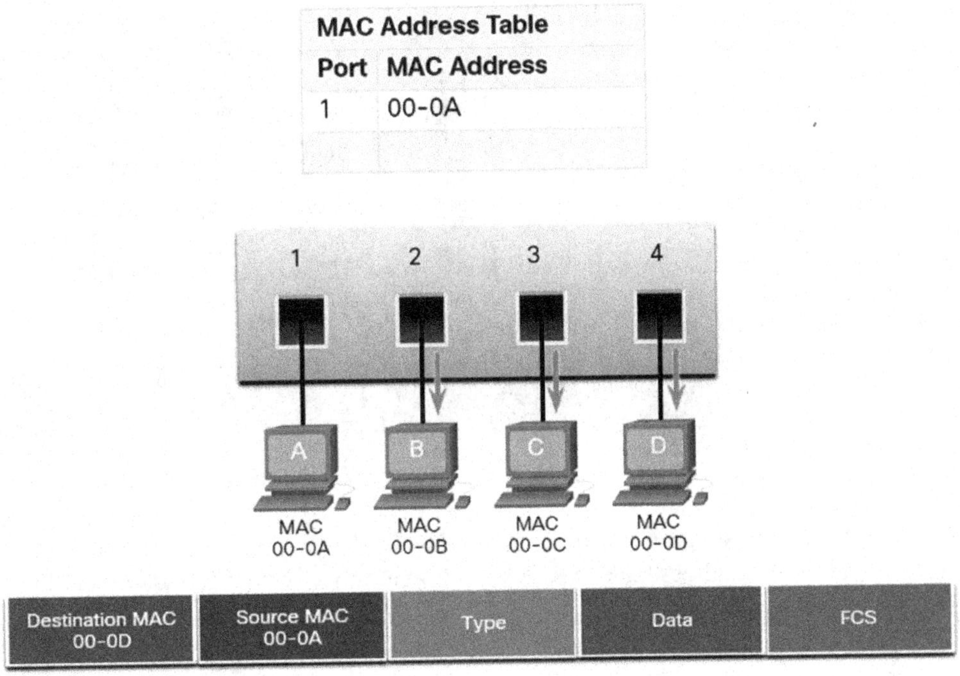

Figure 21-13 Switch Forwards the Frame Out All Other Ports

1. The destination MAC address is not in the table.
2. The switch forwards the frame out all other ports.

Filtering Frames (21.4.3)

As a switch receives frames from different devices, it is able to populate its MAC address table by examining the source MAC address of every frame. When the MAC address table of the switch contains the destination MAC address, the switch can filter the frame and forward it out a single port.

In Figure 21-14, PC-D is replying to PC-A. The switch sees the MAC address of PC-D in the incoming frame on port 4. The switch then puts the MAC address of PC-D associated with port 4 into the MAC address table.

MAC Address Table	
Port	**MAC Address**
1	00-0A
4	00-0D

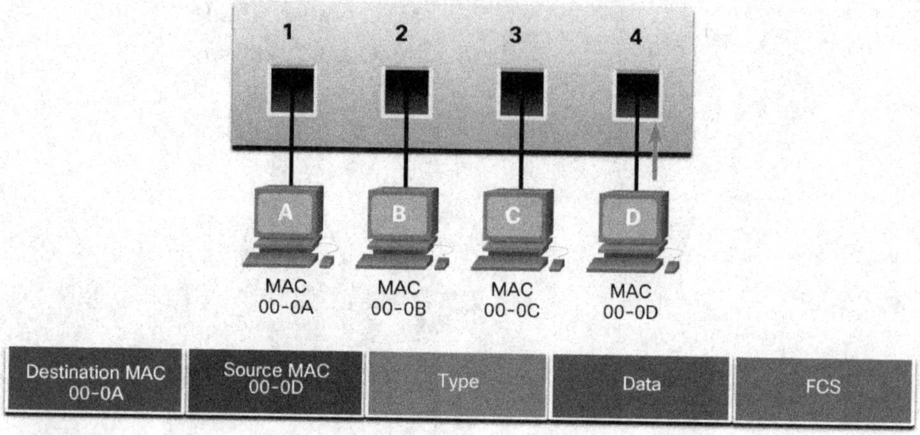

Figure 21-14 Switch Learns the MAC Address for PC-D

Next, because the switch has the destination MAC address for PC-A in the MAC address table, it sends the frame only out port 1, as shown in Figure 21-15.

MAC Address Table	
Port	**MAC Address**
1	00-0A
4	00-0D

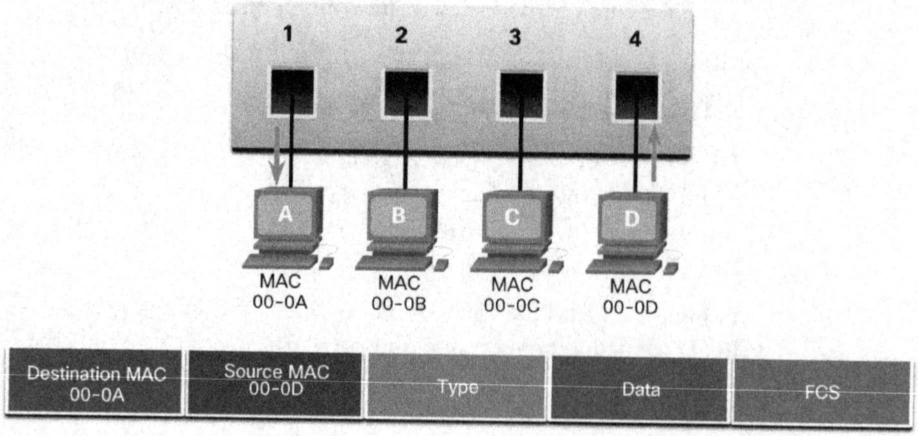

Figure 21-15 Switch Forwards the Frame Out the Port Belonging to PC-A

1. The switch has a MAC address entry for the destination.
2. The switch filters the frame, sending it only out port 1.

Next, PC-A sends another frame to PC-D, as shown in Figure 21-16. The MAC address table already contains the MAC address for PC-A; therefore, the 5-minute refresh timer for that entry is reset. Next, because the switch table contains the destination MAC address for PC-D, it sends the frame only out port 4.

MAC Address Table	
Port	**MAC Address**
1	00-0A
4	00-0D

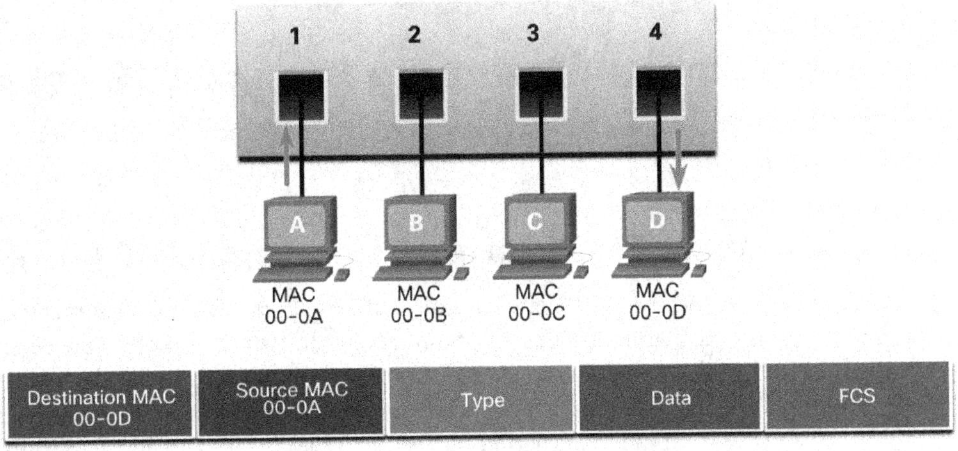

Figure 21-16 Switch Forwards the Frame Out the Port Belonging to PC-D

1. The switch receives another frame from PC-A and refreshes the timer for the MAC address entry for port 1.
2. The switch has a recent entry for the destination MAC address and filters the frame, forwarding it only out port 4.

Video

Video—MAC Address Tables on Connected Switches (21.4.4)

A switch can have multiple MAC addresses associated with a single port. This is common when the switch is connected to another switch. The switch will have a separate MAC address table entry for each frame received with a different source MAC address.

Refer to the online course to view this video.

Video

Video—Sending the Frame to the Default Gateway (21.4.5)

When a device has an IP address that is on a remote network, the Ethernet frame cannot be sent directly to the destination device. Instead, the Ethernet frame is sent to the MAC address of the default gateway, the router.

Refer to the online course to view this video.

Interactive Graphic

Activity—Switch It! (21.4.6)

Use this activity to check your understanding of how a switch learns and forwards frames.

Refer to the online course to complete this activity.

Ethernet Switching Summary (21.5)

The following is a summary of each topic in the chapter and some questions for your reflection.

What Did I Learn in This Chapter? (21.5.1)

- **Ethernet**—There is no official local area networking standard protocol, but Ethernet has become more common than the others. Ethernet protocols define how data is formatted and how it is transmitted over the wired network. The Ethernet standards specify protocols that operate at Layer 1 and Layer 2 of the OSI model. Ethernet has become the de facto standard used by almost all wired LANs.

  IEEE maintains the networking standards, including Ethernet and wireless standards. Each technology standard is assigned a number that refers to the committee that is responsible for approving and maintaining the standard. The 802.3 Ethernet standard has improved over time.

  Ethernet switches can send a frame out all ports (excluding the port it was received from). Each host that receives this frame examines the destination MAC address and compares it to its own MAC address. It is the Ethernet NIC that examines and compares the MAC address. If it does not match the host MAC address, the rest of the frame is ignored. When it is a match, that host receives the rest of the frame and the message it contains.

- **Ethernet Frames**—Ethernet is defined by data link layer 802.2 and 802.3 protocols. Ethernet supports data bandwidths from 10 Mbps up to 100 Gbps.

IEEE 802 LAN/MAN protocols, including Ethernet, use two separate sublayers of the data link layer to operate:

- **LLC sublayer**—This IEEE 802.2 sublayer communicates between the networking software at the upper layers and the device hardware at the lower layers. It places information in the frame that identifies which network layer protocol is being used for the frame. This information allows multiple Layer 3 protocols, such as IPv4 and IPv6, to use the same network interface and media.
- **MAC sublayer**—This sublayer (IEEE 802.3, 802.11, or 802.15, for example) is implemented in hardware and is responsible for data encapsulation and media access control. It provides data link layer addressing and is integrated with various physical layer technologies. Data encapsulation includes the Ethernet frame, Ethernet addressing, and Ethernet error detection.

Ethernet LANs of today use switches that operate in full-duplex. Full-duplex communications with Ethernet switches do not require access control through CSMA/CD. The minimum Ethernet frame size is 64 bytes, and the expected maximum is 1518 bytes. The fields are Preamble and Start Frame Delimiter, Destination MAC Address, Source MAC Address, Type/Length, Data, and FCS. This includes all bytes from the Destination MAC Address field through the FCS field.

- **Ethernet MAC Address**—An Ethernet MAC address consists of a 48-bit binary value. Hexadecimal is used to identify an Ethernet address because a single hexadecimal digit represents 4 binary bits. Therefore, a 48-bit Ethernet MAC address can be expressed using only 12 hexadecimal values.

  A unicast MAC address is the unique address that is used when a frame is sent from a single transmitting device to a single destination device. A source host uses ARP to determine the destination MAC address associated with an IPv4 address. A source host uses Neighbor Discovery to determine the destination MAC address associated with an IPv6 address.

  The features of an Ethernet broadcast are as follows:

  - It has a destination MAC address of FF-FF-FF-FF-FF-FF in hexadecimal (48 1s in binary).
  - It is flooded out all Ethernet switch ports except the incoming port.
  - It is not forwarded by a router.

  The features of an Ethernet multicast are as follows:

  - There is a destination MAC address of 01-00-5E when the encapsulated data is an IPv4 multicast packet and a destination MAC address of 33-33 when the encapsulated data is an IPv6 multicast packet.

- There are other reserved multicast destination MAC addresses for when the encapsulated data is not IP, such as STP and LLDP.
- It is flooded out all Ethernet switch ports except the incoming port, unless the switch is configured for multicast snooping.
- It is not forwarded by a router unless the router is configured to route multicast packets.

- **The MAC Address Table**—A Layer 2 Ethernet switch uses Layer 2 MAC addresses to make forwarding decisions. It is completely unaware of the data (protocol) being carried in the data portion of the frame. An Ethernet switch examines its MAC address table (or CAM table) to make a forwarding decision for each frame.

  A switch dynamically builds its MAC address table by examining the source MAC addresses of the frames received on a port. The switch forwards frames by searching for a match between the destination MAC address in the frame and an entry in the MAC address table. If the destination MAC address is a unicast address, the switch looks for a match between the destination MAC address of the frame and an entry in its MAC address table. If the destination MAC address is in the table, the switch forwards the frame out the specified port. If the destination MAC address is not in the table, the switch forwards the frame out all ports except the incoming port. This is called an unknown unicast.

  As a switch receives frames from different devices, it is able to populate its MAC address table by examining the source MAC address of every frame. When the MAC address table of the switch contains the destination MAC address, the switch can filter the frame and forward it out a single port. A switch can have multiple MAC addresses associated with a single port, which is common when the switch is connected to another switch. The switch will have a separate MAC address table entry for each frame received with a different source MAC address. When a device has an IP address that is on a remote network, the Ethernet frame cannot be sent directly to the destination device. Instead, the Ethernet frame is sent to the MAC address of the default gateway, the router.

Reflection Questions (21.5.2)

Marcy and Vincent previously had no idea how their small business network operates. It's not much more complicated than my own home network. Until recently, I did not realize that protocols ensure how my devices interact with each other and with the Internet. Think about your home network, or the network at school or work. Do you understand the difference between your device's IP address and its MAC address? How does this knowledge help you better understand how your network operates?

Practice

The following lab activities provide practice with the topics introduced in this chapter.

Labs

Lab—Determine the MAC Address of a Host (21.1.4)

Lab—View Captured Traffic in Wireshark (21.2.6)

Lab—Use Wireshark to Examine Ethernet Frames (21.2.7)

Check Your Understanding Questions

Complete all the review questions listed here to test your understanding of the topics and concepts in this chapter. Appendix A, "Answers to 'Check Your Understanding' Questions," lists the answers.

1. What is encapsulated in the Data field of an Ethernet frame?

   a. The Layer 3 PDU
   b. A cyclic redundancy check value
   c. The encoded physical layer bits
   d. The source and destination MAC addresses

2. What is the length restriction of the Data field in an Ethernet frame?

   a. Between 0 to 1500 bytes
   b. Between 46 to 1500 bytes
   c. Between 64 to 1518 bytes
   d. Between 64 to 1548 bytes

3. Refer to the following figure. What is the MAC address of this computer?

```
C:\>ipconfig /all

Windows IP Configuration

   Host Name . . . . . . . . . . . . : PC
   Primary Dns Suffix  . . . . . . . :
   Node Type . . . . . . . . . . . . : Hybrid
   IP Routing Enabled. . . . . . . . : No
   WINS Proxy Enabled. . . . . . . . : No
   DNS Suffix Search List. . . . . . : farfaraway.com

Ethernet adapter Local:

   Connection-specific DNS Suffix  . : farfaraway.com
   Description . . . . . . . . . . . : Ethernet Family Controller
   Physical Address. . . . . . . . . : 87-52-25-78-0F-3A
   DHCP Enabled. . . . . . . . . . . : Yes
   Autoconfiguration Enabled . . . . : Yes
   Link-local IPv6 Address . . . . . : fe80::740c:63a6:e9df:c700%10(Preferred)
   IPv4 Address. . . . . . . . . . . : 10.0.0.24(Preferred)
   Subnet Mask . . . . . . . . . . . : 255.255.255.0
   Lease Obtained. . . . . . . . . . : Sunday, September 25, 2013 09:00:08 AM
   Lease Expires . . . . . . . . . . : Monday, September 26, 2149 07:38:39 PM
   Default Gateway . . . . . . . . . : 10.0.0.1
   DHCP Server . . . . . . . . . . . : 10.0.0.1
   DHCPv6 IAID . . . . . . . . . . . : 239622969
   DHCPv6 Client DUID. . . . . . . . : 00-01-00-01-15-15-BD-53-48-5B-39-A6-0F-3A
   DNS Servers . . . . . . . . . . . : fec0:0:0:ffff::1%1
   NetBIOS over Tcpip. . . . . . . . : Enabled
```

a. 00-01-00-01-15-15-BD-53-48-5B-39-A6-0F-3A

b. 87-52-25-78-0F-3A

c. fe80::740c:63a6:e9df:c700

d. fec0:0:0:ffff::1

4. Which Ethernet sublayer is used to control network access using CSMA/CD?

a. LLC

b. MAC

c. Data link

d. Physical

5. What addressing information is recorded by a switch to build its MAC address table?

a. The destination Layer 3 address of incoming packets

b. The destination Layer 2 address of outgoing frames

c. The source Layer 3 address of outgoing packets

d. The source Layer 2 address of incoming frames

6. What important information does a Layer 2 device examine in the Ethernet frame header in order to forward the data onward?

a. Source MAC address

b. Source IP address

c. Destination MAC address

d. Ethernet type
e. Destination IP address

7. What happens to a runt frame received by a Cisco Ethernet switch?
   a. The frame is dropped.
   b. The frame is returned to the originating network device.
   c. The frame is broadcast to all other devices on the same network.
   d. The frame is sent to the default gateway.

8. What is indicated by the 100 in the 100BASE-T standard?
   a. Meters
   b. Feet
   c. Megabits per second
   d. Twists per meter

9. Which three fields are found in an 802.3 Ethernet frame? (Choose three.)
   a. Source MAC Address
   b. Source Logical Address
   c. Media Type Identifier
   d. Frame Check Sequence
   e. Destination MAC Address
   f. Destination Logical Address

10. Match the components in the notation 100BASE-T to the specification.
   - 100
   - BASE
   - T

   a. Baseband transmission
   b. Twisted-pair cable
   c. Speed in Mbps

11. Which two characteristics describe Ethernet technology? (Choose two.)
   a. It is supported by IEEE 802.3 standards.
   b. It is supported by IEEE 802.5 standards.
   c. It typically uses an average of 16 Mbps for data transfer rates.

d. It uses unique MAC addresses to ensure that data is sent to the appropriate destination.

e. It uses a ring topology.

12. What does a host on an Ethernet network do if it receives a frame with a unicast destination MAC address that does not match its own MAC address?

a. It discards the frame.

b. It forwards the frame to the next host.

c. It sends an error message to the sender.

d. It strips off the data-link frame to check the destination IP address.

CHAPTER 22

Network Layer

Objectives

Upon completion of this chapter, you will be able to answer the following questions:

- How does the network layer use IP protocols for reliable communications?
- What is the role of the major header fields in the IPv4 packet?
- What is the role of the major header fields in the IPv6 packet?

Key Terms

This chapter uses the following key terms. You can find the definitions in the Glossary.

best effort Page 347

connectionless Page 347

fragmentation Page 350

Internet Control Message Protocol (ICMP) Page 351

maximum transmission unit (MTU) Page 350

media independent Page 347

routing Page 345

Introduction (22.0)

Hi again! Bob also had to learn a lot about the network layer in his courses before he became an IT specialist. The network layer, or OSI Layer 3, provides services that allow end devices to exchange data across networks. IPv4 and IPv6 are the principal network layer communication protocols. Network layer protocols perform four operations: addressing end devices, encapsulation, routing, and de-encapsulation.

That sounds like a lot of information to people who do not have much knowledge of networking, such as Marcy and Vincent! Does it sound overwhelming to you? This chapter will help you to understand the network layer.

Network Layer Characteristics (22.1)

This section introduces the protocols and elementary functions of the network layer. The primary function of the network layer is to facilitate the transport of data from one network to another.

Video

Video—Data Encapsulation (22.1.1)

Refer to the online course to view this video.

The Network Layer (22.1.2)

The network layer, or OSI Layer 3, provides services that allow end devices to exchange data across networks. As shown in Figure 22-1, IP version 4 (IPv4) and IP version 6 (IPv6) are the principle network layer communication protocols. Other network layer protocols include routing protocols such as Open Shortest Path First (OSPF) and messaging protocols such as Internet Control Message Protocol (ICMP).

To accomplish end-to-end communications across network boundaries, network layer protocols perform four basic operations:

- **Addressing end devices**—Each end device must be configured with a unique IP address for identification on the network.
- **Encapsulation**—The network layer encapsulates the protocol data unit (PDU) from the transport layer into a packet. The encapsulation process adds IP packet header information, such as the IP address of the source (sending) and destination (receiving) hosts. The encapsulation process is performed by the source of the IP packet.

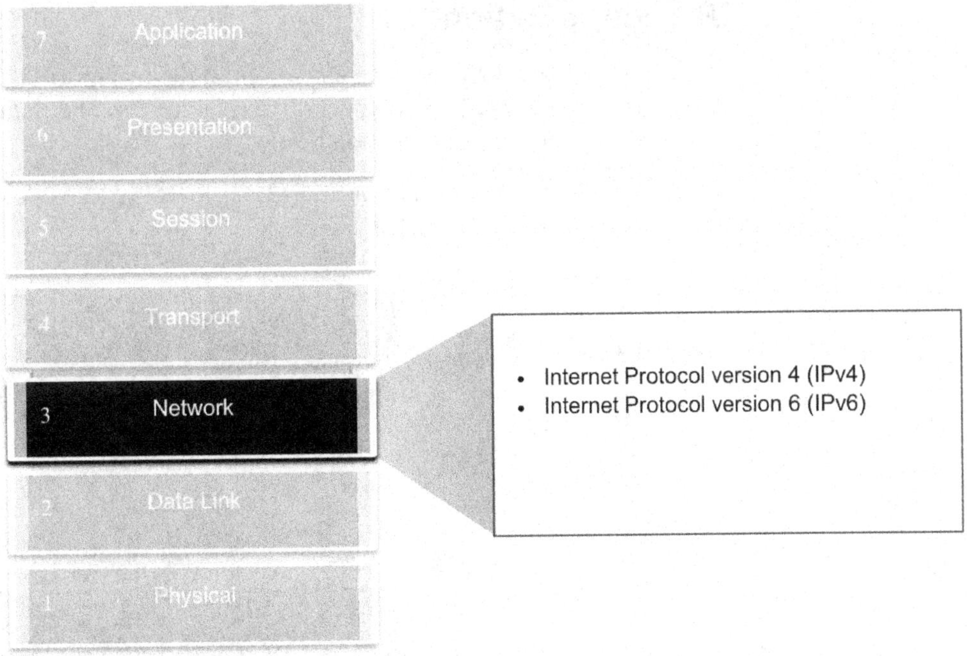

Figure 22-1 Network Layer of the OSI Model

- *Routing*—The network layer provides services to direct the packets to a destination host on another network. To travel to other networks, the packet must be processed by a router. The role of the router is to select the best path and direct packets toward the destination host in a process known as *routing*. A packet may cross many routers before reaching the destination host. Each router a packet crosses to reach the destination host is called a *hop*.
- **De-encapsulation**—When the packet arrives at the network layer of the destination host, the host checks the IP header of the packet. If the destination IP address in the header matches its own IP address, the IP header is removed from the packet. After the packet is de-encapsulated by the network layer, the resulting Layer 4 PDU is passed up to the appropriate service at the transport layer. The de-encapsulation process is performed by the destination host of the IP packet.

Unlike the transport layer (OSI Layer 4), which manages the data transport between the processes running on each host, network layer communication protocols (that is, IPv4 and IPv6) specify the packet structure and the processing used to carry the data from one host to another host. Operating without regard to the data carried in each packet allows the network layer to carry packets for multiple types of communications between multiple hosts.

IP Encapsulation (22.1.3)

IP encapsulates the segment or other data from the transport layer (the layer just above the network layer) by adding an IP packet header. The IP header is used to deliver the packet to the destination host.

Figure 22-2 illustrates how the transport layer PDU is encapsulated by the network layer PDU to create an IP packet.

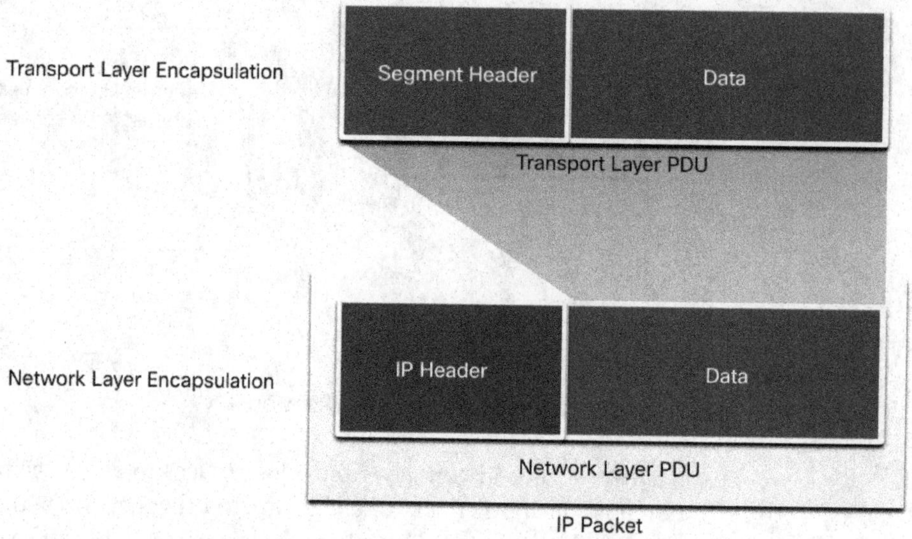

Figure 22-2 Transport Layer Encapsulated in the Network Layer

The process of encapsulating data layer by layer enables the services at the different layers to develop and scale without affecting the other layers. This means the transport layer segments can be readily packaged by IPv4 or IPv6 or by any new protocol that might be developed in the future.

The IP header is examined by Layer 3 devices (that is, routers and Layer 3 switches) as it travels across a network to its destination. It is important to note that the IP addressing information remains the same from the time the packet leaves the source host until it arrives at the destination host, except when translated by the device performing Network Address Translation (NAT) for IPv4.

Note

NAT is discussed in Chapter 12.

Routers implement routing protocols to route packets between networks. The routing performed by these intermediary devices examines the network layer addressing in the packet header. In all cases, the data portion of the packet (that is, the encapsulated transport layer PDU or other data) remains unchanged during the network layer processes.

Characteristics of IP (22.1.4)

IP was designed as a protocol with low overhead. It provides only the functions that are necessary to deliver a packet from a source to a destination over an interconnected system of networks. The protocol was not designed to track and manage the flow of packets. These functions, if required, are performed by other protocols at other layers, primarily TCP at Layer 4.

These are the basic characteristics of IP:

- *Connectionless*—No connection is established with the destination before sending data packets.
- *Best effort*—IP is inherently unreliable because packet delivery is not guaranteed.
- *Media independent*—Operation is independent of the medium (that is, copper, fiber-optic, or wireless) carrying the data.

Connectionless (22.1.5)

IP is connectionless, meaning that no dedicated end-to-end connection is created by IP before data is sent. Connectionless communication is conceptually similar to sending a letter to someone without notifying the recipient in advance, as depicted in Figure 22-3.

Connectionless data communications work on the same principle. As shown in Figure 22-4, IP requires no initial exchange of control information to establish an end-to-end connection before packets are forwarded.

Figure 22-3 Letter Analogy of Connectionless Communication

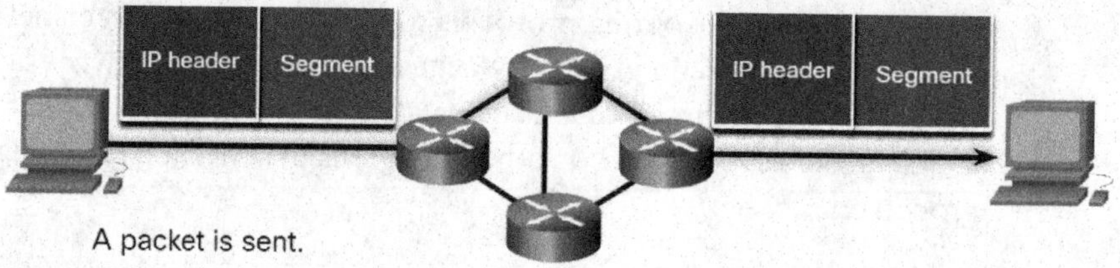

Figure 22-4 IP Is Connectionless

Best Effort (22.1.6)

IP does not require additional fields in the header to maintain an established connection. This process greatly reduces the overhead of IP. However, with no pre-established end-to-end connection, senders are unaware of whether destination devices are present and functional when sending packets, nor are they aware of whether the destination receives the packet or can access and read the packet.

IP does not guarantee that all packets that are delivered are, in fact, received. Figure 22-5 illustrates the unreliable, best-effort delivery characteristic of IP. As an unreliable network layer protocol, IP does not guarantee that all packets that are sent will be received. Other protocols manage the process of tracking packets and ensuring their delivery.

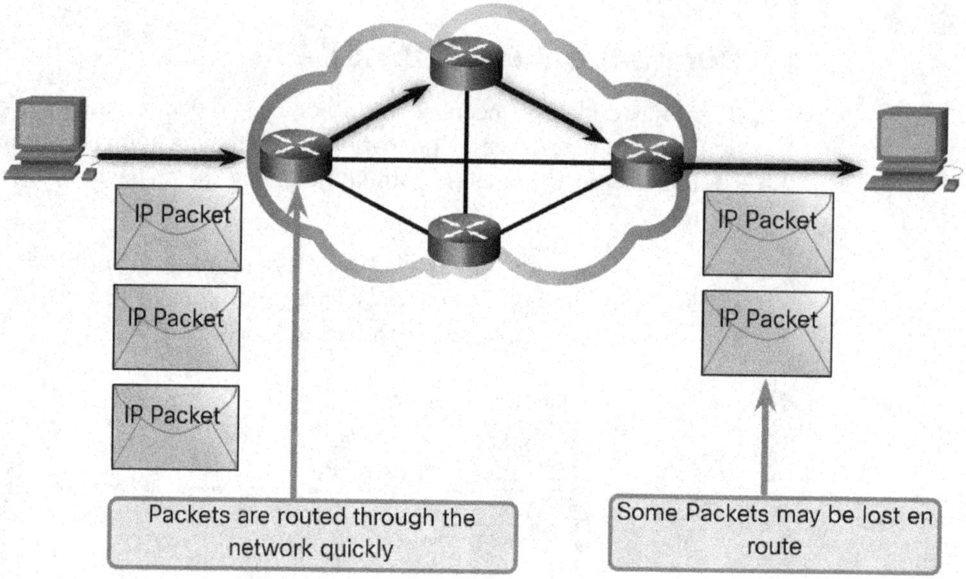

Figure 22-5 Best-Effort Delivery

Media Independent (22.1.7)

Unreliable means that IP does not have the capability to manage and recover from undelivered or corrupt packets. Although IP packets are sent with information about the location of delivery, they do not contain information that can be processed to inform the sender whether delivery was successful. Packets may arrive at the destination corrupted or out of sequence, or not arrive at all. IP provides no capability for packet retransmissions if errors occur.

If out-of-order packets are delivered, or if packets are missing, then applications using the data, or upper-layer services, must resolve these issues. This allows IP to function very efficiently. In the TCP/IP protocol suite, reliability is the role of the TCP protocol at the transport layer.

IP operates independently of the media that carry the data at lower layers of the protocol stack. As shown in Figure 22-6, IP packets can travel over different media. IP packets can be communicated as electronic signals over copper cable, as optical signals over fiber, or wirelessly as radio signals.

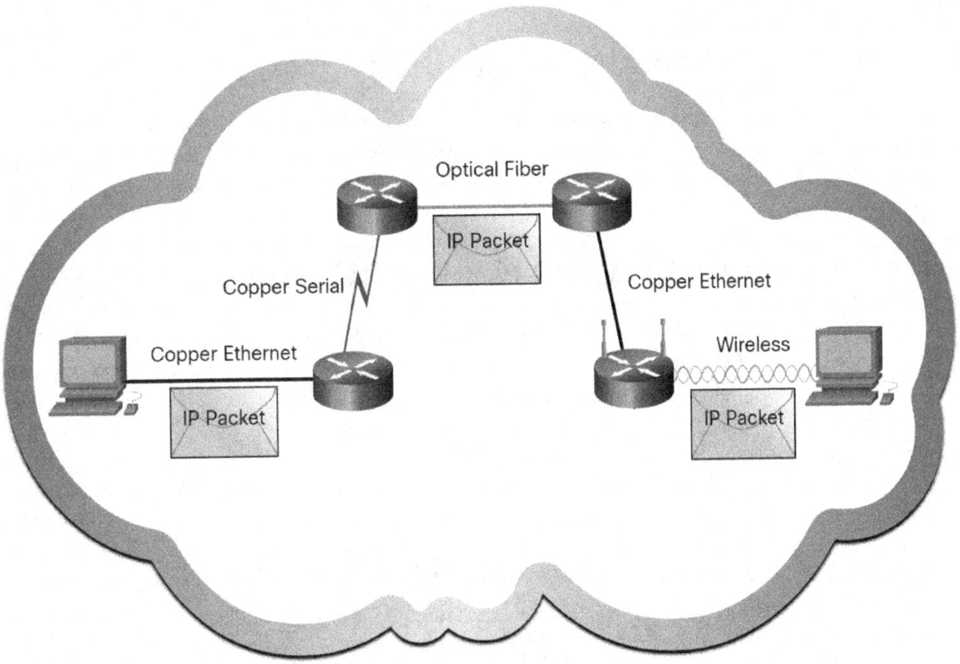

Figure 22-6 IP Packets Cross Multiple Media Types

The OSI data link layer is responsible for preparing an IP packet for transmission over the communications medium. This means that the delivery of IP packets is not limited to any particular medium. However, the network layer does consider one major characteristic of the media: the maximum size of the PDU that each medium can transport. This characteristic is referred to as the *maximum transmission unit (MTU)*. Part of the control communication between the data link layer and the network layer is the establishment of a maximum size for the packet. The data link layer passes the MTU value up to the network layer. The network layer then determines how large packets can be.

In some cases, an intermediate device, usually a router, must split up an IPv4 packet when forwarding it from one medium to another medium with a smaller MTU. This process is called *fragmentation*, or fragmenting the packet. Fragmentation causes latency. IPv6 packets cannot be fragmented by the router.

Interactive Graphic

Check Your Understanding—IP Characteristics (22.1.8)

Refer to the online course to complete this activity.

IPv4 Packet (22.2)

The ability to provide the end-to-end transfer of data by the network layer is based on the content and interpretation of the Layer 3 header. This section examines the structure and contents of the IPv4 packet header.

IPv4 Packet Header (22.2.1)

IPv4 is one of the primary network layer communication protocols. The IPv4 packet header is used to ensure that this packet is delivered to its next stop on the way to its destination end device.

An IPv4 packet header consists of fields containing important information about the packet. These fields contain binary numbers, which are examined by the Layer 3 process.

IPv4 Packet Header Fields (22.2.2)

The binary values of each IPv4 packet header field identify various settings of the IP packet. Protocol header diagrams, which are read left to right and top to bottom, provide a visual to refer to when discussing protocol fields. The IP protocol header diagram in Figure 22-7 identifies the fields of an IPv4 packet.

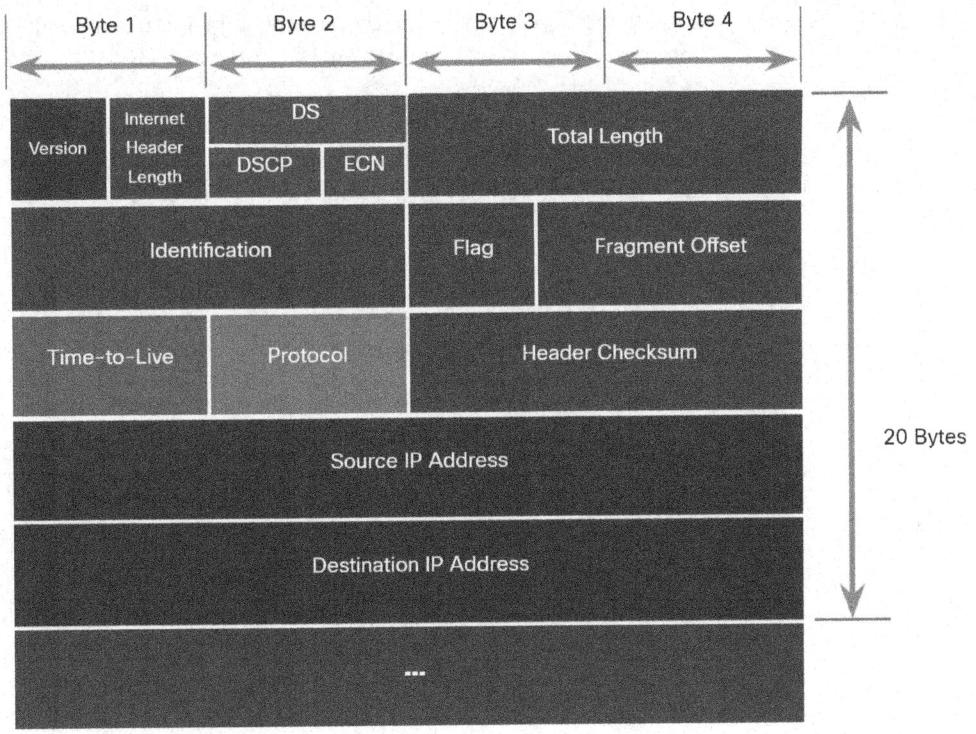

Figure 22-7 IPv4 Packet Header Fields

Significant fields in the IPv4 header include the following:

- **Version**—This field contains a 4-bit binary value set to 0100 that identifies this as an IPv4 packet.
- **Differentiated Services or DiffServ (DS)**—Formerly called the Type of Service (ToS) field, the DS field is an 8-bit field used to determine the priority of each packet. The 6 most significant bits of the DS field are the differentiated services code point (DSCP) bits, and the last 2 bits are the explicit congestion notification (ECN) bits.
- **Time-to-Live (TTL)**—The TTL field contains an 8-bit binary value that is used to limit the lifetime of a packet. The source device of the IPv4 packet sets the initial TTL value. It is decreased by one each time the packet is processed by a router. If the TTL field decrements to 0, the router discards the packet and sends an *Internet Control Message Protocol (ICMP)* Time Exceeded message to the source IP address. Because the router decrements the TTL of each packet, the router must also recalculate the value of the Header Checksum field.
- **Protocol**—This field is used to identify the next-level protocol. This 8-bit binary value indicates the data payload type that the packet is carrying, which enables

the network layer to pass the data to the appropriate upper-layer protocol. Common values include ICMP (1), TCP (6), and UDP (17).

- **Header Checksum**—This field is used to detect corruption in the IPv4 header.
- **Source IPv4 Address**—This field contains a 32-bit binary value that represents the source IPv4 address of the packet. The source IPv4 address is always a unicast address.
- **Destination IPv4 Address**—This field contains a 32-bit binary value that represents the destination IPv4 address of the packet. The destination IPv4 address is a unicast, multicast, or broadcast address.

The two most commonly referenced fields are the Source IP Address and Destination IP Address fields, which identify where the packet is coming from and where it is going. Typically, these addresses do not change while the packet is traveling from the source to the destination.

The Internet Header Length (IHL), Total Length, and Header Checksum fields are used to identify and validate the packet.

Other fields are used to reorder a fragmented packet. Specifically, the IPv4 packet uses Identification, Flags, and Fragment Offset fields to keep track of the fragments. A router may have to fragment an IPv4 packet when forwarding it from one medium to another with a smaller MTU.

The Options and Padding fields are rarely used and are beyond the scope of this chapter.

Video

Video—Sample IPv4 Headers in Wireshark (22.2.3)

Refer to the online course to view this video.

Interactive Graphic

Check Your Understanding—IPv4 Packet (22.2.4)

Refer to the online course to complete this activity.

IPv6 Packet (22.3)

This section introduces the successor of IPv4: IPv6.

Limitations of IPv4 (22.3.1)

IPv4 is still in use today, but IPv6 will eventually replace IPv4. To better understand why you need to know the IPv6 protocol, it helps to know the limitations of IPv4 and the advantages of IPv6.

Through the years, additional protocols and processes have been developed to address new challenges. However, even with changes, IPv4 still has three major issues:

- **IPv4 address depletion**—IPv4 has a limited number of unique public addresses available. Although there are approximately 4 billion IPv4 addresses, the increasing number of new IP-enabled devices, always-on connections, and the potential growth of less-developed regions have increased the need for more addresses.
- **Lack of end-to-end connectivity**—NAT is commonly implemented in IPv4 networks and provides a way for multiple devices to share a single public IPv4 address. However, because the public IPv4 address is shared, the IPv4 address of an internal network host is hidden. This can be problematic for technologies that require end-to-end connectivity.
- **Increased network complexity**—While NAT has extended the lifespan of IPv4, it was designed only as a transition mechanism to IPv6. NAT in its various implementations creates additional complexity in the network, creating latency and making troubleshooting more difficult.

IPv6 Overview (22.3.2)

In the early 1990s, the Internet Engineering Task Force (IETF) grew concerned about the issues with IPv4 and began to look for a replacement. This activity led to the development of IP version 6 (IPv6). IPv6 overcomes the limitations of IPv4 and is a powerful enhancement with features that better suit current and foreseeable network demands.

Improvements that IPv6 provides include the following:

- **Increased address space**—IPv6 addresses are based on 128-bit hierarchical addressing, whereas IPv4 addresses have 32 bits.
- **Improved packet handling**—The IPv6 packet header has been simplified so that it has fewer fields than the IPv4 packet header.
- **Eliminates the need for NAT**—With such a large number of public IPv6 addresses (described next), NAT between a private IPv4 address and a public IPv4 is not needed. This avoids some of the NAT-induced problems experienced by applications that require end-to-end connectivity.

The 32-bit IPv4 address space provides approximately 4,294,967,296 unique addresses. IPv6 address space provides 340,282,366,920,938,463,463,374,607,431, 768,211,456, or 340 undecillion addresses. This is roughly equivalent to every grain of sand on Earth.

Figure 22-8 provides a visual to compare the sizes of the IPv4 address space and IPv6 address space.

Number Name	Scientific Notation	Number of Zeros
1 Thousand	10^3	1,000
1 Million	10^6	1,000,000
1 Billion	10^9	1,000,000,000
1 Trillion	10^12	1,000,000,000,000
1 Quadrillion	10^15	1,000,000,000,000,000
1 Quintillion	10^18	1,000,000,000,000,000,000
1 Sextillion	10^21	1,000,000,000,000,000,000,000
1 Septillion	10^24	1,000,000,000,000,000,000,000,000
1 Octillion	10^27	1,000,000,000,000,000,000,000,000,000
1 Nonillion	10^30	1,000,000,000,000,000,000,000,000,000,000
1 Decillion	10^33	1,000,000,000,000,000,000,000,000,000,000,000
1 Undecillion	10^36	1,000,000,000,000,000,000,000,000,000,000,000,000

Legend

There are 4 billion IPv4 addresses

There are 340 undecillion IPv6 addresses

Figure 22-8 Relative Sizes of IPv4 and IPv6 Address Spaces

IPv4 Packet Header Fields in the IPv6 Packet Header (22.3.3)

One of the major design improvements of IPv6 over IPv4 is the simplified IPv6 packet header.

The IPv4 header consists of a variable-length header of 20 octets (up to 60 bytes if the Options field is used) and 12 basic header fields, not including the Options field and the Padding field.

For the IPv6 packet header, some fields have remained the same, some fields have changed names and positions, and some IPv4 fields are no longer required, as highlighted in Figure 22-9.

In contrast, the simplified IPv6 header shown in Figure 22-10 consists of a fixed-length header of 40 octets (largely due to the length of the source and destination IPv6 addresses).

The IPv6 simplified header allows for more efficient processing of IPv6 headers.

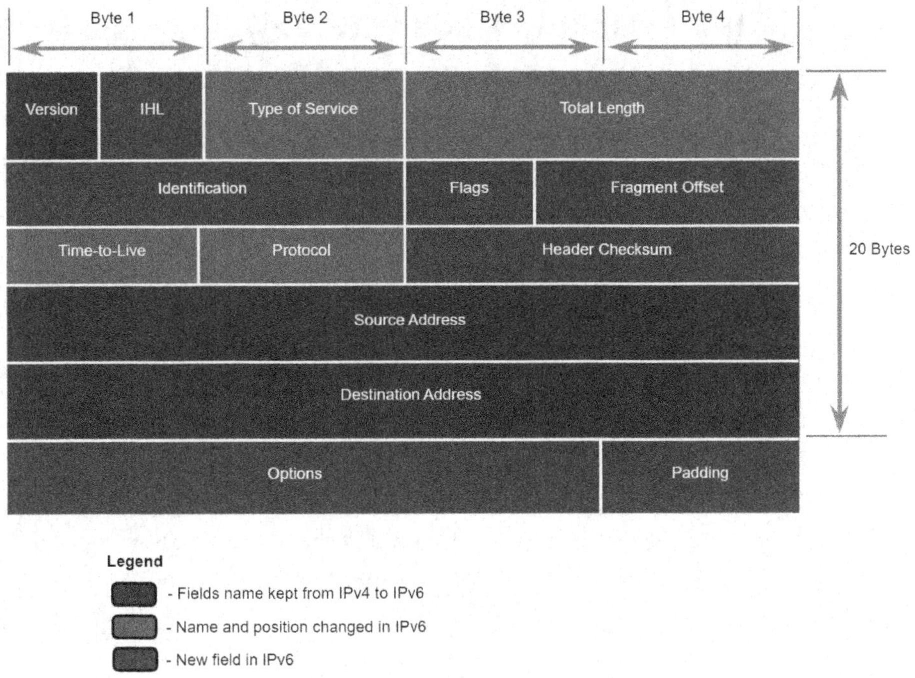

Figure 22-9 IPv4 Fields Kept, Changed, or Removed

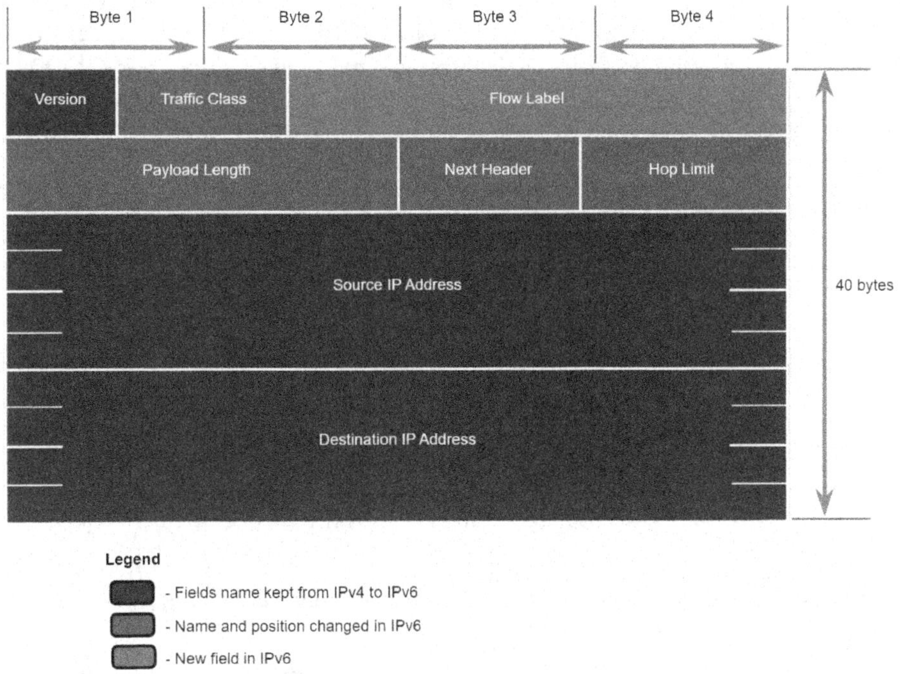

Figure 22-10 IPv6 Packet Header Fields

IPv6 Packet Header (22.3.4)

The fields for the IPv6 packet header, shown in Figure 22-10, are as follows:

- **Version**—This field contains a 4-bit binary value set to 0110 that identifies this as an IPv6 packet.
- **Traffic Class**—This 8-bit field is equivalent to the IPv4 Differentiated Services (DS) field.
- **Flow Label**—This 20-bit field (new in IPv6) suggests that all packets with the same flow label receive the same type of handling by routers.
- **Payload Length**—This 16-bit field indicates the length of the data portion, or payload, of the IPv6 packet. This does not include the length of the IPv6 header, which is a fixed 40-byte header.
- **Next Header**—This 8-bit field is equivalent to the IPv4 Protocol field. It indicates the data payload type that the packet is carrying, enabling the network layer to pass the data to the appropriate upper-layer protocol.
- **Hop Limit**—This 8-bit field replaces the IPv4 TTL field. This value is decremented by a value of 1 by each router that forwards the packet. When the counter reaches 0, the packet is discarded, and an ICMPv6 Time Exceeded message is forwarded to the sending host. This message indicates that the packet did not reach its destination because the hop limit was exceeded. Unlike IPv4, IPv6 does not include an IPv6 Header Checksum field, because this function is performed at both the lower and upper layers. This means the checksum does not need to be recalculated by each router when it decrements the Hop Limit field, which also improves network performance.
- **Source IPv6 Address**—This 128-bit field identifies the IPv6 address of the sending host.
- **Destination IPv6 Address**—This 128-bit field identifies the IPv6 address of the receiving host.

An IPv6 packet may also contain extension headers (EHs), which provide optional network layer information. Extension headers are optional and are placed between the IPv6 header and the payload. EHs are used for fragmentation, security, to support mobility, and more.

Unlike IPv4 packets, routers do not fragment routed IPv6 packets.

Video

Video—Sample IPv6 Headers in Wireshark (22.3.5)

Refer to the online course to view this video.

Interactive Graphic

Check Your Understanding—IPv6 Packet (22.3.6)

Refer to the online course to complete this activity.

Network Layer Summary (22.4)

The following is a summary of each topic in the chapter and some questions for your reflection.

What Did I Learn in This Chapter? (22.4.1)

- **Network Layer Characteristics**—The network layer, or OSI Layer 3, provides services to allow end devices to exchange data across networks. IPv4 and IPv6 are the principal network layer communication protocols. Other network layer protocols include routing protocols such as OSPF and messaging protocols such as ICMP.

  Network layer protocols perform four operations: addressing end devices, encapsulation, routing, and de-encapsulation. IPv4 and IPv6 specify the packet structure and processing used to carry the data from one host to another host. Operating without regard to the data carried in each packet allows the network layer to carry packets for multiple types of communications between multiple hosts.

  IP encapsulates the transport layer segment or other data by adding an IP header. The IP header is used to deliver the packet to the destination host. The IP header is examined by routers and Layer 3 switches as it travels across a network to its destination. IP addressing information remains the same from the time the packet leaves the source host until it arrives at the destination host, except when translated by the device performing NAT for IPv4.

  The basic characteristics of IP are that it is connectionless, best effort, and media independent. Connectionless means that no dedicated end-to-end connection is created by IP before data is sent. IP does not require additional fields in the header to maintain an established connection. This reduces the overhead of IP. IP is best effort because senders are unaware of whether destination devices are present and functional when sending packets, nor are they aware of whether the destination receives the packet or is able to access and read the packet. IP operates independently of the media that carry the data at lower layers of the protocol stack. IP packets can be communicated as electronic signals over copper cable, as optical signals over fiber, or wirelessly as radio signals. One characteristic of the media that the network layer considers is the maximum size of the PDU that each medium can transport, or the MTU.

- **IPv4 Packet**—The IPv4 packet header is used to ensure that a packet is delivered to its next stop on the way to its destination end device. An IPv4 packet header consists of fields containing binary numbers, which are examined by the Layer 3 process. Significant fields in the IPv4 header include Version, DS, TTL, Protocol, Header Checksum, Source IPv4 Address, and Destination IPv4 Address.

  The IHL, Total Length, and Header Checksum fields are used to identify and validate the packet. The IPv4 packet uses Identification, Flags, and Fragment Offset fields to keep track of the fragments. A router may have to fragment an IPv4 packet when forwarding it from one medium to another with a smaller MTU.

- **IPv6 Packet**—IPv4 limitations include IPv4 address depletion, lack of end-to-end connectivity, and increased network complexity. IPv6 overcomes these limitations through improvements that include the following: increased address space, improved packet handling, and elimination of the need for NAT.

  The 32-bit IPv4 address space provides approximately 4,294,967,296 unique addresses. The IPv6 address space provides 340,282,366,920,938,463,463,374,607,431,768,211,456, or 340 undecillion addresses, roughly equivalent to every grain of sand on Earth.

  The IPv6 simplified header fields include Version, Traffic Class, Flow Label, Payload Length, Next Header, Hop Limit, Source IP Address, and Destination IP Address. An IPv6 packet may also contain extension headers (EHs), which provide optional network layer information. EHs are placed between the IPv6 header and the payload. EHs are used for fragmentation, security, to support mobility, and more. Unlike IPv4 packets, routers do not fragment routed IPv6 packets.

Reflection Questions (22.4.2)

More protocols! I am beginning to understand that a great deal of work was done to create these protocols. At the network layer, protocols handle addressing, encapsulating the data, routing the packets, and then de-encapsulating the packets so they can be read. Marcy and Vincent are not IT professionals, so a working network seems a bit mysterious to them. But it does help to know about what happens at the network layer of the OSI model. How can this knowledge help you to troubleshoot your own network?

Practice

There are no labs or Packet Tracer activities in this chapter.

Check Your Understanding Questions

Complete all the review questions listed here to test your understanding of the topics and concepts in this chapter. Appendix A, "Answers to 'Check Your Understanding' Questions," lists the answers.

1. Which value contained in an IPv4 header field is decremented by each router that receives a packet?
   a. Differentiated Services
   b. Fragment Offset
   c. Header Length
   d. Time-to-Live
2. Which statement accurately describes a characteristic of IPv4?
   a. All IPv4 addresses are assignable to hosts.
   b. IPv4 has a 32-bit address space.
   c. An IPv4 header has fewer fields than an IPv6 header has.
   d. IPv4 natively supports IPsec.
3. Which technology provides a solution to IPv4 address depletion by allowing multiple devices to share one public IP address?
   a. ARP
   b. DNS
   c. NAT
   d. SMB
   e. DHCP
   f. HTTP
4. Why is IPv6 designed to replace IPv4?
   a. Because most computers have a 64-bit processor
   b. Because the IPv4 address space will soon be depleted
   c. To allow computers to address more memory
   d. To address compatibility issues with mobile devices

5. Which characteristic of the network layer in the OSI model allows packets for multiple types of communications to be carried among many hosts?

   a. De-encapsulation of headers from lower layers
   b. Selection of paths for and direct packets toward the destination
   c. Capability to operate without regard to the data that is carried in each packet
   d. Capability to manage the data transport between processes running on hosts

6. Which statement describes a characteristic of the network layer in the OSI model?

   a. It manages the data transport between the processes running on each host.
   b. In the encapsulation process, the network layer adds source and destination port numbers to the IP header.
   c. When a packet arrives at the destination host, its IP header is checked by the network layer to determine where the packet has to be routed.
   d. Its protocols specify the packet structure and processing used to carry the data from one host to another.

7. Which layer of the OSI model is responsible for the logical addressing of packets?

   a. Data link
   b. Network
   c. Session
   d. Transport

8. What is the order of encapsulation for the protocol data units passing from the user application down the stack?

   a. Bits, segments, packets, frames, data
   b. Data, segments, packets, frames, bits
   c. Segments, data, packets, frames, bits
   d. Segments, packets, frames, bits, data

9. What process involves placing one PDU inside of another PDU?

   a. Encapsulation
   b. Encoding
   c. Segmentation
   d. Flow control

10. What information is added during encapsulation at OSI Layer 3?

    a. Source and destination MAC addresses
    b. Source and destination application protocols
    c. Source and destination port numbers
    d. Source and destination IP addresses

11. How does the network layer use the MTU value?

    a. The network layer depends on the higher-level layers to determine the MTU.
    b. The network layer depends on the data link layer to set the MTU, and adjusts the speed of transmission to accommodate it.
    c. The MTU is passed to the network layer by the data link layer.
    d. To increase speed of delivery, the network layer ignores the MTU.

CHAPTER 23

IPv4 Address Structure

Objectives

Upon completion of this chapter, you will be able to answer the following question:

- What is the structure of an IPv4 address, including the network portion, the host portion, and the subnet mask?

Key Terms

This chapter uses the following key term. You can find the definition in the Glossary.

prefix length *Page 366*

Introduction (23.0)

Bob has investigated the current network of the furniture business and has assured Marcy and Vincent that they can use it until he makes the upgrades. Bob has convinced Marcy and Vincent to create a new hierarchical network that will use cloud services. With Bob's research and explanations of networking, they are sure this is the best move for them. They really appreciate Bob's knowledge and advice!

You might have a long way to go before you have all of Bob's knowledge and skill, but I think you are on the right path! This chapter will dive deeper into IPv4 addressing. Ready? Keep reading.

IPv4 Address Structure (23.1)

This section presents the IPv4 address structure.

Network and Host Portions (23.1.1)

An IPv4 address is a 32-bit hierarchical address that is made up of a network portion and a host portion. When determining the network portion versus the host portion, you must look at the 32-bit stream, as shown in Figure 23-1.

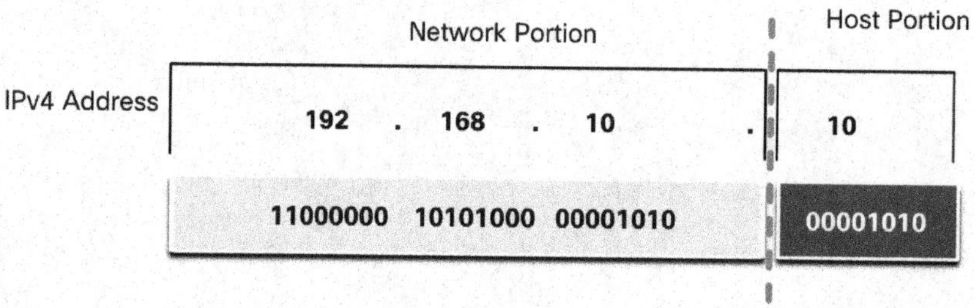

Figure 23-1 Network and Host Portions of an IPv4 Address

The bits in the network portion of the address must be identical for all devices that reside in the same network. The bits in the host portion of the address must be unique to identify a specific host within the network. If two hosts have the same bit pattern in the specified network portion of the 32-bit stream, those two hosts reside in the same network.

But how do hosts know which portion of the 32 bits identifies the network and which identifies the host? That is the role of the subnet mask.

The Subnet Mask (23.1.2)

As shown in Figure 23-2, assigning an IPv4 address to a host requires the following:

- **IPv4 address**—This is the unique IPv4 address of the host.
- **Subnet mask**—This is used to identify the network/host portion of the IPv4 address.

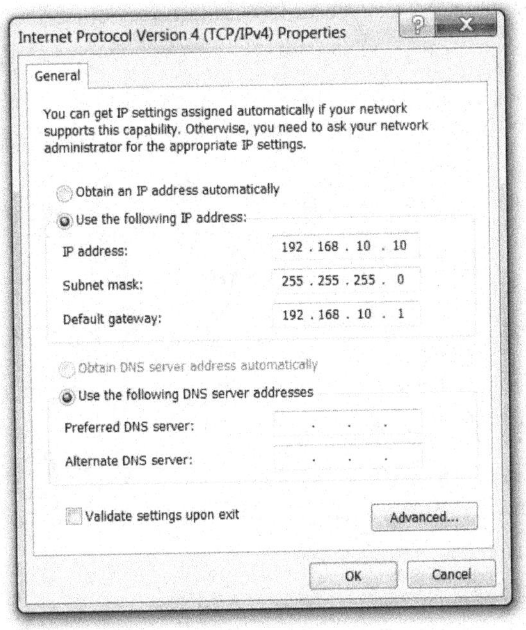

Figure 23-2 IPv4 Addressing on a Windows PC

Note

A default gateway IPv4 address is required to reach remote networks, and DNS server IPv4 addresses are required to translate domain names to IPv4 addresses.

The IPv4 subnet mask is used to differentiate the network portion from the host portion of an IPv4 address. When an IPv4 address is assigned to a device, the subnet mask is used to determine the network address of the device. The network address represents all the devices on the same network.

Figure 23-3 displays the 32-bit subnet mask in dotted decimal and binary formats.

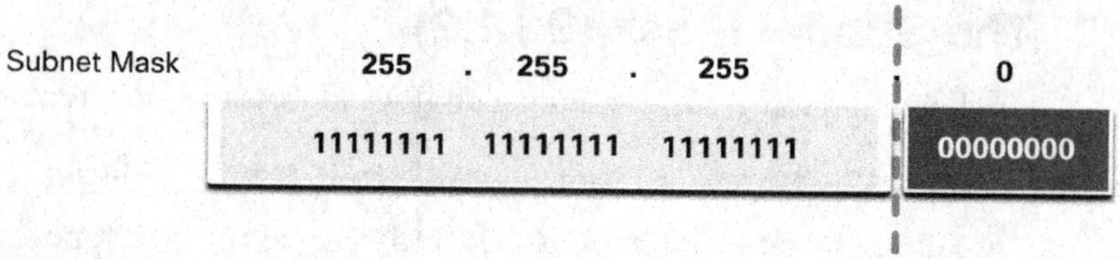

Figure 23-3 32-Bit Subnet Mask

Notice that the subnet mask is a consecutive sequence of 1 bits followed by a consecutive sequence of 0 bits.

To identify the network and host portions of an IPv4 address, the subnet mask is compared to the IPv4 address bit for bit, from left to right, as shown in Figure 23-4.

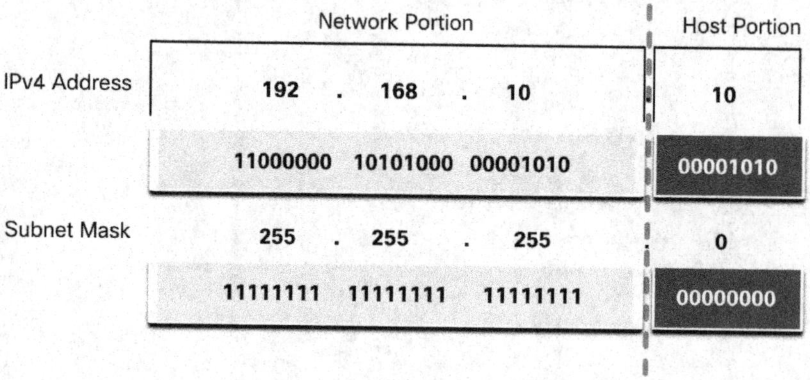

Figure 23-4 Subnet Mask Compared to IPv4 Address

Note that the subnet mask does not actually contain the network or host portion of an IPv4 address; it just tells the computer where to look for the part of the IPv4 address that is the network portion and where to look for the part that is the host portion.

The actual process used to identify the network portion and host portion is called ANDing.

The Prefix Length (23.1.3)

Expressing network addresses and host addresses with the dotted decimal subnet mask address can become cumbersome. Fortunately, the *prefix length* provides an alternative method of identifying a subnet mask. The prefix length is the number of bits set to 1 in the subnet mask. It is written in "slash notation," with a forward slash (/) followed by the number of bits set to 1. Therefore, to determine the prefix length, count the number of 1 bits in the subnet mask and prepend that number with a slash.

Table 23-1 shows several examples. The first column lists various subnet masks that can be used with a host address. The second column displays the converted 32-bit binary address. The last column displays the resulting prefix length.

Table 23-1 Comparing the Subnet Mask and Prefix Length

Subnet Mask	32-Bit Address	Prefix Length
255.0.0.0	11111111.00000000.00000000.00000000	/8
255.255.0.0	11111111.11111111.00000000.00000000	/16
255.255.255.0	11111111.11111111.11111111.00000000	/24
255.255.255.128	11111111.11111111.11111111.10000000	/25
255.255.255.192	11111111.11111111.11111111.11000000	/26
255.255.255.224	11111111.11111111.11111111.11100000	/27
255.255.255.240	11111111.11111111.11111111.11110000	/28
255.255.255.248	11111111.11111111.11111111.11111000	/29
255.255.255.252	11111111.11111111.11111111.11111100	/30

Note

A network address is also referred to as a *prefix* or *network prefix*. Therefore, the prefix length is the number of 1 bits in the subnet mask.

When representing an IPv4 address using a prefix length, the IPv4 address is written followed by the prefix length with no spaces. For example, 192.168.10.10 255.255.255.0 would be written as 192.168.10.10/24. Using various types of prefix lengths will be discussed later. For now, the focus is on the /24 (that is, 255.255.255.0) prefix.

Determining the Network: Logical AND (23.1.4)

A logical AND is one of three Boolean operations used in Boolean or digital logic. The other two are OR and NOT. The AND operation is used in determining the network address.

Logical AND operations compare two bits and produce the following results:

- 1 AND 1 = 1
- 0 AND 1 = 0

- 1 AND 0 = 0
- 0 AND 0 = 0

Note that only 1 AND 1 produces 1. Any other combination results in 0.

Note

In digital logic, 1 represents true and 0 represents false. When using an AND operation, both input values must be true (1) for the result to be true (1).

To identify the network address of an IPv4 host, the IPv4 address is logically ANDed, bit by bit, with the subnet mask. ANDing between the address and the subnet mask yields the network address.

To illustrate how AND is used to discover a network address, consider a host with IPv4 address 192.168.10.10 and subnet mask 255.255.255.0, as shown in Figure 23-5:

- **IPv4 host address (192.168.10.10)**—The IPv4 address of the host in dotted decimal and binary formats.
- **Subnet mask (255.255.255.0)**—The subnet mask of the host in dotted decimal and binary formats.
- **Network address (192.168.10.0)**—The logical AND operation between the IPv4 address and subnet mask results in an IPv4 network address shown in dotted decimal and binary formats.

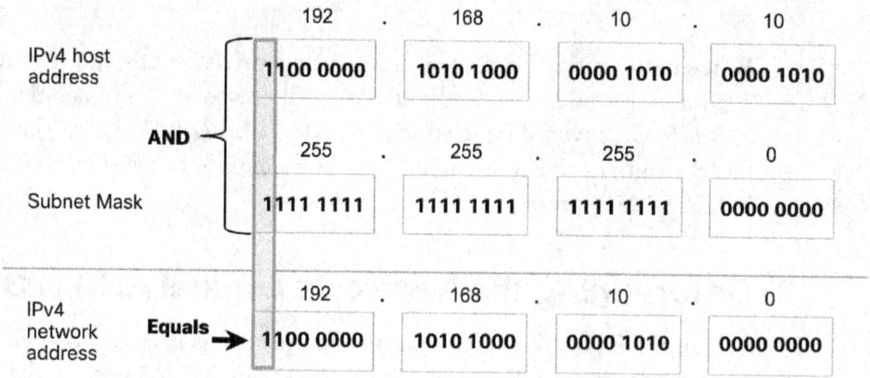

Figure 23-5 ANDing Example

Using the first sequence of bits as an example, notice that the AND operation is performed on the 1 bit of the host address with the 1 bit of the subnet mask. This results in a 1 bit for the network address: 1 AND 1 = 1.

The AND operation between an IPv4 host address and subnet mask results in the IPv4 network address for this host. In this example, the AND operation between the host address 192.168.10.10 and the subnet mask 255.255.255.0 (/24) results in the IPv4 network address 192.168.10.0/24. This is an important IPv4 operation because it tells the host which network it belongs to.

Video

Video—Network, Host, and Broadcast Addresses (23.1.5)

Refer to the online course to view this video.

Interactive Graphic

Activity—ANDing to Determine the Network Address (23.1.6)

Refer to the online course to complete this activity.

IPv4 Address Structure Summary (23.2)

The following is a summary of each topic in the chapter and some questions for your reflection.

What Did I Learn in This Chapter? (23.2.1)

An IPv4 address is a 32-bit hierarchical address that is made up of a network portion and a host portion. When determining the network portion versus the host portion, you must look at the 32-bit stream. The bits in the network portion of the address must be identical for all devices that reside in the same network. The bits in the host portion of the address must be unique to identify a specific host within a network. If two hosts have the same bit pattern in the specified network portion of the 32-bit stream, those two hosts reside in the same network.

The IPv4 subnet mask is used to differentiate the network portion from the host portion of an IPv4 address. When an IPv4 address is assigned to a device, the subnet mask is used to determine the network address of the device. The network address represents all the devices on the same network.

The prefix length is an alternative method of identifying a subnet mask. The prefix length is the number of bits set to 1 in the subnet mask. It is written in "slash notation," with a forward slash (/) followed by the number of bits set to 1. For example, 192.168.10.10 255.255.255.0 would be written as 192.168.10.10/24.

The AND operation is used in determining the network address. Logical AND operations compare two bits, and only 1 AND 1 produces 1:

- 1 AND 1 = 1
- 0 AND 1 = 0
- 1 AND 0 = 0
- 0 AND 0 = 0

To identify the network address of an IPv4 host, the IPv4 address is logically ANDed, bit by bit, with the subnet mask. ANDing between the address and the subnet mask yields the network address.

Reflection Questions (23.2.2)

Before reading this chapter, I was feeling like Marcy and Vincent. I did not have a good grasp of why the numbers in the IPv4 address are important. Did you know the 32-bit hierarchical address is made up of a network portion and a host portion? Are you able to explore this on your own network? And who knew about ANDing and the subnet mask?

I am feeling a little more like Bob after this chapter, and I hope you are too.

Practice

There are no labs or Packet Tracer activities in this chapter.

Check Your Understanding Questions

Complete all the review questions listed here to test your understanding of the topics and concepts in this chapter. Appendix A, "Answers to 'Check Your Understanding' Questions," lists the answers.

1. Which statement describes IPv4 addressing?
   a. Routers use the full 32-bit IP address to determine the location of each individual host.
   b. The network portion of a destination IP address is obtained by performing an AND operation between a host IP address and a subnet mask.
   c. An IPv4 address contains two parts: a network portion and a subnet portion.
   d. Two hosts with the same subnet mask are in the same network.

2. Which statement describes one purpose of the subnet mask setting for a host?
   a. It is used to describe the type of the subnet.
   b. It is used to identify the default gateway.
   c. It is used to determine to which network the host is connected.
   d. It is used to determine the maximum number of bits within one packet that can be placed on a particular network.

3. How many octets exist in an IPv4 address?
   a. 4
   b. 8
   c. 16
   d. 32

4. Which full range of decimal values is valid in one octet of an IPv4 address?
   a. 0 through 31
   b. 1 through 64
   c. 0 through 128
   d. 0 through 255
   e. 1 through 256

5. For what purpose are IPv4 addresses utilized?
   a. An IPv4 address is used to uniquely identify a device on an IP network.
   b. An IPv4 address is burned into the network card to uniquely identify a device.
   c. An IPv4 address is used to uniquely identify the application that requested the information from a remote device.
   d. An IPv4 address is used to identify the number of IP networks available.
6. What is the prefix length notation for the subnet mask 255.255.255.224?
   a. /25
   b. /26
   c. /27
   d. /28
7. Which two parts are components of an IPv4 address? (Choose two.)
   a. Subnet portion
   b. Network portion
   c. Logical portion
   d. Host portion
   e. Physical portion
   f. Broadcast portion
8. What is obtained when ANDing the address 192.168.65.3/18 with its subnet mask?
   a. 192.168.0.0
   b. 192.168.16.0
   c. 192.168.32.0
   d. 192.168.64.0
9. What do devices on the same IPv4 subnet have in common?
   a. They all use the same default gateway.
   b. They all have a subnet mask of /8, /16, or /24.
   c. They all have the same last octet in their IPv4 addresses.
   d. They all have the same number in the first three octets of their IPv4 address.

10. How many unique addresses are available for assignment to hosts in the network 10.100.16.0 with subnet mask 255.255.252.0?

    a. 254
    b. 510
    c. 1022
    d. 4094

11. Which is a valid default gateway address for a host configured with IPv4 address 10.25.1.110 and subnet mask 255.255.255.192?

    a. 10.25.1.65
    b. 10.25.1.1
    c. 10.0.0.1
    d. 10.25.1.127

12. When IPv4 addressing is manually configured on a web server, which property of the IPv4 configuration identifies the network portion and host portion for an IPv4 address?

    a. DNS server address
    b. Subnet mask
    c. Default gateway
    d. DHCP server address

CHAPTER 24

Address Resolution

Objectives

Upon completion of this chapter, you will be able to answer the following question:

- What is the purpose of ARP?

Key Terms

This chapter uses the following key terms. You can find the definitions in the Glossary.

ARP cache *Page 377*

ARP table *Page 377*

Introduction (24.0)

Webster here again! I have another friend to introduce to you, Olcay, an IT professional at a power company in Türkiye. She is mentoring a new hire named Abay. Abay will be shadowing Olcay for the next month to become more proficient in networking in the power company. Olcay asks Abay what he knows about address resolution. Abay responds that he knows that for a host to send a packet to another host on the same local IPv4 network, the source host must know the IPv4 address and the MAC address of the destination device. He also knows that a device uses ARP to determine the destination MAC address of a local device when it knows its IPv4 address.

If Abay is going to be successful at his new job, he needs to learn a little more about address resolution. If you do too, check out this chapter on address resolution.

ARP (24.1)

This section discusses the relationship between MAC and IPv4 addresses, and how the *Address Resolution Protocol (ARP)* is used to map the two addresses.

ARP Overview (24.1.1)

If your network is using the IPv4 communications protocol, you need the Address Resolution Protocol to map IPv4 addresses to MAC addresses. This section explains how ARP works.

Every IP device on an Ethernet network has a unique Ethernet MAC address. When a device sends an Ethernet Layer 2 frame, it contains these two addresses:

- **Destination MAC address**—The Ethernet MAC address of the destination device on the same local network segment. If the destination host is on another network, then the destination address in the frame would be that of the default gateway (that is, the router).
- **Source MAC address**—The MAC address of the Ethernet NIC on the source host.

Figure 24-1 illustrates the problem when sending a frame to another host on the same segment on an IPv4 network.

To send a packet to another host on the same local IPv4 network, a host must know the IPv4 address and the MAC address of the destination device. Device destination IPv4 addresses are either known or resolved by device name. However, MAC addresses must be discovered.

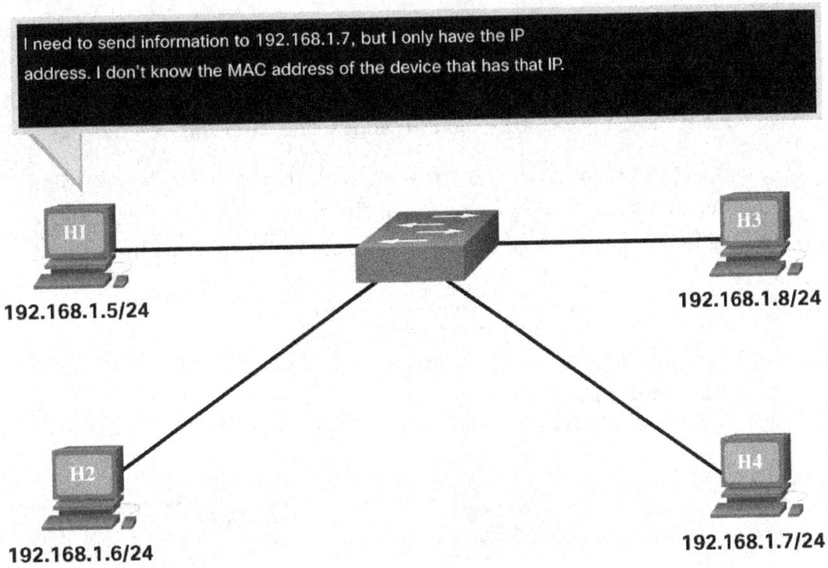

Figure 24-1 A Host Does Not Know the MAC Address for a Destination

A device uses ARP to determine the destination MAC address of a local device when it knows its IPv4 address.

ARP provides two basic functions:

- Resolving IPv4 addresses to MAC addresses
- Maintaining a table of IPv4-to-MAC address mappings

ARP Functions (24.1.2)

Before a packet is sent to the data link layer to be encapsulated into an Ethernet frame, the device refers to a table in its memory to find the MAC address that is mapped to the IPv4 address. This table is stored temporarily in RAM memory and is called the *ARP table* or the *ARP cache*.

The sending device searches its ARP table for a destination IPv4 address and a corresponding MAC address.

- If the packet's destination IPv4 address is on the same network as the source IPv4 address, the device searches the ARP table for the destination IPv4 address.
- If the packet's destination IPv4 address is on a different network than the source IPv4 address, the device searches the ARP table for the IPv4 address of the default gateway.

In both cases, the search is for an IPv4 address and a corresponding MAC address for the device.

Each entry, or row, of the ARP table binds an IPv4 address with a MAC address. The relationship between the two values is called a *map*. This simply means that you can locate an IPv4 address in the table and discover the corresponding MAC address. The ARP table temporarily saves (caches) the mapping for the devices on the LAN.

If the device locates the IPv4 address, it uses its corresponding MAC address as the destination MAC address in the frame. If the device finds no entry for the IPv4 address, it sends a broadcast ARP request, as shown in Figure 24-2.

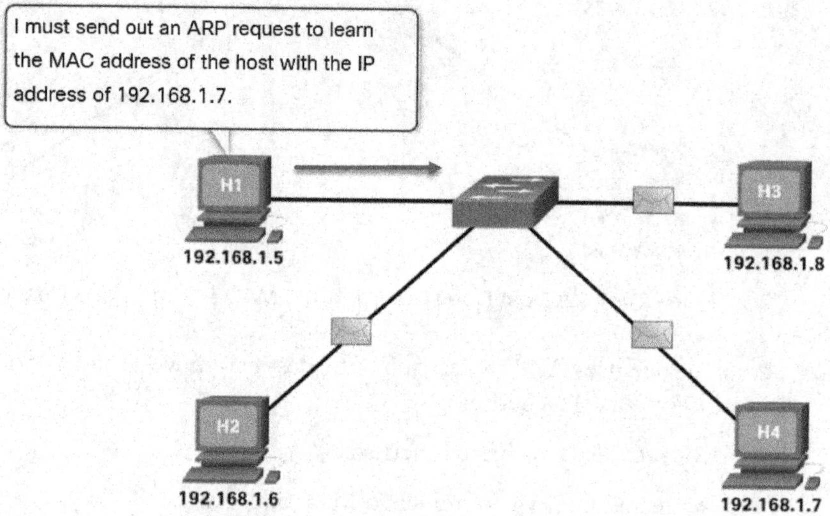

Figure 24-2 H1 Sends a Broadcast ARP Request

The destination responds with a unicast ARP reply, as shown in Figure 24-3.

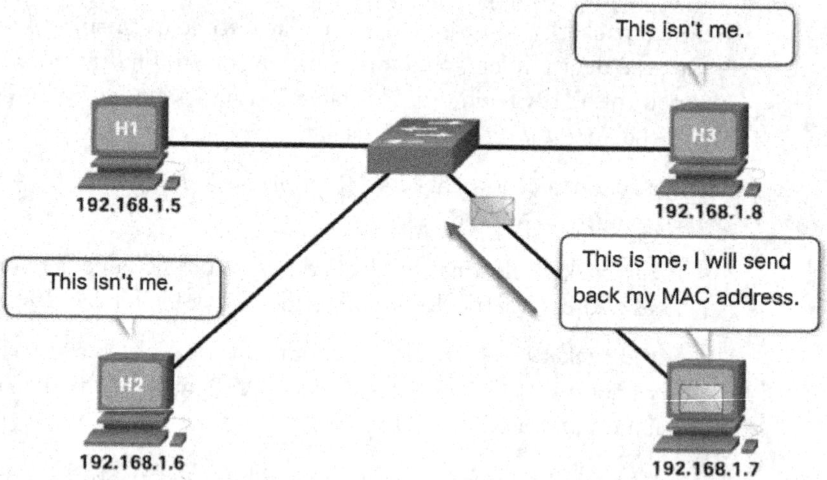

Figure 24-3 H4 Sends a Unicast ARP Reply

Video

Video—ARP Request (24.1.3)

A device sends an ARP request when it needs to determine the MAC address that is associated with an IPv4 address and it does not have an entry for the IPv4 address in its ARP table.

ARP messages are encapsulated directly within an Ethernet frame. There is no IPv4 header. The ARP request is encapsulated in an Ethernet frame using the following header information:

- **Destination MAC Address**—This is a broadcast address FF-FF-FF-FF-FF-FF requiring all Ethernet NICs on the LAN to accept and process the ARP request.
- **Source MAC Address**—This is the MAC address of the sender of the ARP request.
- **Type**—ARP messages have a Type field of 0x806, which informs the receiving NIC that the data portion of the frame needs to be passed to the ARP process.

Because ARP requests are broadcasts, the switch floods them out all ports except the receiving port. All Ethernet NICs on the LAN process broadcasts and each NIC must deliver the ARP request to its operating system for processing. Every device must process the ARP request to see if the target IPv4 address matches its own. A router does not forward broadcasts out other interfaces.

Only one device on the LAN has an IPv4 address that matches the target IPv4 address in the ARP request. That device is the only device that replies to the ARP request.

Refer to the online course to view this video.

Video

Video—ARP Operation—ARP Reply (24.1.4)

Only the device with the target IPv4 address associated with the ARP request responds with an ARP reply. The ARP reply is encapsulated in an Ethernet frame using the following header information:

- **Destination MAC Address**—This is the MAC address of the sender of the ARP request.
- **Source MAC Address**—This is the MAC address of the sender of the ARP reply.
- **Type**—ARP messages have a Type field of 0x806, which informs the receiving NIC that the data portion of the frame needs to be passed to the ARP process.

Only the device that originally sent the ARP request receives the unicast ARP reply. After the ARP reply is received, the device adds the IPv4 address and the corresponding MAC address to its ARP table. Packets destined for that IPv4 address can now be encapsulated in frames using its corresponding MAC address.

If no device responds to the ARP request, the packet is dropped because a frame cannot be created.

Entries in the ARP table are timestamped. If a device does not receive a frame from a particular device before the timestamp expires, the entry for this device is removed from the ARP table.

Additionally, static map entries can be entered in an ARP table, but this is rarely done. Static ARP table entries do not expire over time and must be manually removed.

Refer to the online course to view this video.

Video

Video—ARP Role in Remote Communications (24.1.5)

When the destination IPv4 address is not on the same network as the source IPv4 address, the source device needs to send the frame to its default gateway. This is the interface of the local router. Whenever a source device has a packet with an IPv4 address on another network, it encapsulates that packet in a frame, using the destination MAC address of the router.

The IPv4 address of the default gateway is stored in the IPv4 configuration of the hosts. When a host creates a packet for a destination, it compares the destination IPv4 address and its own IPv4 address to determine if the two IPv4 addresses are located on the same Layer 3 network. If the destination host is not on its same network, the source checks its ARP table for an entry with the IPv4 address of the default gateway. If there is not an entry, the source uses the ARP process to determine a MAC address of the default gateway.

Refer to the online course to view this video.

Removing Entries from an ARP Table (24.1.6)

For each device, an ARP cache timer removes ARP entries that have not been used for a specified period of time. The period of time differs depending on the operating system of the device. For example, newer Windows operating systems store ARP table entries for 15 to 45 seconds, as illustrated in the Figure 24-4.

Commands may also be used to manually remove some or all of the entries in the ARP table. After an entry has been removed, the process for sending an ARP request and receiving an ARP reply must occur again to enter the map in the ARP table.

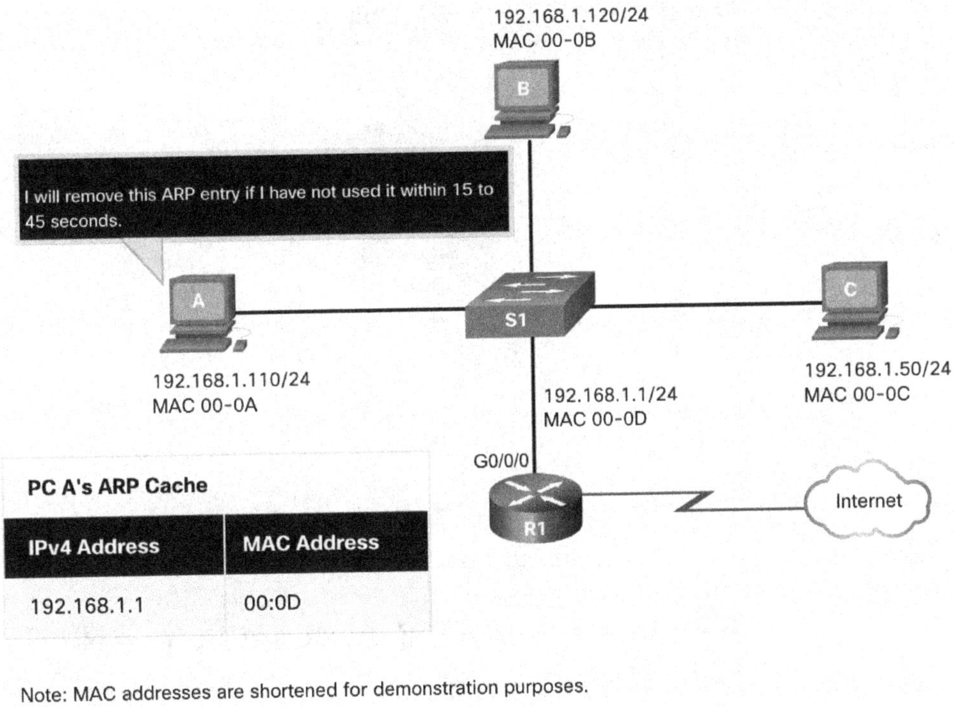

Figure 24-4 Removing MAC-to-IP Address Mappings

ARP Tables on Devices (24.1.7)

On a Cisco router, the **show ip arp** command is used to display the ARP table, as shown Example 24-1.

Example 24-1 R1 ARP Table

```
R1# show ip arp
Protocol  Address          Age (min)  Hardware Addr   Type   Interface
Internet  192.168.10.1             -  a0e0.af0d.e140  ARPA   GigabitEthernet0/0/0
Internet  209.165.200.225          -  a0e0.af0d.e141  ARPA   GigabitEthernet0/0/1
Internet  209.165.200.226          1  a03d.6fe1.9d91  ARPA   GigabitEthernet0/0/1
R1#
```

On a Windows 10 PC, the **arp -a** command is used to display the ARP table, as shown in Example 24-2.

Example 24-2 Windows 10 PC ARP Table

```
C:\Users\PC> arp -a
Interface: 192.168.1.124 --- 0x10
  Internet Address      Physical Address      Type
  192.168.1.1           c8-d7-19-cc-a0-86     dynamic
  192.168.1.101         08-3e-0c-f5-f7-77     dynamic
  192.168.1.110         08-3e-0c-f5-f7-56     dynamic
  192.168.1.112         ac-b3-13-4a-bd-d0     dynamic
  192.168.1.117         08-3e-0c-f5-f7-5c     dynamic
  192.168.1.126         24-77-03-45-5d-c4     dynamic
  192.168.1.146         94-57-a5-0c-5b-02     dynamic
  192.168.1.255         ff-ff-ff-ff-ff-ff     static
  224.0.0.22            01-00-5e-00-00-16     static
  224.0.0.251           01-00-5e-00-00-fb     static
  239.255.255.250       01-00-5e-7f-ff-fa     static
  255.255.255.255       ff-ff-ff-ff-ff-ff     static
C:\Users\PC>
```

ARP Issues—ARP Broadcasts and ARP Spoofing (24.1.8)

As a broadcast frame, an ARP request is received and processed by every device on the local network. On a typical business network, these broadcasts would probably have minimal impact on network performance. However, if a large number of devices were to be powered up and all start accessing network services at the same time, there could be some reduction in performance for a short period of time, as shown in Figure 24-5. After the devices send out the initial ARP broadcasts and have learned the necessary MAC addresses, any impact on the network will be minimized.

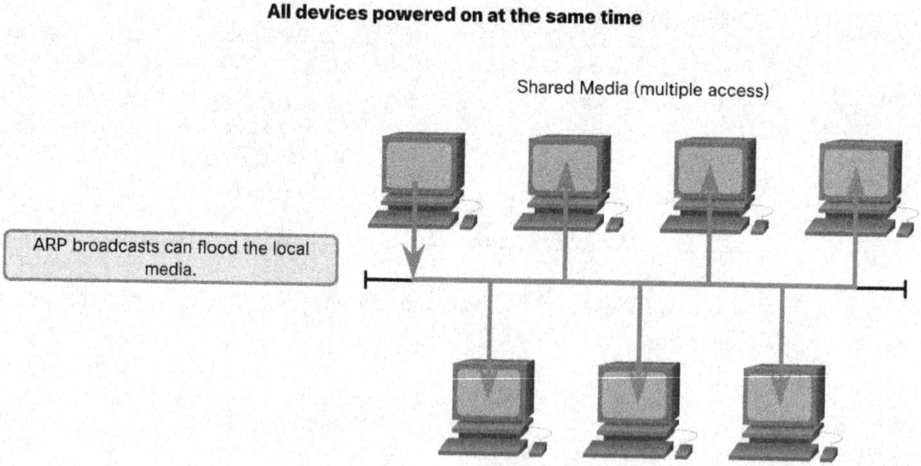

Figure 24-5 ARP Broadcasts Flooding a Network

In some cases, the use of ARP can lead to a potential security risk. A threat actor can use ARP spoofing to perform an ARP poisoning attack. *ARP spoofing* is a technique used by a threat actor to reply to an ARP request for an IPv4 address that belongs to another device, such as the default gateway, as shown in Figure 24-6. The threat actor sends an ARP reply with its own MAC address. The receiver of the ARP reply adds the wrong MAC address to its ARP table and sends these packets to the threat actor.

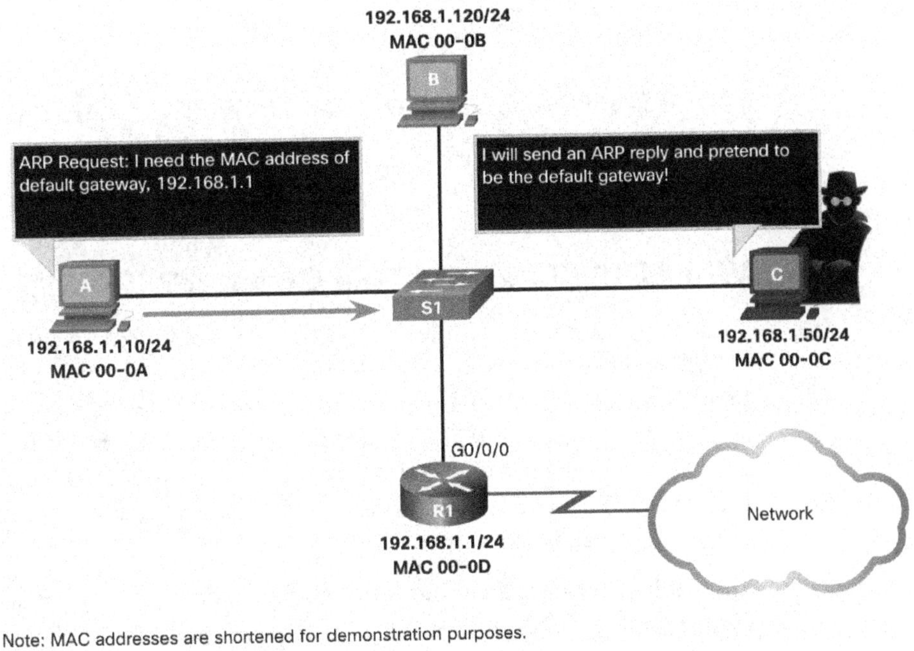

Figure 24-6 Threat Actor Spoofing an ARP Reply

Enterprise-level switches include mitigation techniques known as dynamic ARP inspection (DAI). DAI is beyond the scope of this course.

Packet Tracer
☐ Activity

Packet Tracer—Examine the ARP Table (24.1.9)

In this Packet Tracer activity, you will complete the following objectives:

- Examine an ARP Request
- Examine a Switch MAC Address Table
- Examine the ARP Process in Remote Communications

This activity is optimized for viewing PDUs. The devices are already configured. You will gather PDU information in simulation mode and answer a series of questions about the data you collect.

Refer to the online course to complete this activity.

Lab—View ARP Traffic in Wireshark (24.1.10)

In this activity, you will complete the following objectives:

- Part 1: Capture and Analyze ARP Data in Wireshark
- Part 2: View the ARP cache entries on the PC

Refer to the online course to complete this lab.

Address Resolution Summary (24.2)

The following is a summary of each topic in the chapter and some questions for your reflection.

What Did I Learn in This Chapter? (24.2.1)

To send a packet to another host on the same local IPv4 network, a host must know the IPv4 address and the MAC address of the destination device. Device destination IPv4 addresses are either known or resolved by device name. However, MAC addresses must be discovered. A device uses ARP to determine the destination MAC address of a local device when it knows its IPv4 address. ARP provides two basic functions: resolving IPv4 addresses to MAC addresses, and maintaining a table of IPv4-to-MAC address mappings.

The sending device searches its ARP table for a destination IPv4 address and a corresponding MAC address.

- If the packet's destination IPv4 address is on the same network as the source IPv4 address, the device searches the ARP table for the destination IPv4 address.
- If the packet's destination IPv4 address is on a different network than the source IPv4 address, the device searches the ARP table for the IPv4 address of the default gateway.

Each entry, or row, of the ARP table binds an IPv4 address with a MAC address. The relationship between the two values is called a *map*. ARP messages are encapsulated directly within an Ethernet frame. There is no IPv4 header. The ARP request is encapsulated in an Ethernet frame using the following header information:

- **Destination MAC Address**—This is a broadcast address FF-FF-FF-FF-FF-FF, requiring all Ethernet NICs on the LAN to accept and process the ARP request.
- **Source MAC Address**—This is the MAC address of the sender of the ARP request.

- **Type**—ARP messages have a Type field of 0x806, which informs the receiving NIC that the data portion of the frame needs to be passed to the ARP process.

Because ARP requests are broadcasts, the switch floods them out all ports except the receiving port. Only the device with the target IPv4 address associated with the ARP request responds with an ARP reply. After the ARP reply is received, the device adds the IPv4 address and the corresponding MAC address to its ARP table.

When the destination IPv4 address is not on the same network as the source IPv4 address, the source device needs to send the frame to its default gateway, which is the interface of the local router. Whenever a source device has a packet with an IPv4 address on another network, it encapsulates that packet in a frame using the destination MAC address of the router. The IPv4 address of the default gateway is stored in the IPv4 configuration of the hosts. If the destination host is not on its same network, the source checks its ARP table for an entry with the IPv4 address of the default gateway. If there is not an entry, the source uses the ARP process to determine a MAC address of the default gateway.

For each device, an ARP cache timer removes ARP entries that have not been used for a specified period of time. The period of time differs depending on the operating system of the device. Commands may be used to manually remove some or all of the entries in the ARP table.

On a Cisco router, the **show ip arp** command is used to display the ARP table. On a Windows 10 PC, the **arp -a** command is used to display the ARP table.

As a broadcast frame, an ARP request is received and processed by every device on the local network. If a large number of devices were to be powered up and all start accessing network services at the same time, there could be some reduction in performance for a short period of time.

In some cases, the use of ARP can lead to a potential security risk. A threat actor can use ARP spoofing to perform an ARP poisoning attack. This is a technique used by a threat actor to reply to an ARP request for an IPv4 address that belongs to another device, such as the default gateway. The threat actor sends an ARP reply with its own MAC address. The receiver of the ARP reply adds the wrong MAC address to its ARP table and sends these packets to the threat actor.

Reflection Questions (24.2.2)

Abay now knows a lot more about networking, including address resolution. Before this chapter, did you understand ARP and ARP tables? I had never thought about a threat actor using ARP spoofing to perform an ARP poisoning attack! Had you?

Practice

The following activities provide practice with the topics introduced in this chapter.

Labs

Lab—View ARP Traffic in Wireshark (24.1.10)

Packet Tracer Activity

Packet Tracer Activities

Packet Tracer—Examine the ARP Table (24.1.9)

Check Your Understanding Questions

Complete all the review questions listed here to test your understanding of the topics and concepts in this chapter. Appendix A, "Answers to 'Check Your Understanding' Questions," lists the answers.

1. Which protocol is used to discover the destination address that needs to be added to an Ethernet frame?

   a. ARP

   b. DNS

   c. DHCP

   d. HTTP

2. What is one function of the ARP protocol?

   a. Obtaining an IPv4 address automatically

   b. Mapping a domain name to its IP address

   c. Resolving an IPv4 address to a MAC address

   d. Maintaining a table of domain names with their resolved IP addresses

3. PC1 has IPv4 address 192.168.10.17/24 and wants to communicate with PC2 with IPv4 address 192.168.20.34. PC1 determines PC2 is on another network and sends an ARP request to its default gateway, GW1. How does the default gateway respond?

   a. It sends an ICMP message to PC1 informing the host that it cannot reach PC2.

   b. It responds with an ARP reply to PC1 with the MAC address of PC2.

c. It forwards the ARP request from PC1 to PC2.

d. It responds with an ARP reply to PC1 with its own MAC address.

4. What action does the ARP process take when a host needs to build a frame but the ARP cache does not contain an address mapping?

   a. The ARP process sends out an ARP request to the Ethernet broadcast address to discover the IPv4 address of the destination device.

   b. The ARP process sends out an ARP request to the IPv4 broadcast address to discover the MAC address of the destination device.

   c. The ARP process sends out an ARP request to the IPv4 broadcast address to discover the IPv4 address of the destination device.

   d. The ARP process sends out an ARP request to the Ethernet broadcast address to discover the MAC address associated with the device to receive the Ethernet frame.

5. Which statement describes the treatment of ARP requests on the local link?

   a. They must be forwarded by all routers on the local network.

   b. They are received and processed by every device on the local network.

   c. They are dropped by all switches on the local network.

   d. They are received and processed only by the target device.

6. What is the aim of an ARP spoofing attack?

   a. To flood the network with ARP reply broadcasts

   b. To fill switch MAC address tables with bogus addresses

   c. To associate IP addresses to the wrong MAC address

   d. To overwhelm network hosts with ARP requests

7. A cybersecurity analyst believes that an attacker is announcing a forged MAC address to network hosts in an attempt to spoof the default gateway. Which command could the analyst use on the network hosts to see which MAC address the hosts are using to reach the default gateway?

   a. **netsat -r**

   b. **route print**

   c. **ipconfig /all**

   d. **arp -a**

8. What does a host do first when preparing a Layer 2 PDU for transmission to a host on the same Ethernet network?

   a. It sends the PDU to the router directly connected to the network.

   b. It queries the local DNS server for the name of the destination host.

   c. It searches the ARP table for the MAC address of the destination host.

   d. It initiates an ARP request to find the MAC address of the destination host.

9. Which destination address is used in an ARP request frame?

   a. 0.0.0.0

   b. 255.255.255.255

   c. FFFF.FFFF.FFFF

   d. 127.0.0.1

   e. 01-00-5E-00-AA-23

10. Which protocol is used by a computer to find the MAC address of the default gateway on an Ethernet network?

    a. ARP

    b. TCP

    c. UDP

    d. DHCP

11. Refer to the following figure. PC1 attempts to connect to File_server1 and sends an ARP request to obtain a destination MAC address. Which MAC address will PC1 receive in the ARP reply?

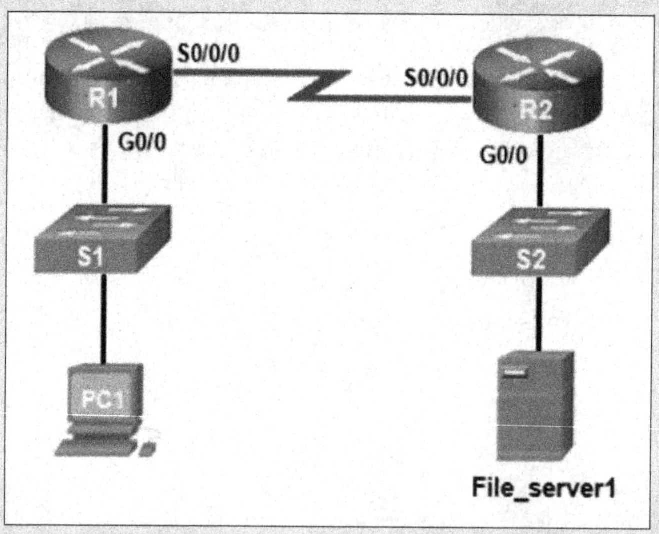

a. The MAC address of S1
b. The MAC address of the G0/0 interface on R1
c. The MAC address of the G0/0 interface on R2
d. The MAC address of S2
e. The MAC address of File_server1

CHAPTER 25

IP Addressing Services

Objectives

Upon completion of this chapter, you will be able to answer the following questions:

- How does DNS operate?
- How does DHCP operate?

Key Terms

This chapter uses the following key terms. You can find the definitions in the Glossary.

Domain Name System (DNS) *Page 392*

Dynamic Host Configuration Protocol (DHCP) *Page 398*

fully qualified domain names (FQDNs) *Page 392*

Introduction (25.0)

Hi there. While Olcay and Abay are working together, Olcay needs to use the **nslookup** command to verify the current status of the name servers. Olcay takes this opportunity to ask Abay what he knows about DNS and DHCP services. Abay explains that the DNS protocol defines an automated service that matches resource names with the required numeric network address. He also explains that using DHCP to assign IPv4 addresses automatically is more efficient than using static addressing for each connection. Olcay is impressed with Abay's knowledge! He has really been doing his homework.

Are you able to explain how DNS and DHCP services operate? If not, this chapter will help you. Keep reading!

DNS Services (25.1)

There are other application layer–specific protocols designed to make it easier to obtain addresses for network devices. These services are essential because it would be very time consuming to remember IP addresses instead of URLs or manually configure all of the devices in a medium to large network. This section goes into more detail about the IP addressing services, DNS and DHCP.

Video

Video—Domain Name System (25.1.1)

Refer to the online course to view this video.

Domain Name System (25.1.2)

In data networks, devices are labeled with numeric IP addresses to send and receive data over networks. Domain names were created to convert the numeric address into a simple, recognizable name.

On the Internet, *fully qualified domain names (FQDNs)*, such as https://www.cisco.com, are much easier for people to remember than 198.133.219.25, which is the actual numeric address for this server. If Cisco were to decide to change the numeric address of www.cisco.com, the change would be transparent to users because the domain name would remain the same. The new numeric address simply would be linked to the existing domain name and connectivity would be maintained.

The *Domain Name System (DNS)* protocol defines an automated service that matches resource names with the required numeric network addresses. It includes the format for queries, responses, and data. DNS communications use a single format

called a *message*. This message format is used for all types of client queries and server responses, error messages, and the transfer of resource record information between servers.

The following are the steps in the DNS process:

Step 1. The user types an FQDN into a browser application Address field, as shown in Figure 25-1.

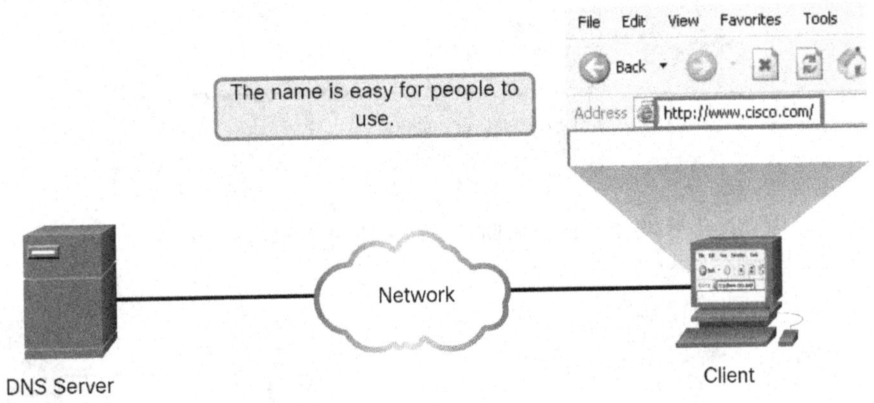

Figure 25-1 Step 1: URL Entered in a Browser

Step 2. A DNS query is sent to the designated DNS server for the client computer, as shown in Figure 25-2. This server is known as the local DNS server.

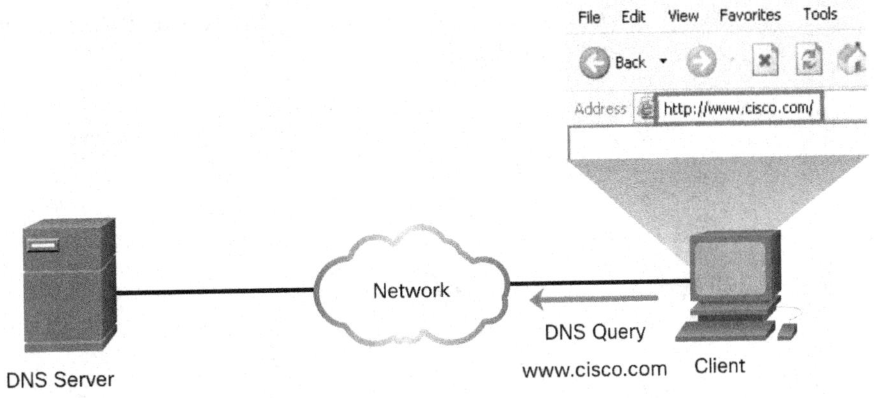

Figure 25-2 Step 2: DNS Query Sent to DNS Server

Step 3. The DNS server matches the FQDN with its IP address, as shown in Figure 25-3.

Step 4. The DNS query response is sent back to the client with the IP address for the FQDN, as shown in Figure 25-4.

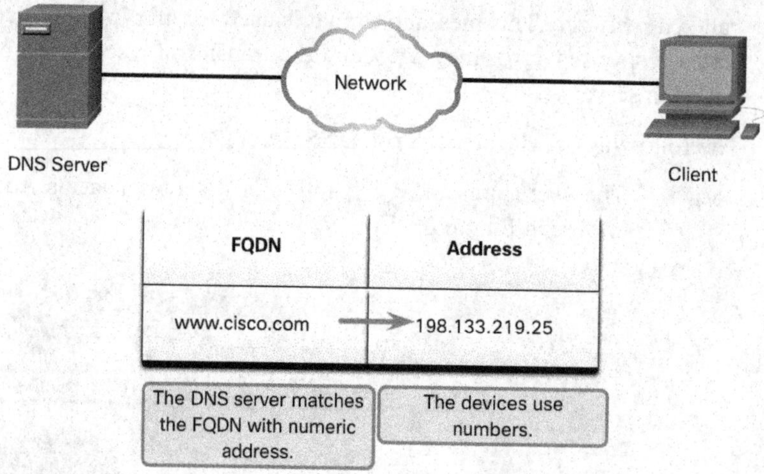

Figure 25-3 Step 3: DNS Server Matches FQDN to an IP Address

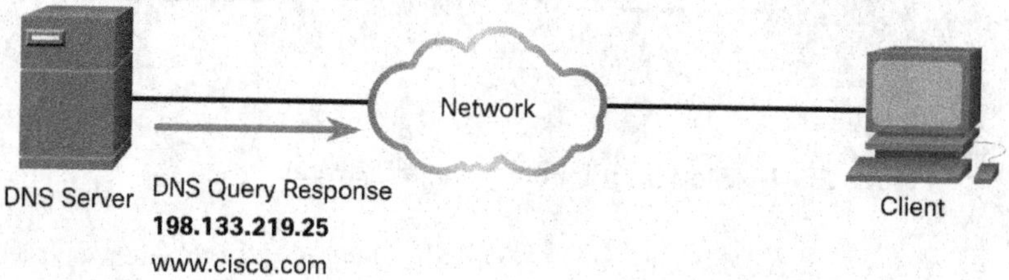

Figure 25-4 Step 4: DNS Server Responds to DNS Query

Step 5. The client computer uses the IP address to make requests of the server, as shown in Figure 25-5.

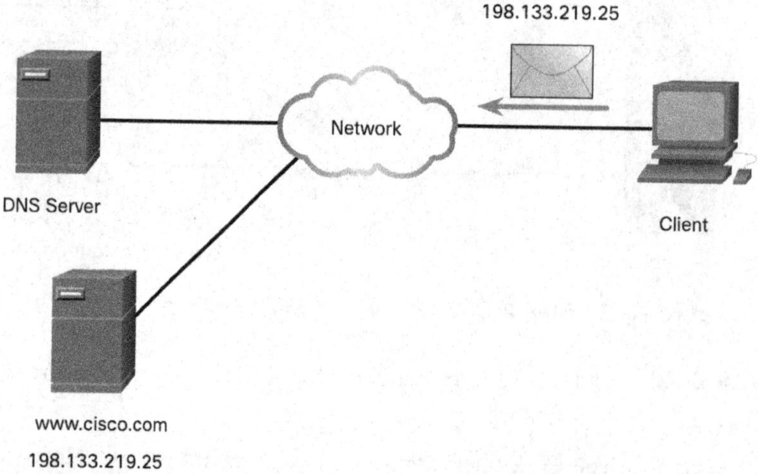

Figure 25-5 Step 5: Client Sends Web Request Using IP Address

DNS Message Format (25.1.3)

The DNS server stores different types of resource records that are used to resolve names. These records contain the name, address, and type of record. Some of these record types are as follows:

- A—An end device IPv4 address
- NS—An authoritative name server
- AAAA—An end device IPv6 address (pronounced quad-A)
- MX—A mail exchange record

When a client makes a query, the server DNS process first looks at its own records to resolve the name. If it is unable to resolve the name by using its stored records, it contacts other servers to resolve the name. After a match is found and returned to the original requesting server, the server temporarily stores the numbered address in the event that the same name is requested again.

The DNS client service on Windows PCs also stores previously resolved names in memory. The **ipconfig /displaydns** command displays all of the cached DNS entries.

As shown Table 25-1, DNS uses the same message format between servers, consisting of a question, an answer, an authority, and additional information for all types of client queries and server responses, error messages, and transfer of resource record information.

Table 25-1 DNS Message

DNS Message Section	Description
Question	The question for the name server
Answer	Resource records answering the question
Authority	Resource records pointing toward an authority
Additional	Resource records holding additional information

DNS Hierarchy (25.1.4)

The DNS protocol uses a hierarchical system to create a database to provide name resolution, as shown in Figure 25-6. DNS uses domain names to form the hierarchy.

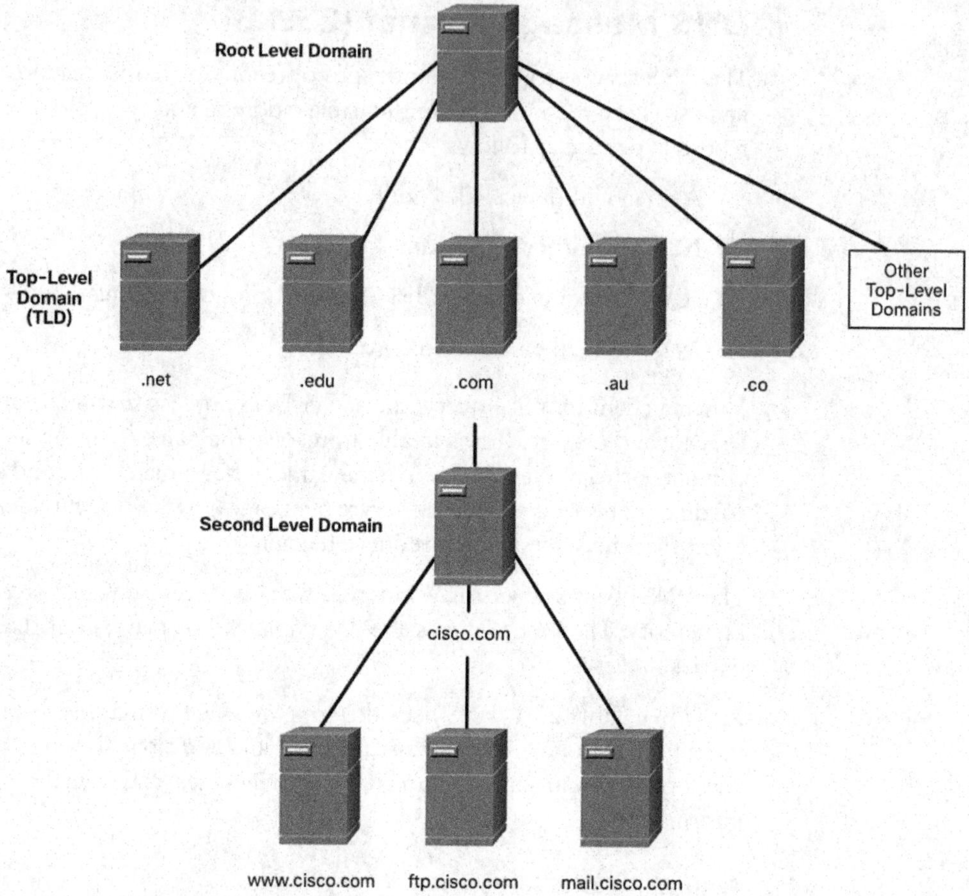

Figure 25-6 DNS Hierarchy

The naming structure is broken down into small, manageable zones. Each DNS server maintains a specific database file and is responsible for managing name-to-IP mappings only for that small portion of the entire DNS structure. When a DNS server receives a request for a name translation that is not within its DNS zone, the DNS server forwards the request to another DNS server within the proper zone for translation. DNS is scalable because hostname resolution is spread across multiple servers.

The different top-level domains represent either the type of organization or the country of origin. Examples of top-level domains are the following:

- **.com**—A business or industry
- **.org**—A nonprofit organization
- **.au**—Australia
- **.co**—Colombia

The nslookup Command (25.1.5)

When configuring a network device, one or more DNS server addresses are provided that the DNS client can use for name resolution. Usually the ISP provides the addresses to use for the DNS servers. When a user's application requests to connect to a remote device by name, the requesting DNS client queries the name server to resolve the name to a numeric address.

Computer operating systems also have a utility called **nslookup** that allows the user to manually query the name servers to resolve a given host name. This utility can also be used to troubleshoot name resolution issues and to verify the current status of the name servers.

When the **nslookup** command is issued, the default DNS server configured for the host is displayed, as shown in Example 25-1. The name of a host or domain can be entered at the **nslookup** prompt. The **nslookup** utility has many options available for extensive testing and verification of the DNS process.

Example 25-1 The **nslookup** Command on a Windows Host

```
C:\Users> nslookup
Default Server:  dns-sj.cisco.com
Address:  171.70.168.183
> www.cisco.com
Server:  dns-sj.cisco.com
Address:  171.70.168.183
Name:    origin-www.cisco.com
Addresses:  2001:420:1101:1::a
          173.37.145.84
Aliases:  www.cisco.com
> cisco.netacad.net
Server:  dns-sj.cisco.com
Address:  171.70.168.183
Name:    cisco.netacad.net
Address:  72.163.6.223
>
```

Interactive Graphic

Syntax Checker—The nslookup Command (25.1.6)

Practice entering the **nslookup** command in both Windows and Linux.

Refer to the online course to complete this activity.

Lab—Observe DNS Resolution (25.1.8)

In this lab, you will complete the following objectives:

- Part 1: Observe the DNS Conversion of a URL to an IP Address
- Part 2: Observe DNS Lookup Using the **nslookup** Command on a Website
- Part 3: Observe DNS Lookup Using the **nslookup** Command on Mail Servers

Refer to the online course to complete this lab.

DHCP Services (25.2)

Dynamic Host Configuration Protocol (25.2.1)

The *Dynamic Host Configuration Protocol (DHCP)* for IPv4 service automates the assignment of IPv4 addresses, subnet masks, gateways, and other IPv4 networking parameters. This is referred to as *dynamic addressing*. The alternative to dynamic addressing is *static addressing*, in which the network administrator manually enters IP address information on hosts.

When a host connects to the network, the host contacts the DHCP to request an address. The DHCP server chooses an address from a configured range of addresses called a *pool* and assigns (leases) it to the host.

On larger networks, or networks where the user population changes frequently, DHCP is preferred for address assignment. New users may arrive and need connections; others may have new computers that must be connected. Assigning IPv4 addresses automatically using DHCP is more efficient than using static addressing for each connection.

DHCP can allocate IP addresses for a configurable period of time, called a *lease period*. The lease period is an important DHCP setting. When the lease period expires or the DHCP server receives a DHCPRELEASE message, the address is returned to the DHCP pool for reuse. Users can freely move from location to location and easily reestablish network connections through DHCP.

As Figure 25-7 shows, various types of devices can be DHCP servers. The DHCP server in most medium-to-large networks is usually a local, dedicated PC-based server. With home networks, the DHCP server is usually located on the local router that connects the home network to the ISP.

Many networks use both DHCP and static addressing. DHCP is used for general-purpose hosts, such as end-user devices, and static addressing is used for network devices, such as gateway routers, switches, servers, and printers.

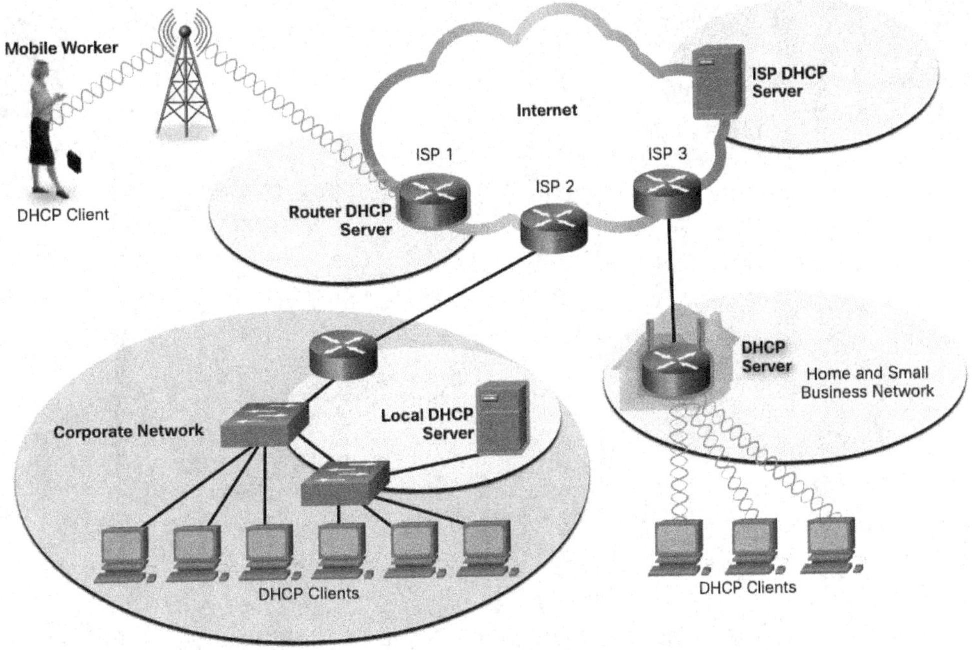

Figure 25-7 Examples of Different DHCP Servers and Clients

DHCP for IPv6 (DHCPv6) provides similar services for IPv6 clients. One important difference is that DHCPv6 does not provide a default gateway address. This can only be obtained dynamically from the Router Advertisement message of the router.

Video

Video—DHCP Operation in a Home Router (25.2.2)

Refer to the online course to view this video.

DHCP Messages (25.2.3)

As shown in Figure 25-8, when an IPv4, DHCP-configured device boots up or connects to the network, the client broadcasts a DHCP Discover (DHCPDISCOVER) message to identify any available DHCP servers on the network. A DHCP server replies with a DHCP Offer (DHCPOFFER) message, which offers a lease to the client. The Offer message contains the IPv4 address and subnet mask to be assigned, the IPv4 address of the DNS server, and the IPv4 address of the default gateway. The lease offer also includes the duration of the lease.

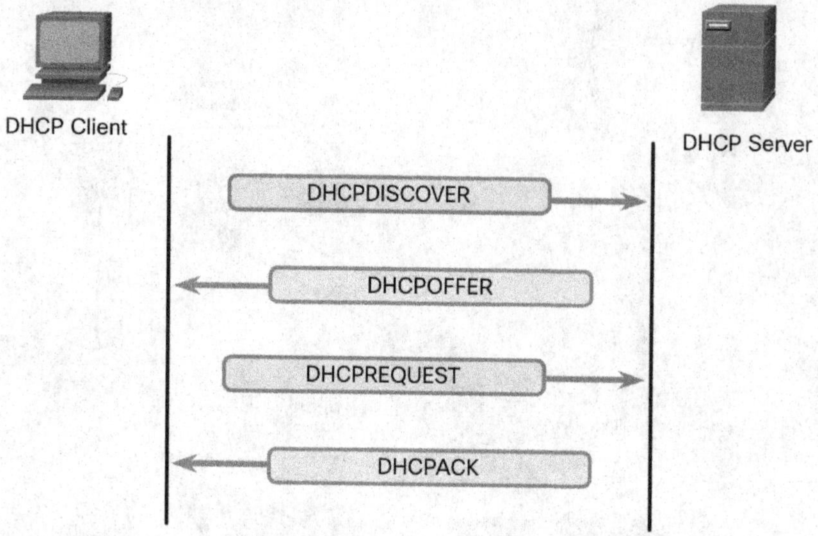

Figure 25-8 DHCP Messages

The client may receive multiple DHCPOFFER messages if there is more than one DHCP server on the local network. Therefore, the client must choose between them and send a DHCP Request (DHCPREQUEST) message that identifies the explicit server and lease offer that the client is accepting. A client may also choose to request an address that it had previously been allocated by the server.

Assuming that the IPv4 address requested by the client, or offered by the server, is still available, the server returns a DHCP Acknowledgment (DHCPACK) message that acknowledges to the client that the lease has been finalized. If the offer is no longer valid, then the selected server responds with a DHCP Negative Acknowledgment (DHCPNAK) message. If a DHCPNAK message is returned, then the selection process must begin again with a new DHCPDISCOVER message being transmitted. After the client has the lease, it must be renewed prior to the lease expiration through another DHCPREQUEST message.

The DHCP server ensures that all IP addresses are unique (the same IP address cannot be assigned to two different network devices simultaneously). Most ISPs use DHCP to allocate addresses to their customers.

DHCPv6 has a set of messages that is similar to those for DHCPv4. The DHCPv6 messages are SOLICIT, ADVERTISE, INFORMATION REQUEST, and REPLY.

Interactive Graphic

Check Your Understanding—DHCP Services (25.2.4)

Refer to the online course to complete this activity.

IP Addressing Services Summary (25.3)

The following is a summary of each topic in the chapter and some questions for your reflection.

What Did I Learn in This Chapter? (25.3.1)

In data networks, devices are labeled with numeric IP addresses to send and receive data over networks. Domain names were created to convert the numeric address into a simple, recognizable name. The DNS protocol defines an automated service that matches resource names with the required numeric network address. DNS communications use a single message format for all types of client queries and server responses, error messages, and the transfer of resource record information between servers.

The DNS server stores different types of resource records that are used to resolve names. These records contain the name, address, and type of record. DNS uses the same message format between servers, consisting of a question, an answer, an authority, and additional information for all types of client queries and server responses, error messages, and transfer of resource record information.

DNS uses domain names to form the hierarchy. The naming structure is broken down into small, manageable zones. Each DNS server maintains a specific database file and is responsible only for managing name-to-IP mappings for that small portion of the entire DNS structure. When a DNS server receives a request for a name translation that is not within its DNS zone, the DNS server forwards the request to another DNS server within the proper zone for translation. DNS is scalable because hostname resolution is spread across multiple servers.

Computer operating systems have a utility called **nslookup** that allows the user to manually query the name servers to resolve a given host name. This utility can also be used to troubleshoot name resolution issues and to verify the current status of the name servers. When the **nslookup** command is issued, the default DNS server configured for the host is displayed. The name of a host or domain can be entered at the **nslookup** prompt.

On larger networks, DHCP is preferred for address assignment. Assigning IPv4 addresses automatically using DHCP is more efficient than using static addressing for each connection. DHCP can allocate IP addresses for a configurable period of time, called a lease period. When the lease period expires or the DHCP server gets a DHCPRELEASE message, the address is returned to the DHCP pool for reuse. Users can freely move from location to location and easily reestablish network connections through DHCP.

DHCPv6 provides similar services for IPv6 clients. One important difference is that DHCPv6 does not provide a default gateway address. This can only be obtained dynamically from the Router Advertisement message of the router.

When an IPv4, DHCP-configured device boots up or connects to the network, the client broadcasts a DHCPDISCOVER message to identify any available DHCP servers on the network. A DHCP server replies with a DHCPOFFER message, which offers a lease to the client. The client sends a DHCPREQUEST message that identifies the explicit server and lease offer that the client is accepting. Assuming that the IPv4 address requested by the client, or offered by the server, is still available, the server returns a DHCPACK message that acknowledges to the client that the lease has been finalized. If the offer is no longer valid, then the selected server responds with a DHCPNAK message. If a DHCPNAK message is returned, then the selection process must begin again with a new DHCPDISCOVER message being transmitted.

DHCPv6 has a set of messages that is similar to those for DHCPv4: SOLICIT, ADVERTISE, INFORMATION REQUEST, and REPLY.

Reflection Questions (25.3.2)

What did you learn in this chapter about IP addressing services? Before reading this chapter, did you think about the DNS protocol defining an automated service that matches resource names with the required numeric network address? Did you know the difference between static addressing and DHCP? I really learned a lot, and I hope you did too!

Practice

The following lab provides practice with the topics introduced in this chapter.

Labs

Lab—Observe DNS Resolution (25.1.8)

Check Your Understanding Questions

Complete all the review questions listed here to test your understanding of the topics and concepts in this chapter. Appendix A, "Answers to 'Check Your Understanding' Questions," lists the answers.

1. Which network service automatically assigns IP addresses to devices on the network?
   a. DHCP
   b. Telnet
   c. DNS
   d. **traceroute**
2. A host PC has just booted and is attempting to lease an address through DHCP. Which two messages will the client typically broadcast on the network? (Choose two.)
   a. DHCPDISCOVER
   b. DHCPOFFER
   c. DHCPREQUEST
   d. DHCPACK
   e. DHCPNACK
3. The client computer, Host A, is trying to resolve the name www.internal.cisco.com to an IP address. The IP address is not in its DNS cache. Which DNS server will Host A communicate with to resolve the domain name to an IP address?
   a. Host A's local DNS server; the IP address Host A has for a DNS server
   b. The root DNS server
   c. The top-level DNS server for .com
   d. The web server www.cisco.com

4. Which statement is true about DHCP operation?

   a. A client confirms the IP addressing information offered by the DHCP server by sending it a DHCPACK message.

   b. A client must wait for lease expiration before it sends a DHCPREQUEST message.

   c. When a device that is configured to use DHCP boots, the client broadcasts a DHCPDISCOVER message to identify any available DHCP servers on the network.

   d. The DHCPDISCOVER message contains the IP address and subnet mask to be assigned, the IP address of the DNS server, and the IP address of the default gateway.

5. Which DHCPv4 message does a client send to accept an IPv4 address that is offered by a DHCP server?

   a. DHCPOFFER

   b. DHCPACK

   c. DHCPREQUEST

   d. DHCPDISCOVER

6. Which protocol translates a website name such as www.cisco.com into a network address?

   a. HTTP

   b. FTP

   c. DHCP

   d. DNS

7. What type of information is contained in a DNS MX record?

   a. The FQDN of the alias used to identify a service

   b. The IP address for an FQDN entry

   c. The domain name mapped to mail exchange servers

   d. The IP address of an authoritative name server

8. A technician is adding a new PC to a LAN. After unpacking the components and making all the connections, the technician starts the PC. After the OS loads, the technician opens a browser and verifies that the PC can reach the Internet. Why was the PC able to connect to the network with no additional configuration?

   a. The PC does not require any additional information to function on the network.

   b. The PC came preconfigured with IP addressing information from the factory.

c. The PC was preconfigured to use DHCP.
d. The PC used DNS to automatically receive IP addressing information from a server.
e. The PC virtual interface is compatible with any network.

9. Which network server is malfunctioning if a user can ping the IP address of a web server but cannot ping the web server host name (domain name)?
   a. DNS server
   b. DHCP server
   c. FTP server
   d. HTTP server

10. Which protocol allows a user to type www.cisco.com instead of an IP address to access the web server?
   a. DNS
   b. FTP
   c. HTML
   d. HTTP
   e. SNMP

11. What action does a local DNS server, the server a client has for its DNS address, take if it does not have an entry for a requested URL?
   a. The server drops the request.
   b. The server returns a "page not found" response to the client.
   c. The server checks with another DNS server to see whether it has an entry.
   d. The server assigns a temporary IP address to the name and sends this IP address to the client.

CHAPTER 26

Transport Layer

Objectives

Upon completion of this chapter, you will be able to answer the following questions:

- What is the purpose of the transport layer in managing the transportation of data in end-to-end communication?
- What are the characteristics of TCP?
- What are the characteristics of UDP?
- How do TCP and UDP use port numbers?
- How do the TCP session establishment and termination processes facilitate reliable communication?
- How are TCP protocol data units transmitted and acknowledged to guarantee delivery?
- What are the operations of transport layer protocols in supporting end-to-end communication?

Key Terms

This chapter uses the following key terms. You can find the definitions in the Glossary.

connection-oriented protocol Page 417

expectational acknowledgment Page 435

initial sequence number (ISN) Page 434

port numbers Page 423

segments Page 409

selective acknowledgment (SACK) Page 435

socket Page 423

socket pair Page 424

stateful Page 418

three-way handshake Page 430

Transmission Control Protocol (TCP) Page 408

User Datagram Protocol (UDP) Page 408

window size Page 438

Introduction (26.0)

Looks like Olcay and Abay are finishing their shift at the utilities plant. Olcay tells Abay to have a good night. She tells him to be prepared to talk about all things that have to do with the transport layer in the morning.

Abay might want to read this chapter before he talks to Olcay in the morning. Are you familiar with the transport layer? You should be if you want to understand networking. The transport layer is responsible for logical communications between applications running on different hosts. Let's get started!

Transportation of Data (26.1)

As previously discussed, for communication to occur between source and destination, a set of rules or protocols must be followed. This section focuses on the protocols at the transport layer.

Role of the Transport Layer (26.1.1)

Application layer programs generate data that must be exchanged between source and destination hosts. The transport layer is responsible for logical communications between applications running on different hosts. This may include services such as establishing a temporary session between two hosts and the reliable transmission of information for an application.

As shown in Figure 26-1, the transport layer is the link between the application layer and the lower layers that are responsible for network transmission.

The transport layer has no knowledge of the destination host type, the type of media over which the data must travel, the path taken by the data, the congestion on a link, or the size of the network.

The transport layer includes two protocols:

- *Transmission Control Protocol (TCP)*
- *User Datagram Protocol (UDP)*

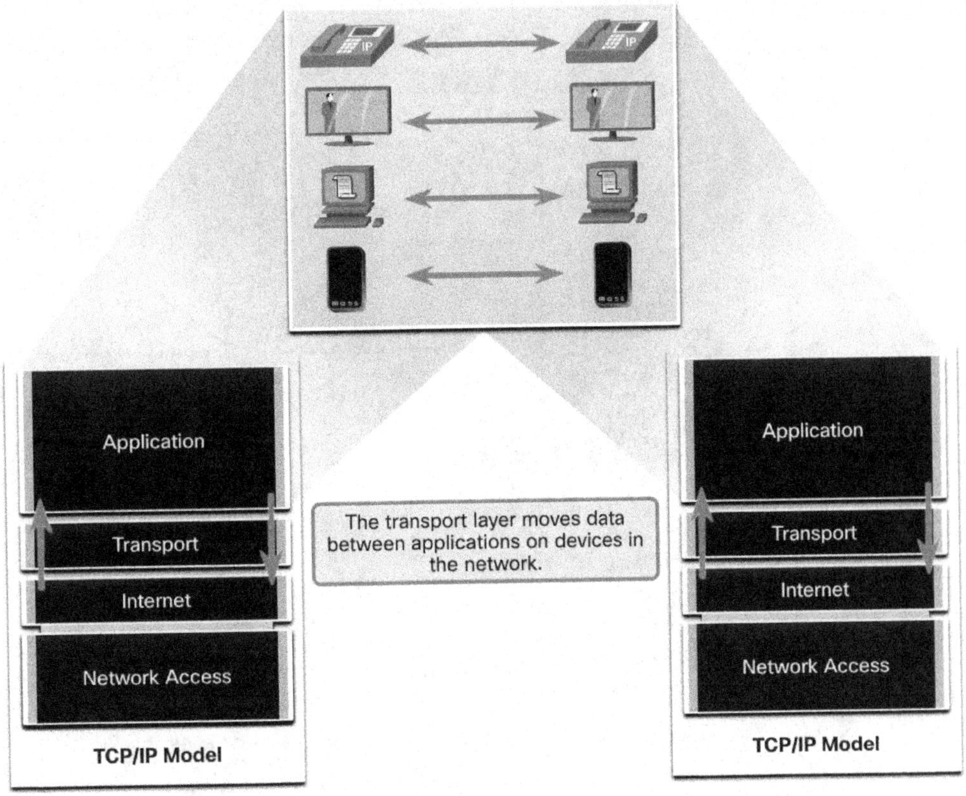

Figure 26-1 The Transport Layer in the TCP/IP Model

Transport Layer Responsibilities (26.1.2)

The transport layer has many responsibilities.

At the transport layer, each set of data flowing between a source application and a destination application is known as a *conversation* and is tracked separately. It is the responsibility of the transport layer to maintain and track these multiple conversations. As illustrated in Figure 26-2, a host may have multiple applications that are communicating across the network simultaneously.

Most networks have a limitation on the amount of data that can be included in a single packet. Therefore, data must be divided into manageable pieces.

It is the transport layer's responsibility to divide the application data into appropriately sized blocks that are easier to manage and transport. Depending on the transport layer protocol used, the transport layer blocks are called either *segments* or *datagrams*. Figure 26-3 illustrates the transport layer using different blocks for each conversation.

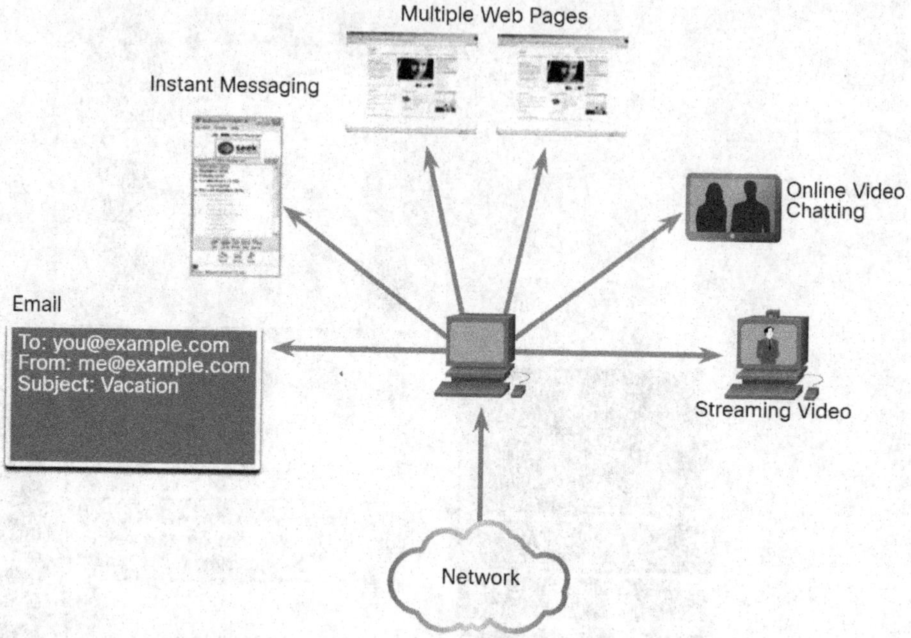

Figure 26-2 Tracking Individual Conversations

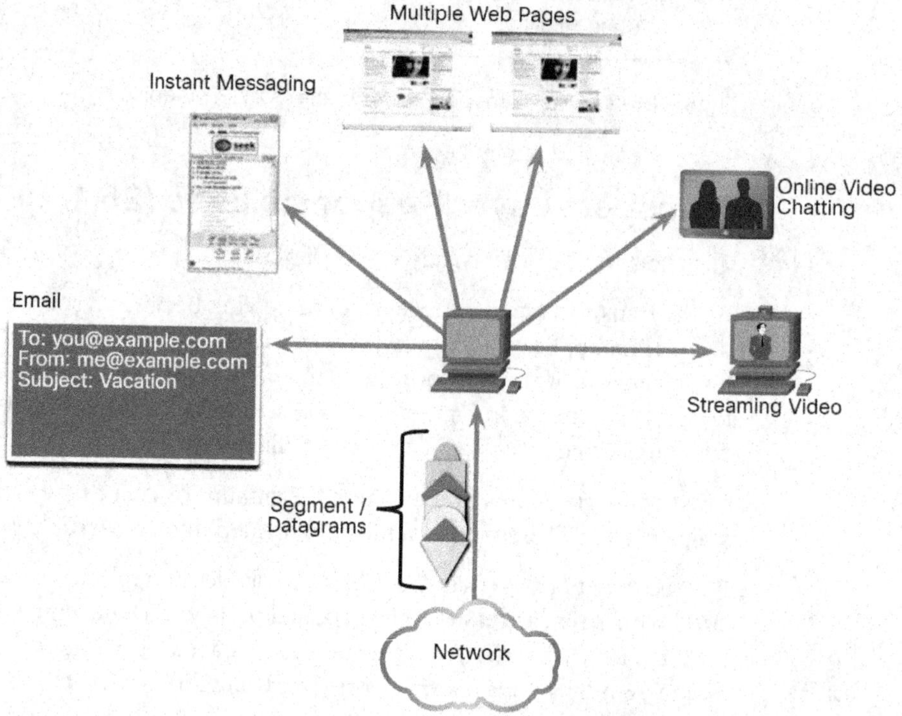

Figure 26-3 Segmenting Data and Reassembling Segments

The transport layer protocol also adds header information containing binary data organized into several fields to each block of data. The values in these fields enable various transport layer protocols to perform different functions in managing data communication. For instance, the header information is used by the receiving host to reassemble the blocks of data into a complete data stream for the receiving application layer program, as shown in Figure 26-4.

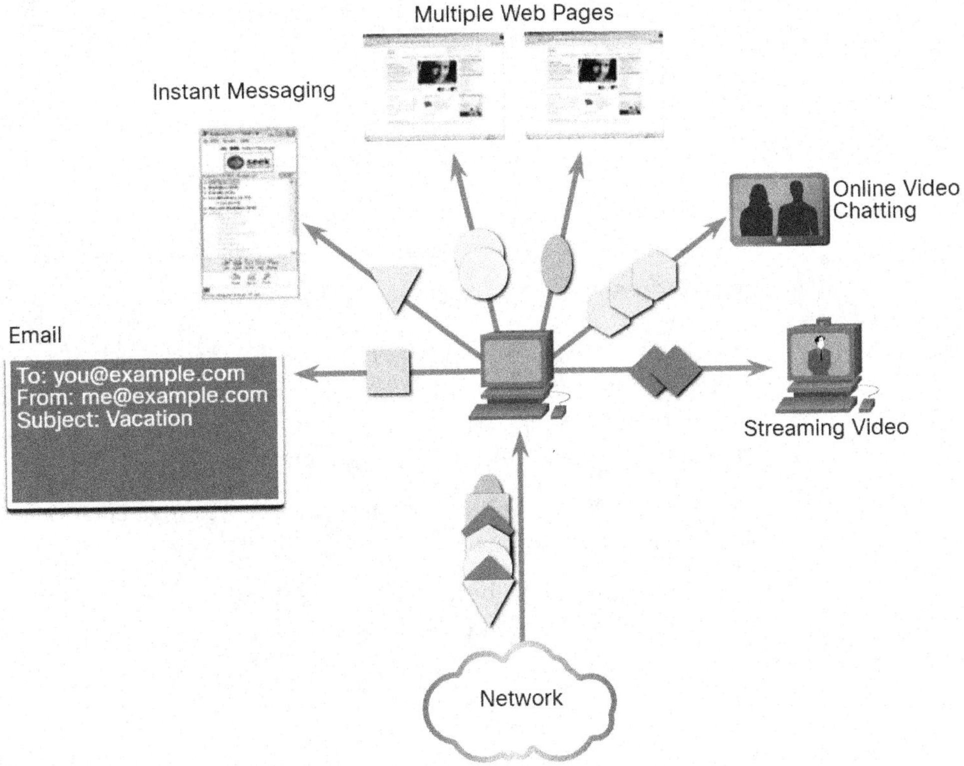

Figure 26-4 Adding Header Information

The transport layer ensures that even with multiple applications running on a device, all applications receive the correct data.

The transport layer must be able to separate and manage multiple communications with different transport requirement needs. To pass data streams to the proper applications, the transport layer identifies the target application using an identifier called a *port number* (see "Port Numbers" later in this chapter). As illustrated in Figure 26-5, each software process that needs to access the network is assigned a port number unique to that host.

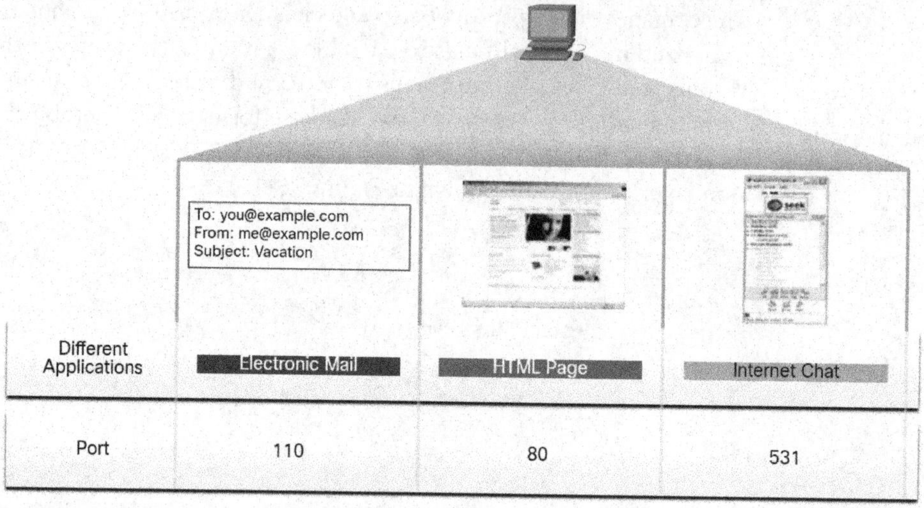

Figure 26-5 Identifying the Applications

Sending some types of data (for example, a streaming video) across a network as one complete communication stream could consume all the available bandwidth. This would prevent other communication conversations from occurring at the same time. It would also make error recovery and retransmission of damaged data difficult.

As shown in Figure 26-6, the transport layer uses segmentation and multiplexing to enable different communication conversations to be interleaved on the same network.

Error checking can be performed on the data in the segment to determine whether the segment was altered during transmission.

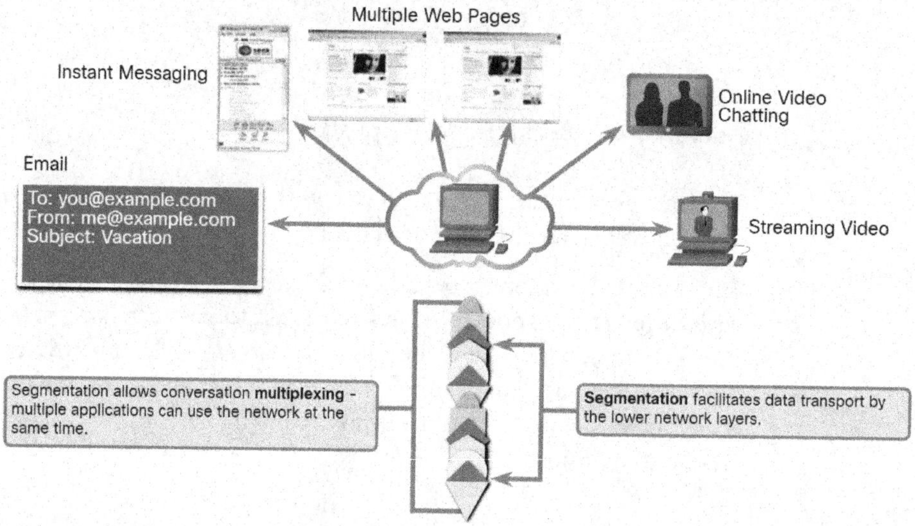

Figure 26-6 Conversation Multiplexing

Transport Layer Protocols (26.1.3)

IP is concerned only with the structure, addressing, and routing of packets. IP does not specify how the delivery or transportation of the packets takes place.

Transport layer protocols specify how to transfer messages between hosts and are responsible for managing reliability requirements of a conversation. The transport layer includes the TCP and UDP protocols.

Different applications have different transport reliability requirements. Therefore, TCP/IP provides two transport layer protocols, as shown in Figure 26-7.

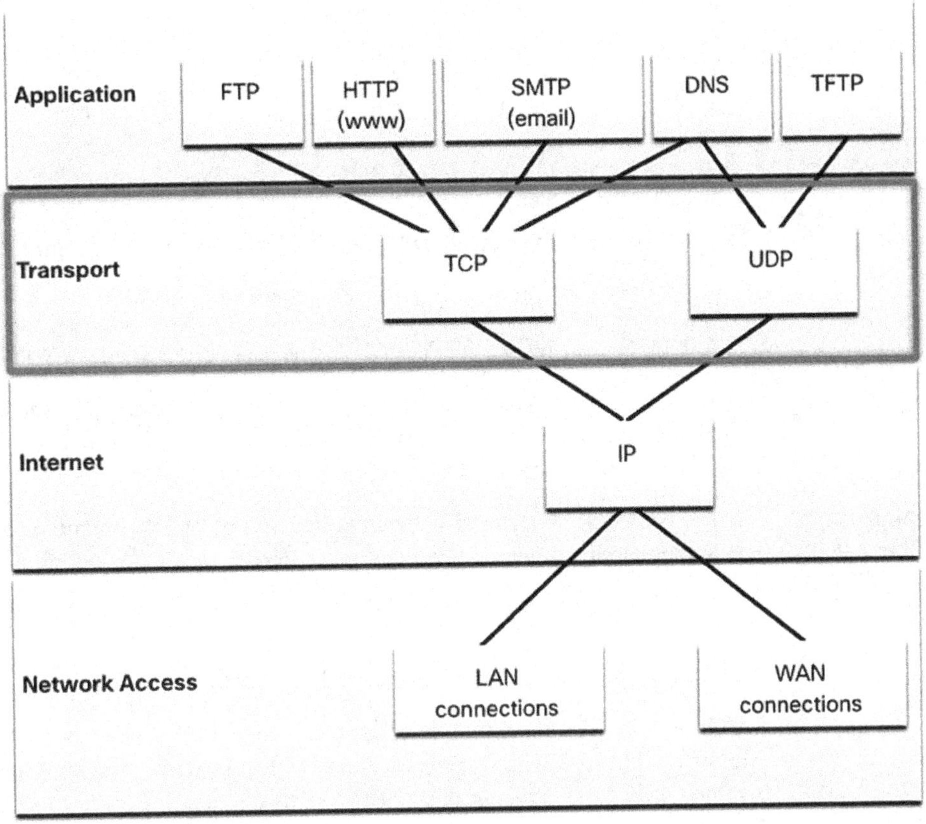

Figure 26-7 Transport Layer Protocols

Transmission Control Protocol (TCP) (26.1.4)

IP is concerned only with the structure, addressing, and routing of packets, from original sender to final destination. IP is not responsible for guaranteeing delivery or determining whether a connection between the sender and receiver needs to be established.

TCP is considered a reliable, full-featured transport layer protocol, which ensures that all of the data arrives at the destination. TCP includes fields that ensure the delivery of the application data. These fields require additional processing by the sending and receiving hosts.

Note

TCP divides data into segments.

TCP transport is analogous to sending packages that are tracked from source to destination. If a shipping order is broken up into several packages, a customer can check online to see the order of the delivery.

TCP provides reliability and flow control using these basic operations:

- Number and track data segments transmitted to a specific host from a specific application
- Acknowledge received data
- Retransmit any unacknowledged data after a certain amount of time
- Sequence data that might arrive in the wrong order
- Send data at an efficient rate that is acceptable by the receiver

To maintain the state of a conversation and track the information, TCP must first establish a connection between the sender and the receiver. This is why TCP is known as a *connection-oriented protocol.*

Interactive Graphic

Go to the online course to view an animation of TCP segments and acknowledgments being transmitted between sender and receiver.

User Datagram Protocol (UDP) (26.1.5)

UDP is a simpler transport layer protocol than TCP. It does not provide reliability and flow control, which means it requires fewer header fields. Because the sender and the receiver UDP processes do not have to manage reliability and flow control, UDP datagrams can be processed faster than TCP segments. UDP provides the basic functions for delivering datagrams between the appropriate applications, with very little overhead and data checking.

Note

UDP divides data into datagrams, also referred to as segments.

UDP is a *connectionless protocol*. Because UDP does not provide reliability or flow control, it does not require an established connection. Because UDP does not track information sent or received between the client and server, UDP is also known as a *stateless protocol*.

UDP is also known as a *best-effort delivery protocol* because there is no acknowledgment that the data is received at the destination. With UDP, there are no transport layer processes that inform the sender of a successful delivery.

UDP is like placing a regular, nonregistered, letter in the mail. The sender of the letter is not aware of the availability of the receiver to receive the letter. Nor is the post office responsible for tracking the letter or informing the sender if the letter does not arrive at the final destination.

Interactive Graphic

Go to the online course to view an animation of UDP segments being transmitted from sender to receiver.

The Right Transport Layer Protocol for the Right Application (26.1.6)

Some applications can tolerate some data loss during transmission over the network but cannot tolerate delays in transmission. For these applications, UDP is the better choice because it requires less network overhead. UDP is preferable for applications such as voice over IP (VoIP). Acknowledgments and retransmission would slow down delivery and make the voice conversation unacceptable.

UDP is also used by request-and-reply applications where the data is minimal and retransmission can be done quickly. For example, DNS uses UDP for this type of transaction. The client requests IPv4 and IPv6 addresses for a known domain name from a DNS server. If the client does not receive a response in a predetermined amount of time, it simply sends the request again.

For example, if one or two segments of a live video stream fail to arrive, it creates a momentary disruption in the stream. This may appear as distortion in the image or sound, but may not be noticeable to the user. If the destination device had to account for lost data, the stream could be delayed while waiting for retransmissions, therefore causing the image or sound to be greatly degraded. In this case, it is better to render the best media possible with the segments received and forgo reliability.

For other applications, it is important that all the data arrives and that it can be processed in its proper sequence. For these types of applications, TCP is used as the transport protocol. For example, applications such as databases, web browsers, and email clients require that all data that is sent arrives at the destination in its original condition. Any missing data could corrupt a communication, making it either

incomplete or unreadable. For example, it is important when accessing banking information over the web to make sure all the information is sent and received correctly.

Application developers must choose which transport protocol type is appropriate based on the requirements of the application. Video may be sent over TCP or UDP. Applications that stream stored audio and video typically use TCP. For example, the application uses TCP to perform buffering, bandwidth probing, and congestion control to provide a better user experience.

Real-time video and voice usually use UDP, but may also use TCP, or both UDP and TCP. A video conferencing application may use UDP by default, but because many firewalls block UDP, the application may also be sent over TCP.

Applications that stream stored audio and video use TCP. For example, if your network suddenly cannot support the bandwidth needed to watch an on-demand movie, the application pauses the playback. During the pause, you might see a "buffering..." message while TCP works to reestablish the stream. When all the segments are in order and a minimum level of bandwidth is restored, your TCP session resumes, and the movie resumes playing.

Figure 26-8 summarizes differences between UDP and TCP.

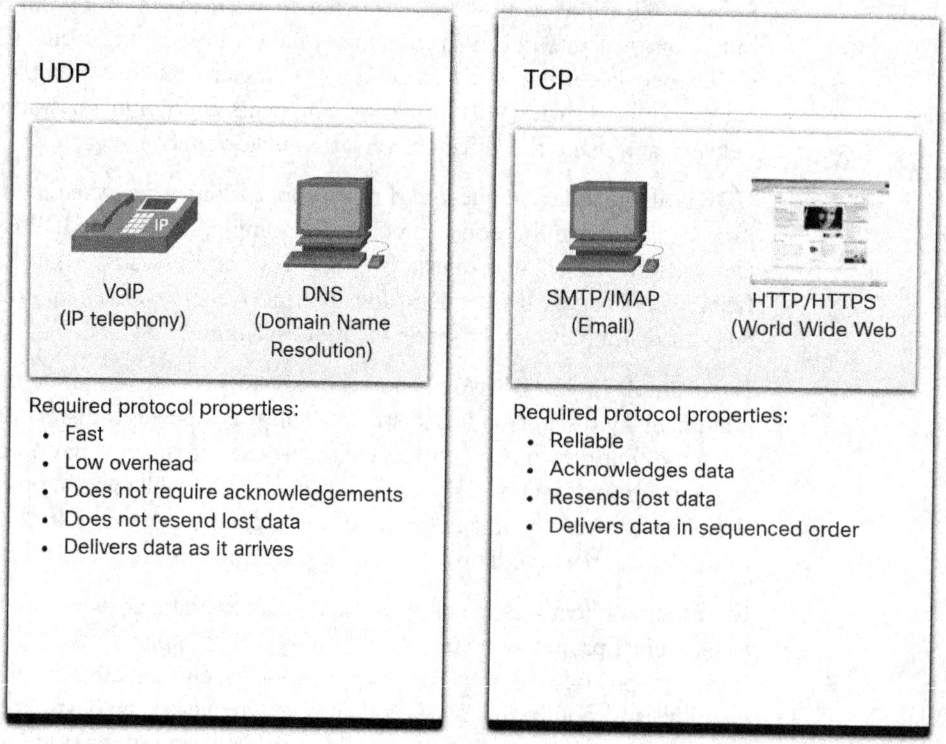

Figure 26-8 UDP and TCP Uses

Interactive Graphic

Check Your Understanding—Transportation of Data (26.1.7)

Refer to the online course to complete this activity.

TCP Overview (26.2)

As previously mentioned, both TCP and UDP are transport layer protocols. It is up to the developer to determine which of these protocols best matches the requirements of the application being developed. TCP establishes a connection proving reliability and flow control.

TCP Features (26.2.1)

This section gives more details about what TCP does and when it is a good idea to use it instead of UDP.

To understand the differences between TCP and UDP, it is important to understand how each protocol implements specific reliability features and how each protocol tracks conversations.

In addition to supporting the basic functions of data segmentation and reassembly, TCP also provides the following services:

- **Establishes a session**—TCP is a *connection-oriented protocol* that negotiates and establishes a permanent connection (or session) between source and destination devices prior to forwarding any traffic. Through session establishment, the devices negotiate the amount of traffic that can be forwarded at a given time, and the communication data between the two can be closely managed.
- **Ensures reliable delivery**—As a segment is transmitted over the network, it could be corrupted or lost completely, for various reasons. TCP ensures that each segment that is sent by the source arrives at the destination.
- **Provides same-order delivery**—Because networks may provide multiple routes that can have different transmission rates, data can arrive in the wrong order. By numbering and sequencing the segments, TCP ensures segments are reassembled into the proper order.
- **Supports flow control**—Network hosts have limited resources (that is, memory and processing power). When TCP is aware that these resources are overtaxed, it can request that the sending application reduce the rate of data flow. This is done by TCP regulating the amount of data the source transmits. Flow control can prevent the need for retransmission of the data when the resources of the receiving host are overwhelmed.

For more information on TCP, search the Internet for RFC 9293.

TCP Header (26.2.2)

TCP is a *stateful* protocol, which means it keeps track of the state of the communication session. To track the state of a session, TCP records which information it has sent and which information has been acknowledged. The stateful session begins with the session establishment and ends with the session termination.

A TCP segment adds 20 bytes (160 bits) of overhead when encapsulating the application layer data. Figure 26-9 shows the fields in a TCP header.

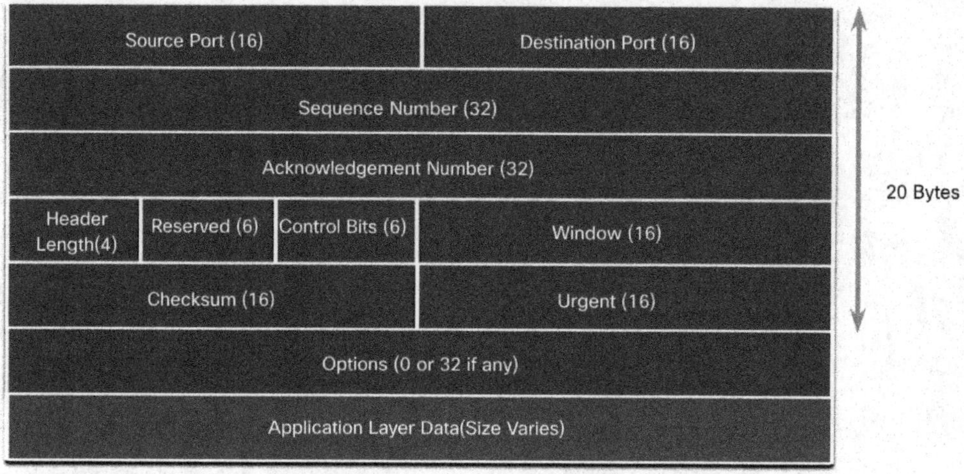

Figure 26-9 Fields of the TCP Header

TCP Header Fields (26.2.3)

Table 26-1 identifies and describes the ten fields in a TCP header.

Table 26-1 Details of the TCP Header Fields

TCP Header Field	Description
Source Port	A 16-bit field used to identify the source application by port number
Destination Port	A 16-bit field used to identify the destination application by port number
Sequence Number	A 32-bit field used for data reassembly purposes
Acknowledgment Number	A 32-bit field used to indicate that data has been received and the next byte expected from the source

TCP Header Field	Description
Header Length	A 4-bit field known as "data offset" that indicates the length of the TCP segment header
Reserved	A 6-bit field that is reserved for future use
Control Bits	A 6-bit field that includes bit codes, or flags, used to indicate the purpose and function of the TCP segment
Window Size	A 16-bit field used to indicate the number of bytes that can be accepted at one time
Checksum	A 16-bit field used for error checking of the segment header and data
Urgent	A 16-bit field used to indicate if the contained data is urgent

Applications That Use TCP (26.2.4)

TCP is a good example of how the different layers of the TCP/IP protocol suite have specific roles. TCP handles all tasks associated with dividing the data stream into segments, providing reliability, controlling data flow, and reordering segments. TCP frees the application from having to manage any of these tasks. Applications, like those shown in Figure 26-10, can simply send the data stream to the transport layer and use the services of TCP.

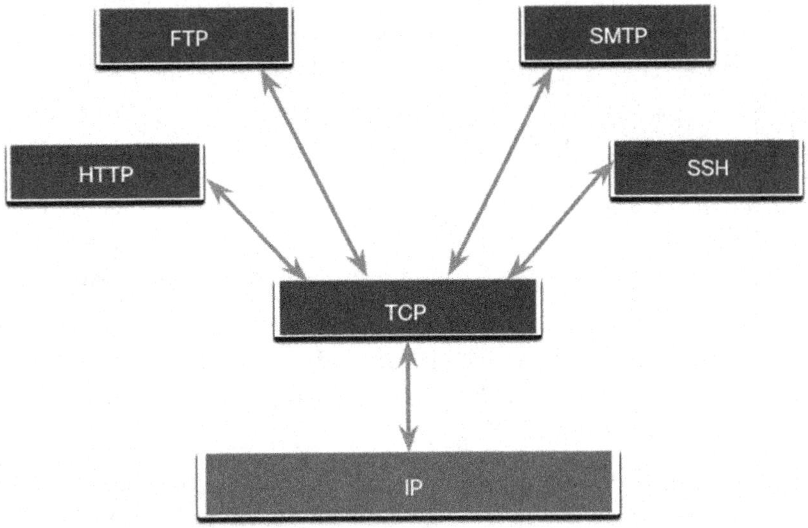

Figure 26-10 Applications That Use TCP

Interactive Graphic

Check Your Understanding—TCP Overview (26.2.5)

Refer to the online course to complete this activity.

UDP Overview (26.3)

The reliability and flow control features provided by TCP come with additional overhead related to the connection establishment and tracking whether or not segments were received. UDP is a transport layer protocol that is used when this kind of overhead creates unnecessary delay; for example, transaction-based protocols such as DNS or DHCP, and delay-sensitive such as Voice over IP.

UDP Features (26.3.1)

This section covers what UDP does and when it is a good idea to use it instead of TCP. UDP is a best-effort, lightweight transport protocol that offers the same data segmentation and reassembly as TCP but without TCP's reliability and flow control.

UDP features include the following:

- Data is reconstructed in the order that it is received.
- Any segments that are lost are not resent.
- There is no session establishment.
- The sender is not informed about resource availability.

For more information on UDP, search the Internet for RFC 768.

UDP Header (26.3.2)

UDP is a *stateless* protocol, which means that neither the client nor the server tracks the state of the communication session. If reliability is required when using UDP as the transport protocol, it must be handled by the application.

One of the most important requirements for delivering live video and voice over the network is that the data continues to flow quickly. Live video and voice applications can tolerate some data loss with minimal or no noticeable effect, making them perfectly suited to UDP.

The blocks of communication in UDP are called *datagrams*, or *segments*. These datagrams are sent as best effort by the transport layer protocol.

The UDP header is far simpler than the TCP header because it only has four fields and requires 8 bytes (64 bits). Figure 26-11 shows the fields in a TCP header.

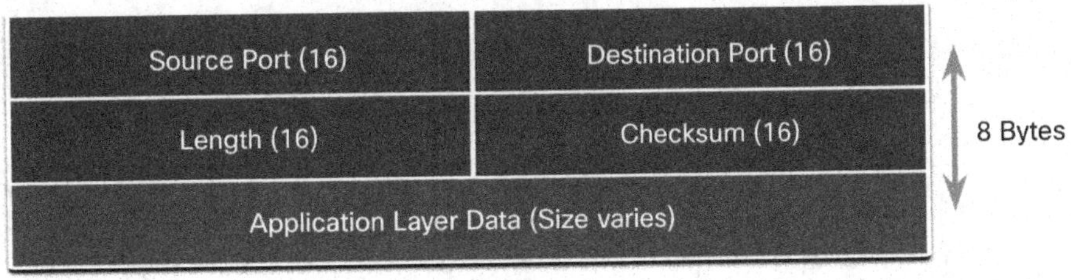

Figure 26-11 Fields of the UDP Header

UDP Header Fields (26.3.3)

Table 26-2 identifies and describes the four fields in a UDP header.

Table 26-2 Details of the UDP Header Fields

UDP Header Field	Description
Source Port	A 16-bit field used to identify the source application by port number
Destination Port	A 16-bit field used to identify the destination application by port number
Length	A 16-bit field that indicates the length of the UDP datagram header
Checksum	A 16-bit field used for error checking of the datagram header and data

Applications That Use UDP (26.3.4)

Three types of applications are best suited for UDP:

- **Live video and multimedia applications**—Applications that can tolerate some data loss but require little or no delay. Examples include VoIP and live streaming video.
- **Simple request and reply applications**—Applications with simple transactions where a host sends a request and may or may not receive a reply. Examples include DNS and DHCP.
- **Applications that handle reliability themselves**—Unidirectional communications where flow control, error detection, acknowledgments, and error recovery are not required or can be handled by the application. Examples include SNMP and TFTP.

Figure 26-12 identifies applications that require UDP.

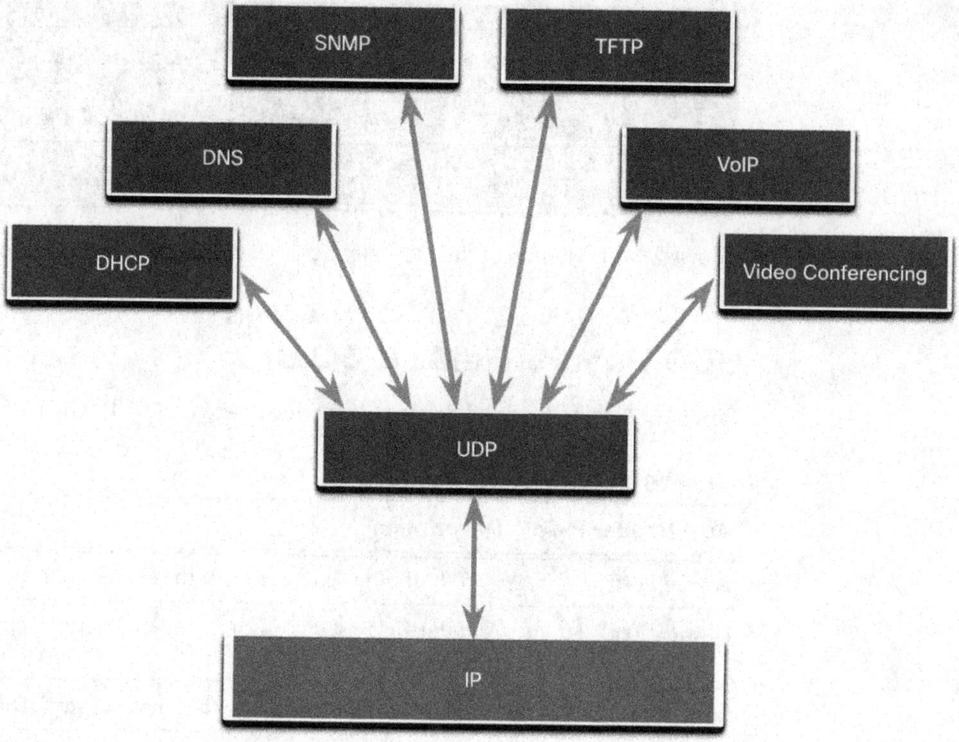

Figure 26-12 Applications That Use UDP

Although DNS and SNMP use UDP by default, they both also use TCP. DNS uses TCP if the DNS request or DNS response is more than 512 bytes, such as when a DNS response includes many name resolutions. Similarly, under some situations, a network administrator may want to configure SNMP to use TCP.

Interactive Graphic

Check Your Understanding—UDP Overview (26.3.5)

Refer to the online course to complete this activity.

Port Numbers (26.4)

This section covers how both TCP and UDP use port numbers to identify the proper application layer process.

Multiple Separate Communications (26.4.1)

As you have learned, there are some situations in which TCP is the right protocol for the job, and other situations in which UDP should be used. No matter what type of

data is being transported, the TCP and UDP transport layer protocols use *port numbers* to manage multiple, simultaneous conversations. As shown in Figure 26-13, the TCP and UDP header fields identify a source application port number and a destination application port number.

Figure 26-13 Source and Destination Port Fields

The source port number is associated with the originating application on the local host, whereas the destination port number is associated with the destination application on the remote host.

For instance, when a host initiates a web page request from a web server, the source port number is dynamically generated by the host to uniquely identify the conversation. Each request generated by a host uses a different dynamically created source port number. This process allows multiple conversations to occur simultaneously.

In the request, the destination port number identifies the type of service being requested of the destination web server. For example, when a client specifies port 80 in the destination port, the server that receives the message knows that web services are being requested.

A server can offer more than one service simultaneously, such as web services on port 80 and File Transfer Protocol (FTP) connection establishment on port 21.

Socket Pairs (26.4.2)

The source and destination ports are placed within the segment. The segments are then encapsulated within an IP packet. The IP packet contains the IP addresses of the source and destination. The combination of the source IP address and source port number, or the destination IP address and destination port number, is known as a *socket*.

In the example in Figure 26-14, the PC is simultaneously requesting FTP and web services from the destination server.

In Figure 26-14, the FTP request generated by the PC includes the Layer 2 MAC addresses and the Layer 3 IP addresses. The request also identifies the source port number 1305 (dynamically generated by the host) and destination port, identifying the FTP services on port 21. The host also has requested a web page from the server using the same Layer 2 and Layer 3 addresses. However, it is using the source port number 1099 (dynamically generated by the host) and destination port identifying the web service on port 80.

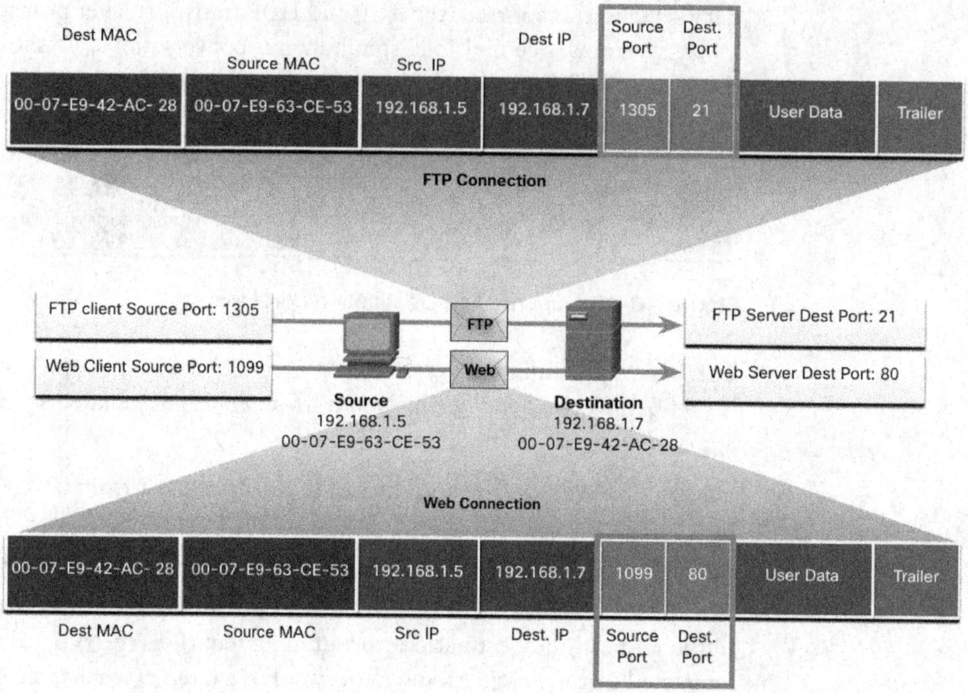

Figure 26-14 Host Sending Multiple Simultaneous Communications

The socket is used to identify the server and service being requested by the client. A client socket might look like this, with 1099 representing the source port number: 192.168.1.5:1099.

The socket on a web server might be 192.168.1.7:80.

Together, these two sockets combine to form a *socket pair*: 192.168.1.5:1099, 192.168.1.7:80.

Sockets enable multiple processes, running on a client, to distinguish themselves from each other, and enable multiple connections to a server process to be distinguished from each other.

The source port number acts as a return address for the requesting application. The transport layer keeps track of this port and the application that initiated the request so that when a response is returned, it can be forwarded to the correct application.

Port Number Groups (26.4.3)

The Internet Assigned Numbers Authority (IANA) is the standards organization responsible for assigning various addressing standards, including the 16-bit port

numbers. The 16 bits used to identify the source and destination port numbers provide a range of ports from 0 through 65535.

The IANA has divided the range of numbers into the three port groups shown in Table 26-3.

Table 26-3 Details of Port Number Groups

Port Group	Number Range	Description
Well-known ports	0 to 1023	These port numbers are reserved for common or popular services and applications such as web browsers, email clients, and remote access clients. The use of defined well-known ports for common server applications enables clients to easily identify the associated service required.
Registered ports	1024 to 49151	These port numbers are assigned by IANA to a requesting entity to use with specific processes or applications. These processes are primarily individual applications that a user has chosen to install, rather than common applications that would receive a well-known port number. For example, Cisco has registered port 1812 for its RADIUS server authentication process.
Private and/or dynamic ports	49152 to 65535	These ports are also known as *ephemeral ports*. The client's OS usually assigns port numbers dynamically when a connection to a service is initiated. The dynamic port is then used to identify the client application during communication.

Note

Some client operating systems may use registered port numbers instead of dynamic port numbers for assigning source ports.

Table 26-4 displays some common well-known port numbers and their associated applications.

Table 26-4 Well-Known Port Numbers

Port Number	Protocol	Application
20	TCP	File Transfer Protocol (FTP)—Data
21	TCP	File Transfer Protocol (FTP)—Control
22	TCP	Secure Shell (SSH)

Port Number	Protocol	Application
23	TCP	Telnet
25	TCP	Simple Mail Transfer Protocol (SMTP)
53	UDP, TCP	Domain Name Service (DNS)
67	UDP	Dynamic Host Configuration Protocol (DHCP)—Server
68	UDP	Dynamic Host Configuration Protocol—Client
69	UDP	Trivial File Transfer Protocol (TFTP)
80	TCP	Hypertext Transfer Protocol (HTTP)
110	TCP	Post Office Protocol version 3 (POP3)
143	TCP	Internet Message Access Protocol (IMAP)
161	UDP	Simple Network Management Protocol (SNMP)
443	TCP	Hypertext Transfer Protocol Secure (HTTPS)

Some applications may use both TCP and UDP. For example, DNS uses UDP when clients send requests to a DNS server. However, communication between two DNS servers always uses TCP.

Search the IANA website for port registry to view the full list of port numbers and associated applications.

The netstat Command (26.4.4)

Unexplained TCP connections can pose a major security threat. They can indicate that something or someone is connected to the local host. Sometimes it is necessary to know which active TCP connections are open and running on a networked host. Netstat is an important network utility that can be used to verify those connections. As shown in Example 26-1, enter the command **netstat** to list the protocols in use, the local address and port numbers, the foreign address and port numbers, and the connection state.

Example 26-1 The **netstat** Command on a Windows Host

```
C:\> netstat
Active Connections
Proto  Local Address          Foreign Address          State
TCP    192.168.1.124:3126     192.168.0.2:netbios-ssn  ESTABLISHED
TCP    192.168.1.124:3158     207.138.126.152:http     ESTABLISHED
TCP    192.168.1.124:3159     207.138.126.169:http     ESTABLISHED
```

```
TCP    192.168.1.124:3160    207.138.126.169:http    ESTABLISHED
TCP    192.168.1.124:3161    sc.msn.com:http         ESTABLISHED
TCP    192.168.1.124:3166    www.cisco.com:http      ESTABLISHED
```

By default, the **netstat** command attempts to resolve IP addresses to domain names and port numbers to well-known applications. Adding the **-n** option displays IP addresses and port numbers in their numerical form.

Interactive Graphic

Check Your Understanding—Port Numbers (26.4.5)

Refer to the online course to complete this activity.

TCP Communication Process (26.5)

TCP is considered a stateful protocol because it establishes a session between source and destination and keeps track of the data within that session. This section covers how TCP establishes this connection to ensure reliability and flow control.

TCP Server Processes (26.5.1)

You already know the fundamentals of TCP. Understanding the role of port numbers will help you to grasp the details of the TCP communication process. In this section, you will also learn about the TCP three-way handshake and session termination processes.

Each application process running on a server is configured to use a port number. The port number is either automatically assigned or configured manually by a system administrator.

An individual server cannot have two services assigned to the same port number within the same transport layer services. For example, a host running a web server application and a file transfer application cannot have both configured to use the same port, such as TCP port 80.

An active server application assigned to a specific port is considered open, which means that the transport layer accepts and processes segments addressed to that port. Any incoming client request addressed to the correct socket is accepted, and the data is passed to the server application. There can be many ports open simultaneously on a server, one for each active server application.

The following details information about TCP server processes.

In Figure 26-15, Client 1 is requesting web services and Client 2 is requesting email service from the same server.

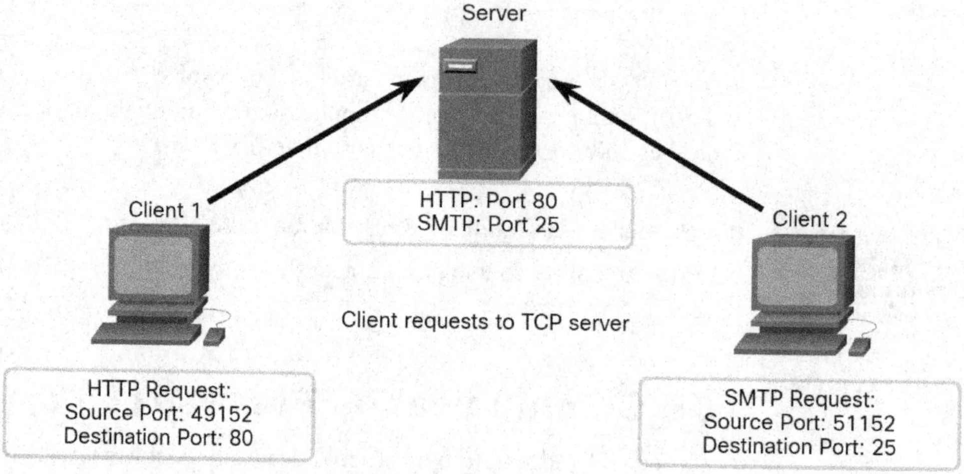

Figure 26-15 Clients Sending TCP Requests

In Figure 26-16, Client 1 is requesting web services using well-known destination port 80 (HTTP) and Client 2 is requesting email service using well-known port 25 (SMTP).

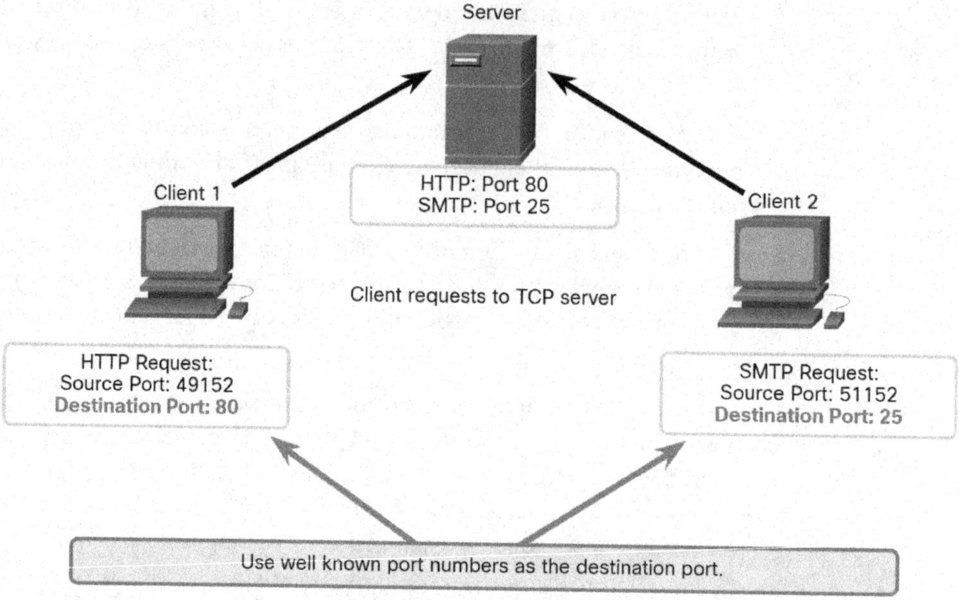

Figure 26-16 Request Destination Ports

Client requests dynamically generate a source port number. In Figure 26-17, Client 1 is using source port 49152 and Client 2 is using source port 51152.

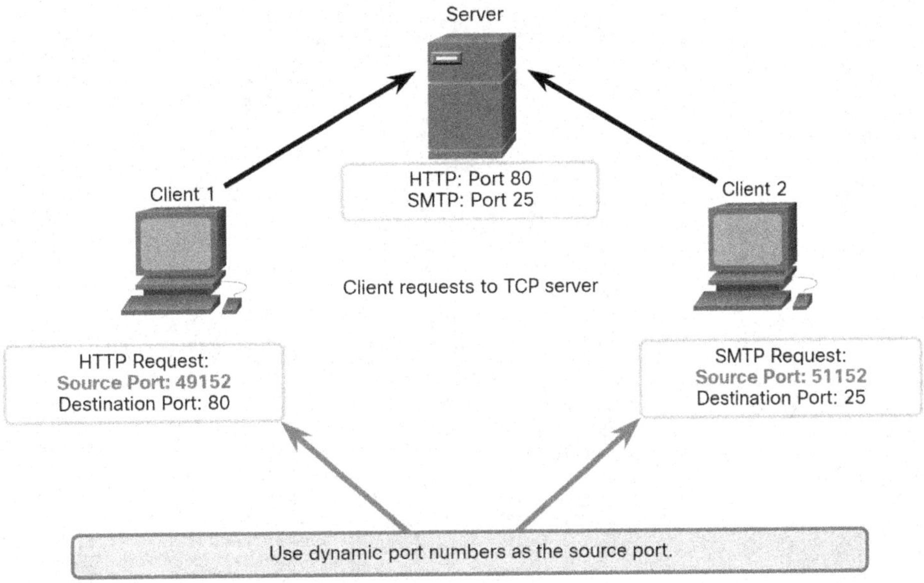

Figure 26-17 Request Source Ports

When the server responds to the client requests, it reverses the destination and source ports of the initial request, as shown in Figures 26-18 and 26-19. Notice that the server response to the web request now has destination port 49152 and the email response now has destination port 51152, as shown in Figure 26-18.

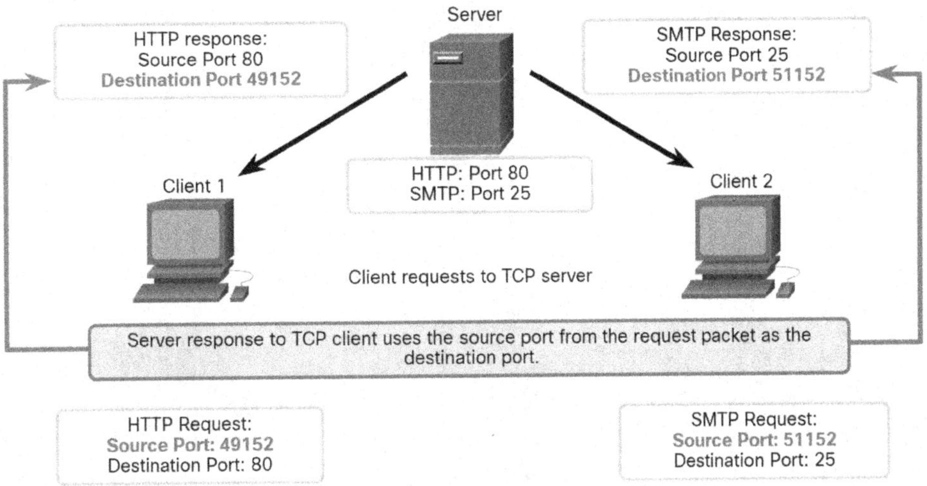

Figure 26-18 Response Destination Ports

The source port in the server response is the original destination port in the initial requests, as shown in Figure 26-19.

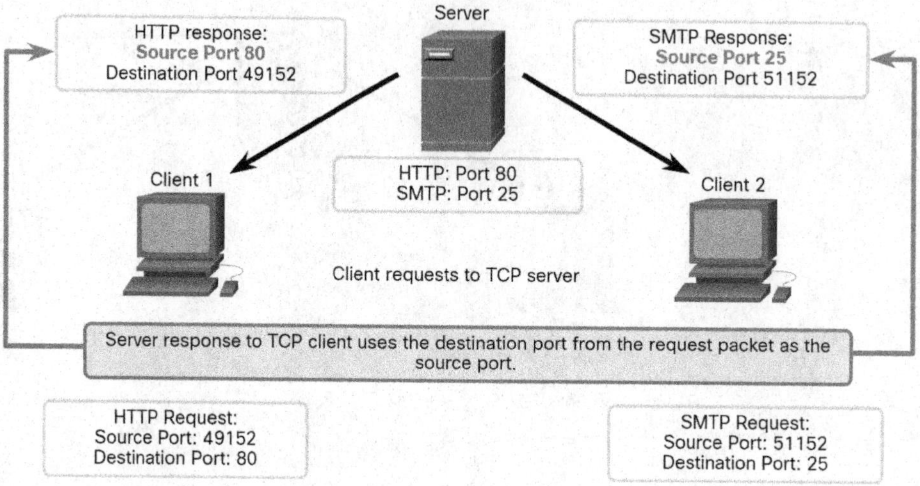

Figure 26-19 Response Source Ports

TCP Connection Establishment (26.5.2)

In some cultures, when two persons meet, they often greet each other by shaking hands. Both parties understand the act of shaking hands as a signal for a friendly greeting. Connections on the network are similar. In TCP connections, the host client establishes the connection with the server using the *three-way handshake* process.

The steps for the TCP connection establishment process are shown in Figure 26-20 and described here:

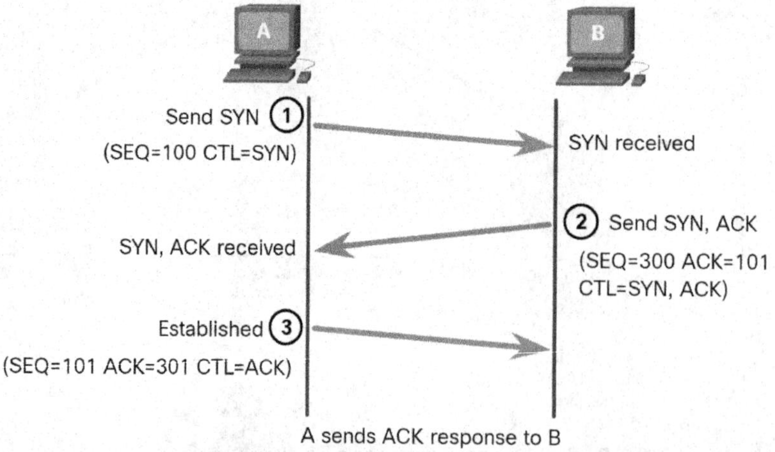

Figure 26-20 Steps in the TCP Connection Establishment Process

Step 1. SYN—The initiating client requests a client-to-server communication session with the server.

Step 2. ACK and SYN—The server acknowledges the client-to-server communication session and requests a server-to-client communication session.

Step 3. ACK—The initiating client acknowledges the server-to-client communication session.

The three-way handshake validates that the destination host is available to communicate. In this example, host A has validated that host B is available.

Session Termination (26.5.3)

To close a connection, the Finish (FIN) control flag must be set in the segment header. To end each one-way TCP session, a two-way handshake, consisting of a FIN segment and an Acknowledgment (ACK) segment, is used. Therefore, to terminate a single conversation supported by TCP, four exchanges are needed to end both sessions. Either the client or the server can initiate the termination.

Note

For simplicity, the terms *client* and *server* are used in the following steps, but any two hosts that have an open session can initiate the termination process.

The steps for the TCP session termination process are shown in Figure 26-21.

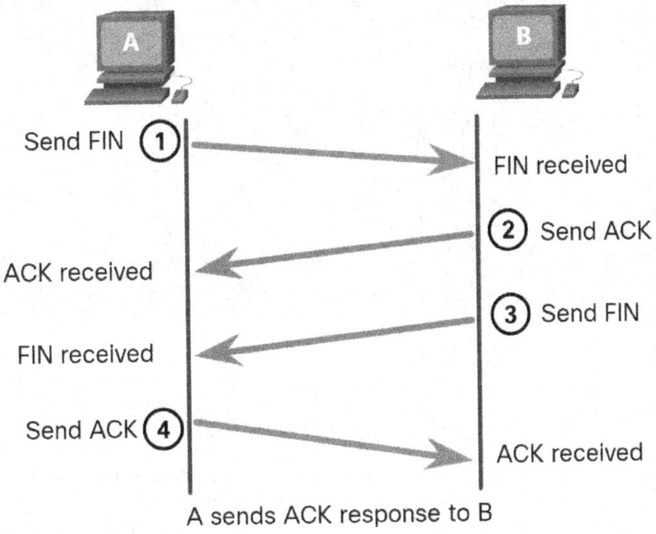

Figure 26-21 Steps in the TCP Session Termination Process

Step 1. FIN—When the client has no more data to send in the stream, it sends a segment with the FIN flag set.

Step 2. ACK—The server sends an ACK to acknowledge the receipt of the FIN to terminate the session from client to server.

Step 3. FIN—The server sends a FIN to the client to terminate the server-to-client session.

Step 4. ACK—The client responds with an ACK to acknowledge the FIN from the server.

When all segments have been acknowledged, the session is closed.

TCP Three-Way Handshake Analysis (26.5.4)

Hosts maintain state, track each data segment within a session, and exchange information about what data is received using the information in the TCP header. TCP is a full-duplex protocol, where each connection represents two one-way communication sessions. To establish the connection, the hosts perform a three-way handshake. As shown in Figure 26-22, control bits in the TCP header indicate the progress and status of the connection.

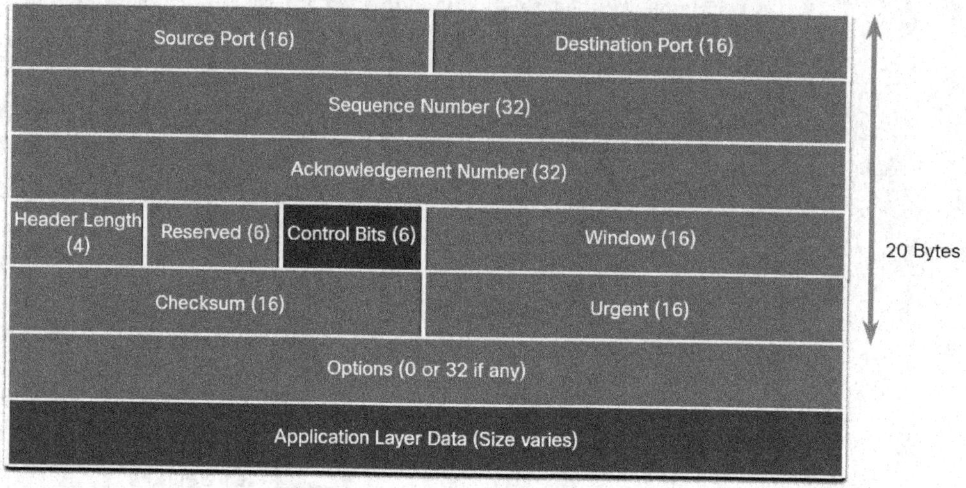

Figure 26-22 Control Bits Field

These are the functions of the three-way handshake:

- It establishes that the destination device is present on the network.
- It verifies that the destination device has an active service and is accepting requests on the destination port number that the initiating client intends to use.

- It informs the destination device that the source client intends to establish a communication session on that port number.

After the communication is completed, the sessions are closed and the connection is terminated. The connection and session mechanisms enable TCP's reliability function.

The 6 bits in the Control Bits field of the TCP segment header are also known as *flags*. A flag is a bit that is set to either on or off. The six control bit flags are as follows:

- URG—Urgent pointer field significant
- ACK—Acknowledgment flag used in connection establishment and session termination
- PSH—Push function
- RST—Reset the connection when an error or timeout occurs
- SYN—Synchronize sequence numbers used in connection establishment
- FIN—No more data from sender, and used in session termination

Search the Internet to learn more about the PSH and URG flags.

Video

Video—TCP Three-Way Handshake (26.5.5)

Refer to the online course to view this video.

Interactive Graphic

Check Your Understanding—TCP Communication Process (26.5.6)

Refer to the online course to complete this activity.

Reliability and Flow Control (26.6)

Reliability and flow control are two of the main features of TCP, not present in UDP.

TCP Reliability—Guaranteed and Ordered Delivery (26.6.1)

The reason that TCP is the better protocol for some applications is that, unlike UDP, it resends dropped packets and numbers packets to indicate their proper order before delivery. TCP can also help maintain the flow of packets so that devices do not become overloaded. This section covers these features of TCP in detail.

Sometimes TCP segments do not arrive at their destination. Other times, TCP segments arrive out of order. For the original message to be understood by the recipient, all the data must be received and the data in these segments must be reassembled into the original order. Sequence numbers are assigned in the header of each packet to achieve this goal. The sequence number represents the first data byte of the TCP segment.

During session setup, an *initial sequence number (ISN)* is set. This ISN represents the starting value of the bytes that are transmitted to the receiving application. As data is transmitted during the session, the sequence number is incremented by the number of bytes that have been transmitted. This data byte tracking enables each segment to be uniquely identified and acknowledged. Missing segments can then be identified.

The ISN does not begin at 1 but is effectively a random number. This is to prevent certain types of malicious attacks. For simplicity, we will use an ISN of 1 for the examples in this chapter.

Segment sequence numbers indicate how to reassemble and reorder received segments, as shown in Figure 26-23.

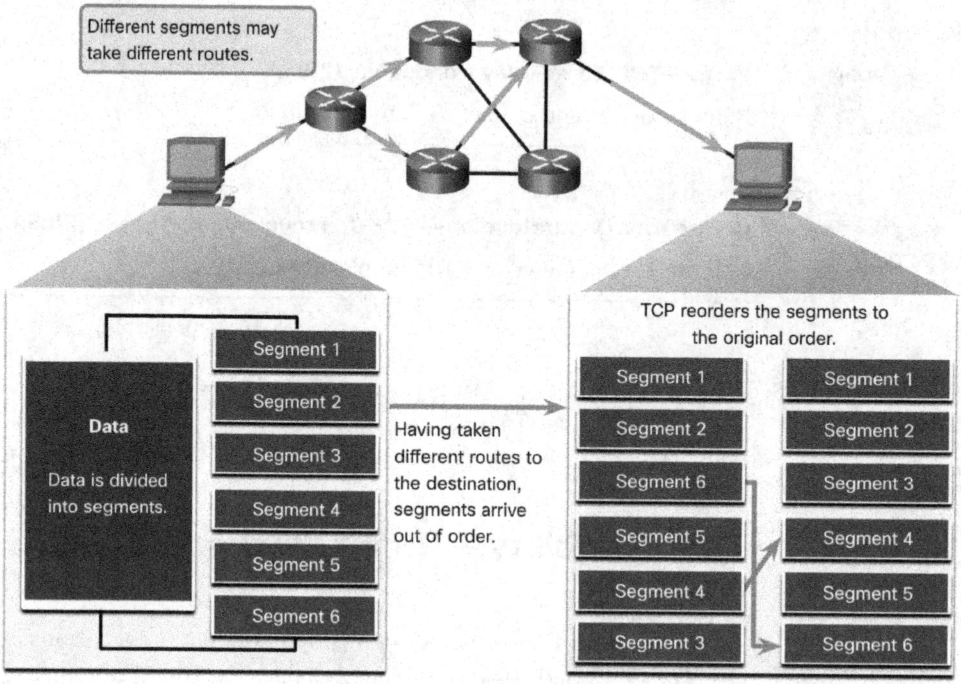

Figure 26-23 TCP Segments Are Reordered at the Destination

The receiving TCP process places the data from a segment into a receiving buffer. Segments are then placed in the proper sequence order and passed to the application

layer when reassembled. Any segments that arrive with sequence numbers that are out of order are held for later processing. Then, when the segments with the missing bytes arrive, these segments are processed in order.

Video

Video—TCP Reliability—Sequence Numbers and Acknowledgments (26.6.2)

Refer to the online course to view this video.

TCP Reliability—Data Loss and Retransmission (26.6.3)

No matter how well designed a network is, data loss occasionally occurs. TCP provides methods of managing these segment losses. Among these methods is a mechanism to retransmit segments for unacknowledged data.

The sequence (SEQ) number and acknowledgment (ACK) number are used together to confirm receipt of the bytes of data contained in the transmitted segments. The SEQ number identifies the first byte of data in the segment being transmitted. TCP uses the ACK number sent back to the source to indicate the next byte that the receiver expects to receive. This is called *expectational acknowledgment*.

Prior to later enhancements, TCP could only acknowledge the next byte expected. For example, in Figure 26-24, using segment numbers for simplicity, Host A sends segments 1 through 10 to Host B. If all the segments arrive except for segments 3 and 4, Host B would reply with acknowledgment specifying that the next segment expected is segment 3. Host A has no idea if any other segments arrived or not. Host A would, therefore, resend segments 3 through 10. If all the resent segments arrived successfully, segments 5 through 10 would be duplicates. This can lead to delays, congestion, and inefficiencies.

Note

For simplicity, segment numbers are being used instead of the byte numbers.

Host operating systems today typically employ an optional TCP feature called *selective acknowledgment (SACK)*, negotiated during the three-way handshake. If both hosts support SACK, the receiver can explicitly acknowledge which segments (bytes) were received, including any discontinuous segments. That way, the sending host needs to retransmit only the missing data. For example, in Figure 26-25, again using segment numbers for simplicity, Host A sends segments 1 through 10 to Host B. If all the segments arrive except for segments 3 and 4, Host B can acknowledge that it has received segments 1 and 2 (ACK 3) and selectively acknowledge that it has received segments 5 through 10 (SACK 5-10). Host A now knows that it needs to resend only segments 3 and 4.

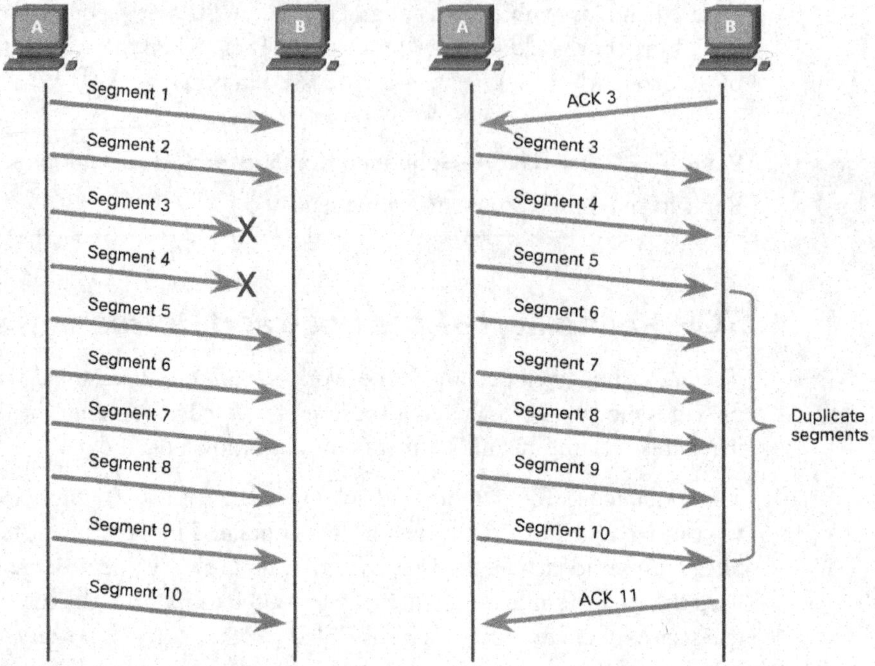

Figure 26-24 Data Retransmission

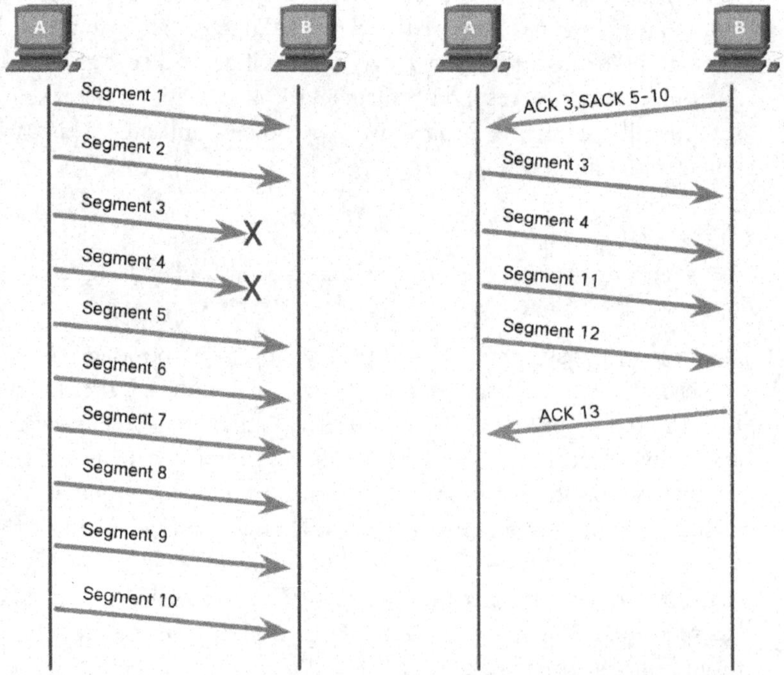

Figure 26-25 Selective Acknowledgment

Note

TCP typically sends ACKs for every other packet, but other factors beyond the scope of this topic may alter this behavior.

Video

Video—TCP Reliability—Data Loss and Retransmission (26.6.4)

Refer to the online course to view this video.

TCP Flow Control—Window Size and Acknowledgments (26.6.5)

TCP also provides mechanisms for flow control. Flow control is the amount of data that the destination can receive and process reliably. Flow control helps maintain the reliability of TCP transmission by adjusting the rate of data flow between source and destination for a given session. To accomplish this, the TCP header includes a 16-bit field called the window size.

Figure 26-26 shows an example of window size and acknowledgments.

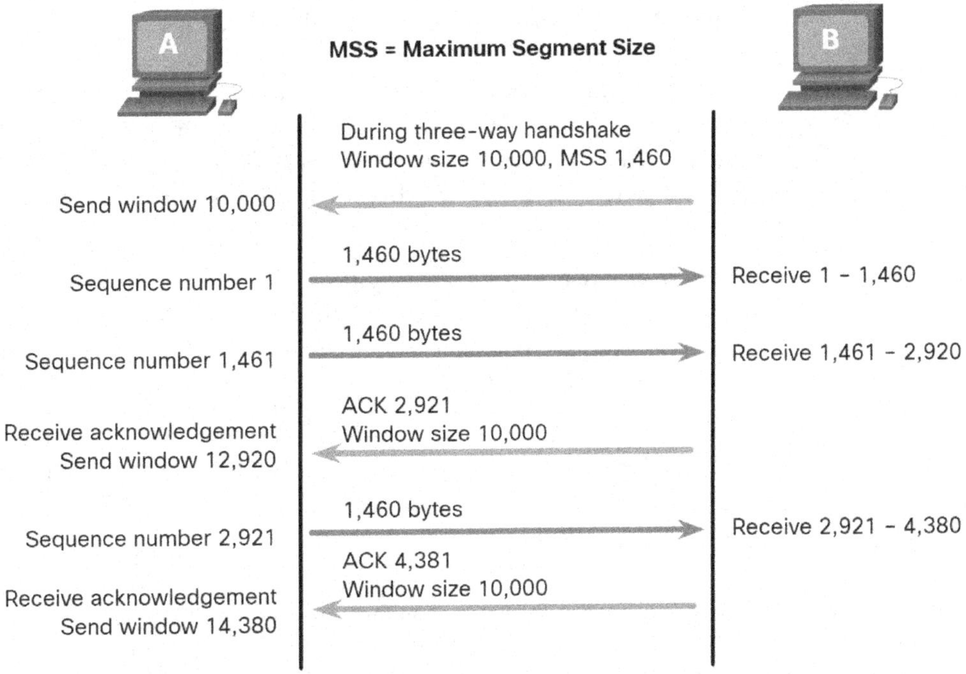

Figure 26-26 TCP Window Size Example

The *window size* determines the number of bytes that can be sent before expecting an acknowledgment. The acknowledgment number is the number of the next expected byte.

The window size is the number of bytes that the destination device of a TCP session can accept and process at one time. In the example shown in Figure 26-26, the PC B initial window size for the TCP session is 10,000 bytes. Starting with the first byte, byte number 1, the last byte PC A can send without receiving an acknowledgment is byte 10,000. This is known as the *send window* of PC A. The window size is included in every TCP segment, so the destination can modify the window size at any time depending on buffer availability.

The initial window size is agreed upon when the TCP session is established during the three-way handshake. The source device must limit the number of bytes sent to the destination device based on the window size of the destination. Only after the source device receives an acknowledgment that the bytes have been received can it continue sending more data for the session. Typically, the destination does not wait for all the bytes for its window size to be received before replying with an acknowledgment. As the bytes are received and processed, the destination sends acknowledgments to inform the source that it can continue to send additional bytes.

For example, PC B typically would not wait until all 10,000 bytes have been received before sending an acknowledgment. This means PC A can adjust its send window as it receives acknowledgments from PC B. As shown in Figure 26-26, when PC A receives an acknowledgment with the acknowledgment number 2,921, which is the next expected byte, the PC A send window increments 2,920 bytes. This changes the send window from 10,000 bytes to 12,920. PC A can now continue to send up to another 10,000 bytes to PC B as long as it does not send more than its new send window at 12,920.

A destination sending acknowledgments as it processes bytes received, and the continual adjustment of the source send window, is known as *sliding windows*. In the previous example, the send window of PC A increments or slides over another 2,921 bytes from 10,000 to 12,920.

If the availability of the destination's buffer space decreases, it may reduce its window size to inform the source to reduce the number of bytes it should send without receiving an acknowledgment.

Note

Devices today use the sliding windows protocol. The receiver typically sends an acknowledgment after every two segments it receives. The number of segments received before being acknowledged may vary. The advantage of sliding windows is that it allows the sender to continuously transmit segments, as long as the receiver is acknowledging previous segments. The details of sliding windows are beyond the scope of this course.

TCP Flow Control—Maximum Segment Size (MSS) (26.6.6)

In Figure 26-27, the source is transmitting 1,460 bytes of data within each TCP segment. This is typically the Maximum Segment Size (MSS) that the destination device can receive. The MSS is part of the Options field in the TCP header that specifies the largest amount of data, in bytes, that a device can receive in a single TCP segment. The MSS size does not include the TCP header. The MSS is typically included during the three-way handshake.

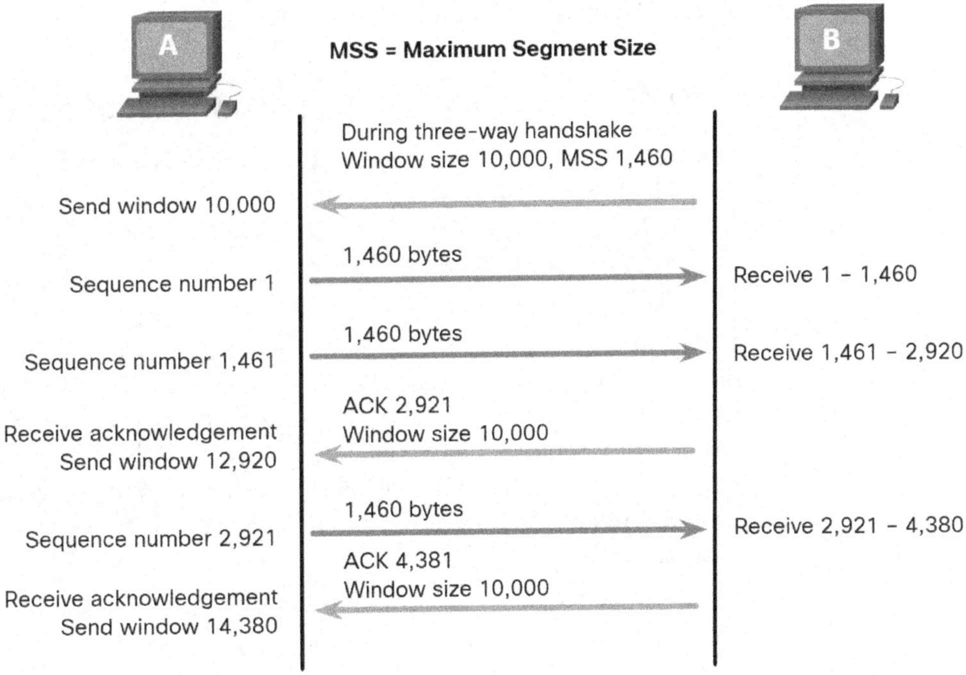

Figure 26-27 Maximum Segment Size

A common MSS is 1,460 bytes when using IPv4. A host determines the value of its MSS field by subtracting the IP and TCP headers from the Ethernet maximum transmission unit (MTU). On an Ethernet interface, the default MTU is 1,500 bytes. Subtracting the IPv4 header of 20 bytes and the TCP header of 20 bytes, the default MSS size is 1,460 bytes, as shown in Figure 26-28.

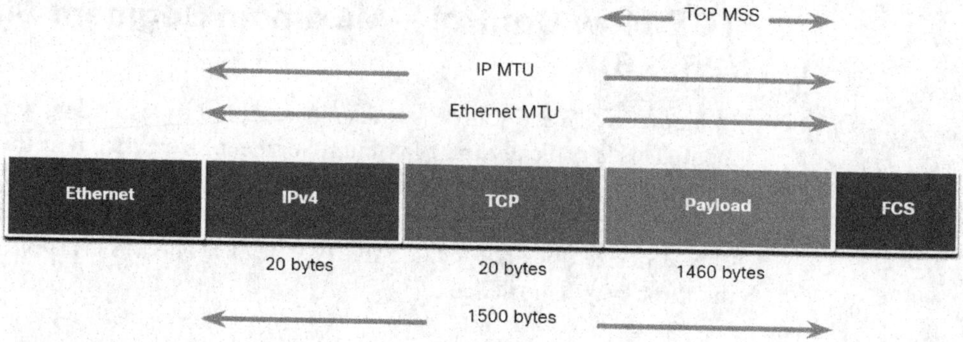

Figure 26-28 1,460 Byte MSS

TCP Flow Control—Congestion Avoidance (26.6.7)

When congestion occurs on a network, it results in packets being discarded by the overloaded router. When packets containing TCP segments do not reach their destination, they are left unacknowledged. By determining the rate at which TCP segments are sent but not acknowledged, the source can assume a certain level of network congestion.

Whenever there is congestion, retransmission of lost TCP segments from the source occurs. If the retransmission is not properly controlled, the additional retransmission of the TCP segments can make the congestion even worse. Not only are new packets with TCP segments introduced into the network, but also the feedback effect of the retransmitted TCP segments that were lost also adds to the congestion. To avoid and control congestion, TCP employs several congestion handling mechanisms, timers, and algorithms.

If the source determines that the TCP segments are either not being acknowledged or not acknowledged in a timely manner, then it can reduce the number of bytes it sends before receiving an acknowledgment. As illustrated in Figure 26-29, PC A senses there is congestion and therefore reduces the number of bytes it sends before receiving an acknowledgment from PC B.

Notice that it is the source that is reducing the number of unacknowledged bytes it sends and not the window size determined by the destination.

Note

Explanations of actual congestion handling mechanisms, timers, and algorithms are beyond the scope of this course.

Interactive Graphic

Check Your Understanding—Reliability and Flow Control (26.6.8)

Refer to the online course to complete this activity.

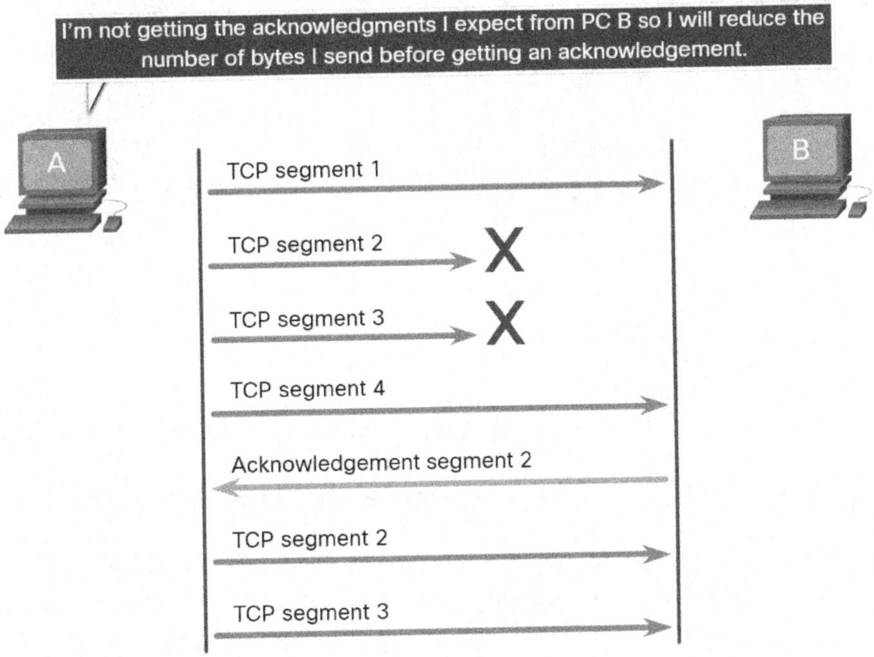

Figure 26-29 TCP Congestion Control

UDP Communication (26.7)

Sometimes the reliability associated with TCP is not required or the overhead associated with providing this reliability is not suitable for the application. This is where UDP is used.

UDP Low Overhead Versus Reliability (26.7.1)

As previously explained, UDP is perfect for communications that need to be fast, like VoIP. This topic explains in detail why UDP is perfect for some types of transmissions. As shown in Figure 26-30, UDP does not establish a connection. UDP provides low-overhead data transport because it has a small datagram header and no network management traffic.

UDP Datagram Reassembly (26.7.2)

Like segments with TCP, when UDP datagrams are sent to a destination, they often take different paths and arrive in the wrong order. UDP does not track sequence numbers the way TCP does. UDP has no way to reorder the datagrams into their transmission order, as shown in Figure 26-31.

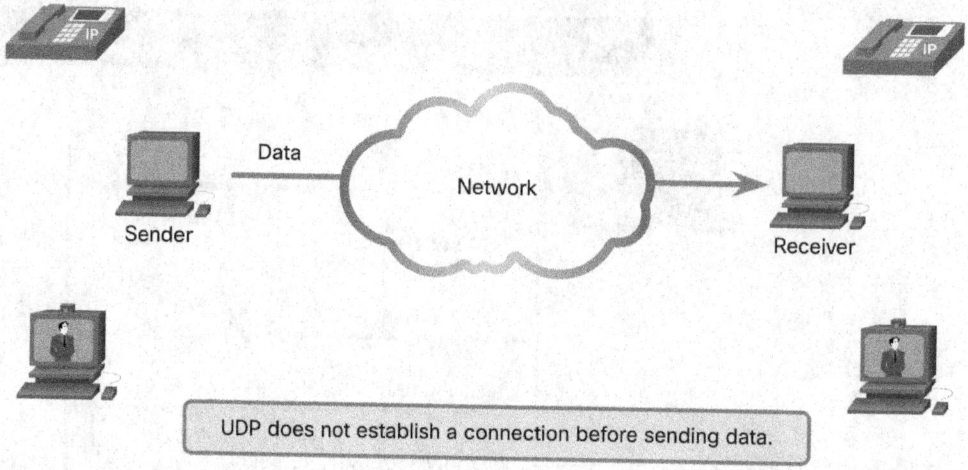

Figure 26-30 Connectionless Transport Between Sender and Receiver

Therefore, UDP simply reassembles the data in the order that it was received and forwards it to the application. If the data sequence is important to the application, the application must identify the proper sequence and determine how the data should be processed.

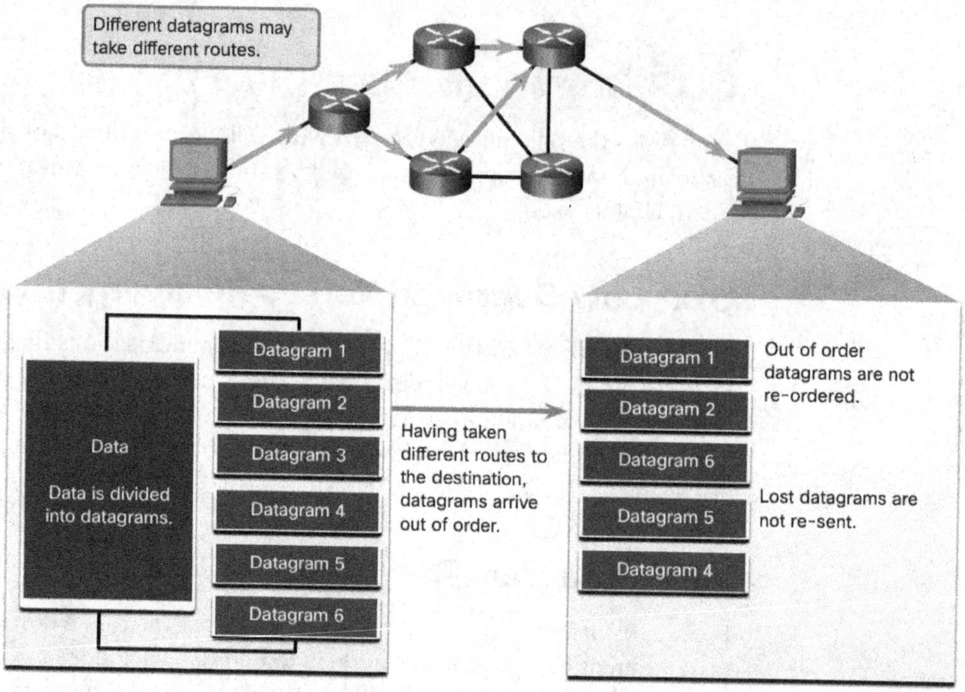

Figure 26-31 UDP: Connectionless and Unreliable

UDP Server Processes and Requests (26.7.3)

Like TCP-based applications, UDP-based server applications are assigned well-known or registered port numbers, as shown in Figure 26-32. When these applications or processes are running on a server, they accept the data matched with the assigned port number. When UDP receives a datagram destined for one of these ports, it forwards the application data to the appropriate application based on its port number.

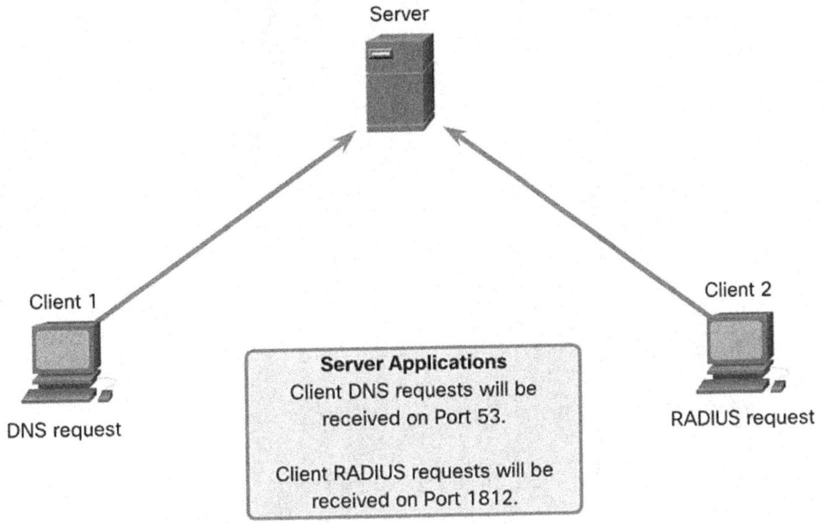

Figure 26-32 UDP Server Listening for Requests

Note

The Remote Authentication Dial-In User Service (RADIUS) server shown Figure 26-32 provides authentication, authorization, and accounting services to manage user access. The operation of RADIUS is beyond the scope of this book.

UDP Client Processes (26.7.4)

As with TCP, client/server communication is initiated by a client application that requests data from a server process. The UDP client process dynamically selects a port number from the range of port numbers and uses this as the source port for the conversation. The destination port is usually the well-known or registered port number assigned to the server process.

After a client has selected the source and destination ports, the same pair of ports is used in the header of all datagrams in the transaction. For the data returning to the client from the server, the source and destination port numbers in the datagram header are reversed.

The example presented in Figures 26-33 through 26-37 demonstrates the sequence that occurs when two hosts are simultaneously requesting services from the DNS and RADIUS authentication server.

In Figure 26-33, Client 1 is sending a DNS request to the server and Client 2 is requesting RADIUS authentication services from the same server.

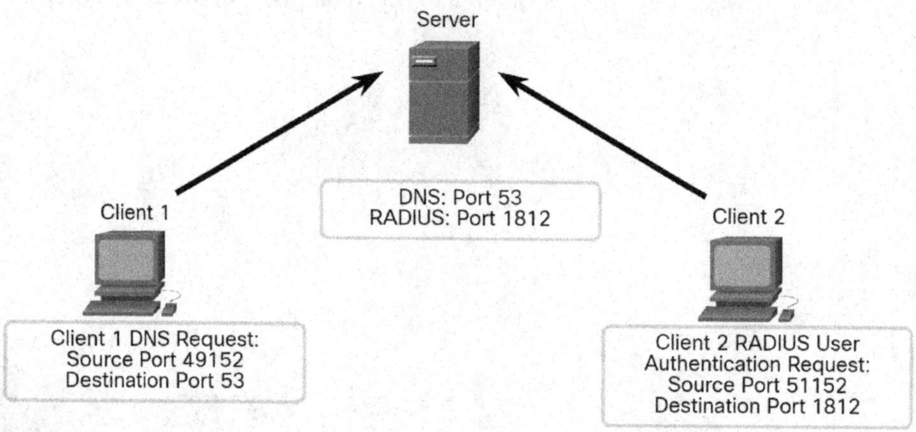

Figure 26-33 Clients Sending UDP Requests

In Figure 26-34, Client 1 is sending a DNS request using the well-known destination port 53 while Client 2 is requesting RADIUS authentication services using the registered destination port 1812.

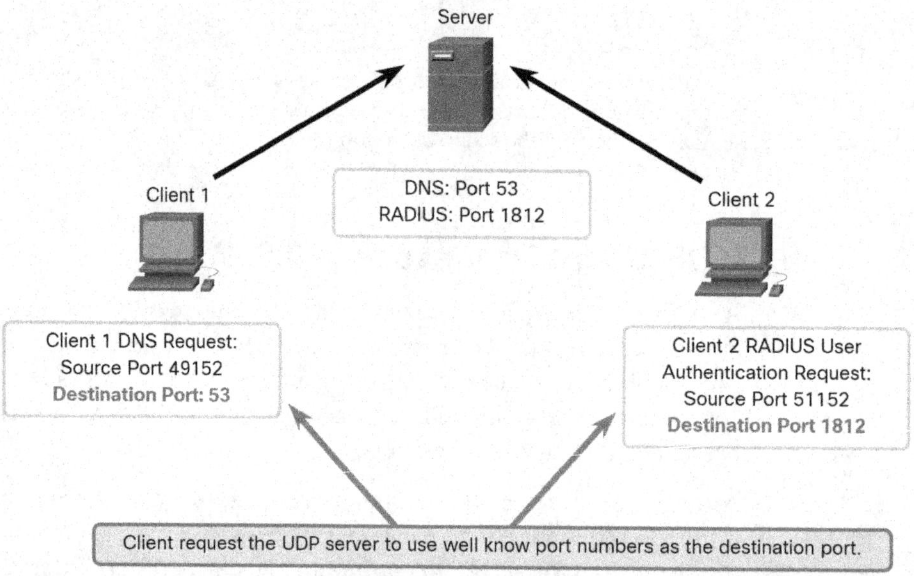

Figure 26-34 UDP Request Destination Ports

The requests of the clients dynamically generate source port numbers. In this case, Client 1 is using source port 49152 and Client 2 is using source port 51152, as shown in Figure 26-35.

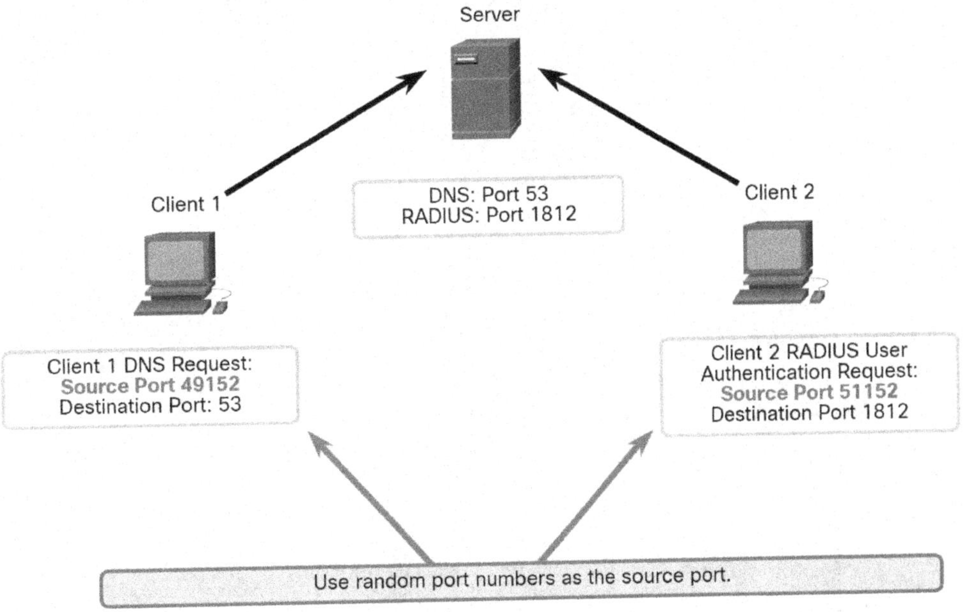

Figure 26-35 UDP Request Source Ports

When the server responds to the client requests, it reverses the destination and source ports of the initial request, as shown in Figures 26-36 and 26-37. In the server response to the DNS request, the destination port now is 49152, and in the server response to the RADIUS authentication request, the destination port now is 51152, as shown in Figure 26-36.

The source ports in the server response are the original destination ports in the initial requests, as shown in Figure 26-37.

Interactive Graphic

Check Your Understanding—UDP Communication (26.7.5)

Refer to the online course to complete this activity.

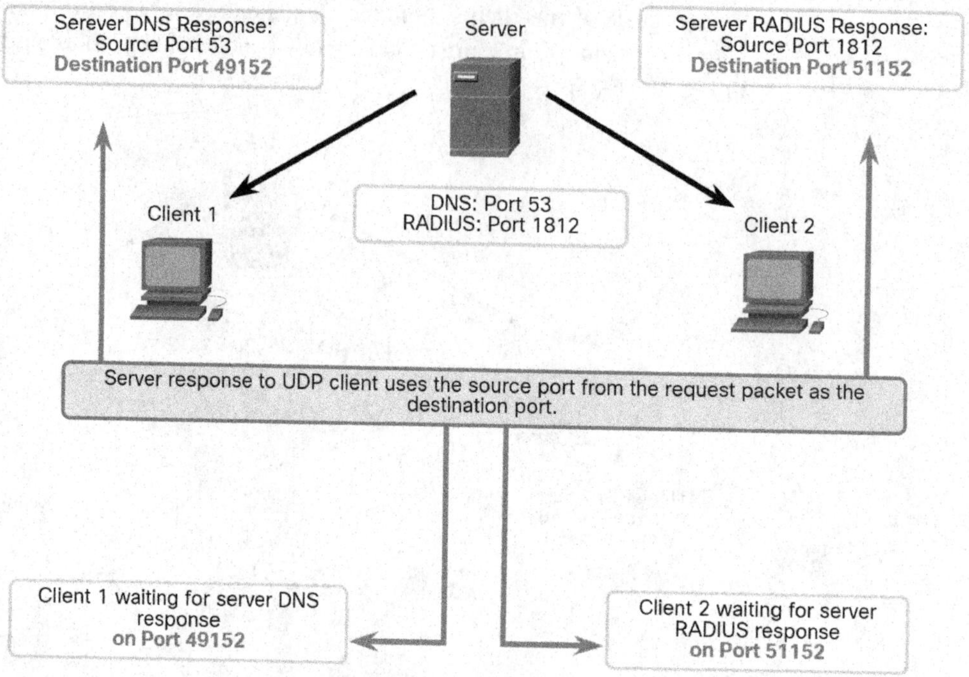

Figure 26-36 UDP Response Destination

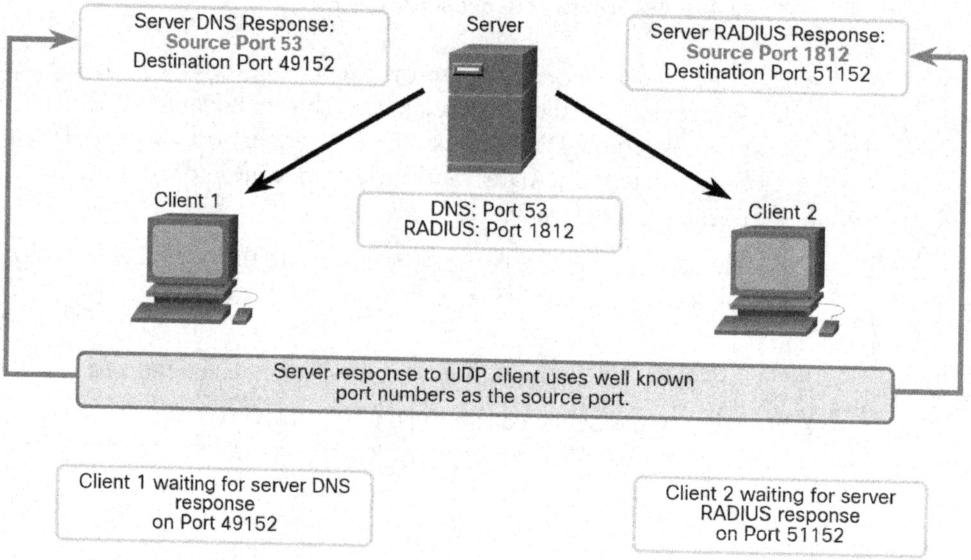

Figure 26-37 UDP Response Source Ports

Transport Layer Summary (26.8)

The following is a summary of each topic in the chapter and some questions for your reflection.

Packet Tracer
☐ Activity

Packet Tracer—TCP and UDP Communications (26.8.1)

In this activity, you will explore the functionality of the TCP and UDP protocols, multiplexing, and the function of port numbers in determining which local application requested the data or is sending the data.

What Did I Learn in This Chapter? (26.8.2)

- **Transportation of Data**—The transport layer is the link between the application layer and the lower layers that are responsible for network transmission. The transport layer is responsible for logical communications between applications running on different hosts. The transport layer includes TCP and UDP. Transport layer protocols specify how to transfer messages between hosts and are responsible for managing reliability requirements of a conversation. The transport layer is responsible for tracking conversations (sessions), segmenting data and reassembling segments, adding header information, identifying applications, and conversation multiplexing. TCP is stateful, reliable, acknowledges data, resends lost data, and delivers data in sequenced order. TCP is used for email and the web. UDP is stateless, fast, has low overhead, does not requires acknowledgments, does not resend lost data, and delivers data in the order it arrives. Use UDP for VoIP and DNS.
- **TCP Overview**—TCP establishes sessions, ensures reliability, provides same-order delivery, and supports flow control. A TCP segment adds 20 bytes of overhead as header information when encapsulating the application layer data. TCP header fields are the Source Port, Destination Port, Sequence Number, Acknowledgment Number, Header Length, Reserved, Control Bits, Window Size, Checksum, and Urgent. Applications that use TCP are HTTP, FTP, SMTP, and Telnet.
- **UPD Overview**—UDP reconstructs data in the order it is received, does not resend lost segments, does not establish a session, and does not inform the sender of resource availability. UDP header fields are Source Port, Destination Port, Length, and Checksum. Applications that use UDP are DHCP, DNS, SNMP, TFTP, VoIP, and video conferencing.
- **Port Numbers**—The TCP and UDP transport layer protocols use port numbers to manage multiple, simultaneous conversations. This is why the TCP and UDP

header fields identify a source application port number and a destination application port number. The source and destination ports are placed within the segment. The segments are then encapsulated within an IP packet. The IP packet contains the IP addresses of the source and destination. The combination of the source IP address and source port number, or the destination IP address and destination port number, is known as a socket. The socket is used to identify the server and service being requested by the client. The range of port numbers is 0 through 65535. This range is divided into groups: well-known ports, registered ports, and private and/or dynamic ports. Some well-known port numbers are reserved for common applications such as FTP, SSH, DNS, HTTP, and others. Sometimes it is necessary to know which active TCP connections are open and running on a networked host. Netstat is an important network utility that can be used to verify those connections.

- **TCP Communications Process**—Each application process running on a server is configured to use a port number. The port number is either automatically assigned or configured manually by a system administrator. TCP server processes are as follows: clients sending TCP requests, clients requesting destination ports, clients requesting source ports, and the server responding to destination port and source port requests. To terminate a single conversation supported by TCP, four exchanges are needed to end both sessions. Either the client or the server can initiate the termination. The three-way handshake establishes that the destination device is present on the network, verifies that the destination device has an active service and is accepting requests on the destination port number that the initiating client intends to use, and informs the destination device that the source client intends to establish a communication session on that port number. The six control bits flags are URG, ACK, PSH, RST, SYN, and FIN.
- **Reliability and Flow Control**—For the original message to be understood by the recipient, all the data must be received and the data in these segments must be reassembled into the original order. Sequence numbers are assigned in the header of each packet. No matter how well designed a network is, data loss occasionally occurs. TCP provides ways to manage segment losses, including a mechanism to retransmit segments for unacknowledged data. Host operating systems today typically employ an optional TCP feature called selective acknowledgment (SACK), negotiated during the three-way handshake. If both hosts support SACK, the receiver can explicitly acknowledge which segments (bytes) were received, including any discontinuous segments. That way, the sending host needs to retransmit only the missing data. Flow control helps maintain the reliability of TCP transmission by adjusting the rate of data flow between source and destination. To accomplish this, the TCP header includes a 16-bit field called the Window Size. The process of the destination sending acknowledgments as

it processes bytes received and the continual adjustment of the source's send window is known as sliding windows. A source might be transmitting 1,460 bytes of data within each TCP segment. This is the typical maximum segment size (MSS) that a destination device can receive. To avoid and control congestion, TCP employs several congestion handling mechanisms. The source reduces the number of unacknowledged bytes it sends, not the window size determined by the destination.

- **UPD Communication**—UDP is a simple protocol that provides the basic transport layer functions. When UDP datagrams are sent to a destination, they often take different paths and arrive in the wrong order. UDP does not track sequence numbers the way TCP does. UDP has no way to reorder the datagrams into their transmission order. UDP simply reassembles the data in the order that it was received and forwards it to the application. If the data sequence is important to the application, the application must identify the proper sequence and determine how the data should be processed. UDP-based server applications are assigned well-known or registered port numbers. When UDP receives a datagram destined for one of these ports, it forwards the application data to the appropriate application based on its port number. The UDP client process dynamically selects a port number from the range of port numbers and uses this as the source port for the conversation. The destination port is usually the well-known or registered port number assigned to the server process. After a client has selected the source and destination ports, the same pair of ports is used in the header of all datagrams used in the transaction. For the data returning to the client from the server, the source and destination port numbers in the datagram header are reversed.

Reflection Questions (26.8.3)

This chapter had a lot of information about the transport layer. I never knew so much happened here! Did you? When going to a website or sending an email, did you ever think about how that was different than joining a video call? Did you wonder why you always receive every word in an email message but sometimes lose a word on your video call? Now you should have some knowledge about the differences between TCP and UDP and why TCP is more reliable than UDP. I am excited to be taking this course, and I hope you are too!

Practice

The following activities provide practice with the topics introduced in this chapter.

Packet Tracer Activity

Packet Tracer Activities

Packet Tracer 26.8.1: TCP and UDP Communications

Check Your Understanding Questions

Complete all the review questions listed here to test your understanding of the topics and concepts in this chapter. Appendix A, "Answers to 'Check Your Understanding' Questions," lists the answers.

1. Match the characteristics to the correct protocol, TCP or UDP.
   a. Flow control
   b. Application dependent for error correction
   c. Reliable delivery
   d. Sequence number
   e. Fastest delivery
   f. Less overhead

2. Which statement correctly describes data transmission at the transport layer?
   a. Retransmission of lost packets is provided by both TCP and UDP.
   b. Segmentation is provided by the Window Size field when the TCP protocol is used.
   c. A single segment can include both a TCP and a UDP header.
   d. Both UDP and TCP use port numbers.
   e. Segmentation is provided by sequence numbers when UDP is used.

3. Which three fields are used in a UDP segment header? (Choose three.)
   a. Window Size
   b. Length
   c. Source Port
   d. Acknowledgment Number
   e. Checksum
   f. Sequence Number

4. What is the last segment sent to complete the termination process of a TCP session that was initiated by a client?

   a. A segment with the ACK flag set to 1 from the client

   b. A segment with the FIN flag set to 1 from the server

   c. A segment with the SYN flag set to 1 from the client

   d. A segment with the ACK flag set to 1 from the server

5. What is a characteristic of a TCP server process?

   a. Every application process running on the server is assigned to use a dynamic port number.

   b. A server may have many ports open (listening on several ports), one port for each active server application.

   c. An individual server can have two services assigned to the same port number within the same transport layer services.

   d. A client running two different types of network applications can both use the same destination port.

6. Network congestion has resulted in the source learning of the loss of TCP segments that were sent to the destination. What is one way that the TCP protocol addresses this?

   a. The source decreases the amount of data that it transmits before it receives an acknowledgment from the destination.

   b. The source decreases the window size to decrease the rate of transmission from the destination.

   c. The destination decreases the window size.

   d. The destination sends fewer acknowledgment messages in order to conserve bandwidth.

7. Which field in the TCP header indicates the status of the three-way handshake process?

   a. Window

   b. Reserved

   c. Checksum

   d. Control Bits

8. What are two features of protocols used in the TCP/IP protocol stack? (Choose two.)

   a. The Internet layer IP protocol has built-in mechanisms for ensuring the reliable transmission and receipt of data.
   b. UDP is used when an application must be delivered as quickly as possible and some loss of data can be tolerated.
   c. TCP and UDP destination port numbers are dynamically generated by the sending device in order to track the responses to requests.
   d. TCP mechanisms retransmit data when an acknowledgment is not received from the destination system within a set period of time.
   e. The same transport layer source port is used for all of the tabs opened at the same time within a web browser.

9. Match each TCP mechanism with the corresponding description.

   - Window size
   - Maximum segment size
   - Acknowledgment message
   - Sequence number

   a. The largest amount of data encapsulated in a segment that a device can receive
   b. Used to identify each segment of data
   c. Used to inform the source of the number of bytes it can send before waiting for an acknowledgment
   d. Must be received by a sender before transmitting more segments larger than the window size

10. Match the description to either TCP or UDP.

    a. Is connection-oriented
    b. Is connectionless
    c. Uses acknowledgments
    d. Has a larger header
    e. Is suitable for delay-intolerant applications
    f. Best-effort delivery protocol

11. What is a characteristic of the UDP protocol?

    a. Low overhead
    b. Guaranteed delivery
    c. Error correction
    d. End-to-end establishment before delivery

12. Which two flags in the Layer 4 PDU header are set by a client and server to terminate a TCP conversation? (Choose two.)

    a. URG
    b. SYN
    c. RST
    d. FIN
    e. ACK

CHAPTER 27

The Cisco IOS Command Line

Objectives

Upon completion of this chapter, you will be able to answer the following questions:

- How do you navigate to the different Cisco IOS modes?
- How do you navigate the Cisco IOS to configure network devices?
- How do you use **show** commands to monitor device operations?

Key Terms

This chapter uses the following key terms. You can find the definitions in the Glossary.

privileged EXEC mode Page 457

user EXEC mode Page 457

Introduction (27.0)

Hello! I have another friend I want you to meet. Diego was just hired as a junior member of a new IT department for a small manufacturing firm in Cusco, Peru. This firm creates parts for agricultural and milling equipment. They have recently updated and expanded their operations. They need a network in the second location that is connected to their new network at headquarters. Most of the equipment is made by Cisco, so Diego needs to quickly learn the Cisco IOS command-line functions. Fortunately, this chapter explains the basics of the Cisco IOS command-line functions that Diego (and you) needs to know to get up and running in no time!

Navigate the IOS (27.1)

The Cisco IOS command-line interface (CLI) is a text-based program that enables you to enter and execute Cisco IOS commands to configure, monitor, and maintain Cisco devices. The Cisco CLI can be used with either in-band or out-of-band management tasks.

The Cisco IOS Command-Line Interface (27.1.1)

CLI commands are used to alter the configuration of the device and to display the current status of processes on the router. For experienced users, the CLI offers many time-saving features for creating both simple and complex configurations. Almost all Cisco networking devices use a similar CLI. When the router has completed the power-up sequence and the Router> prompt appears, the CLI can be used to enter Cisco IOS commands, as shown in Example 27-1.

Example 27-1 Enter Configuration Mode After Router Power-Up

```
Router con0 is now available



Press RETURN to get started!




Router> enable
Router# configure terminal
Enter configuration commands, one per line.  End with CNTL/Z.
Router(config)# hostname R1
R1(config)# interface gigabitethernet 0/0/0
R1(config-if)#
```

Technicians familiar with the IOS commands and operation of the CLI find it easy to monitor and configure a variety of different networking devices because the same basic commands are used for configuring a switch and a router. The CLI has an extensive help system that assists users in setting up and monitoring devices.

Primary Command Modes (27.1.2)

Many network administrators find that using the CLI provides more precise control and flexibility than using the GUI. This section discusses using the CLI to navigate the Cisco IOS.

As a security feature, Cisco IOS software separates management access into the following two command modes:

- *User EXEC mode*—This mode has limited capabilities but is useful for basic operations. It allows only a limited number of basic monitoring commands. It does not allow the execution of any commands that might change the configuration of the device. User EXEC mode is identified by the CLI prompt that ends with the > symbol.
- *Privileged EXEC mode*—To execute configuration commands, a network administrator must access privileged EXEC mode. Higher configuration modes, like global configuration mode, can be reached only from privileged EXEC mode. Privileged EXEC mode is identified by the prompt ending with the # symbol.

Table 27-1 summarizes the two modes and displays the default CLI prompts of a Cisco switch and router.

Table 27-1 Primary Command Modes

Command Mode	Description	Default Device Prompt
User EXEC mode	■ Allows access to only a limited number of basic monitoring commands. ■ Often referred to as "view-only" mode.	`Switch>` `Router>`
Privileged EXEC mode	■ Allows access to all commands and features. ■ The user can use any monitoring commands and execute configuration and management commands.	`Switch#` `Router#`

Video

Video—IOS CLI Primary Command Modes (27.1.3)

Refer to the online course to view this video.

Video

Video—Navigate Between IOS Modes (27.1.4)

Refer to the online course to view this video.

A Note About Syntax Checker Activities (27.1.5)

When you are learning how to modify device configurations, consider starting in a safe, nonproduction environment before trying it on real equipment. Cisco Networking Academy (NetAcad) gives you different simulation tools to help build your configuration and troubleshooting skills. Because these are simulation tools, they typically do not have all the functionality of real equipment. One such tool is the Syntax Checker. In each Syntax Checker, you are given a set of instructions to enter a specific set of commands. You cannot progress in Syntax Checker unless the exact and full command is entered as specified. More advanced simulation tools, such as Packet Tracer, let you enter abbreviated commands, much as you would do on real equipment.

Interactive Graphic

Syntax Checker—Navigate Between IOS Modes (27.1.6)

Refer to the online course to complete this activity.

The Command Structure (27.2)

A network administrator must know the basic IOS command structure to be able to use the CLI for device configuration.

Basic IOS Command Structure (27.2.1)

A Cisco IOS device supports many commands. Each IOS command has a specific format, or syntax, and can be executed only in the appropriate mode. The general syntax for a command, shown in Figure 27-1, is the command followed by any appropriate keywords and arguments.

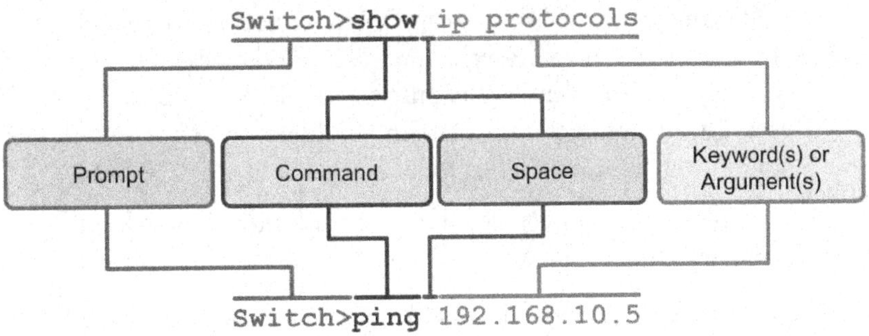

Figure 27-1 Basic Command Syntax

- **Keyword**—This is a specific parameter defined in the operating system (**ip protocols** in Figure 27-1).
- **Argument**—This is not predefined; it is a value or variable defined by the user (**192.168.10.5** in Figure 27-1).

After entering each complete command, including any keywords and arguments, press Enter to submit the command to the command interpreter.

IOS Command Syntax (27.2.2)

A command might require one or more arguments. To determine the keywords and arguments required for a command, refer to the command syntax. The syntax provides the pattern, or format, that must be used when entering a command.

As identified in Table 27-2, boldface text indicates commands and keywords that are entered as shown. Italic text indicates an argument for which the user provides the value.

Table 27-2 Syntax Conventions

Convention	Description
boldface	Boldface text indicates commands and keywords that you enter literally as shown.
italics	Italic text indicates arguments for which you supply values.
[x]	Square brackets indicate an optional element (keyword or argument).
{x}	Braces indicate a required element (keyword or argument).
[x {y | z }]	Braces and vertical lines within square brackets indicate a required choice within an optional element. Spaces are used to clearly delineate parts of the command.

For instance, the syntax for using the **description** command is **description** *string*. The argument is a *string* value provided by the user. The **description** command is typically used to identify the purpose of an interface. For example, the command **description Connects to the main headquarter office switch** describes where the other device is at the end of the connection.

The following examples demonstrate conventions used to document and use IOS commands:

- **ping** *ip-address*—The command is **ping** and the user-defined argument *ip-address* is the IP address of the destination device. For example, **ping 10.10.10.5**.
- **traceroute** *ip-address*—The command is **traceroute** and the user-defined argument *ip-address* is the IP address of the destination device. For example, **traceroute 192.168.254.254**.

If a command is complex with multiple arguments, you may see it represented like this:

```
Switch(config-if)# switchport port-security aging { static | time time | type
   {absolute | inactivity}}
```

The command typically is followed with a detailed description of the command and each argument in the Cisco IOS Command Reference. The Cisco IOS Command Reference is the ultimate source of online information for a particular IOS command.

Video

Video—Context-Sensitive Help and Command Syntax Check (27.2.3)

Refer to the online course to view this video.

Hotkeys and Shortcuts (27.2.4)

The IOS CLI provides hotkeys and shortcuts that make configuring, monitoring, and troubleshooting easier.

Commands and keywords can be shortened to the minimum number of characters that identify a unique selection. For example, the **configure** command can be shortened to **conf** because **configure** is the only command that begins with **conf**. An even shorter version, **con**, does not work because more than one command begins with **con**. Keywords can also be shortened.

Table 27-3 lists keystrokes to enhance command-line editing.

Table 27-3 Keystroke Shortcuts

Keystroke	Description
Tab	Completes a partial command or keyword name entry.
Backspace	Erases the character to the left of the cursor.
Ctrl-D	Erases the character at the cursor.
Ctrl-K	Erases all characters from the cursor to the end of the command line.
Esc D	Erases all characters from the cursor to the end of the word.
Ctrl-U or **Ctrl-X**	Erases all characters from the cursor back to the beginning of the command line.
Ctrl-W	Erases the word to the left of the cursor.
Ctrl-A	Moves the cursor to the beginning of the line.
Left Arrow or **Ctrl-B**	Moves the cursor one character to the left.
Esc B	Moves the cursor back one word to the left.
Esc F	Moves the cursor forward one word to the right.
Right Arrow or **Ctrl-F**	Moves the cursor one character to the right.
Ctrl-E	Moves the cursor to the end of the command line.
Up Arrow or **Ctrl-P**	Recalls the previous command in the history buffer, beginning with the most recent command.
Down Arrow or **Ctrl-N**	Goes to the next line in the history buffer.
Ctrl-R or **Ctrl-I** or **Ctrl-L**	Redisplays the system prompt and command line after a console message is received.

Note

Although the **Delete** key typically deletes the character to the right of the prompt, the IOS command structure does not recognize the **Delete** key.

When a command output produces more text than can be displayed in a terminal window, the IOS displays a --More-- prompt. Table 27-4 describes the keystrokes that can be used when this prompt is displayed.

Table 27-4 Keystrokes for Navigating the --More-- Prompt

Keystroke	Description
Enter	Displays the next line.
Space	Displays the next screen.
Any other key*	Ends the display string, returning to previous prompt. *Except **y**, which answers "yes" to the --More-- prompt and acts like the **Space**.

Table 27-5 lists commands used to exit an operation.

Table 27-5 Keystrokes for Exiting a Command Mode

Keystroke	Description
Ctrl-C	When in any configuration mode, ends the configuration mode and returns to privileged EXEC mode. When in setup mode, aborts back to the command prompt.
Ctrl-Z	When in any configuration mode, ends the configuration mode and returns to privileged EXEC mode.
Ctrl-Shift-6	All-purpose break sequence used to abort DNS lookups, traceroutes, and pings, and to interrupt an IOS process.

Video

Video—Hot Keys and Shortcuts (27.2.5)

Refer to the online course to view this video.

Packet Tracer Activity

Packet Tracer—Navigate the IOS (27.2.6)

In this activity, you will practice skills necessary for navigating the Cisco IOS, including different user access modes, various configuration modes, and common commands used on a regular basis. You will also practice accessing the context-sensitive help by configuring the **clock** command.

Refer to the online course to complete this Packet Tracer.

View Device Information (27.3)

The Cisco IOS provides commands to verify the operation of router and switch interfaces. The commands are commonly known as **show** commands.

Video

Video—Cisco IOS show Commands (27.3.1)

Refer to the online course to view this video.

show Commands (27.3.2)

The Cisco IOS CLI **show** commands display relevant information about the configuration and operation of the device. Network technicians use **show** commands extensively for viewing configuration files, checking the status of device interfaces and processes, and verifying the device operational status. The status of nearly every process or function of the router can be displayed using a **show** command.

Commonly used **show** commands and when to use them are listed in Table 27-6.

Table 27-6 Common **show** Commands

Command	Used to
show running-config	Verify the current configuration and settings.
show interfaces	Verify the interface status and see if there are any error messages.
show ip interface	Verify the Layer 3 information of an interface.
show arp	Verify the list of known hosts on the local Ethernet LANs.
show ip route	Verify the Layer 3 routing information.
show protocols	Verify which protocols are operational.
show version	Verify the memory, interfaces, and licenses of the device.

Examples 27-2 through 27-8 display the output from each of these **show** commands.

Example 27-2 show running-config

```
R1# show running-config

(Output omitted)

!
version 15.5
service timestamps debug datetime msec
service timestamps log datetime msec
```

```
service password-encryption
!
hostname R1
!
interface GigabitEthernet0/0/0
 description Link to R2
 ip address 209.165.200.225 255.255.255.252
 negotiation auto
!
interface GigabitEthernet0/0/1
 description Link to LAN
 ip address 192.168.10.1 255.255.255.0
 negotiation auto
!
router ospf 10
 network 192.168.10.0 0.0.0.255 area 0
 network 209.165.200.224 0.0.0.3 area 0
!
banner motd ^C Authorized access only! ^C
!
line con 0
 password 7 14141B180F0B
 login
line vty 0 4
 password 7 00071A150754
 login
 transport input telnet ssh
!
end
R1#
```

Example 27-3 show interfaces

```
R1# show interfaces
GigabitEthernet0/0/0 is up, line protocol is up
  Hardware is ISR4321-2x1GE, address is a0e0.af0d.e140 (bia a0e0.af0d.e140)
  Description: Link to R2
  Internet address is 209.165.200.225/30
  MTU 1500 bytes, BW 100000 Kbit/sec, DLY 100 usec,
```

```
     reliability 255/255, txload 1/255, rxload 1/255
  Encapsulation ARPA, loopback not set
  Keepalive not supported
  Full Duplex, 100Mbps, link type is auto, media type is RJ45
  output flow-control is off, input flow-control is off
  ARP type: ARPA, ARP Timeout 04:00:00
  Last input 00:00:01, output 00:00:21, output hang never
  Last clearing of "show interface" counters never
  Input queue: 0/375/0/0 (size/max/drops/flushes); Total output drops: 0
  Queueing strategy: fifo
  Output queue: 0/40 (size/max)
  5 minute input rate 0 bits/sec, 0 packets/sec
  5 minute output rate 0 bits/sec, 0 packets/sec
     5127 packets input, 590285 bytes, 0 no buffer
     Received 29 broadcasts (0 IP multicasts)
     0 runts, 0 giants, 0 throttles
     0 input errors, 0 CRC, 0 frame, 0 overrun, 0 ignored
     0 watchdog, 5043 multicast, 0 pause input
     1150 packets output, 153999 bytes, 0 underruns
     0 output errors, 0 collisions, 2 interface resets
     0 unknown protocol drops
     0 babbles, 0 late collision, 0 deferred
     1 lost carrier, 0 no carrier, 0 pause output
     0 output buffer failures, 0 output buffers swapped out
```

Example 27-4 show ip interface

```
R1# show ip interface
GigabitEthernet0/0/0 is up, line protocol is up
  Internet address is 209.165.200.225/30
  Broadcast address is 255.255.255.255
  Address determined by setup command
  MTU is 1500 bytes
  Helper address is not set
  Directed broadcast forwarding is disabled
  Multicast reserved groups joined: 224.0.0.5 224.0.0.6
  Outgoing Common access list is not set
  Outgoing access list is not set
  Inbound Common access list is not set
  Inbound  access list is not set
```

```
   Proxy ARP is enabled
   Local Proxy ARP is disabled
   Security level is default
   Split horizon is enabled
   ICMP redirects are always sent
   ICMP unreachables are always sent
   ICMP mask replies are never sent
   IP fast switching is enabled
   IP Flow switching is disabled
   IP CEF switching is enabled
   IP CEF switching turbo vector
   IP Null turbo vector
   Associated unicast routing topologies:
         Topology "base", operation state is UP
   IP multicast fast switching is enabled
   IP multicast distributed fast switching is disabled
   IP route-cache flags are Fast, CEF
   Router Discovery is disabled
   IP output packet accounting is disabled
   IP access violation accounting is disabled
   TCP/IP header compression is disabled
   RTP/IP header compression is disabled
   Probe proxy name replies are disabled
   Policy routing is disabled
   Network address translation is disabled
   BGP Policy Mapping is disabled
   Input features: MCI Check
   IPv4 WCCP Redirect outbound is disabled
   IPv4 WCCP Redirect inbound is disabled
   IPv4 WCCP Redirect exclude is disabled

(Output omitted)
```

Example 27-5 show arp

```
R1# show arp
Protocol  Address          Age (min)  Hardware Addr   Type   Interface
Internet  192.168.10.1             -   a0e0.af0d.e141  ARPA   GigabitEthernet0/0/1
Internet  192.168.10.10           95   c07b.bcc4.a9c0  ARPA   GigabitEthernet0/0/1
Internet  209.165.200.225          -   a0e0.af0d.e140  ARPA   GigabitEthernet0/0/0
Internet  209.165.200.226        138   a03d.6fe1.9d90  ARPA   GigabitEthernet0/0/0
R1#
```

Example 27-6 show ip route

```
R1# show ip route
Codes: L - local, C - connected, S - static, R - RIP, M - mobile, B - BGP
       D - EIGRP, EX - EIGRP external, O - OSPF, IA - OSPF inter area
       N1 - OSPF NSSA external type 1, N2 - OSPF NSSA external type 2
       E1 - OSPF external type 1, E2 - OSPF external type 2
       i - IS-IS, su - IS-IS summary, L1 - IS-IS level-1, L2 - IS-IS level-2
       ia - IS-IS inter area, * - candidate default, U - per-user static route
       o - ODR, P - periodic downloaded static route, H - NHRP, l - LISP
       a - application route
       + - replicated route, % - next hop override, p - overrides from PfR
Gateway of last resort is 209.165.200.226 to network 0.0.0.0
O*E2  0.0.0.0/0 [110/1] via 209.165.200.226, 02:19:50, GigabitEthernet0/0/0
      10.0.0.0/24 is subnetted, 1 subnets
O        10.1.1.0 [110/3] via 209.165.200.226, 02:05:42, GigabitEthernet0/0/0
      192.168.10.0/24 is variably subnetted, 2 subnets, 2 masks
C        192.168.10.0/24 is directly connected, GigabitEthernet0/0/1
L        192.168.10.1/32 is directly connected, GigabitEthernet0/0/1
      209.165.200.0/24 is variably subnetted, 3 subnets, 2 masks
C        209.165.200.224/30 is directly connected, GigabitEthernet0/0/0
L        209.165.200.225/32 is directly connected, GigabitEthernet0/0/0
O        209.165.200.228/30 [110/2] via 209.165.200.226, 02:07:19,
  GigabitEthernet0/0/0
R1#
```

Example 27-7 show protocols

```
R1# show protocols
Global values:
  Internet Protocol routing is enabled
GigabitEthernet0/0/0 is up, line protocol is up
  Internet address is 209.165.200.225/30
GigabitEthernet0/0/1 is up, line protocol is up
  Internet address is 192.168.10.1/24
Serial0/1/0 is down, line protocol is down
Serial0/1/1 is down, line protocol is down
GigabitEthernet0 is administratively down, line protocol is down
R1#
```

Example 27-8 show version

```
R1# show version
Cisco IOS XE Software, Version 03.16.08.S - Extended Support Release
Cisco IOS Software, ISR Software (X86_64_LINUX_IOSD-UNIVERSALK9-M), Version 15.5(3)
  S8, RELEASE SOFTWARE (fc2)
Technical Support: http://www.cisco.com/techsupport
Copyright (c) 1986-2018 by Cisco Systems, Inc.
Compiled Wed 08-Aug-18 10:48 by mcpre

(Output omitted)

ROM: IOS-XE ROMMON
R1 uptime is 2 hours, 25 minutes
Uptime for this control processor is 2 hours, 27 minutes
System returned to ROM by reload
System image file is "bootflash:/isr4300-universalk9.03.16.08.S.155-3.S8-ext.SPA.
  bin"
Last reload reason: LocalSoft

(Output omitted)

Technology Package License Information:
-----------------------------------------------------------------
Technology    Technology-package            Technology-package
              Current        Type            Next reboot
------------------------------------------------------------------
appxk9        appxk9         RightToUse      appxk9
uck9          None           None            None
securityk9    securityk9     Permanent       securityk9
ipbase        ipbasek9       Permanent       ipbasek9
cisco ISR4321/K9 (1RU) processor with 1647778K/6147K bytes of memory.
Processor board ID FLM2044W0LT
2 Gigabit Ethernet interfaces
2 Serial interfaces
32768K bytes of non-volatile configuration memory.
4194304K bytes of physical memory.
3207167K bytes of flash memory at bootflash:.
978928K bytes of USB flash at usb0:.
Configuration register is 0x2102
R1#
```

Packet Tracer Activity

Packet Tracer—Use Cisco IOS show Commands (27.3.3)

In this activity, you will explore some Cisco IOS **show** commands.

Refer to the online course to complete this Packet Tracer.

The Cisco IOS Command Line Summary (27.4)

The following is a summary of each topic in the chapter and some questions for your reflection.

What Did I Learn in This Chapter? (27.4.1)

- **Navigate the Cisco IOS**—The Cisco IOS CLI is a text-based program that enables you to enter and execute Cisco IOS commands to configure, monitor, and maintain Cisco devices. The Cisco CLI can be used with either in-band or out-of-band management tasks.

  CLI commands are used to alter the configuration of the device and to display the current status of processes on the router. When the router has completed the power-up sequence and the Router> prompt appears, the CLI can be used to enter Cisco IOS commands.

  As a security feature, the Cisco IOS software separates management access into the following two command modes:

  - **User EXEC mode**—This mode is useful for basic operations and allows only a limited number of basic monitoring commands. It does not allow the execution of any commands that might change the configuration of the device. User EXEC mode is identified by the CLI prompt that ends with the > symbol.
  - **Privileged EXEC mode**—To execute configuration commands, a network administrator must access privileged EXEC mode. Privileged EXEC mode can be identified by the prompt ending with the # symbol. Higher configuration modes, like global configuration mode, can be reached only from privileged EXEC mode. Global configuration mode is identified by the CLI prompt that ends with (config)#.

  The following commands are used to navigate between the different IOS command modes:

  - **enable**
  - **disable**
  - **configure terminal**

- **exit**
- **end**
- **Ctrl-Z**
- **line console 0**
- **line vty 0 15**
- **interface vlan 1**

- **The Command Structure**—Each IOS command has a specific format or syntax and can be executed only in the appropriate mode. The general syntax for a command is the command followed by any appropriate keywords and one or more arguments:
  - Boldface text indicates commands and keywords.
  - Italic text indicates an argument for which the user provides the value.
  - Square brackets, [x], indicate an optional element.
  - Braces, {x}, indicate a required element.
  - Braces and vertical lines within square brackets, [x {y | z}], indicate a required choice within an optional element.

  The IOS CLI provides hotkeys (for example, **Tab**, **Backspace**, **Ctrl-C**, and so forth) and shortcuts (for example, **conf** for **configure**) to make configuring, monitoring, and troubleshooting easier.

- **View Device Information**—A typical **show** command can provide information about the configuration, operation, and status of parts of a Cisco switch or router. Some of the more popular **show** commands are
  - **show running-config**
  - **show interfaces**
  - **show ip interface**
  - **show arp**
  - **show ip route**
  - **show protocols**
  - **show version**

Reflection Questions (27.4.2)

Have you ever watched a movie or television program in which some smart person was typing away at a computer to circumvent a security measure and gain unauthorized access to files? They weren't typing a novel; they were using the command-line interface. While you can employ a user interface to configure most network devices, becoming familiar with and using commands is so much faster. If you must troubleshoot your network, you'll need to use commands. Yes, it's a bit like learning a new language, but you know right away if you did it correctly or not. Once you start to use commands, you may never go back to the user interface. What would you like to be able to do with commands?

Practice

The following activities provide practice with the topics introduced in this chapter.

Packet Tracer
Activity

Packet Tracer Activities

Packet Tracer—Navigate the IOS (27.2.6)

Packet Tracer—Use Cisco IOS show Commands (27.3.3)

Check Your Understanding Questions

Complete all the review questions listed here to test your understanding of the topics and concepts in this chapter. Appendix A, "Answers to 'Check Your Understanding' Questions," lists the answers.

1. Which Cisco IOS mode displays the prompt Router#?
   a. Privileged EXEC mode
   b. User EXEC mode
   c. Global configuration mode
   d. Setup mode

2. While troubleshooting a network problem, a network administrator issues the **show version** command on a router. What information can be found by using this command?
   a. The version of the routing protocol that is running on the router
   b. Differences between the backup configuration and the current running configuration
   c. The amount of NVRAM, DRAM, and flash memory installed on the router
   d. The bandwidth, encapsulation, and I/O statistics on the interfaces

3. What is the difference between the terms *keyword* and *argument* in the IOS command structure?
   a. A keyword is required to complete a command. An argument is not.
   b. A keyword always appears directly after a command. An argument does not.
   c. A keyword is a specific parameter. An argument is not a predefined variable.
   d. A keyword is entered with a predefined length. An argument can be any length.

4. Which command or key combination always allows a user to return to the previous level in the command hierarchy?

   a. **exit**
   b. **Ctrl-Z**
   c. **Ctrl-C**
   d. **end**

5. An administrator uses the **Ctrl-Shift-6** key combination on a switch after issuing the **traceroute** command. What is the purpose of using these keystrokes?

   a. To allow the user to complete the command
   b. To interrupt the traceroute process
   c. To restart the ping process
   d. To exit a different configuration mode

6. Refer to the exhibit. An administrator is trying to configure the switch but receives the error message that is displayed in the exhibit. What is the problem?

```
Switch1> config t
                ^
% Invalid input detected at '^' marker.
```

   a. The administrator must use the entire command **configure terminal.**
   b. The administrator must connect via the console port to access global configuration mode.
   c. The administrator must first enter privileged EXEC mode before issuing the command.
   d. The administrator is already in global configuration mode.

7. What function does pressing the **Tab** key have when an IOS command is entered?

   a. It exits configuration mode and returns to user EXEC mode.
   b. It aborts the current command and returns to configuration mode.
   c. It completes the remainder of a partially typed word in a command.
   d. It moves the cursor to the beginning of the next line.

8. In the **show running-config** command, which part of the syntax is represented by **running-config**?

   a. The command
   b. A prompt
   c. A keyword
   d. A variable

9. Which two statements are true about user EXEC mode? (Choose two.)
   a. All router commands are available.
   b. Interfaces and routing protocols can be configured.
   c. The device prompt for this mode ends with the > symbol.
   d. Global configuration mode can be accessed by entering the **enable** command.
   e. Only some aspects of the router configuration can be viewed.

10. Immediately after a router completes its boot sequence, the network administrator wants to check the configuration of the router. From privileged EXEC mode, which of the following commands can the administrator use for this purpose? (Choose two.)
    a. **show version**
    b. **show running-config**
    c. **show flash**
    d. **show nvram**
    e. **show startup-config**

CHAPTER 28

Build a Small Cisco Network

Objectives

Upon completion of this chapter, you will be able to answer the following questions:

- How do you configure initial settings on a Cisco switch?
- How do you configure initial settings on a router?
- How do you configure devices for secure remote management?
- How do you build a network that includes a switch and router?

Key Term

This chapter uses the following key term. You can find the definition in the Glossary.

switch virtual interface (SVI) *Page 478*

Introduction (28.0)

Hi, it's me, Webster. Now that Diego has a good grasp of the Cisco IOS command-line functions, his next task will be much easier. At the new location that his employer is opening, he is tasked with setting up and configuring all the new Cisco devices, including host devices, switches, and routers, and all the wiring needed. This new network must be able to communicate with the network at headquarters, as well as access the Internet. This is a bit more complicated than my home network, but I feel like I might be able to do it, with a little help. That is why I'm going to take this chapter. I hope you'll join me!

Basic Switch Configuration (28.1)

The Cisco switch comes preconfigured and needs to be assigned only basic security information before being connected to the network. Elements that are usually configured on a LAN switch include host name, management IP address information, passwords, and descriptive information.

Basic Switch Configuration Steps (28.1.1)

The switch host name is the configured name of the device. Just like each computer or printer is assigned a name, networking equipment should be configured with a descriptive name. It is helpful to include in the device name the location where the switch will be installed; for example, SW_Bldg_R-Room_216.

A management IP address is necessary only if you plan to configure and manage the switch through an in-band connection on the network. A management address enables you to reach the device through Telnet, SSH, or HTTP clients. The IP address information that must be configured on a switch is essentially the same as you configure on a PC: IP address, subnet mask, and default gateway.

To secure a Cisco LAN switch, it is necessary to configure passwords on each of the various methods of access to the command line. The minimum requirements include assigning passwords to remote-access methods, such as Telnet, SSH, and the console connection. You must also assign a password to the privileged mode in which configuration changes can be made.

Note

Telnet sends the username and password in plaintext and is not considered secure. SSH encrypts the username and password and thus is a more secure method.

To configure the initial settings on a switch, follow these steps:

Step 1. Configure the device name:

```
hostname name
```

Step 2. Secure user EXEC mode:

```
line console 0
password password
login
```

Step 3. Secure remote Telnet/SSH access:

```
line vty 0 15
password password
login
```

Step 4. Secure privileged EXEC mode:

```
enable secret password
```

Step 5. Secure all passwords in the config file:

```
service password-encryption
```

Step 6. Provide legal notification:

```
banner motd delimiter message delimiter
```

Step 7. Configure the management SVI (discussed further in the next section):

```
interface vlan 1
ip address ip-address subnet-mask
no shutdown
```

Step 8. Save the configuration:

```
copy running-config startup-config
```

Example 28-1 shows a sample switch configuration using the preceding commands.

Example 28-1 Sample Switch Configuration

```
Switch> enable
Switch# configure terminal
Switch(config)# hostname S1
S1(config)# enable secret class
S1(config)# line console 0
S1(config-line)# password cisco
S1(config-line)# login
```

```
S1(config-line)# line vty 0 15
S1(config-line)# password cisco
S1(config-line)# login
S1(config-line)# exit
S1(config)# service password-encryption
S1(config)# banner motd #No unauthorized access allowed!#
S1(config)# interface vlan1
S1(config-if)# ip address 192.168.1.20 255.255.255.0
S1(config-if)# no shutdown
S1(config-if)# end
S1# copy running-config startup-config
Destination filename [startup-config]?
Building configuration...
[OK]
S1#
```

Switch Virtual Interface Configuration (28.1.2)

To access the switch remotely, you first need to configure an IP address and a subnet mask on the *switch virtual interface (SVI)*. To configure an SVI on a switch, use the **interface vlan 1** global configuration command. (VLAN 1 is not an actual physical interface but a virtual one.) Next, assign an IPv4 address using the **ip address** *ip-address subnet-mask* interface configuration command. Finally, enable the SVI using the **no shutdown** interface configuration command.

After the switch is configured with these commands, shown in Example 28-2, the switch has all the IPv4 elements ready for communication over the network.

Note

Similar to Windows hosts, switches configured with an IPv4 address typically also need to have a default gateway assigned. To do this, use the **ip default-gateway** *ip-address* global configuration command, where *ip-address* is the IPv4 address of the local router on the network, as shown in Example 28-2. However, in this section you will only be configuring a network with switches and hosts. Routers will be configured later.

Example 28-2 SVI Configuration

```
Sw-Floor-1# configure terminal
Sw-Floor-1(config)# interface vlan 1
Sw-Floor-1(config-if)# ip address 192.168.1.20 255.255.255.0
Sw-Floor-1(config-if)# no shutdown
Sw-Floor-1(config-if)# exit
Sw-Floor-1(config)# ip default-gateway 192.168.1.1
```

Interactive Graphic

Syntax Checker—Configure a Switch Virtual Interface (28.1.3)

Refer to the online course to complete this activity.

Packet Tracer Activity

Packet Tracer—Implement Basic Connectivity (28.1.4)

In this activity, you will complete the following objectives:

- Perform a Basic Configuration on S1 and S2
- Configure the PCs
- Configure the Switch Management Interface

Refer to the online course to complete this Packet Tracer.

Configure Initial Router Settings (28.2)

The basic router configuration is similar to that of the switch. However, because the function and interfaces of a router are different, there are some differences in its configuration.

Basic Router Configuration Steps (28.2.1)

To configure the initial settings on a router, follow these steps:

Step 1. Configure the device name:

```
Router(config)# hostname hostname
```

Step 2. Secure privileged EXEC mode:

```
Router(config)# enable secret password
```

Step 3. Secure user EXEC mode:

```
Router(config)# line console 0
Router(config-line)# password password
Router(config-line)# login
```

Step 4. Secure remote Telnet/SSH access:

```
Router(config-line)# line vty 0 4
Router(config-line)# password password
```

```
Router(config-line)# login
Router(config-line)# transport input {ssh | telnet | none | all}
```

Step 5. Secure all passwords in the config file:

```
Router(config-line)# exit
Router(config)# service password-encryption
```

Step 6. Provide legal notification:

```
Router(config)# banner motd delimiter message delimiter
```

Step 7. Save the configuration:

```
Router(config)# copy running-config startup-config
```

Basic Router Configuration Example (28.2.2)

In Example 28-3, router R1 is configured with initial settings. To configure the device name for R1, use the following commands.

Example 28-3 Device Name Configuration

```
Router> enable
Router# configure terminal
Enter configuration commands, one per line.
End with CNTL/Z.
Router(config)# hostname R1
R1(config)#
```

Note

Notice that the router prompt now displays the router host name.

All router access should be secured. Privileged EXEC mode provides users with complete access to the device and its configuration, so you must secure it.

The commands in Example 28-4 secure privileged EXEC mode and user EXEC mode, enable Telnet and SSH remote access, and encrypt all plaintext (that is, user EXEC and vty line) passwords. It is very important to use a strong password when securing privileged EXEC mode because this mode allows access to the configuration of the device.

Example 28-4 Basic Router Security

```
R1(config)# enable secret class
R1(config)#
R1(config)# line console 0
R1(config-line)# password cisco
R1(config-line)# login
R1(config-line)# exit
R1(config)#
R1(config)# line vty 0 4
R1(config-line)# password cisco
R1(config-line)# login
R1(config-line)# transport input ssh telnet
R1(config-line)# exit
R1(config)#
R1(config)# service password-encryption
R1(config)#
```

The legal notification warns users that the device can be accessed only by permitted users. Legal notification can be configured as shown in Example 28-5.

Example 28-5 Banner Configuration

```
R1(config)# banner motd #
Enter TEXT message. End with a new line and the # **********************************
  **************  WARNING: Unauthorized access is prohibited! *********************
  ************************** #
R1(config)#
```

If the router were to be configured with the previous commands and it accidently lost power, the router configuration would be lost. For this reason, it is important to save the configuration when changes are implemented. Example 28-6 shows how to save the configuration to NVRAM.

Example 28-6 Saving the Configuration

```
R1# copy running-config startup-config
Destination filename [startup-config]?
Building configuration...
[OK]
R1#
```

Interactive Graphic

Syntax Checker—Configure Initial Router Settings (28.2.3)

Use this Syntax Checker to practice configuring the initial settings on a router.

- Configure the device name.
- Secure the privileged EXEC mode.
- Secure and enable remote SSH and Telnet access.
- Secure all plaintext passwords.
- Provide legal notification.

Refer to the online course to complete this activity.

Packet Tracer Activity

Packet Tracer—Configure Initial Router Settings (28.2.4)

In this activity, you will complete the following objectives:

- Verify the Default Router Configuration
- Configure and Verify the Initial Router Configuration
- Save the Running-Configuration File

Refer to the online course to complete this Packet Tracer.

Secure the Devices (28.3)

Properly securing a device should always be done before putting the device into the production network.

Password Recommendations (28.3.1)

To protect network devices, it is important to use strong passwords. Here are standard guidelines to follow:

- Use a password length of at least 8 characters, preferably 10 or more characters. A longer password is a more secure password.
- Make passwords complex. Include a mix of uppercase and lowercase letters, numbers, symbols, and spaces, if allowed.
- Avoid passwords based on repetition, common dictionary words, letter or number sequences, usernames, relative or pet names, or biographical information

such as birthdates, ID numbers, ancestor names, or other easily identifiable pieces of information.

- Deliberately misspell a password. For example, Smith = Smyth = 5mYth or Security = 5ecur1ty.
- Change passwords often. If a password is unknowingly compromised, the window of opportunity for the threat actor to use the password is limited.
- Do not write down passwords and leave them in obvious places such as on the desk or monitor.

Tables 28-1 and 28-2 show examples of strong and weak passwords.

Table 28-1 Weak Password Examples

Weak Password	Why It Is Weak
secret	Simple dictionary password
smith	Maiden name of mother
toyota	Make of a car
bob1967	Name and birthday of the user
Blueleaf23	Simple words and numbers

Table 28-2 Strong Password Examples

Strong Password	Why It Is Strong
b67n42d39c	Combines alphanumeric characters
12^h u4@1p7	Combines alphanumeric characters, symbols, and a space

On Cisco routers, leading spaces are ignored for passwords, but spaces after the first character are not. Therefore, one method to create a strong password is to create a *passphrase* made of many words with spaces in between them. A passphrase is often easier to remember than a simple password. It is also longer and harder to guess.

Secure Remote Access (28.3.2)

There are multiple ways to access a device to perform configuration tasks. One of these ways is to use a PC attached to the console port on the device. This type of connection is frequently used for initial device configuration.

Setting a password for console connection access is done in global configuration mode. These commands prevent unauthorized users from accessing user mode from the console port:

```
Switch(config)# line console 0
Switch(config)# password password
Switch(config)# login
```

When the device is connected to the network, it can be accessed over the network connection using SSH or Telnet. SSH is the preferred method because it is more secure. When the device is accessed through the network, it is considered a vty connection. The password must be assigned to the vty port. The following configuration is used to enable SSH access to the switch:

```
Switch(config)# line vty 0 15
Switch(config)# password password
Switch(config)# transport input ssh
Switch(config)# login
```

Example 28-7 shows a sample configuration.

Example 28-7 Secure Remote Access with Passwords

```
S1(config)# line console 0
S1(config-line)# password cisco
S1(config-line)# login
S1(config-line)# exit
S1(config)#
S1(config)# line vty 0 15
S1(config-line)# password cisco
S1(config-line)# login
S1(config-line)#
```

By default, many Cisco switches support up to 16 vty lines, numbered 0 to 15. The number of vty lines supported on a Cisco router varies with the type of router and the IOS version. However, the most common number of vty lines configured on a router is five. These lines are numbered 0 to 4 by default, though additional lines can be configured. A password needs to be set for all available vty lines. The same password can be set for all connections.

To verify that the passwords are set correctly, use the **show running-config** command. These passwords are stored in the running-configuration file in plaintext. It is possible to set encryption on all passwords stored within the router so that unauthorized individuals can't read them easily. The global configuration command **service password-encryption** ensures that all passwords are encrypted.

With remote access secured on the switch, you can now configure SSH.

Enable SSH (28.3.3)

Before you configure SSH, you must minimally configure the switch with a unique host name and the correct network connectivity settings. Follow these steps:

Step 1. Verify SSH support.

Use the **show ip ssh** command to verify that the switch supports SSH. If the switch is not running an IOS that supports cryptographic features, this command is unrecognized.

Step 2. Configure the IP domain name.

Configure the IP domain name of the network using the **ip domain-name** *domain-name* global configuration mode command. In Example 28-8, the *domain-name* value is **cisco.com**.

Step 3. Generate RSA key pairs.

Not all versions of the IOS default to SSH version 2, and SSH version 1 has known security flaws. To configure SSH version 2, issue the **ip ssh version 2** global configuration mode command. Generating an RSA key pair automatically enables SSH. Use the **crypto key generate rsa** global configuration mode command to enable the SSH server on the switch and generate an RSA key pair. When generating RSA keys, the administrator is prompted to enter a modulus length. The configuration in Example 28-8 uses a modulus size of 1,024 bits. A longer modulus length is more secure but takes more time to generate and to use.

Note

To delete the RSA key pair, use the **crypto key zeroize rsa** global configuration mode command. After the RSA key pair is deleted, the SSH server is automatically disabled.

Step 4. Configure user authentication.

The SSH server can authenticate users locally or use an authentication server. To use the local authentication method, create a username and password pair with the **username** *username* **secret** *password* global configuration mode command. In Example 28-8, the user **admin** is assigned the password **ccna**.

Step 5. Configure the vty lines.

Enable the SSH protocol on the vty lines using the **transport input ssh** line configuration mode command. The Catalyst 2960 in Example 28-8 has vty lines ranging from 0 to 15. This configuration prevents non-SSH (such as Telnet) connections and limits the switch to accept only SSH connections. Use the **line vty** global configuration mode command and then the **login local** line configuration mode command to require local authentication for SSH connections from the local username database.

Step 6. Enable SSH version 2.

By default, SSH supports both versions 1 and 2. When supporting both versions, this is shown in the **show ip ssh** output as supporting version 1.99. Version 1 has known vulnerabilities. For this reason, it is recommended to enable only version 2. Enable SSH version using the **ip ssh version 2** global configuration command.

Example 28-8 shows a sample SSH configuration.

Example 28-8 Configuring S1 with SSHv2

```
S1# show ip ssh
SSH Disabled - version 1.99
%Please create RSA keys (of at least 768 bits size) to enable SSH v2.
Authentication timeout: 120 secs; Authentication retries: 3
S1# configure terminal
S1(config)# ip domain-name cisco.com
S1(config)# crypto key generate rsa
The name for the keys will be: S1.cisco.com
...
How many bits in the modulus [512]: 1024
...
S1(config)# username admin secret ccna
S1(config-line)# line vty 0 15
S1(config-line)# transport input ssh
S1(config-line)# login local
S1(config-line)# exit
S1(config)# ip ssh version 2
S1(config)# exit
S1#
```

Interactive Graphic

Syntax Checker—Configure SSH (28.3.4)

Use this Syntax Checker to configure SSH on switch S1.

Refer to the online course to complete this activity.

Verify SSH (28.3.5)

On a PC, an SSH client such as PuTTY is used to connect to an SSH server. In the next example, the following have been configured:

- SSH enabled on switch S1
- Interface VLAN 99 (SVI) with IPv4 address 172.17.99.11 on switch S1
- PC1 with IPv4 address 172.17.99.21

In Figure 28-1, the technician is initiating an SSH connection to the SVI VLAN IPv4 address of S1 using the terminal software PuTTY.

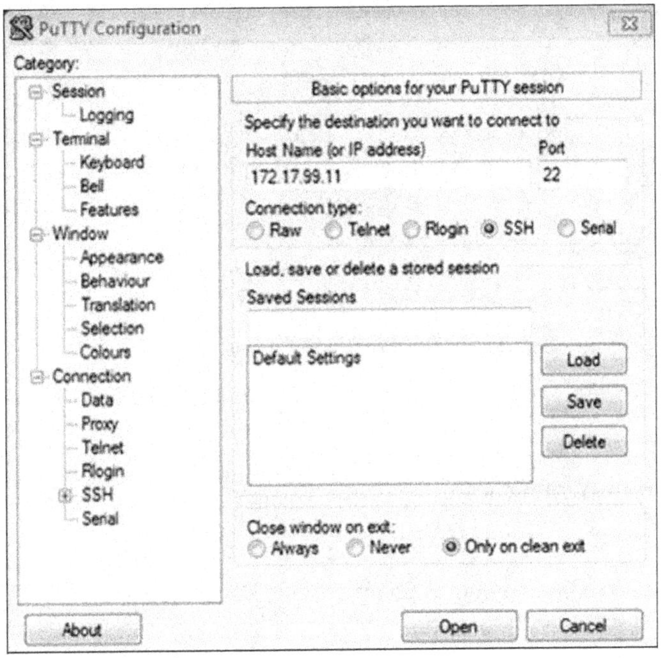

Figure 28-1 SSH Connection with PuTTY

After clicking Open in PuTTY, the user is prompted for a username and password. Using the configuration from Example 28-8, the username **admin** and password **ccna** are entered. After entering the correct combination, the user is connected via SSH to the CLI on the Catalyst 2960 switch.

To display the version and configuration data for SSH on the device that you configured as an SSH server, use the **show ip ssh** command. In Example 28-9, SSH version 2 is enabled. To check the SSH connections to the device, use the **show ssh** command.

Example 28-9 Establishing a Remote SSH Session

```
Login as: admin
Using keyboard-interactive authentication.
Password: <ccna>
S1> enable
Password: <class>
S1# show ip ssh
SSH Enabled - version 2.0
Authentication timeout: 90 secs; Authentication retries: 2
Minimum expected Diffie Hellman key size : 1024 bits
IOS Keys in SECSH format(ssh-rsa, base64 encoded):
ssh-rsa AAAAB3NzaC1yc2EAAAADAQABAAAAgQCdLksVz2QlREsoZt2f2scJHbW3aMDM8 /8jg/srGFNL
i+f+qJWwxt26BWmy694+6ZIQ/j7wUfIVNlQhI8GUOVIuKNqVMOMtLg8Ud4qAiLbGJfAaP3fyrKmViPpO
eOZof6tnKgKKvJz18Mz22XAf2u/7Jq2JnEFXycGMO88OUJQL3Q==

S1# show ssh
Connection Version Mode Encryption  Hmac        State           Username
0          2.0      IN   aes256-cbc  hmac-sha1 Session started admin
0          2.0      OUT  aes256-cbc  hmac-sha1 Session started admin
%No SSHv1 server connections running.
S1#
```

Packet Tracer
☐ Activity

Packet Tracer—Configure SSH (28.3.6)

In this activity, you will complete the following objectives:

- Secure Passwords
- Encrypt Communications
- Verify SSH Implementation

Refer to the online course to complete this Packet Tracer.

Connecting the Switch to the Router (28.4)

Most local networks have only one router. This router is the gateway router, and all hosts and switches on the local network must be configured with this information. This section explains how to configure the default gateway on hosts and switches.

Default Gateway for a Host (28.4.1)

For an end device to communicate over the network, it must be configured with the correct IP address information, including the default gateway address. The default

gateway is used only when the host wants to send a packet to a device on another network. The default gateway address is generally the router interface address attached to the local network of the host. The IP address of the host device and the router interface address must be in the same network.

For example, assume an IPv4 network topology consists of a router interconnecting two separate LANs. G0/0/0 is connected to network 192.168.10.0, while G0/0/1 is connected to network 192.168.11.0. Each host device is configured with the appropriate default gateway address.

In Figure 28-2, if PC1 sends a packet to PC2, the default gateway is not used because they are on the same LAN. Instead, PC1 addresses the packet with the IPv4 address of PC2 and forwards the packet directly to PC2 through the switch.

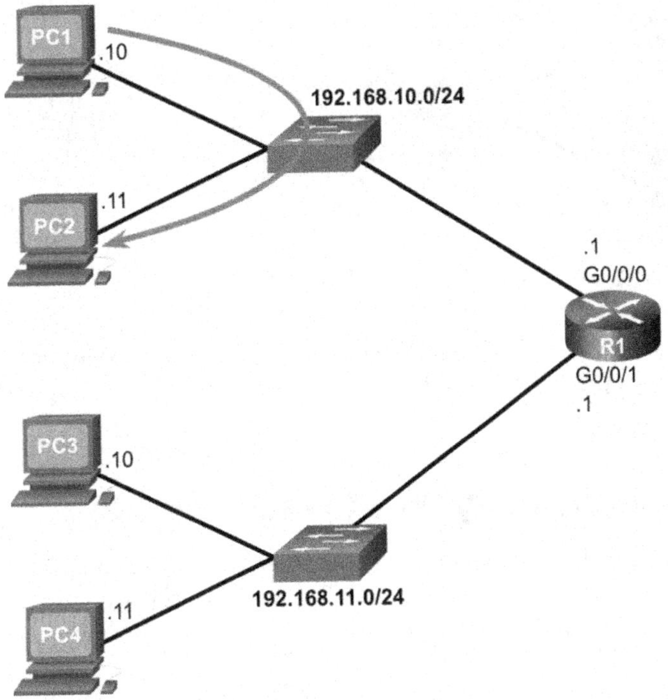

Figure 28-2 PC1 Sending a Packet to PC2

If PC1 wants to send a packet to PC3 on a different LAN, PC1 addresses the packet with the IPv4 address of PC3 but forwards the packet to its default gateway, which is the G0/0/0 interface of R1, as shown in Figure 28-3. The router accepts the packet and accesses its routing table to determine that G0/0/1 is the appropriate exit interface based on the destination address. R1 then forwards the packet out of the appropriate interface to reach PC3.

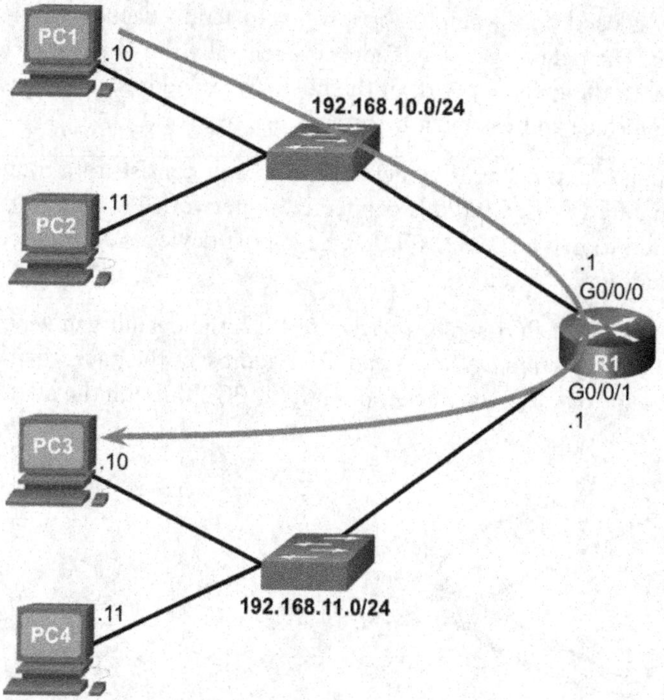

Figure 28-3 PC1 Sending a Packet to PC3

The same process would occur on an IPv6 network, although this is not shown in the topology. Devices would use the IPv6 address of the local router as their default gateway.

Default Gateway on a Switch (28.4.2)

A switch that interconnects client computers is typically a Layer 2 device. As such, a Layer 2 switch does not require an IP address to function properly. However, an IP configuration can be configured on a switch to give an administrator remote access to the switch.

To connect to and manage a switch over a local IP network, the switch must have an SVI configured. The SVI is configured with an IPv4 address and subnet mask on the local LAN. The switch must also have a default gateway address configured so that it can be remotely managed from another network. The default gateway address is typically configured on all devices that will communicate beyond their local network.

To configure an IPv4 default gateway on a switch, use the **ip default-gateway** *ip-address* global configuration command. The *ip-address* that is configured is the IPv4 address of the local router interface connected to the switch.

Figure 28-4 shows an administrator establishing a remote connection to switch S1 on another network.

Figure 28-4 Administrator Establishing a Remote Connection to Switch S1

In this example, the administrator host would use its default gateway to send the packet to the G0/0/1 interface of R1. R1 would forward the packet to S1 out of its G0/0/0 interface. Because the packet source IPv4 address came from another network, S1 would require a default gateway to forward the packet to the G0/0/0 interface of R1. Therefore, S1 must be configured with a default gateway to be able to reply and establish an SSH connection with the administrative host.

Note

Packets originating from host computers connected to the switch must already have the default gateway address configured on their host computer operating system.

A workgroup switch can also be configured with an IPv6 address on an SVI. However, the switch does not require the IPv6 address of the default gateway to be configured manually. The switch automatically receives its default gateway from the ICMPv6 Router Advertisement message from the router.

Interactive Graphic

Syntax Checker—Configure the Default Gateway (28.4.3)

Use this Syntax Checker to practice configuring the default gateway of a Layer 2 switch.

Refer to the online course to complete this activity.

Packet Tracer ☐ Activity

Packet Tracer—Build a Switch and Router Network (28.4.4)

This Packet Tracer Tutored Activity includes a hinting system and a built-in tutorial. You will connect the devices, configure the PCs, configure the router, configure the switch, and verify end-to-end connectivity.

Refer to the online course to complete this Packet Tracer.

Packet Tracer ☐ Activity

Packet Tracer—Troubleshoot Default Gateway Issues (28.4.5)

In this activity, you will complete the following objectives:

- Verify Network Documentation and Isolate Problems
- Implement, Verify, and Document Solutions

Refer to the online course to complete this Packet Tracer.

Build a Small Cisco Network Summary (28.5)

The following is a summary of each topic in the chapter and some questions for your reflection.

What Did I Learn in This Chapter? (28.5.1)

- **Basic Switch Configuration**—Elements that are usually configured on a LAN switch include host name, management IP address information, passwords, and descriptive information. Configure switches with descriptive host names, including the location where the switch will be installed.

  A management IP address is necessary only if you plan to configure and manage the switch through an in-band connection on the network.

  To secure a Cisco LAN switch, assign passwords for each of the various access methods to the command line. The minimum requirements include assigning passwords to remote-access methods, such as Telnet, SSH, and the console

connection. You must also assign a password to the privileged mode in which configuration changes can be made.

To access the switch remotely, you first need to configure an IP address and a subnet mask on the SVI. To configure an SVI on a switch, use the **interface vlan 1** global configuration command. (VLAN 1 is a virtual interface.) Next, assign an IPv4 address using the **ip address** *ip-address subnet-mask* interface configuration command. Finally, enable the virtual interface using the **no shutdown** interface configuration command.

After the switch has been configured with these commands, the switch has all the IPv4 elements ready for communication over the network.

- **Configure Initial Router Settings**—Steps to configure a router:

  Step 1. Configure the device name.

  Step 2. Secure privileged EXEC mode.

  Step 3. Secure user EXEC mode.

  Step 4. Secure remote Telnet/SSH access.

  Step 5. Secure all passwords in the config file.

  Step 6. Provide legal notification.

  Step 7. Save the configuration.

- **Secure the Devices**—To protect network devices, it is important to use strong passwords. Here are standard guidelines to follow:

  - Use a password length of at least 8 characters, preferably 10 or more characters.
  - Include a mix of uppercase and lowercase letters, numbers, symbols, and spaces, if allowed.
  - Avoid passwords based on repetition, common dictionary words, letter or number sequences, usernames, relative or pet names, or biographical information.
  - Deliberately misspell a password.
  - Change passwords often.
  - Do not write down passwords and leave them in obvious places such as on the desk or monitor.

  Passphrases, which are made up of many words with spaces in between them, are generally more difficult to crack than passwords and tend to be easier to remember.

Among the multiple ways to access a device to perform configuration tasks is to use a PC attached to the console port on the device. This type of connection is frequently used for initial device configuration. Setting a password for console connection access is done in global configuration mode.

When the device is connected to the network, it can be accessed over the network connection using SSH or Telnet. SSH is the preferred method because it is more secure. When the device is accessed through the network, it is considered a vty connection. A password needs to be set for all available vty lines. The same password can be set for all connections. The global configuration command **service password-encryption** ensures that all passwords are encrypted.

To configure a Cisco device to support SSH, use the following six steps:

Step 1. Configure a unique device host name. A device must have a unique host name other than the default.

Step 2. Configure the IP domain name of the network by using the global configuration mode command **ip domain-name** *name*.

Step 3. Generate a key to encrypt SSH traffic. SSH encrypts traffic between source and destination. However, to do so, a unique authentication key must be generated by using the global configuration command **crypto key generate rsa general-keys modulus** *bits*.

Step 4. Verify or create a local database entry. Create a local database username entry using the **username** global configuration command.

Step 5. Authenticate against the local database. Use the **login local** line configuration command to authenticate the vty line against the local database.

Step 6. Enable vty inbound SSH sessions. By default, no input session is allowed on vty lines. You can specify multiple input protocols including Telnet and SSH using the **transport input** {**ssh** | **telnet**} command.

To display the version and configuration data for SSH on the device that you configured as an SSH server, use the **show ip ssh** command. To check the SSH connections to the device, use the **show ssh** command.

- **Connecting the Switch to the Router**—If your local network has only one router, it is the gateway router, and all hosts and switches on your network must be configured with this information.

  For an end device to communicate over the network, it must be configured with the correct IP address information, including the default gateway address. The default gateway address is generally the router interface address attached to the local network of the host. The IP address of the host device and the router interface address must be in the same network.

To connect the switch and administratively manage it over multiple networks, configure the switch virtual interface (SVI) with an IPv4 address, subnet mask, and default gateway address.

To remotely access the switch from another network using SSH, the switch must have an SVI with an IPv4 address, subnet mask, and default gateway address configured. The IP address configured is that of the router interface of the connected switch. To configure an IPv4 default gateway on a switch, use the **ip default-gateway** *ip-address* global configuration command. The IP address that is configured is the IPv4 address of the local router interface connected to the switch.

A workgroup switch can also be configured with an IPv6 address on an SVI. The switch automatically receives its default gateway from the ICMPv6 Router Advertisement message from the router.

Reflection Questions (28.5.2)

It's nice to have some help when you have a big project, like Diego has. This chapter has almost everything I would need to know to set up a branch network. Based on what you have learned in this course so far, I bet you could have helped Diego. Do you have access to a network that is large enough to contain switches and more than one router? If so, ask your IT department if you could have a tour. You might be surprised at how much you already understand!

Practice

The following activities provide practice with the topics introduced in this chapter.

Packet Tracer Activities

Packet Tracer
Activity

Packet Tracer—Implement Basic Connectivity (28.1.4)

Packet Tracer—Configure Initial Router Settings (28.2.4)

Packet Tracer—Configure SSH (28.3.6)

Packet Tracer—Build a Switch and Router Network (28.4.4)

Packet Tracer—Troubleshoot Default Gateway Issues (28.4.5)

Check Your Understanding Questions

Complete all the review questions listed here to test your understanding of the topics and concepts in this chapter. Appendix A, "Answers to 'Check Your Understanding' Questions," lists the answers.

1. Which connection provides a secure CLI session with encryption to a Cisco switch?
   a. A console connection
   b. A Telnet connection
   c. An AUX connection
   d. An SSH connection
2. Which interface is the default SVI on a Cisco switch?
   a. VLAN 1
   b. FastEthernet 0/1
   c. VLAN 99
   d. GigabitEthernet 0/1

3. On which switch interface would an administrator configure an IP address so that the switch can be managed remotely?

   a. VLAN 1
   b. Console 0
   c. FastEthernet 0/1
   d. vty 0

4. What is the effect of using the Router# **copy running-config startup-config** command on a router?

   a. The contents of flash will change.
   b. The contents of ROM will change.
   c. The contents of NVRAM will change.
   d. The contents of RAM will change.

5. What is one difference between using Telnet or SSH to connect to a network device for management purposes?

   a. Telnet uses UDP as the transport protocol, whereas SSH uses TCP.
   b. Telnet does not provide authentication, whereas SSH provides authentication.
   c. Telnet sends the username and password in plaintext, whereas SSH encrypts the username and password.
   d. Telnet supports a host GUI, whereas SSH only supports a host CLI.

6. A network technician is statically assigning an IP address to a PC. The subnet mask is 255.255.255.0. The default gateway is 172.16.10.1. What would be a valid IP address to assign to the host?

   a. 172.16.1.10
   b. 172.16.10.1
   c. 172.16.10.100
   d. 172.16.10.255

7. What happens when the **transport input ssh** command is entered on the switch vty lines?

   a. The switch requires a username/password combination for remote access.
   b. The switch requires remote connection via proprietary client software.
   c. The SSH client on the switch is enabled.
   d. Communication between the switch and remote users is encrypted.

8. Company policy requires using the most secure method to safeguard access to the privileged EXEC and configuration mode on the routers. The privileged EXEC password is *trustknow1*. Which of the following router commands achieves the goal of providing the highest level of security?

   a. **enable password trustknow1**

   b. **secret password trustknow1**

   c. **service password-encryption**

   d. **enable secret trustknow1**

9. Which command can be used to encrypt all passwords in the configuration file?

   a. **enable secret**

   b. **password**

   c. **service password-encryption**

   d. **enable password**

CHAPTER 29

ICMP

Objectives

Upon completion of this chapter, you will be able to answer the following questions:

- How is ICMP used to test network connectivity?
- How do you use ping and traceroute utilities to test network connectivity?

Introduction (29.0)

Welcome to ICMP! Imagine that you have an intricate model train set. Your tracks and trains are all connected and powered up and ready to go. You throw the switch. The train goes halfway around the track and stops. You know right away that the problem is most likely located where the train has stopped, so you look there first. It is not as easy to visualize this with a network. Like a train, packets might not make it to their destination. Fortunately, there are tools to help you locate problem areas in your network, *and* they work with both IPv4 and IPv6 networks! You will be happy to know that this chapter has a couple Packet Tracer activities to help you practice using these tools, so let's get testing!

ICMP Messages (29.1)

In this section, you will learn about the different types of Internet Control Message Protocol (ICMP) messages and the tools that are used to send them.

ICMPv4 and ICMPv6 Messages (29.1.1)

Although IP is only a best-effort protocol, the TCP/IP suite does provide for error messages and informational messages when communicating with another IP device. These messages are sent using the services of ICMP. The purpose of these messages is to provide feedback about issues related to the processing of IP packets under certain conditions, not to make IP reliable. ICMP messages are not required and are often not allowed within a network for security reasons.

ICMP is available for both IPv4 and IPv6. ICMPv4 is the messaging protocol for IPv4. ICMPv6 provides these same services for IPv6 but includes additional functionality. In this chapter, the term ICMP is used when referring to both ICMPv4 and ICMPv6.

The types of ICMP messages, and the reasons why they are sent, are extensive. The ICMP messages common to both ICMPv4 and ICMPv6 and discussed in this section include

- Host reachability messages
- Destination Unreachable
- Time Exceeded

Host Reachability (29.1.2)

An ICMP Echo message can be used to test whether a host on an IP network is reachable. The local host sends an ICMP Echo Request to a host. If the destination

host is available, it responds with an Echo Reply, as shown in Figure 29-1. This use of the ICMP Echo messages is the basis of the **ping** utility.

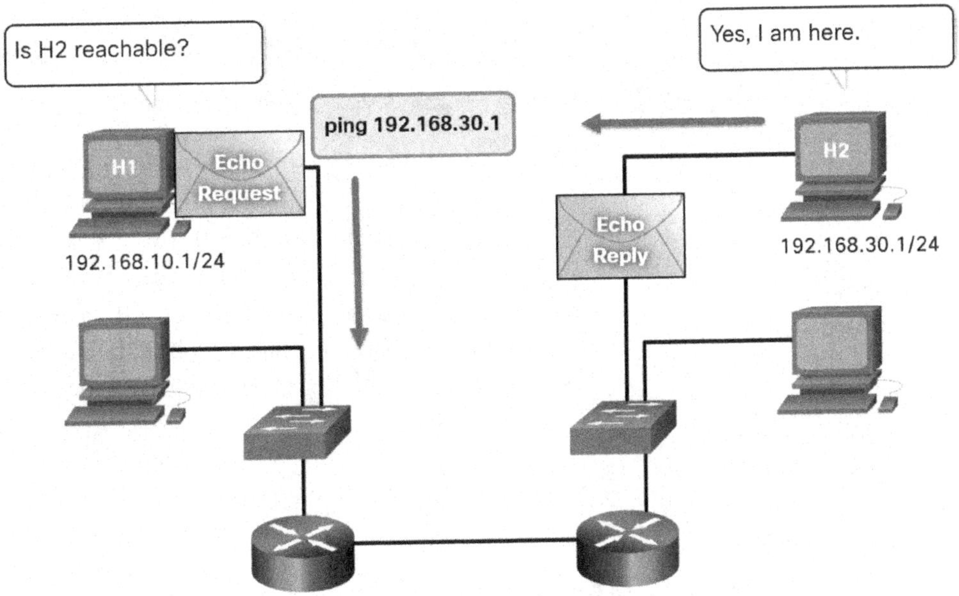

Figure 29-1 Echo Request and Echo Reply

Destination or Service Unreachable (29.1.3)

When a host or gateway receives a packet that it cannot deliver, it can use an ICMP Destination Unreachable message to notify the source that the destination or service is unreachable. The message includes a code that indicates why the packet could not be delivered.

Some of the Destination Unreachable codes for ICMPv4 are as follows:

- 0—Net unreachable
- 1—Host unreachable
- 2—Protocol unreachable
- 3—Port unreachable

Some of the Destination Unreachable codes for ICMPv6 are as follows:

- 0—No route to destination
- 1—Communication with the destination is administratively prohibited (for example, by a firewall)

- 2—Beyond scope of the source address
- 3—Address unreachable
- 4—Port unreachable

Time Exceeded (29.1.4)

An ICMPv4 Time Exceeded message is used by a router to indicate that a packet cannot be forwarded because the Time-to-Live (TTL) field of the packet was decremented to 0. If a router receives a packet and decrements the TTL field in the IPv4 packet to 0, it discards the packet and sends a Time Exceeded message to the source host.

ICMPv6 also sends a Time Exceeded message if the router cannot forward an IPv6 packet because the packet has expired. Unlike IPv4, IPv6 doesn't have a TTL field; ICMPv6 uses the IPv6 Hop Limit field to determine if the packet has expired.

Note

Time Exceeded messages are used by the **traceroute** tool.

ICMPv6 Messages (29.1.5)

The informational and error messages found in ICMPv6 are very similar to the control and error messages implemented by ICMPv4. However, ICMPv6 has new features and improved functionality not found in ICMPv4. ICMPv6 messages are encapsulated in IPv6.

ICMPv6 includes four new protocols as part of the Neighbor Discovery Protocol (ND or NDP).

Messaging between an IPv6 router and an IPv6 device, including dynamic address allocation, is as follows:

- Router Solicitation (RS) message
- Router Advertisement (RA) message

Messaging between IPv6 devices, including duplicate address detection and address resolution, is as follows:

- Neighbor Solicitation (NS) message
- Neighbor Advertisement (NA) message

Note

ICMPv6 ND also includes the Redirect message, which has a similar function to the Redirect message used in ICMPv4.

RA messages are sent by IPv6-enabled routers every 200 seconds to provide addressing information to IPv6-enabled hosts. The RA message can include addressing information for the host such as the prefix, prefix length, DNS address, and domain name. A host using Stateless Address Autoconfiguration (SLAAC) sets its default gateway to the link-local address of the router that sent the RA.

In Figure 29-2, R1 sends the following RA message to FF02::1, the all-nodes multicast address that will reach PC1:

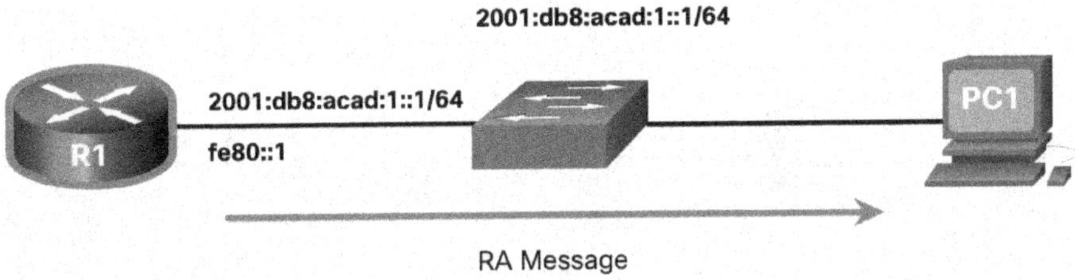

Figure 29-2 RA Message

An IPv6-enabled router also sends out an RA message in response to an RS message. In Figure 29-3, PC1 sends an RS message to determine how to receive its IPv6 address information dynamically. R1 replies to the RS message with an RA message. The exchange goes something like this:

1. PC1 sends an RS message: "Hi, I just booted up. Is there an IPv6 router on the network? I need to know how to get my IPv6 address information dynamically."
2. R1 replies with an RA message: "Hi, all IPv6-enabled devices. I'm R1, and you can use SLAAC to create an IPv6 global unicast address. The prefix is 2001:db8:acad:1::/64. By the way, use my link-local address fe80::1 as your default gateway."

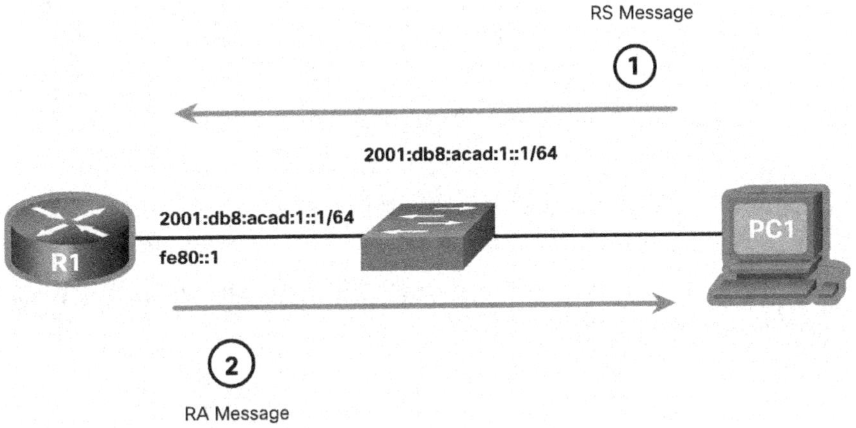

Figure 29-3 RS Message

When a device is assigned a global IPv6 unicast or link-local unicast address, it may perform duplicate address detection (DAD) to ensure that the IPv6 address is unique. To check the uniqueness of an address, the device sends an NS message with its own IPv6 address as the targeted IPv6 address, as shown in Figure 29-4. The NS message from PC1 states, in effect, "Will whoever has the IPv6 address 2001:db8:acad:1::10 send me your MAC address?"

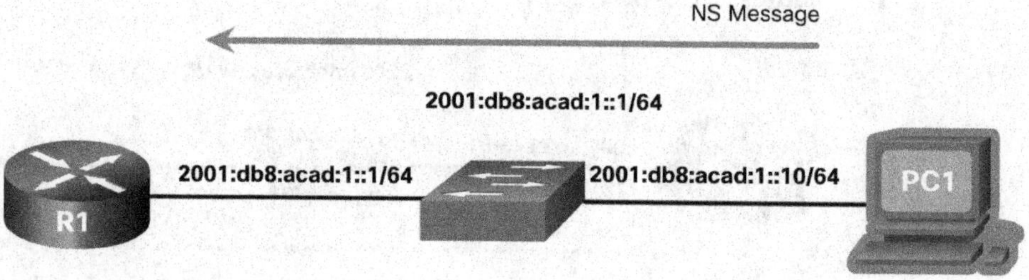

Figure 29-4 NS Message

If another device on the network has this address, it responds with an NA message, which notifies the sending device that the address is in use. If a corresponding NA message is not returned within a certain amount of time, the unicast address is unique and acceptable for use.

Note

DAD is not required, but RFC 4861 recommends that DAD be performed on unicast addresses.

Address resolution is used when a device on the LAN knows the IPv6 unicast address of a destination but does not know its Ethernet MAC address. To determine the MAC address for the destination, the device sends an NS message to the solicited node address. The message includes the known (targeted) IPv6 address. The device that has the targeted IPv6 address responds with an NA message containing its Ethernet MAC address.

Figure 29-5 shows an example of address resolution: R1 sends an NS message to 2001:db8:acad:1::10 asking for its MAC address.

1. R1 sends an address resolution NS message: "Will whoever has the IPv6 address 2001:db8:acad:1::10 send me your MAC address?"
2. PC1 replies with an NA message: "I'm 2001:db8:acad:1::10 and my MAC address is 00:aa:bb:cc:dd:ee."

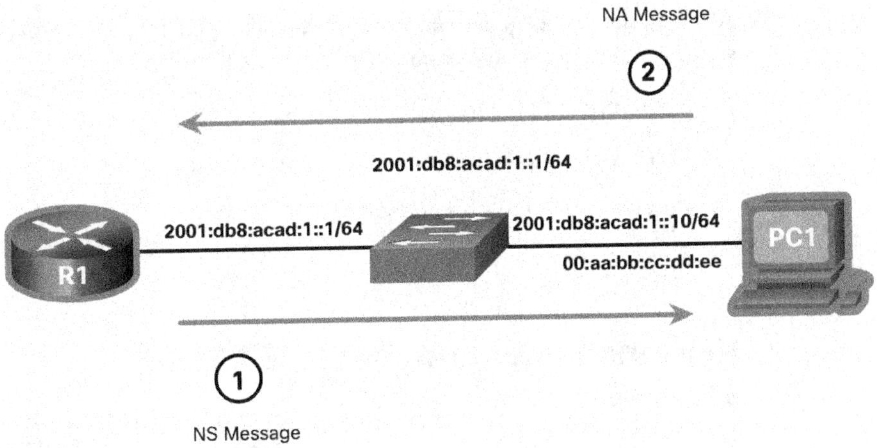

Figure 29-5 NA Message

Interactive Graphic

Check Your Understanding—ICMP Messages (29.1.6)

Refer to the online course to complete this activity.

Ping and Traceroute Tests (29.2)

This section discusses two important tools that are used to verify Layer 3 connectivity: ping and traceroute.

Ping—Test Connectivity (29.2.1)

This section explains when to use the **ping** and **traceroute** (**tracert** in Windows) tools and how to use them. Ping is an IPv4 and IPv6 testing utility that uses ICMP Echo Request and Echo Reply messages to test connectivity between hosts.

To test connectivity to another host on a network, an Echo Request is sent to the host address using the **ping** command. If the host at the specified address receives the Echo Request, it responds with an Echo Reply. As each Echo Reply is received, **ping** provides feedback on the time between when the request was sent and when the reply was received. This can provide a measure of network performance.

Ping has a timeout value for the reply. If a reply is not received within the timeout, ping provides a message indicating that a response was not received. This may indicate that there is a problem, but could also indicate that security features blocking ping messages have been enabled on the network. It is common for the first ping to time out if address resolution (ARP or ND) needs to be performed before sending the ICMP Echo Request.

After all the requests are sent, the **ping** utility provides a summary that includes the success rate and average round-trip time to the destination.

Types of connectivity tests performed with **ping** include the following:

- Pinging the local loopback
- Pinging the default gateway
- Pinging a remote host

Ping the Local Loopback (29.2.2)

Ping can be used to test the internal configuration of IPv4 or IPv6 on the local host. To perform this test, **ping** the local loopback address of 127.0.0.1 for IPv4 (::1 for IPv6), as shown in Figure 29-6.

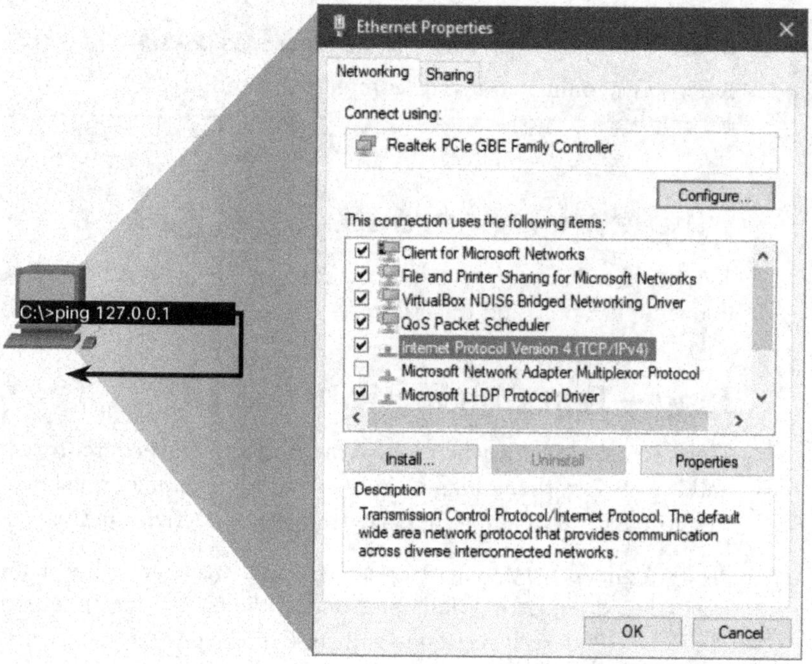

Figure 29-6 Pinging the Local Loopback on a Windows Host

A response from 127.0.0.1 for IPv4, or ::1 for IPv6, indicates that IP is properly installed on the host. This response comes from the network layer. This response is not, however, an indication that the addresses, masks, or gateways are properly configured. Nor does it indicate anything about the status of the lower layers of the network stack. This simply tests IP down through the network layer of IP. An error message indicates that TCP/IP is not operational on the host.

Ping the Default Gateway (29.2.3)

You can also use **ping** to test the ability of a host to communicate on the local network. This is generally done by pinging the IP address of the default gateway of the host, as shown in Figure 29-7. A successful **ping** to the default gateway indicates that both the host and the router interface serving as the default gateway are operational on the local network.

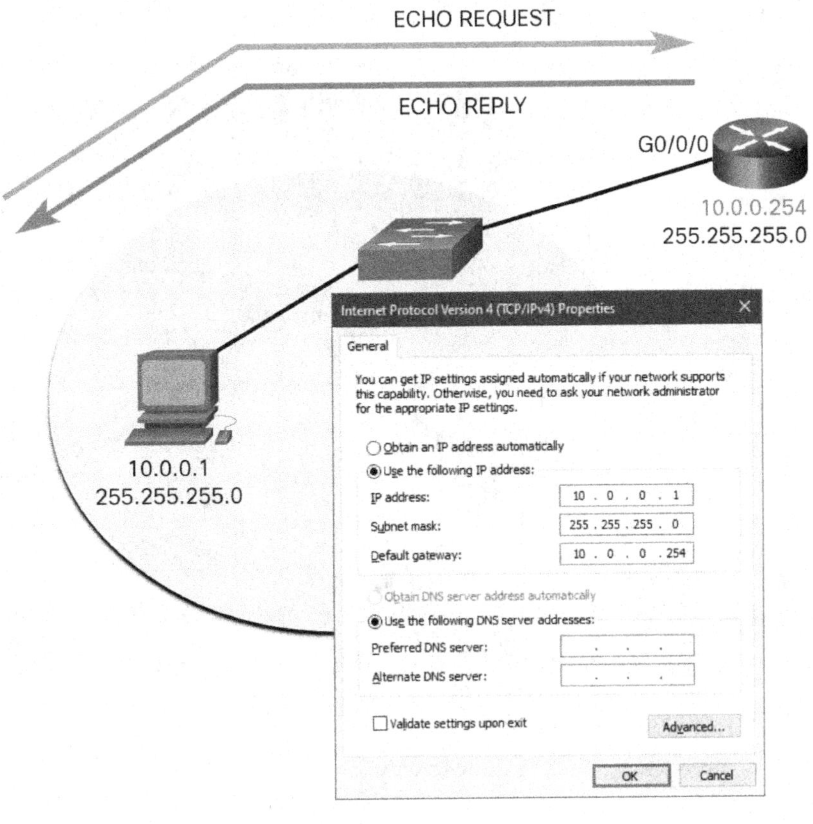

Figure 29-7 Pinging the Default Gateway

For this test, the default gateway address is most often used because the router is normally always operational. If the default gateway address does not respond, a **ping** can be sent to the IP address of another host on the local network that is known to be operational.

If either the default gateway or another host responds, this confirms that the local host can successfully communicate over the local network. If the default gateway does not respond but another host does, this could indicate a problem with the router interface serving as the default gateway. One possibility is that the wrong default gateway address has been configured on the host. Another possibility is that the

router interface is fully operational but has security applied to it that prevents it from processing or responding to ping requests.

Ping a Remote Host (29.2.4)

Ping can also be used to test the ability of a local host to communicate across an internetwork. The local host can ping an operational IPv4 host of a remote network, as shown in Figure 29-8. The router uses its IP routing table to forward the packets.

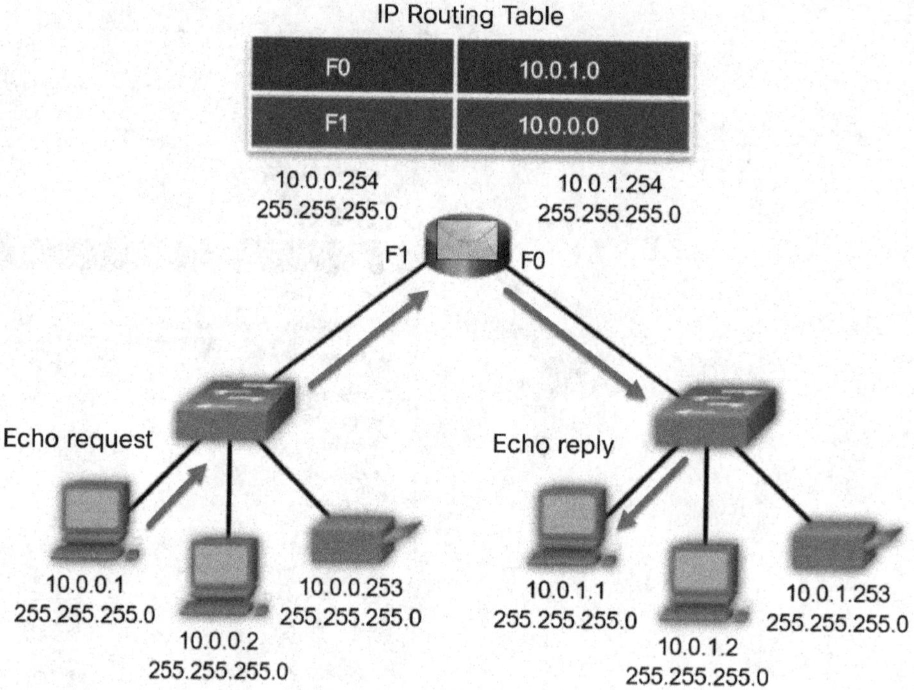

Figure 29-8 Testing Connectivity to a Remote LAN

Interactive Graphic

Go to the online course to view an animation of pinging a device on a remote LAN.

If this ping is successful, the operation of a large piece of the internetwork can be verified. A successful **ping** across the internetwork confirms communication on the local network, the operation of the router serving as the default gateway, and the operation of all other routers that might be in the path between the local network and the network of the remote host.

Additionally, the functionality of the remote host can be verified. If the remote host could not communicate outside of its local network, it would not have responded.

Note

Many network administrators limit or prohibit the entry of ICMP messages into the corporate network; therefore, the lack of a **ping** response could be due to security restrictions.

Traceroute—Test the Path (29.2.5)

Ping is used to test connectivity between two hosts but does not provide information about the details of devices between the hosts. The **traceroute** (**tracert**) utility is used to generate a list of hops that were successfully reached along the path. This list can provide important verification and troubleshooting information. If the data reaches the destination, the trace lists the interface of every router in the path between the hosts. If the data fails at some hop along the way, the address of the last router that responded to the trace provides an indication of where the problem or security restrictions are found.

Round-Trip Time (RTT)

Using traceroute provides the round-trip time for each hop along the path and indicates if a hop fails to respond. The round-trip time is the time a packet takes to reach the remote host and for the response from the host to return. An asterisk (*) is used to indicate a lost or unreplied packet.

This information can be used to locate a problematic router in the path, or it may indicate that the router is configured not to reply. If the display shows high response times or data losses from a particular hop, this is an indication that the resources of the router or its connections might be stressed.

IPv4 TTL and IPv6 Hop Limit

Traceroute makes use of a function of the TTL field in IPv4 and the Hop Limit field in IPv6 in the Layer 3 headers, along with the ICMP Time Exceeded message.

The first sequence of messages sent from traceroute has a TTL field value of 1. This causes the TTL to time out the IPv4 packet at the first router. This router then responds with an ICMPv4 Time Exceeded message. Traceroute now has the address of the first hop.

Traceroute then progressively increments the TTL field (2, 3, 4, and so on) for each sequence of messages. This provides the trace with the address of each hop as the packets time out further down the path. The TTL field continues to be increased until the destination is reached or a predefined maximum TTL value is reached.

After the final destination is reached, the host responds with either an ICMP Port Unreachable message or an ICMP Echo Reply message instead of the ICMP Time Exceeded message.

In Figure 29-9, the host at 10.0.0.1 has sent three ICMPv4 messages. The next ICMPv4 message sent by that host will reach 192.168.1.2. The host at 192.168.1.2 will respond with an ICMP Echo Reply message.

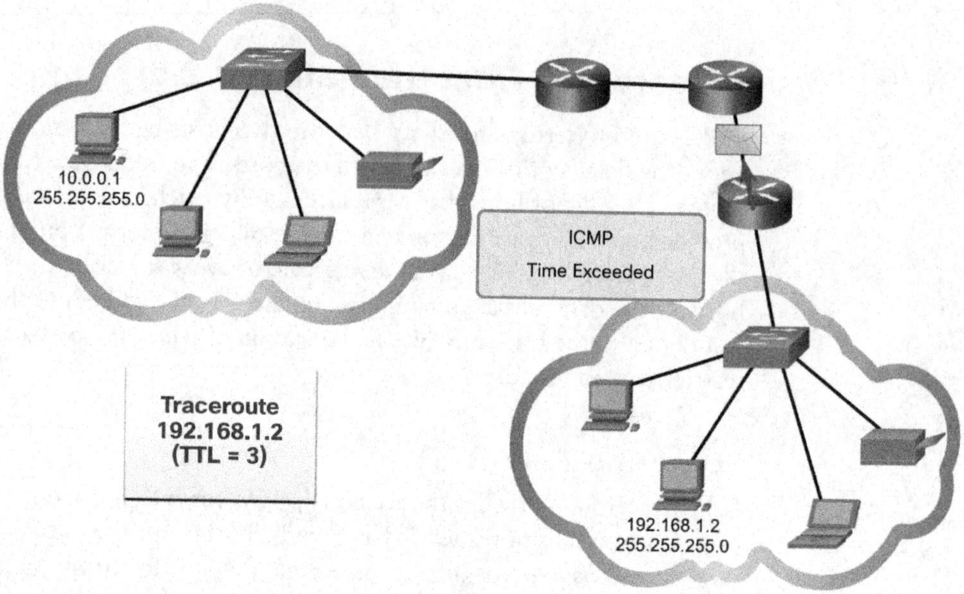

Figure 29-9 Tracing the Route to a Destination

Interactive Graphic

Go to the online course to view an animation of Figure 29-9.

Packet Tracer Activity

Packet Tracer—Verify IPv4 and IPv6 Addressing (29.2.6)

IPv4 and IPv6 can coexist on the same network. From the command prompt of a PC, there are some differences in the way commands are issued and in the way output is displayed.

Refer to the online course to complete this Packet Tracer.

Packet Tracer Activity

Packet Tracer—Use Ping and Traceroute to Test Network Connectivity (29.2.7)

There are connectivity issues in this activity. In addition to gathering and documenting information about the network, you will locate the problems and implement acceptable solutions to restore connectivity.

Refer to the online course to complete this Packet Tracer.

Packet Tracer
☐ Activity

Packet Tracer—Use ICMP to Test and Correct Network Connectivity (29.3.1)

In this Packet Tracer activity, you will use ICMP to test network connectivity and locate network problems. You will also correct simple configuration issues and restore connectivity to the network.

- Use ICMP to locate connectivity issues.
- Configure network devices to correct connectivity issues.

Refer to the online course to complete this Packet Tracer.

ICMP Summary (29.3)

The following is a summary of each topic in the chapter and some questions for your reflection.

What Did I Learn in This Chapter? (29.3.2)

- **ICMP Messages**—Although IP is only a best-effort protocol, the TCP/IP suite does provide for error messages and informational messages when communicating with another IP device. These messages are sent using the services of ICMP. The purpose of these messages is to provide feedback about issues related to the processing of IP packets under certain conditions, not to make IP reliable. ICMP is available for both IPv4 and IPv6. ICMPv4 is the messaging protocol for IPv4. ICMPv6 provides these same services for IPv6 but includes additional functionality.

  An ICMP Echo message can be used to test the reachability of a host on an IP network. The local host sends an ICMP Echo Request to a host. If the host is available, the destination host responds with an Echo Reply.

  When a host or gateway receives a packet that it cannot deliver, it can use an ICMP Destination Unreachable message to notify the source that the destination or service is unreachable. The message includes a code that indicates why the packet could not be delivered.

  An ICMPv4 Time Exceeded message is used by a router to indicate that a packet cannot be forwarded because the TTL field of the packet was decremented to 0. If a router receives a packet and decrements the TTL field in the IPv4 packet to 0, it discards the packet and sends a Time Exceeded message to the source host.

  ICMPv6 also sends a Time Exceeded message if the router cannot forward an IPv6 packet because the packet has expired. The informational and error messages found in ICMPv6 are very similar to the control and error messages

implemented by ICMPv4. However, ICMPv6 includes four new protocols as part of the Neighbor Discovery Protocol, as follows:

  - RS message
  - RA message
  - NS message
  - NA message

- **Ping and Traceroute Tests**—To test connectivity to another host on a network, an Echo Request is sent to the host address using the **ping** command. If the host at the specified address receives the Echo Request, it responds with an Echo Reply. As each Echo Reply is received, ping provides feedback on the time between when the request was sent and when the reply was received. This can provide a measure of network performance. Ping has a timeout value for the reply. If a reply is not received within the timeout, ping provides a message indicating that a response was not received.

  Types of connectivity tests performed with **ping** include the following:

  - **Pinging the local loopback**—Ping can be used to test the internal configuration of IPv4 or IPv6 on the local host. To perform this test, ping the local loopback address.
  - **Pinging the default gateway**—This is generally done by pinging the IP address of the default gateway of the host. A successful ping to the default gateway indicates that both the host and the router interface serving as the default gateway are operational on the local network.
  - **Pinging the remote host**—A successful ping across the internetwork confirms communication on the local network, the operation of the router serving as the default gateway, and the operation of all other routers that might be in the path between the local network and the network of the remote host.

  The **traceroute (tracert)** utility is used to generate a list of hops that were successfully reached along the path. This list can provide important verification and troubleshooting information. If the data reaches the destination, the trace lists the interface of every router in the path between the hosts. If the data fails at some hop along the way, the address of the last router that responded to the trace provides an indication of where the problem or security restrictions are found.

  The round-trip time is the time a packet takes to reach the remote host and for the response from the host to return. An asterisk (*) is used to indicate a lost or unreplied packet. Traceroute makes use of a function of the TTL field in IPv4 and the Hop Limit field in IPv6 in the Layer 3 headers, along with the ICMP Time Exceeded message.

Reflection Questions (29.3.3)

There's not much point in setting up a network if you don't test it to make sure it is operating properly. Diego needs to ensure that his network is working and that it connects to the network at headquarters and to the Internet. This chapter provided some of the most common troubleshooting tools used by network administrators the world over. You can even use these tools on your home network. Try it and see!

Practice

The following activities provide practice with the topics introduced in this chapter.

Packet Tracer Activities

Packet Tracer Activity

Packet Tracer 29.2.6: Verify IPv4 and IPv6 Addressing

Packet Tracer 29.2.7: Use Ping and Traceroute to Test Network Connectivity

Packet Tracer 29.3.1: Use ICMP to Test and Correct Network Connectivity

Check Your Understanding Questions

Complete all the review questions listed here to test your understanding of the topics and concepts in this chapter. Appendix A, "Answers to 'Check Your Understanding' Questions," lists the answers.

1. A user calls to report that a PC cannot access the Internet. The network technician asks the user to issue the command ping 127.0.0.1 in a command prompt window. The user reports that the result is four positive replies. What conclusion can be drawn based on this connectivity test?

   a. The PC can access the network. The problem exists beyond the local network.

   b. The IP address obtained from the DHCP server is correct.

   c. The PC can access the Internet. However, the web browser may not work.

   d. The TCP/IP implementation is functional.

2. Which command can be used to test connectivity between two devices using Echo Request and Echo Reply messages?

   a. **netstat**

   b. **ipconfig**

   c. **ICMP**

   d. **ping**

3. What IPv6 field does a router use to determine that a packet has expired?

   a. TTL field

   b. CRC field

c. Hop Limit field
d. Time Exceeded field

4. Which protocol provides feedback from the destination host to the source host about errors in packet delivery?

a. ARP
b. BOOTP
c. DNS
d. ICMP

5. Which utility uses the Internet Control Messaging Protocol (ICMP)?

a. RIP
b. DNS
c. Ping
d. NTP

6. A network administrator can successfully ping the server at www.cisco.com but cannot ping the company web server located at an ISP in another city. Which tool or command would help identify the specific router where the packet was lost or delayed?

a. **ipconfig**
b. **netstat**
c. **telnet**
d. **traceroute**

7. Which protocol is used by IPv4 and IPv6 to provide error messaging?

a. ICMP
b. NDP
c. ARP
d. DHCP

8. What message can be sent by a host to check the uniqueness of an IPv6 address before using that address?

a. Neighbor Solicitation
b. ARP Request
c. Echo Request
d. Router Solicitation

9. A technician is troubleshooting a network where it is suspected that a defective node in the network path is causing packets to be dropped. The technician has only the IP address of the end point device and does not have any details of the intermediate devices. Which Windows command can the technician use to identify the faulty node?

   a. **tracert**

   b. **ping**

   c. **ipconfig /flushdns**

   d. **ipconfig /displaydns**

10. A user who is unable to connect to the file server contacts the help desk. The help desk technician asks the user to ping the IP address of the default gateway that is configured on the workstation. What is the purpose for this ping command?

    a. To obtain a dynamic IP address from the server

    b. To request that the gateway forward the connection request to the file server

    c. To test that the host has the capability to reach hosts on other networks

    d. To resolve the domain name of the file server to its IP address

11. What is a function of the Windows **tracert** command that differs from the **ping** command when they are used on a workstation?

    a. The **tracert** command reaches the destination faster.

    b. The **tracert** command shows information about the routers in the path.

    c. The **tracert** command sends one ICMP message to each hop in the path.

    d. The **tracert** command is used to test the connectivity between two devices.

12. Which ICMP message is used by the traceroute utility during the process of finding the path between two end hosts?

    a. Redirect

    b. Ping

    c. Time Exceeded

    d. Destination Unreachable

13. Which two things can be determined by using the **ping** command? (Choose two.)

    a. The number of routers between the source and destination device

    b. The IP address of the route nearest the destination device

    c. The average time it takes a packet to reach the destination and for the response to return to the source

d. The destination device is reachable through the network

e. The average time it takes each router in the path between the source and the destination to respond

14. Which statement describes a characteristic of the traceroute utility?

a. It sends four Echo Request messages.

b. It utilizes three ICMP Source Quench messages.

c. It is primarily used to test connectivity between two hosts.

d. It identifies the routers in the path from a source host to a destination host.

CHAPTER 30

Physical Layer

Objectives

Upon completion of this chapter, you will be able to answer the following questions:

- What are the purpose and functions of the physical layer in the network?
- What are characteristics of the physical layer?
- What are the basic characteristics of copper cabling?
- How is UTP cable used in Ethernet networks?
- What is fiber-optic cabling and what are its main advantages over other media?

Key Terms

This chapter uses the following key terms. You can find the definitions in the Glossary.

American National Standards Institute (ANSI) Page 524

bandwidth Page 527

coaxial cable Page 533

crosstalk Page 530

electromagnetic interference (EMI) Page 530

encoding Page 525

fiber-optic cable Page 534

goodput Page 529

International Organization for Standardization (ISO) Page 524

International Telecommunication Union (ITU) Page 524

Institute of Electrical and Electronics Engineers (IEEE) Page 524

Manchester encoding Page 525

network interface card (NIC) Page 521

shielded twisted-pair (STP) Page 533

Telecommunications Industry Association/Electronic Industries Association (TIA/EIA) Page 524

throughput Page 529

unshielded twisted-pair (UTP) Page 531

wireless access point (AP) Page 520

Introduction (30.0)

I have a friend I'd like you to meet. Her name is Halimah. She just started working as a junior member of the IT department of a large oil and gas firm that specializes in exploration and production. Her company has a multi-building headquarters in Lagos, Nigeria, and several branch offices throughout Nigeria.

In this chapter, you will learn about the physical layer of networks. Halimah already knows this information and she needs to use it to better understand the way the network at headquarters is constructed.

Are you ready to get started?

Purpose of the Physical Layer (30.1)

All data being transferred over a network must be represented on a medium by the sending node and interpreted on a medium by the receiving node. The physical layer is responsible for these functions. This section explores the physical layer.

The Physical Connection (30.1.1)

Whether connecting to a local printer in the home or a website in another country, before any network communications can occur, a physical connection to a local network must be established. A physical connection can be a wired connection using a cable or a wireless connection using radio waves.

The type of physical connection used depends on the setup of the network. For example, in many corporate offices, employees have desktop or laptop computers that are physically connected, via cable, to a shared switch. This type of setup is a wired network. Data is transmitted through a physical cable.

In addition to wired connections, many businesses also offer wireless connections for laptops, tablets, and smartphones. With wireless devices, data is transmitted using radio waves. Wireless connectivity is common because individuals and businesses alike are aware of its advantages. Devices on a wireless network must be connected to a *wireless access point (AP)* or wireless router like the one shown in Figure 30-1.

The numbers in Figure 30-1 correspond to the following components of an access point:

1. The wireless antennas (embedded inside the router version shown in Figure 30-1)
2. Several Ethernet switch ports
3. An Internet port

Figure 30-1 Wireless Router

Similar to corporate offices, most homes have both wired and wireless connectivity to the network. Figure 30-2 shows a home router and a laptop connecting to the local area network (LAN).

Figure 30-2 Wired Connection to a Wireless Router

A ***network interface card (NIC)*** connects a device to a network. An Ethernet NIC is used for a wired connection, as shown in Figure 30-3, whereas a wireless local area network (WLAN) NIC is used for wireless. An end-user device may include one or both types of NICs. A network printer, for example, might have only an Ethernet NIC, requiring that it connect to the network using an Ethernet cable. Other devices, such as tablets and smartphones, might contain only a WLAN NIC, requiring use of a wireless connection.

Not all physical connections are equal, in terms of the performance level, when connecting to a network.

Figure 30-3 Wired Connection Using an Ethernet NIC

The Physical Layer Process (30.1.2)

The OSI physical layer provides the means to transport the bits that make up a data link layer frame across the network media. This layer accepts a complete frame from the data link layer and encodes it as a series of signals that is transmitted to the local media. The encoded bits that comprise a frame are received by either an end device or an intermediate device.

Figure 30-4 show an example of the encapsulation process. The last part of this process shows the bits being sent over the physical medium. The physical layer encodes the frames and creates the electrical, optical, or radio wave signals that represent the bits in each frame. These signals are then sent over the media, one at a time.

The destination node physical layer retrieves these individual signals from the media, restores them to their bit representations, and passes the bits up to the data link layer as a complete frame.

Interactive Graphic

Refer to the online course to view an animation of the encapsulation process.

Interactive Graphic

Check Your Understanding—Purpose of the Physical Layer (30.1.3)

Refer to the online course to complete this activity.

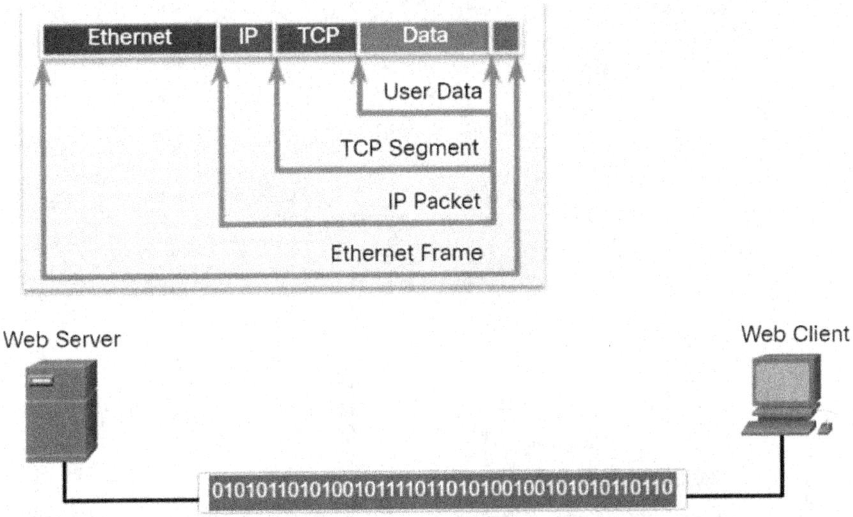

Figure 30-4 Bits Transported over the Medium

Physical Layer Characteristics (30.2)

At the foundation of network communications is the physical layer, Layer 1. This section examines standards and components that make up the physical layer.

Physical Layer Standards (30.2.1)

In the previous section, you gained a high-level overview of the physical layer and its place in a network. This section dives a bit deeper into the specifics of the physical layer. This includes the standards that are required so that everything works together.

The protocols and operations of the upper OSI layers are performed using software designed by software engineers and computer scientists. The services and protocols in the TCP/IP suite are defined by the Internet Engineering Task Force (IETF), as depicted in Figure 30-5.

The physical layer consists of electronic circuitry, media, and connectors developed by engineers. Therefore, it is appropriate that the standards governing this hardware are defined by the relevant electrical and communications engineering organizations.

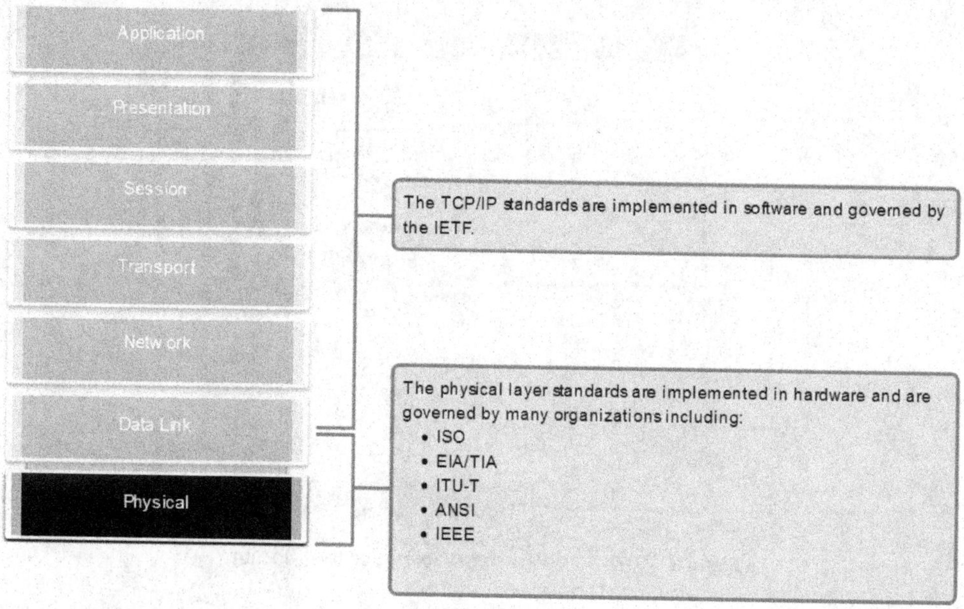

Figure 30-5 Physical Layer Standards Organizations

Many different international and national organizations, regulatory government organizations, and private companies are involved in establishing and maintaining physical layer standards. For instance, the physical layer hardware, media, encoding, and signaling standards are defined and governed by these standards organizations, also depicted in Figure 30-5:

- *International Organization for Standardization (ISO)*
- *Telecommunications Industry Association/Electronic Industries Association (TIA/EIA)*
- *International Telecommunication Union (ITU)*
- *American National Standards Institute (ANSI)*
- *Institute of Electrical and Electronics Engineers (IEEE)*
- National telecommunications regulatory authorities including the U.S. Federal Communication Commission (FCC) and the European Telecommunications Standards Institute (ETSI)

In addition to these organization, there are often regional cabling standards groups such as CSA (Canadian Standards Association), CENELEC (European Committee for Electrotechnical Standardization), and JSA/JIS (Japanese Standards Association) that develop local specifications.

Physical Components (30.2.2)

The physical layer standards address three functional areas:

- Physical components
- Encoding
- Signaling

The physical components are the electronic hardware devices, media, and other connectors that transmit the signals that represent the bits. Hardware components such as NICs, interfaces and connectors, and cables (including cable materials and cable designs) are all specified in standards associated with the physical layer. The various ports and interfaces on a Cisco 1941 router (for example) are also physical components with specific connectors and pinouts resulting from standards.

Encoding (30.2.3)

Encoding or line encoding is a method of converting a stream of data bits into a predefined "code." Codes are groupings of bits used to provide a predictable pattern that can be recognized by both sender and receiver. In other words, encoding is the method or pattern used to represent digital information. This is similar to how Morse code encodes a message using a series of dots and dashes.

For example, *Manchester encoding* represents a 0 bit by a transition from high voltage to low voltage and represents a 1 bit by a transition from low voltage to high voltage. An example of Manchester encoding is illustrated in Figure 30-6. The transition occurs at the middle of each bit period. This type of encoding is used in 10 Mbps Ethernet. Faster data rates require more complex encoding. Manchester encoding is used in older Ethernet standards such as 10BASE-T. Ethernet 100BASE-TX uses 4B/5B encoding and 1000BASE-T uses 8B/10B encoding.

Signaling (30.2.4)

The physical layer must generate the electrical, optical, or wireless signals that represent the 1s and 0s on the media. The way that bits are represented is called the *signaling method*. The physical layer standards must define what type of signal represents a 1 and what type of signal represents a 0. This can be as simple as a change in the level of an electrical signal or optical pulse. For example, a long pulse might represent a 1, whereas a short pulse might represent a 0.

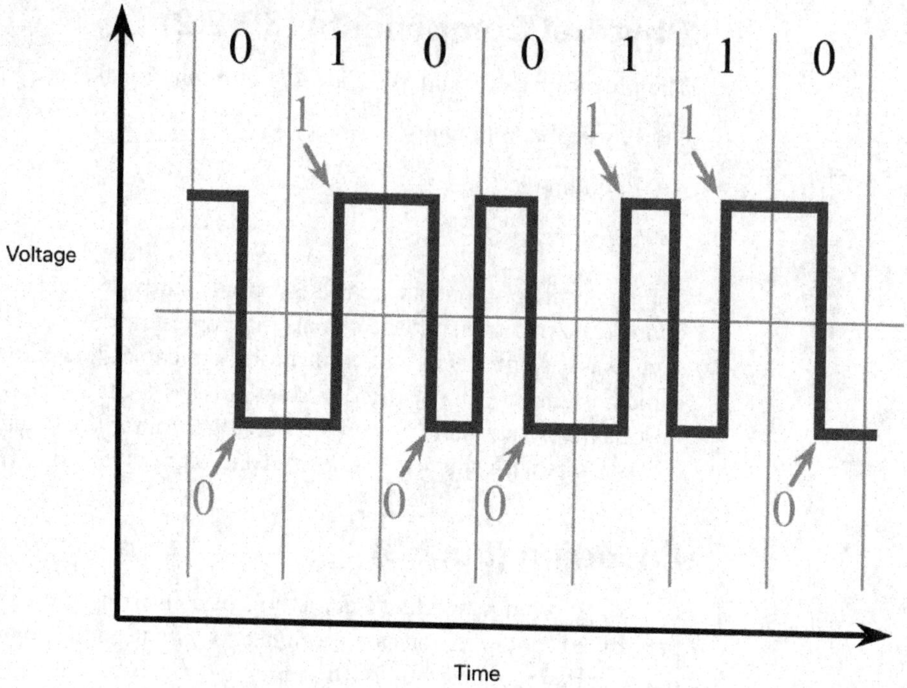

The transition occurs at the middle of each bit period.

Figure 30-6 Manchester Encoding

This is similar to the signaling method used in Morse code, which may use a series of on/off tones, lights, or clicks to send text over telephone wires or between ships at sea.

Figures 30-7 through 30-9 show illustrations of signaling for copper cable, fiber-optic cable, and wireless media.

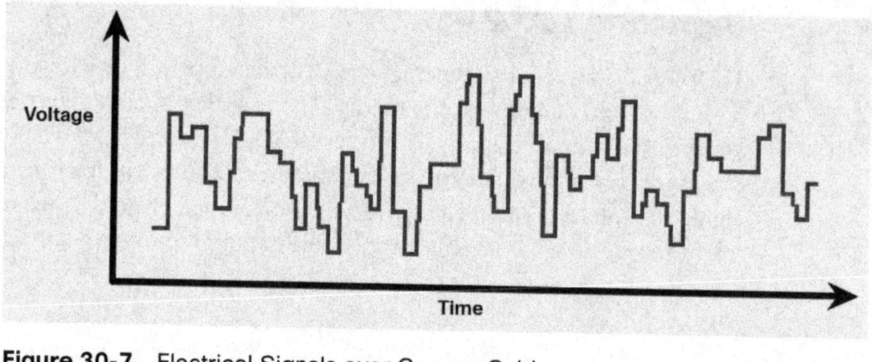

Figure 30-7 Electrical Signals over Copper Cable

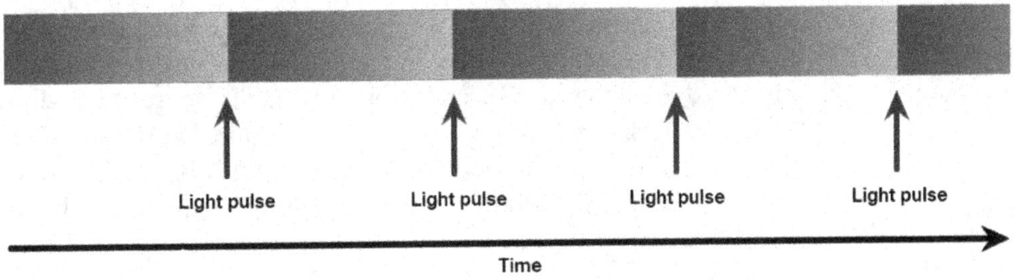

Figure 30-8 Light Pulses over Fiber-Optic Cable

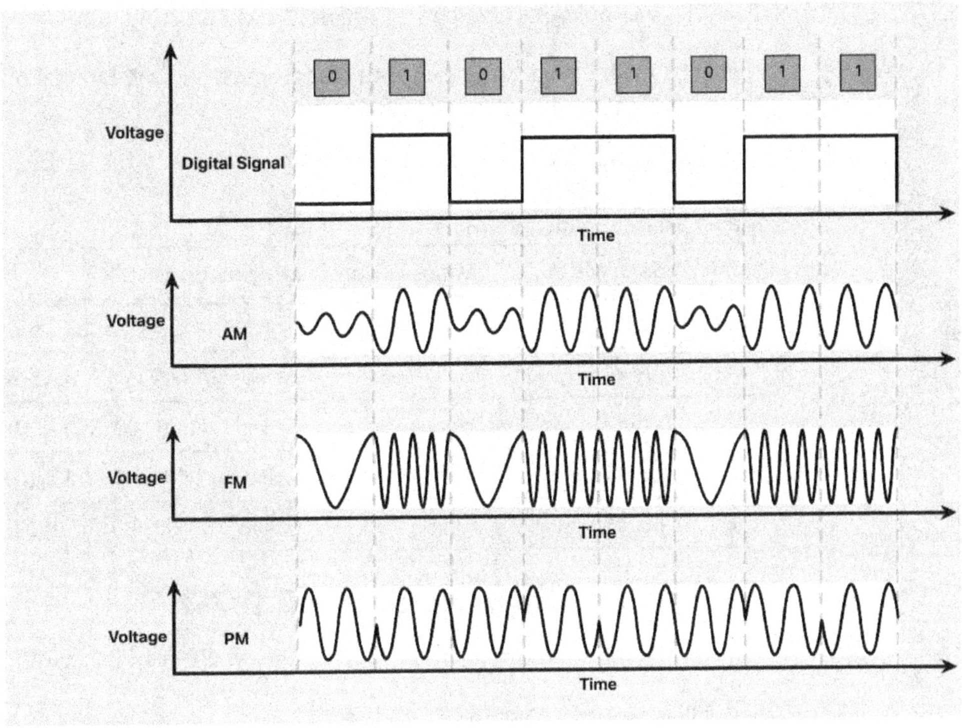

Figure 30-9 Microwave Signals over Wireless

Video

Video—Bandwidth (30.2.5)

Refer to the online course to view this video.

Bandwidth (30.2.6)

Different physical media support the transfer of bits at different rates. Data transfer is usually discussed in terms of bandwidth. *Bandwidth* is the capacity at which a

medium can carry data. Digital bandwidth measures the amount of data that can flow from one place to another in a given amount of time. Bandwidth is typically measured in kilobits per second (Kbps), megabits per second (Mbps), or gigabits per second (Gbps). Bandwidth is sometimes thought of as the speed at which bits travel, but this is not accurate. For example, in both 10 Mbps and 100 Mbps Ethernet, the bits are sent at the speed of electricity; they differ in the number of bits that are transmitted per second.

A combination of factors determines the practical bandwidth of a network:

- The properties of the physical media
- The technologies chosen for signaling and detecting network signals

Physical media properties, current technologies, and the laws of physics all play roles in determining the available bandwidth.

Table 30-1 shows the commonly used units of measure for bandwidth.

Table 30-1 Bandwidth Units

Unit of Bandwidth	Abbreviation	Equivalence
Bits per second	bps	1 bps = fundamental unit of bandwidth
Kilobits per second	Kbps	1 Kbps = 1,000 bps = 10^3 bps
Megabits per second	Mbps	1 Mbps = 1,000,000 bps = 10^6 bps
Gigabits per second	Gbps	1 Gbps = 1,000,000,000 bps = 10^9 bps
Terabits per second	Tbps	1 Tbps = 1,000,000,000,000 bps = 10^{12} bps

Bandwidth Terminology (30.2.7)

The following terms are used to measure the quality of bandwidth:

- Latency
- Throughput
- Goodput

Latency

Latency refers to the amount of time, including delays, for data to travel from one given point to another.

In an internetwork, or a network with multiple segments, throughput cannot be faster than the slowest link in the path from source to destination. Even if all, or most, of

the segments have high bandwidth, it takes only one segment in the path with low throughput to create a bottleneck in the throughput of the entire network.

Throughput

Throughput is the measure of the transfer of bits across the media over a given period of time.

Due to a number of factors, throughput usually does not match the specified bandwidth in physical layer implementations. Throughput is usually lower than the bandwidth. Many factors influence throughput, including the following:

- The amount of traffic
- The type of traffic
- The latency created by the number of network devices encountered between source and destination

There are many online speed tests that can reveal the throughput of an Internet connection.

Goodput

Goodput is the measure of usable data transferred over a given period of time. Goodput is throughput minus traffic overhead for establishing sessions, sending acknowledgments, performing encapsulation, and retransmitting bits. Goodput is always lower than throughput, which is generally lower than the bandwidth.

Interactive Graphic

Check Your Understanding—Physical Layer Characteristics (30.2.8)

Refer to the online course to complete this activity.

Copper Cabling (30.3)

Copper cabling is one of the oldest and most commonly used cabling for communications. Copper cabling actually comes in three different types, each of which is used in specific situations. This section describes the characteristics and use of copper cabling in data networks.

Characteristics of Copper Cabling (30.3.1)

Copper cabling is the most common type of cabling used in networks today. Networks use copper cabling because it is inexpensive, easy to install, and has low

resistance to electrical current. However, copper cabling is limited by distance and signal interference.

Data is transmitted on copper cables as electrical pulses. A detector in the network interface of a destination device must receive a signal that can be successfully decoded to match the signal sent. However, the farther the signal travels, the more it deteriorates. This is referred to as *signal attenuation*. For this reason, all copper cabling must follow strict distance limitations, as specified by the guiding standards.

The timing and voltage values of the electrical pulses are also susceptible to interference from two sources:

- *Electromagnetic interference (EMI)* **or radio frequency interference (RFI)**—EMI and RFI signals can distort and corrupt the data signals being carried by copper cabling. Potential sources of EMI and RFI include radio waves and electromagnetic devices, such as fluorescent lights or electric motors.
- *Crosstalk*—Crosstalk is a disturbance caused by the electric or magnetic fields of a signal on one wire to the signal in an adjacent wire. In telephone circuits, crosstalk can result in hearing part of another voice conversation from an adjacent circuit. Specifically, when an electrical current flows through a wire, it creates a small, circular magnetic field around the wire, which can be picked up by an adjacent wire.

Figure 30-10 shows how data transmission can be affected by interference:

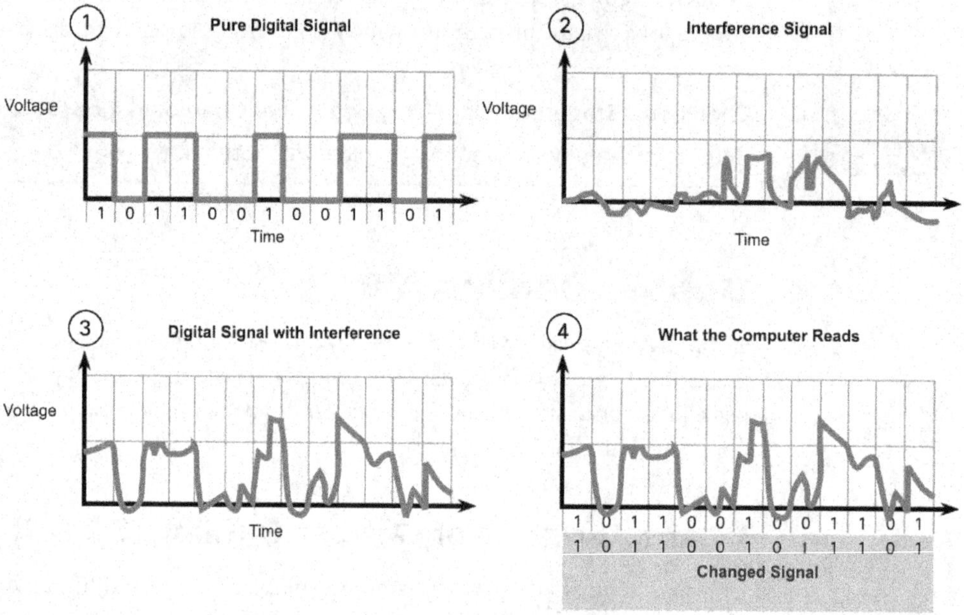

Figure 30-10 Effect of Interference on Data Transmission

1. A pure digital signal is transmitted.
2. On the medium, there is an interference signal.
3. The digital signal is corrupted by the interference signal.
4. The receiving computer reads a changed signal. Notice that a 0 bit is now interpreted as a 1 bit.

To counter the negative effects of EMI and RFI, some types of copper cables are wrapped in metallic shielding and require proper grounding connections.

To counter the negative effects of crosstalk, some types of copper cables have opposing circuit wire pairs twisted together, which effectively cancels the crosstalk.

The susceptibility of copper cables to electronic noise can also be limited by using these recommendations:

- Select the cable type or category most suited to a given networking environment.
- Design a cable infrastructure to avoid known and potential sources of interference in the building structure.
- Use cabling techniques that include the proper handling and termination of the cables.

Types of Copper Cabling (30.3.2)

The three main types of copper cabling used in networking are shown in Figure 30-11 and described next in turn.

Unshielded Twisted-Pair (UTP) (30.3.3)

Unshielded twisted-pair (UTP) cabling is the most common networking medium. UTP cabling, terminated with RJ-45 connectors, is used for interconnecting network hosts with intermediary networking devices, such as switches and routers.

In LANs, UTP cable consists of four pairs of color-coded wires that have been twisted together and then encased in a flexible plastic sheath that protects from minor physical damage, as shown in Figure 30-12. The twisting of wires helps protect against signal interference from other wires.

The color codes identify the individual pairs and wires and aid in cable termination.

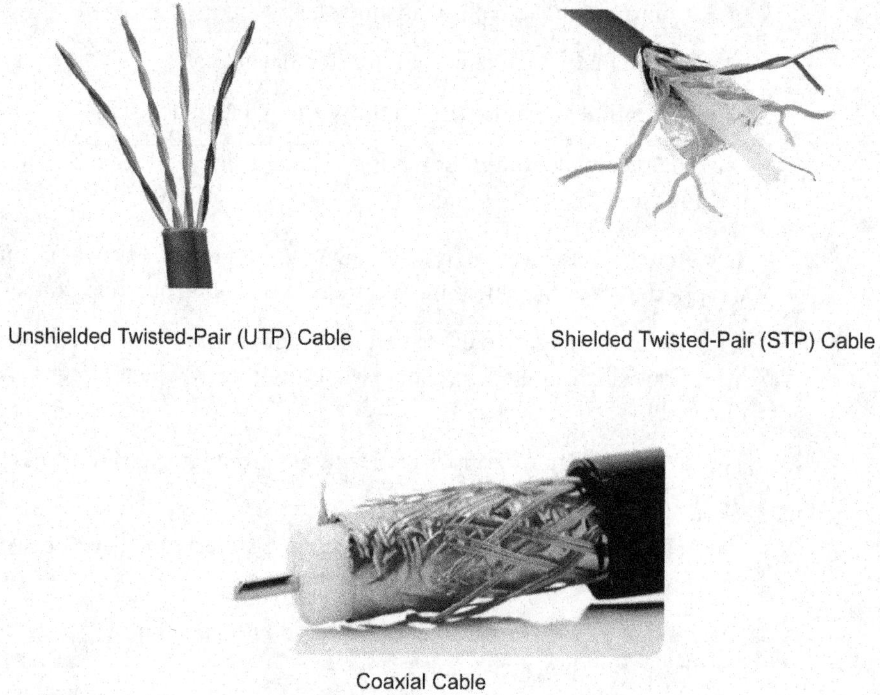

Figure 30-11 Types of Copper Cabling

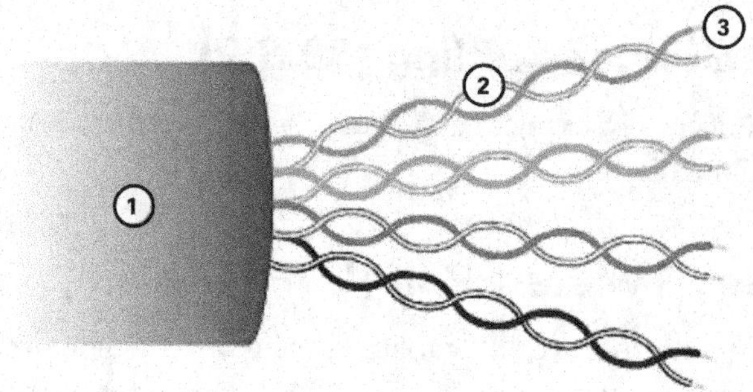

Figure 30-12 UTP Cable

The numbers in Figure 30-12 identify some key features of UTP cable:

1. The outer jacket protects the copper wires from physical damage.
2. Twisted pairs protect the signal from interference.
3. Color-coded plastic insulation electrically isolates wires from each other and identifies each pair.

Shielded Twisted-Pair (STP) (30.3.4)

Shielded twisted-pair (STP) cabling provides better noise protection than UTP cabling. However, compared to UTP cable, STP cable is significantly more expensive and difficult to install. Like UTP cable, STP cable uses an RJ-45 connector.

STP cables combine the techniques of shielding to counter EMI and RFI and wire twisting to counter crosstalk. To gain the full benefit of the shielding, STP cables are terminated with special shielded STP data connectors. If the cable is improperly grounded, the shield may act as an antenna and pick up unwanted signals.

The STP cable shown in Figure 30-13 uses four pairs of wires, each wrapped in a foil shield, which are then wrapped in an overall metallic braid or foil.

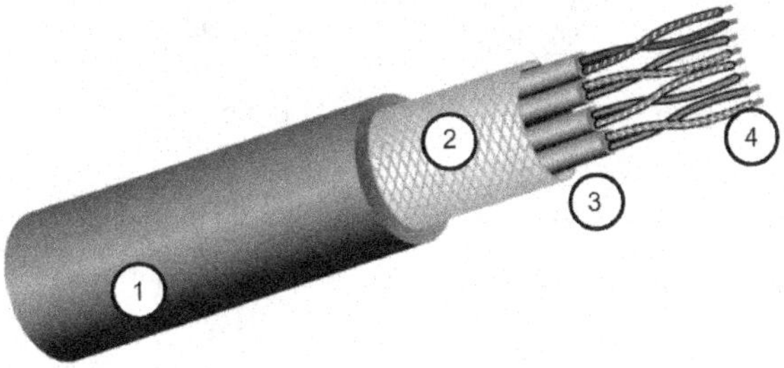

Figure 30-13 STP Cable

The numbers in Figure 30-13 identify some key features of STP cable:

1. Outer jacket
2. Braided or foil shield
3. Foil shields
4. Twisted pairs

Coaxial Cable (30.3.5)

Coaxial cable, or *coax* for short, gets its name from the fact that there are two conductors that share the same axis. As shown in the upper portion of Figure 30-14, coaxial cable consists of the following key features:

1. The entire cable is covered with a cable jacket to prevent minor physical damage.
2. The insulating material is surrounded in a woven copper braid, or metallic foil, that acts as the second wire in the circuit and as a shield for the inner conductor. This second layer, or shield, also reduces the amount of outside EMI.
3. A layer of flexible plastic insulation surrounds a copper conductor.
4. A copper conductor is used to transmit the electronic signals.

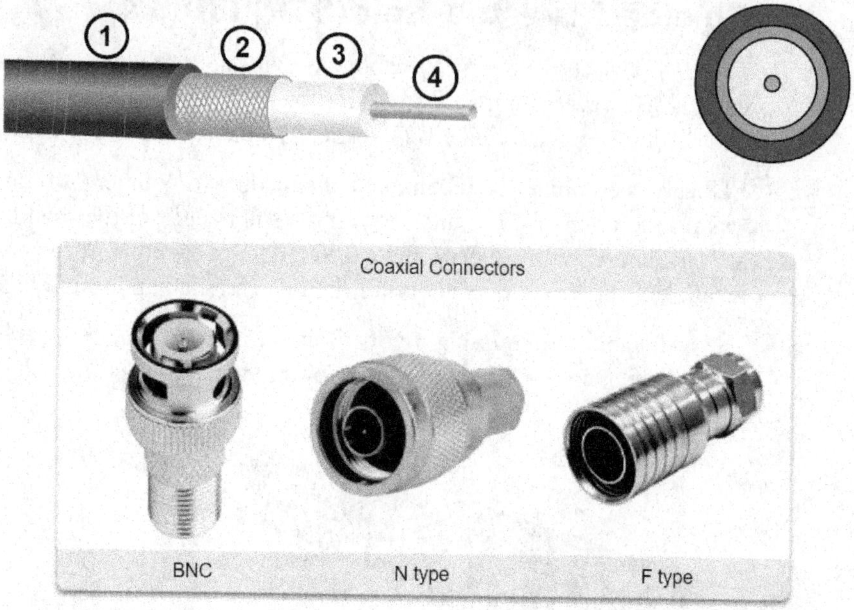

Figure 30-14 Coaxial Cable and Connectors

Different types of connectors are used with coax cable. The Bayonet Neill–Concelman (BNC), N type, and F type connectors are shown in Figure 30-14.

The numbers in Figure 30-14 identify some key features of coaxial cable:

1. Outer jacket
2. Braided copper shielding
3. Plastic insulation
4. Copper conductor

Although UTP cable has essentially replaced coaxial cable in modern Ethernet installations, the coaxial cable design is used in the following situations:

- **Wireless installations**—Coaxial cables attach antennas to wireless devices. The coaxial cable carries radio frequency (RF) energy between the antennas and the radio equipment.
- **Cable Internet installations**—Cable service providers provide Internet connectivity to their customers by replacing portions of the coaxial cable and supporting amplification elements with *fiber-optic cable*. However, the wiring inside the customer's premises is still coax cable.

Interactive Graphic

Check Your Understanding—Copper Cabling (30.3.6)

Refer to the online course to complete this activity.

UTP Cabling (30.4)

In the previous section, you learned a bit about unshielded twisted-pair (UTP) copper cabling. Because UTP cabling is the standard for use in LANs, this section goes into detail about its advantages and limitations, and what can be done to avoid problems.

Properties of UTP Cabling (30.4.1)

Copper cabling has some inherent issues. Twisting the internal pairs of the copper cabling, as used in UTP, is a low-cost solution to improve some of the cabling performance.

When used as a networking medium, UTP cabling consists of four pairs of color-coded copper wires that have been twisted together and then encased in a flexible plastic sheath (as previously shown in Figure 30-12). Its small size can be advantageous during installation.

UTP cable does not use shielding to counter the effects of EMI and RFI. Instead, cable designers have discovered other ways to limit the negative effect of crosstalk:

- **Cancellation**—Designers now pair wires in a circuit. When two wires in an electrical circuit are placed close together, their magnetic fields are the exact opposite of each other. Therefore, the two magnetic fields cancel each other and also cancel out any outside EMI and RFI signals.
- **Varying the number of twists per wire pair**—To further enhance the cancellation effect of paired circuit wires, designers vary the number of twists of each wire pair in a cable. UTP cable must follow precise specifications governing how many twists or braids are permitted per meter (3.28 feet) of cable. Notice in Figure 30-15 that the orange/orange white pair at the bottom is twisted less than the blue/blue white pair. Each colored pair is twisted a different number of times.

UTP cable relies solely on the cancellation effect produced by the twisted wire pairs to limit signal degradation and effectively provide self-shielding for wire pairs within the network cabling.

Figure 30-15 Different Number of Twists in Each UTP Pair

UTP Cabling Standards and Connectors (30.4.2)

UTP cabling conforms to the standards established jointly by the TIA/EIA. Specifically, TIA/EIA-568 stipulates the commercial cabling standards for LAN installations and is the standard most commonly used in LAN cabling environments. Some of the elements defined in TIA/EIA-568 are as follows:

- Cable types
- Cable lengths
- Connectors
- Cable termination
- Methods of testing cable

The electrical characteristics of copper cabling are defined by the Institute of Electrical and Electronics Engineers (IEEE). IEEE rates UTP cabling according to its performance. Cables are placed into categories based on their ability to carry higher bandwidth rates. For example, Category 5 cable is used commonly in 100BASE-TX Fast Ethernet installations. Other categories include Enhanced Category 5 cable, Category 6, and Category 6a.

Cables in higher categories are designed and constructed to support higher data rates. As new gigabit speed Ethernet technologies are being developed and adopted, Category 5e is now the minimally acceptable cable type, with Category 6 being the recommended type for new building installations.

Figure 30-16 shows three of the following categories of UTP cable:

- Category 3 was originally used for voice communication over voice lines but later was also used for data transmission.
- Category 5 and 5e are used for data transmission. Category 5 supports 100 Mbps, and Category 5e supports 1000 Mbps.

- Category 6 has an added separator between each wire pair to support higher speeds. Category 6 supports up to 10 Gbps.
- Category 7 also supports 10 Gbps.
- Category 8 supports 40 Gbps.

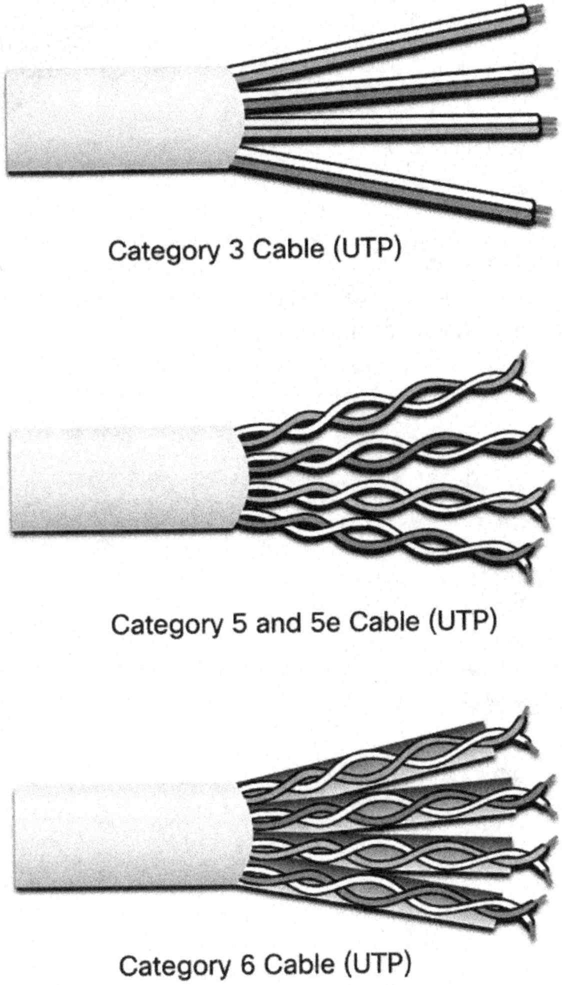

Figure 30-16 Categories of UTP

Some manufacturers are making cables exceeding the TIA/EIA Category 6a specifications and refer to these as Category 7.

UTP cable is usually terminated with an RJ-45 connector. The TIA/EIA-568 standard describes the wire color codes to pin assignments (pinouts) for Ethernet cables.

As shown in Figure 30-17, the RJ-45 connector is crimped at the end of the cable.

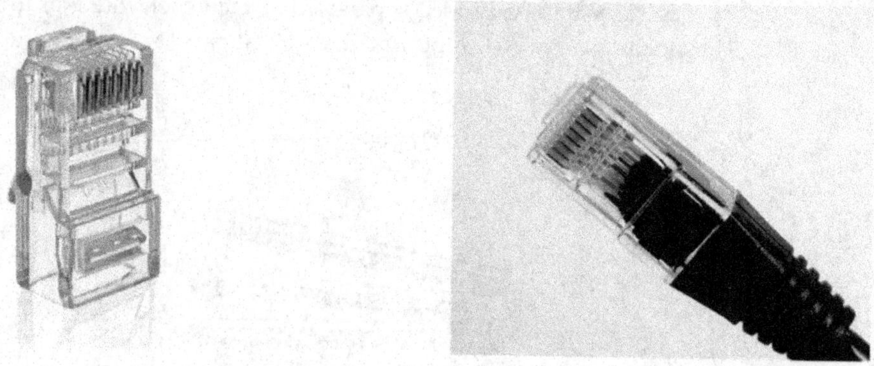

Figure 30-17 RJ-45 UTP Plugs

The socket, shown in Figure 30-18, is the network device, wall, cubicle partition outlet, or patch panel. When terminated improperly, each cable is a potential source of physical layer performance degradation.

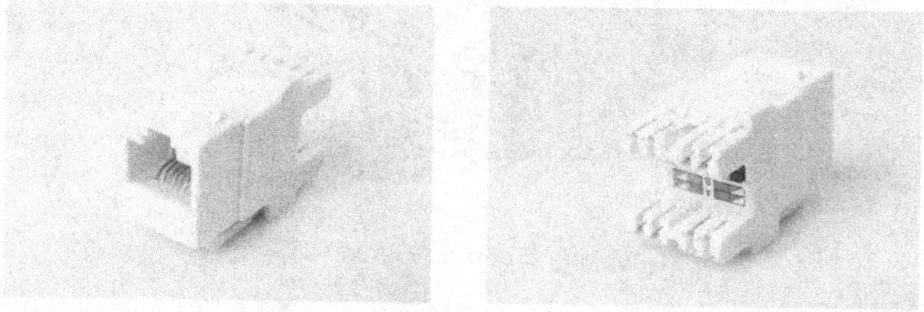

Figure 30-18 RJ-45 UTP Sockets

Figure 30-19 shows an example of a badly terminated UTP cable. This bad connector has wires that are exposed, untwisted, and not entirely covered by the sheath.

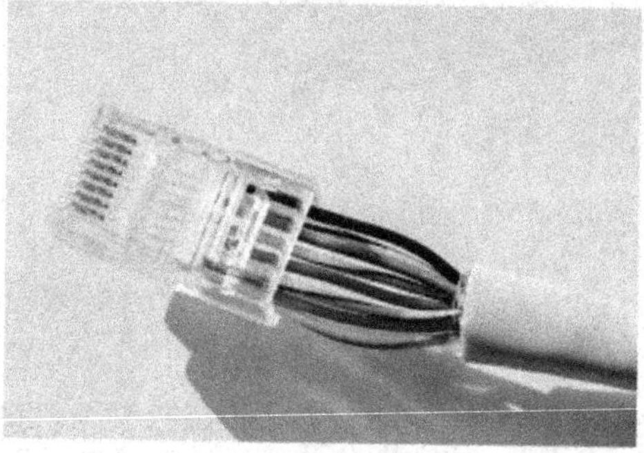

Figure 30-19 Poorly Terminated UTP Cable

Figure 30-20 shows a properly terminated UTP cable. It is a good connector with wires that are untwisted only to the extent necessary to attach the connector.

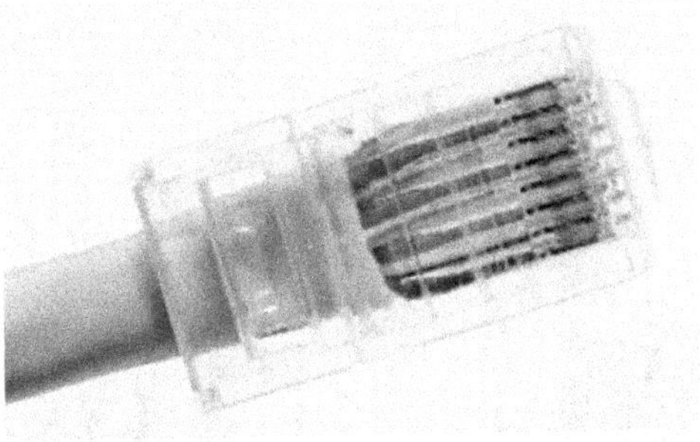

Figure 30-20 Properly Terminated UTP Cable

Note

Improper cable termination can impact transmission performance.

Straight-Through and Crossover UTP Cables (30.4.3)

Different situations may require UTP cables to be wired according to different wiring conventions. This means that the individual wires in the cable have to be connected in different orders to different sets of pins in the RJ-45 connectors.

The following are the main cable types that are obtained by using specific wiring conventions:

- **Ethernet straight-through**—This is the most common type of networking cable, commonly used to interconnect a host to a switch and a switch to a router.
- **Ethernet crossover**—This type of cable is used to interconnect similar devices; for example, to connect a switch to a switch, a host to a host, or a router to a router. However, crossover cables are now considered legacy because NICs use medium-dependent interface crossover (auto-MDIX) to automatically detect the cable type and make the internal connection.

Note

Another type of cable is the Cisco-proprietary rollover cable, which is used to connect a workstation to a router or switch console port.

Using a crossover or straight-through cable incorrectly between devices may not damage the devices, but connectivity and communication between the devices will

not take place. This is a common error, and checking that the device connections are correct should be the first troubleshooting action if connectivity is not achieved.

Figure 30-21 identifies the individual wire pairs for the T568A and T568B standards.

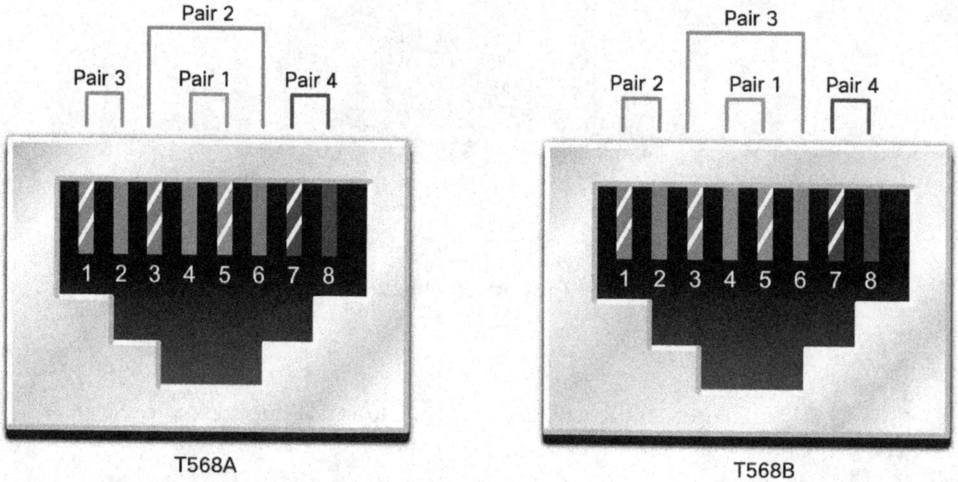

Figure 30-21 T568A and T568B Standards

Table 30-2 shows the UTP cable type, related standards, and typical application of these cables.

Table 30-2 Cable Types and Standards

Cable Type	Standard	Application
Ethernet straight-through	Both ends T568A or both ends T568B	Connects a network host to a network device such as a switch or hub
Ethernet crossover	One end T568A, other end T568B	Connects two network hosts Connects two network intermediary devices (switch to switch or router to router)
Rollover	Cisco proprietary	Connects a workstation serial port to a router console port, using an adapter

Interactive Graphic

Activity—Cable Pinouts (30.4.4)

For this activity, correctly order the wire colors to a TIA/EIA cable pinout. Select a wire case color by clicking it. Then click a wire to apply that casing to it.

Refer to the online course to complete this activity.

Fiber-Optic Cabling (30.5)

Networking media selection is being driven by the growing needs for network bandwidth. The distance and performance of fiber-optic cable make it a good media choice to support these network needs. This section examines the characteristics of fiber-optic cabling use in data networks.

Properties of Fiber-Optic Cabling (30.5.1)

As you have learned, fiber-optic cabling is the other type of cabling used in networks. Because it is expensive, it is not as commonly used as the various types of copper cabling. But fiber-optic cabling has certain properties that make it the best option in certain situations, as described in this section.

Optical fiber cable transmits data over longer distances and at higher bandwidths than any other networking media. Fiber-optic cable can transmit signals with less attenuation than copper wire and is completely immune to EMI and RFI. Optical fiber is commonly used to interconnect network devices.

Optical fiber contains a flexible, extremely thin, transparent strand of very pure glass, not much bigger than a human hair. Bits are encoded on the fiber as light impulses. The fiber-optic cable acts as a waveguide, or "light pipe," to transmit light between the two ends with minimal loss of signal.

As an analogy, consider an empty paper towel roll with the inside coated like a mirror. Imagine that it is 1,000 meters in length and that a small laser pointer is used to send Morse code signals through it at the speed of light. Essentially, that is how a fiber-optic cable operates, except that it is smaller in diameter and uses sophisticated light technologies.

Types of Fiber Media (30.5.2)

Fiber-optic cables are broadly classified into two types: single-mode fiber and multimode fiber.

Single-Mode Fiber

Single-mode fiber (SMF) consists of a very small core and uses expensive laser technology to send a single ray of light, as shown in Figure 30-22. SMF is popular in long-distance situations spanning hundreds of kilometers, such as those required in long-haul telephony and cable TV applications.

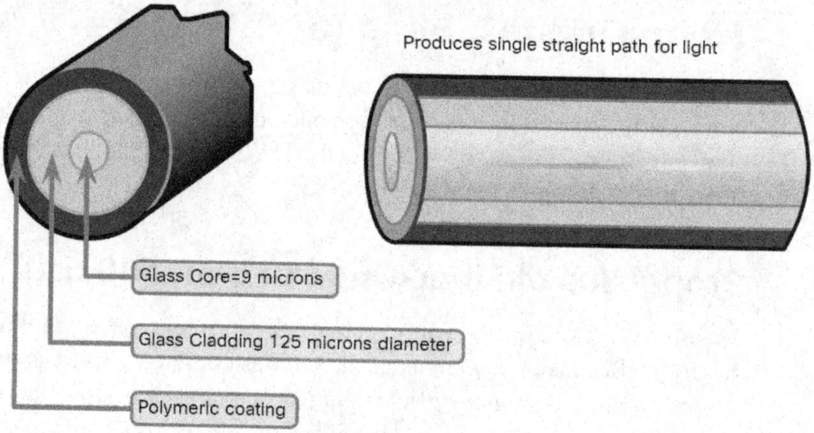

Figure 30-22 Single-Mode Fiber

Multimode Fiber

Multimode fiber (MMF) consists of a larger core and uses LED emitters to send light pulses. Specifically, light from an LED enters the MMF at different angles, as shown in Figure 30-23. Its use is popular in LANs because they can be powered by low-cost LEDs. It provides bandwidth up to 10 Gbps over link lengths of up to 550 meters.

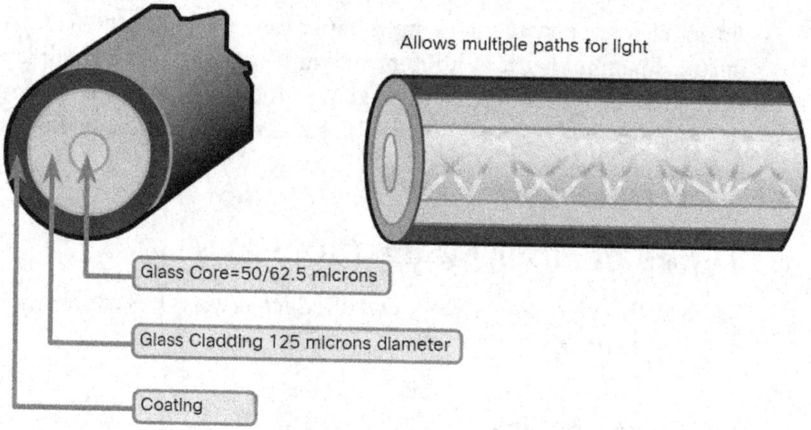

Figure 30-23 Multimode Fiber

One of the highlighted differences between MMF and SMF is the amount of dispersion. Dispersion refers to the spreading out of a light pulse over time. Increased dispersion means increased loss of signal strength. MMF has a greater dispersion than SMF. That is why MMF can only travel up to 500 meters before signal loss.

Fiber-Optic Cabling Usage (30.5.3)

Fiber-optic cabling is now being used in four types of industry:

- **Enterprise networks**—Fiber is used for backbone cabling applications and interconnecting infrastructure devices.
- **Fiber-to-the-home (FTTH)**—Fiber is used to provide always-on broadband services to homes and small businesses.
- **Long-haul networks**—Fiber is used by service providers to connect countries and cities.
- **Submarine cable networks**—Fiber is used to provide reliable high-speed, high-capacity solutions capable of surviving in harsh undersea environments at up to transoceanic distances. Search the Internet for "submarine cables telegeography map" to view various maps online.

Our focus in this book is the use of fiber within the enterprise.

Fiber-Optic Connectors (30.5.4)

An optical-fiber connector terminates the end of an optical fiber. A variety of optical-fiber connectors are available. The main differences among the types of connectors are their dimensions and their methods of coupling. Businesses decide on the types of connectors that will be used, based on their equipment.

Note

Some switches and routers have ports that support fiber-optic connectors through a small form-factor pluggable (SFP) transceiver. Search the Internet for various types of SFP transceivers.

The straight-tip (ST) connector (see Figure 30-24) was one of the first connector types used. The connector locks securely with a "twist-on/twist-off" bayonet-style mechanism.

Figure 30-24 Straight-Tip (ST) Connectors

The subscriber connector (SC) connector (see Figure 30-25), sometimes referred to as square connector or standard connector, is a widely adopted LAN and WAN connector type that uses a push-pull mechanism to ensure positive insertion. This connector type is used with multimode and single-mode fiber.

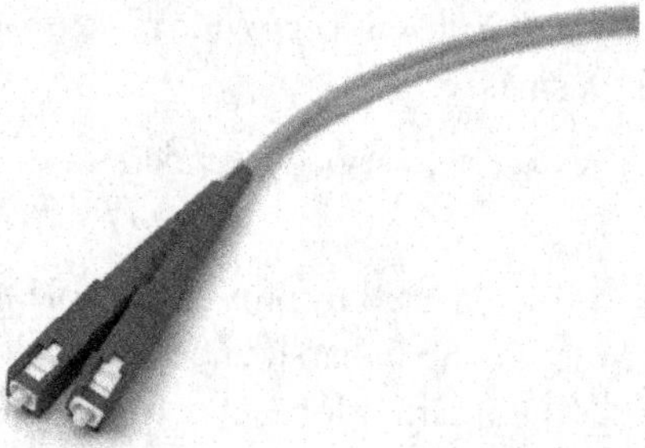

Figure 30-25 Subscriber Connector (SC) Connectors

The Lucent Connector (LC) simplex connector (see Figure 30-26) is a smaller version of the SC connector. LC connectors are sometimes called little connectors or local connectors, and they are quickly growing in popularity due to their smaller size.

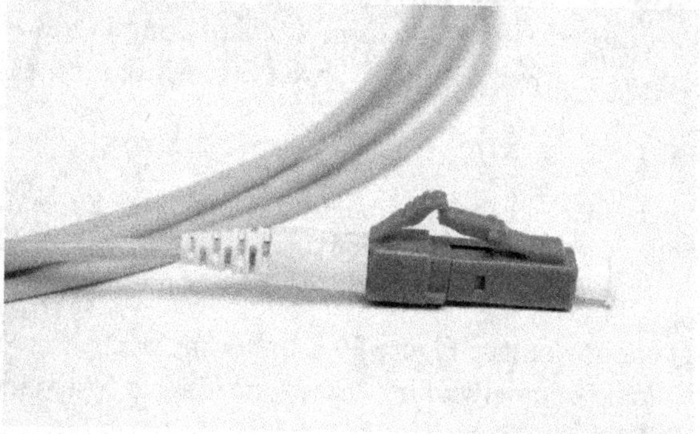

Figure 30-26 Lucent Connector (LC) Simplex Connector

A duplex multimode LC connector (see Figure 30-27) is similar to an LC simplex connector but uses a duplex connector.

Until recently, light could travel in only one direction over optical fiber. Many standards require two fibers to support full-duplex operation. Therefore, fiber-optic patch cables bundle together two optical fiber cables and terminate them with a pair of standard, single-fiber connectors. Some fiber connectors accept both the transmitting and receiving fibers in a single connector known as a duplex connector, as shown in Figure 30-27. Now, BX standards such as 100BASE-BX use different wavelengths for sending and receiving over a single fiber.

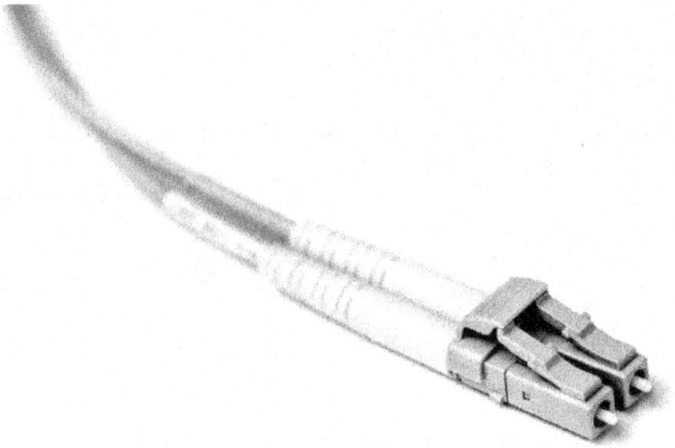

Figure 30-27 Duplex Multimode LC Connectors

Fiber Patch Cords (30.5.5)

Fiber patch cords are required for interconnecting infrastructure devices. The use of different jacket colors distinguishes between single-mode (yellow) and multimode (orange or aqua) patch cords.

Figures 30-28 through 30-31 show four types of fiber patch cords.

Figure 30-28 SC-SC Multimode Patch Cord

Figure 30-29 LC-LC Single-Mode Patch Cord

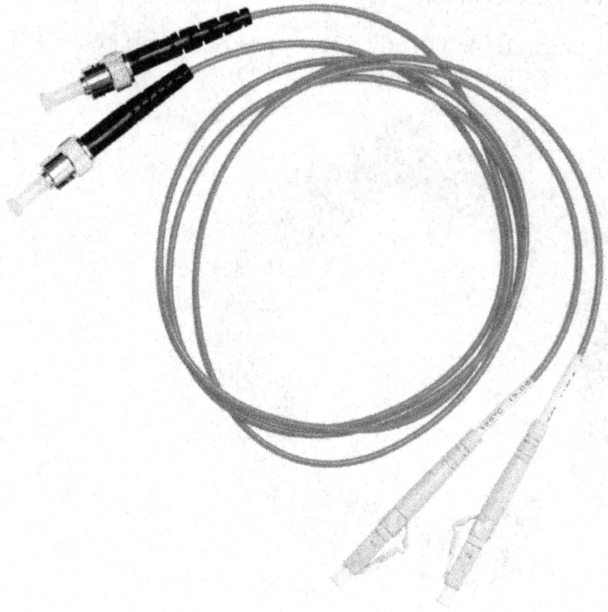

Figure 30-30 ST-LC Multimode Patch Cord

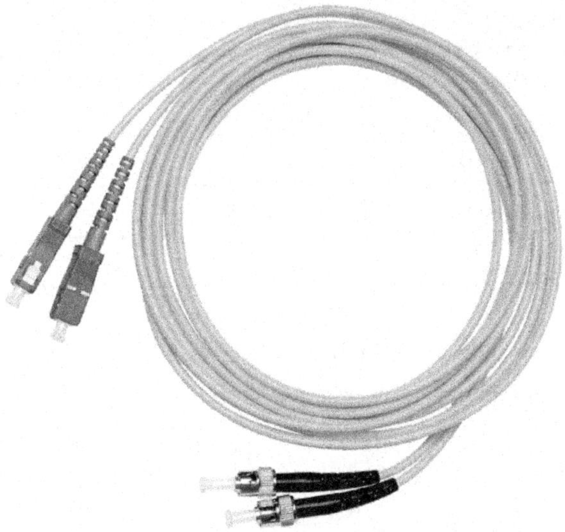

Figure 30-31 SC-ST Single-Mode Patch Cord

Note

Fiber cables should be protected with a small plastic cap when not in use.

Fiber Versus Copper (30.5.6)

There are many advantages to using fiber-optic cable compared to copper cables. Table 30-3 highlights some of the differences between these cable types.

At present, in most enterprise environments, optical fiber is primarily used as backbone cabling for high-traffic, point-to-point connections between data distribution facilities. It is also used to interconnect buildings in multi-building campuses. Because fiber-optic cables do not conduct electricity and have a low signal loss, they are well suited for these uses.

Table 30-3 UTP and Fiber-Optic Cabling Comparison

Implementation Issue	UTP Cabling	Fiber-Optic Cabling
Bandwidth supported	10 Mbps–10 Gbps	10 Mbps–100 Gbps
Distance	Relatively short (1–100 meters)	Relatively long (1–100,000 meters)
Immunity to EMI and RFI	Low	High (completely immune)

Implementation Issue	UTP Cabling	Fiber-Optic Cabling
Immunity to electrical hazards	Low	High (completely immune)
Media and connector costs	Lowest	Highest
Installation skills required	Lowest	Highest
Safety precautions	Lowest	Highest

Interactive Graphic

Check Your Understanding—Fiber-Optic Cabling (30.5.7)

Refer to the online course to complete this activity.

Summary (30.6)

The following is a summary of each topic in the chapter and some questions for your reflection.

What Did I Learn in This Chapter? (30.6.1)

- **Purpose of the Physical Layer**—Before any network communications can occur, a physical connection to a local network must be established. A physical connection can be a wired connection using a cable or a wireless connection using radio waves. Network interface cards (NICs) connect devices to the network. Ethernet NICs are used for wired connections, whereas WLAN (wireless LAN) NICs are used for wireless connections. The OSI physical layer provides the means to transport the bits that make up a data link layer frame across the network media. The physical layer accepts a complete frame from the data link layer and encodes it as a series of signals that is transmitted onto the local media. The encoded bits that comprise a frame are received by either an end device or an intermediary device.
- **Physical Layer Characteristics**—The physical layer consists of electronic circuitry, media, and connectors developed by engineers. The physical layer standards address three functional areas: physical components, encoding, and signaling. Bandwidth is the capacity at which a medium can carry data. Digital bandwidth measures the amount of data that can flow from one place to another in a given amount of time. Throughput is the measure of the transfer of bits across the media over a given period of time and is usually lower than bandwidth. Latency refers to the amount of time, including delays, for data to travel from one given point to another. Goodput is the measure of usable data

transferred over a given period of time. The physical layer produces the representation and groupings of bits for each type of media as follows:

  - **Copper cable**—The signals are patterns of electrical pulses.
  - **Fiber-optic cable**—The signals are patterns of light.
  - **Wireless**—The signals are patterns of microwave transmissions.

- **Copper Cabling**—Networks use copper media because it is inexpensive, easy to install, and has low resistance to electrical current. However, copper media is limited by distance and signal interference. The timing and voltage values of the electrical pulses are also susceptible to interference from two sources: EMI and crosstalk. Three types of copper cabling are UTP, STP, and coaxial cable (coax). UTP has an outer jacket to protect the copper wires from physical damage, twisted pairs to protect the signal from interference, and color-coded plastic insulation that electrically isolates wires from each other and identifies each pair. The STP cable uses four pairs of wires, each wrapped in a foil shield, which are then wrapped in an overall metallic braid or foil. Coaxial cable gets its name from the fact that there are two conductors that share the same axis. Coax is used to attach antennas to wireless devices. Cable Internet providers use coax inside their customers' premises.
- **UTP Cabling**—UTP cabling consists of four pairs of color-coded copper wires that have been twisted together and then encased in a flexible plastic sheath. UTP cable does not use shielding to counter the effects of EMI and RFI. Instead, it limits the negative effect of crosstalk by using cancellation and by varying the number of twists per wire pair. UTP cabling conforms to the standards established jointly by the TIA/EIA. The electrical characteristics of copper cabling are defined by the IEEE. UTP cable is usually terminated with an RJ-45 connector. The main cable types that are obtained by using specific wiring conventions are Ethernet straight-through and Ethernet crossover. Cisco has a proprietary UTP cable called a rollover cable that connects a workstation to a router console port.
- **Fiber-Optic Cabling**—Optical fiber cable transmits data over longer distances and at higher bandwidths than any other networking media. Fiber-optic cable can transmit signals with less attenuation than copper wire and is completely immune to EMI and RFI. Optical fiber contains a flexible, extremely thin, transparent strand of very pure glass, not much bigger than a human hair. Bits are encoded on the fiber as light impulses. Fiber-optic cabling is now being used in four types of industry: enterprise networks, fiber-to-the-home (FTTH), long-haul networks, and submarine cable networks. There are four types of fiber-optic connectors: ST, SC, LC simplex, and duplex multimode LC. Fiber-optic patch cords include SC-SC multimode, LC-LC single-mode, ST-LC multimode, and SC-ST single-mode. In most enterprise environments, optical fiber is primarily used as backbone cabling for high-traffic point-to-point connections between data distribution facilities and to interconnect buildings in multi-building campuses.

Reflection Questions (30.6.2)

Halimah already knew about the physical layer in the network. Did you?

In this chapter, you learned that a physical connection can be a wired connection using a cable or a wireless connection using radio waves. You also learned about media types.

Consider these reflection questions:

- Have you ever thought about the difference between copper cable, fiber-optic cable, and wireless?
- Which media types are used in your home?
- What are the advantages and disadvantages of those media types you have in your home?
- Where might you find fiber-optic cables being used?
- What advantages do fiber-optic cables offer?

Practice

There are no labs or Packet Tracer activities in this chapter.

Check Your Understanding Questions

Complete all the review questions listed here to test your understanding of the topics and concepts in this chapter. Appendix A, "Answers to 'Check Your Understanding' Questions," lists the answers.

1. What is the purpose of the OSI physical layer?
   a. To control access to media
   b. To transmit bits across the local media
   c. To perform error detection on received frames
   d. To exchange frames between nodes over physical network media

2. Why are two strands of fiber used for a single fiber-optic connection?
   a. They allow the data to travel for longer distances without degrading.
   b. They prevent crosstalk from causing interference on the connection.
   c. They increase the speed at which the data can travel.
   d. They allow for full-duplex connectivity.

3. Which statement describes crosstalk?
   a. The distortion of a network signal due to fluorescent lighting
   b. The distortion of a transmitted message due to signals carried in adjacent wires
   c. The weakening of a network signal over long cable lengths
   d. The loss of wireless signal over excessive distance from an access point

4. Which procedure is used to reduce the effect of crosstalk in copper cables?
   a. Requiring proper grounding connections
   b. Twisting opposing-circuit wire pairs together
   c. Wrapping a bundle of wires with metallic shielding
   d. Designing a cable infrastructure to avoid crosstalk interference
   e. Avoiding sharp bends during installation

5. Which type of UTP cable is used to connect a PC to a switch port?
   a. Console
   b. Rollover
   c. Crossover
   d. Straight-through

6. What is the definition of bandwidth?
   a. The speed of bits across the media over a given period of time
   b. The speed at which bits travel on the network
   c. The amount of data that can flow from one place to another in a given amount of time
   d. The measure of usable data transferred over a given period of time

7. Which statement correctly describes frame encoding?
   a. It uses the characteristic of one wave to modify another wave.
   b. It transmits data signals along with a clock signal that occurs at evenly spaced time durations.
   c. It generates the electrical, optical, or wireless signals that represent the binary numbers of the frame.
   d. It converts bits into a predefined code in order to provide a predictable pattern to help distinguish data bits from control bits.

8. What is a characteristic of UTP cabling?
   a. Cancellation
   b. Cladding
   c. Immunity to electrical hazards
   d. Woven copper braid or metallic foil

9. What is indicated by the term *throughput*?
   a. The guaranteed data transfer rate offered by an ISP
   b. The capacity of a particular medium to carry data
   c. The measure of the usable data transferred across the media over a given period of time
   d. The measure of transfer of bits across the media over a given period of time

10. What is one advantage of using fiber-optic cabling rather than copper cabling?
    a. It is usually cheaper than copper cabling.
    b. It is able to be installed around sharp bends.

c. It is easier to terminate and install than copper cabling.

d. It is able to carry signals much farther than copper cabling.

11. A network administrator is troubleshooting connectivity issues on a server. Using a tester, the administrator notices that the signals generated by the server NIC are distorted and not usable. In which layer of the OSI model is the error categorized?

   a. Presentation layer
   b. Network layer
   c. Physical layer
   d. Data link layer

12. What type of cable is used to connect a workstation serial port to a Cisco router console port?

   a. Crossover
   b. Rollover
   c. Straight-through
   d. Coaxial

CHAPTER 31

Data Link Layer

Objectives

Upon completion of this chapter, you will be able to answer the following questions:

- What are the characteristics of physical and logical topologies?
- How do devices access a LAN in order to send frames?

Key Terms

This chapter uses the following key terms. You can find the definitions in the Glossary.

bus topology Page 560

Carrier Sense Multiple Access with Collision Avoidance (CSMA/CA) Page 563

Carrier Sense Multiple Access with Collision Detection (CSMA/CD) Page 563

extended star topology Page 560

full-duplex Page 562

half-duplex Page 562

logical topology Page 556

physical topology Page 556

ring topology Page 561

star topology Page 560

Introduction (31.0)

How will Halimah familiarize herself with the network at headquarters?

She will examine some topologies that have been created by the IT department. These will help her understand how the various end and intermediary devices are connected and what media is used to connect them. Logical topologies will help her understand the type of network framing and media access control that are being used. Physical topologies serve as a sort of map that tells Halimah what devices are found in which rooms of each of the buildings on campus.

Learning how to read topologies is a very important part of becoming an IT professional.

Let's get going!

Topologies (31.1)

Nodes on a network can be interconnected in numerous ways. How these nodes are physically connected is described by the topology of the network. This section provides an overview of network topologies.

Physical and Logical Topologies (31.1.1)

As you learned in the previous chapter, the data link layer prepares network data for the physical network. It must know the logical topology of a network in order to be able to determine what is needed to transfer frames from one device to another. This section explains the ways in which the data link layer works with different logical network topologies.

The topology of a network is the arrangement, or the relationship, of the network devices and the interconnections between them.

There are two types of topologies used when describing LAN and WAN networks:

- *Physical topology*—Identifies the physical connections and how end devices and intermediary devices (i.e., routers, switches, and wireless access points) are interconnected. The topology may also include specific device location such as room number and location on the equipment rack. Physical topologies are usually point-to-point or star.
- *Logical topology*—Refers to the way a network transfers frames from one node to the next. This topology identifies virtual connections using device interfaces and Layer 3 IP addressing schemes.

The data link layer "sees" the logical topology of a network when controlling data access to the media. It is the logical topology that influences the type of network framing and media access control used.

Figure 31-1 displays a sample physical topology for a small sample network.

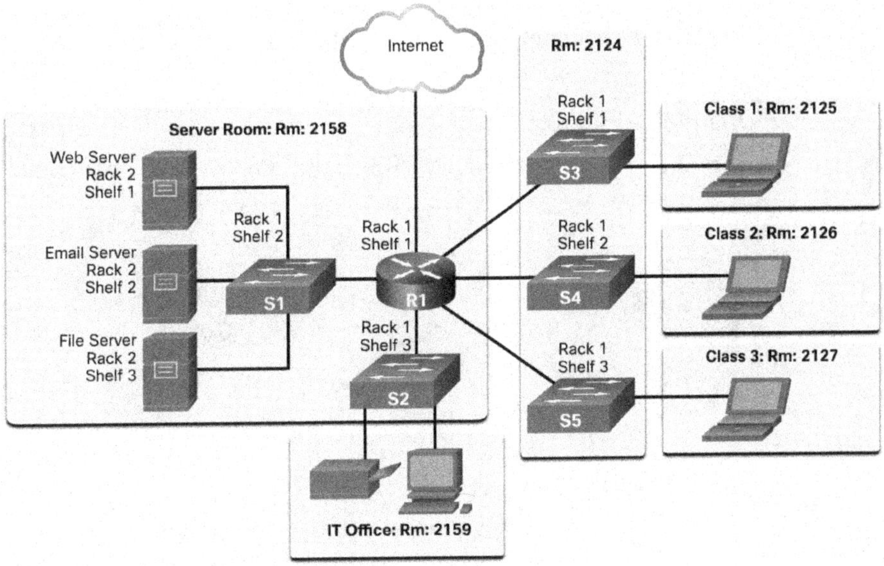

Figure 31-1 Example of a Physical Topology

Figure 31-2 displays a sample logical topology for the same network.

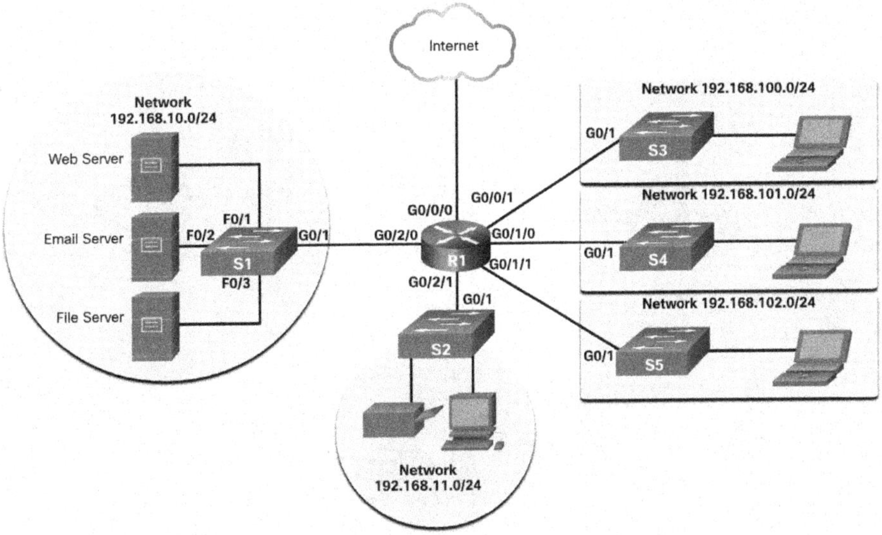

Figure 31-2 Example of a Logical Topology

Video

Video—The Logical Topology (31.1.2)

Refer to the online course to view this video.

WAN Topologies (31.1.2)

WANs are commonly interconnected using three common physical WAN topologies.

Point-to-Point

A point-to-point link (Figure 31-3) is the simplest and most common WAN topology. It consists of a permanent link between two endpoints.

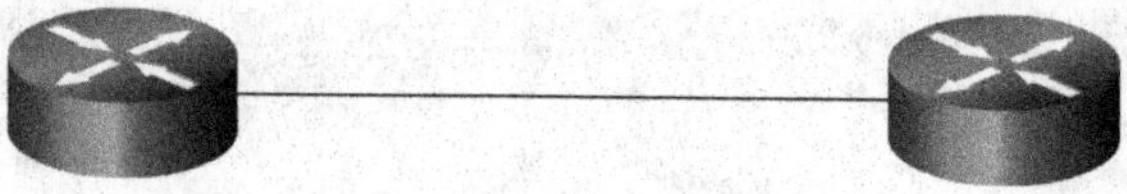

Figure 31-3 Point-to-Point Topology

Hub and Spoke

Figure 31-4 shows a WAN version of the star topology in which a central site interconnects branch sites through the use of point-to-point links. Branch sites cannot exchange data with other branch sites without going through the central site.

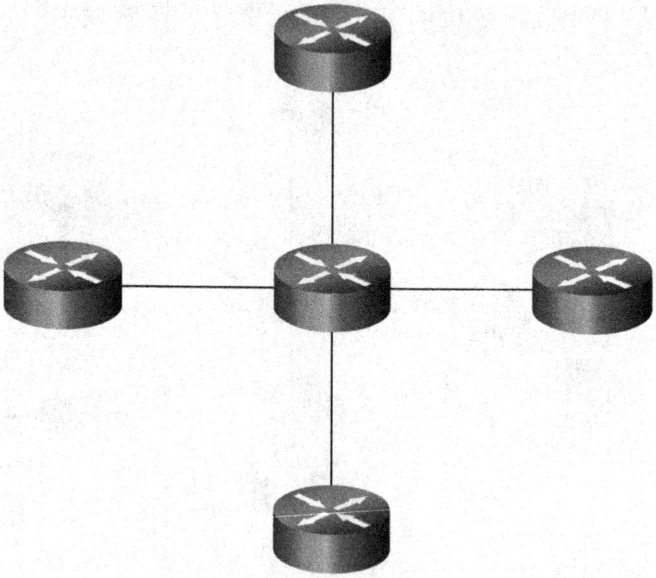

Figure 31-4 Hub and Spoke Topology

Mesh

A mesh topology (Figure 31-5) provides high availability but requires that every end system is interconnected to every other system. Therefore, the administrative and physical costs can be significant. Each link is essentially a point-to-point link to the other node.

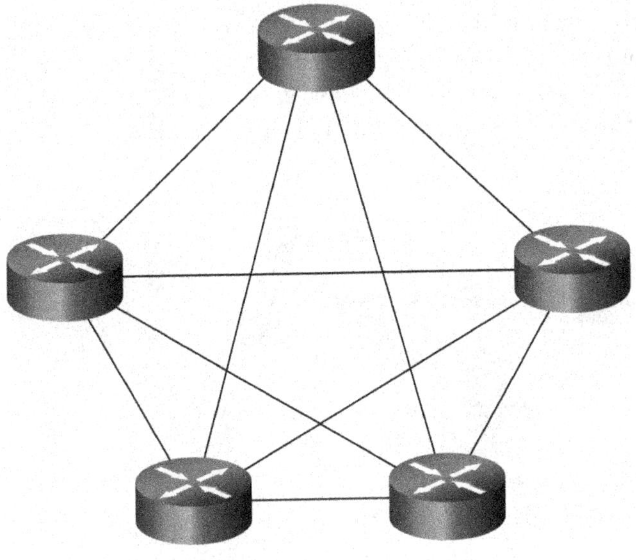

Figure 31-5 Mesh Topology

A hybrid is a variation or combination of any topologies. For example, a partial mesh is a hybrid topology in which some, but not all, end devices are interconnected.

Point-to-Point WAN Topology (31.1.4)

Physical point-to-point topologies directly connect two nodes, as shown in Figure 31-6. In this arrangement, two nodes do not have to share the media with other hosts. Additionally, when using a serial communications protocol such as Point-to-Point Protocol (PPP), a node does not have to make any determination about whether an incoming frame is destined for it or another node. Therefore, the logical data link protocols can be very simple, as all frames on the media can only travel to or from the two nodes. The node places the frames on the media at one end and those frames are taken from the media by the node at the other end of the point-to-point circuit.

Figure 31-6 Point-to-Point WAN Topology

Note

A point-to-point connection over Ethernet requires the device to determine if the incoming frame is destined for this node.

A source node and destination node may be indirectly connected to each other over some geographical distance using multiple intermediary devices. However, the use of physical devices in the network does not affect the logical topology. As shown in Figure 31-7, adding intermediary physical connections may not change the logical topology. The logical point-to-point connection is the same.

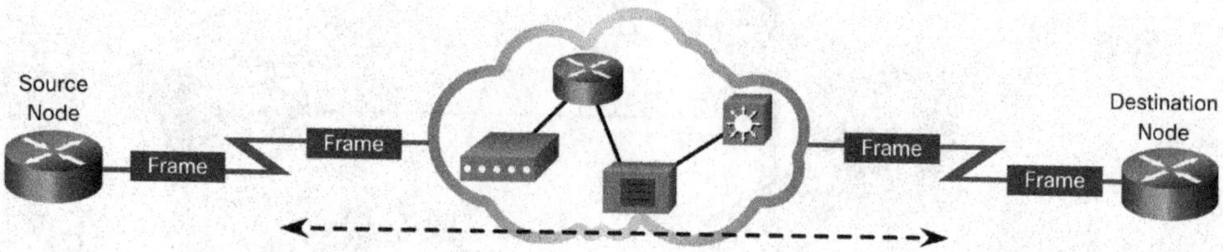

Figure 31-7 Logical and Physical WAN Topology

LAN Topologies (31.1.5)

In multiaccess LANs, end devices (i.e., nodes) are interconnected using *star* or *extended star topologies*, as shown in Figure 31-8. In this type of topology, end devices are connected to a central intermediary device, in this case, an Ethernet switch. An extended star extends this topology by interconnecting multiple Ethernet switches. The star and extended star topologies are easy to install, very scalable (easy to add and remove end devices), and easy to troubleshoot. Early star topologies interconnected end devices using Ethernet hubs.

At times there may be only two devices connected on the Ethernet LAN. An example is two interconnected routers. This would be an example of Ethernet used on a point-to-point topology.

Legacy LAN Topologies

Early Ethernet and legacy Token Ring LAN technologies included two other types of topologies:

- *Bus topology*—All end systems are chained to each other and terminated in some form on each end. Infrastructure devices such as switches are not required to interconnect the end devices. Legacy Ethernet networks were often bus topologies using coax cables because it was inexpensive and easy to set up.

- *Ring topology*—End systems are connected to their respective neighbor forming a ring. The ring does not need to be terminated, unlike in the bus topology. Legacy Fiber Distributed Data Interface (FDDI) and Token Ring networks used ring topologies.

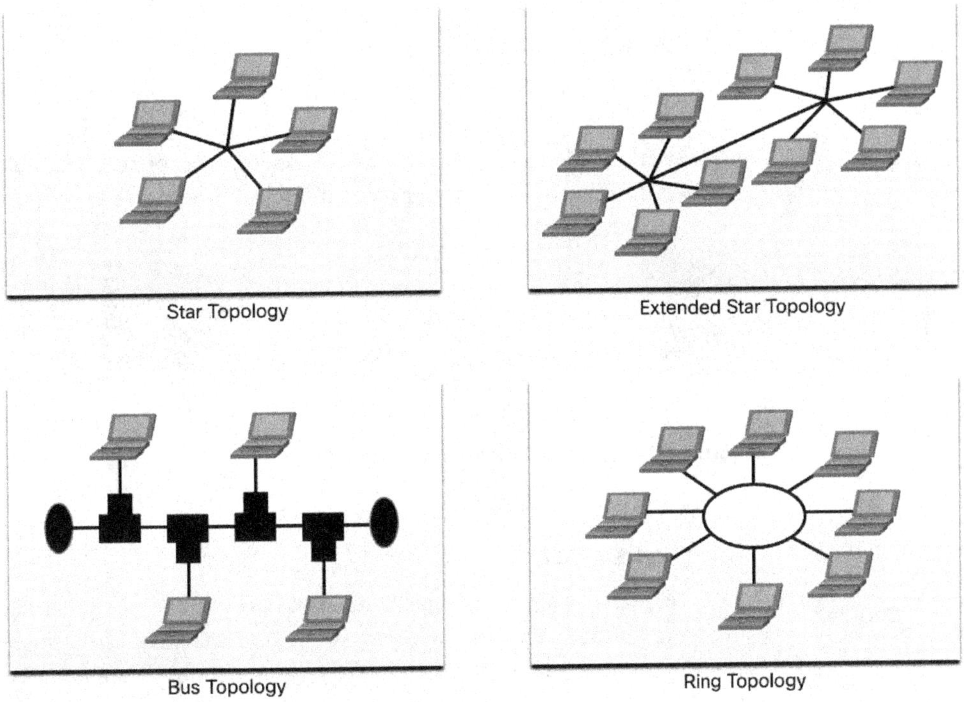

Figure 31-8 LAN Physical Topologies

Figure 31-8 illustrates how end devices are interconnected on LANs. It is common for a straight line in networking graphics to represent an Ethernet LAN including a simple star and an extended star.

Interactive Graphic

Check Your Understanding—Topologies (31.1.6)

Refer to the online course to complete this activity.

Media Access Control Methods (31.2)

How nodes on a network communicate is determined by the topology of the network. This section provides an overview of how data access to the media is regulated.

Half- and Full-Duplex Communication (31.2.1)

Understanding duplex communication is important when discussing LAN topologies because it refers to the direction of data transmission between two devices. There are two common modes of duplex.

Half-Duplex Communication

Both devices can transmit and receive on the media but cannot do so simultaneously. WLANs and legacy bus topologies with Ethernet hubs use the half-duplex mode. *Half-duplex* allows only one device to send or receive at a time on the shared medium. In Figure 31-9, the server and hub are operating in half-duplex.

Figure 31-9 Half-Duplex Communication

Full-Duplex Communication

Both devices can simultaneously transmit and receive on the shared media. The data link layer assumes that the media is available for transmission for both nodes at any time. Ethernet switches operate in *full-duplex* mode by default, but they can operate in half-duplex if connecting to a device such as an Ethernet hub. Figure 31-10 shows an example of full-duplex communication.

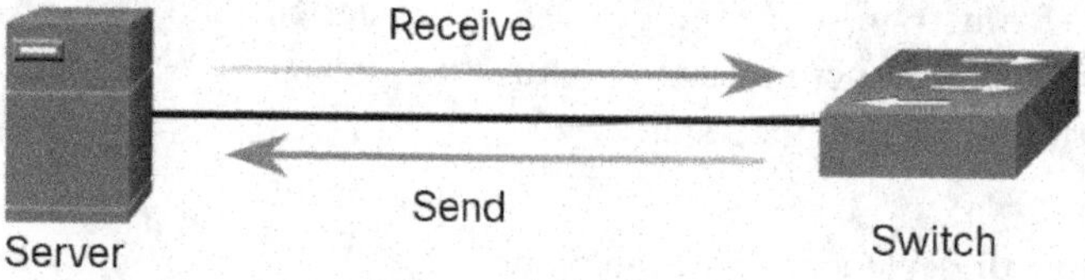

Figure 31-10 Full-Duplex Communication

In summary, half-duplex communications restrict the exchange of data to one direction at a time. Full-duplex allows the sending and receiving of data to happen simultaneously.

It is important that two interconnected interfaces, such as a host NIC and an interface on an Ethernet switch, operate using the same duplex mode. Otherwise, there will be a duplex mismatch creating inefficiency and latency on the link.

Access Control Methods (31.2.2)

Ethernet LANs and WLANs are examples of multiaccess networks. A multiaccess network is a network that can have two or more end devices attempting to access the network simultaneously.

Some multiaccess networks require rules to govern how devices share the physical media. There are two basic access control methods for shared media:

- Contention-based access
- Controlled access

Contention-Based Access

In contention-based multiaccess networks, all nodes are operating in half-duplex, competing for the use of the medium. However, only one device can send at a time. Therefore, there is a process if more than one device transmits at the same time. Examples of contention-based access methods include the following:

- *Carrier Sense Multiple Access with Collision Detection (CSMA/CD)*—Used on legacy bus-topology Ethernet LANs, as shown in Figure 31-11.
- *Carrier Sense Multiple Access with Collision Avoidance (CSMA/CA)*—Used on wireless LANs.

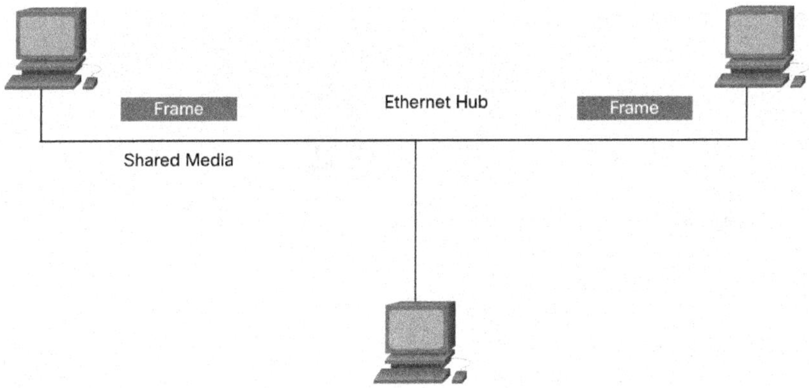

Figure 31-11 Contention-Based Access on Shared Media

Controlled Access

In a controlled-based multiaccess network, each node has its own time to use the medium. These deterministic types of legacy networks are inefficient because a device must wait its turn to access the medium. Examples of multiaccess networks that use controlled access include the following:

- Legacy Token Ring (Figure 31-12)
- Legacy ARCNET

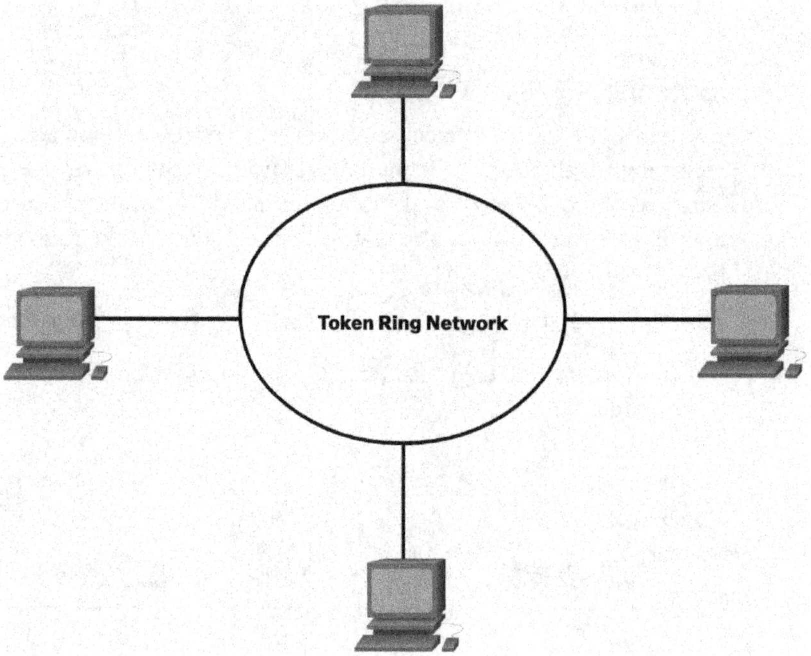

Figure 31-12 Controlled Access on Token Ring

> **Note**
>
> Today, Ethernet networks operate in full-duplex and do not require an access method.

Contention-Based Access—CSMA/CD (31.2.3)

Examples of contention-based access networks include the following:

- Wireless LAN (uses CSMA/CA)
- Legacy bus-topology Ethernet LAN (uses CSMA/CD)
- Legacy Ethernet LAN using a hub (uses CSMA/CD)

These networks operate in half-duplex mode, meaning only one device can send or receive at a time. This requires a process to govern when a device can send and what happens when multiple devices send at the same time.

If two devices transmit at the same time, a collision will occur. For legacy Ethernet LANs, both devices will detect the collision on the network. This is the collision detection (CD) portion of CSMA/CD. The NIC compares data transmitted with data received, or by recognizing that the signal amplitude is higher than normal on the media. The data sent by both devices will be corrupted and will need to be resent.

Figures 31-13 through 31-15 demonstrate the CSMA/CD process in legacy Ethernet LANs that use a hub.

In Figure 31-13, PC1 has an Ethernet frame to send to PC3. The PC1 NIC needs to determine if any device is transmitting on the medium. If it does not detect a carrier signal (in other words, it is not receiving transmissions from another device), it will assume the network is available to send.

The PC1 NIC sends the Ethernet frame when the medium is available.

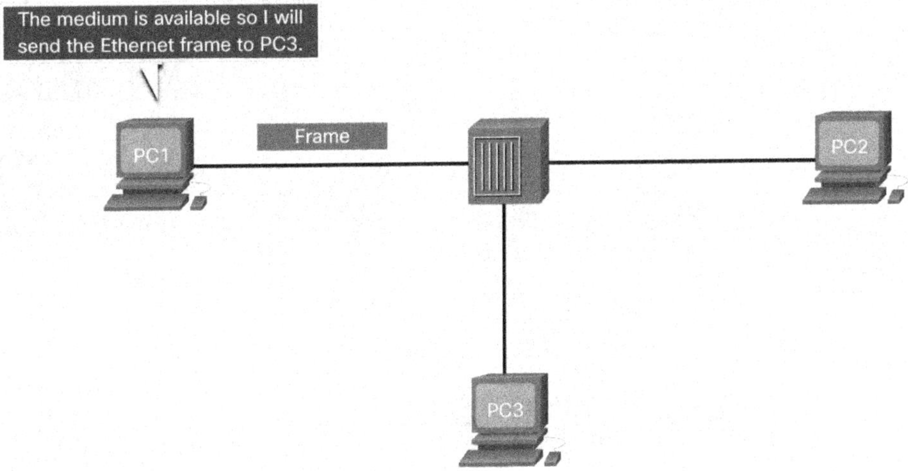

Figure 31-13 PC1 Sends a Frame

In Figure 31-14, the Ethernet hub receives and sends the frame. An Ethernet hub is also known as a multiport repeater. Any bits received on an incoming port are regenerated and sent out all other ports, as shown in the figure.

If another device, such as PC2, wants to transmit but is currently receiving a frame, it must wait until the channel is clear.

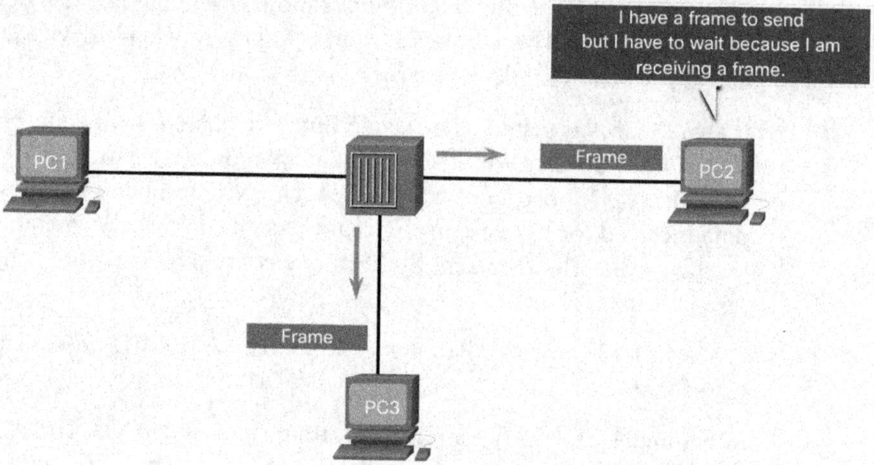

Figure 31-14 The Hub Receives the Frame

In Figure 31-15, all devices attached to the hub will receive the frame. However, because the frame has a destination data link address for PC3, only that device will accept and copy in the entire frame. All other device NICs will ignore the frame.

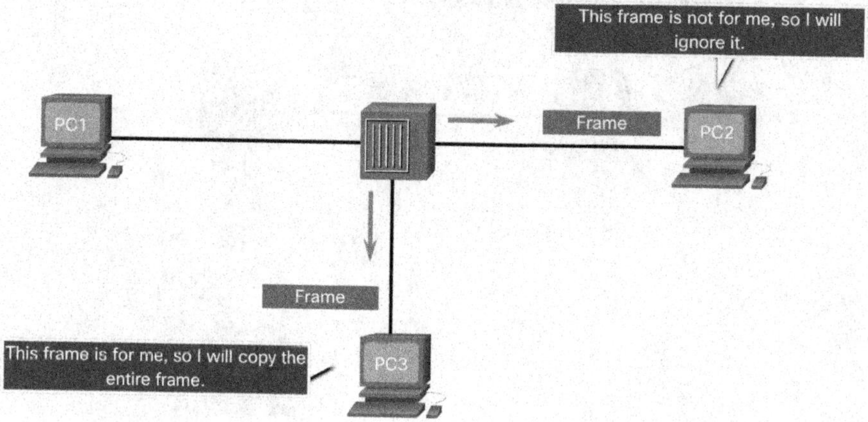

Figure 31-15 The Hub Sends the Frame

Contention-Based Access—CSMA/CA (31.2.4)

Another form of CSMA used by IEEE 802.11 WLANs is Carrier Sense Multiple Access with Collision Avoidance (CSMA/CA).

CMSA/CA uses a method similar to CSMA/CD to detect if the media is clear. CMSA/CA uses additional techniques. In wireless environments it may not be

possible for a device to detect a collision. CMSA/CA does not detect collisions but attempts to avoid them by waiting before transmitting. Each device that transmits includes the time duration that it needs for the transmission. All other wireless devices receive this information and know how long the medium will be unavailable.

In Figure 31-16, if host A is receiving a wireless frame from the access point, hosts B and C will also see the frame and how long the medium will be unavailable.

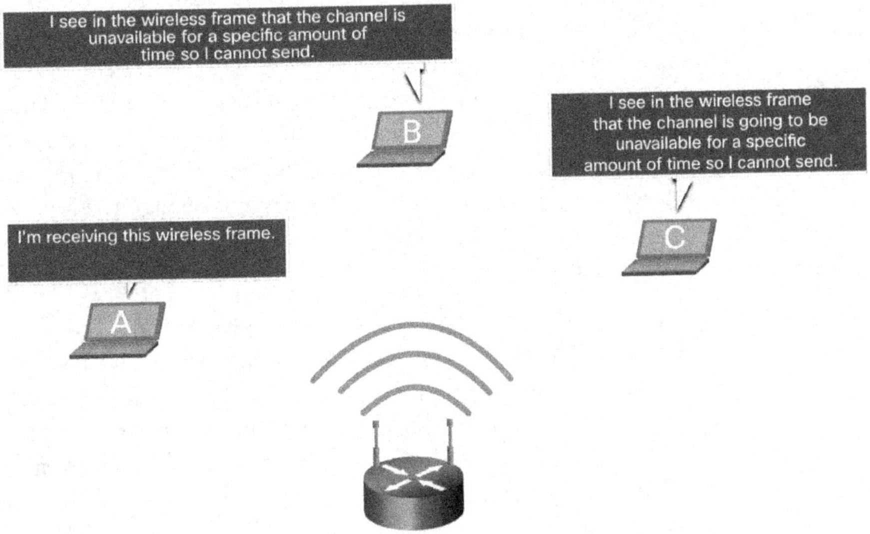

Figure 31-16 CSMA/CA

After a wireless device sends an 802.11 frame, the receiver returns an acknowledgment so that the sender knows the frame arrived.

Whether it is an Ethernet LAN using hubs or a WLAN, contention-based systems do not scale well under heavy media use.

Note

Ethernet LANs using switches do not use a contention-based system because the switch and the host NIC operate in full-duplex mode.

Interactive Graphic

Check Your Understanding—Media Access Control Methods (31.2.5)

Refer to the online course to complete this activity.

Summary (31.3)

The following is a summary of each topic in the chapter and some questions for your reflection.

What Did I Learn in This Chapter? (31.3.1)

- **Topologies**—The two types of topologies used in LAN and WAN networks are physical and logical. The data link layer "sees" the logical topology of a network when controlling data access to the media. The logical topology influences the type of network framing and media access control used. Three common types of physical WAN topologies are point-to-point, hub and spoke, and mesh. Physical point-to-point topologies directly connect two end devices (nodes). Adding intermediate physical connections may not change the logical topology. In multiaccess LANs, nodes are interconnected using star or extended star topologies. In this type of topology, nodes are connected to a central intermediary device.

  Physical LAN topologies include star, extended star, bus, and ring. Half-duplex communications exchange data in one direction at a time. Full-duplex sends and receives data simultaneously. Two interconnected interfaces must use the same duplex mode or there will be a duplex mismatch creating inefficiency and latency on the link. Ethernet LANs and WLANs are examples of multiaccess networks. A multiaccess network is a network that can have multiple nodes accessing the network simultaneously.

- **Media Access Control Methods**—Some multiaccess networks require rules to govern how devices share the physical media. There are two basic access control methods for shared media: contention-based access and controlled access. In contention-based multiaccess networks, all nodes are operating in half-duplex. There is a process if more than one device transmits at the same time. Examples of contention-based access methods include CSMA/CD for bus-topology Ethernet LANs and CSMA/CA for WLANs.

Reflection Questions (31.3.2)

Halimah had to examine the network at her headquarters in Nigeria. She is very experienced with creating topologies. The two types of topologies used in LAN and WAN networks are physical and logical. Halimah can easily create and interpret topologies.

- Can you draw a topology of your home network? That may be a bit simpler than the topology in your office building.
- What type of topology do you think your office building has? Consider asking someone in your IT department if you can look at the topology.

Practice

There are no labs or Packet Tracer activities in this chapter.

Check Your Understanding Questions

Complete all the review questions listed here to test your understanding of the topics and concepts in this chapter. Appendix A, "Answers to 'Check Your Understanding' Questions," lists the answers.

1. What is true concerning physical and logical topologies?
   a. The logical topology is always the same as the physical topology.
   b. Physical topologies are concerned with how a network transfers frames.
   c. Physical topologies display the IP addressing scheme of each network.
   d. Logical topologies refer to how a network transfers data between devices.
2. What type of physical topology can be created by connecting all Ethernet cables to a central device?
   a. Bus
   b. Ring
   c. Star
   d. Mesh
3. A technician has been asked to develop a physical topology for a network that provides a high level of redundancy. Which physical topology requires that every node is attached to every other node on the network?
   a. Bus
   b. Hierarchical
   c. Mesh
   d. Ring
   e. Star
4. Which statement describes the half-duplex mode of data transmission?
   a. Data transmitted over the network can only flow in one direction.
   b. Data transmitted over the network flows in one direction at a time.
   c. Data transmitted over the network flows in one direction to many different destinations simultaneously.
   d. Data transmitted over the network flows in both directions at the same time.

5. Which data link layer media access control method does Ethernet use with legacy Ethernet hubs?

   a. CSMA/CD
   b. Determinism
   c. Turn taking
   d. Token passing

6. What method is used to manage contention-based access on a wireless network?

   a. CSMA/CD
   b. Priority ordering
   c. CSMA/CA
   d. Token passing

7. Although CSMA/CD is still a feature of Ethernet, why is it no longer necessary?

   a. The virtually unlimited availability of IPv6 addresses
   b. The use of CSMA/CA
   c. The use of full-duplex capable Layer 2 Ethernet switches
   d. The development of half-duplex switch operation
   e. The use of Gigabit Ethernet speeds

CHAPTER 32

Routing at the Network Layer

Objectives

Upon completion of this chapter, you will be able to answer the following questions:

- How do network devices use routing tables to direct packets to a destination network?
- What is the function of fields in the routing table of a router?

Key Terms

This chapter uses the following key terms. You can find the definitions in the Glossary.

default gateway Page 574

default route Page 578

directly connected network Page 578

dynamic routing protocol Page 580

loopback interface Page 572

remote network Page 578

static route Page 579

Introduction (32.0)

Halimah is getting a good picture of the network at headquarters and at the other branches. She understands better how these networks are, in fact, just one connected network.

The network layer is where end-to-end connectivity occurs. Connectivity is what lets you send an email to a friend, access a website, stream a podcast, and retrieve a document from a central location. Like so much about networking, protocols and services are involved.

Are you intrigued? I know I am!

How a Host Routes (32.1)

Hosts need to communicate with hosts that might be on networks other than the local network. This section examines how communication from hosts is able to reach hosts on remote networks.

Host Forwarding Decision (32.1.1)

With both IPv4 and IPv6, packets are always created at the source host. The source host must be able to direct the packet to the destination host. To do this, host end devices create their own routing table. This section discusses how end devices use routing tables.

Another role of the network layer is to direct packets between hosts. A host can send a packet to the following:

- **Itself**—A host can ping itself by sending a packet to a special IPv4 address of 127.0.0.1 or an IPv6 address ::/1, which is referred to as the *loopback interface*. Pinging the loopback interface tests the TCP/IP protocol stack on the host.
- **Local host**—This is a destination host that is on the same local network as the sending host. The source and destination hosts share the same network address.
- **Remote host**—This is a destination host on a remote network. The source and destination hosts do not share the same network address.

Figure 32-1 illustrates PC1 connecting to a local host on the same network and to a remote host located on another network.

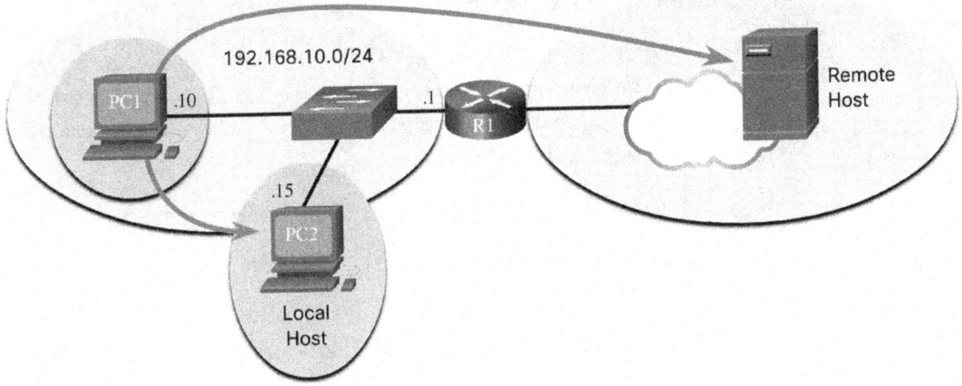

Figure 32-1 Hosts Can Connect to Local and Remote Networks

Whether a packet is destined for a local host or a remote host is determined by the source end device. The source end device determines whether the destination IP address is on the same network that the source device itself is on. The method of determination varies by IP version:

- **In IPv4**—The source device uses its own subnet mask along with its own IPv4 address and the destination IPv4 address to make this determination.
- **In IPv6**—The local router advertises the local network address (prefix) to all devices on the network.

In a home or business network, you may have several wired and wireless devices interconnected together using an intermediary device, such as a LAN switch or a wireless access point (WAP). This intermediary device provides interconnections between local hosts on the local network. Local hosts can reach each other and share information without the need for any additional devices. If a host is sending a packet to a device that is configured with the same IP network as the host device, the packet is simply forwarded out of the host interface, through the intermediary device, and to the destination device directly.

Of course, in most situations we want our devices to be able to connect beyond the local network segment, such as out to other homes, businesses, and the Internet. Devices that are beyond the local network segment are known as remote hosts. When a source device sends a packet to a remote destination device, then the help of routers and routing is needed. Routing is the process of identifying the best path to a destination. The router connected to the local network segment is referred to as the default gateway.

Default Gateway (32.1.2)

The *default gateway* is the network device (i.e., router or Layer 3 switch) that can route traffic to other networks. If you use the analogy that a network is like a room, then the default gateway is like a doorway. If you want to get to another room or network you need to find the doorway.

On a network, a default gateway is usually a router with these features:

- It has a local IP address in the same address range as other hosts on the local network.
- It can accept data into the local network and forward data out of the local network.
- It routes traffic to other networks.

A default gateway is required to send traffic outside of the local network. Traffic cannot be forwarded outside the local network if there is no default gateway, the default gateway address is not configured, or the default gateway is down.

A Host Routes to the Default Gateway (32.1.3)

A host routing table will typically include a default gateway. In IPv4, the host receives the IPv4 address of the default gateway either dynamically from Dynamic Host Configuration Protocol (DHCP) or configured manually. In IPv6, the router advertises the default gateway address or the host can be configured manually.

In Figure 32-2, PC1 and PC2 are configured with the IPv4 address of 192.168.10.1 as the default gateway.

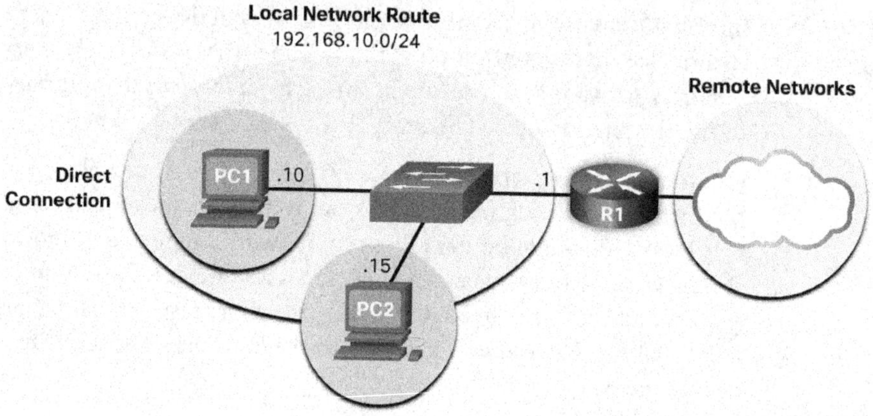

Figure 32-2 Hosts Use a Default Gateway for Remote Network Access

Having a default gateway configured creates a default route in the routing table of the PC. A default route is the route or pathway your computer will take when it tries to contact a remote network.

Both PC1 and PC2 will have a default route to send all traffic destined to remote networks to R1.

Host Routing Tables (32.1.4)

On a Windows host, the **route print** or **netstat -r** command can be used to display the host routing table. Both commands generate the same output. The output may seem overwhelming at first but is fairly simple to understand.

Figure 32-3 displays a sample topology for host routes.

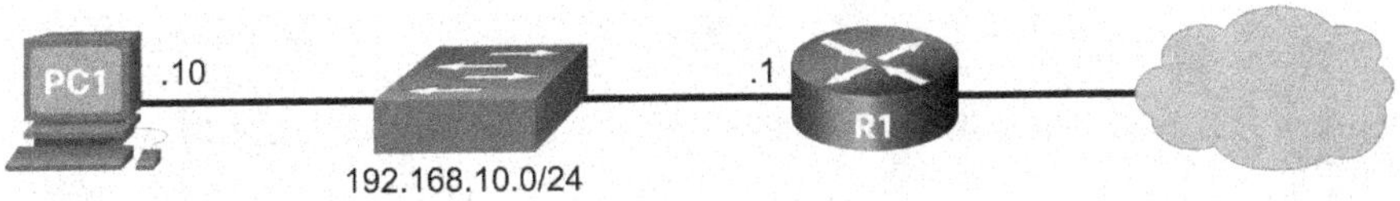

Figure 32-3 Host Route Topology

The output generated by the **netstat -r** command is shown in Example 32-1.

Example 32-1 IPv4 Routing Table for PC1

```
C:\Users\PC1> netstat -r

IPv4 Route Table
===========================================================================
Active Routes:
Network Destination        Netmask          Gateway       Interface  Metric
          0.0.0.0          0.0.0.0     192.168.10.1    192.168.10.10     25
        127.0.0.0        255.0.0.0         On-link         127.0.0.1    306
        127.0.0.1  255.255.255.255         On-link         127.0.0.1    306
  127.255.255.255  255.255.255.255         On-link         127.0.0.1    306
     192.168.10.0    255.255.255.0         On-link     192.168.10.10    281
    192.168.10.10  255.255.255.255         On-link     192.168.10.10    281
   192.168.10.255  255.255.255.255         On-link     192.168.10.10    281
        224.0.0.0        240.0.0.0         On-link         127.0.0.1    306
        224.0.0.0        240.0.0.0         On-link     192.168.10.10    281
  255.255.255.255  255.255.255.255         On-link         127.0.0.1    306
  255.255.255.255  255.255.255.255         On-link     192.168.10.10    281
```

Note

The output only displays the IPv4 route table.

Entering the **netstat -r** command or the equivalent **route print** command displays three sections related to the current TCP/IP network connections:

- **Interface List**—Lists the Media Access Control (MAC) address and assigned interface number of every network-capable interface on the host, including Ethernet, Wi-Fi, and Bluetooth adapters.
- **IPv4 Route Table**—Lists all known IPv4 routes, including direct connections, local network, and local default routes.
- **IPv6 Route Table**—Lists all known IPv6 routes, including direct connections, local network, and local default routes.

Interactive Graphic

Check Your Understanding—How a Host Routes (32.4.5)

Refer to the online course to complete this activity.

Routing Tables (32.2)

This section introduces the role of the router in the routing process and the router's use of routing tables for forwarding packets.

Router Packet Forwarding Decision (32.2.1)

The previous section discussed host routing tables. Most networks also contain routers, which are intermediary devices. Routers also contain routing tables. This section covers router operations at the network layer. When a host sends a packet to another host, it consults its routing table to determine where to send the packet. If the destination host is on a remote network, the packet is forwarded to the default gateway, which is usually the local router.

What happens when a packet arrives on a router interface?

The router examines the destination IP address of the packet and searches its routing table to determine where to forward the packet. The routing table contains a list of all known network addresses (prefixes) and where to forward the packet. These entries are known as route entries or routes. The router will forward the packet using

the best (longest) matching route entry. Refer to Figure 32-4 for an example of this forwarding process:

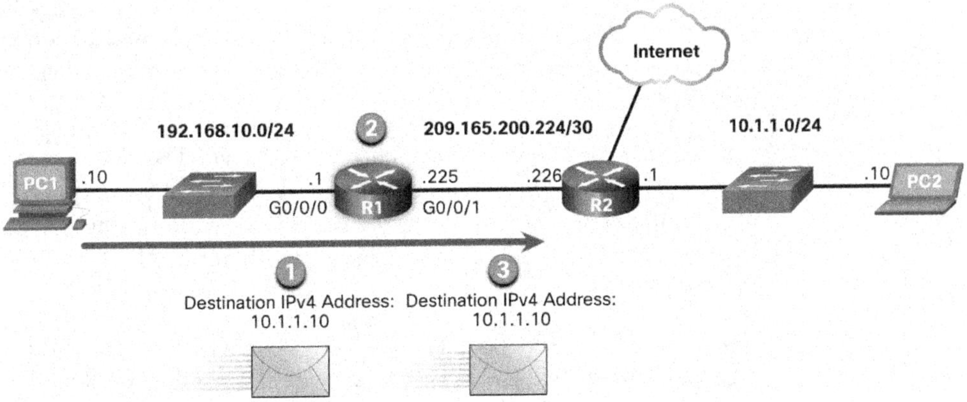

Figure 32-4 Packet Forwarding Process

1. Packet arrives on the Gigabit Ethernet 0/0/0 interface of router R1. R1 de-encapsulates the Layer 2 Ethernet header and trailer.
2. Router R1 examines the destination IPv4 address of the packet and searches for the best match in its IPv4 routing table. The route entry indicates that this packet is to be forwarded to router R2.
3. Router R1 encapsulates the packet into a new Ethernet header and trailer, and forwards the packet to the next hop router R2.

Table 32-1 shows the pertinent information from the R1 routing table.

Table 32-1 R1 Routing Table

Route	Next Hop or Exit Interface
192.168.10.0 /24	G0/0/0
209.165.200.224/30	G0/0/1
10.1.1.0/24	via R2
Default Route 0.0.0.0/0	via R2

IP Router Routing Table (32.2.2)

The routing table of the router contains network route entries listing all the possible known network destinations.

The routing table stores three types of route entries:

- *Directly connected networks*—These network route entries are active router interfaces. Routers add a directly connected route when an interface is configured with an IP address and is activated. Each router interface is connected to a different network segment. In Figure 32-5, the directly connected networks in the R1 IPv4 routing table would be 192.168.10.0/24 and 209.165.200.224/30.
- *Remote networks*—These network route entries are connected to other routers. Routers learn about remote networks either by being explicitly configured by an administrator or by exchanging route information using a dynamic routing protocol. In Figure 32-5, the remote network in the R1 IPv4 routing table would be 10.1.1.0/24.
- *Default route*—Like a host, most routers also include a default route entry, a gateway of last resort. The default route is used when there is no better (longer) match in the IP routing table. In Figure 32-5, the R1 IPv4 routing table would most likely include a default route to forward all packets to router R2.

Figure 32-5 identifies the directly connected and remote networks of router R1.

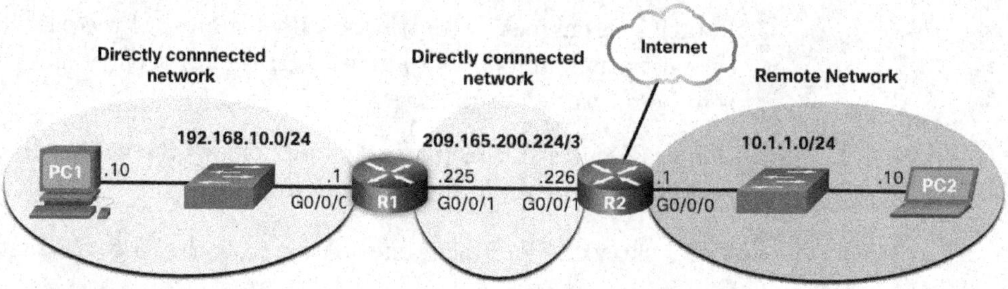

Figure 32-5 Example Topology of Directly Connected and Remote Networks

In Figure 32-5, R1 has two directly connected networks:

- 192.168.10.0/24
- 209.165.200.224/30

R1 also has remote networks (i.e., 10.1.1.0/24 and the Internet) that it can learn about.

A router can learn about remote networks in one of two ways:

- **Manually**—Remote networks are manually entered into the route table using static routes.
- **Dynamically**—Remote routes are automatically learned using a dynamic routing protocol.

Static Routing (32.2.3)

Static routes are route entries that are manually configured. Figure 32-6 shows an example of a static route that was manually configured on router R1. The static route includes the remote network address and the IP address of the next hop router.

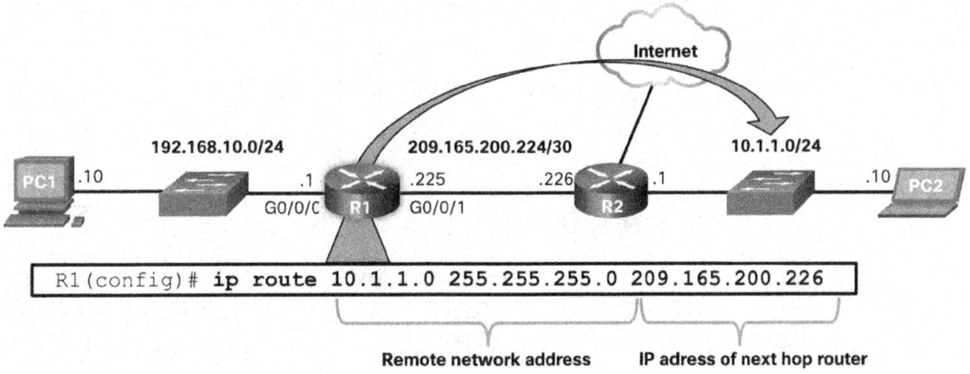

Figure 32-6 Static Routing Example

If there is a change in the network topology, the static route is not automatically updated and must be manually reconfigured. For example, in Figure 32-7 R1 has a static route to reach the 10.1.1.0/24 network via R2. If that path is no longer available, R1 would need to be reconfigured with a new static route to the 10.1.1.0/24 network via R3. Router R3 would therefore need to have a route entry in its routing table to send packets destined for 10.1.1.0/24 to R2.

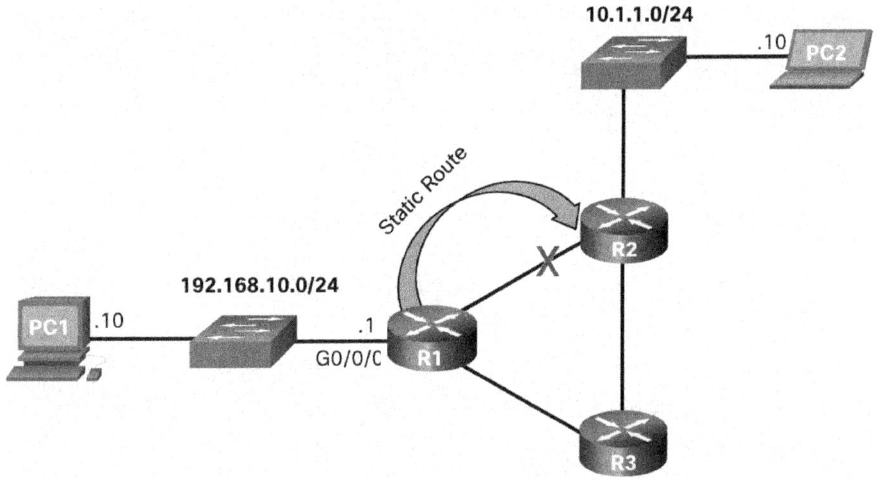

Figure 32-7 Static Routing Does Not Automatically Update to Topology Changes

Static routing has the following characteristics:

- A static route must be configured manually.
- The administrator needs to reconfigure a static route if there is a change in the topology and the static route is no longer viable.
- A static route is appropriate for a small network and when there are few or no redundant links.
- A static route is commonly used with a dynamic routing protocol for configuring a default route.

Dynamic Routing (32.2.4)

A *dynamic routing protocol* allows the routers to automatically learn about remote networks, including a default route, from other routers. Routers that use dynamic routing protocols automatically share routing information with other routers and compensate for any topology changes without involving the network administrator. If there is a change in the network topology, routers share this information using the dynamic routing protocol and automatically update their routing tables.

Dynamic routing protocols include OSPF and Enhanced Interior Gateway Routing Protocol (EIGRP). Figure 32-8 shows an example of routers R1 and R2 automatically sharing network information using the routing protocol OSPF.

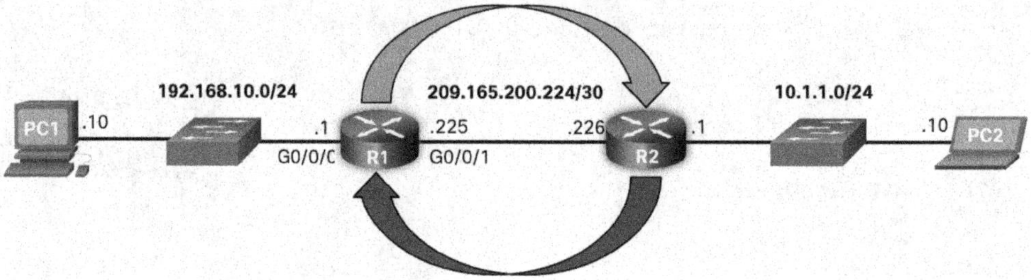

Figure 32-8 Dynamic Routing Example

- R1 is using the routing protocol OSPF to let R2 know about the 192.168.10.0/24 network.
- R2 is using the routing protocol OSPF to let R1 know about the 10.1.1.0/24 network.

Basic configuration only requires the network administrator to enable the directly connected networks within the dynamic routing protocol. The dynamic routing protocol will automatically do as follows:

- Discover remote networks
- Maintain up-to-date routing information
- Choose the best path to destination networks
- Attempt to find a new best path if the current path is no longer available

When a router is manually configured with a static route or learns about a remote network dynamically using a dynamic routing protocol, the remote network address and next hop address are entered into the IP routing table. As shown Figure 32-9, if there is a change in the network topology, the routers will automatically adjust and attempt to find a new best path.

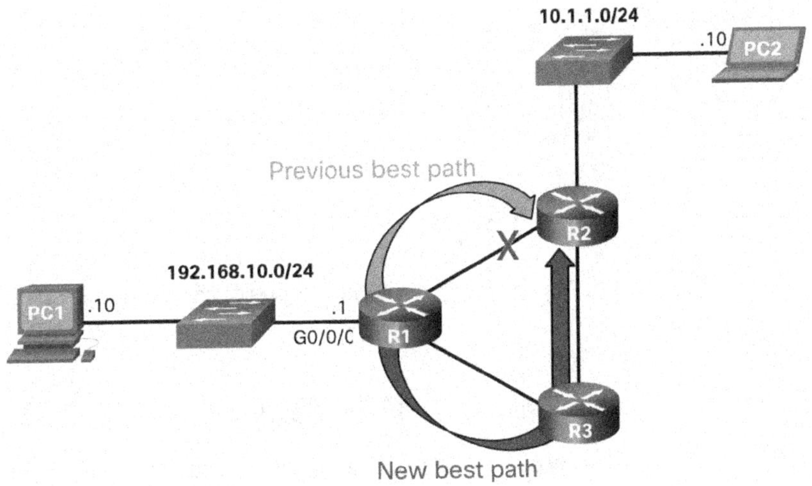

Figure 32-9 Dynamic Routing Automatically Updates to Topology Changes

Note

It is common for some routers to use a combination of both static routes and a dynamic routing protocol.

Video

Video—IPv4 Router Routing Tables (32.2.5)

Refer to the online course to view this video.

Introduction to an IPv4 Routing Table (32.2.6)

Notice in Figure 32-10 that R2 is connected to the Internet. Therefore, the administrator configured R1 with a default static route sending packets to R2 when there is no specific entry in the routing table that matches the destination IP address. R1 and R2 are also using OSPF routing to advertise directly connected networks.

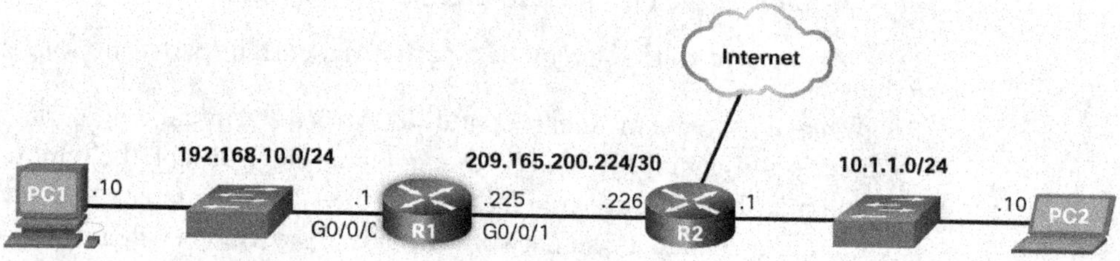

Figure 32-10 Example Topology for IPv4 Routing Table

Interactive Graphic

Check Your Understanding—Introduction to Routing (32.2.7)

Refer to the online course to complete this activity.

Summary (32.3)

The following is a summary of each topic in the chapter and some questions for your reflection.

What Did I Learn in This Chapter? (32.3.1)

- **How a Host Routes**—A host can send a packet to itself, another local host, and a remote host. In IPv4, the source device uses its own subnet mask along with its own IPv4 address and the destination IPv4 address to determine whether the destination host is on the same network. In IPv6, the local router advertises the local network address (prefix) to all devices on the network to make this determination. The default gateway is the network device (i.e., router) that can route traffic to other networks. On a network, a default gateway is usually a router that has a local IP address in the same address range as other hosts on the local network, can accept data into the local network and forward data out of the local network, and route traffic to other networks. A host routing table will typically include a default gateway. In IPv4, the host receives the IPv4 address of the default gateway either dynamically via DHCP or it is configured manually. In IPv6, the router advertises the default gateway address, or the host can be configured manually.

On a Windows host, the **route print** or **netstat -r** command can be used to display the host routing table.

- **Routing Tables**—When a host sends a packet to another host, it consults its routing table to determine where to send the packet. If the destination host is on a remote network, the packet is forwarded to the default gateway, which is usually the local router. What happens when a packet arrives on a router interface? The router examines the packet's destination IP address and searches its routing table to determine where to forward the packet. The routing table contains a list of all known network addresses (prefixes) and where to forward the packet. These entries are known as route entries or routes. The router will forward the packet using the best (longest) matching route entry.

  The routing table of a router stores three types of route entries: directly connected networks, remote networks, and a default route. Routers learn about remote networks manually or dynamically using a dynamic routing protocol. Static routes are route entries that are manually configured. Static routes include the remote network address and the IP address of the next hop router. OSPF and EIGRP are two dynamic routing protocols. The **show ip route** privileged EXEC mode command is used to view the IPv4 routing table on a Cisco IOS router. At the beginning of an IPv4 routing table is a code that is used to identify the type of route or how the route was learned. Common route sources (codes) include

  - **L**—Directly connected local interface IP address
  - **C**—Directly connected network
  - **S**—Static route manually configured by an administrator
  - **O**—Open Shortest Path First (OSPF)
  - **D**—Enhanced Interior Gateway Routing Protocol (EIGRP)

Reflection Questions (32.3.2)

Maybe you don't work in a hospital, but if you are here now it's because, like Kishori, you use computers and want to know more about networks.

Did you know that the Internet is a massive network of networks that are connected, either directly or indirectly, to each other? It's kind of like this web that I live in. One part can be broken but my web doesn't fall apart; I can fix it, and even make it stronger.

Would you like to be able to do that for your network?

Practice

There are no labs or Packet Tracer activities in this chapter.

Check Your Understanding Questions

Complete all the review questions listed here to test your understanding of the topics and concepts in this chapter. Appendix A, "Answers to 'Check Your Understanding' Questions," lists the answers.

1. Which information is used by routers to forward a data packet toward its destination?
   a. Source IP address
   b. Destination IP address
   c. Source data-link address
   d. Destination data-link address
2. A computer has to send a packet to a destination host in the same LAN. How will the packet be sent?
   a. The packet will be sent to the default gateway first, and then, depending on the response from the gateway, it may be sent to the destination host.
   b. The packet will be sent directly to the destination host.
   c. The packet will first be sent to the default gateway, and then from the default gateway it will be sent directly to the destination host.
   d. The packet will be sent only to the default gateway.
3. A router receives a packet from the Gigabit Ethernet 0/0 interface and determines that the packet needs to be forwarded out the Gigabit Ethernet 0/1 interface. What will the router do next?
   a. Route the packet out the Gigabit Ethernet 0/1 interface
   b. Create a new Layer 2 Ethernet frame to be sent to the destination
   c. Look into the ARP cache to determine the destination IP address
   d. Look into the routing table to determine if the destination network is in the routing table
4. Which IPv4 address can a host use to ping the loopback interface?
   a. 126.0.0.1
   b. 127.0.0.0
   c. 126.0.0.0
   d. 127.0.0.1

5. When a router receives a packet, what information must be examined in order for the packet to be forwarded to a remote destination?

   a. Destination MAC address
   b. Source IP address
   c. Destination IP address
   d. Source MAC address

6. Which command can be used on a Windows host to display the routing table?

   a. **netstat -s**
   b. **show ip route**
   c. **netstat -r**
   d. **tracert**

7. What type of route is created when a network administrator manually configures a route that has a next hop IP address to the remote network?

   a. Static
   b. Directly connected
   c. Local
   d. Dynamic

8. If a company has decided not to use static routing for the four routers inside the company, what would be an alternative solution?

   a. Use DHCP.
   b. Install a routing protocol.
   c. Use automatic flow labels.
   d. Allow the Internet provider to do the routing.

9. Which statement describes a feature of an IPv4 routing table on a router?

   a. The **netstat -r** command can be used to display the routing table of a router.
   b. Directly connected interfaces will have the source code in the routing table of **D**.
   c. If a default static route is configured in the router, an entry will be included in the routing table with source code **S**.
   d. The routing table lists the MAC addresses of each active interface.

10. Which address should be configured as the default gateway address of an end device on a LAN?

    a. The Layer 2 address of the switch management interface

    b. The Layer 2 address of the switch port that is connected to the workstation

    c. The IPv4 address of the router interface that is connected to the same LAN

    d. The IPv4 address of the router interface that is connected to the Internet

CHAPTER 33

IPv6 Addressing

Objectives

Upon completion of this chapter, you will be able to answer the following questions:

- What are the types of IPv6 network addresses?
- How do you configure static global unicast and link-local IPv6 network addresses?
- How do you configure global unicast addresses dynamically?
- How do you configure link-local addresses dynamically?
- How do you identify IPv6 addresses?

Key Terms

This chapter uses the following key terms. You can find the definitions in the Glossary.

Extended Unique Identifier (EUI-64) Page 605

global routing prefix Page 592

global unicast address (GUA) Page 589

interface ID Page 593

link-local address (LLA) Page 589

Router Advertisement (RA) message Page 599

Router Solicitation (RS) message Page 599

solicited-node multicast address Page 614

Stateless Address Autoconfiguration (SLAAC) Page 601

stateful DHCPv6 Page 603

stateless DHCPv6 Page 602

Subnet ID Page 592

well-known IPv6 multicast address Page 613

Introduction (33.0)

Hi, it's Webster. Well, that last chapter was a lot of new information for me. And now there is a whole new type of IP address—IPv6! But I'm feeling confident that I can learn this.

Halimah knows a lot about IPv6 addressing and she is happy to see that it is incorporated into her company's network strategically. This will help the company's network continue to grow and change.

Here's your chance to get up to speed on IPv6, too!

IPv6 Address Types (33.1)

This section introduces the different types and uses of IPv6 addresses.

Unicast, Multicast, Anycast (33.1.1)

As with IPv4, there are different types of IPv6 addresses. In fact, there are three broad categories of IPv6 addresses:

- **Unicast**—An IPv6 unicast address uniquely identifies an interface on an IPv6-enabled device.
- **Multicast**—An IPv6 multicast address is used to send a single IPv6 packet to multiple destinations.
- **Anycast**—An IPv6 anycast address is any IPv6 unicast address that can be assigned to multiple devices. A packet sent to an anycast address is routed to the nearest device having that address. Anycast addresses are beyond the scope of this course.

Unlike IPv4, IPv6 does not have a broadcast address. However, there is an IPv6 all-nodes multicast address that essentially gives the same result.

IPv6 Prefix Length (33.1.2)

The prefix, or network portion, of an IPv4 address can be identified by a dotted-decimal subnet mask or prefix length (slash notation). For example, an IPv4 address of 192.168.1.10 with dotted-decimal subnet mask 255.255.255.0 is equivalent to 192.168.1.10/24.

In IPv4 the /24 is called the prefix. In IPv6 it is called the prefix length. IPv6 does not use the dotted-decimal subnet mask notation. Like IPv4, the prefix length is

represented in slash notation and is used to indicate the network portion of an IPv6 address.

The prefix length can range from 0 to 128. The recommended IPv6 prefix length for LANs and most other types of networks is /64, as shown in Figure 33-1.

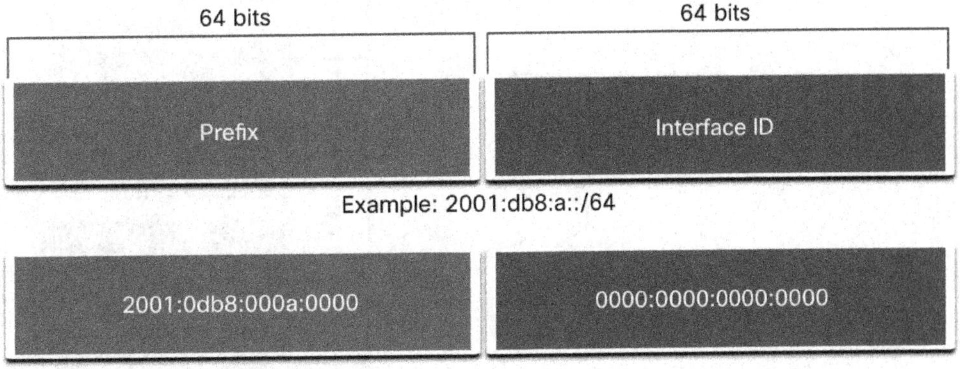

Figure 33-1 IPv6 Prefix Length

It is strongly recommended to use a 64-bit Interface ID for most networks. This is because Stateless Address Autoconfiguration (SLAAC) uses 64 bits for the Interface ID. It also makes subnetting easier to create and manage.

Types of IPv6 Unicast Addresses (33.1.3)

An IPv6 unicast address uniquely identifies an interface on an IPv6-enabled device. A packet sent to a unicast address is received by the interface that is assigned that address. Similar to IPv4, a source IPv6 address must be a unicast address. The destination IPv6 address can be either a unicast or a multicast address. Figure 33-2 shows the different types of IPv6 unicast addresses.

Unlike IPv4 devices that have only a single address, IPv6 addresses typically have two unicast addresses:

- *Global unicast address (GUA)*—This is similar to a public IPv4 address. GUAs are globally unique, Internet-routable addresses. GUAs can be configured statically or assigned dynamically.
- *Link-local address (LLA)*—This is required for every IPv6-enabled device. LLAs are used to communicate with other devices on the same local link. With IPv6, the term *link* refers to a subnet. LLAs are confined to a single link. Their uniqueness must only be confirmed on that link because they are not routable beyond the link. In other words, routers will not forward packets with a link-local source or destination address.

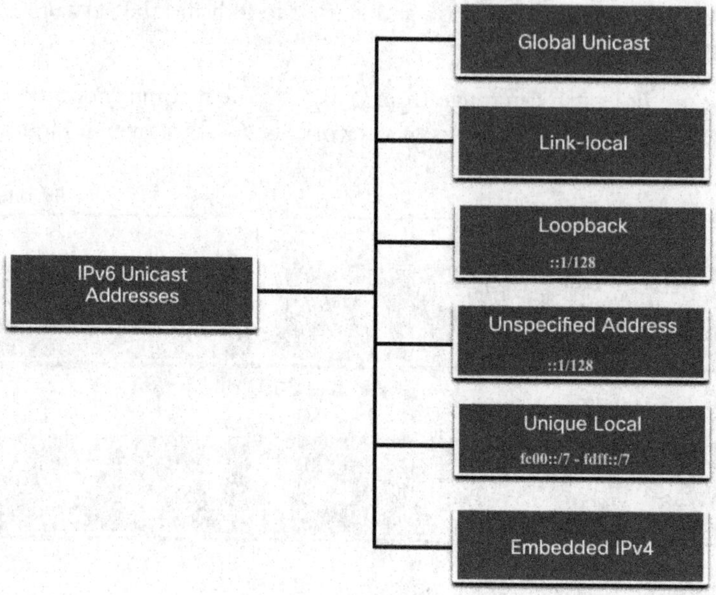

Figure 33-2 IPv6 Unicast Addresses

A Note About the Unique Local Address (33.1.4)

Unique local addresses (range fc00::/7 to fdff::/7) are not yet commonly implemented. Therefore, this chapter only covers GUA and LLA configuration. However, unique local addresses may eventually be used to address devices that should not be accessible from the outside, such as internal servers and printers.

The IPv6 unique local addresses have some similarity to RFC 1918 private addresses for IPv4, but there are significant differences:

- Unique local addresses are used for local addressing within a site or between a limited number of sites.
- Unique local addresses can be used for devices that will never need to access another network.
- Unique local addresses are not globally routed or translated to a global IPv6 address.

Note

Many sites also use the private nature of RFC 1918 addresses to attempt to secure or hide their network from potential security risks. However, this was never the intended use of these technologies, and the IETF has always recommended that sites take the proper security precautions on their Internet-facing router.

IPv6 GUA (33.1.5)

IPv6 global unicast addresses (GUAs) are globally unique and routable on the IPv6 Internet. These addresses are equivalent to public IPv4 addresses. The Internet Committee for Assigned Names and Numbers (ICANN), the operator for IANA, allocates IPv6 address blocks to the five RIRs. Currently, only GUAs with the first three bits of 001 or 2000::/3 are being assigned, as shown in Figure 33-3.

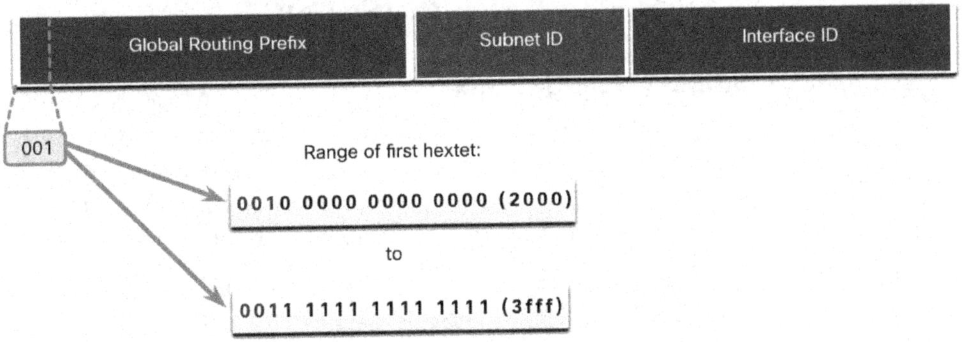

Figure 33-3 Range of First Hextet Values for GUAs

Figure 33-3 shows the range of values for the first hextet where the first hexadecimal digit for currently available GUAs begins with a 2 or a 3. This is only 1/8th of the total available IPv6 address space, excluding only a very small portion for other types of unicast and multicast addresses.

Note

The 2001:db8::/32 address has been reserved for documentation purposes, including use in examples.

Figure 33-4 shows the structure and range of a GUA.

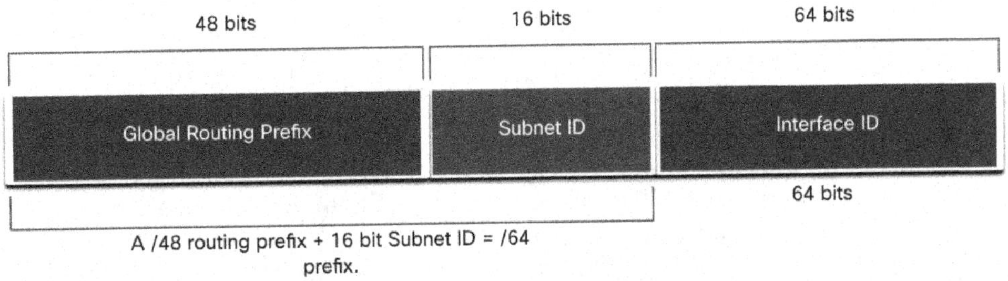

Figure 33-4 IPv6 Address with a /48 Global Routing Prefix and /64 Prefix

A GUA has three parts:

- Global Routing Prefix
- Subnet ID
- Interface ID

IPv6 GUA Structure (33.1.6)

Global Routing Prefix

The *global routing prefix* is the prefix, or network, portion of the address that is assigned by the provider, such as an ISP, to a customer or site. For example, it is common for an ISP to assign a /48 global routing prefix to its customers. The global routing prefix will usually vary depending on the policies of the ISP.

Figure 33-4 shows a GUA using a /48 global routing prefix. /48 prefixes are a common global routing prefix that is assigned and will be used in most of the examples throughout this course.

For example, the IPv6 address 2001:db8:acad::/48 has a global routing prefix that indicates that the first 48 bits (3 hextets) (2001:db8:acad) is how the ISP knows of this prefix (network). The double colon (::) following the /48 prefix length means the rest of the address contains all 0s. The size of the global routing prefix determines the size of the Subnet ID.

Subnet ID

The *Subnet ID* field is the area between the Global Routing Prefix and the Interface ID. Unlike IPv4 where you must borrow bits from the host portion to create subnets, IPv6 was designed with subnetting in mind. The Subnet ID is used by an organization to identify subnets within its site. The larger the Subnet ID, the more subnets available.

Note

Many organizations are receiving a /32 global routing prefix. Using the recommended /64 prefix in order to create a 64-bit Interface ID leaves a 32-bit Subnet ID. This means an organization with a /32 global routing prefix and a 32-bit Subnet ID will have 4.3 billion subnets, each with 18 quintillion devices per subnet. That is as many subnets as there are public IPv4 addresses!

The IPv6 address in Figure 33-4 has a /48 Global Routing Prefix, which is common among many enterprise networks. This makes it especially easy to examine the

different parts of the address. Using a typical /64 prefix length, the first four hextets are for the network portion of the address, with the fourth hextet indicating the Subnet ID. The remaining four hextets are for the Interface ID.

Interface ID

The IPv6 *interface ID* is equivalent to the host portion of an IPv4 address. The term *Interface ID* is used because a single host may have multiple interfaces, each having one or more IPv6 addresses. The figure shows an example of the structure of an IPv6 GUA. It is strongly recommended that in most cases /64 subnets should be used, which creates a 64-bit interface ID. A 64-bit interface ID allows for 18 quintillion devices or hosts per subnet.

A /64 subnet or prefix (Global Routing Prefix + Subnet ID) leaves 64 bits for the interface ID. This is recommended to allow SLAAC-enabled devices to create their own 64-bit interface ID. It also makes developing an IPv6 addressing plan simple and effective.

Note

Unlike IPv4, in IPv6, the all-0s and all-1s host addresses can be assigned to a device. The all-1s address can be used because broadcast addresses are not used within IPv6. The all-0s address can also be used, but is reserved as a Subnet-Router anycast address, and should be assigned only to routers.

IPv6 LLA (33.1.7)

An IPv6 link-local address (LLA) enables a device to communicate with other IPv6-enabled devices on the same link and only on that link (subnet). Packets with a source or destination LLA cannot be routed beyond the link from which the packet originated.

The GUA is not a requirement. However, every IPv6-enabled network interface must have an LLA.

If an LLA is not configured manually on an interface, the device will automatically create its own without communicating with a DHCP server. IPv6-enabled hosts create an IPv6 LLA even if the device has not been assigned a global unicast IPv6 address. This allows IPv6-enabled devices to communicate with other IPv6-enabled devices on the same subnet. This includes communication with the default gateway (router).

IPv6 LLAs are in the fe80::/10 range. The /10 indicates that the first 10 bits are 1111 1110 10xx xxxx. The first hextet has a range of 1111 1110 10**00 0000** (fe80) to 1111 1110 10**11 1111** (febf).

Figure 33-5 shows an example of communication using IPv6 LLAs. The PC is able to communicate directly with the printer using the LLAs.

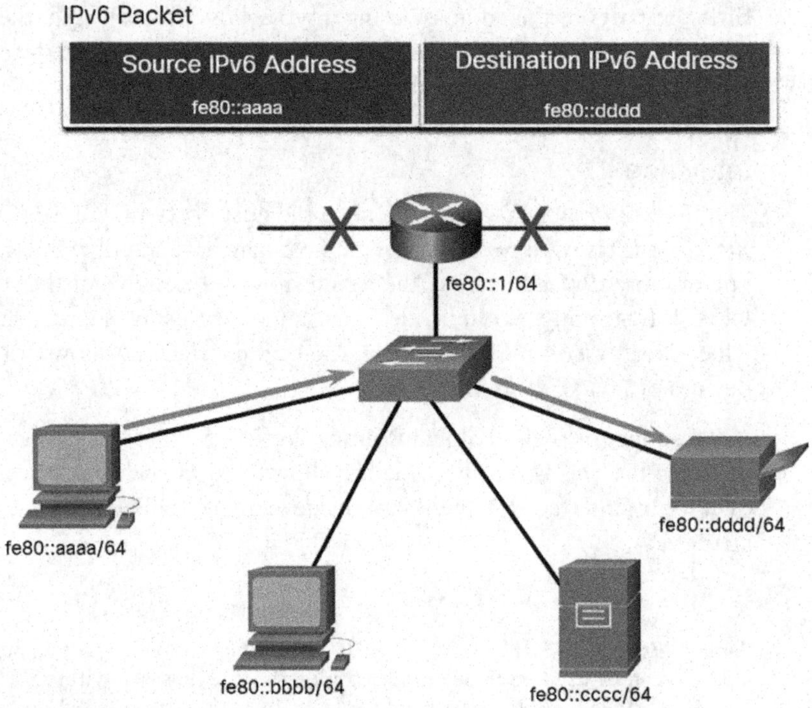

Figure 33-5 IPv6 Link-Local Communications

Figure 33-6 shows some of the uses for IPv6 LLAs.

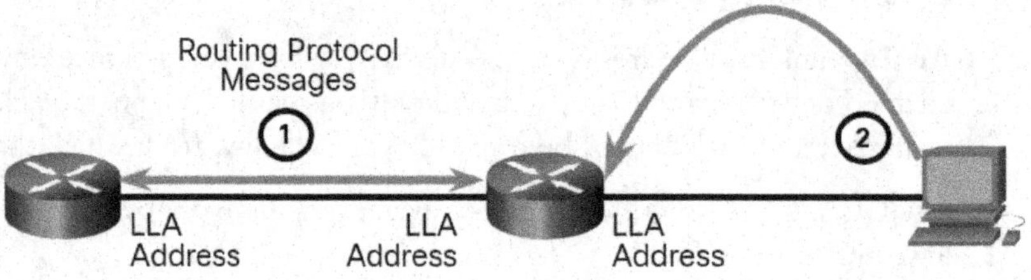

Figure 33-6 Example of Using IPv6 LLAs

1. Routers use the LLAs of neighbor routers to send routing updates.
2. Hosts use the LLA of a local router as the default-gateway.

Note

Typically, it is the LLA of the router, and not the GUA, that is used as the default gateway for other devices on the link.

There are two ways that a device can obtain an LLA:

- **Statically**—This means the device has been manually configured.
- **Dynamically**—This means the device creates its own interface ID by using randomly generated values or using the Extended Unique Identifier (EUI) method, which uses the client MAC address along with additional bits.

Interactive Graphic

Check Your Understanding—IPv6 Address Types (33.1.8)

Refer to the online course to complete this activity.

GUA and LLA Static Configuration (33.2)

This section discusses the static configuration of IPv6 global unicast (GUA) and link-local addresses.

Static GUA Configuration on a Router (33.2.1)

As you learned in the previous section, IPv6 GUAs are the same as public IPv4 addresses. They are globally unique and routable on the IPv6 Internet. An IPv6 LLA lets two IPv6-enabled devices communicate with each other on the same link (subnet). It is easy to statically configure IPv6 GUAs and LLAs on routers to help you create an IPv6 network. This section teaches you how to do just that!

Most IPv6 configuration and verification commands in the Cisco IOS are similar to their IPv4 counterparts. In many cases, the only difference is the use of **ipv6** in place of **ip** within the commands.

For example, the Cisco IOS command to configure an IPv4 address on an interface is **ip address** *ip-address subnet-mask*. In contrast, the command to configure an IPv6 GUA on an interface is **ipv6 address** *ipv6-address/prefix-length*.

Notice that there is no space between *ipv6-address* and *prefix-length*.

The example configuration uses the topology shown in Figure 33-7 and these IPv6 subnets:

- 2001:db8:acad:1:/64
- 2001:db8:acad:2:/64
- 2001:db8:acad:3:/64

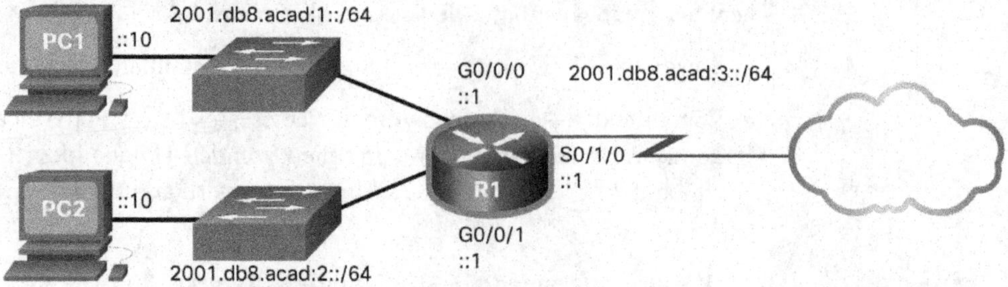

Figure 33-7 IPv6 Addressing Topology

Example 33-1 shows the commands required to configure the IPv6 GUA on GigabitEthernet 0/0/0, GigabitEthernet 0/0/1, and the Serial 0/1/0 interface of R1.

Example 33-1 IPv6 GUA Configuration on Router R1

```
R1(config)# interface gigabitethernet 0/0/0
R1(config-if)# ipv6 address 2001:db8:acad:1::1/64
R1(config-if)# no shutdown
R1(config-if)# exit
R1(config)# interface gigabitethernet 0/0/1
R1(config-if)# ipv6 address 2001:db8:acad:2::1/64
R1(config-if)# no shutdown
R1(config-if)# exit
R1(config)# interface serial 0/1/0
R1(config-if)# ipv6 address 2001:db8:acad:3::1/64
R1(config-if)# no shutdown
```

Static GUA Configuration on a Windows Host (33.2.2)

Manually configuring the IPv6 address on a host is similar to configuring an IPv4 address.

As shown in Figure 33-8, the default gateway address configured for PC1 is 2001:db8:acad:1::1. This is the GUA of the R1 GigabitEthernet interface on the same network. Alternatively, the default gateway address can be configured to match the LLA of the GigabitEthernet interface. Using the LLA of the router as the default gateway address is considered best practice. Either configuration will work.

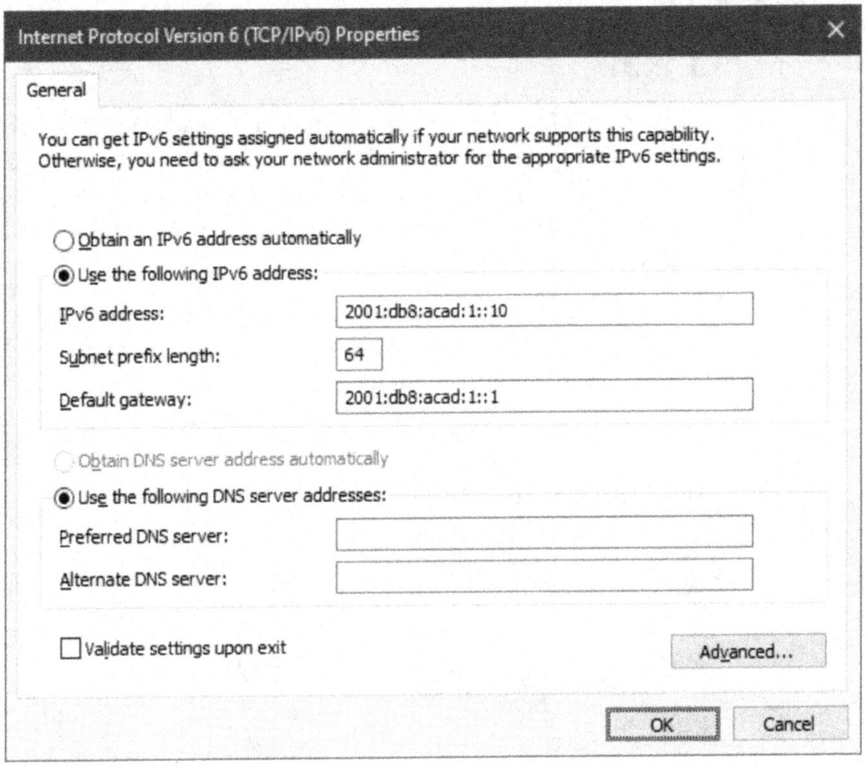

Figure 33-8 Manually Configuring IPv6 Addressing on a Windows Host

Just as with IPv4, configuring static IPv6 addresses on clients does not scale to larger environments. For this reason, most network administrators in an IPv6 network will enable dynamic assignment of IPv6 addresses.

There are two ways in which a device can obtain an IPv6 GUA automatically:

- Stateless Address Autoconfiguration (SLAAC)
- Stateful DHCPv6

SLAAC and DHCPv6 are covered in the next section.

Note

When DHCPv6 or SLAAC is used, the LLA of the router will automatically be specified as the default gateway address.

Static Configuration of a Link-Local Unicast Address (33.2.3)

Configuring the LLA manually lets you create an address that is recognizable and easier to remember. Typically, it is only necessary to create recognizable LLAs on routers. This is beneficial because router LLAs are used as default gateway addresses and in routing advertisement messages, the messages sent by dynamic routing protocols.

LLAs can be configured manually using the **ipv6 address** *ipv6-link-local-address* **link-local** command. When an address begins with this hextet within the range of fe80 to febf, the **link-local** parameter must follow the address.

Figure 33-9 shows an example topology with LLAs on each interface.

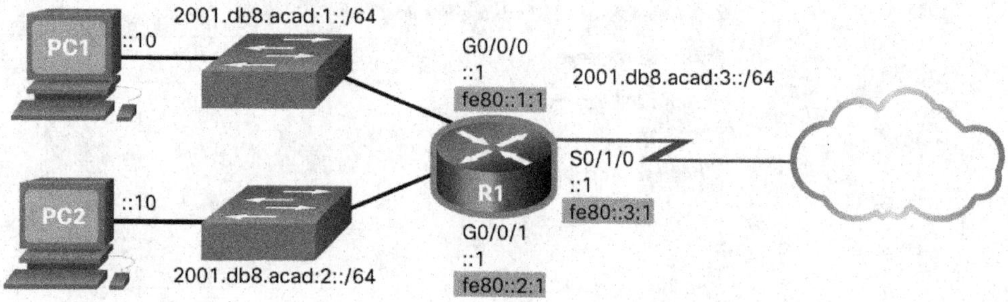

Figure 33-9 IPv6 Addressing Topology with LLAs

Example 33-2 shows the configuration of an LLA on router R1.

Example 33-2 R1 Static LLA Configuration

```
R1(config)# interface gigabitethernet 0/0/0
R1(config-if)# ipv6 address fe80::1:1 link-local
R1(config-if)# exit
R1(config)# interface gigabitethernet 0/0/1
R1(config-if)# ipv6 address fe80::1:2 link-local
R1(config-if)# exit
R1(config)# interface serial 0/1/0
R1(config-if)# ipv6 address fe80::1:3 link-local
R1(config-if)# exit
```

Statically configured LLAs are used to make them more easily recognizable as belonging to router R1. In this example, all the interfaces of router R1 have been

configured with an LLA that begins with **fe80::1:*n*** and a unique right-most digit ***n***. The **1** represents router R1.

Following the same syntax as router R1, if the topology included router R2, it would have its three interfaces configured with the LLAs fe80::2:1, fe80::2:2, and fe80::2:3.

Note

The exact same LLA could be configured on each link as long as it is unique on that link. This is because LLAs only have to be unique on that link. However, common practice is to create a different LLA on each interface of the router to make it easy to identify the router and the specific interface.

Interactive Graphic

Syntax Checker—GUA and LLA Static Configuration (33.2.4)

Refer to the online course to complete this activity.

Dynamic Addressing for IPv6 GUAs (33.3)

This section discusses the different methods of how a device can automatically create or receive an IPv6 GUA.

RS and RA Messages (33.3.1)

If you do not want to statically configure IPv6 GUAs, no need to worry. Most devices obtain their IPv6 GUAs dynamically. This topic explains how this process works using *Router Advertisement (RA)* and *Router Solicitation (RS) messages*. This topic gets rather technical, but when you understand the difference between the three methods that a router advertisement can use, as well as how the EUI-64 process for creating an interface ID differs from a randomly generated process, you will have made a huge leap in your IPv6 expertise!

For the GUA, a device obtains the address dynamically through Internet Control Message Protocol version 6 (ICMPv6) messages. IPv6 routers periodically send out ICMPv6 RA messages, every 200 seconds, to all IPv6-enabled devices on the network. An RA message will also be sent in response to a host sending an ICMPv6 RS message, which is a request for an RA message. Both messages are shown in Figure 33-10.

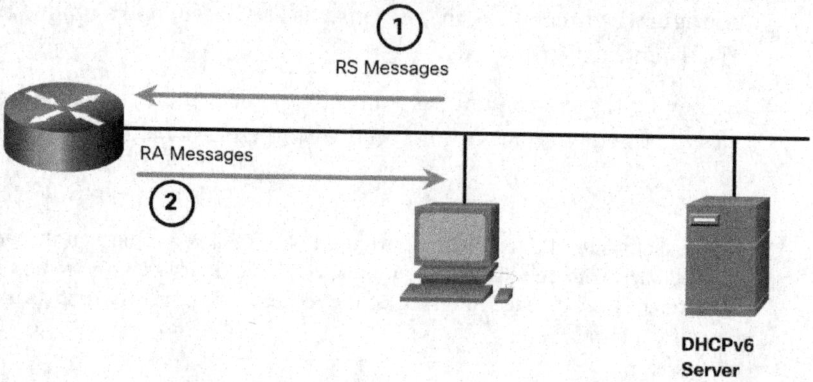

Figure 33-10 ICMPv6 RS and RA Messages

1. RS messages are sent to all IPv6 routers by hosts requesting addressing information.

2. RA messages are sent to all IPv6 nodes. If Method 1 (SLAAC only) is used, the RA includes network prefix, prefix length, and default gateway information.

RA messages are on IPv6 router Ethernet interfaces. The router must be enabled for IPv6 routing, which is not enabled by default. To enable a router as an IPv6 router, the **ipv6 unicast-routing** global configuration command must be used.

The ICMPv6 RA message is a suggestion to a device on how to obtain an IPv6 GUA. The ultimate decision is up to the device operating system. The ICMPv6 RA message includes the following:

- **Network prefix and prefix length**—This tells the device which network it belongs to.
- **Default gateway address**—This is an IPv6 LLA, the source IPv6 address of the RA message.
- **DNS addresses and domain name**—These are the addresses of DNS servers and a domain name.

There are three methods for RA messages:

- **Method 1: SLAAC**—"I have everything you need including the prefix, prefix length, and default gateway address."
- **Method 2: SLAAC with a stateless DHCPv6 server**—"Here is my information but you need to get other information such as DNS addresses from a stateless DHCPv6 server."

- **Method 3: Stateful DHCPv6 (no SLAAC)**—"I can give you your default gateway address. You need to ask a stateful DHCPv6 server for all your other information."

Method 1: SLAAC (33.3.2)

Stateless Address Autoconfiguration (SLAAC) is a method that allows a device to create its own GUA without the services of DHCPv6. Using SLAAC, devices rely on the ICMPv6 RA messages of the local router to obtain the necessary information.

By default, the RA message suggests that the receiving device use the information in the RA message to create its own IPv6 GUA and all other necessary information. The services of a DHCPv6 server are not required.

SLAAC is stateless, which means there is no central server (for example, a stateful DHCPv6 server) allocating GUAs and keeping a list of devices and their addresses. With SLAAC, the client device uses the information in the RA message to create its own GUA. As shown in Figure 33-11, the two parts of the address are created as follows:

- **Prefix**—This is advertised in the RA message.
- **Interface ID**—This uses the EUI-64 process or by generating a random 64-bit number, depending on the device operating system.

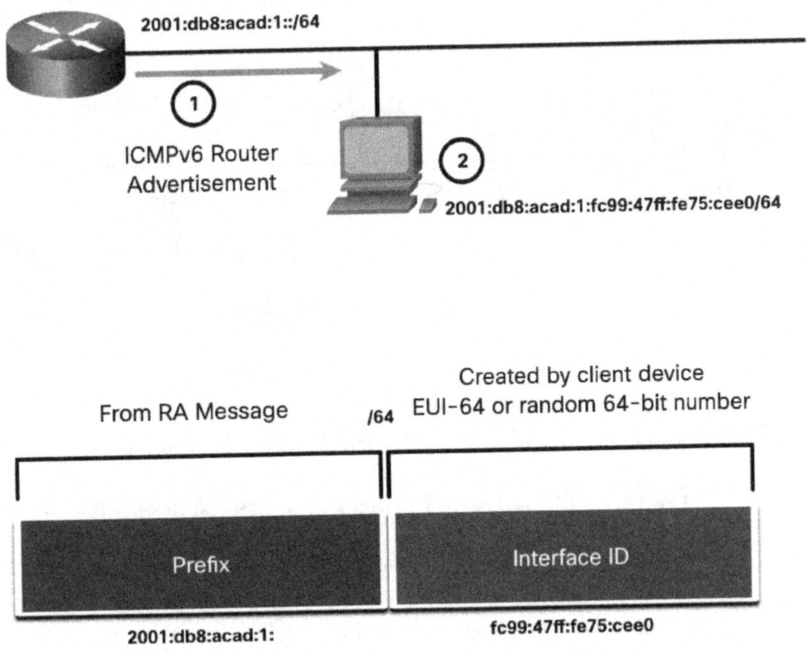

Figure 33-11 SLAAC Example

1. The router sends an RA message with the prefix for the local link.
2. The PC uses SLAAC to obtain a prefix from the RA message and creates its own Interface ID.

Method 2: SLAAC and Stateless DHCPv6 (33.3.3)

A router interface can be configured to send a router advertisement using SLAAC and *stateless DHCPv6*.

As shown in Figure 33-12, with this method, the RA message suggests devices use the following:

- SLAAC to create their own IPv6 GUA
- The router LLA, which is the RA source IPv6 address, as the default gateway address
- A stateless DHCPv6 server to obtain other information such as a DNS server address and a domain name

Note

A stateless DHCPv6 server distributes DNS server addresses and domain names. It does not allocate GUAs.

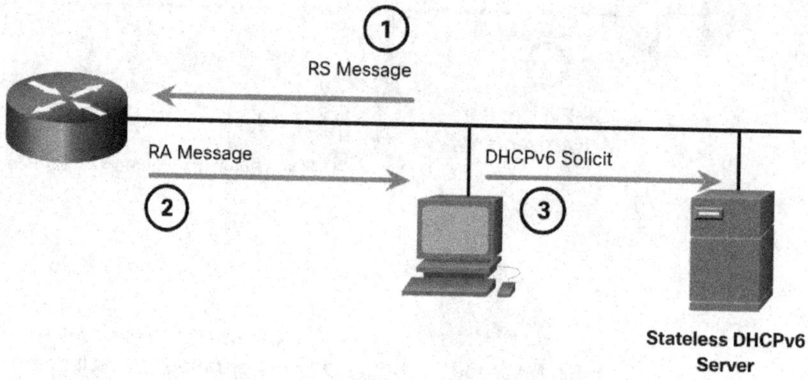

Figure 33-12 SLAAC and Stateless DHCPv6 Example

1. The PC sends an RS to all IPv6 routers, "I need addressing information."
2. The router sends an RA message to all IPv6 nodes with Method 2 (SLAAC and DHCPv6) specified. "Here is your prefix, prefix length, and default gateway information. But you will need to get DNS information from a DHCPv6 server."

3. The PC sends a DHCPv6 Solicit message to all DHCPv6 servers. "I used SLAAC to create my IPv6 address and get my default gateway address, but I need other information from a stateless DHCPv6 server."

Method 3: Stateful DHCPv6 (33.3.4)

A router interface can be configured to send an RA using stateful DHCPv6 only.

Stateful DHCPv6 is similar to DHCP for IPv4. A device can automatically receive its addressing information including a GUA, prefix length, and the addresses of DNS servers from a stateful DHCPv6 server.

As shown in Figure 33-13, with this method, the RA message suggests devices use the following:

- The router LLA, which is the RA source IPv6 address, for the default gateway address.
- A stateful DHCPv6 server to obtain a GUA, DNS server address, domain name, and other necessary information.

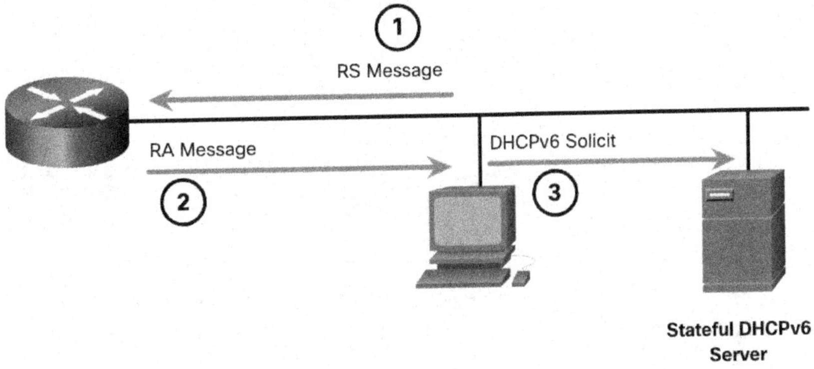

Figure 33-13 Stateful DHCPv6 Example

1. The PC sends an RS to all IPv6 routers, "I need addressing information."
2. The router sends an RA message to all IPv6 nodes with Method 3 (Stateful DHCPv6) specified, "I am your default gateway, but you need to ask a stateful DHCPv6 server for your IPv6 address and other addressing information."
3. The PC sends a DHCPv6 Solicit message to all DHCPv6 servers, "I received my default gateway address from the RA message, but I need an IPv6 address and all other addressing information from a stateful DHCPv6 server."

A stateful DHCPv6 server allocates and maintains a list of which device receives which IPv6 address. DHCP for IPv4 is stateful.

Note

The default gateway address can only be obtained dynamically from the RA message. The stateless or stateful DHCPv6 server does not provide the default gateway address.

EUI-64 Process vs. Randomly Generated (33.3.5)

When the RA message is either SLAAC or SLAAC with stateless DHCPv6, the client must generate its own interface ID. The client knows the prefix portion of the address from the RA message but must create its own interface ID. The interface ID can be created using the EUI-64 process or a randomly generated 64-bit number, as shown in Figure 33-14.

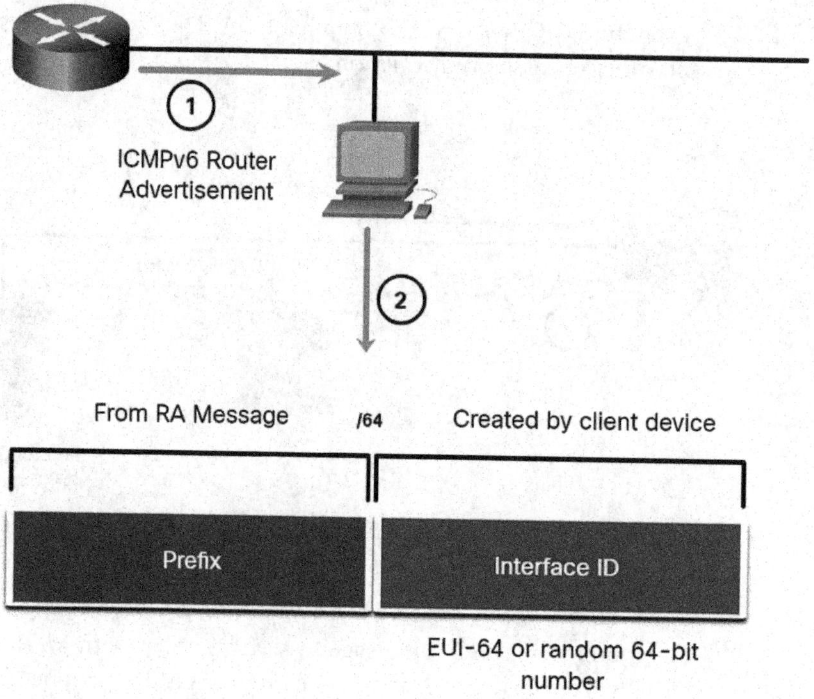

Figure 33-14 Dynamically Creating an Interface ID

1. The router sends an RA message.
2. The PC uses the prefix in the RA message and uses either EUI-64 or a random 64-bit number to generate an interface ID.

EUI-64 Process (33.3.6)

IEEE defined the *Extended Unique Identifier (EUI-64)* or modified EUI-64 process. This process uses the 48-bit Ethernet MAC address of a client, and inserts another 16 bits in the middle of the 48-bit MAC address to create a 64-bit interface ID.

Ethernet MAC addresses are usually represented in hexadecimal and are made up of two parts:

- **Organizationally Unique Identifier (OUI)**—The OUI is a 24-bit (six hexadecimal digits) vendor code assigned by IEEE.
- **Device Identifier**—The device identifier is a unique 24-bit (six hexadecimal digits) value within a common OUI.

An EUI-64 Interface ID is represented in binary and is made up of three parts:

- 24-bit OUI from the client MAC address, but the 7th bit (the Universally/Locally [U/L] bit) is reversed. This means that if the 7th bit is a 0, it becomes a 1, and vice versa.
- The inserted 16-bit value fffe (in hexadecimal).
- 24-bit Device Identifier from the client MAC address.

The EUI-64 process is illustrated in Figure 33-15, using the R1 GigabitEthernet MAC address of fc99:4775:cee0.

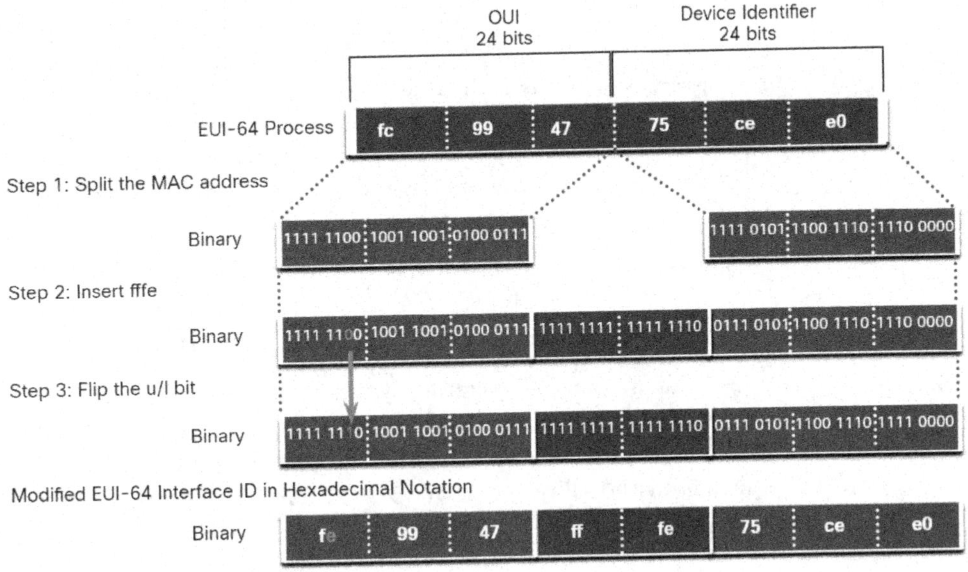

Figure 33-15 The EUI-64 Process

Step 1. Divide the MAC address between the OUI and device identifier.

Step 2. Insert the hexadecimal value fffe, which in binary is 1111 1111 1111 1110.

Step 3. Convert the first two hexadecimal values of the OUI to binary and flip the U/L bit (bit 7). In this example, the 0 in bit 7 is changed to a 1.

The result is an EUI-64 generated interface ID of fe99:47ff:fe75:cee0.

Note

The use of the U/L bit and the reasons for reversing its value are discussed in RFC 5342.

The output in Example 33-3 for the **ipconfig** command shows the IPv6 GUA being dynamically created using SLAAC and the EUI-64 process. An easy way to identify that an address was probably created using EUI-64 is the **fffe** located in the middle of the interface ID.

The advantage of EUI-64 is that the Ethernet MAC address can be used to determine the interface ID. It also allows network administrators to easily track an IPv6 address to an end device using the unique MAC address. However, this has caused privacy concerns among many users who worried that their packets could be traced to the actual physical computer. Due to these concerns, a randomly generated interface ID may be used instead.

Example 33-3 EUI-64 Generated Interface ID

```
C:\> ipconfig
Windows IP Configuration
Ethernet adapter Local Area Connection:
   Connection-specific DNS Suffix  . :
   IPv6 Address. . . . . . . . . . . : 2001:db8:acad:1:fc99:47ff:fe75:cee0
   Link-local IPv6 Address . . . . . : fe80::fc99:47ff:fe75:cee0
   Default Gateway . . . . . . . . . : fe80::1
C:\>
```

Randomly Generated Interface IDs (33.3.7)

Depending upon the operating system, a device may use a randomly generated interface ID instead of using the MAC address and the EUI-64 process. Beginning with Windows Vista, Windows uses a randomly generated interface ID instead of one created with EUI-64. Windows XP and previous Windows operating systems used EUI-64.

After the interface ID is established, either through the EUI-64 process or through random generation, it can be combined with an IPv6 prefix in the RA message to create a GUA, as shown in Example 33-4.

Example 33-4 Random 64-bit Generated Interface ID

```
C:\> ipconfig
Windows IP Configuration
Ethernet adapter Local Area Connection:
   Connection-specific DNS Suffix  . :
   IPv6 Address. . . . . . . . . . . : 2001:db8:acad:1:50a5:8a35:a5bb:66e1
   Link-local IPv6 Address . . . . . : fe80::50a5:8a35:a5bb:66e1
   Default Gateway . . . . . . . . . : fe80::1
C:\>
```

Note

To ensure the uniqueness of any IPv6 unicast address, the client may use a process known as duplicate address detection (DAD). This is similar to an ARP request for its own address. If there is no reply, then the address is unique.

Interactive Graphic

Check Your Understanding—Dynamic Addressing for IPv6 GUAs (33.3.8)

Refer to the online course to complete this activity.

Dynamic Addressing for IPv6 LLAs (33.4)

This section discusses how a device automatically creates an IPv6 link-local address.

Dynamic LLAs (33.4.1)

All IPv6 devices must have an IPv6 LLA. Like IPv6 GUAs, you can also create LLAs dynamically. Regardless of how you create your LLAs (and your GUAs), it is important that you verify all IPv6 address configuration. This topic explains dynamically generated LLAs and IPv6 configuration verification.

Figure 33-16 shows the LLA is dynamically created using the fe80::/10 prefix and the interface ID using the EUI-64 process, or a randomly generated 64-bit number.

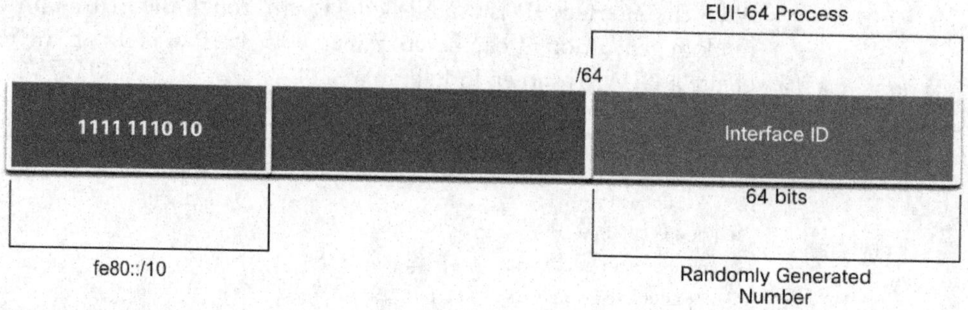

Figure 33-16 Dynamic Creation of an LLA

Dynamic LLAs on Windows (33.4.2)

Operating systems, such as Windows, will typically use the same method for both a SLAAC-created GUA and a dynamically assigned LLA. See the highlighted areas in Examples 33-5 and 33-6 that were shown previously.

Example 33-5 EUI-64 Generated Interface ID

```
C:\> ipconfig
Windows IP Configuration
Ethernet adapter Local Area Connection:
Connection-specific DNS Suffix . :
IPv6 Address. . . . . . . . . . . . : 2001:db8:acad:1:fc99:47ff:fe75:cee0
Link-local IPv6 Address . . . . . . : fe80::fc99:47ff:fe75:cee0
Default Gateway . . . . . . . . . . : fe80::1
C:\>
```

Example 33-6 Random 64-bit Generated Interface ID

```
C:\> ipconfig
Windows IP Configuration
Ethernet adapter Local Area Connection:
   Connection-specific DNS Suffix  . :
   IPv6 Address. . . . . . . . . . . . : 2001:db8:acad:1:50a5:8a35:a5bb:66e1
   Link-local IPv6 Address . . . . . : fe80::50a5:8a35:a5bb:66e1
   Default Gateway . . . . . . . . . : fe80::1
C:\>
```

Dynamic LLAs on Cisco Routers (33.4.3)

Cisco routers automatically create an IPv6 LLA whenever a GUA is assigned to the interface. By default, Cisco IOS routers use EUI-64 to generate the interface ID for all LLAs on IPv6 interfaces. For serial interfaces, the router will use the MAC address of an Ethernet interface. Recall that an LLA must be unique only on that link or network. However, a drawback to using the dynamically assigned LLA is its long interface ID, which makes it challenging to identify and remember assigned addresses. Example 33-7 displays the MAC address on the GigabitEthernet 0/0/0 interface of router R1. This address is used to dynamically create the LLA on the same interface, and also for the Serial 0/1/0 interface.

To make it easier to recognize and remember these addresses on routers, it is common to statically configure IPv6 LLAs on routers.

Example 33-7 IPv6 LLA Using EUI-64 on Router R1

```
R1# show interface gigabitEthernet 0/0/0
GigabitEthernet0/0/0 is up, line protocol is up
  Hardware is ISR4221-2x1GE, address is 7079.b392.3640 (bia 7079.b392.3640)
(Output omitted)
R1# show ipv6 interface brief
GigabitEthernet0/0/0    [up/up]
    FE80::7279:B3FF:FE92:3640
    2001:DB8:ACAD:1::1
GigabitEthernet0/0/1    [up/up]
    FE80::7279:B3FF:FE92:3641
    2001:DB8:ACAD:2::1
Serial0/1/0              [up/up]
    FE80::7279:B3FF:FE92:3640
    2001:DB8:ACAD:3::1
Serial0/1/1              [down/down]
    unassigned
R1#
```

Verify IPv6 Address Configuration (33.4.4)

Figure 33-17 shows the example topology.

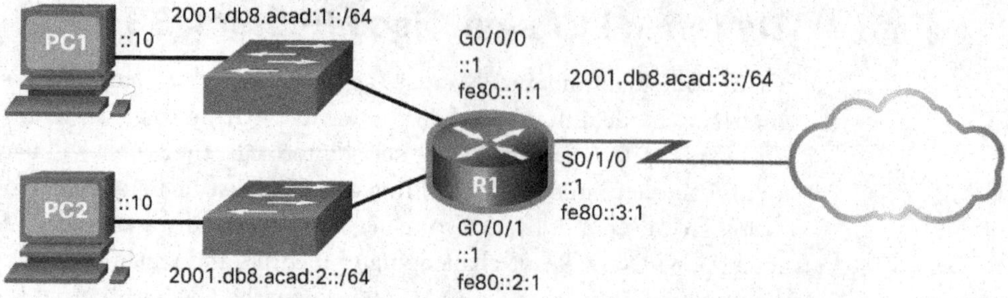

Figure 33-17 IPv6 Addressing Topology

The **show ipv6 interface brief** command in Example 33-8 displays the MAC address of the Ethernet interfaces. EUI-64 uses this MAC address to generate the interface ID for the LLA. Additionally, the **show ipv6 interface brief** command displays abbreviated output for each of the interfaces. The [up/up] output on the same line as the interface indicates the Layer 1/Layer 2 interface state. This is the same as the Status and Protocol columns in the equivalent IPv4 command.

Example 33-8 The **show ipv6 interface brief** Command on R1

```
R1# show ipv6 interface brief
GigabitEthernet0/0/0    [up/up]
    FE80::1:1
    2001:DB8:ACAD:1::1
GigabitEthernet0/0/1    [up/up]
    FE80::1:2
    2001:DB8:ACAD:2::1
Serial0/1/0             [up/up]
    FE80::1:3
    2001:DB8:ACAD:3::1
Serial0/1/1             [down/down]
    unassigned
R1#
```

Notice that each interface has two IPv6 addresses. The second address for each interface is the GUA that was configured. The first address, the one that begins with fe80, is the link-local unicast address for the interface. Recall that the LLA is automatically added to the interface when a GUA is assigned.

Also, notice that the R1 Serial 0/1/0 LLA is the same as its GigabitEthernet 0/0/0 interface. Serial interfaces do not have Ethernet MAC addresses, so Cisco IOS uses the MAC address of the first available Ethernet interface. This is possible because link-local interfaces only have to be unique on that link.

As shown in Example 33-9, the **show ipv6 route** command can be used to verify that IPv6 networks and specific IPv6 interface addresses have been installed in the IPv6 routing table. The **show ipv6 route** command will only display IPv6 networks, not IPv4 networks.

Example 33-9 The **show ipv6 route** Command on R1

```
R1# show ipv6 route
IPv6 Routing Table - default - 7 entries
Codes: C - Connected, L - Local, S - Static, U - Per-user Static route

C    2001:DB8:ACAD:1::/64 [0/0]
      via GigabitEthernet0/0/0, directly connected
L    2001:DB8:ACAD:1::1/128 [0/0]
      via GigabitEthernet0/0/0, receive
C    2001:DB8:ACAD:2::/64 [0/0]
      via GigabitEthernet0/0/1, directly connected
L    2001:DB8:ACAD:2::1/128 [0/0]
      via GigabitEthernet0/0/1, receive
C    2001:DB8:ACAD:3::/64 [0/0]
      via Serial0/1/0, directly connected
L    2001:DB8:ACAD:3::1/128 [0/0]
      via Serial0/1/0, receive
L    FF00::/8 [0/0]
      via Null0, receive
R1#
```

Within the route table, a **C** next to a route indicates that this is a directly connected network. When the router interface is configured with a GUA and is in the "up/up" state, the IPv6 prefix and prefix length are added to the IPv6 routing table as a connected route.

Note

The **L** indicates a Local route, the specific IPv6 address assigned to the interface. This is not an LLA. LLAs are not included in the routing table of the router because they are not routable addresses.

The IPv6 GUA configured on the interface is also installed in the routing table as a local route. The local route has a /128 prefix. Local routes are used by the routing table to efficiently process packets with a destination address of the router interface address.

The **ping** command for IPv6 is identical to the command used with IPv4, except that an IPv6 address is used. As shown in Example 33-10, the command is used to verify Layer 3 connectivity between R1 and PC1. When pinging an LLA from a router, Cisco IOS will prompt the user for the exit interface. Because the destination LLA can be on one or more of its links or networks, the router needs to know which interface to send the ping to.

Example 33-10 The **ping** Command on R1

```
R1# ping 2001:db8:acad:1::10
Type escape sequence to abort.
Sending 5, 100-byte ICMP Echos to 2001:DB8:ACAD:1::10, timeout is 2 seconds:
!!!!!
Success rate is 100 percent (5/5), round-trip min/avg/max = 1/1/1 ms
R1#
```

Interactive Graphic

Syntax Checker—Verify IPv6 Address Configuration (33.4.5)

Refer to the online course to complete this activity.

Packet Tracer Activity

Packet Tracer—Configure IPv6 Addressing (33.4.6)

In this activity, you will practice configuring IPv6 addresses on a router, servers, and clients. You will also practice verifying your IPv6 addressing implementation.

Refer to the online course to complete this activity.

IPv6 Multicast Addresses (33.5)

This section introduces the two types of IPv6 multicast addresses: well-known multicast and solicited-node multicast addresses.

Assigned IPv6 Multicast Addresses (33.5.1)

Earlier in this chapter, you learned that there are three broad categories of IPv6 addresses: unicast, anycast, and multicast. This section goes into more detail about multicast addresses.

IPv6 multicast addresses are similar to IPv4 multicast addresses. Recall that a multicast address is used to send a single packet to one or more destinations (multicast group). IPv6 multicast addresses have the prefix ff00::/8.

Note

Multicast addresses can only be destination addresses and not source addresses.

There are two types of IPv6 multicast addresses:

- Well-known multicast addresses
- Solicited-node multicast addresses

Well-Known IPv6 Multicast Addresses (33.5.2)

Well-known IPv6 multicast addresses are assigned. Assigned multicast addresses are reserved multicast addresses for predefined groups of devices. An assigned multicast address is a single address used to reach a group of devices running a common protocol or service. Assigned multicast addresses are used in context with specific protocols such as DHCPv6.

These are two common IPv6 assigned multicast groups:

- **ff02::1 All-nodes multicast group**—This is a multicast group that all IPv6-enabled devices join. A packet sent to this group is received and processed by all IPv6 interfaces on the link or network. This has the same effect as a broadcast address in IPv4. Figure 33-18 shows an example of communication using the all-nodes multicast address. An IPv6 router sends ICMPv6 RA messages to the all-nodes multicast group.
- **ff02::2 All-routers multicast group**—This is a multicast group that all IPv6 routers join. A router becomes a member of this group when it is enabled as an IPv6 router with the **ipv6 unicast-routing** global configuration command. A packet sent to this group is received and processed by all IPv6 routers on the link or network.

The fourth digit in the address refers to the scope. A 2 for the scope indicates that these addresses have "link-local scope," meaning packets with this destination address are not be routed off this link or network.

IPv6-enabled devices send ICMPv6 RS messages to the all-routers multicast address. The RS message requests an RA message from the IPv6 router to assist the device in its address configuration. The IPv6 router responds with an RA message, as shown in Figure 33-18.

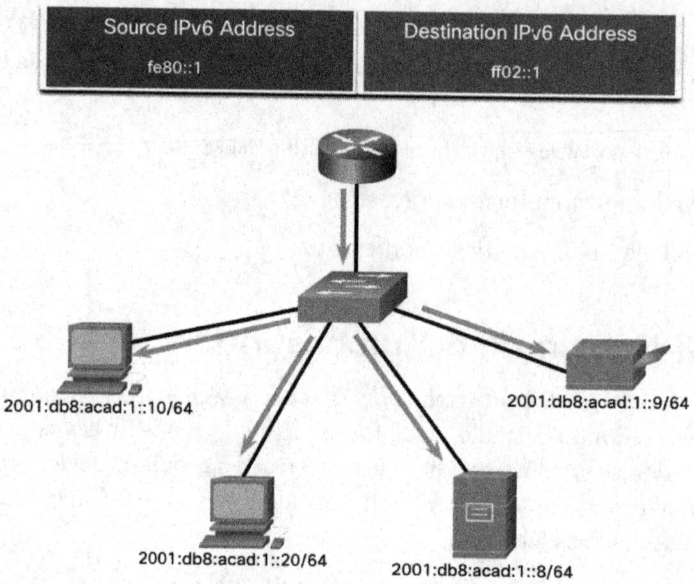

Figure 33-18 IPv6 All-Nodes Multicast: RA Message

Solicited-Node IPv6 Multicast Addresses (33.5.3)

A *solicited-node multicast address* is similar to the all-nodes multicast address. The advantage of a solicited-node multicast address is that it is mapped to a special Ethernet multicast address. This allows the Ethernet NIC to filter the frame by examining the destination MAC address without sending it to the IPv6 process to see if the device is the intended target of the IPv6 packet, as shown in Figure 33-19.

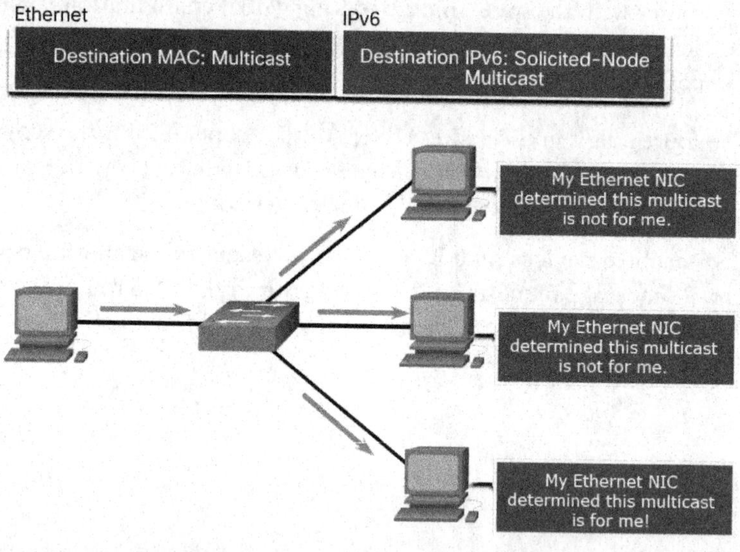

Figure 33-19 Solicited-Node IPv6 Multicast Example

Summary (33.6)

The following is a summary of each topic in the chapter and some questions for your reflection.

What Did I Learn in This Chapter? (33.6.1)

- **IPv6 Address Types**—There are three types of IPv6 addresses: unicast, multicast, and anycast. IPv6 does not use the dotted-decimal subnet mask notation. Like IPv4, the prefix length is represented in slash notation and is used to indicate the network portion of an IPv6 address. An IPv6 unicast address uniquely identifies an interface on an IPv6-enabled device. IPv6 addresses typically have two unicast addresses: global unique address (GUA) and link-local address (LLA). IPv6 unique local addresses have the following uses: they are used for local addressing within a site or between a limited number of sites, they can be used for devices that will never need to access another network, and they are not globally routed or translated to a global IPv6 address. IPv6 GUAs are globally unique and routable on the IPv6 Internet. These addresses are equivalent to public IPv4 addresses. A GUA has three parts: a global routing prefix, a Subnet ID, and an interface ID. An IPv6 LLA enables a device to communicate with other IPv6-enabled devices on the same link and only on that link (subnet). Devices can obtain an LLA either statically or dynamically.
- **GUA and LLA Static Configuration**—The Cisco IOS command to configure an IPv4 address on an interface is **ip address** *ip-address subnet-mask*. In contrast, the command to configure an IPv6 GUA on an interface is **ipv6 address** *ipv6-address/prefix-length*. Just as with IPv4, configuring static addresses on clients does not scale to larger environments. For this reason, most network administrators in an IPv6 network will enable dynamic assignment of IPv6 addresses. Configuring the LLA manually lets you create an address that is recognizable and easier to remember. Typically, it is only necessary to create recognizable LLAs on routers. LLAs can be configured manually using the **ipv6 address** *ipv6-link-local-address* **link-local** command.
- **Dynamic Addressing for IPv6 GUAs**—A device obtains a GUA dynamically through ICMPv6 messages. IPv6 routers periodically send out ICMPv6 RA messages, every 200 seconds, to all IPv6-enabled devices on the network. An RA message will also be sent in response to a host sending an ICMPv6 RS message, which is a request for an RA message. The ICMPv6 RA message includes: network prefix and prefix length, default gateway address, and the DNS addresses and domain name. RA messages have three methods: SLAAC, SLAAC with a stateless DHCPv6 server, and stateful DHCPv6 (no SLAAC). With SLAAC, the client device uses the information in the RA message to create its own GUA

because the message contains the prefix and the interface ID. With SLAAC with stateless DHCPv6 the RA message suggests devices use SLAAC to create their own IPv6 GUA, use the router LLA as the default gateway address, and use a stateless DHCPv6 server to obtain other necessary information.

With stateful DHCPv6 the RA suggests that devices use the router LLA as the default gateway address, and the stateful DHCPv6 server to obtain a GUA, a DNS server address, domain name, and all other necessary information. The interface ID can be created using the EUI-64 process or a randomly generated 64-bit number. The EUIs process uses the 48-bit Ethernet MAC address of the client and inserts another 16 bits in the middle of the MAC address to create a 64-bit interface ID. Depending upon the operating system, a device may use a randomly generated interface ID.

- **Dynamic Addressing for IPv6 LLAs**—All IPv6 devices must have an IPv6 LLA. An LLA can be configured manually or created dynamically. Operating systems, such as Windows, will typically use the same method for both a SLAAC-created GUA and a dynamically assigned LLA. Cisco routers automatically create an IPv6 LLA whenever a GUA is assigned to the interface. By default, Cisco IOS routers use EUI-64 to generate the interface ID for all LLAs on IPv6 interfaces. For serial interfaces, the router will use the MAC address of an Ethernet interface. To make it easier to recognize and remember these addresses on routers, it is common to statically configure IPv6 LLAs on routers. To verify IPv6 address configuration, use the following three commands: **show ipv6 interface brief**, **show ipv6 route**, and **ping**.

- **IPv6 Multicast Addresses**—There are two types of IPv6 multicast addresses: well-known multicast addresses and solicited-node multicast addresses. Assigned multicast addresses are reserved multicast addresses for predefined groups of devices. Well-known multicast addresses are assigned. Two common IPv6 assigned multicast groups are: ff02::1 All-nodes multicast group and ff02::2 All-routers multicast group. A solicited-node multicast address is similar to the all-nodes multicast address. The advantage of a solicited-node multicast address is that it is mapped to a special Ethernet multicast address.

Reflection Questions (33.6.2)

This chapter had a lot of information about IPv6! You learned that there are three types of IPv6 addresses: unicast, multicast, and anycast. IPv6 does not use the dotted-decimal subnet mask notation.

- What did you learn about static addressing for LLA and GUA?
- What is an advantage in static addressing?
- At your office or university, what would be a disadvantage of static addressing?

Practice

The following activity provides practice with the topics introduced in this chapter.

Packet Tracer Activity

Packet Tracer Activities

Packet Tracer 33.6.6: Configure IPv6 Addressing

Check Your Understanding Questions

Complete all the review questions listed here to test your understanding of the topics and concepts in this chapter. Appendix A, "Answers to 'Check Your Understanding' Questions," lists the answers.

1. What is indicated by a successful ping to the ::1 IPv6 address?

   a. The host is cabled correctly.

   b. The default gateway address is configured correctly.

   c. All hosts on the local link are available.

   d. The link-local address is correctly configured.

   e. IP is properly installed on the host.

2. What is the most compressed representation of the IPv6 address 2001:0db8:0000:abcd:0000:0000:0000:0001?

   a. 2001:0db8:abcd::1

   b. 2001:db8:0:abcd::1

   c. 2001:0db8:abcd::1

   d. 2001:0db8:0000:abcd::1

   e. 2001:db8::abcd:0:1

3. At a minimum, which address is required on IPv6-enabled interfaces?

   a. Link-local

   b. Unique local

   c. Site local

   d. Global unicast

4. What is the interface ID of the IPv6 address 2001:db8::1000:a9cd:47ff:fe57:fe94/64?
   a. fe94
   b. fe57:fe94
   c. 47ff:fe57:fe94
   d. a9cd:47ff:fe57:fe94
   e. 1000:a9cd:47ff:fe57:fe94

5. What is the valid most compressed format possible of the IPv6 address 2001:0db8:0000:ab00:0000:0000:0000:1234?
   a. 2001:db8:0:ab00::1234
   b. 2001:db8:0:ab::1234
   c. 2001:db8:0000:ab::1234
   d. 2001:db8:0:ab:0::1234

6. What is the prefix associated with the IPv6 address 2001:db8:d15:ea:cc44::1/64?
   a. 2001::/64
   b. 2001:db8::/64
   c. 2001:db8:d15:ea::/64
   d. 2001:db8:d15:ea:cc44::/64

7. What type of address is automatically assigned to an interface when IPv6 is enabled on that interface?
   a. Global unicast
   b. Link-local
   c. Loopback
   d. Unique local

8. Your organization is issued the IPv6 prefix of 2001:0:130f::/48 by your service provider. With this prefix, how many bits are available for your organization to create /64 subnetworks if interface ID bits are not borrowed?
   a. 8
   b. 16
   c. 80
   d. 128

9. What is the network address for the IPv6 address 2001:db8:aa04:b5::1/64?

   a. 2001::/64
   b. 2001:db8::/64
   c. 2001:db8:aa04::/64
   d. 2001:db8:aa04:b5::/64

10. Which type of IPv6 address is not routable and is used only for communication on a single subnet?

   a. Global unicast address
   b. Link-local address
   c. Loopback address
   d. Unique local address
   e. Unspecified address

11. Which address type is not supported in IPv6?

   a. Private
   b. Multicast
   c. Unicast
   d. Broadcast

CHAPTER 34

IPv6 Neighbor Discovery

Objectives

Upon completion of this chapter, you will be able to answer the following question:

- What is the operation of IPv6 neighbor discovery?

Key Terms

There are no new terms in this chapter.

Introduction (34.0)

Webster here! Halimah is still investigating her company's network. She is impressed with the way the IT team has structured it. She knows about IPv6 Neighbor Discovery (ND) and, in this chapter, you will learn about it too.

IPv6 ND is how IPv6-addressed devices resolve MAC addresses. IPv6 ND lets devices with IPv6 addresses communicate with other devices on a network, which is, let's face it, the whole reason for having a network.

So, given how important this subject is, let's get started!

Neighbor Discovery Operation (34.1)

This section discusses the relationship between MAC and IPv6 addresses and how the Neighbor Discovery (ND) protocol is used to map the two addresses.

Video

Video—IPv6 Neighbor Discovery (34.1.1)

If your network is using the IPv6 communications protocol, the Neighbor Discovery protocol, or ND, is what you need to match IPv6 addresses to MAC addresses. This topic explains how ND works.

Refer to the online course to view this video.

IPv6 Neighbor Discovery Messages (34.1.2)

IPv6 Neighbor Discovery protocol is sometimes referred to as ND or NDP. In this course, we will refer to it as ND. ND provides address resolution, router discovery, and redirection services for IPv6 using ICMPv6. ICMPv6 ND uses five ICMPv6 messages to perform these services:

- Neighbor Solicitation messages
- Neighbor Advertisement messages
- Router Solicitation messages
- Router Advertisement messages
- Redirect message

Neighbor Solicitation and Neighbor Advertisement messages are used for device-to-device messaging such as address resolution (similar to ARP for IPv4). Devices include both host computers and routers, as shown in Figures 34-1 and 34-2.

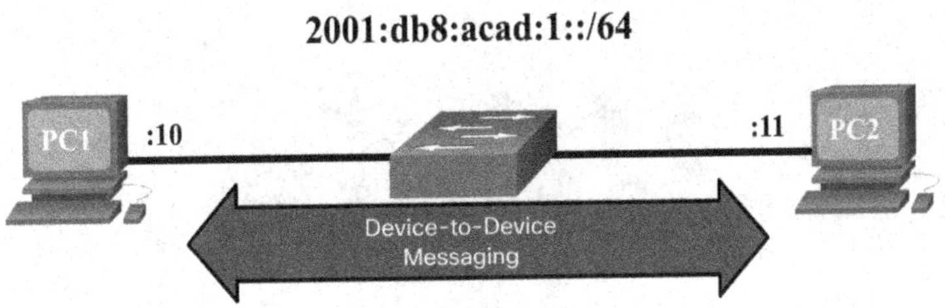

Figure 34-1 Device-to-Device Messaging

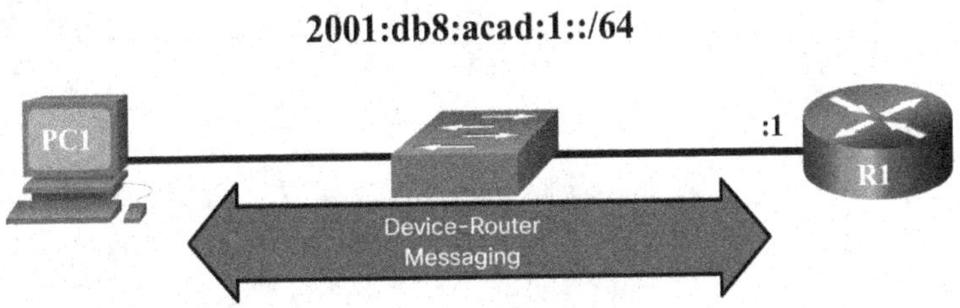

Figure 34-2 Device-Router Messaging

Router Solicitation and Router Advertisement messages are for messaging between devices and routers. Typically router discovery is used for dynamic address allocation and Stateless Address Autoconfiguration (SLAAC).

Note

The fifth ICMPv6 ND message is a Redirect message, which is used for better next-hop selection. This is beyond the scope of this course.

IPv6 ND is defined in the IETF RFC 4861.

IPv6 Neighbor Discovery—Address Resolution (34.1.3)

Much like ARP for IPv4, IPv6 devices use IPv6 ND to determine the MAC address of a device that has a known IPv6 address.

ICMPv6 Neighbor Solicitation and Neighbor Advertisement messages are used for MAC address resolution. This is similar to ARP requests and ARP replies used by ARP for IPv4. For example, assume PC1 wants to ping PC2 at IPv6 address 2001:db8:acad::11. To determine the MAC address for the known IPv6 address, PC1 sends an ICMPv6 Neighbor Solicitation message as illustrated in Figure 34-3.

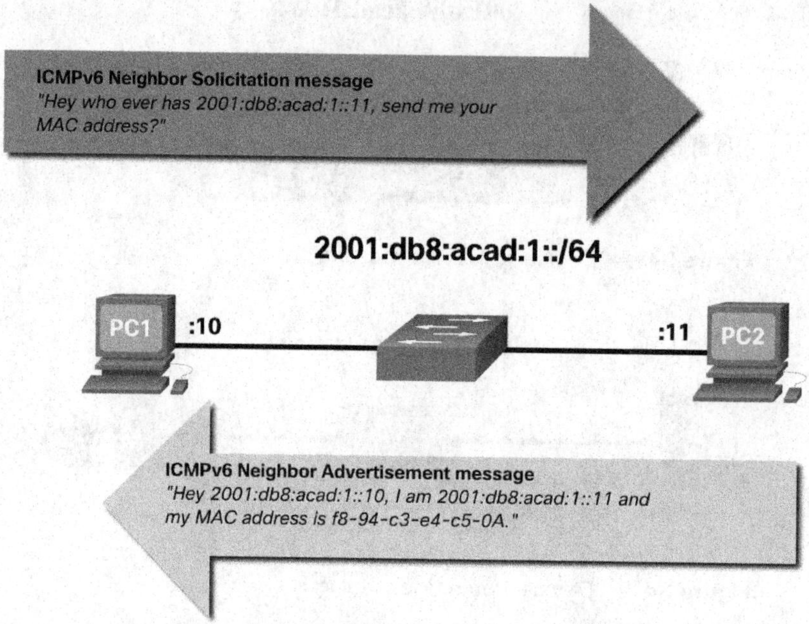

Figure 34-3 IPv6 Neighbor Discovery Process

ICMPv6 Neighbor Solicitation messages are sent using special Ethernet and IPv6 multicast addresses. This allows the Ethernet NIC of the receiving device to determine whether the Neighbor Solicitation message is for itself without having to send it to the operating system for processing.

PC2 replies to the request with an ICMPv6 Neighbor Advertisement message, which includes its MAC address.

Packet Tracer Activity

Packet Tracer—IPv6 Neighbor Discovery (34.1.4)

In order for a device to communicate with another device, the MAC address of the destination device must be known. With IPv6, a process called Neighbor Discovery is responsible for determining the destination MAC address. You will gather PDU information in simulation mode to better understand the process. There is no Packet Tracer scoring for this activity.

Refer to the online course to complete this activity.

Interactive Graphic

Check Your Understanding—Neighbor Discovery (34.1.5)

Refer to the online course to complete this activity.

Summary (34.2)

The following is a summary of each topic in the chapter.

What Did I Learn in This Chapter? (34.2.1)

IPv6 does not use ARP; it uses the ND protocol to resolve MAC addresses. ND provides address resolution, router discovery, and redirection services for IPv6 using ICMPv6. ICMPv6 ND uses five ICMPv6 messages to perform these services: Neighbor Solicitation, Neighbor Advertisement, Router Solicitation, Router Advertisement, and Redirect. Much like ARP for IPv4, IPv6 devices use IPv6 ND to resolve the MAC address of a device to a known IPv6 address.

Practice

The following activity provides practice with the topics introduced in this chapter.

Packet Tracer Activities

Packet Tracer Activity

Packet Tracer 34.1.4—IPv6 Neighbor Discovery

Check Your Understanding Questions

Complete all the review questions listed here to test your understanding of the topics and concepts in this chapter. Appendix A, "Answers to 'Check Your Understanding' Questions," lists the answers.

1. What address scope is used in the IPv6 frame to ensure that an IPv6 Neighbor Solicitation message would not be forwarded by routers?

   a. Site-local scope
   b. Link-local scope
   c. Subnet-local scope
   d. Interface-local scope

2. What type of data transmission does an IPv6 host use to send a Neighbor Solicitation message?

   a. Unicast
   b. Anycast
   c. Multicast
   d. Broadcast

3. Which protocol provides messages to support IPv6 address resolution?

   a. DNS
   b. ARP
   c. ICMPv6
   d. DHCPv6

4. Which method would an IPv6-enabled host using SLAAC employ to learn the address of the default gateway?

   a. Router Advertisement messages received from the local router
   b. Neighbor Solicitation messages sent to link neighbors

c. Neighbor Advertisement messages received from link neighbors
d. Router Solicitation messages received from the link router

5. Which message should an IPv6 host send in response to a request of its MAC address?

a. Router Solicitation message
b. Neighbor Solicitation message
c. Router Advertisement message
d. Neighbor Advertisement message

6. IPv6 host A is sending a Neighbor Solicitation message to IPv6 host B on the same Ethernet network. What address type is used in the Destination MAC field of the Ethernet frame header?

a. Unicast MAC address
b. Anycast MAC address
c. Multicast MAC address
d. Broadcast MAC address

7. Which two ICMPv6 messages are used during the Ethernet MAC address resolution process? (Choose two.)

a. Router Solicitation
b. Router Advertisement
c. Neighbor Solicitation
d. Neighbor Advertisement
e. Echo Request

CHAPTER 35

Cisco Switches and Routers

Objectives

Upon completion of this chapter, you will be able to answer the following questions:

- What are Cisco LAN switches?
- What are the available switch forwarding methods and port settings on Layer 2 switch ports?
- What is the Cisco LAN switch boot process?
- What are Cisco small business routers?
- What is the Cisco router boot process?

Key Terms

This chapter uses the following key terms. You can find the definitions in the Glossary.

automatic medium-dependent interface crossover (auto-MDIX) Page 641

cut-through switching Page 635

fast-forward switching Page 637

fragment-free switching Page 637

store-and-forward switching Page 635

Introduction (35.0)

I'm back! Halimah told me that she has been given her first assignment. She will be helping to design and set up a new branch network. She is very excited about this opportunity!

If I had this task, I'm not sure I'd know quite where to start. I know about the devices and media needed, and about addressing schemes. But I have never set up a switch, let alone more than one switch. I've set up my home network router, but an enterprise router is probably a bit more complex.

I think this chapter is exactly what I need. How about you?

Cisco Switches (35.1)

Ethernet switches are Layer 2 devices that forward Ethernet frames. Switches can be interconnected to allow more devices to be connected.

Connect More Devices (35.1.1)

Home and small business networks usually do not require more than one or two networking devices in order to function efficiently. A wireless router, equipped with wireless connections and a few wired connections, is the only piece of networking equipment that is necessary in order to provide sufficient connectivity for the average small group of users. These routers are configured through a web browser and have an easy-to-use graphical user interface (GUI) that guides you through the most common configuration items.

Wireless routers that are designed primarily for home use are not appropriate for most business networks that must support more than a few users. Modern networks use a variety of devices for connectivity. Each device has certain capabilities for controlling the flow of data across a network. A general rule is that the higher the device is in the OSI model, the more intelligent it is. What this means is that a higher-level device can better analyze the data traffic and forward it based on information not available at lower layers. As an example, a Layer 2 switch can filter the data and send it only out of the port that is connected to the destination, based on the MAC address.

As switches and routers evolve, the distinction between them may seem blurred. One simple distinction remains: LAN switches provide connectivity within the local area networks of the organization, while routers interconnect local networks and are needed in a wide area network (WAN) environment. In other words, a switch is used to connect devices on the same network. A router is used to connect multiple networks to each other.

Figure 35-1 shows a series of Cisco switches.

Figure 35-1 Cisco Catalyst 9300 Series Switches

Figure 35-2 shows a series of Cisco routers.

Figure 35-2 Cisco 4300 Series Routers

In addition to switches and routers, there are other connectivity options available for LANs. Wireless access points that are deployed in enterprises enable computers and other devices, such as IP phones, to wirelessly connect to the network, or share broadband connectivity. Firewalls guard against network threats and provide security, network control, and containment.

Cisco LAN Switches (35.1.2)

When a LAN grows to the point where the four Ethernet ports provided by the wireless router are not enough for all of the devices that need to attach to the wired network, it is time to add a LAN switch to the network. A switch can provide connectivity at the access layer of a network, connecting devices to a LAN. A switch can allow the network to grow without replacing central devices. When choosing a switch, there are a number of factors to consider, including the following:

- Type of ports
- Speed required

- Expandability
- Manageability

Type of Ports

When selecting a switch for your LAN, choosing the appropriate number and type of ports is critical. Most lower-cost switches support only copper twisted-pair interface ports. Higher-priced switches may have fiber-optic connections. These are used to link the switch to other switches that may be located over long distances. The Cisco Catalyst 9300 series (Figure 35-3) has a variety of options depending on your environment.

Figure 35-3 The Cisco Catalyst 9300 Series

Speed Required

Ethernet twisted-pair interfaces on a switch have defined speeds. A 10/100 Ethernet port can only function at either 10 megabits per second (Mbps) or 100 Mbps. What this means is that even if the device that you are connecting to the 10/100 switch interface port is capable of connecting at gigabit speeds, the maximum speed at which it will be able to communicate will be 100 Mbps. Switches may also include Gigabit Ethernet ports. If your Internet connection is more than 100 Mbps, then a Gigabit Ethernet port is necessary to take advantage of the higher Internet bandwidth. Gigabit Ethernet ports will also operate at 10/100 Mbps. Gigabit Ethernet is sometimes represented as 1000 Mbps. The Cisco Catalyst 9300 48S switch in Figure 35-4 has two 40 Gbps uplink ports to provide a fast path for the 48 ports to access the rest of the network and the Internet.

Figure 35-4 The Cisco Catalyst 9300 48S Switch

Similar to a switch port, Ethernet NICs operate at specific bandwidths such as 10/100 or 10/100/1000 Mbps. The actual bandwidth of the attached device will be the highest common bandwidth between the NIC on the device and the switch port.

Expandability

Networking devices come in both fixed and modular physical configurations. Fixed configurations have a specific type and number of ports or interfaces. Modular devices have expansion slots that provide the flexibility to add new modules as required. Figure 35-5 shows a Cisco Catalyst 9600 chassis in which you can install different configurations of hardware to address your particular environment.

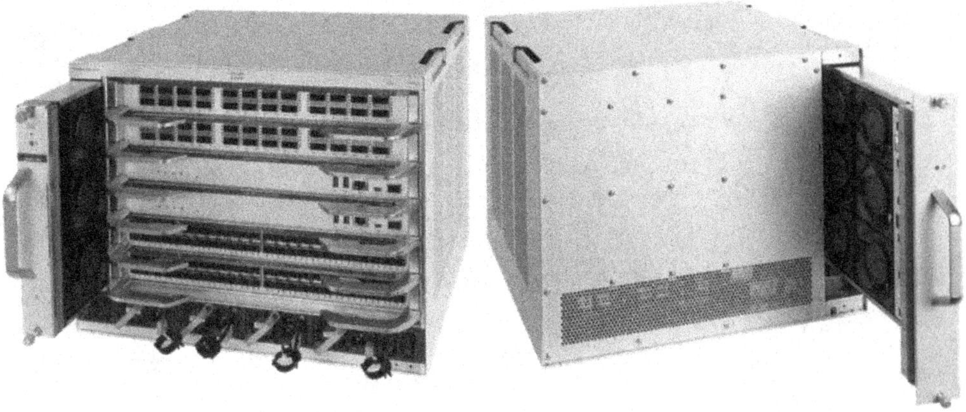

Figure 35-5 Cisco Catalyst 9600 Chassis

Manageability

Many basic, inexpensive switches are not configurable. A managed switch that uses a Cisco operating system enables control over individual ports or over the switch as a whole. Controls include the ability to change the settings for a device, add port security, and monitor performance. The network administrator in Figure 35-6 is directly connecting to a Cisco Catalyst switch using a console cable.

Figure 35-6 Network Administrator Managing Network Switches

Video

Video—Components of a LAN Switch—Part 1 (35.1.3)

Refer to the online course to view this video.

Video

Video—Components of a LAN Switch—Part 2 (35.1.4)

Refer to the online course to view this video.

LAN Switch Components (35.1.5)

The Cisco Catalyst 9300 switch shown in Figure 35-7 is suitable for small- and medium-sized networks. It provides 24 1 Gbps data ports with Power over Ethernet (PoE) so that some device types can be directly powered from the switch. It also has two modular 40 Gbps uplink ports. The LEDs indicate the port and system status of the switch. The switch is equipped with a console and storage ports for device management.

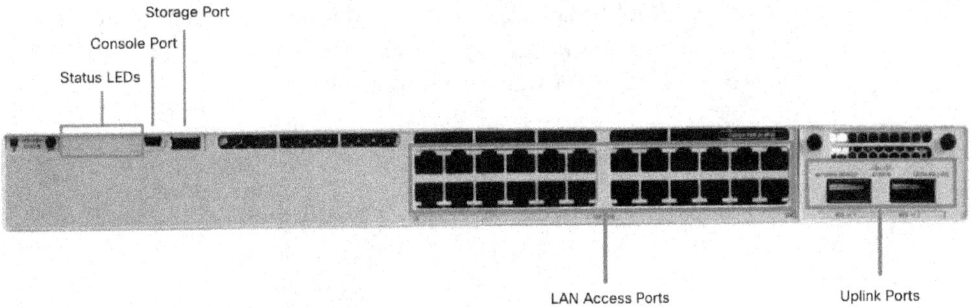

Figure 35-7 Cisco Catalyst 9300 24 UPOE Switch

Switch Speeds and Forwarding Methods (35.2)

Switches may have the capability to implement various forwarding methods to increase performance.

Frame Forwarding Methods on Cisco Switches (35.2.1)

As you learned previously, switches use their MAC address tables to determine which port to use to forward frames. With Cisco switches, there are actually two frame forwarding methods and there are good reasons to use one instead of the other, depending on the situation.

Switches use one of the following forwarding methods for switching data between network ports:

- *Store-and-forward switching*—This frame forwarding method receives the entire frame and computes the CRC. CRC uses a mathematical formula, based on the number of bits (1s) in the frame, to determine whether the received frame has an error. If the CRC is valid, the switch looks up the destination address, which determines the outgoing interface. Then the frame is forwarded out of the correct port.
- *Cut-through switching*—This frame forwarding method forwards the frame before it is entirely received. At a minimum, the destination address of the frame must be read before the frame can be forwarded.

A big advantage of store-and-forward switching is that it determines if a frame has errors before propagating the frame. When an error is detected in a frame, the switch discards the frame. Discarding frames with errors reduces the amount of bandwidth consumed by corrupt data. Store-and-forward switching is required for quality of

service (QoS) analysis on converged networks where frame classification for traffic prioritization is necessary. For example, voice over IP (VoIP) data streams need to have priority over web-browsing traffic.

Figure 35-8 shows the store-and-forward process.

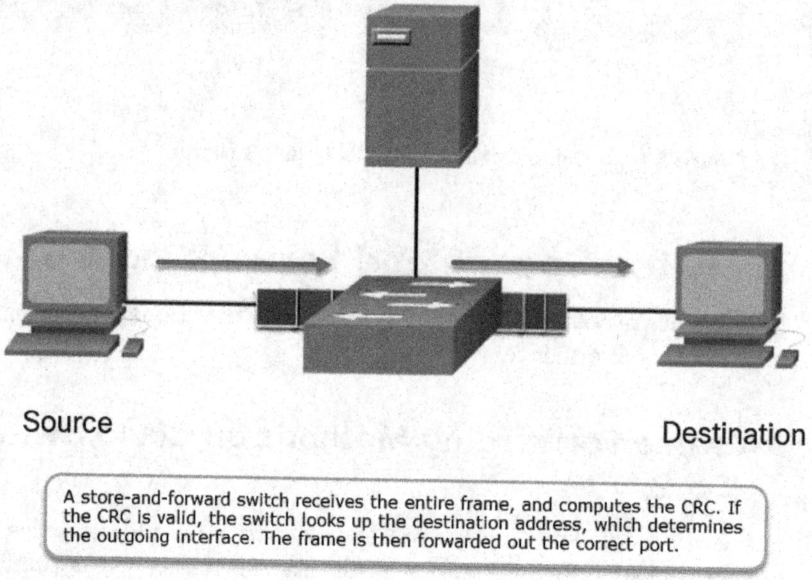

Figure 35-8 Store-and-Forward Switching

Cut-Through Switching (35.2.2)

In cut-through switching, the switch acts upon the data as soon as it is received, even if the transmission is not complete. The switch buffers just enough of the frame to read the destination MAC address so that it can determine to which port it should forward out the data. The destination MAC address is located in the first 6 bytes of the frame following the preamble. The switch looks up the destination MAC address in its switching table, determines the outgoing interface port, and forwards the frame onto its destination through the designated switch port. The switch does not perform any error checking on the frame.

Figure 35-9 shows the cut-through switching process.

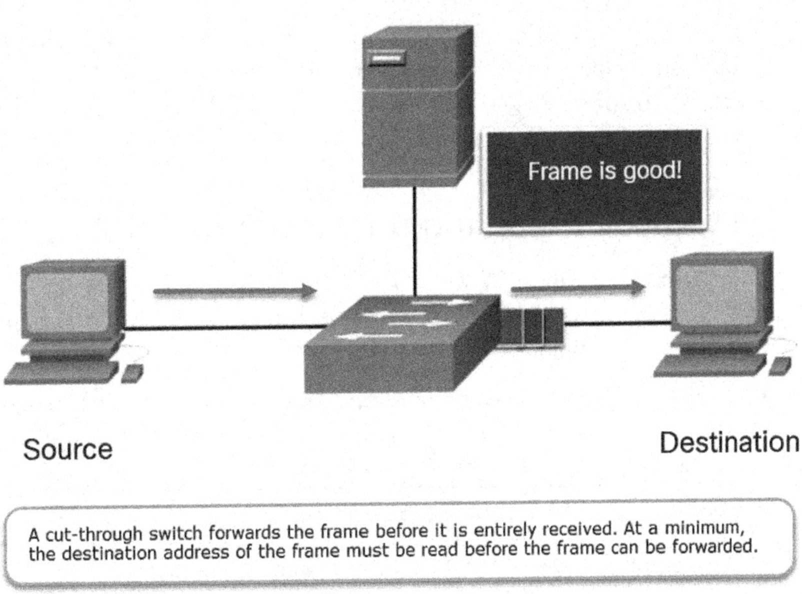

Figure 35-9 Cut-Through Switching

There are two variants of cut-through switching:

- *Fast-forward switching*—Fast-forward switching offers the lowest level of latency. Fast-forward switching immediately forwards a packet after reading the destination address. Because fast-forward switching starts forwarding before the entire packet has been received, there may be times when packets are relayed with errors. This occurs infrequently, and the destination NIC discards the faulty packet upon receipt. In fast-forward mode, latency is measured from the first bit received to the first bit transmitted. Fast-forward switching is the typical cut-through method of switching.
- *Fragment-free switching*—In fragment-free switching, the switch stores the first 64 bytes of the frame before forwarding. Fragment-free switching can be viewed as a compromise between store-and-forward switching and fast-forward switching. The reason fragment-free switching stores only the first 64 bytes of the frame is that most network errors and collisions occur during the first 64 bytes. Fragment-free switching tries to enhance fast-forward switching by performing a small error check on the first 64 bytes of the frame to ensure that a collision has not occurred before forwarding the frame. Fragment-free switching is a compromise between the high latency and high integrity of store-and-forward switching and the low latency and reduced integrity of fast-forward switching.

Some switches are configured to perform cut-through switching on a per-port basis until a user-defined error threshold is reached, and then they automatically change to store-and-forward. When the error rate falls below the threshold, the port automatically changes back to cut-through switching.

Memory Buffering on Switches (35.2.3)

An Ethernet switch may use a buffering technique to store frames before forwarding them. Buffering may also be used when the destination port is busy because of congestion. The switch stores the frame until it can be transmitted.

As shown in Table 35-1, there are two methods of memory buffering.

Table 35-1 Memory Buffering Methods

Method	Description
Port-based memory	■ Frames are stored in queues that are linked to specific incoming and outgoing ports. ■ A frame is transmitted to the outgoing port only when all the frames ahead in the queue have been successfully transmitted. ■ It is possible for a single frame to delay the transmission of all the frames in memory because of a busy destination port. ■ This delay occurs even if the other frames could be transmitted to open destination ports.
Shared memory	■ All frames are deposited into a common memory buffer shared by all switch ports and the amount of buffer memory required by a port is dynamically allocated. ■ The frames in the buffer are dynamically linked to the destination port, enabling a packet to be received on one port and then transmitted on another port, without moving it to a different queue.

Shared memory buffering also results in the ability to store larger frames with potentially fewer dropped frames. This is important with asymmetric switching, which allows for different data rates on different ports such as when connecting a server to a 10 Gbps switch port and PCs to 1 Gbps ports.

Duplex and Speed Settings (35.2.4)

Two of the most basic settings on a switch are the bandwidth (sometimes referred to as "speed") and duplex settings for each individual switch port. It is critical that the

duplex and bandwidth settings match between the switch port and the connected devices, such as a computer or another switch.

There are two types of duplex settings used for communications on an Ethernet network:

- **Full-duplex**—Both ends of the connection can send and receive simultaneously.
- **Half-duplex**—Only one end of the connection can send at a time.

Autonegotiation is an optional function found on most Ethernet switches and NICs. It enables two devices to automatically negotiate the best speed and duplex capabilities. Full-duplex is chosen if both devices have the capability along with their highest common bandwidth.

In Figure 35-10, the Ethernet NIC for PC-A can operate in full-duplex or half-duplex, and in 10 Mbps or 100 Mbps. PC-A is connected to switch S2 on port 1, which can operate in full-duplex or half-duplex, and in 10 Mbps, 100 Mbps, or 1000 Mbps (1 Gbps). If both devices are using autonegotiation, the operating mode will be full-duplex and 100 Mbps.

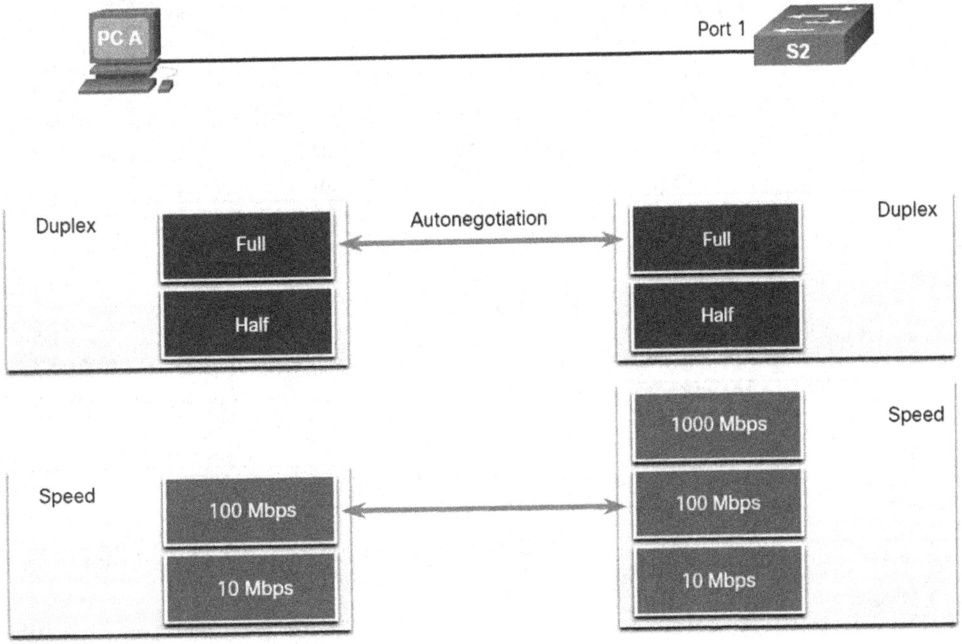

Figure 35-10 Duplex and Speed Settings

Note

Most Cisco switches and Ethernet NICs default to autonegotiation for speed and duplex. Gigabit Ethernet ports only operate in full-duplex.

Duplex mismatch is one of the most common causes of performance issues on 10/100 Mbps Ethernet links. It occurs when one port on the link operates at half-duplex while the other port operates at full-duplex, as shown in Figure 35-11. S2 will continually experience collisions because S1 keeps sending frames any time it has something to send.

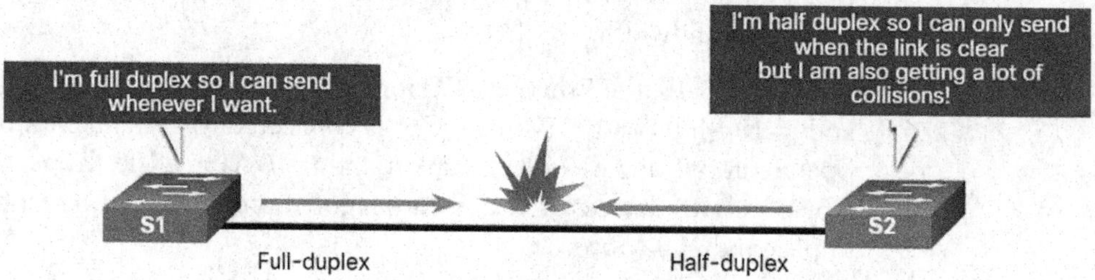

Figure 35-11 Duplex Mismatch

Duplex mismatch occurs when one or both ports on a link are reset, and the autonegotiation process does not result in both link partners having the same configuration. It also can occur when users reconfigure one side of a link and forget to reconfigure the other. Both sides of a link should have autonegotiation on, or both sides should have it off. Best practice is to configure both Ethernet switch ports as full-duplex.

Auto-MDIX (35.2.5)

Connections between devices once required the use of either a crossover or straight-through cable. The type of cable required depended on the type of interconnecting devices.

For example, Figure 35-12 identifies the correct cable type required to interconnect switch-to-switch, switch-to-router, switch-to-host, or router-to-host devices. A crossover cable is used when connecting like devices, and a straight-through cable is used for connecting unlike devices.

Note

A direct connection between a router and a host requires a crossover connection.

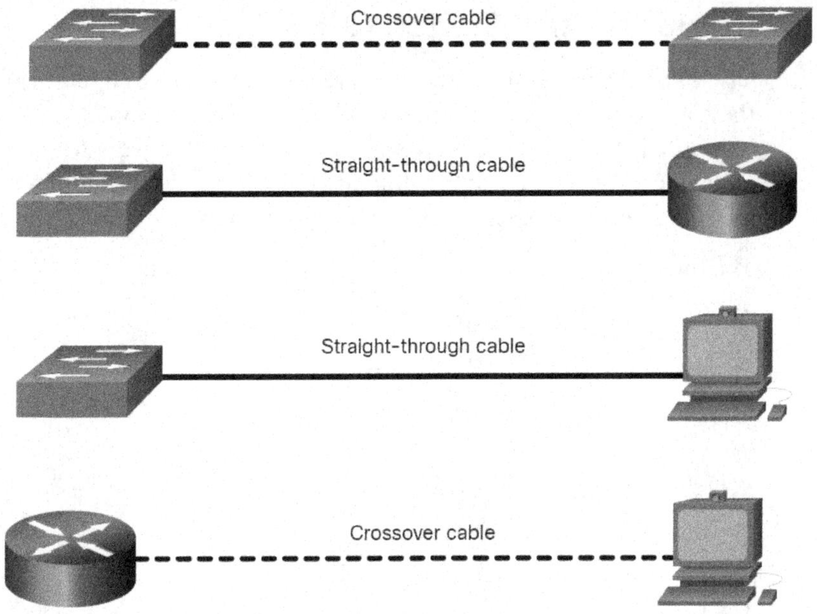

Figure 35-12 Auto-MDIX

Most switch devices now support the *automatic medium-dependent interface crossover (auto-MDIX)* feature. When enabled, the switch automatically detects the type of cable attached to the port and configures the interfaces accordingly. Therefore, you can use either a crossover or a straight-through cable for connections to a copper 10/100/1000 port on the switch, regardless of the type of device on the other end of the connection.

The auto-MDIX feature is enabled by default on switches running Cisco IOS Release 12.2(18)SE or later. However, the feature could be disabled. For this reason, you should always use the correct cable type and not rely on the auto-MDIX feature. Auto-MDIX can be re-enabled using the **mdix auto** interface configuration command.

Interactive Graphic

Check Your Understanding—Switch Speeds and Forwarding Methods (35.2.6)

Refer to the online course to complete this activity.

Switch Boot Process (35.3)

Cisco switches go through a boot process similar to that of your computer or smartphone. Ethernet switches in small networks usually do not require any configuration. They are designed to work "right out of the box."

Power Up the Switch (35.3.1)

Cisco switches, like most switches, are preconfigured to operate in a LAN as soon as they are powered on. All of the interface ports on the switch are active and will begin forwarding traffic immediately when devices are plugged into them. It is important to remember that no security settings are enabled by default. You will need to configure the basic security settings before placing the switch into the network.

The three basic steps for powering up a switch are as follows:

Step 1. Check the components.

Step 2. Connect the cables to the switch.

Step 3. Power up the switch.

Note

You can also attach cables after power is applied.

When the switch is on, the power-on self-test (POST) begins. During POST, the LEDs blink while a series of tests determines that the switch is functioning properly.

POST is completed when the SYST LED rapidly blinks green. If the switch fails POST, the SYST LED turns amber. When a switch fails POST, it is necessary to return the switch for repairs.

When all startup procedures are finished, the Cisco switch is ready to configure.

Step 1. Check the components.

Ensure all the components that came with the switch are available (Figure 35-13). These could include a console cable, power cord, Ethernet cable, and switch documentation.

Step 2. Connect the cables to the switch.

As shown in Figure 35-14, connect the PC to the switch with a console cable and start a terminal emulation session. Connect the AC power cord to the switch and to a grounded AC outlet.

Step 3. Power up the switch.

Some Cisco switch models do not have an on/off switch, like the Cisco Catalyst 9300 48S switch shown in Figure 35-15. To power on the switch, plug one end of the AC power cord into the switch AC power connector, and plug the other end into an AC power outlet.

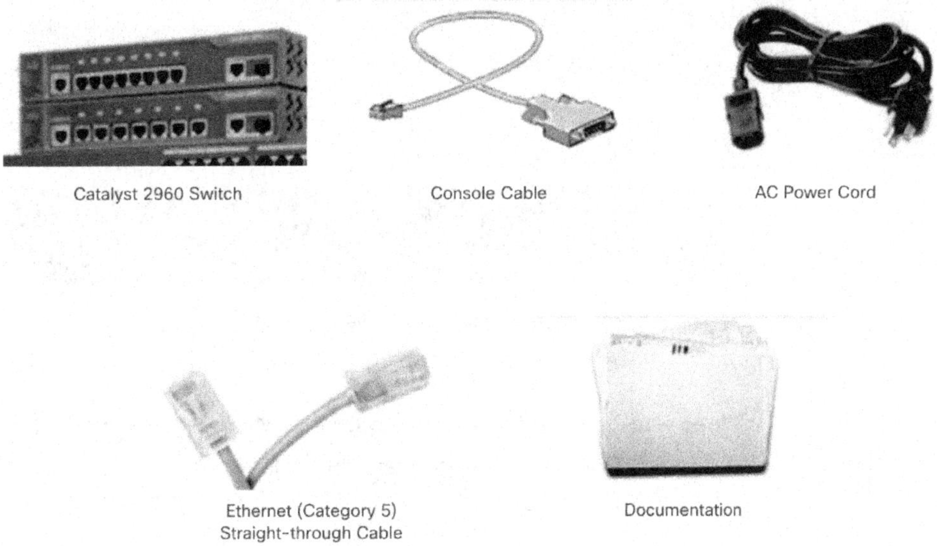

Figure 35-13 Components for Connecting to a Switch

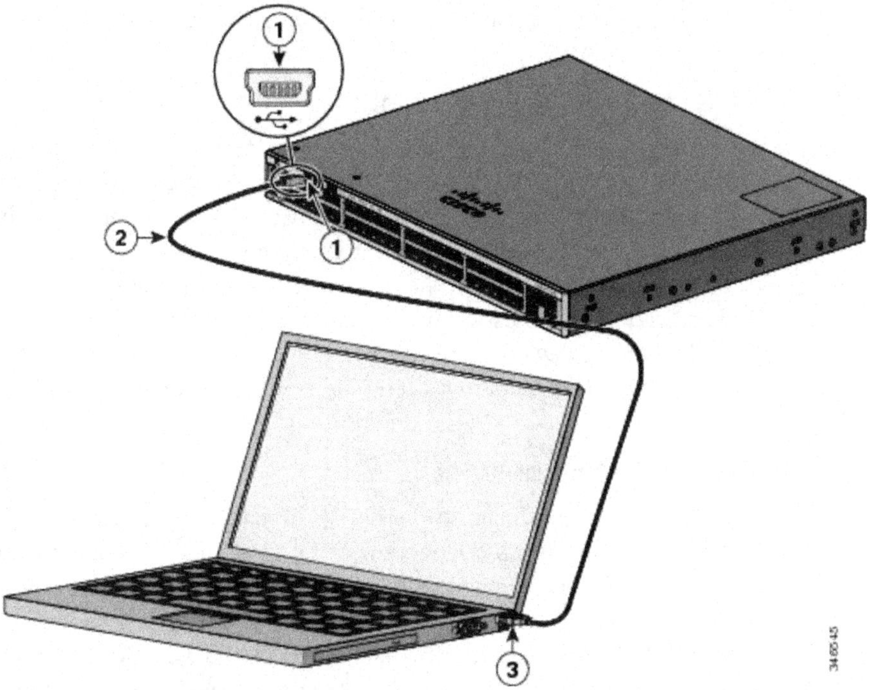

Figure 35-14 Switch to Laptop Console Connection

Note

The Cisco Catalyst 9300 switch in Figure 35-15 has redundant power supplies in case one fails.

Figure 35-15 Back Panel of the Cisco Catalyst 9300 48S

Video

Video—In-Band and Out-of-Band Device Management (35.3.2)

Refer to the online course to view this video.

In-Band and Out-of-Band Management (35.3.3)

There are two methods to connect a PC to a network device to perform configuration and monitoring tasks: out-of-band management and in-band management.

Out-of-Band Management

Out-of-band management requires a computer to be directly connected to the console port of the network device that is being configured. This type of connection does not require the local network connections on the device to be active. Technicians use out-of-band management to initially configure a network device, because until properly configured, the device cannot participate in the network. Out-of-band management is also useful when the network connectivity is not functioning correctly, and the device cannot be reached over the network. Performing out-of-band management tasks requires a terminal emulation client installed on the PC.

In-Band Management

Use in-band management to monitor and make configuration changes to a network device over a network connection. For a computer to connect to the device and perform in-band management tasks, at least one network interface on the device must be connected to the network and have an IP address configured on it. Either Telnet, SSH, HTTP, or HTTPS can be used to access a Cisco device for in-band management, monitor the network device, or make configuration changes. Telnet and HTTP send

all data, including passwords, in clear text and therefore should only be used in a lab environment.

IOS Startup Files (35.3.4)

As shown in Figure 35-16, a Cisco device loads the following two files into RAM when it is booted:

- **IOS image file**—The IOS facilitates the basic operation of the device's hardware components. The IOS image file is stored in flash memory.
- **Startup configuration file**—The startup configuration file contains commands that are used to initially configure a router and switch and create the running configuration file stored in RAM. The startup configuration file is stored in NVRAM. All configuration changes are stored in the running configuration file and are implemented immediately by the IOS.

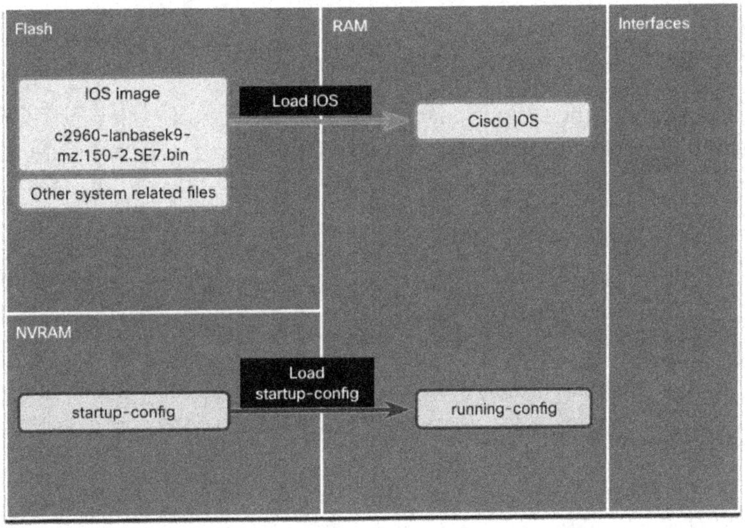

Figure 35-16 Memory Location of IOS and Startup Configuration

The running configuration file is modified when the network administrator performs device configuration. When changes are made to the running-config file, it should be saved to NVRAM as the startup configuration file in case the router is restarted or loses power.

Video

Video—Establish a Console Connection (35.3.5)

Refer to the online course to view this video.

Cisco Routers (35.4)

A router is a computer with specialized hardware and a network operating system. A computer, such as a PC running Linux, could even be configured as a router for a small network. Cisco routers have specialized hardware and software designed to provide the features and performance needed for enterprise and service provider networks.

Video

Video—Cisco Router Components (35.4.1)

Refer to the online course to view this video.

Router Components (35.4.2)

Regardless of their function, size, or complexity, all router models are essentially computers. Just like computers, tablets, and smart devices, routers also require the following:

- Operating system (OS)
- Central processing unit (CPU)
- Random-access memory (RAM)
- Read-only memory (ROM)
- Nonvolatile random-access memory (NVRAM)

Like all computers, tablets, and smart devices, Cisco routers require a CPU to execute OS instructions, such as system initialization, routing functions, and switching functions.

The CPU requires an OS to provide routing and switching functions. The Cisco Internetwork Operating System (IOS) is the system software used for most Cisco devices, regardless of the size and type of the device. It is used for routers, LAN switches, small wireless access points, large routers with dozens of interfaces, and many other devices.

Router Interface Ports (35.4.3)

Although there are several different types and models of routers, every Cisco router has the same general hardware components.

Figure 35-17 shows a Cisco 4321 Integrated Services Router (ISR).

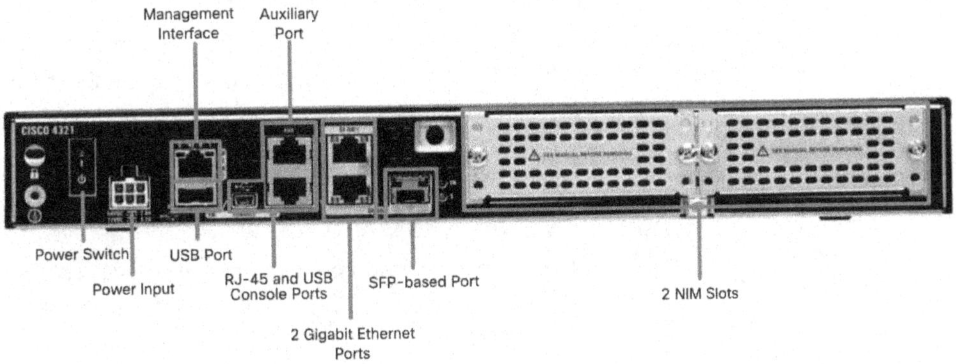

Figure 35-17 Connections on the Cisco 4321 ISR

The router includes the following connections:

- **Console ports**—Two console ports for the initial configuration and command-line interface (CLI) management access using a regular RJ-45 port and a USB Type-B (mini-B USB) connector.
- **Two LAN interfaces**—Two Gigabit Ethernet interfaces for LAN access labeled GE 0/0/0 and GE 0/0/1. The GE 0/0/0 port can be accessed through an RJ-45 connection or by using a small form-factor pluggable (SFP) attachment to provide a fiber-optic connection.
- **Network Interface Modules (NIMs)**—Two NIM expansion slots that provide modularity and flexibility by enabling the router to support different types of interface modules, including serial, digital subscriber line (DSL), switch ports, and wireless.

The Cisco 4321 ISR also has a USB port, a management interface, and an auxiliary port. The USB port can be used for file transfers. The management port can be used for remote management access when the two Gigabit Ethernet interfaces are unavailable. The auxiliary port provides legacy support for a method for connecting a dial-up modem to the router for remote access. The auxiliary port is rarely used in networks today.

Router Boot Process (35.5)

Since the router is just a specialized computer, the boot process is the same as most computers.

Power Up the Router (35.5.1)

Before beginning any equipment installation, it is important to be sure to read the Quick Start guide and other documentation that is included with the device. The documentation contains important safety and procedural information.

Step 1. Securely mount the device to the rack (Figure 35-18).

Note

Figure 35-18 shows a typical scenario of mounting the chassis in a rack.

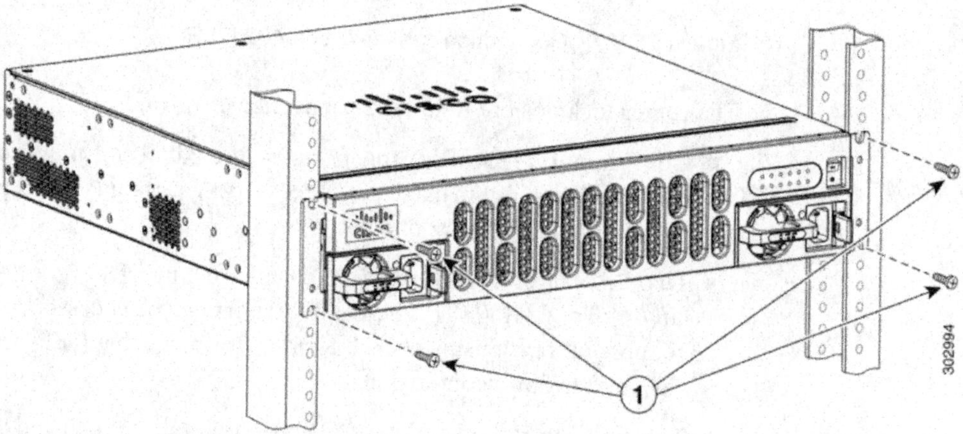

Figure 35-18 Mounting the Chassis in a Rack

Step 2. Ground the device (Figure 35-19).

Step 3. Connect the power cable (Figure 35-20).

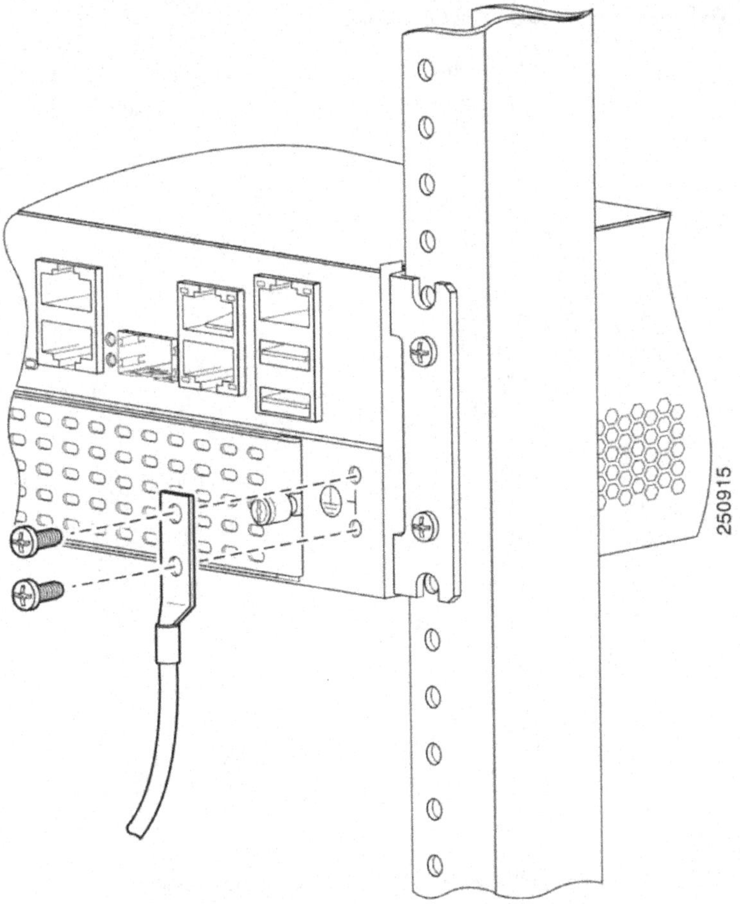

Figure 35-19 Attaching the Ground Wire to the Chassis

Figure 35-20 Power Input Connector

Step 4. Connect a console cable.

Configure the terminal emulation software on the laptop and connect the laptop to the console port, as shown in Figure 35-21.

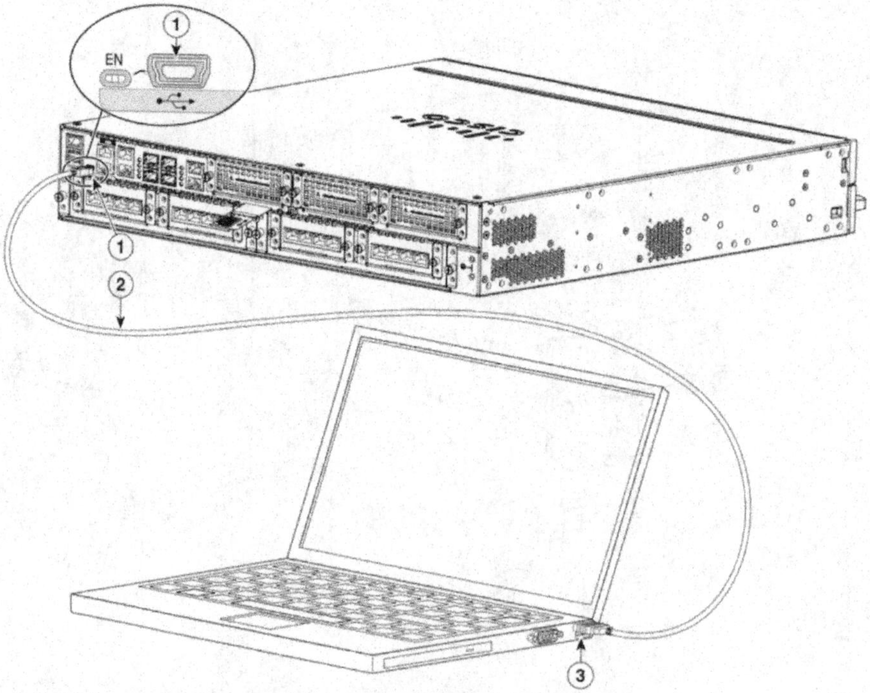

Figure 35-21 Attaching a Console Cable to the Device

Step 5. Turn on the router (Figure 35-22).

Figure 35-22 The Power Switch

Step 6. Observe the startup messages on the laptop as the router boots up, as shown in Example 35-1.

Example 35-1 Cisco 4200 ISR Bootup Messages

```
Located isr4200-universalk9_ias.16.09.04.SPA.bin
###################################################....
(output omitted)

Package header rev 3 structure detected
IsoSize = 486723584
Calculating SHA-1 hash...Validate package: SHA-1 hash:
         calculated 4155409B:CC0DB23E:6D72A6AE:EA887F82:AC94DC6A
         expected   4155409B:CC0DB23E:6D72A6AE:EA887F82:AC94DC6A
RSA Signed RELEASE Image Signature Verification Successful.
Image validated

                Restricted Rights Legend

Use, duplication, or disclosure by the Government is
subject to restrictions as set forth in subparagraph
(c) of the Commercial Computer Software - Restricted
Rights clause at FAR sec. 52.227-19 and subparagraph
(c) (1) (ii) of the Rights in Technical Data and Computer
Software clause at DFARS sec. 252.227-7013.

             Cisco Systems, Inc.
             170 West Tasman Drive
             San Jose, California 95134-1706



Cisco IOS Software [Fuji], ISR Software (X86_64_LINUX_IOSD-UNIVERSALK9_IAS-M),
  Version 16.9.4, RELEASE SOFTWARE (fc2)
Technical Support: http://www.cisco.com/techsupport
Copyright (c) 1986-2019 by Cisco Systems, Inc.
Compiled Thu 22-Aug-19 18:09 by mcpre

(output omitted)
```

Management Ports (35.5.2)

Similar to a Cisco switch, there are several ways to access the command-line interface on a Cisco router. The most common methods are as follows:

- **Console**—Uses a low-speed serial or USB connection to provide direct connect, out-of-band management access to a Cisco device.

- **SSH**—Method for remotely accessing a CLI session across an active network interface, including the management interface.
- **AUX port**—Used for remote management of the router using a dial-up telephone line and modem.

The console port is a physical port located on the router. When using SSH, there must be an active network interface that is configured with a valid IP address for the network. This can be one of the active network interfaces used for network traffic or it can be the management interface. Figure 35-23 shows ports available for management access.

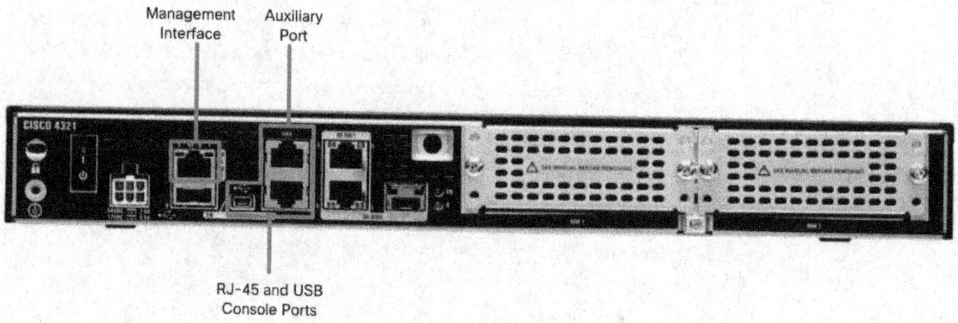

Figure 35-23 Management Configuration Access

In addition to these management ports, routers also have network interfaces to receive and forward IP packets. Most routers have multiple interfaces that are used to connect to multiple networks. Typically, the interfaces connect to various types of networks, as shown in Figure 35-24, which means that different types of media and connectors are required.

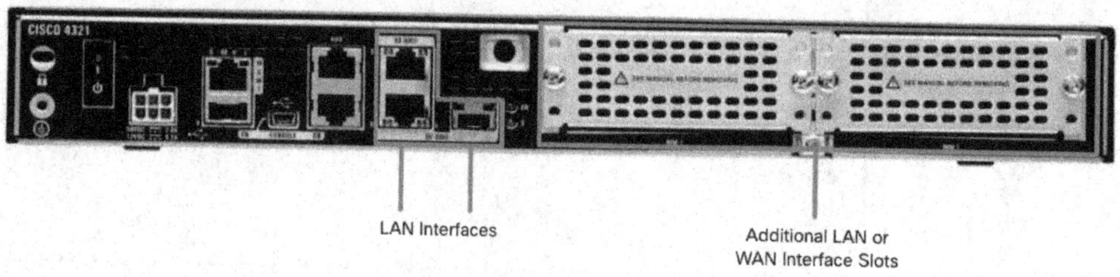

Figure 35-24 LAN and WAN Interfaces

Video

Video—The Cisco Router Boot Process (35.5.3)

Refer to the online course to view this video.

Summary (35.6)

The following is a summary of each topic in the chapter and some questions for your reflection.

What Did I Learn in This Chapter? (35.6.1)

- **Cisco Switches**—A switch is used to connect devices on the same network. A router is used to connect multiple networks to each other. When selecting a switch for your LAN, choosing the appropriate number and type of ports is critical. Lower-cost switches may support only copper twisted-pair interface ports. Higher-priced switches may have fiber-optic connections. These are used to link the switch to other switches that may be located over long distances.

  Similar to a switch port, Ethernet NICs operate at specific bandwidths such as 10/100 or 10/100/1000 Mbps. The actual bandwidth of the attached device will be the highest common bandwidth between the device NIC and the switch port. Networking devices come in both fixed and modular physical configurations. A managed switch that uses a Cisco operating system enables control over individual ports or over the switch as a whole. Cisco Catalyst 2960 Series Ethernet switches are suitable for small- and medium-sized networks.

- **Switch Speeds and Forwarding Methods**—Switches use one of the following forwarding methods for switching data between network ports: store-and-forward switching or cut-through switching. Two variants of cut-through switching are fast-forward and fragment-free. Two methods of memory buffering are port-based memory and shared memory. There are two types of duplex settings used for communications on an Ethernet network: full-duplex and half-duplex.

  Autonegotiation is an optional function found on most Ethernet switches and NICs. It enables two devices to automatically negotiate the best speed and duplex capabilities. Full-duplex is chosen if both devices have the capability along with their highest common bandwidth. Most switch devices now support the automatic medium-dependent interface crossover (auto-MDIX) feature. When enabled, the switch automatically detects the type of cable attached to the port and configures the interfaces accordingly.

- **Switch Boot Process**—Cisco switches are preconfigured to operate in a LAN as soon as they are powered on. Configure the basic security settings before placing the switch into the network. The three basic steps for powering up a switch are as follows: (1) check the components, (2) connect the cables to the switch, and (3) power up the switch. When the switch is on, the power-on self-test (POST) begins.

There are two methods to connect a PC to a network device to perform configuration and monitoring tasks: out-of-band management and in-band management. Out-of-band management requires a computer to be directly connected to the console port of the network device that is being configured. Use in-band management to monitor and make configuration changes to a network device over a network connection.

A Cisco device loads the following two files into RAM when it is booted: the IOS image file and the startup configuration file. The IOS image file is stored in flash memory. The startup configuration file is stored in NVRAM.

- **Cisco Routers**—Routers require an OS, a CPU, RAM, ROM, and NVRAM. Every Cisco router has the same general hardware components: console ports, LAN interfaces, expansion slots for different types of interface modules (e.g., EHWIC, Serial, DSL, switch ports, wireless), and storage slots for expanded capabilities (e.g., compact flash memory, USB ports).
- **Router Boot Process**—Follow these steps to power up a Cisco router:

  Step 1. Securely mount the device to the rack.

  Step 2. Ground the device.

  Step 3. Connect the power cable.

  Step 4. Connect a console cable.

  Step 5. Turn on the router.

  Step 6. Observe the startup messages on the PC within the terminal window as the router boots.

  The most common methods to access the command-line interface on a Cisco router are console, SSH, and Aux ports. Routers also have network interfaces to receive and forward IP packets.

Reflection Questions (35.6.2)

I found this chapter very helpful and I hope you did too. Now I want to go back to my office network and tour it again. Knowing how to set up multiple switches and routers will help me better understand why our network is set up the way it is.

Now that you know how to set up a multi-switch, multi-router network, see if you can tour your office or school network.

- What are the advantages of having the network set up the way it is?
- How might it change if the network were to double in size?

Practice

There are no labs or Packet Tracer activities in this chapter.

Check Your Understanding Questions

Complete all the review questions listed here to test your understanding of the topics and concepts in this chapter. Appendix A, "Answers to 'Check Your Understanding' Questions," lists the answers.

1. A technician is setting up a network in a new room. What is the best device to use to connect the PCs to each other and to the rest of the LAN?

   a. Gateway

   b. Firewall

   c. Switch

   d. Router

2. Which advantage does the store-and-forward switching method have compared with the cut-through switching method?

   a. Collision detecting

   b. Frame error checking

   c. Faster frame forwarding

   d. Frame forwarding using IPv4 Layer 3 and 4 information

3. A technician is setting up a network in a new room. What is the best device to use to connect the PCs to each other and to the rest of the LAN?

   a. Router

   b. Switch

   c. Gateway

   d. Firewall

4. During normal operation, from which location do most Cisco switches run the IOS?

   a. Disk drive

   b. Flash

   c. NVRAM

   d. RAM

5. When a router is powered on, where will the router first search for a valid IOS image to load by default?

   a. RAM
   b. Flash memory
   c. NVRAM
   d. ROM

6. Which two protocols can be used to access a Cisco switch for in-band management? (Choose two.)

   a. DHCP
   b. FTP
   c. Telnet
   d. SSH
   e. SMTP

7. During troubleshooting procedures, from which location will most Cisco routers load a limited IOS?

   a. NVRAM
   b. Flash
   c. ROM
   d. RAM

8. Which two networking devices are used in enterprise networks for providing network connectivity to end devices? (Choose two.)

   a. Firewall
   b. LAN switch
   c. Web server
   d. Router
   e. Wireless access point

9. What is required for a network administrator to perform out-of-band management tasks on a Cisco device?

   a. An active network connection available to the device
   b. A computer directly connected to the console port of the device
   c. A valid IP address configured on VLAN 1
   d. SSH enabled and functional on the device

10. What is the first action in the boot sequence when a switch is powered on?

    a. Load boot loader software
    b. Low-level CPU initialization
    c. Load the default Cisco IOS software
    d. Load a power-on self-test program

11. What are two functions of NVRAM? (Choose two.)

    a. To store the startup configuration file
    b. To store the ARP table
    c. To store the routing table
    d. To retain content when power is removed
    e. To contain the running configuration file

12. Which two ports can be used for the initial configuration of a Cisco router? (Choose two.)

    a. Flash slot
    b. AUX
    c. WAN interface
    d. Console
    e. LAN interface

13. Which two files are loaded into RAM of a Cisco switch when it is booted? (Choose two.)

    a. File that contains customer settings
    b. Startup configuration file
    c. IOS image file
    d. Routing table
    e. The contents of the saved configuration file in NVRAM

14. Which information does the **show startup-config** command display?

    a. The bootstrap program in ROM
    b. The contents of the current running configuration file in RAM
    c. The IOS image copied into RAM
    d. The contents of the saved configuration file in NVRAM

CHAPTER 36

Troubleshoot Common Network Problems

Objectives

Upon completion of this chapter, you will be able to answer the following questions:

- What are some of the approaches used to troubleshoot networks?
- What is the process of detecting physical layer problems?
- How do you troubleshoot a wireless network problem?
- What are the common Internet connectivity problems?
- What outside sources and Internet resources are available for troubleshooting?

Introduction (36.0)

Diego has completed their task of designing and setting up a new branch network. They will need to test it, and if there are problems, they will diagnose and fix them. I want to know how to test, diagnose, and fix network problems too. Being able to do this is a sure sign that you are ready to become a networking professional.

Let's do this together!

The Troubleshooting Process (36.1)

Troubleshooting is the process of identifying, locating, and correcting problems. Experienced individuals often rely on instinct to troubleshoot. However, there are structured techniques that can be used to determine the most probable cause and solution.

Video

Video—Network Troubleshooting (36.1.1)

Refer to the online course to view this video.

Network Troubleshooting Overview (36.1.2)

When troubleshooting, proper documentation must be maintained. This documentation should include as much information as possible about the following:

- The problem encountered
- Steps taken to determine the cause of the problem
- Steps to correct the problem and ensure that it will not reoccur

Document all steps taken in troubleshooting, even the ones that did not solve the issue. This documentation becomes a valuable reference should the same or similar problem occur again. Even in a small home network, good documentation saves hours of trying to remember how a problem was fixed in the past.

Gather Information (36.1.3)

When a problem is first discovered in the network, it is important to verify it and determine how much of the network is affected by it. After the problem is confirmed, the first step in troubleshooting is to gather information. The following checklist provides some of the important information you should check.

- **Nature of Problem**
  - End-user reports
  - Problem verification report
- **Equipment**
  - Manufacturer
  - Make/model
  - Firmware version
  - Operating system version
  - Ownership/warranty information
- **Configuration and Topology**
  - Physical and logical topology
  - Configuration files
  - Log files
- **Previous Troubleshooting**
  - Steps taken
  - Results achieved

One of the first ways to gather information is to question the individual who reported the problem, as well as any other affected users. Questions can include end-user experiences, observed symptoms, error messages, and information about recent configuration changes to devices or applications.

Next, collect information about any equipment that may be affected. This can be gathered from documentation. A copy of all log files and a listing of any recent changes made to equipment configurations are also necessary. Log files are generated by the equipment itself and are usually obtainable through the management software. Other information on the equipment includes the manufacturer, make, and model of devices affected, as well as ownership and warranty information. The version of any firmware or software on the device is also important because there may be compatibility problems with particular hardware platforms.

Information about the network can also be gathered using network monitoring tools. Network monitoring tools are complex applications often used on large networks to continually gather information about the state of the network and network devices. These tools may not be available for smaller networks.

After all necessary information is gathered, start the troubleshooting process.

Structured Troubleshooting Methods (36.1.4)

There are several structured troubleshooting approaches that can be used. Which one to use will depend on the situation. Each approach has its advantages and disadvantages. This section describes methods and provides guidelines for choosing the best method for a specific situation.

Bottom-Up

In bottom-up troubleshooting, you start with the physical layer and the physical components of the network, as shown in Figure 36-1, and move up through the layers of the OSI model until the cause of the problem is identified.

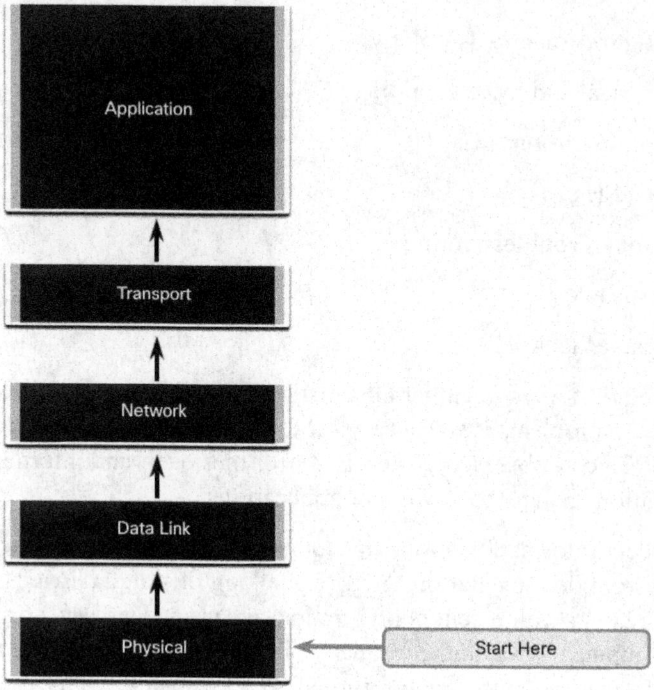

Figure 36-1 Bottom-Up Troubleshooting

Bottom-up troubleshooting is a good approach to use when the problem is suspected to be a physical one. Most networking problems reside at the lower levels, so implementing the bottom-up approach is often effective.

The disadvantage with the bottom-up troubleshooting approach is it requires that you check every device and interface on the network until the possible cause of the problem is found. Remember that each conclusion and possibility must be

documented, so there can be a lot of paperwork associated with this approach. A further challenge is to determine which devices to start examining first.

Top-Down

As shown in Figure 36-2, top-down troubleshooting starts with the end-user applications and moves down through the layers of the OSI model until the cause of the problem has been identified.

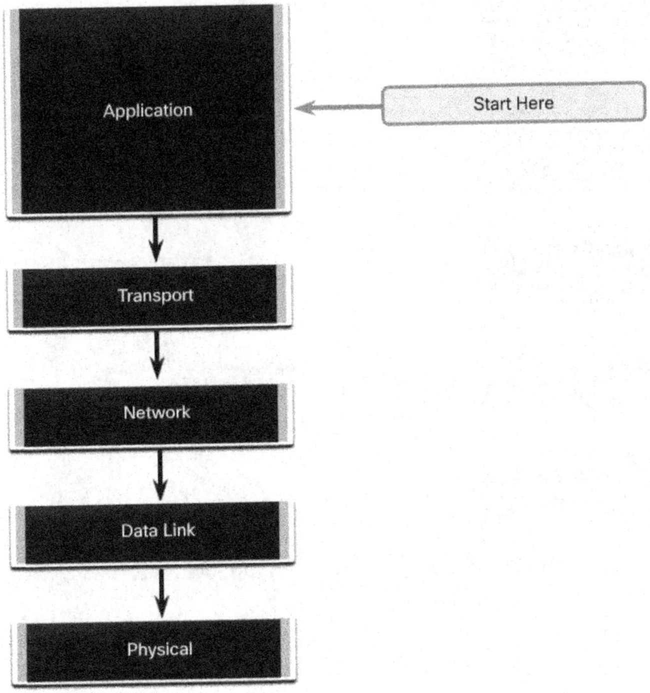

Figure 36-2 Top-Down Troubleshooting

End-user applications of an end system are tested before tackling the more specific networking pieces. Use this approach for simpler problems, or when you think the problem is with a piece of software.

The disadvantage with the top-down approach is it requires checking every network application until the possible cause of the problem is found. Each conclusion and possibility must be documented. The challenge is to determine which application to start examining first.

Divide-and-Conquer

Figure 36-3 shows the divide-and-conquer approach to troubleshooting a networking problem. The network administrator selects a layer and tests in both directions from that layer.

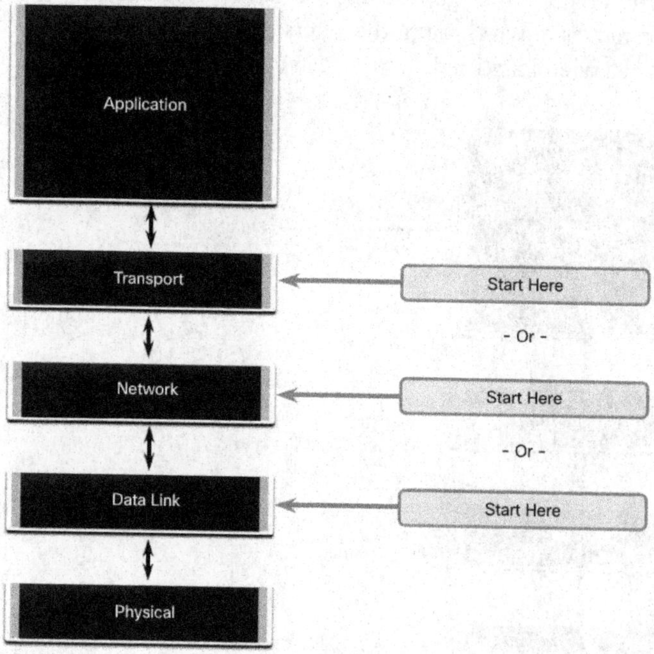

Figure 36-3 Divide-and-Conquer Troubleshooting

In divide-and-conquer troubleshooting, you start by collecting user experiences of the problem, document the symptoms, and then, using that information, make an informed guess as to which OSI layer to start your investigation. When a layer is verified to be functioning properly, it can be assumed that the layers below it are functioning. The administrator can work up the OSI layers. If an OSI layer is not functioning properly, the administrator can work down the OSI layer model.

For example, if users cannot access the web server, but they can ping the server, then the problem is above Layer 3. If pinging the server is unsuccessful, then the problem is likely at a lower OSI layer.

Follow-the-Path

This is one of the most basic troubleshooting techniques. The approach first discovers the traffic path all the way from source to destination. The scope of troubleshooting is reduced to just the links and devices that are in the forwarding path.

The objective is to eliminate the links and devices that are irrelevant to the troubleshooting task at hand. This approach usually complements one of the other approaches.

Substitution

This approach is also called swap-the-component because you physically swap the problematic device with a known, working one. If the problem is fixed, then the problem is with the removed device. If the problem remains, then the cause may be elsewhere.

In specific situations, this can be an ideal method for quick problem resolution, such as with a critical single point of failure. For example, a border router goes down. It may be more beneficial to simply replace the device and restore service rather than to troubleshoot the issue.

If the problem lies within multiple devices, it may not be possible to correctly isolate the problem.

Comparison

This approach is also called the spot-the-differences approach and attempts to resolve the problem by changing the nonoperational elements to be consistent with the working ones. You compare configurations, software versions, hardware, or other device properties, links, or processes between working and nonworking situations and spot significant differences between them.

The weakness of this method is that it might lead to a working solution, without clearly revealing the root cause of the problem.

Educated Guess

This approach is also called the shoot-from-the-hip troubleshooting approach. This is a less-structured troubleshooting method that uses an educated guess based on the symptoms of the problem. Success of this method varies based on your troubleshooting experience and ability. Seasoned technicians are more successful because they can rely on their extensive knowledge and experience to decisively isolate and solve network issues. With a less-experienced network administrator, this troubleshooting method may be too random to be effective.

Guidelines for Selecting a Troubleshooting Method (36.1.5)

To quickly resolve network problems, take the time to select the most effective network troubleshooting method.

Figure 36-4 illustrates which method could be used when a certain type of problem is discovered.

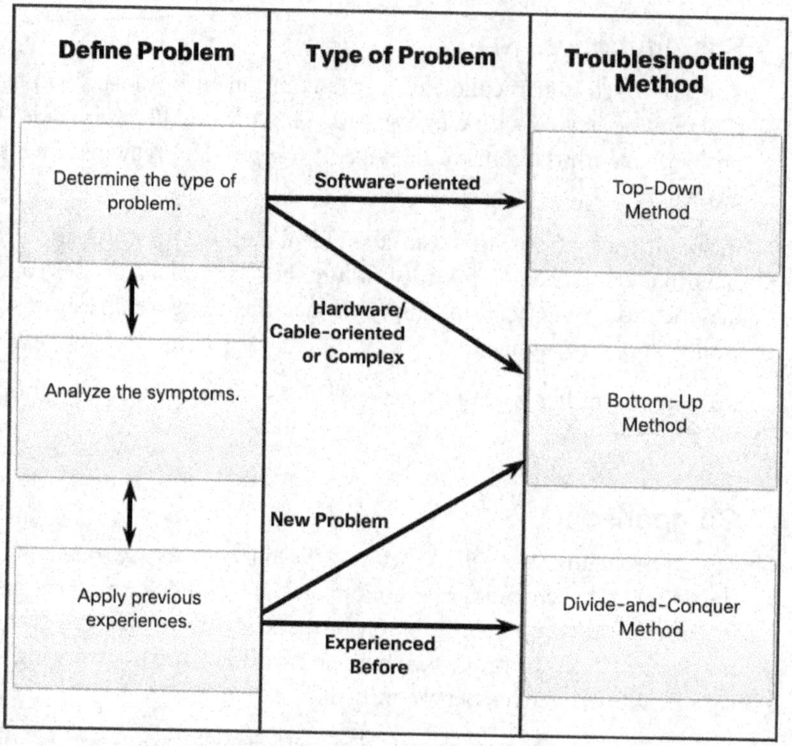

Figure 36-4 Selecting a Troubleshooting Method

For instance, software problems are often solved using a top-down approach, while hardware-based problems are solved using the bottom-up approach. New problems may be solved by an experienced technician using the divide-and-conquer method. Otherwise, the bottom-up approach may be used.

Troubleshooting is a skill that is developed by doing it. Every network problem you identify and solve adds to your skill set.

Interactive Graphic

Check Your Understanding—The Troubleshooting Process (36.1.6)

Refer to the online course to complete this activity.

Physical Layer Problems (36.2)

A large proportion of networking problems are related to physical components or problems with the physical layer. Physical problems are concerned mainly with the hardware aspects of computers and networking devices, and the cables that interconnect them. Physical problems do not include the logical (software) configuration of devices.

Common Layer 1 Problems (36.2.1)

Remember, the physical layer (Layer 1) deals with the physical connectivity of the network devices. Some of the more common Layer 1 problems include the following:

- Device power turned off
- Device power unplugged
- Loose network cable connection
- Incorrect cable type
- Faulty network cable
- Faulty wireless access point

To troubleshoot at Layer 1, first check that all devices have the proper power supplied and that the devices are turned on. This may seem to be an obvious solution, but many times the person reporting the problem may overlook a device that is within the network path from source to destination. Ensure there are no errors showing on any LEDs that display the connectivity status. If you're on site, visually inspect all network cabling and reconnect cables to ensure a proper connection. If the problem is with wireless, verify that the wireless access point is operational and that wireless settings are configured correctly.

The Sense of Sight

Vision is used to detect problems such as improperly connected or poorly constructed cables:

- Cables that are not connected
- Cables connected to the wrong port
- Loose cable connections

- Damaged cables and connectors
- Use of the wrong type of cable

Vision also allows us to view the condition and function of various network devices with LEDs.

The Senses of Smell and Taste

Smell can alert troubleshooters to components that are overheating. The smell of burning insulation or components is very distinct and is a sure sign that something is seriously wrong.

The sense of taste is directly related to the sense of smell because both use the same receptors. You may also taste the acridness of something burning.

The Sense of Touch

Troubleshooters can use touch to feel for overheated components as well as to detect mechanical problems with devices such as cooling fans. These devices usually create a small vibration in the component that can be detected using touch. The absence of this vibration or the presence of excessive amounts of vibration can indicate that the cooling fan has failed or is about to do so.

The Sense of Hearing

Hearing is used to detect major problems such as electrical issues and the proper operation of cooling fans and disk drives. All devices have characteristic sounds, and any change from the normal sounds usually indicates a problem of some sort.

Wireless Router LEDs (36.2.2)

Regardless of whether the fault is present on the wireless or wired network, one of the first steps in a bottom-up strategy of troubleshooting should be to examine the LEDs, which indicate the current state or activity of a piece of equipment or connection. LEDs may change color or flash to convey information. The exact configuration and meaning of LEDs varies between manufacturers and devices. Figure 36-5 shows a typical wireless router with LEDs indicating power, system, WLAN, wired ports, and Internet (labeled WAN in Figure 36-5), USB, and Quick Security Setup (QSS, also known as Wi-Fi Protected Setup [WPS]).

Note

WPS/QSS has known vulnerabilities that allow a threat actor to gain access to your network. Therefore, it is a security best practice to disable this feature. Refer to documentation to learn how to disable WPS or QSS.

Figure 36-5 LED Lights on a Wireless Router

On some devices, a single LED may convey multiple pieces of information depending on the current status of the device. It is important to check the equipment documentation for the exact meaning of all indicators, but some commonality does exist.

Most devices will have activity LEDs, which are often called link lights. A normal condition is for these LEDs to flash, indicating that traffic is flowing through the port. A solid green light typically indicates that a device is plugged into the port, but no traffic is flowing. No light typically indicates one or more of the following:

- Nothing is plugged into the port.
- There is an issue with the wired or wireless connection.
- A device or port has failed.

- There is a cabling issue.
- The wireless router is improperly configured; for example, a port was administratively shut down.
- The wireless router has a hardware fault.
- The device does not have power.

Whether the network is wired or wireless, verify that the device and ports are up and functional before spending large amounts of time trying to troubleshoot other issues.

Cabling Problems (36.2.3)

If the wired client is unable to connect to the wireless router, one of the first things to check is the physical connectivity and cabling. Cabling is the central nervous system of wired networks and one of the most common issues when experiencing inactivity.

There are several issues to watch for when cabling:

- Be sure to use the correct type of cable. Two types of UTP cables are commonly encountered in networking: straight-through cables and crossover cables. Using the wrong type of cable may prevent connectivity.
- Improper cable termination is one of the main problems encountered in networks. To avoid this, cables should be terminated according to standards. Terminate cables via the T568A or the T568B termination standard. Avoid untwisting too much of the wire pairs during termination. Crimp connectors on the cable jacket to provide strain relief.
- Maximum cable run lengths exist based on characteristics of the different cables. Exceeding these run lengths can have a serious negative impact on network performance.
- If connectivity is a problem, verify that the correct ports are being used between the networking devices.
- Protect cables and connectors from physical damage. Support cables to prevent strain on connectors and run cable through areas that will not be in the way.

Interactive Graphic

Check Your Understanding—Physical Layer Problems (36.2.4)

Refer to the online course to complete this activity.

Troubleshoot Wireless Issues (36.3)

Troubleshooting a wireless LAN is similar to troubleshooting a wired LAN, but there are some important differences associated with the wireless signal and the access point.

Causes of Wireless Issues (36.3.1)

If the wireless client is unable to connect to the AP, it may be because of wireless connectivity problems. Wireless communications rely on radio frequency (RF) signals to carry data. Many factors can affect our ability to connect hosts using RF:

- Not all wireless standards are compatible. The 802.11ac (5 GHz band) is not compatible with the 802.11b/g/n standards (2.4 GHz band). Within the 2.4 GHz band, each standard uses different technology. Unless specifically configured, equipment that conforms to one standard may not function with equipment that conforms to another. In Figure 36-6, the 2.4 GHz network is configured to support legacy devices.
- Each wireless conversation must occur on a separate, nonoverlapping channel. Some AP devices can be configured to select the least congested or highest throughput channel. Although automatic settings work, manual setting of the AP channel provides greater control and may be necessary in some environments.
- The strength of an RF signal decreases with distance. If the signal strength is too low, devices will be unable to reliably associate and move data. The signal may be dropped. The NIC client utility can be used to display the signal strength and connection quality.
- RF signals are susceptible to interference from outside sources, including other devices functioning on the same frequency. A site survey should be used to detect for this.
- APs share the available bandwidth between devices. As more devices associate with the AP, the bandwidth for each individual device will decrease, causing network performance problems. The solution is to reduce the number of wireless clients using each channel.

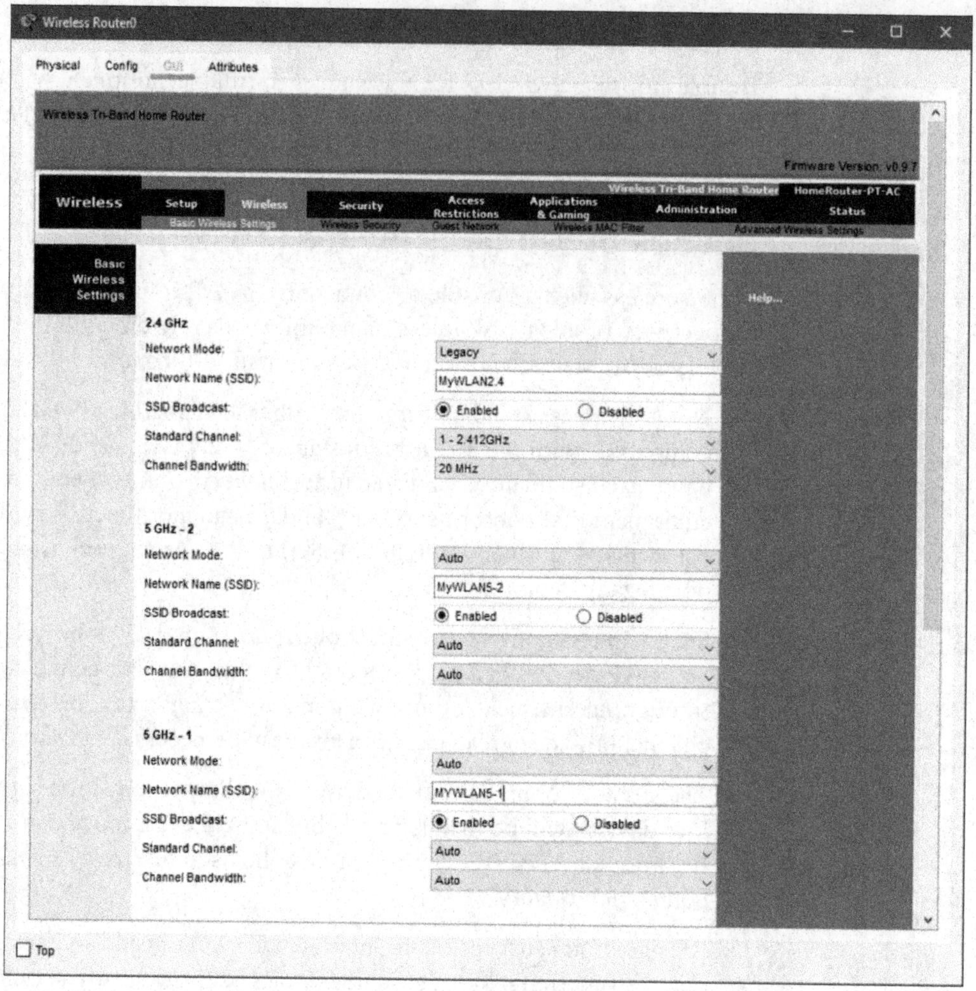

Figure 36-6 Basic Wireless Settings on a Wireless Router

Authentication and Association Errors (36.3.2)

Modern WLANs incorporate various technologies to help secure the data on the WLAN. Incorrect configuration of any of these can prevent communication. Some of the most common settings that are configured incorrectly include the SSID, authentication, and encryption.

- The SSID is a case-sensitive, alphanumeric string that is up to 32 characters. It must match on both the AP and client. If the SSID is broadcast and detected, this is not an issue. If the SSID is not broadcast, it must be manually entered onto the client. If the client is configured with the wrong SSID, it will not associate with

the AP. Additionally, if another AP is present that has broadcasted the SSID, the client may automatically associate to it.

- On most APs, open authentication is configured by default, allowing all devices to connect. If a more secure form of authentication is configured, a key is necessary. Both the client and the AP must be configured with the same key. If the keys do not match, authentication will fail, and the devices will not associate.
- Encryption is the process of altering the data so that it is not usable by anyone without the proper encryption key. If encryption is enabled, the same encryption key must be configured on both the AP and the client. If the client associates with the AP but cannot send or receive data, the encryption key may be the issue, as shown in Figure 36-7.

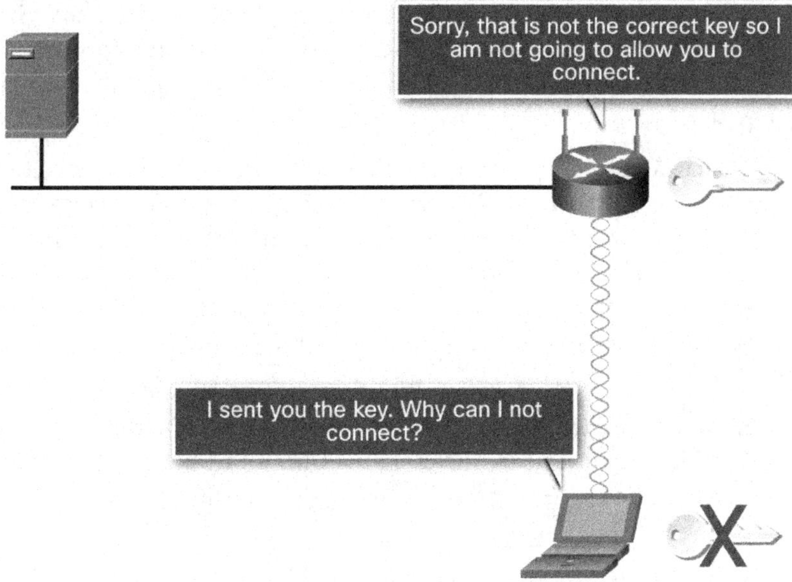

Figure 36-7 Failed Authentication

Packet Tracer Activity

Packet Tracer—Troubleshoot a Wireless Connection (36.3.3)

In this activity, you will be given a scenario. You will determine the reason why a wireless client is unable to connect to a wireless router and correct the problem.

Refer to the online course to complete this Packet Tracer.

Common Internet Connectivity Issues (36.4)

There are several connectivity issues that can be attributed to other devices such as the DHCP server or with reaching the ISP.

DHCP Server Configuration Errors (36.4.1)

If the physical connection to the wired or wireless host appears to be connecting as expected but the host cannot communicate on remote networks or the Internet, then check the IP configuration of the client.

The IP configuration can have a major impact on the ability for a host to connect to the network. A wireless router acts as a DHCP server for local wired and wireless clients and provides IP configuration, including the IP address, subnet mask, default gateway, and commonly the IP addresses of DNS servers. The DHCP server binds the IP address to a client MAC address and stores that information in a client table. It is usually possible to view this table using the configuration GUI included with the router.

The client table information should match the local host information, which you can see using the **ipconfig /all** command. Additionally, the IP address on the client must be on the same network as the LAN interface of the wireless router. The LAN interface of the wireless router should be set as the default gateway. If the client configuration information does not agree with information in the client table, the address should be released (**ipconfig /release**) and renewed (**ipconfig /renew**) to form a new binding.

In most cases, the wireless router receives its own IP address through DHCP from the ISP. Check to make sure that the router has an IP address (Figure 36-8), and attempt to release and renew the address using the GUI utility.

Check Internet Configuration (36.4.2)

If hosts on the wired and wireless local network can connect to the wireless router and with other hosts on the local network, but not to the Internet, as shown in Example 36-1 and Figure 36-9, the problem may be in the connection between the router and the ISP.

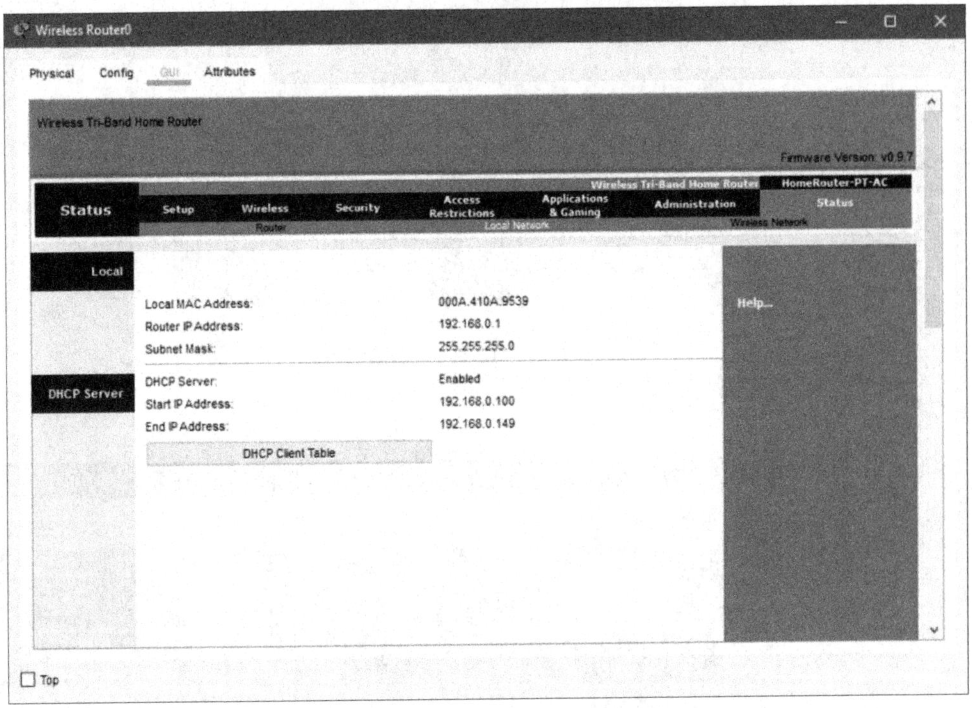

Figure 36-8 DHCP Configuration Received from the ISP

Example 36-1 A Failed Ping

```
C:\> ping 10.18.32.12
Pinging 10.18.32.12 with 32 bytes of data:
Request timed out.
Request timed out.
Request timed out.
Request timed out.

Ping statistics for 10.18.32.12:
     Packets: Sent = 4, Received = 0, Lost = 4 (100% loss),
```

There are many ways to verify connectivity between the router and the ISP. Using the GUI, one way to check connectivity is to examine the router status page. As shown in Figure 36-10, it should show the IP address assigned by the ISP (64.100.0.11 in this example).

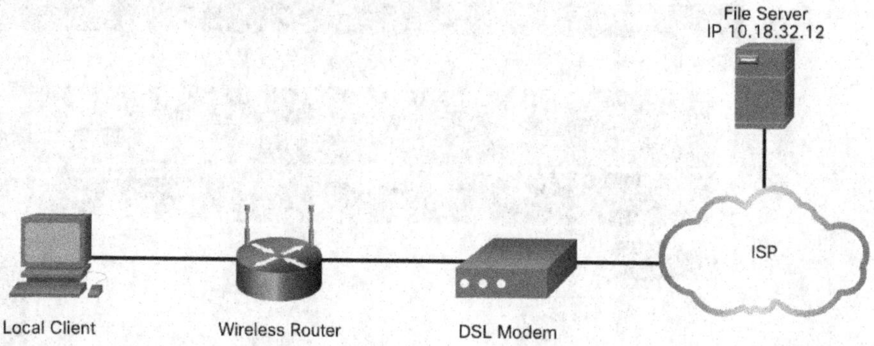

Figure 36-9 Example Topology

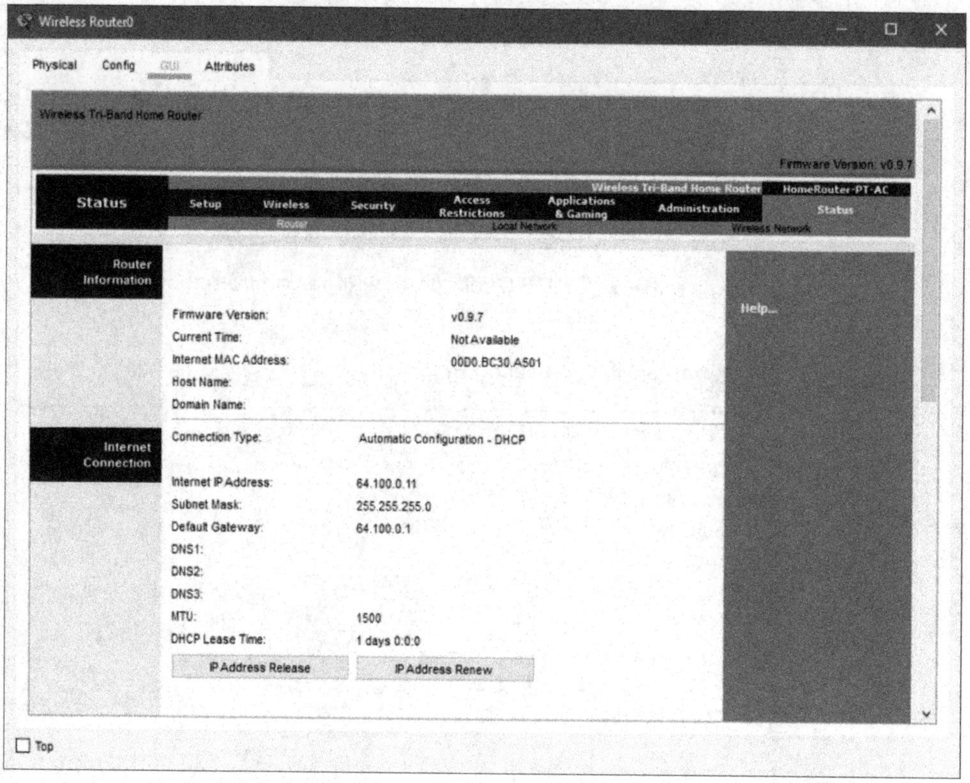

Figure 36-10 ISP Configuration

If this page shows no connection, the wireless router may not be connected. Check all physical connections and LED indicators. If the DSL or cable modem is a separate device, check those connections and indicators as well. If the ISP requires a login name and password, check that they are configured to match those given by the ISP.

Using the GUI, password configurations can normally be located on the Setup configuration page. Next, try to reestablish connectivity by clicking the Connect, or IP Address Renew, button on the status page. If the wireless router will still not connect, contact the ISP to see if the issue is occurring from their end.

Check Firewall Settings (36.4.3)

If Layers 1 through 3 all appear to be operating normally and you can successfully ping the IP address of the remote server, it is time to check the higher layers. For example, if a network firewall is used along the path (Figure 36-11), it is important to check that the application TCP or UDP port is open and no filter lists are blocking traffic to that port.

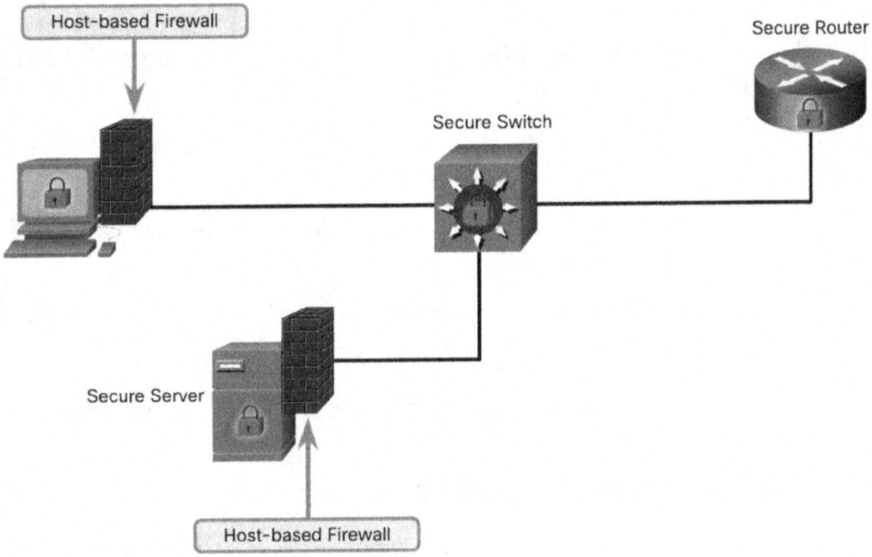

Figure 36-11 Example of Firewalls in a Small Topology

If all clients are obtaining the correct IP configuration and can connect to the wireless router but are unable to ping each other or cannot access a remote server or application, the problem may be with rules on the router. Check all settings on the router to ensure no security restrictions could be causing the issue. Verify that the local firewalls on the client devices are not preventing network functionality.

Interactive Graphic

Check Your Understanding—Common Internet Connectivity Issues (36.4.4)

Refer to the online course to complete this activity.

Divide and Conquer with ping (36.4.5)

Connectivity problems occur on wireless networks, wired networks, and networks that use both. When troubleshooting a network with both wired and wireless connections, it is often best to troubleshoot using a divide-and-conquer technique to isolate the problem to either the wired or the wireless network.

A number of software utility programs are available that can help identify the cause and location of network problems. Some of the available utilities include

- **netstat**—Displays network connections.
- **tracert**—Displays the route taken to the destination.
- **nslookup**—Directly queries the name server for information on a destination domain.

The easiest way to determine if the problem is with the wired or the wireless network is to do the following:

- Ping from a wireless client to the default gateway. This verifies if the wireless client is connecting as expected.
- Ping from a wired client to the default gateway. This verifies if the wired client is connecting as expected.
- Ping from the wireless client to a wired client. This verifies if the wireless router is functioning as expected.

After the problem is isolated, it can be corrected.

The tracert Command (36.4.6)

Although **ping** is the most commonly used network troubleshooting command, there are other useful commands that are available on Windows devices.

The **ping** command can verify end-to-end connectivity. However, if a problem exists and the device cannot ping the destination, the **ping** command does not indicate where the connection was really dropped. To pinpoint this, another command known as **traceroute** or **tracert** must be used. Microsoft Windows uses the **tracert** command, while other operating systems commonly use the command **traceroute**.

The **tracert** utility provides connectivity information about the path a packet takes to reach the destination and about every router (hop) along the way. It also indicates how long a packet takes to get from the source to each hop and back (round-trip

time). The **tracert** utility can help identify where a packet may have been lost or delayed due to bottlenecks or slowdowns in the network.

In Example 36-2, the user is tracing the path to Cisco. The path is unique to this user. Your path will have a different listing of hops and may be shorter or longer (number of hops).

Note

Notice in the output that the second hop failed. This is most likely due to a firewall configuration on that device that does not permit responding to packets from the **tracert** command. However, the device does forward the packets to the next hop.

Example 36-2 Tracing a Route to Cisco

```
C:\> tracert www.cisco.com

Tracing route to e2867.dsca.someispedge.net [104.95.63.78]
over a maximum of 30 hops:

  1     1 ms     1 ms    <1 ms  10.10.10.1
  2      *        *        *     Request timed out.
  3     8 ms     8 ms     8 ms  24-155-250-94.dyn.yourisp.net [172.30.250.94]
  4    22 ms    23 ms    23 ms  24-155-121-218.static.yourisp.net [172.30.121.218]
  5    23 ms    24 ms    25 ms  dls-b22-link.anotherisp.net [64.0.70.170]
  6    25 ms    24 ms    25 ms  dls-b23-link.anotherisp.net [192.168.137.106]
  7    24 ms    23 ms    21 ms  someisp-ic-341035-dls-b1.c.anotherisp.net
  [192.168.169.47]
  8    25 ms    24 ms    23 ms  ae3.databank-dfw5.netarch.someisp.com
  [10.250.230.195]
  9    25 ms    24 ms    24 ms  a104-95-63-78.deploy.static.someisptechnologies.
  com [104.95.63.78]

Trace complete.

C:\>
```

The basic **tracert** command will only allow up to 30 hops between a source and destination device before it assumes that the destination is unreachable. This number is adjustable by using the **-h** parameter. Other modifiers, displayed as options in Example 36-3, are also available.

Example 36-3 The Options for the **tracert** Command

```
C:\> tracert

Usage: tracert [-d] [-h maximum_hops] [-j host-list] [-w timeout]
               [-R] [-S srcaddr] [-4] [-6] target_name

Options:
    -d                  Do not resolve addresses to hostnames.
    -h maximum_hops     Maximum number of hops to search for target.
    -j host-list        Loose source route along host-list (IPv4-only).
    -w timeout          Wait timeout milliseconds for each reply.
    -R                  Trace round-trip path (IPv6-only).
    -S srcaddr          Source address to use (IPv6-only).
    -4                  Force using IPv4.
    -6                  Force using IPv6.

C:\>
```

The netstat Command (36.4.7)

Sometimes it is necessary to know which active TCP connections are open and running on a networked host. The **netstat** command is an important network utility that can be used to verify those connections. As shown in Example 36-4, the **netstat** command lists the protocol in use, the local address and port number, the foreign address and port number, and the state of the connection.

Example 36-4 The **netstat** Command

```
C:\> netstat

Active Connections

  Proto  Local Address          Foreign Address          State
  TCP    10.10.10.130:58520     dfw28s01-in-f14:https    ESTABLISHED
  TCP    10.10.10.130:58522     dfw25s25-in-f14:https    ESTABLISHED
  TCP    10.10.10.130:58523     dfw25s25-in-f14:https    ESTABLISHED
  TCP    10.10.10.130:58525     ec2-3-13-132-189:https   ESTABLISHED
  TCP    10.10.10.130:58579     203.104.160.12:https     ESTABLISHED
  TCP    10.10.10.130:58580     104.16.249.249:https     ESTABLISHED
  TCP    10.10.10.130:58624     52.242.211.89:https      ESTABLISHED
  TCP    10.10.10.130:58628     24-155-92-110:https      ESTABLISHED
  TCP    10.10.10.130:58651     ec2-18-211-133-65:https  ESTABLISHED
  TCP    10.10.10.130:58686     do-33:https              ESTABLISHED
```

```
  TCP    10.10.10.130:58720     172.253.119.189:https  ESTABLISHED
  TCP    10.10.10.130:58751     ec2-35-170-0-145:https  ESTABLISHED
  TCP    10.10.10.130:58753     ec2-44-224-80-214:https  ESTABLISHED
  TCP    10.10.10.130:58755     a23-65-237-228:https   ESTABLISHED

C:\>
```

Unexplained TCP connections can pose a major security threat. This is because they can indicate that something or someone is connected to the local host. Additionally, unnecessary TCP connections can consume valuable system resources, thus slowing down the performance of the host. Netstat should be used to examine the open connections on a host when performance appears to be compromised.

Many useful options are available for the **netstat** command. These options can be viewed by typing **netstat /?** at the command prompt, as shown in Example 36-5.

Example 36-5 Options for the **netstat** Command

```
C:\> netstat /?

Displays protocol statistics and current TCP/IP network connections.

NETSTAT [-a] [-b] [-e] [-f] [-n] [-o] [-p proto] [-r] [-s] [-t] [-x] [-y]
  [interval]

  -a            Displays all connections and listening ports.
  -b            Displays the executable involved in creating each connection or
                listening port. In some cases well-known executables host
                multiple independent components, and in these cases the
                sequence of components involved in creating the connection
                or listening port is displayed. In this case the executable
                name is in [] at the bottom, on top is the component it called,
                and so forth until TCP/IP was reached. Note that this option
                can be time-consuming and will fail unless you have sufficient
                permissions.
  -e            Displays Ethernet statistics. This may be combined with the -s
                option.
  -f            Displays Fully Qualified Domain Names (FQDN) for foreign
                addresses.
  -n            Displays addresses and port numbers in numerical form.
  -o            Displays the owning process ID associated with each connection.
```

```
  -p proto      Shows connections for the protocol specified by proto; proto
                may be any of: TCP, UDP, TCPv6, or UDPv6.  If used with the -s
                option to display per-protocol statistics, proto may be any of:
                IP, IPv6, ICMP, ICMPv6, TCP, TCPv6, UDP, or UDPv6.
  -q            Displays all connections, listening ports, and bound
                nonlistening TCP ports. Bound nonlistening ports may or may not
                be associated with an active connection.
  -r            Displays the routing table.
  -s            Displays per-protocol statistics.  By default, statistics are
                shown for IP, IPv6, ICMP, ICMPv6, TCP, TCPv6, UDP, and UDPv6;
                the -p option may be used to specify a subset of the default.
  -t            Displays the current connection offload state.
  -x            Displays NetworkDirect connections, listeners, and shared
                endpoints.
  -y            Displays the TCP connection template for all connections.
                Cannot be combined with the other options.
  interval      Redisplays selected statistics, pausing interval seconds
                between each display.  Press CTRL+C to stop redisplaying
                statistics.  If omitted, netstat will print the current
                configuration information once.

C:\>
```

The nslookup Command (36.4.8)

When a network device is being configured, one or more DNS server addresses are provided that the DNS client can use for name resolution. Usually, the ISP provides the addresses to use for the DNS servers. When a user application requests to connect to a remote device by name, the requesting DNS client queries the name server to resolve the name to a numeric address.

Computer operating systems also have a utility called **nslookup** that allows the user to manually query the name servers to resolve a given host name. This utility can also be used to troubleshoot name resolution issues and to verify the current status of the name servers.

In Example 36-6, when the **nslookup** command is issued, the default DNS server configured for your host is displayed. The name of a host or domain can be entered at the **nslookup** prompt. The **nslookup** utility has many options available for extensive testing and verification of the DNS process.

Example 36-6 Looking Up Cisco Information with the **nslookup** Command

```
C:\Users> nslookup
Default Server:  dns-sj.cisco.com
Address:  171.70.168.183
> www.cisco.com
Server:  dns-sj.cisco.com
Address:  171.70.168.183
Name:     origin-www.cisco.com
Addresses:  2001:420:1101:1::a
            173.37.145.84
Aliases:  www.cisco.com
> cisco.netacad.net
Server:  dns-sj.cisco.com
Address:  171.70.168.183
Name:     cisco.netacad.net
Address:  72.163.6.223
>
```

Interactive Graphic

Syntax Checker—The nslookup Command (36.4.9)

Practice entering the **nslookup** command in both Windows and Linux.

Refer to the online course to complete this activity.

Lab—Troubleshoot Using Network Utilities (36.4.10)

In this lab, you will complete the following objectives:

- Interpret the output of commonly used network command-line utilities.
- Determine which network utility can provide the necessary information to perform troubleshooting activities in a bottom-up troubleshooting strategy.

Customer Support (36.5)

Knowing where to find help when needed is an important part of being able to solve networking issues.

Sources of Help (36.5.1)

If, during the troubleshooting process, you are unable to determine the problem and its resolution, it might be necessary to obtain assistance from outside sources. Some of the most common sources for help include these:

- **Documentation**—Good documentation can save a great deal of time and effort by directing the troubleshooter to the most likely cause of the problem. It can also provide the technical information required to isolate, verify, and correct the issue. The documentation provided with many networking devices, however, often does not provide sufficient information to troubleshoot anything except the most basic issues.
- **Online FAQs (Frequently Asked Questions)**—Most manufacturers provide a series of FAQs about their product or technology on their website. Usually based on previous requests for help, FAQs are a good source of current information and should be consulted whenever possible.
- **Internet searches**—With the increased availability of support forums, troubleshooters can now obtain assistance from people around the world in real time.
- **Colleagues**—Colleagues are often a wealth of information; there is no substitute for troubleshooting experience.

When to Call for Help (36.5.2)

Sometimes we cannot solve networking issues by ourselves. It may be necessary to contact the vendor or ISP support desk for assistance, as shown in Figure 36-12. The customer support line or support desk is the first stop for end-user assistance. The support desk is a group of individuals with the knowledge and tools required to help diagnose and correct common problems. It provides assistance for the end user to determine if a problem exists, the nature of the problem, and the solution.

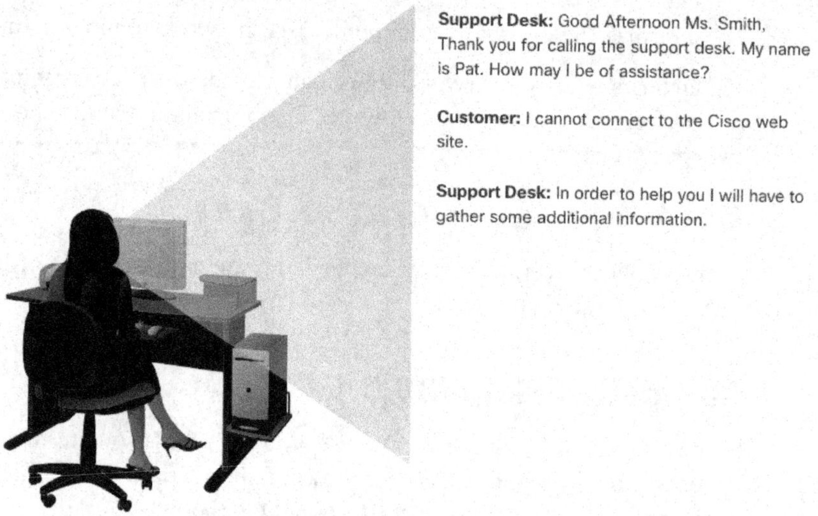

Figure 36-12 An Example of a Customer Support Call

Many companies and ISPs establish support desks to assist their users with networking problems. Most large IT companies run support desks for their individual products or technologies. For example, Cisco Systems offers support desk assistance for problems integrating Cisco equipment into a network or problems that may occur after installation.

There are many ways to contact a support desk, including email, live chat, and phone. While email is good for non-urgent problems, phone or live chat is better for network emergencies. This is especially important in organizations such as banks where small amounts of downtime can cost large amounts of money.

If necessary, the support desk can take control of a local host through remote-access software. This allows support desk technicians to run diagnostic programs and interact with the host and network without having to physically travel to a job site. This greatly reduces the wait time for problem resolution and allows the support desk to assist more users.

Support Desk Interaction (36.5.3)

As an end user, it is important to give the support desk as much information as possible, as shown in Figure 36-13. The support desk will require information on any service or support plans that are in place along with specific details of the affected equipment. This can include make, model, and serial number along with the version of firmware or operating system running on the device. They may also require the IP and MAC addresses of the malfunctioning device. The support desk will require information specific to the problem:

- What symptoms were encountered?
- Who encountered the problem?
- When did the problem manifest?
- What steps have been taken to identify the problem?
- What were the results of steps taken?

If this is a follow-up call, be prepared to provide the date and time of the previous call, the ticket number, and name of the technician. Be at the affected equipment, and be prepared to provide the support desk staff with access to the equipment if requested.

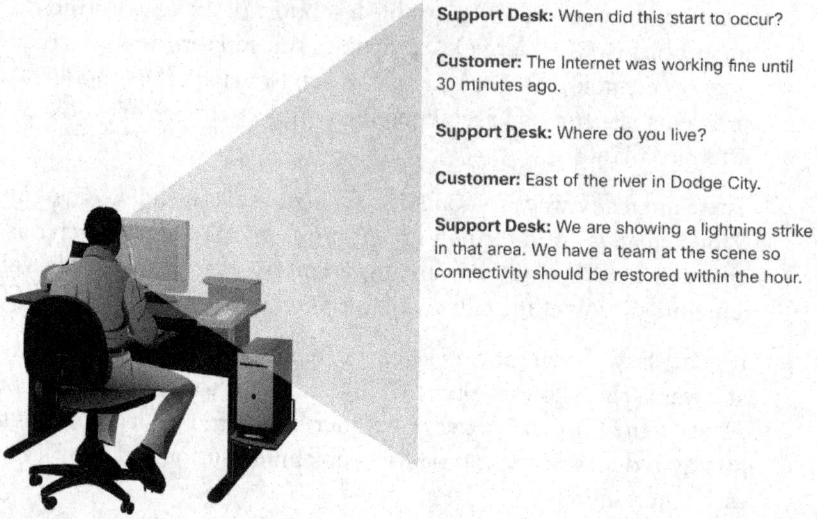

Figure 36-13 Providing Information to Customer Support

Issue Resolution (36.5.4)

A support desk is generally organized in a series of levels of experience and knowledge. If the first-level support desk staff is unable to solve the problem they may escalate the problem to a higher level. Higher-level staff are generally more knowledgeable and have access to resources and tools that the first-level support desk does not.

Record all information regarding the interaction with the support desk, such as

- Time/date of call
- Name/ID of technician
- Problem reported
- Course of action taken
- Resolution/escalation
- Next steps (follow-up)

By working together with the support desk, most problems can be resolved quickly and easily. When resolved, be sure to update all documentation accordingly for future reference.

Support Desk Tickets and Work Orders (36.5.5)

When a Level 1 support desk technician receives a call, there is a process followed to gather information. There are also specific systems for storing and retrieving relevant

information. It is extremely important to gather the information correctly in the event that a call has to be escalated to a Level 2 technician or require an onsite visit.

The information gathering and recording process starts as soon as the technician answers the phone. After customer identification, the technician accesses the relevant customer information. Typically, a database application is used to manage the customer information.

The information is transferred to a trouble ticket, or incident report. This document can be a piece of paper in a paper filing system or an electronic tracking system designed to follow the troubleshooting process from beginning to end. Each person who works on the problem is expected to record what was done on the trouble ticket. When an onsite call is required, the trouble ticket information can be converted to a work order that the onsite technician can take to the customer site.

When a problem is resolved, the solution is documented in the customer work order (Figure 36-14) or trouble ticket and in a knowledge base document for future reference.

Work Order

Student Technician Sheet

Company Name:	JH Travel, Inc.
Contact:	Dan Handy
Company Address:	204 N. Main Street
Company Phone:	1-866-555-0998

Generating a New Ticket

Category:	Hardware	**Closure Code:**	N/A	**Status:**	Open
Type:	N/A	**Escalated:**	Yes	**Pending:**	N/A
Item:	N/A			**Pending Until Date:**	N/A
Business Impacting? (Yes / No)	Yes				
Summary	The computer will not turn on or the computer beeps constantly.				
Case ID#:	47	**Connection Type:**	N/A		
Priority:	2	**Environment:**	N/A		
User Platform:	Windows 10				

Problem Description:

Computer will not boot. Customer does not know the manufacturer of the BIOS. Customer cannot identify error from beep sequence. Customer did not hear any strange sounds from the computer. Customer does not smell smoke or burning electronics.

Problem Solution:

Verified external cable connections. Mouse and keyboard connections were reversed (if applicable). Connections were corrected. Internal hardware and cable connections were verified. RAM was not installed. Customer installed RAM. Optical drive power cable was disconnected. Optical drive power cable was reconnected. Hard drive data cable was disconnected from the motherboard. Hard drive data cable was reconnected to the motherboard. Computer displayed "Non-system disk or disk error" upon reboot. Computer was shut down and rebooted to confirm the solution. Front panel power on switch cable was unplugged from the motherboard. Front panel power on switch cable was reconnected to the motherboard.

Figure 36-14 An Example of a Work Order

Interactive Graphic

Check Your Understanding—Customer Support (36.5.6)

Refer to the online course to complete this activity.

Troubleshoot Common Network Problems Summary (36.6)

The following is a summary of each topic in the chapter.

What Did I Learn in This Chapter? (36.6.1)

- **The Troubleshooting Process**—Troubleshooting is the process of identifying, locating, and correcting problems that occur. There are structured techniques that can be used to determine the most probable cause and solution. Document all steps taken in troubleshooting, even the ones that did not solve the issue.

  To gather information about a problem, start by talking to the individual who reported the problem as well as any other affected users. Next, collect information about any equipment that may be affected. This can be gathered from documentation. A copy of all log files and a listing of any recent changes made to equipment configurations are also necessary. Information about the network can also be gathered using network monitoring tools.

  Choose a troubleshooting approach to organize your efforts to fix the problem. Here are three structured troubleshooting techniques: top-down, divide-and-conquer, and bottom-up. All of these structured approaches assume a layered concept of networking. Other good approaches are follow-the-path, substitution, comparison, and educated guess.

- **Physical Layer Problems**—Physical layer problems are concerned mainly with the hardware aspects of computers and networking devices and the cables that interconnect them. To troubleshoot at Layer 1, first check that all devices have power supplied, and that the devices are turned on. If the problem is with wireless, verify that the wireless access point is operational and that wireless settings are configured correctly.

  Regardless of whether the fault is present on the wireless or wired network, one of the first steps in a bottom-up strategy of troubleshooting should be to examine the LEDs, which indicate the current state or activity of a piece of equipment or connection. Cabling is the central nervous system of wired networks and one of the most common causes of connectivity problems. Be sure to use the correct type of cable. Improper cable termination is one of the main problems encountered in networks. To avoid this, cables should be terminated according to

standards. Maximum cable run lengths exist based on characteristics of the different cables. Verify that the correct ports are being used between the networking devices. Protect cables and connectors from physical damage.

- **Troubleshoot Wireless Issues**—Wireless communications rely on RF signals to carry data. Many factors can affect our ability to connect hosts using RF:
  - Not all wireless standards are compatible.
  - Each wireless conversation must occur on a separate, non-overlapping channel.
  - The strength of an RF signal decreases with distance.
  - RF signals are susceptible to interference from outside sources, including other devices functioning on the same frequency.
  - APs share the available bandwidth between devices.

  Modern WLANs incorporate various technologies to help secure the data on the WLAN. Incorrect configuration of any of these can prevent communication. Some of the most common settings that are configured incorrectly include the SSID, authentication, and encryption.

- **Common Internet Connectivity Issues**—A number of software utility programs are available that can help identify network problems. Some of the available utilities include **ipconfig**, **ping**, **netstat**, **tracert**, and **nslookup**.

  On Windows devices, you can view the IP configuration information with the **ipconfig** command at the command prompt. If the IP configuration appears to be correctly configured on the local host, then test network connectivity by using ping. Ping is used to test if a destination host is reachable.

  When troubleshooting a network with both wired and wireless connections, use a divide-and-conquer technique to isolate the problem to either the wired or wireless network. The easiest way to determine if the problem is with the wired or the wireless network is to
  - Ping from a wireless client to the default gateway, which verifies if the wireless client is connecting as expected.
  - Ping from a wired client to the default gateway, which verifies if the wired client is connecting as expected.
  - Ping from the wireless client to a wired client, which verifies if the wireless router is functioning as expected.

  The **tracert** utility provides connectivity information about the path a packet takes to reach the destination and about every router (hop) along the way. It also indicates how long a packet takes to get from the source to each hop and back

(round-trip time). Tracert can help identify where a packet may have been lost or delayed due to bottlenecks or slowdowns in the network.

Sometimes it is necessary to know which active TCP connections are open and running on a networked host. Netstat is an important network utility that can be used to verify those connections. Netstat lists the protocol in use, the local address and port number, the foreign address and port number, and the state of the connection.

The **nslookup** utility allows an end user to look up information about a particular DNS name in the DNS server. When the **nslookup** command is issued, the information returned includes the IP address of the DNS server being used as well as the IP address associated with the specified DNS name. Nslookup is often used as a troubleshooting tool for determining if the DNS server is performing name resolution as expected.

If the physical connection to the wired or wireless host appears to be connecting as expected, then check the IP configuration of the client. In most cases, the wireless router receives its own IP address through DHCP from the ISP. Check to make sure that the router has an IP address, and attempt to release and renew the address using the GUI utility.

If hosts on the wired and wireless local network can connect to the wireless router and with other hosts on the local network, but not to the Internet, the problem may be in the connection between the router and the ISP. Using the GUI, one way to check connectivity is to examine the router Status page. It should show the IP address assigned by the ISP and should indicate if the connection is established. If this page shows no connection, the wireless router may not be connected. If the wireless router will still not connect, contact the ISP to see if the issue is occurring from their end.

If a network firewall is used along the path, it is important to check that the application TCP or UDP port is open and no filter lists are blocking traffic to that port. If all clients are obtaining the correct IP configuration and can connect to the wireless router but are unable to ping each other, or cannot access a remote server or application, the problem may be with rules on the router. Check all settings on the router to ensure no security restrictions could be causing the issue. Verify that the local firewalls on the client devices are not preventing network functionality.

- **Customer Support**—Some of the most common sources for help include previously kept documentation, online FAQs, colleagues and other network professionals, and Internet sources including forums, articles, and blogs. The support desk is a group of individuals with the knowledge and tools required to help diagnose and correct common problems. If necessary, the support desk can take

control of a local host through remote-access software. The support desk will require information specific to the problem, including symptoms encountered, who encountered the problem, when the problem manifests, steps taken to identify the problem, and results of steps taken.

If the first-level support desk staff is unable to solve the problem, they may escalate the problem to a higher level. Higher-level staff are generally more knowledgeable and have access to resources and tools that the first-level support desk does not. Record all information regarding the interaction with the support desk, such as time/date of call, name/ID of technician, problem reported, course of action taken, resolution/escalation, and next steps.

When a Level 1 support desk technician receives a call, there is a process followed to gather information. There are also specific systems for storing and retrieving relevant information. It is extremely important to gather the information correctly in the event that a call has to be escalated to Level 2 or require an onsite visit. The information is transferred to a trouble ticket, or incident report. When a problem is resolved, the solution is documented in the customer work order or trouble ticket and in a knowledge base document for future reference.

Practice

The following activity provides practice with the topics introduced in this chapter.

Packet Tracer Activities

Packet Tracer
Activity

Packet Tracer—Troubleshoot a Wireless Connection (36.3.3)

Check Your Understanding Questions

Complete all the review questions listed here to test your understanding of the topics and concepts in this chapter. Appendix A, "Answers to 'Check Your Understanding' Questions," lists the answers.

1. The home computer of a user is working properly. However, the user cannot access the Internet. The Internet connection is provided through a cable company. The user cannot identify the cause of the problem. Whom should the user contact for further help?

   a. The help line of the cable company

   b. The support website of the computer vendor

   c. The help line of the computer manufacturer

   d. The operating system vendor

2. A network technician enters the command **ipconfig /release** followed by **ipconfig /renew** in order to ensure that the DHCP IP configuration on a workstation is updated. However, the workstation does not receive a valid IP configuration for the network. Which two problems may exist on the network? (Choose two.)

   a. The **ipconfig /all** command must be issued to restore all IP configurations.

   b. There is no network connectivity to the DHCP server.

   c. The DHCP lease time is misconfigured.

   d. There is a DHCP server issue.

   e. The gateway router address needs to be updated.

3. Refer to the following figure. The command output is from a wireless DHCP host connected to a Linksys integrated router. What can be determined from the output?

```
C:\>ipconfig
Ethernet adapter Wireless Network Connection:

     Connection-specific DNS Suffix. .:
     IP Address.........................: 192.168.10.100
     Subnet Mask .....................: 255.255.255.0
     Default Gateway ...............: 192.168.1.1

<output omitted>

C:\>ping 192.168.1.1

Pinging 192.168.1.1 with 32 bytes of data:

Request timed out.
Request timed out.
Request timed out.
Request timed out.
```

a. There is a DNS problem.
b. The DHCP configuration needs to be checked.
c. The connection to the SSID needs to be verified.
d. The new wireless NIC needs to be installed.
e. An incorrect cable is being used between the host and the router.

4. A customer called the cable company to report that the Internet connection is unstable. After trying several configuration changes, the technician decided to send the customer a new cable modem to try. What troubleshooting technique does this represent?

   a. Divide-and-conquer
   b. Top-down
   c. Bottom-up
   d. Substitution

5. A small office uses a wireless router to connect to a cable modem for Internet access. The network administrator receives a call that one office computer cannot access external websites. The first troubleshooting step that the network administrator performs is to ping the wireless router from the office computer. Which troubleshooting technique does this represent?

   a. Bottom-up
   b. Substitution
   c. Divide-and-conquer
   d. Top-down

6. A network administrator can successfully ping the server at www.cisco.com, but cannot ping the company web server located at an ISP in another city. Which tool or command would help identify the specific router where the packet was lost or delayed?

   a. **telnet**

   b. **ipconfig**

   c. **traceroute**

   d. **netstat**

7. Which command would a technician use to display network connections on a host computer?

   a. **nslookup**

   b. **tracert**

   c. **ipconfig**

   d. **netstat**

8. Which three items should be documented after troubleshooting an internal web server crash? (Choose three.)

   a. Steps that were performed that failed to identify the cause of the problem

   b. When the problem occurred

   c. Steps that were performed to identify the cause of the problem

   d. The dialogue with the user

   e. The configuration of all hosts on the LAN at the time of the crash

   f. The configuration of all networking devices on the LAN at the time of the crash

9. A user calls the help desk to report a workstation problem. Which three questions would produce the most helpful information for troubleshooting? (Choose three.)

   a. What operating system version is running on your workstation?

   b. Have you performed a backup recently?

   c. What changes have you made to your workstation?

   d. If you received an error message, what was it?

   e. Do you have the warranty for your workstation?

   f. Have you used a network monitoring tool on your workstation?

10. What are two common causes of a physical layer network connectivity problem? (Choose two.)

    a. An Ethernet cable plugged into a wrong port
    b. A faulty Ethernet cable
    c. An incorrect default gateway
    d. An unassigned IP address
    e. A monitor unplugged

11. Refer to the following figure. A web designer calls to report that the web server web-s1.cisco.com is not reachable through a web browser. The technician uses command-line utilities to verify the problem and to begin the troubleshooting process. Which two things can be determined about the problem? (Choose two.)

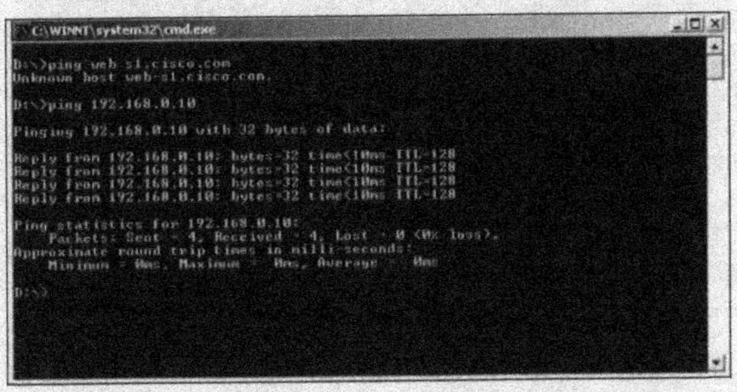

    a. The web server at 192.168.68.106 is reachable from the source host.
    b. There is a problem with the web server software on web-s1.cisco.com.
    c. DNS cannot resolve the IP address for the server web-s1.cisco.com.
    d. The default gateway between the source host and the server at 192.168.68.106 is down.
    e. A router is down between the source host and the server web-s1.cisco.com.

12. Which step should be taken next once a problem is resolved during a troubleshooting process?

    a. Update the documentation.
    b. Consult an FAQ.
    c. Run remote-access software.
    d. Escalate the problem.

CHAPTER 37

Network Support

Objectives

Upon completion of this chapter, you will be able to answer the following questions:

- Can you demonstrate effective troubleshooting methodologies?
- How do you create network documentation?
- What are help desk best practices?
- How do you verify network connectivity in the operating systems of Windows, Linux, MacOS, Android, and Apple iOS devices?
- How do you troubleshoot a network?
- How do you troubleshoot connectivity remotely?

Key Terms

This chapter uses the following key terms. You can find the definitions in the Glossary.

baseline Page 718

bottom-up troubleshooting Page 702

Cisco Discovery Protocol (CDP) Page 719

divide-and-conquer troubleshooting Page 702

top-down troubleshooting Page 702

Introduction (37.0)

Hello! It's Webster. Let me introduce you to my friend Lara! Lara has been working as a help desk technician in the IT department for a small community college in Brisbane, Australia, for just over a year. The help desk receives numerous IT support requests from administrators, faculty, and students. Lara has proven to be an excellent asset to the help desk team, as she is very effective at solving problems. Because of her superb work, Lara was recently promoted and assigned to develop a troubleshooting guide to help new technicians solve everyday IT problems. What approach would you use when diagnosing a reported problem? What documentation would you need to help do your job? How do you keep track of a reported problem? Which commands would be helpful when diagnosing endpoint and network problems? Keep reading, as we will answer these questions in this chapter.

Diagnostics and Troubleshooting Methodologies (37.1)

In this section, you will learn about the general troubleshooting process.

Troubleshooting Process Review (37.1.1)

Troubleshooting is the process of identifying, locating, and correcting problems. This process involves gathering information and using one or more structured troubleshooting methods.

After the problem in the network is first discovered, one of the first steps is to gather information. The following list provides a review of some of the information you may wish to collect.

- **Determine the nature of problem**
  - End-user reports
  - Problem verification report
- **Gather relevant equipment information**
  - Manufacturer
  - Make/model
  - Firmware version
  - Operating system version
  - Ownership/warranty information

- **Gather configuration and topology information**
  - Physical and logical topology
  - Configuration files
  - Log files
- **Determine if there were any similar issues previously**
  - Steps taken
  - Results achieved

Seven-Step Troubleshooting Process (37.1.2)

Figure 37-1 displays a more detailed seven-step troubleshooting process. Notice how some steps interconnect. This is because some technicians may be able to jump between steps based on their level of experience.

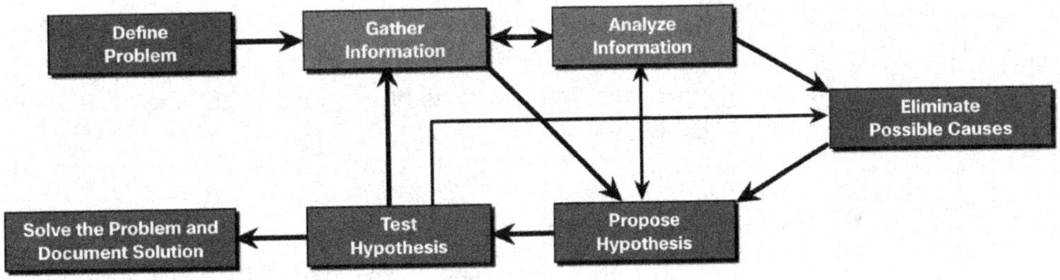

Figure 37-1 A Seven-Step Troubleshooting Process

Define the Problem

The goal of this stage is to verify that there is a problem and then properly define what the problem is. Problems are usually identified by a symptom (e.g., the network is slow or has stopped working). Network symptoms may appear in many different forms, including alerts from the network management system, console messages, and user complaints.

While gathering symptoms, it is important to ask questions and investigate the issue in order to localize the problem to a smaller range of possibilities. For example, is the problem restricted to a single device, a group of devices, or an entire subnet or network of devices?

In an organization, problems are typically assigned to network technicians as trouble tickets. These tickets are created using trouble ticketing software that tracks the progress of each ticket. Trouble ticketing software may also include a self-service

user portal to submit tickets, access to a searchable trouble tickets knowledge base, remote control capabilities to solve end-user issues, and more.

Gather Information

In this step, targets (i.e., hosts, devices) to be investigated must be identified, access to the target devices must be obtained, and information gathered. During this step, the technician may gather and document more symptoms, depending on the characteristics that are identified.

Analyze Information

Possible causes must be identified. The gathered information is interpreted and analyzed by using network documentation and network baselines, searching organizational knowledge bases, searching the Internet, and talking with other technicians.

Eliminate Possible Causes

If multiple causes are identified, then the list must be reduced by progressively eliminating possible causes to eventually identify the most probable cause. Troubleshooting experience is extremely valuable to quickly eliminate causes and identify the most probable cause.

Propose Hypothesis

When the most probable cause has been identified, a solution must be formulated. At this stage, troubleshooting experience is very valuable when proposing a plan.

Test Hypothesis

Before testing the solution, it is important to assess the impact and urgency of the problem. For instance, could the solution have an adverse effect on other systems or processes? The severity of the problem should be weighed against the impact of the solution. For example, if a critical server or router must be offline for a significant amount of time, it may be better to wait until the end of the workday to implement the fix. Sometimes, a workaround can be created until the actual problem is resolved.

Solve the Problem

When the problem is solved, inform the users and anyone involved in the troubleshooting process that the problem has been resolved. Other IT team members should be informed of the solution. It is important to properly document the cause and solution as this can assist other support technicians to prevent and solve similar problems in the future.

Troubleshooting with Layered Models (37.1.3)

The OSI and TCP/IP models can be applied to isolate network problems when troubleshooting. For example, if the symptoms suggest a physical connection problem, the network technician can focus on troubleshooting the cables and their connections at the physical layer.

Figure 37-2 shows some common devices and the OSI layers that must be examined during the troubleshooting process for that device.

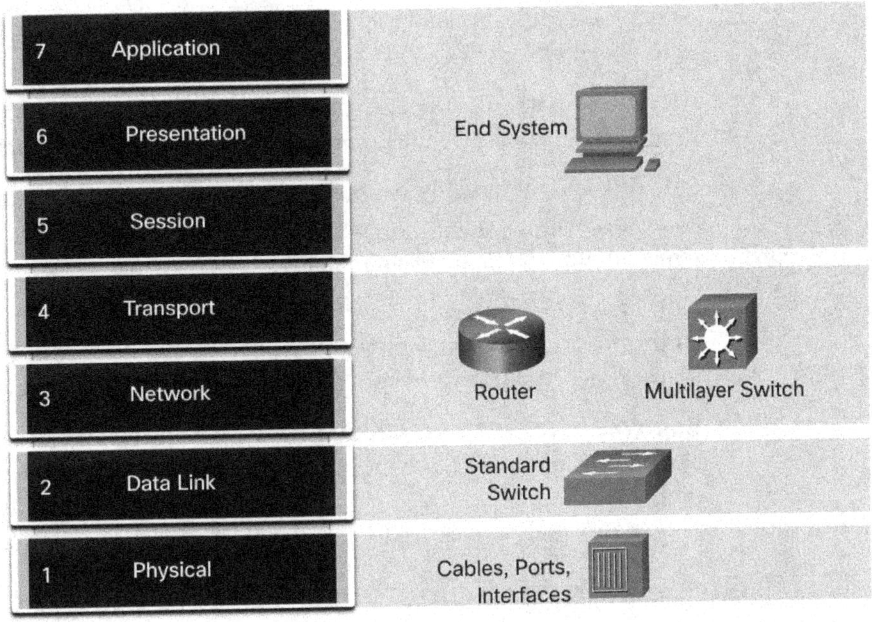

Figure 37-2 Layers of the OSI Model and Where Troubleshooting Typically Starts for Different Devices

Notice that routers and multilayer switches are shown at Layer 4, the transport layer. Although routers and multilayer switches usually make forwarding decisions at Layer 3, ACLs on these devices can be used to make filtering decisions using Layer 4 information.

Structured Troubleshooting Methods (37.1.4)

There are several structured troubleshooting methods that can be used to solve computer and network problems. The troubleshooting method used will vary depending on the type of problem and the personal experience of the technician.

A technician may choose one or more of the following troubleshooting methods to solve a problem:

- *Bottom-up*—Start with the physical layer and the physical components of the network and move up through the layers of the OSI model until the cause of the problem is identified.
- *Top-down*—Start with the end-user applications and move down through the layers of the OSI model until the cause of the problem has been identified.
- *Divide-and-conquer*—Start by collecting user experiences of the problem, document the symptoms, and then, using that information, make an informed guess as to which OSI layer to start your investigation.
- **Follow-the-path**—Discover the traffic path all the way from source to destination. This approach usually complements one of the other approaches.
- **Substitution**—Physically swap the problematic device or component with a known, working one. If the problem is fixed, then the problem is with the removed item. If the problem remains, then the cause is elsewhere.
- **Comparison**—Compare specifics such as configurations, software versions, hardware, or other device properties, links, or processes between working and nonworking situations and spot significant differences between them.
- **Educated guess**—A less-structured troubleshooting method uses an educated guess based on the experience of the technician and their ability to solve problems.

Guidelines for Selecting a Troubleshooting Method (37.1.5)

To quickly resolve network problems, take the time to select the most effective network troubleshooting method.

Figure 37-3 illustrates which method could be used when a certain type of problem is discovered.

For instance, software problems are often solved using a top-down approach while hardware-based problem are solved using the bottom-up approach. New problems may be solved by an experienced technician using the divide-and-conquer method. Otherwise, the bottom-up approach may be used.

Troubleshooting is a skill that is developed by doing it. Every network problem you identify and solve gets added to your skill set.

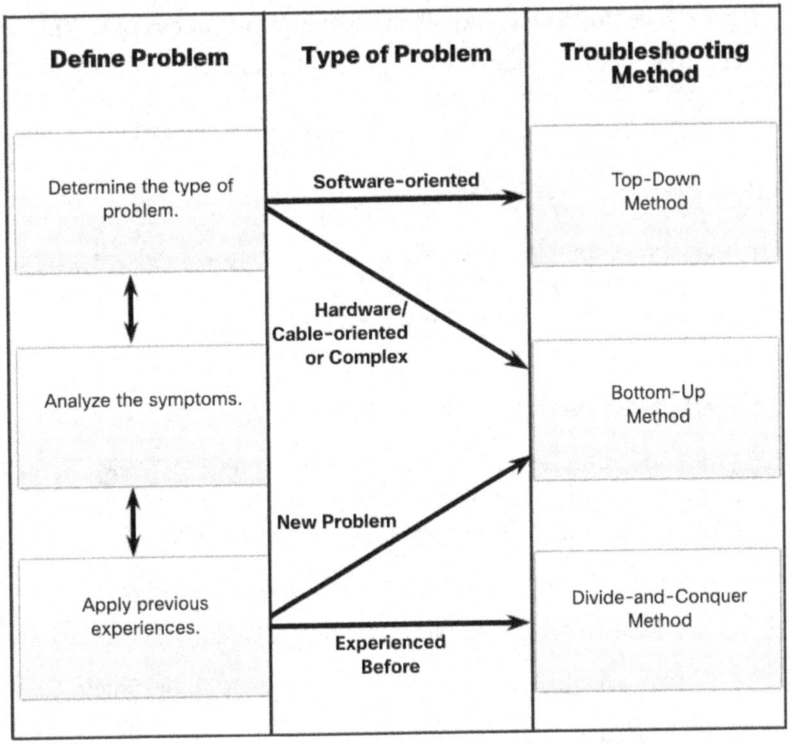

Figure 37-3 Different Troubleshooting Methods Used for Different Types of Problems

Document Findings, Actions, and Outcomes (37.1.6)

After troubleshooting and resolving all issues, it is important to complete the troubleshooting process by documenting all information.

A technician must document the following:

- **Problem**—Includes the initial report of the problem, a description of the symptoms, information gathered, and any other information that would help resolve similar problems.
- **Solution**—Includes the steps taken to resolve the problem.
- **Commands and tools used**—Include the commands and tools used in diagnosing the problem and solving the problem.

Verify the solution with the customer. If the customer is available, demonstrate how the solution has corrected their problem. Have the customer test the solution and try to reproduce the problem. When the customer can verify that the problem has been resolved, you can update the documentation with any new information provided by the customer.

Interactive Graphic

Check Your Understanding—Troubleshooting Process (37.1.7)

Refer to the online course to complete this activity.

Network Documentation (37.2)

Accurate and complete documentation can help you resolve problems with the network more quickly and avoid making additional mistakes. This section discusses the importance of network documentation.

Documentation Overview (37.2.1)

As with any complex activity like network troubleshooting, you will need to start with good documentation. Accurate and complete network documentation is required to effectively monitor and troubleshoot networks.

Common network documentation includes the following:

- Physical and logical network topology diagrams
- Network device documentation that records all pertinent device information
- Network performance baseline documentation

All network documentation should be kept in a single location, either as hard copy or on the network on a protected server. Backup documentation should be maintained and kept in a separate location.

Network Topologies and Descriptions (37.2.2)

Networks vary in size depending on the networking requirement. A technician must be knowledgeable about the different types of networks available to connect end devices and corporate sites, as described by the following sections.

PAN

A personal area network (PAN) is a network that connects devices such as mice, keyboards, printers, smartphones, and tablets within the range of an individual person (Figure 37-4). These devices are most often connected with Bluetooth technology. Bluetooth is a wireless technology that enables devices to communicate over short distances.

Figure 37-4 Example of a PAN Network

LAN

Traditionally, a local area network (LAN) is defined as a network that connects devices using wire cables in a small geographical area, such as the one shown in Figure 37-5. However, the distinguishing characteristic for LANs today is that they are typically owned by an individual, such as in a home or small business, or wholly managed by an IT department, such as in a school or corporation.

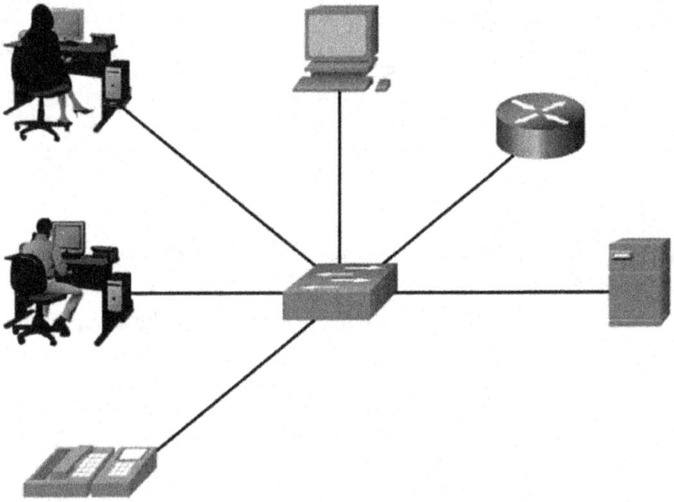

Figure 37-5 Example of a LAN Network

VLAN

A virtual LAN (VLAN) allows an administrator to segment the ports on a single switch as if it were multiple switches. This provides more efficient forwarding of data by isolating traffic to only those ports where it is required. VLANs also allow end devices to be grouped together for administrative purposes. In Figure 37-6, VLAN 2 creates a virtual LAN for IT's computers, even on different floors, and can have different network permissions set than the other VLANs.

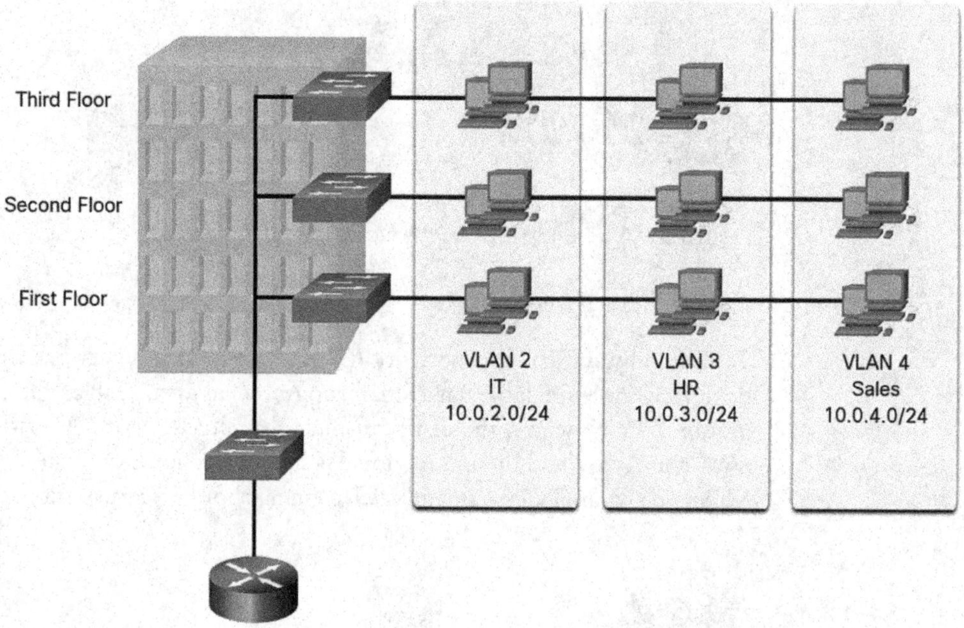

Figure 37-6 Example of VLANs

WLAN

A wireless LAN (WLAN) is similar to a LAN but wirelessly connects users and devices in a small geographical area instead of using a wired connection, as shown in Figure 37-7. A WLAN uses radio waves to transmit data between wireless devices.

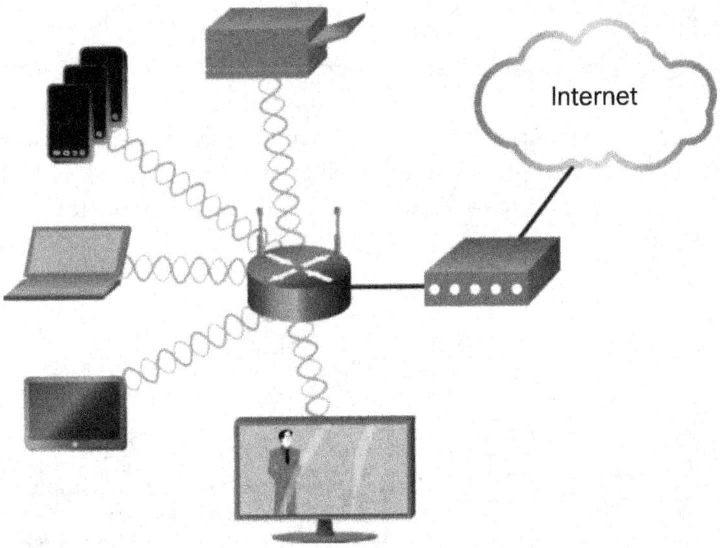

Figure 37-7 Example of a WLAN Network

WMN

A wireless mesh network (WMN) uses multiple access points to extend the WLAN. The topology in Figure 37-8 shows a wireless router. The two wireless APs extend the reach of the WLAN within the home. Similarly, businesses and municipalities can use WMNs to quickly add new areas of coverage.

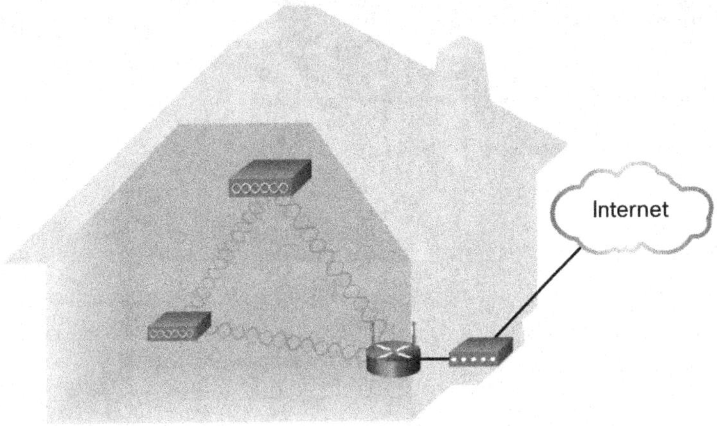

Figure 37-8 Example of a WMN Network

CAN

A campus area network (CAN) is a group of interconnected LANs, belonging to the same organization and operating in a limited geographical area. CANs are found in both academic campuses and business or corporate campuses. Campus area networks typically consist of several buildings interconnected by high-speed Ethernet links using fiber-optic cabling. Figure 37-9 shows three different-sized campus area networks.

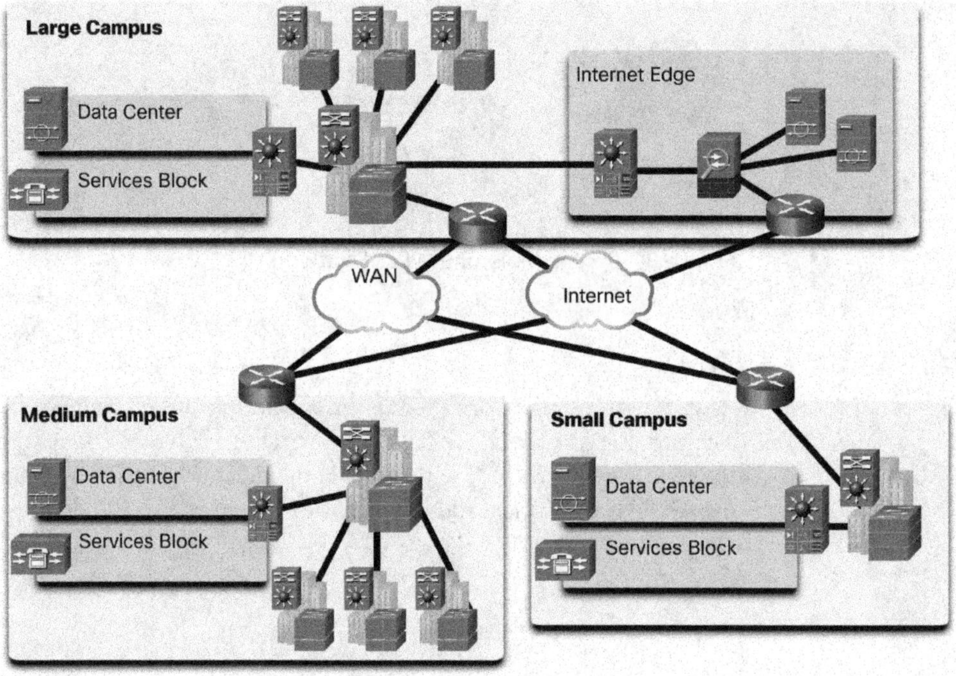

Figure 37-9 Examples of CAN Networks

MAN

A metropolitan area network (MAN) is a network that spans across a large campus or a city, as shown in Figure 37-10. The network consists of various buildings connected through wireless or fiber-optic media.

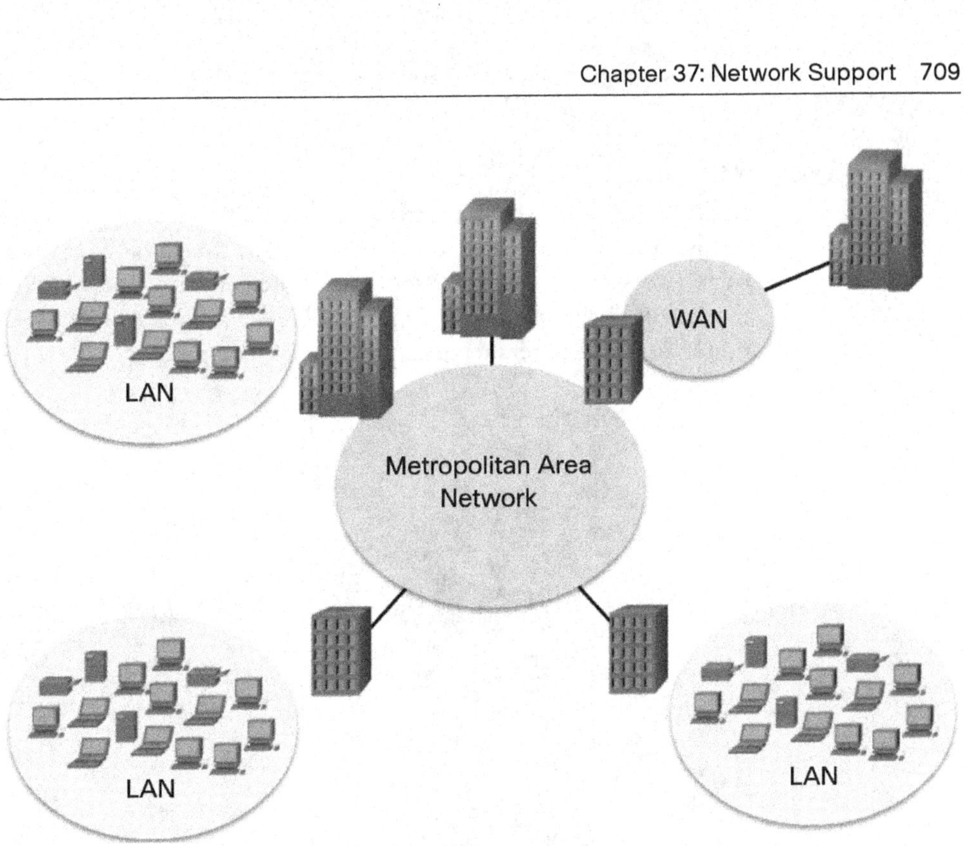

Figure 37-10 Example of a MAN Network

WAN

A wide area network (WAN) connects multiple networks that are in geographically separated locations. Individuals and organizations contract for WAN access from a service provider. Your service provider for your home or mobile device connects you to the largest WAN, the Internet. In Figure 37-11, the Tokyo and Moscow networks are connected through the Internet.

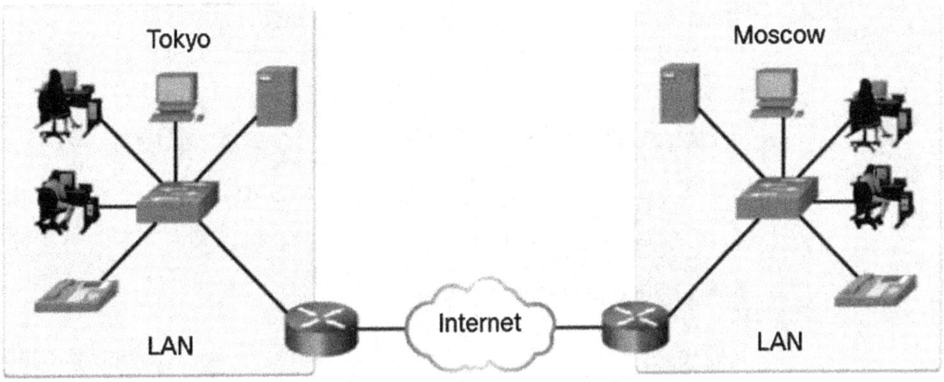

Figure 37-11 Example of a WAN Network

VPN

A virtual private network (VPN) is used to securely connect to another network over an insecure network, such as the Internet. The most common type of VPN is used by teleworkers to access a corporate private network. Teleworkers are network users that are offsite or remote. In Figure 37-12, the fat links between Teleworker 1 and the router at Headquarters represent a VPN connection.

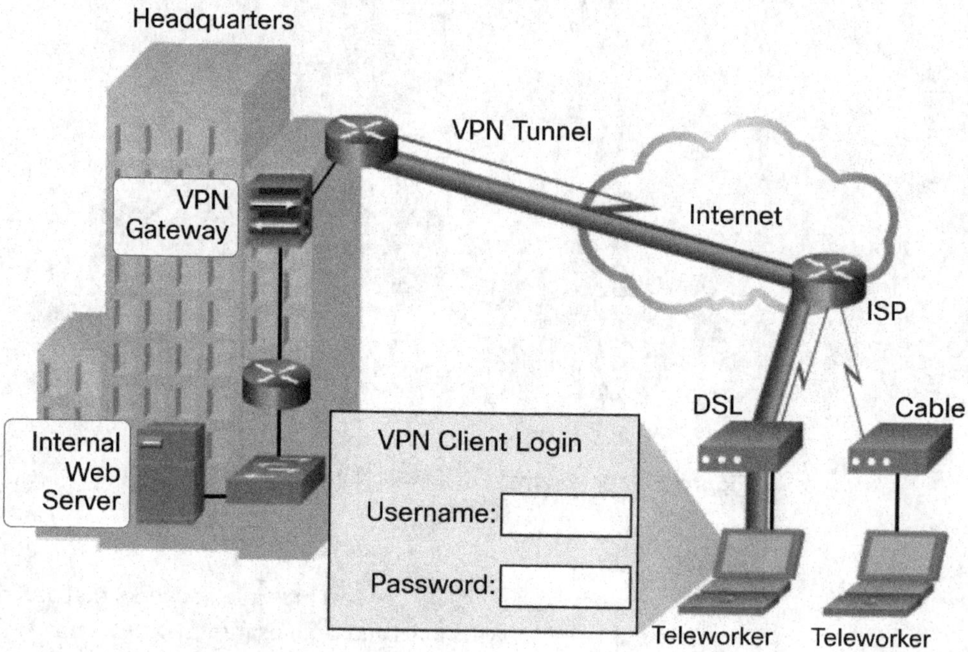

Figure 37-12 Example of a VPN Network

Interactive Graphic

Check Your Understanding—Types of Networks (37.2.3)

Refer to the online course to complete this activity.

Enterprise Network Topologies (37.2.4)

Two types of network topologies that you have learned about are

- Physical network topology
- Logical network topology

Figure 37-13 displays a sample physical topology for a small sample network. The topology identifies the physical location and function of the devices.

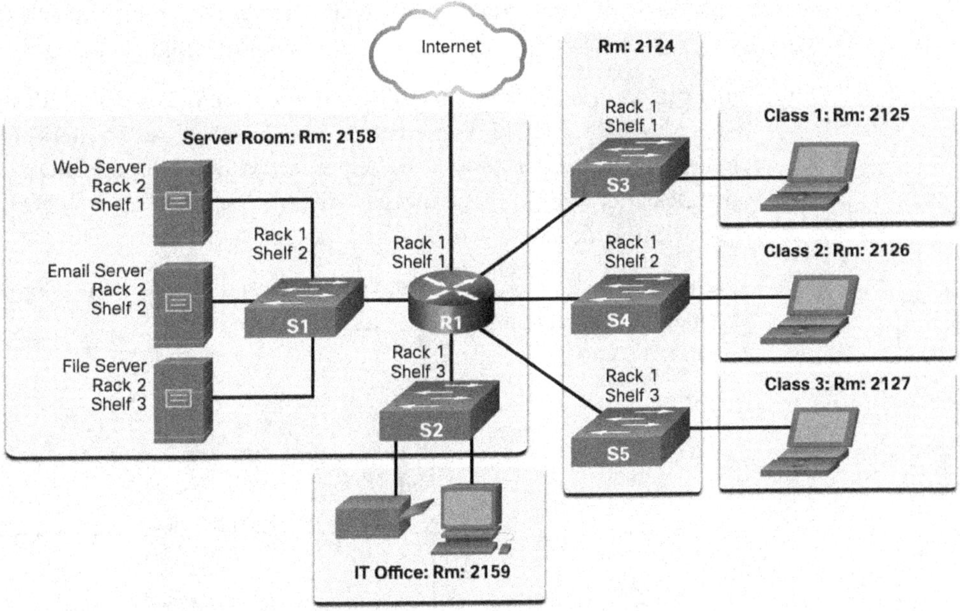

Figure 37-13 A Physical Topology

Figure 37-14 displays a sample logical topology for the same small sample network. Notice Figure 37-14 displays connecting interfaces and the Layer 3 network addressing scheme.

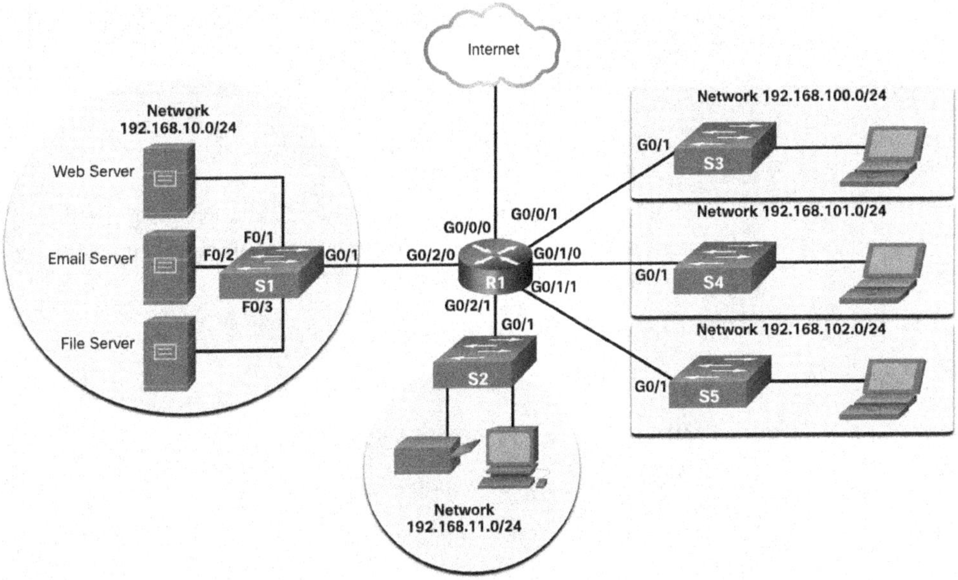

Figure 37-14 A Logical Topology

Enterprise network topologies are similar but larger in scale and complexity. They will also typically include additional network topology diagrams.

In a previous chapter you learned about hierarchical network design including the access, distribution, and core layers. This is one of several architecture models used in enterprise networks that can help guide you in creating and maintaining an effective design strategy. These models are not templates, as each network is different in size, complexity, requirements, and budget.

Figure 37-15 shows a high-level view of how different parts of an enterprise network connect along its connection to its cloud provider.

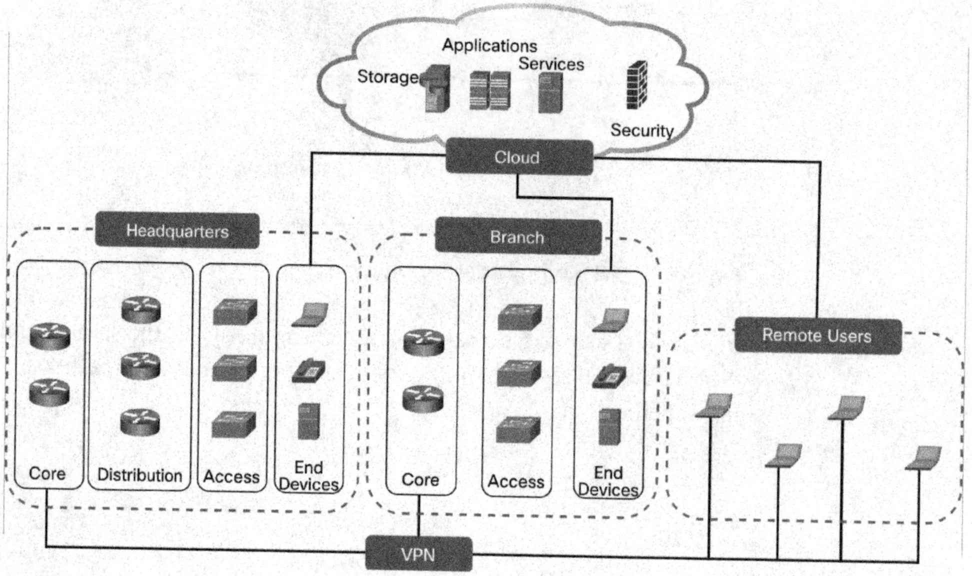

Figure 37-15 A Sample Enterprise Network

For an enterprise network, your network documentation will typically include several network topology diagrams showing different levels of detail and different types of information.

Different topology diagrams may include

- Physical layout and connections
- IP address and VLAN management
- Security and VPN policies
- Cloud services and management

- Routing policies
- Remote-access policies for remote and hybrid workers

Network Cloud Services and Applications (37.2.5)

There are three basic types of cloud computing: SaaS, PaaS, and IaaS.

SaaS (Software as a Service)

SaaS applications are focused on the end user. Instead of the application being installed locally on the end user's computer, the application is accessed over the network, usually using a web browser. In a traditional computing environment, the user would access their word processing application software stored in the local hard disk drive. Using SaaS, the user can use a web browser to access, for example, the Google Docs word processing application in the Google cloud. The user's documents can be stored in Google cloud or exported to the local computer.

Other SaaS applications include

- Google Sheets
- Google Calendar
- Google Maps
- Office 365
- Salesforce

PaaS (Platform as a Service)

PaaS is used primarily by software developers. PaaS allows developers to focus on their code and not on the underlying software and hardware needed to run their programs. The PaaS cloud provides the servers, storage, security, tools, database, and other services to host the consumer's application. PaaS in its simplest form is where the developer only has to write code, and the infrastructure and operations are handled by the PaaS provider.

Some examples of PaaS services include

- Microsoft Azure
- Salesforce Lightning
- AWS Lambda

- AWS Elastic Beanstalk
- Google App Engine

IaaS (Infrastructure as a Service)

IaaS is a service where computing resources are supplied by a cloud services provider. The IaaS cloud provides the virtual machines (VMs) for storage, networking, and other services. The cloud provider is responsible for the uptime requirements, power, and security of the VMs.

IaaS is a service used by both software developers and system administrators. Because the VMs and the applications are managed by the IaaS cloud provider, organizations do not have to host these systems in their own data center.

Some examples of IaaS services include

- Cisco Metacloud
- Microsoft Azure
- DigitalOcean
- Google Compute Engine
- Rackspace

XaaS (Anything/Everything as a Service)

Today, a variety of solutions and technologies can be delivered by cloud providers to clients as a service. XaaS is not a specific cloud service but is defined as the delivery of anything and everything as a service. XaaS includes Saas, PaaS, and IaaS.

Other examples of XaaS include

- Disaster recovery as a service (DRaaS)
- Communications as a service (CaaS)
- Monitoring as a service (MaaS)
- Desktop as a service (DaaS)

Wireless Standards (37.2.6)

The world of wireless communications is vast. However, for particular job-related skills, we want to focus on specific aspects of Wi-Fi. The best place to start is with the IEEE 802.11 WLAN standards. These standards define how radio frequencies are used for wireless links. Most of the standards specify that wireless devices have

one antenna to transmit and receive wireless signals on the specified radio frequency (2.4 GHz, 5 GHz, or 6 GHz). Some of the newer standards that transmit and receive at higher speeds require access points (APs) and wireless clients to have multiple antennas using the multiple-input and multiple-output (MIMO) technology. MIMO uses multiple antennas as both the transmitter and receiver to improve communication performance. Up to eight transmit and receive antennas can be used to increase throughput.

Various implementations of the IEEE 802.11 standards have been developed over the years. Table 37-1 highlights these standards.

Table 37-1 IEEE 802.11 Wireless Standards

IEEE WLAN Standard	Radio Frequency	Description
802.11	2.4 GHz	■ Speeds of up to 2 Mbps
802.11a	5 GHz	■ Speeds of up to 54 Mbps ■ Small coverage area ■ Less effective at penetrating building structures ■ Not interoperable with the 802.11b and 802.11g
802.11b	2.4 GHz	■ Speeds of up to 11 Mbps ■ Longer range than 802.11a ■ Better able to penetrate building structures
802.11g	2.4 GHz	■ Speeds of up to 54 Mbps ■ Backward compatible with 802.11b with reduced bandwidth capacity
802.11n	2.4 GHz, 5 GHz	■ Data rates range from 150 Mbps to 600 Mbps with a distance range of up to 70 m (230 feet) ■ APs and wireless clients require multiple antennas using MIMO technology ■ Backward compatible with 802.11a/b/g devices with limiting data rates
802.11ac	5 GHz	■ Provides data rates ranging from 450 Mbps to 1.3 Gbps (1300 Mbps) using MIMO technology ■ Up to eight antennas can be supported ■ Backward compatible with 802.11a/n devices with limiting data rates

IEEE WLAN Standard	Radio Frequency	Description
802.11ax	2.4 GHz, 5 GHz	■ Released in 2019—latest standard ■ Also known as High-Efficiency Wireless (HEW) ■ Higher data rates ■ Increased capacity ■ Handles many connected devices ■ Improved power efficiency ■ 1 GHz and 7 GHz capable when those frequencies become available ■ Search the Internet for Wi-Fi Generation 6 for more information ■ Wi-Fi 6—Uses 2.4 GHz and 5 GHz bands ■ Wi-Fi 6E—Uses 6 GHz band

Licensed and Unlicensed Bands

Various communications channels transmit signals over the electromagnetic spectrum. The licensed spectrum refers to the bands (range of frequency) that are reserved for radio stations, cellular companies, and broadcast television stations. Media and cellular companies typically pay for the right to transmit over a specific frequency within the licensed spectrum. In the United States, this is done by the Federal Communications Commission (FCC). Other countries have a similar regulatory agency that licenses specific bands for that country.

The unlicensed spectrum is open for anyone to use. The unlicensed spectrum is where we find IEEE 802.11 Wi-Fi technologies and is available free to the public. Anyone can transmit over the unlicensed spectrum.

Packet Tracer
☐ Activity

Packet Tracer—Connect a Network Based on a Network Diagram (37.2.7)

In this activity, you will complete a physical topology based on a provided network diagram.

Refer to the online course to complete this Packet Tracer.

Network Device Documentation (37.2.8)

Network device documentation should contain accurate, up-to-date records of the network hardware and software. Documentation should include all pertinent information about the network devices.

Many organizations create documents with tables or spreadsheets to capture relevant device information.

The following sections provide examples of router, switch, and end-device documentation.

Router Device Documentation

The table in Figure 37-16 displays sample network device documentation for two interconnecting routers.

Device	Model	Description	Location	IOS	License
Central	ISR 4321	Central Edge Router	Building A Rm: 137	Cisco IOS XE Software, Version 16.09.04 flash:isr4300-universalk9_ias.16.09.04.SPA.bin	ipbasek9 securityk9

Interface	Description	IPv4 Address	IPv6 Address	MAC Address	Routing
G0/0/0	Connects to SVR-1	10.0.0.1/30	2001:db8:acad:1::1/64	a03d.6fe1.e180	OSPF
G0/0/1	Connects to Branch-1	10.1.1.1/30	2001:db8:acad:a001::1/64	a03d.6fe1.e181	OSPFv3
G0/1/0	Connects to ISP	209.165.200.226/30	2001:db8:feed:1::2/64	a03d.6fc3.a132	Default
S0/1/1	Connects to Branch-2	10.1.1.2/24	2001:db8:acad:2::1/64	n/a	OSPFv3

Device	Model	Description	Site	IOS	License
Branch-1	ISR 4221	Branch-2 Edge Router	Building B Rm: 107	Cisco IOS XE Software, Version 16.09.04 flash:isr4200-universalk9.16.09.04.SPA.bin	ipbasek9 securityk9

Interface	Description	IPv4 Address	IPv6 Address	MAC Address	Routing
G0/0/0	Connects to S1	Router-on-a-stick	Router-on-a-stick	a03d.6fe1.9d90	OSPF
G0/0/1	Connects to Central	10.1.1.2/30	2001:db8:acad:a001::2/64	a03d.6fe1.9d91	OSPF

Figure 37-16 Router Device Documentation

LAN Switch Device Documentation

The table in Figure 37-17 displays sample device documentation for a LAN switch.

Device	Model	Description	Mgt. IP Address	IOS	VTP
S1	Cisco Catalyst WS-C2960-24TC-L	Branch-1 LAN1 switch	192.168.77.2/24	IOS: 15.0(2)SE7 Image: C2960-LANBASEK9-M	Domain: CCNA Mode: Server

Port	Description	Access	VLAN	Trunk	EtherChannel	Native	Enabled
Fa0/1	Port Channel 1 trunk to S2 Fa0/1	-	-	Yes	Port-Channel 1	99	Yes
Fa0/2	Port Channel 1 trunk to S2 Fa0/2	-	-	Yes	Port-Channel 1	99	Yes
Fa0/3	*** Not in use ***	Yes	999	-	-		Shut
Fa0/4	*** Not in use ***	Yes	999	-	-		Shut
Fa0/5	Access port to user	Yes	10	-	-		Yes
...				-	-		-
Fa0/24	Access port to user	Yes	20	-	-		Yes
Fa0/24	*** Not in use ***	Yes	999	-	-		Shut
G0/1	Trunk link to Branch-1	-	-	Yes	-	99	Yes
G0/2	*** Not in use ***	Yes	999		-		

Figure 37-17 LAN Switch Device Documentation

End-System Documentation

End-system documentation focuses on the hardware and software used in servers, network management consoles, and user workstations. An incorrectly configured end system can have a negative impact on the overall performance of a network. For this reason, having access to end-system device documentation can be very useful when troubleshooting.

The table in Figure 37-18 displays a sample of information that could be recorded in an end-system device document.

Device	OS	Services	MAC Address	IPv4 / IPv6 Addresses	Default Gateway	DNS
SRV1	MS Server 2016	SMTP, POP3, File services, DHCP	5475.d08e.9ad8	10.0.0.2/30	10.0.0.1	10.0.0.1
				2001:db8:acad:1::2/64	2001:db8:acad:1::1	2001:db8:acad:1::1
SRV2	MS Server 2016	HTTP, HTTPS	5475.d07a.5312	209.165.201.10	209.165.201.1	209.165.201.1
				2001:db8:feed:1::10/64	2001:db8:feed:1::1	2001:db8:feed:1::1
PC1	MS Windows 10	HTTP, HTTPS	5475.d017.3133	192.168.10.10/24	192.168.10.1	192.168.10.1
				2001:db8:acad:1::251/64	2001:db8:acad:1::1	2001:db8:acad:1::1
...						

Figure 37-18 End-System Documentation Files

Establish a Network Baseline (37.2.9)

The purpose of network monitoring is to watch network performance in comparison to a predetermined *baseline*. A baseline is used to establish normal network or system performance to determine the "personality" of a network under normal conditions.

Establishing a network performance baseline requires collecting performance data from the ports and devices that are essential to network operation.

A network baseline should answer the following questions:

- How does the network perform during a normal or average day?
- Where are the most errors occurring?
- What part of the network is most heavily used?
- What part of the network is least used?
- Which devices should be monitored and what alert thresholds should be set?
- Can the network meet the identified policies?

Measuring the initial performance and availability of critical network devices and links allows a network administrator to determine the difference between abnormal

behavior and proper network performance as the network grows or traffic patterns change. The baseline also provides insight into whether the current network design can meet business requirements. Without a baseline, no standard exists to measure the optimum nature of network traffic and congestion levels.

Analysis after an initial baseline also tends to reveal hidden problems. The collected data shows the true nature of congestion or potential congestion in a network. It may also reveal areas in the network that are underutilized, and quite often can lead to network redesign efforts, based on quality and capacity observations.

The initial network performance baseline sets the stage for measuring the effects of network changes and subsequent troubleshooting efforts. Therefore, it is important to plan for it carefully.

Cisco Discovery Protocol (CDP) Overview (37.2.10)

The first thing you want to know about your network is what is in it. Where are these components? How are they connected? Basically, you need a map. This section explains how you can use *Cisco Discovery Protocol (CDP)* to create a map of your network.

CDP is a Cisco proprietary Layer 2 protocol that is used to gather information about Cisco devices that share the same data link. CDP is media and protocol independent and runs on all Cisco devices, such as routers, switches, and access servers.

The device sends periodic CDP advertisements to connected devices, as shown in Figure 37-19.

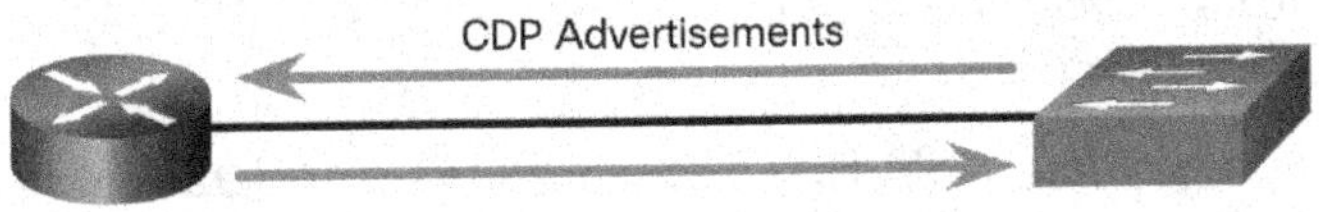

Figure 37-19 CDP Advertisements Sent Between a Router and a Switch

These advertisements share information about the type of device that is discovered, the name of the device, and the number and type of the interfaces.

Because most network devices are connected to other devices, CDP can assist in network design decisions, troubleshooting, and making changes to equipment. CDP can also be used as a network discovery tool to determine the information about the neighboring devices. This information gathered from CDP can help build a logical topology of a network when documentation is missing or lacking in detail.

Discover Devices Using CDP (37.2.11)

Consider the lack of documentation in the topology shown in Figure 37-20. The network administrator only knows that R1 is connected to another device.

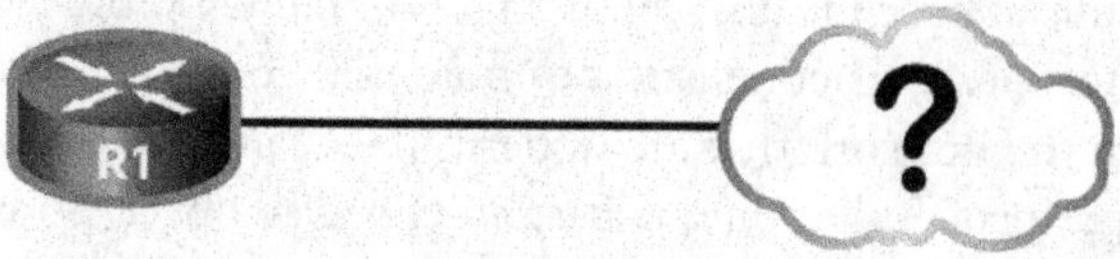

Figure 37-20 R1 Topology Before Discovery

With CDP enabled on the network, the **show cdp neighbors** command can be used to determine the network layout, as shown in Example 37-1.

Example 37-1 Discover Connected CDP Neighbors for R1

```
R1# show cdp neighbors
Capability Codes: R - Router, T - Trans Bridge, B - Source Route Bridge
                  S - Switch, H - Host, I - IGMP, r - Repeater, P - Phone,
                  D - Remote, C - CVTA, M - Two-port Mac Relay

Device ID         Local Intrfce      Holdtme     Capability  Platform   Port ID
S1                Gig 0/0/1          179           S I        WS-C3560- Fas 0/5
R1#
```

No information is available regarding the rest of the network. The **show cdp neighbors** command provides helpful information about each CDP neighbor device, including the following:

- **Device identifiers**—This is the host name of the neighbor device (S1).
- **Port identifier**—This is the name of the local and remote port (G0/0/1 and F0/5, respectively).
- **Capabilities list**—This shows whether the device is a router or a switch (S for switch; I for IGMP is beyond the scope of this course).
- **Platform**—This is the hardware platform of the device (WS-C3560 for Cisco 3560 switch).

The output shows that there is another Cisco device, S1, connected to the G0/0/1 interface on R1. Furthermore, S1 is connected through its F0/5, as shown in Figure 37-21.

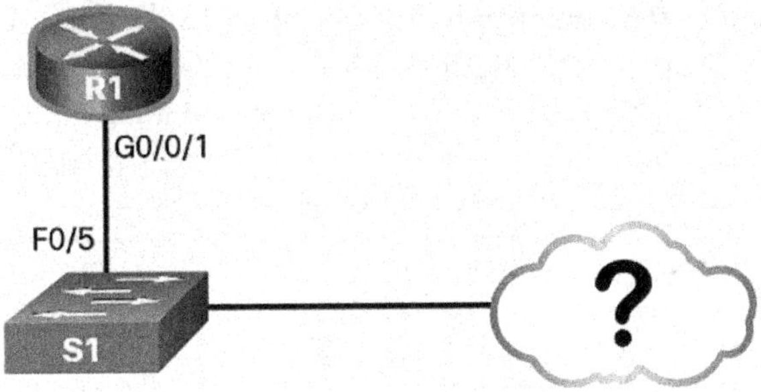

Figure 37-21 Topology from S1

The network administrator uses **show cdp neighbors detail** to discover the IP address for S1. As displayed in Example 37-2, the address for S1 is 192.168.1.2.

Example 37-2 Discover Detailed Information About S1

```
R1# show cdp neighbors detail
-------------------------
Device ID: S1
Entry address(es):
  IP address: 192.168.1.2
Platform: cisco WS-C3560-24TS,  Capabilities: Switch IGMP
Interface: GigabitEthernet0/0/1,  Port ID (outgoing port): FastEthernet0/5
Holdtime : 136 sec

Version :
Cisco IOS Software, C3560 Software (C3560-LANBASEK9-M), Version 15.0(2)SE7, R
RELEASE SOFTWARE (fc1)
Technical Support: http://www.cisco.com/techsupport
Copyright (c) 1986-2014 by Cisco Systems, Inc.
Compiled Thu 23-Oct-14 14:49 by prod_rel_team

advertisement version: 2
Protocol Hello:  OUI=0x00000C, Protocol ID=0x0112; payload len=27,
value=00000000FFFFFFFF010221FF000000000000002291210380FF0000
VTP Management Domain: ''
Native VLAN: 1
Duplex: full
Management address(es):
  IP address: 192.168.1.2

Total cdp entries displayed : 1
R1#
```

By accessing S1 either remotely through SSH or physically through the console port, the network administrator can determine what other devices are connected to S1, as displayed in the output of the **show cdp neighbors** command in Example 37-3.

Example 37-3 Discover Connected CDP Neighbors for S1

```
S1# show cdp neighbors
Capability Codes: R - Router, T - Trans Bridge, B - Source Route Bridge
                   S - Switch, H - Host, I - IGMP, r - Repeater, P - Phone,
                   D - Remote, C - CVTA, M - Two-port Mac Relay
Device ID         Local Intrfce      Holdtme    Capability  Platform  Port ID
S2                 Fas 0/1            150               S I   WS-C2960- Fas 0/1
R1                 Fas 0/5            179             R S I   ISR4331/K Gig 0/0/1
S1#
```

Another switch, S2, is revealed in the output. S2 is using F0/1 to connect to the F0/1 interface on S1, as shown in Figure 37-22.

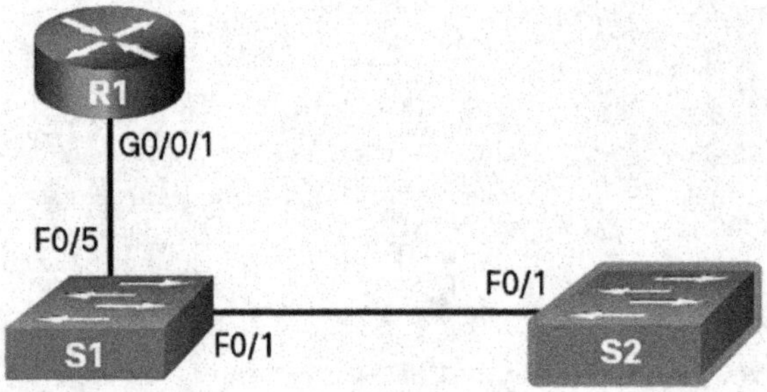

Figure 37-22 Topology from S2

Again, the network administrator can use **show cdp neighbors detail** to discover the IP address for S2, and then remotely access it. After a successful login, the network administrator uses the **show cdp neighbors** command to discover if there are more devices, as shown in Example 37-4.

Example 37-4 Discover Connected CDP Neighbors for S2

```
S2# show cdp neighbors
Capability Codes: R - Router, T - Trans Bridge, B - Source Route Bridge
                   S - Switch, H - Host, I - IGMP, r - Repeater, P - Phone,
                   D - Remote, C - CVTA, M - Two-port Mac Relay
Device ID         Local Intrfce      Holdtme    Capability  Platform  Port ID
S1                 Fas 0/1            141               S I   WS-C3560- Fas 0/1
S2#
```

The only device connected to S2 is S1. Therefore, there are no more devices to discover in the topology. The network administrator can now update the documentation to reflect the discovered devices.

Packet Tracer
☐ Activity

Packet Tracer—Use CDP to Map a Network (37.2.12)

A senior network administrator requires you to map the Remote Branch Office network and discover the name of a recently installed switch that still needs an IPv4 address to be configured. Your task is to create a map of the branch office network. To map the network, you will use SSH for remote access and the Cisco Discovery Protocol (CDP) to discover information about neighboring network devices, like routers and switches.

Refer to the online course to complete this Packet Tracer.

Packet Tracer
☐ Activity

Packet Tracer—Troubleshooting Challenge—Document the Network (37.2.13)

In this Packet Tracer activity, you will document a network that is unknown to you.

- Test network connectivity.
- Compile host addressing information.
- Remotely access default gateway devices.
- Document default gateway device configurations.
- Discover devices on the network.
- Draw the network topology.

Refer to the online course to complete this Packet Tracer.

Help Desks (37.3)

A help desk is typically the first line of support in any organization. This section discusses the structure, operations, and skills needed for an effective help desk organization.

The Security Policy (37.3.1)

Organizations operate with well-defined corporate, employee, and security policies.

The "Security Policy" document contains policies that inform users, IT staff, and managers of the requirements for protecting technology and information assets. As shown Figure 37-23, there are policies for:

- Specifying how users are identified and authenticated
- Setting password length, complexity, and refresh interval
- Defining what behavior is acceptable on the corporate network
- Specifying remote access requirements, etc.

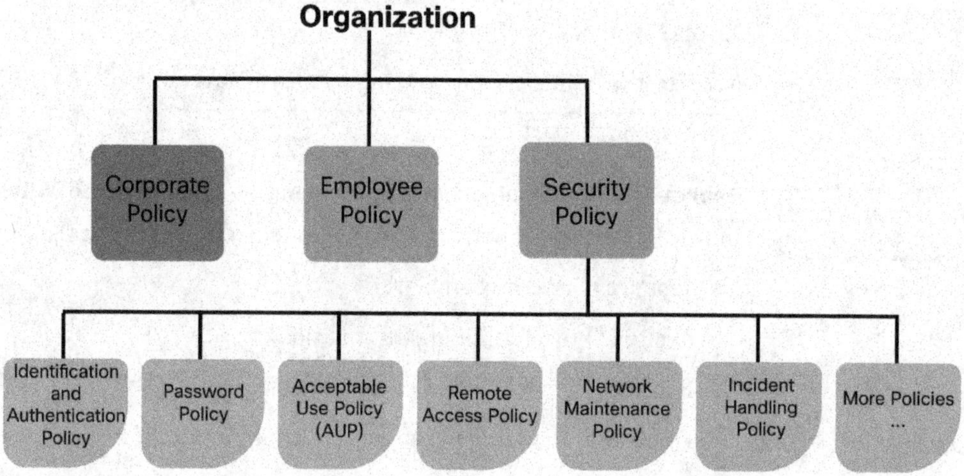

Figure 37-23 Example of How Security Documentation Fits in with the Larger Organizational Policies

The Security Policy document is a constantly evolving document that reacts to changes in the threat landscape, new vulnerabilities, and business and employee requirements. The Security Policy helps the IT team understand what they must do to keep the network operational and secure by using:

- **Standard operating procedures (SOPs)**—These define step-by-step actions that must be completed for any given task to comply with a policy. There are SOPs to follow when replacing network devices, installing (or uninstalling) applications, onboarding new employees, terminating existing employees, and more.
- **Guidelines**—These cover the areas where there are no SOPs defined.

When users encounter a problem or need network support, they must contact a "help desk." The help desk assists users by following the defined SOPs and guidelines. The help desk will use a ticketing system to manage the steps within the troubleshooting life cycle shown in Figure 37-24.

This section will focus on using a ticketing system to complete the first three steps shown in Figure 37-24.

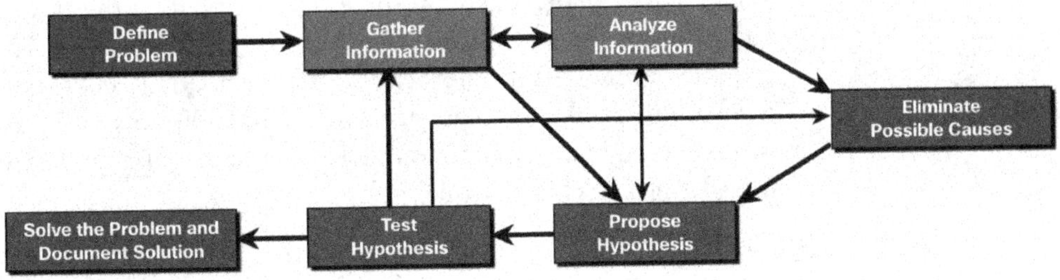

Figure 37-24 Seven-Step Troubleshooting Process

Help Desks (37.3.2)

A help desk is a specialized team in an IT department that is the central point of contact for employees or customers.

When users require support, they must contact the IT help desk. This may be done by using an online reporting tool, live chat, telephone, or email (e.g., IT-support@email.com). Help desks often use a "shared" email account. This means that all help desk technicians can see the email requests and respond to them accordingly.

Note

The online reporting tool could be integrated into the ticketing system.

Often, the help desk technician may be able to quickly answer or solve user issues. For example, if an organization had an Internet network failure, users may contact the help desk asking why they cannot reach external sites. The technician would inform them that the network is down, and that it should be operational within a specific time.

However, if the request for support is valid, then the technician will create a "trouble ticket." This is done using special ticketing system software to manage requests, incidents, and reported problems. These "tickets" can be created by the user using a ticketing system dashboard or by a help desk technician. Typically, a user initiates the ticket, and the help desk technician validates it.

The help desk technician may have to gather additional information about the request. When questioning users, use effective questioning techniques and listen carefully to the user answers. You may also have to physically investigate the device or connect remotely to replicate the problem, execute commands, and check configurations.

The technician would then analyze the collected data and either:

- **Solve the problem**—Once the user problem has been addressed, the technician would update and close the trouble ticket. Updating the ticket solution is important because it can populate the ticketing system database. Therefore, if the same problem is reported by another user, the responding technician can search the database to quickly resolve the problem. In addition, administrators can analyze the tickets to identify common issues and their causes in order to globally eliminate the problem, if possible.
- **Escalate the trouble ticket**—Some problems are more complex or require access to devices which the technician has no credentials for. In these cases, the technician must escalate (i.e., forward) the trouble ticket to a more experienced technician. It is important that all documentation captured from the user is clear, concise, and accurate.

Figure 37-25 summarizes a typical trouble ticket process that a help desk technician would have to perform.

Note

Processes can vary depending on the organization.

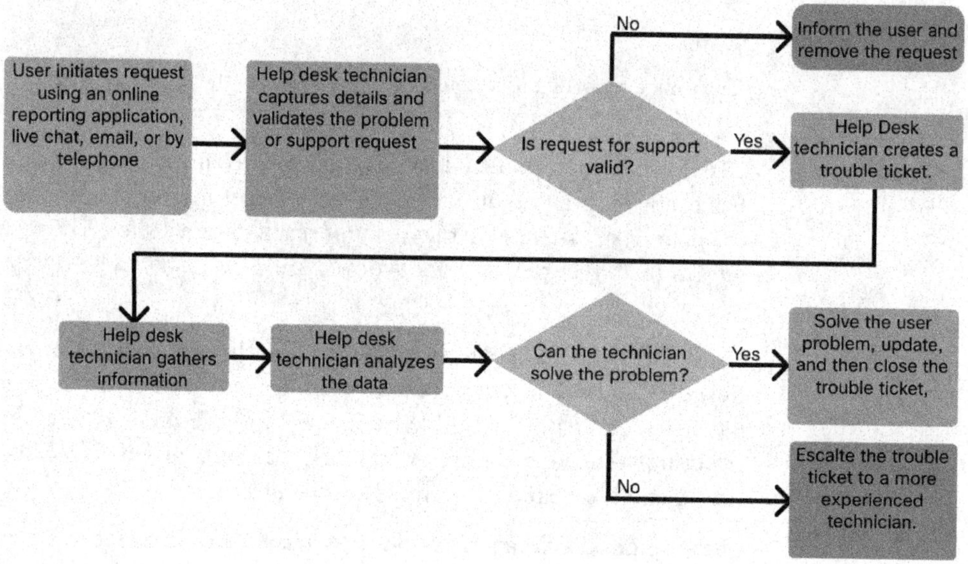

Figure 37-25 Typical Trouble Ticket Process

Ticketing Systems (37.3.3)

Help desk ticketing systems help organizations manage user problems or requests. Ticketing software is specifically designed to ensure that corporate users or clients receive support in a timely and systematic manner. They also ensure that all tickets get noticed and addressed.

A shared mailbox is an alternative method that can be used by an organization to support user requests. Help desk technicians would all share the same mailbox and respond to emails to solve problems.

Ticketing systems vary depending on the need of the organization. For example, there are ticketing systems designed for the needs of internal corporate users and other systems to support service providers or external customers.

Note

A quick Internet search for "help desk software" reveals many different software vendors including Zendesk, HaloITSM, ConnectWise, and more.

Figure 37-26 shows a sample ticket designed to help you understand what information a help desk ticket could capture.

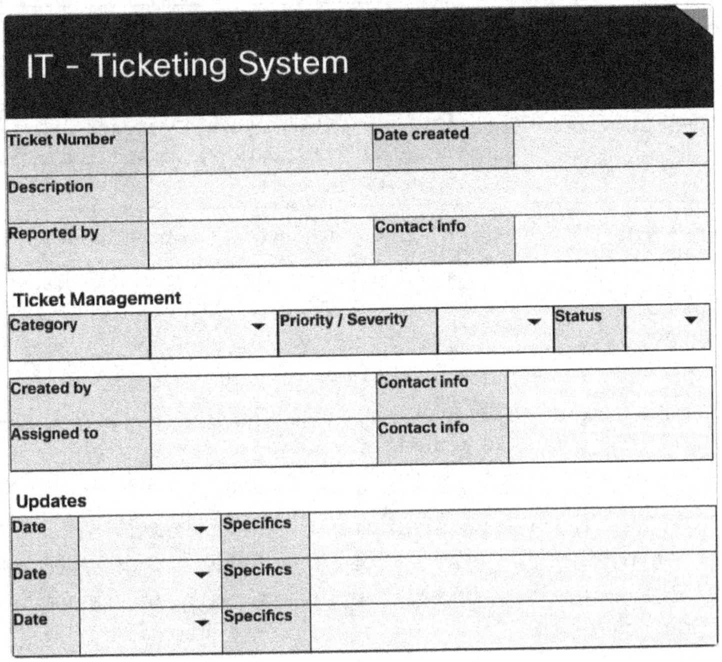

Figure 37-26 A Sample Trouble Ticket

Table 37-2 describes the fields that could be used when a trouble ticket is created.

Table 37-2 Explanation of the Fields in the Trouble Ticket

Filed Name	Field Contains...
Ticket Number	■ A unique number automatically generated by the ticketing system to keep track of the request ■ The ticket number never changes.
Date created	A drop-down list that displays the date the ticket was created
Description	A free-form field that describes the request
Reported by	Free-form fields that identify who requested the support
Category	■ A drop-down list for selecting predetermined categories ■ This is useful to group related tickets together. ■ For example, New Device/App Request, Employee Onboarding/Termination, Support, Report a problem, and Security Incident
Priority / Severity	■ A drop-down list for selecting pre-determined priority levels ■ For example, high, medium, low, or critical, major, and minor
Status	■ A drop-down list for selecting predetermined status levels ■ For example, not started, opened, in progress, completed
Create by, Assigned to	Free-form fields that identify the technician who created the ticket, and who the ticket was assigned to if escalation was required
Date and Specifics	■ A drop-down list that displays the date the ticket was updated ■ A free-form field for updating the ticket

Note

Other fields may also be available, such as platform type and model, operating system version, network connection used, and others.

In the sample ticket, some fields were system generated (in orange), drop-down (in blue), or free-form (in yellow). Drop-down fields make it easier to enter and maintain consistency. The free-form fields are used by the help desk technician to add descriptive information.

Free-form fields will be read by other technicians and managers. Therefore, it is important to use clear and concise written communication. Use plain language and short sentences. Always pay attention to your spelling, grammar, and style.

Question End Users (37.3.4)

When requesting support from a help desk, users often provide vague and sometimes misleading information. For example, users often report problems such as "The network is down," "I cannot access my email," or "My computer is slow." In most cases, additional information is required to fully understand the problem.

When entering the trouble ticket, the help desk technician must discover the "who," "what," and "when" of the problem.

The following recommendations should be employed when communicating with a user:

- Always be considerate and empathize with users while letting them know you will help them solve their problem. Users reporting a problem may be under stress and anxious to resolve the problem as quickly as possible. Never talk down to, belittle, or insult the user or accuse the user of causing the problem.
- Speak at a technical level they can understand. Avoid using complex terminology or industry jargon.
- Always listen to or read carefully what the user is saying. Taking notes can be helpful when documenting a complex problem.

Good interpersonal skills are an asset to the help desk technician. It is important to develop this skill set to better serve and communicate with users and peers. For example, a technician should address a user by their preferred name, attempt to relate to the user, and work to clarify exactly what it is that they are requesting.

Table 37-3 summarizes three general guidelines that help to develop the know, relate, and understand skill set.

Table 37-3 Know, Relate, Understand Skills

Rule	Suggestion	Example
Know	■ Call the user by his or her name. ■ You can ask if there is any name that they prefer that you use.	■ If a user tells you her name is Mrs. Johnson, ask if that is what she prefers to be called by you. ■ She may say yes, or she may give you her first name. ■ In any case, only use the preferred name with your customer.

Rule	Suggestion	Example
Relate	Attempt to create a one-to-one connection with the user.	■ Try to find something you may have in common. ■ If you hear a pet in the background, briefly ask them about it. ■ If you have had to call customer support for your own computer, mention that you understand how frustrating this can be and that you will do everything you can to help them. ■ Do not lose control of the call.
Understand	■ Determine the user's level of technical knowledge. ■ This will help you best communicate with them.	■ A customer who is very new to computers will not be likely to know all the jargon that you use every day, so you should use the most common words you can think of to describe aspects of their computer. ■ A more experienced customer probably knows some of the same jargon that you use.

When interviewing the user, guide the conversation and use effective questioning techniques to quickly ascertain the problem. Two common methods to do so include using

- **Open-ended questions**—These types of questions allow users to explain the details of the problem in their own words and are useful to obtain general information.
- **Closed-ended questions**—These require simple yes, no, or single-word answers that can be used to discover important facts about the network problem.

Table 37-4 provides some questioning guidelines and sample open-ended end-user questions.

Table 37-4 Open-Ended End-User Questions

Guideline	Examples of Open-Ended End-User Questions
Ask pertinent questions.	■ What does not work? ■ What exactly is the problem? ■ What are you trying to accomplish?
Determine the scope of the problem.	■ Who does this issue affect? Is it just you or others? ■ What device is this happening on?

Guideline	Examples of Open-Ended End-User Questions
Determine when the problem occurred/ occurs.	■ When exactly does the problem occur? ■ When was the problem first noticed? ■ Were there any error message(s) displayed?
Determine if the problem is constant or intermittent.	■ Can you reproduce the problem? ■ Can you send me a screenshot or video of the problem?
Determine if anything has changed.	■ What has changed since the last time that it worked?
Use questions to eliminate or discover possible problems.	■ What works? ■ What does not work?

When done interviewing the user, repeat your understanding of the problem to the user to ensure that you both agree on what is being reported.

Interactive Graphic

Check Your Understanding—Closed-Ended and Open-Ended Questions (37.3.5)

Refer to the online course to complete this activity.

Active Listening (37.3.6)

To better understand the problem reported by the user, practice active listening skills. Allow the customer to tell the whole story. During the time that the customer is explaining the problem, occasionally interject some small word or phrase, such as "I understand," "Yes," "I see," or "Okay." This behavior lets the customer know that you are there and that you are listening.

However, a technician should not interrupt the customer to ask a question or make a statement. This is rude, disrespectful, and creates tension. Often in a conversation, you might find yourself thinking of what to say before the other person finishes talking. When you do this, you are not actively listening. Instead, listen carefully when your customers speak, and let them finish their thoughts.

You asked the customer to explain the problem to you. This is an open-ended question. An open-ended question rarely has a simple answer. Usually, it involves information about what the customer was doing, what they were trying to do, and why they are frustrated.

After you have listened to the customer explain the whole problem, summarize what the customer has said. This helps convince the customer that you have heard and understand the situation. A good practice for clarification is to paraphrase the

customer's explanation by beginning with the words, "Let me see if I understand what you have told me." This is a very effective tool that demonstrates to the customer that you have listened and that you understand.

After you have assured the customer that you understand the problem, you will probably have to ask some follow-up questions. Make sure that these questions are pertinent. Do not ask questions that the customer has already answered while describing the problem. Doing this only irritates the customer and shows that you were not listening.

Follow-up questions should be targeted closed-ended questions based on the information that you have already gathered. Closed-ended questions should focus on obtaining specific information. The customer should be able to answer a closed-ended question with a simple "yes" or "no" or with a factual response, such as "Windows 10."

Use all the information that you have gathered from the customer to complete the trouble ticket.

Document the user-provided information in the trouble ticket. Include anything that you think might be important for you or another technician. The small details often lead to the solution of a difficult or complicated problem.

When the ticket has been completed, you should repeat your understanding of the problem to the user to ensure that you both agree on the problem being reported.

Video

Video Demonstration—Active Listening and Summarizing (37.3.7)

Tips for Using Active Listening with a Customer

- Allow the customer to tell their problem.
- Occasionally interject some small word or phrase such as "I understand," "Yes," "I see," or "Okay" to let the customer know that you are listening.
- Summarize the customer's problem when they are done so that you both are certain that you understand.
- Ask clarifying questions.
- Do not interrupt the customer the moment you realize you have a question.

Refer to the online course to view this video.

Gather Information for Host-Related Tickets (37.3.8)

The ticketing system often includes sections for entering host-related information. These fields are often completed during the "Gather Information" step of the troubleshooting life cycle.

Useful host-related information includes

- Host manufacturer, model, serial number
- Operating system version
- Network environment (i.e., wired, wireless, ...)
- Network connectivity test results (ping, tracert, ...)

Additional information that can be captured from a host includes

- Beep codes
- Event Viewer logs
- Device Manager settings
- Task Manager data
- Diagnostic tool results

Beep Codes

Each BIOS manufacturer has a unique beep sequence, a combination of long and short beeps, for hardware failures. When troubleshooting, power on the computer and listen. As the system proceeds through the POST, most computers emit one beep to indicate that the system is booting properly. If there is an error, you might hear multiple beeps. Document the beep code sequence, and research the code to determine the specific problem.

BIOS Information

If the computer boots and stops after the POST, investigate the BIOS settings. A device might not be detected or configured properly. Refer to the motherboard documentation to ensure that the BIOS settings are correct.

Event Viewer

When system, user, or software errors occur on a Windows computer, the Event Viewer, shown in Figure 37-27, is updated with information about the errors.

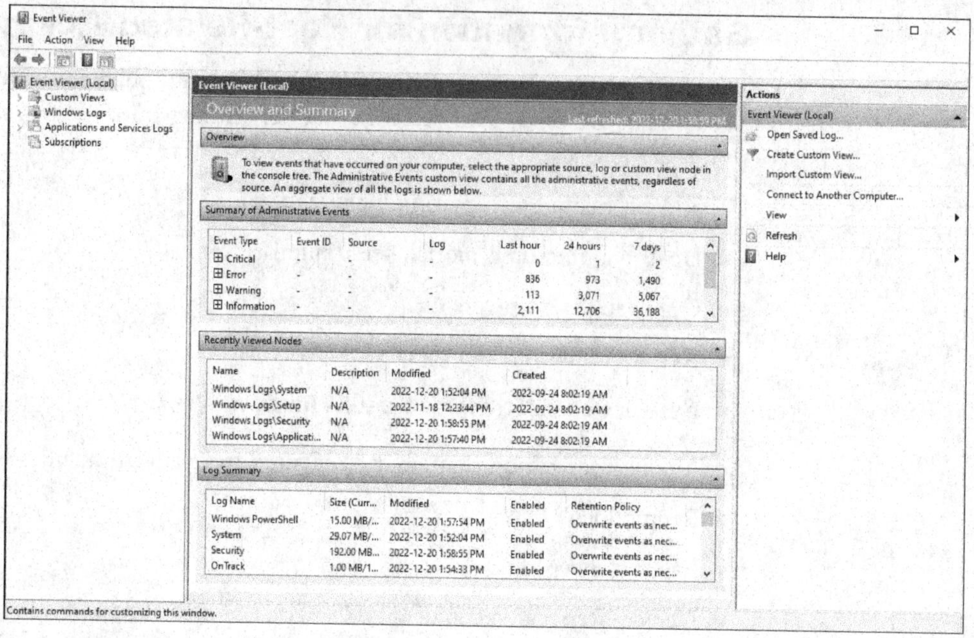

Figure 37-27 Windows Event Viewer

The Event Viewer application records the following information about the problem:

- What problem occurred
- Date and time of the problem
- Severity of the problem
- Source of the problem
- Event ID number
- Which user was logged in when the problem occurred

Although the Event Viewer lists details about the error, you might need to further research the problem to determine a solution.

Device Manager

The Device Manager, shown in Figure 37-28, displays all the devices that are configured on a Windows computer.

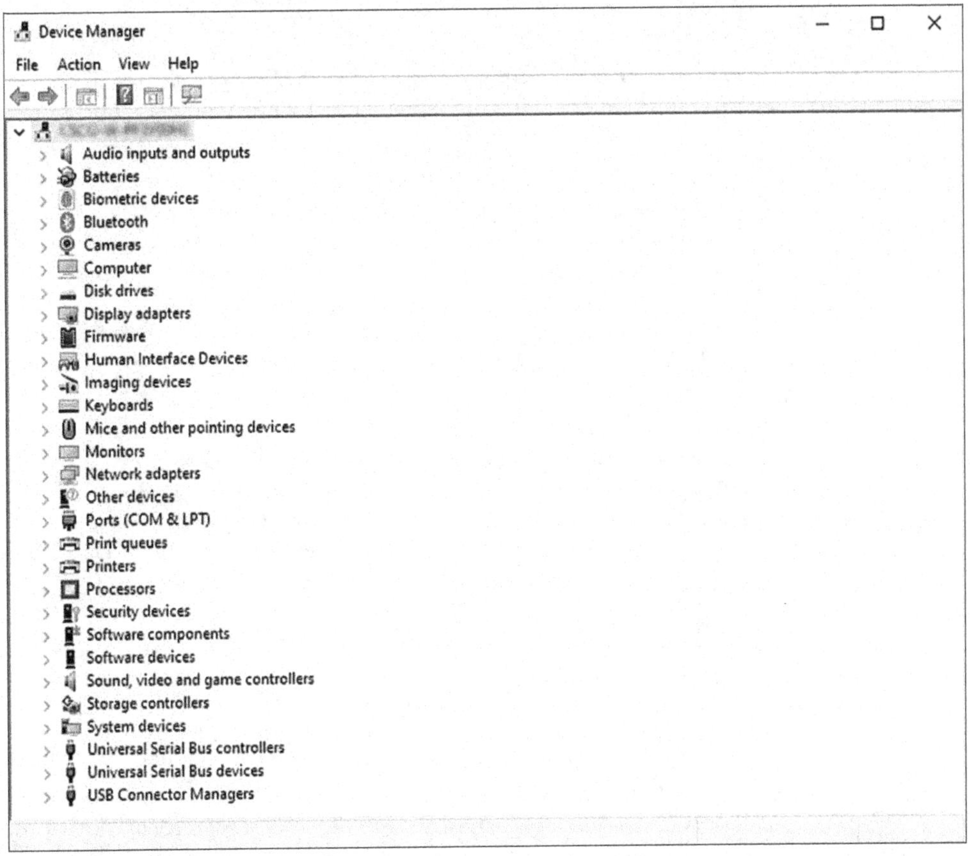

Figure 37-28 Windows Device Manager

The operating system flags the devices that are not operating correctly with an error icon. A yellow triangle with an exclamation point indicates that the device is in a problem state. A red X means that the device is disabled, removed, or Windows can't locate the device. An arrow pointing down means the device has been disabled. A yellow question mark indicates that the system does not know which driver to install for the hardware.

Task Manager

The Task Manager, shown in Figure 37-29, displays the applications and background processes that are currently running on a Windows computer.

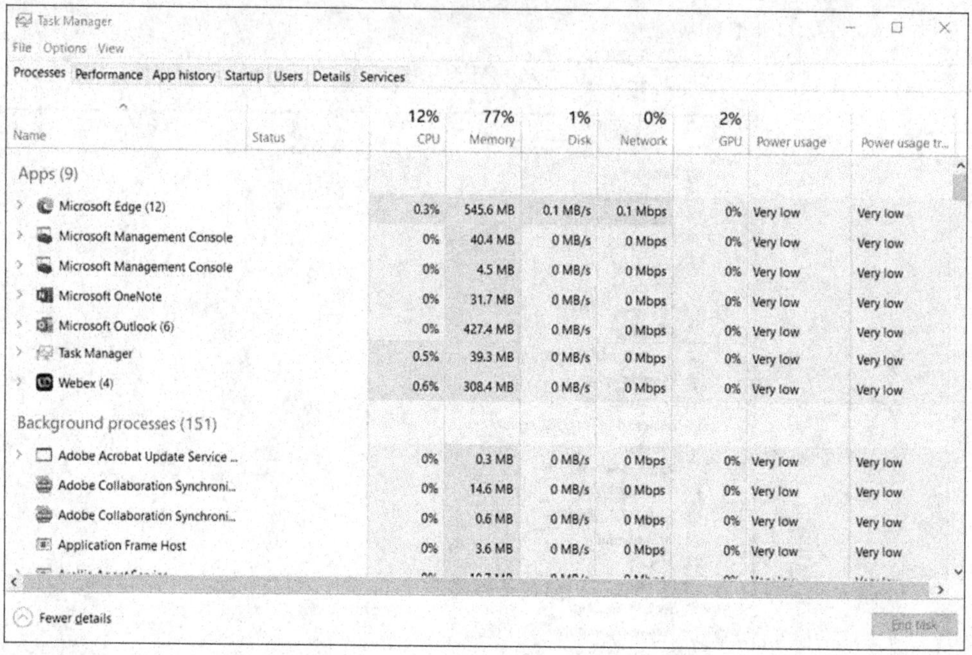

Figure 37-29 Windows Task Manager

With the Task Manager, you can close applications that have stopped responding. You can also monitor the performance of the CPU and virtual memory, view all processes that are currently running, and view information about the network connections.

Diagnostic Tools

Conduct research to determine which software is available to help diagnose and solve problems. There are many programs to help you troubleshoot hardware. Manufacturers of system hardware usually provide diagnostic tools of their own. For instance, a hard drive manufacturer might provide a tool to boot the computer and diagnose why the hard drive does not start the operating system.

Gather Information for Cisco Device-Related Tickets (37.3.9)

To gather symptoms from a networking device that is suspected to have issues, use Cisco IOS commands (see Table 37-5) and other tools such as packet captures and device logs.

Table 37-5 Cisco IOS Commands for Gathering Information

Command	Description
ping {*host* | *ip-address*}	■ Sends an echo request packet to an address, then waits for a reply. ■ The *host* or *ip-address* variable is the IP alias or IP address of the target system.
traceroute *destination*	■ Identifies the path a packet takes through the networks. ■ The *destination* variable is the host name or IP address of the target system.
telnet {*host* | *ip-address*}	■ Connects to an IP address using the Telnet application. ■ Use SSH whenever possible instead of Telnet.
ssh -l *user-id ip-address*	■ Connects to an IP address using SSH. ■ SSH is more secure than Telnet.
show ip interface brief **show ipv6 interface brief**	■ Displays a summary status of all interfaces on a device. ■ Useful for quickly identifying IP addressing on all interfaces
show ip route **show ipv6 route**	Displays the current IPv4 and IPv6 routing tables, which contain the routes to all known network destinations.
show protocols	Displays the configured protocols and shows the global and interface-specific status of any configured Layer 3 protocol.

Analyze the Information (37.3.10)

Now that the trouble ticket has been created and information has been gathered, the technician must analyze the information. To accomplish this, the technician relies on their experience, knowledge bases, and other information sources to decide if they can solve the problem. The technician may also communicate with peers to gain insight on the problem.

Knowledge bases that can be searched include

- **Ticketing software databases**—Most ticketing systems build a repository of previous tickets that can be searched to see if another technician resolved an identical or similar problem.

- **Vendor resources**—Vendors maintain Frequently Asked Questions (FAQs) documents that can be searched and may also offer online tools to help resolve problems. Some offer live chats to solve problems faster.
- **Online Internet searches**—Using search engines to see if a problem has been encountered before.

If the problem cannot be solved, then the ticket must be escalated to a more-experienced IT staff member.

Interactive Graphic

Check Your Understanding—Help Desks (37.3.11)

Refer to the online course to complete this activity.

Troubleshoot Endpoint Connectivity (37.4)

Many support requests begin with a report from the end user. Being able to troubleshoot the endpoints of the network is important in determining the cause and scope of the problem.

Windows Network Setup (37.4.1)

If you have used any of the tools to verify connectivity and found that some part of your network is not working as it should, now is the time to use some commands to troubleshoot your devices. Host and IOS commands can help you determine if the problem is with the IP addressing of your devices, which is a common network problem.

Checking the IP addressing on host devices is a common practice in networking for verifying and troubleshooting end-to-end connectivity. In Windows 10, you can access the IP address details from the **Network and Sharing Center** > *interface* > **Details.** As shown in Figure 37-30, the interface details reveal the host's IP address, subnet mask, default gateway, and known DNS servers.

The preferred method used by technicians to view the IP addressing information on a Windows host is to use the **ipconfig** Windows command as shown in Example 37-5.

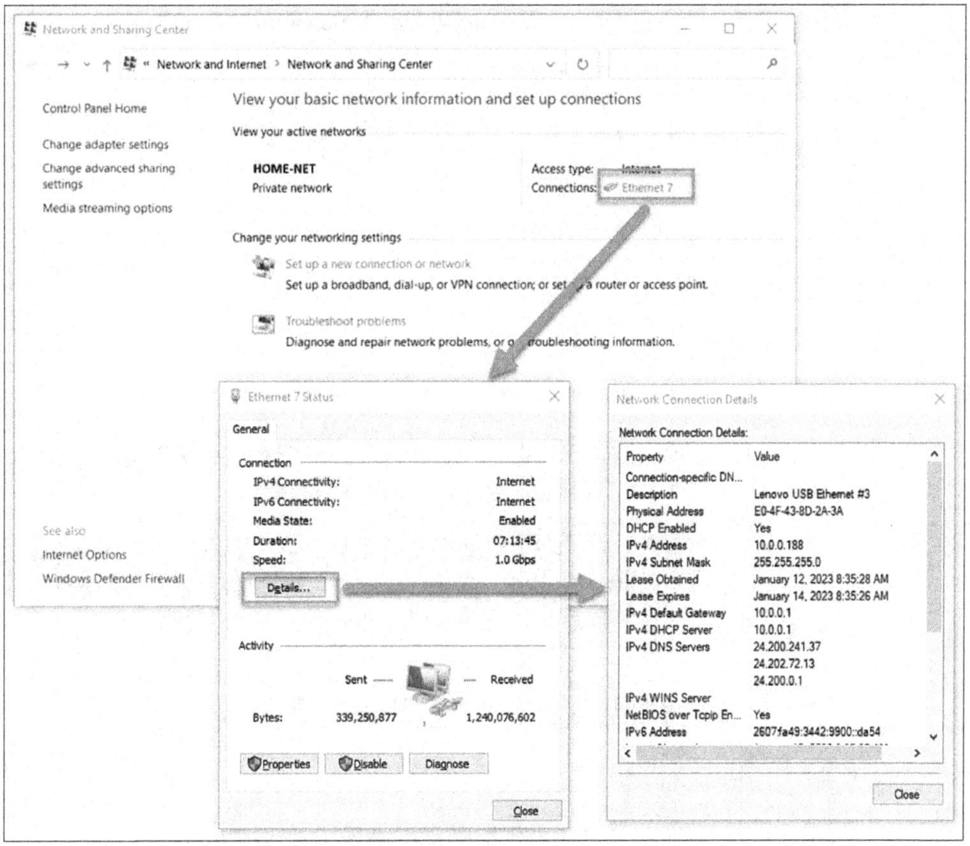

Figure 37-30 Viewing the Details of an Ethernet Connection in Windows

Example 37-5 Output for the **ipconfig** Command

```
C:\Users\PC-A> ipconfig
Windows IP Configuration
(Output omitted)
Wireless LAN adapter Wi-Fi:
   Connection-specific DNS Suffix  . :
   Link-local IPv6 Address . . . . . : fe80::a4aa:2dd1:ae2d:a75e%16
   IPv4 Address. . . . . . . . . . . : 192.168.10.10
   Subnet Mask . . . . . . . . . . . : 255.255.255.0
   Default Gateway . . . . . . . . . : 192.168.10.1
(Output omitted)
```

The **ipconfig /all** command is used to view additional addressing details as shown in Example 37-6.

Example 37-6 Output for the **ipconfig /all** Command

```
C:\Users\PC-A> ipconfig /all
Windows IP Configuration
   Host Name . . . . . . . . . . . . : PC-A-00H20
   Primary Dns Suffix  . . . . . . . : cisco.com
   Node Type . . . . . . . . . . . . : Hybrid
   IP Routing Enabled. . . . . . . . : No
   WINS Proxy Enabled. . . . . . . . : No
   DNS Suffix Search List. . . . . . : cisco.com
(Output omitted)
Wireless LAN adapter Wi-Fi:
   Connection-specific DNS Suffix  . :
   Description . . . . . . . . . . . : Intel(R) Dual Band Wireless-AC 8265
   Physical Address. . . . . . . . . : F8-94-C2-E4-C5-0A
   DHCP Enabled. . . . . . . . . . . : Yes
   Autoconfiguration Enabled . . . . : Yes
   Link-local IPv6 Address . . . . . : fe80::a4aa:2dd1:ae2d:a75e%16(Preferred)
   IPv4 Address. . . . . . . . . . . : 192.168.10.10(Preferred)
   Subnet Mask . . . . . . . . . . . : 255.255.255.0
   Lease Obtained. . . . . . . . . . : August 17, 2019 1:20:17 PM
   Lease Expires . . . . . . . . . . : August 18, 2019 1:20:18 PM
   Default Gateway . . . . . . . . . : 192.168.10.1
   DHCP Server . . . . . . . . . . . : 192.168.10.1
   DHCPv6 IAID . . . . . . . . . . . : 100177090
   DHCPv6 Client DUID. . . . . . . . : 00-01-00-01-21-F3-76-75-54-E1-AD-DE-DA-9A
   DNS Servers . . . . . . . . . . . : 192.168.10.1
   NetBIOS over Tcpip. . . . . . . . : Enabled
```

Verify Connectivity in Windows (37.4.2)

The **ping** command is an effective way to quickly test Layer 3 connectivity between a source and destination IP address. This command, as shown in Example 37-7, also displays various round-trip time statistics.

Example 37-7 Round-Trip Time Statistics in the **ping** Command

```
C:\Users\PC-A> ping 10.1.1.10
Pinging 10.1.1.10 with 32 bytes of data:
Reply from 10.1.1.10: bytes=32 time=47ms TTL=51
Reply from 10.1.1.10: bytes=32 time=60ms TTL=51
Reply from 10.1.1.10: bytes=32 time=53ms TTL=51
Reply from 10.1.1.10: bytes=32 time=50ms TTL=51
Ping statistics for 10.1.1.10:
```

```
    Packets: Sent = 4, Received = 4, Lost = 0 (0% loss),
Approximate round trip times in milli-seconds:
    Minimum = 47ms, Maximum = 60ms, Average = 52ms
C:\Users\PC-A>
```

As shown in Example 37-7, the output validates Layer 3 connectivity between PC A and the device with the IPv4 address 10.1.1.10.

The **traceroute** or Windows **tracert** commands can help locate Layer 3 problem areas in a network. A trace returns a list of hops as a packet is routed through a network. It could be used to identify the point along the path where the problem can be found.

Some firewalls, such as Windows Firewall, will block pings by default. It is important to include this information as part of your network documentation and to be aware of these settings when testing and verifying network connectivity.

Linux Network Setup (37.4.3)

Verifying IP settings using the GUI on a Linux machine will differ depending on the Linux distribution (distro) and desktop interface. Figure 37-31 shows the Connection Information dialog box on the Ubuntu distro running the Gnome desktop.

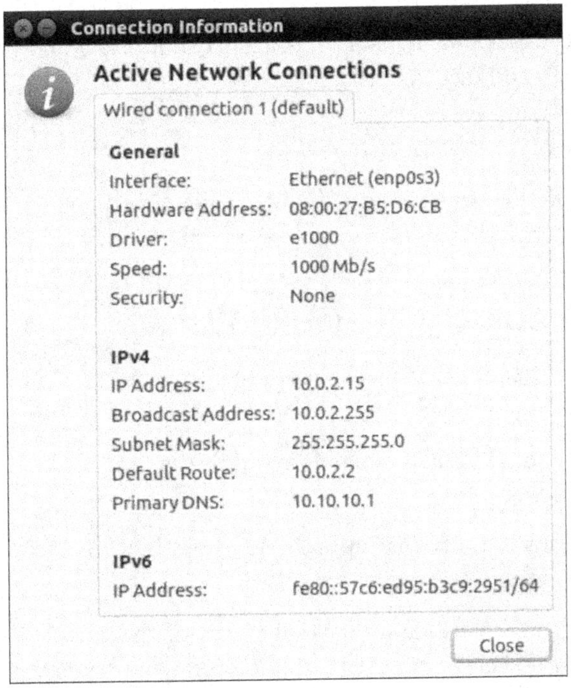

Figure 37-31 Viewing the Ubuntu Connection Information

Technicians most often prefer to use the **ifconfig terminal** window command to display the status of the currently active interfaces and their IP configuration, as shown in Example 37-8.

Example 37-8 Output for the **ifconfig** Command

```
ubuntu@ubuntu2004:~$ ifconfig
enp0s3     Link encap:Ethernet  HWaddr 08:00:27:b5:d6:cb
           inet addr: 10.0.2.15  Bcast:10.0.2.255  Mask: 255.255.255.0
           inet6 addr: fe80::57c6:ed95:b3c9:2951/64 Scope:Link
           UP BROADCAST RUNNING MULTICAST  MTU:1500  Metric:1
           RX packets:1332239 errors:0 dropped:0 overruns:0 frame:0
           TX packets:105910 errors:0 dropped:0 overruns:0 carrier:0
           collisions:0 txqueuelen:1000
           RX bytes:1855455014 (1.8 GB)  TX bytes:13140139 (13.1 MB)
lo: flags=73  mtu 65536
           inet 127.0.0.1  netmask 255.0.0.0
           inet6 ::1  prefixlen 128  scopeid 0x10
           loop  txqueuelen 1000  (Local Loopback)
           RX packets 0  bytes 0 (0.0 B)
           RX errors 0  dropped 0  overruns 0  frame 0
           TX packets 0  bytes 0 (0.0 B)
           TX errors 0  dropped 0 overruns 0  carrier 0  collisions 0
```

The Linux **ip address** command is used to display addresses and their properties. It can also be used to add or delete IP addresses.

Note

The output displayed may vary depending on the Linux distribution.

Verify Connectivity in Linux (37.4.4)

Linux offers the same **ping** and **traceroute** tools as Windows to verify network connectivity.

There are several other Linux command-line tools that are available for most Linux distributions including:

- **speedtest**—This is a tool that tests the bandwidth of your connectivity with your Internet provider.
- **ncat**—Ncat is a networking utility that is part of the nmap suite of networking tools. Ncat, or nc, has many uses including verifying connectivity to a device

using a specific port. Example 37-9 demonstrates using ncat to test HTTPS (port 443) connectivity to two different devices.

Example 37-9 Output for the **ncat** Command

```
ubuntu@ubuntu2004:~$ nc -z -v www.google.com 443
Connection to www.google.com (142.250.138.105) 443 port [tcp/https] succeeded!
  ubuntu@ubuntu2004:~$
ubuntu@ubuntu2004:~$ nc -z -v 10.0.0.122 443
nc: connect to 10.0.0.122 port 443 (tcp) failed: Connection refused
ubuntu@ubuntu2004:~$
```

macOS Network Setup (37.4.5)

In the GUI of a Mac host, open **Network Preferences** > **Advanced** to get the IP addressing information, as shown Figure 37-32.

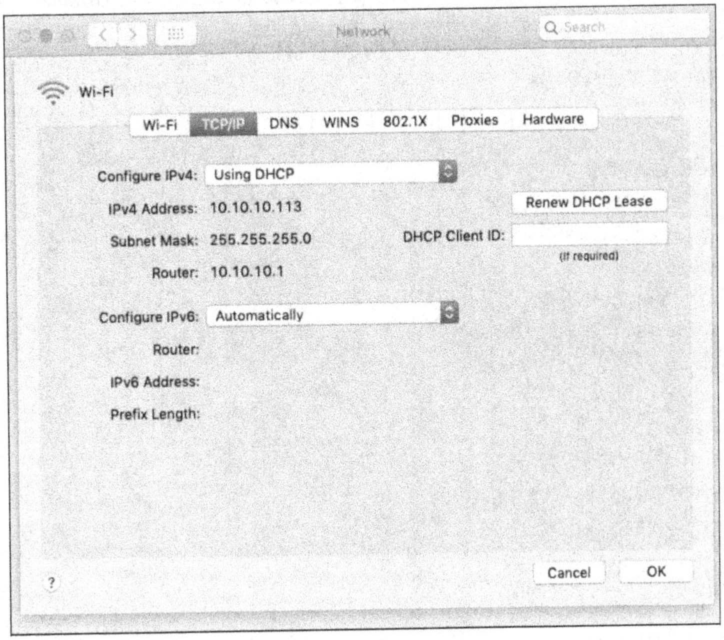

Figure 37-32 Viewing the macOS Network Settings

However, the **ifconfig** command can also be used to verify the interface IP configuration, as shown in Example 37-10.

Example 37-10 Verifying an Interface's Configuration

```
MacBook-Air:~ Admin$ ifconfig en0
en0: flags=8863 mtu 1500
        ether c4:b3:01:a0:64:98
        inet6 fe80::c0f:1bf4:60b1:3adb%en0 prefixlen 64 secured scopeid 0x5
        inet 10.10.10.113 netmask 0xffffff00 broadcast 10.10.10.255
        nd6 options=201
        media: autoselect
        status: active
MacBook-Air:~ Admin$
```

Other useful macOS commands to verify the network settings include **networksetup -listallnetworkservices** and **networksetup -getinfo** *<network service>*, as shown in Example 37-11.

Example 37-11 Additional macOS Commands to Verify Network Settings

```
MacBook-Air:~ Admin$ networksetup -listallnetworkservices
An asterisk (*) denotes that a network service is disabled.
iPhone USB
Wi-Fi
Bluetooth PAN
Thunderbolt Bridge
MacBook-Air:~ Admin$
MacBook-Air:~ Admin$ networksetup -getinfo Wi-Fi
DHCP Configuration
IP address: 10.10.10.113
Subnet mask: 255.255.255.0
Router: 10.10.10.1
Client ID:
IPv6: Automatic
IPv6 IP address: none
IPv6 Router: none
Wi-Fi ID: c4:b3:01:a0:64:98
MacBook-Air:~ Admin$
```

Verify Connectivity in macOS (37.4.6)

The **ping** and **traceroute** commands to verify network connectivity are also available on macOS. Like Linux, macOS is based on the UNIX operating system and therefore shares many of the same network connectivity commands, including **ncat** and **speedtest**.

Additional network verification information can be obtained using the macOS **System Information** tool as shown in Figure 37-33, which displays Wi-Fi information including supported Wi-Fi protocols such as IEEE 802.11ac.

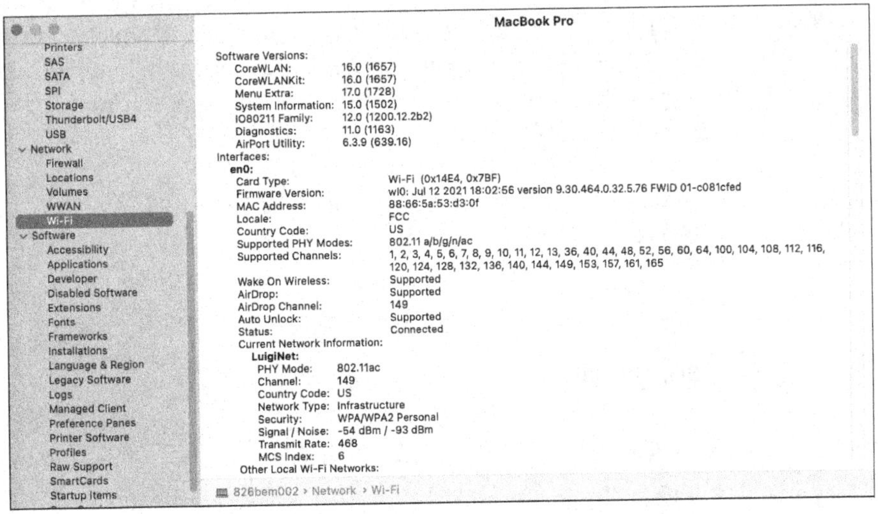

Figure 37-33 Verifying the Wi-Fi Setting in macOS

The macOS Wireless Diagnostics application, shown in Figure 37-34, can be used to troubleshoot and monitor Wi-Fi connectivity. When selecting the option to monitor the network, the application will generate a diagnostics report.

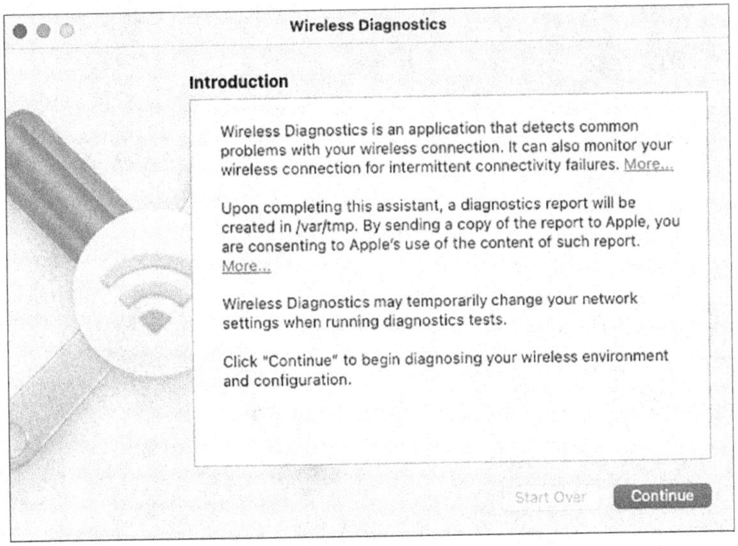

Figure 37-34 macOS Wireless Diagnostic Application

Set Up and Verify Networking in iOS (37.4.7)

Network connectivity on an Apple iOS device can be easily verified by attempting to reach a website or an online application.

You can also verify the IPv4 and IPv6 addressing information including the default gateway (router) on an Apple iOS device, as shown in Figure 37-35. To do so, go to **Settings > Wi-Fi** and select the information icon (i) to the right of the active Wi-Fi network name (SSID).

Figure 37-35 Verifying the Wireless Setting in iOS

Set Up and Verify Networking in Android (37.4.8)

Like Apple iOS, network connectivity on an Android device can be verified by attempting to reach a website or an online application.

If the connection fails, verify that you have a reliable connection to your cellular data provider. If you are attempting to connect over Wi-Fi, be sure that you are connected to a Wi-Fi network and that you have successfully authenticated to that network. Sometimes additional authentication is required through an alternative authentication method, which may require agreement to usage terms or providing additional login information.

With some Android versions, an icon may appear next to the Wi-Fi signal strength indicator in the device status bar that indicates a problem with an Internet connection. Wi-Fi connectivity may be established without access to the Internet. This can indicate a problem with the Internet gateway for the network that you are attached to, or it may indicate that further measures are required to gain access to the network.

The Android interface can vary significantly depending on the Android version and the device manufacturer. Therefore, the process for checking network connections may differ slightly between devices.

To access your network settings, open the **Settings** app on your phone and touch **Connections** or **Network and Internet**. Do the following:

1. If using Wi-Fi, verify that Wi-Fi is active on your phone.
2. Touch **Wi-Fi** and verify that you are connected to a network that you can authenticate to. Check the Available Networks list to see if other networks may be more suitable. You may need to determine the network password for the various networks that you will see. Also verify that signal strength is adequate.
3. If using a mobile cellular data network, verify that you have connectivity to that network in the device status bar. Check the swipe-down Settings menu to ensure that mobile data is active on your device.

IPv4 and IPv6 addressing information including the default gateway (router) can be verified by going to **Settings > About phone > Status**, as shown in Figure 37-36.

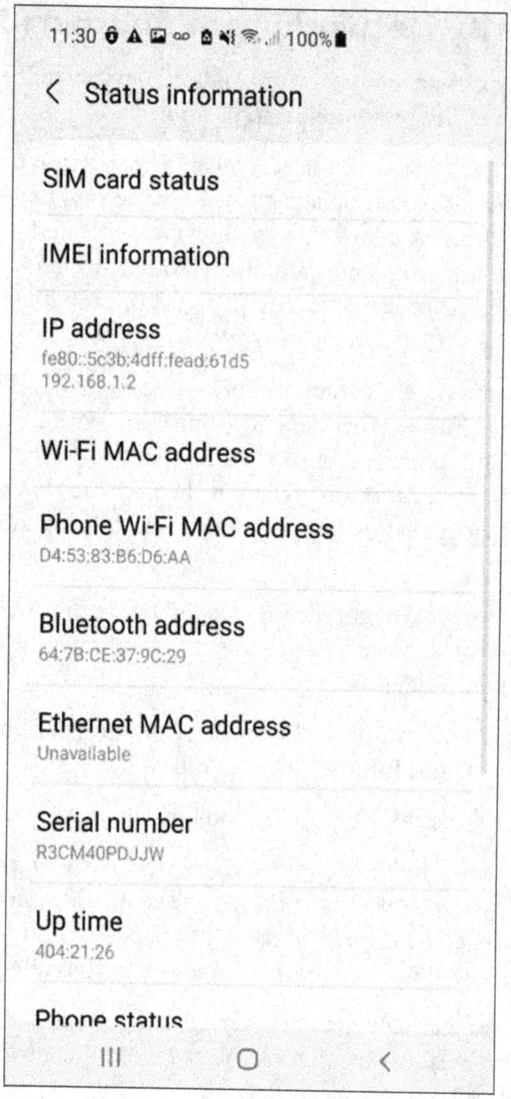

Figure 37-36 Verifying the Network Settings on Android

Third-party network analysis apps that have various functions are available for Android. They may provide more detailed information about the device network settings, allow network testing with **ping** and **trace**, and even perform network port and device scans, as shown in Figure 37-37.

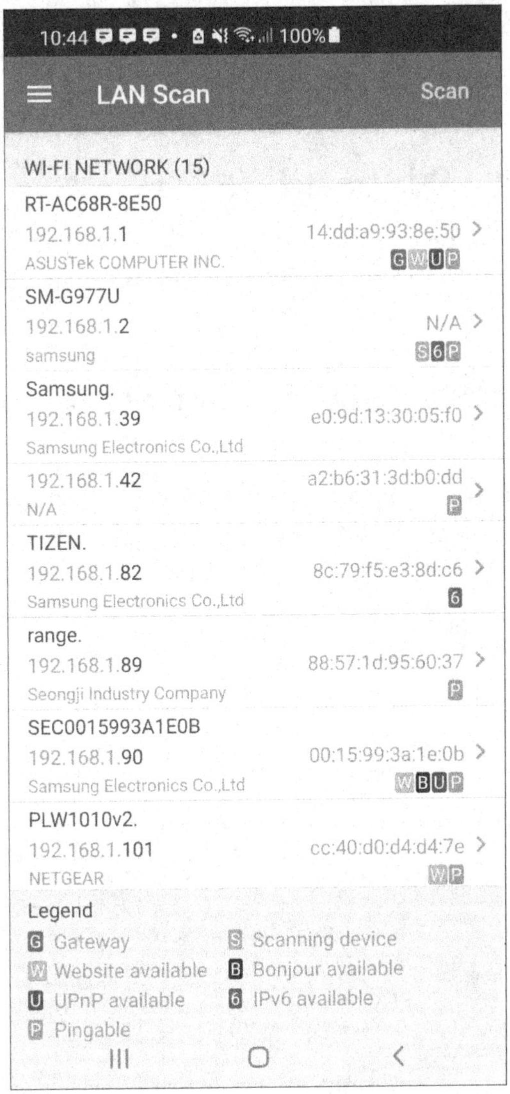

Figure 37-37 Using a Third-Party App to Perform Network Testing and Scans

Lab—Verify Address with a Subnet Calculator (37.4.9)

In this activity, you will determine the IPv4 address and subnet mask of your device and use an online subnet calculator to determine the IPv4 network address.

Refer to the online course to complete this lab.

Interactive Graphic

Check Your Understanding—Troubleshoot Endpoint Connectivity (37.4.10)

Refer to the online course to complete this activity.

Troubleshoot a Network (37.5)

There are many tools that can help you determine the cause and scope of problems affecting the network. This section introduces you to some of those tools and commands.

Network Devices as Sources of Network Information (37.5.1)

When documenting or diagnosing a network problem, it is often necessary to gather information directly from routers and switches. Obvious useful network commands include **ping**, **traceroute**, and **telnet**. There are also many **show** commands available to help verify a device operation.

Table 37-6 lists some of the most common Cisco IOS **show** commands used for data collection.

Table 37-6 Common Cisco ISO **show** Commands for Data Collection

Command	Description
show version	Displays uptime, version information, and licensing information for the device software and hardware.
show ip interface [brief] show ipv6 interface [brief]	■ Displays all the configuration options that are set on an interface. ■ Use the **brief** keyword to only display status and IP address of the IP interfaces.
show interfaces	■ Displays detailed output for each interface. ■ To display detailed output for only a single interface, include the interface type and number in the command (e.g., Gigabit Ethernet 0/0/0).
show ip route show ipv6 route	Displays the routing table content listing directly connected networks and learned remote networks.
show cdp neighbors detail	■ Displays detailed information about directly connected Cisco neighbor devices. ■ Useful to validate that Layers 1 and 2 are operational.

Command	Description
show arp show ipv6 neighbors	Displays the contents of the ARP table (IPv4) and the neighbor table (IPv6).
show running-config	Displays the current device configuration.
show vlan	Displays the status of VLANs on a switch.
show port	Displays the status of ports on a switch.
show mac-address table	Displays contents of switch's MAC address table.
show interface status	Displays statistics and status information for network interfaces.
show inventory	Displays inventory information about the specific components in a Cisco device.
show switch	Displays the switch stack status when switches are grouped together using Cisco StackWise.
show tech-support	■ This command is useful for collecting a large amount of information about the device for troubleshooting purposes. ■ It executes multiple **show** commands, which can be provided to technical support representatives when reporting a problem.

Some of these **show** commands would require privilege EXEC mode access.

As a security feature, the Cisco IOS software separates management access into two privilege levels:

- **User EXEC mode**—This is privilege level 1 and indicated by a device prompt ending with a greater than (>) symbol (e.g., Router> or Switch>). It provides access to limited commands useful to a technician when verifying the basic operation of a device.
- **Privileged EXEC mode**—This is privilege level 15 and indicated by a prompt ending with a number (#) symbol (e.g., Router# or Switch#). It is the highest level available and should only be accessible by a network administrator. In this mode, all device commands are available including the ability to configure or change the configuration settings on the device. Use the **enable** command to enter the mode.

The Cisco IOS also provides command syntax check and context-sensitive help. If you enter a command incorrectly, the IOS will identify where you made an entry error.

Context-sensitive help enables the user to quickly find answers to these questions:

- Which commands are available in each command mode?
- Which commands start with specific characters or group of characters?
- Which arguments and keywords are available to particular commands?

To access context-sensitive help, simply enter a question mark (?) while typing in a command.

Cisco IOS also does not require the entire command, argument, or keyword to be entered. The partial command entry must just be long enough to uniquely identify the full command. For instance, you can use **en** instead of entering the full command **enable**.

To be sure the proper command is being entered, the Tab key can also be used to complete the partial entry of a command, argument, or keyword.

Packet Capture and Protocol Analysis (37.5.2)

Protocol analyzers can investigate packet content while flowing through the network. A protocol analyzer decodes the various protocol layers in a recorded frame and presents this information in a relatively easy-to-use format.

As a technician, you may be tasked to capture traffic from a specific host. Therefore, it is important that you become familiar with the software to complete the assigned task.

Figure 37-38 shows a screen capture of the Wireshark protocol analyzer.

The information displayed by a protocol analyzer includes the physical layer bit data, data link layer information, protocols, and descriptions for each frame. Most protocol analyzers can filter traffic that meets certain criteria so that all traffic to and from a device can be captured. Protocol analyzers such as Wireshark can help troubleshoot network performance problems. It is important to have both a good understanding of TCP/IP and how to use a protocol analyzer to inspect information at each TCP/IP layer.

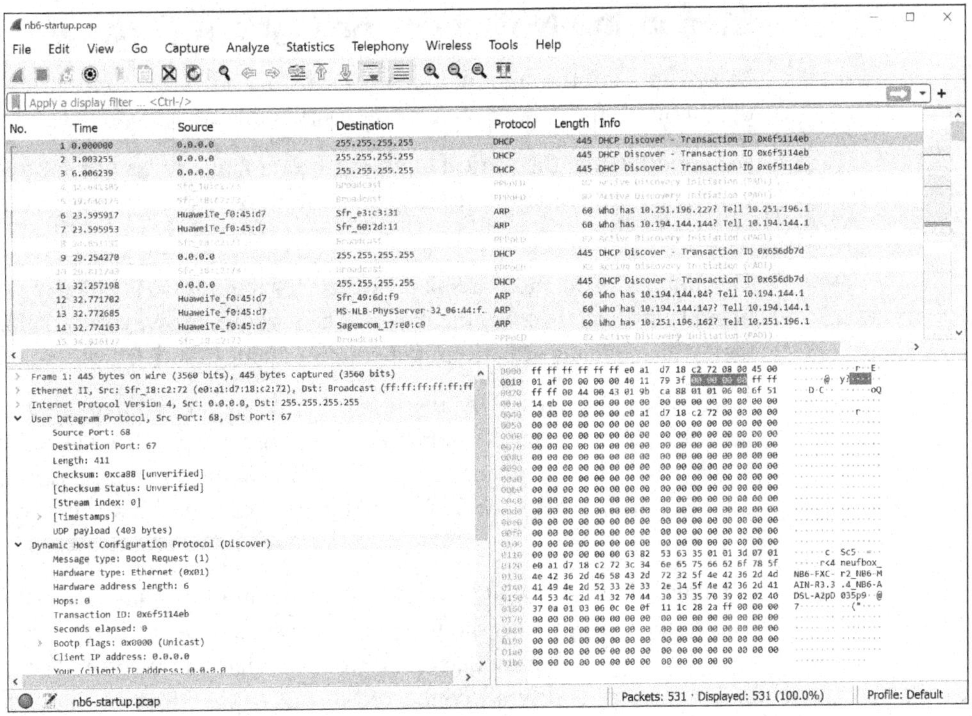

Figure 37-38 Example of Viewing a Wireshark Capture

Lab—Install Wireshark (37.5.3)

Wireshark is a software protocol analyzer, or "packet sniffer" application, used for network troubleshooting, analysis, software and protocol development, and education. Wireshark is used throughout the course to demonstrate network concepts. In this lab, you will download and install Wireshark.

Refer to the online course to complete this lab.

Lab—Use Network Tools to Learn About a Network (37.5.4)

Wireshark is a software protocol analyzer, or "packet sniffer" application, used for network troubleshooting, analysis, software and protocol development, and education. Wireshark is used in this course to demonstrate network concepts. Nmap is a popular network scanning and mapping tool. In this lab, you use Nmap to discover hosts on your network and then use Wireshark to capture traffic between your computer and other hosts.

Refer to the online course to complete this lab.

Measuring Network Throughput (37.5.5)

Bandwidth and throughput are two terms that are commonly used when describing the amount of traffic flowing between two devices.

Bandwidth is the theoretical amount of data that can be transmitted from one device to another in an amount of time. Bandwidth is typically measured in the number of bits per second.

Throughput is the measurement of the actual number of bits per second that are being transmitted across the media. Throughput is always lower than the specified bandwidth because traffic can encounter latency or delay during transmission.

Latency may be caused by any number of issues specifically the physical distance between the source and destination. There are other factors as well, including the number of network devices encountered between source and destination. As data crosses multiple networks, it must be processed and forwarded by switches and routers.

A technician might need to verify the throughput of a link to verify its operation. There are many sites on the Internet that we can use to do so. Searching using **internet speed test** will provide several websites that will measure the connection "speed" and performance of your connected device to the Internet. These sites typically use preselected servers and report both your downloading and upload "speeds."

iPerf is a downloadable Windows tool to measure throughput between a client and a server. iPerf is required to be running on both end devices. Example 37-12 shows the throughput between a client and public iPerf server, speedtest.masnet.ec.

Example 37-12 Output for the **iperf** Command

```
C:\tools\iperf> iperf3 -c speedtest.masnet.ec
Connecting to host speedtest.masnet.ec, port 5201
[  7] local 10.0.0.129 port 58350 connected to 170.83.216.19 port 5201
[ ID] Interval           Transfer     Bitrate
[  7]   0.00-1.00   sec  576 KBytes   4.72 Mbits/sec
[  7]   1.00-2.00   sec  393 KBytes   3.22 Mbits/sec
[  7]   2.00-3.00   sec  775 KBytes   6.35 Mbits/sec
[  7]   3.00-4.00   sec  713 KBytes   5.83 Mbits/sec
[  7]   4.00-5.00   sec  677 KBytes   5.55 Mbits/sec
[  7]   5.00-6.00   sec  701 KBytes   5.75 Mbits/sec
[  7]   6.00-7.00   sec  718 KBytes   5.89 Mbits/sec
[  7]   7.00-8.00   sec  621 KBytes   5.08 Mbits/sec
[  7]   8.00-9.00   sec  749 KBytes   6.13 Mbits/sec
```

```
[  7]   9.00-10.00  sec  738 KBytes   6.05 Mbits/sec
- - - - - - - - - - - - - - - - - - - - - - - - -
[ ID] Interval           Transfer     Bitrate
[  7]   0.00-10.00  sec  6.50 MBytes  5.46 Mbits/sec    sender
[  7]   0.00-10.18  sec  6.38 MBytes  5.26 Mbits/sec    receiver

iperf Done.
C:\tools\iperf>
```

The relevant output is

- **Interval**—The time interval iPerf periodically reports throughput. By default, the time interval is 1 second.
- **Transfer**—The amount of data transferred during each time interval.
- **Bitrate**—The measured throughput in in each time interval.

Packet Tracer Activity

Packet Tracer—Troubleshooting Challenge—Use Documentation to Solve Issues (37.5.6)

In this Packet Tracer activity, you use network documentation to identify and fix network communications problems.

- Use various techniques and tools to identify connectivity issues.
- Use documentation to guide troubleshooting efforts.
- Identify specific network problems.
- Implement solutions to network communication problems.
- Verify network operation.

Refer to the online course to complete this Packet Tracer.

Troubleshoot Connectivity Remotely (37.6)

Quite often the issue is in a remote location. This section discusses the tools at your disposal to help you support remote users and troubleshoot problems from a distance.

Supporting Remote Users (37.6.1)

When assisting remote users, it is often not efficient to verbally walk a user through complicated procedures. Remote-access technologies enable support technicians to take control of a user's desktop to view and configure settings on the user's computer. During a remote desktop session, the user is often unable to control their PC. However, they can watch everything that the technician does.

For example, a user may be having trouble accessing the corporate site. Because this access can depend on multiple conditions regarding the configuration of the computer, a support technician requests remote access to the system. After the user authorizes access, the technician can then check multiple security and access settings on the system to identify and fix the problem.

Remote desktop applications introduce potential security vulnerabilities because they offer complete control of computers by someone other than the authorized user. For example, threat actors could exploit open remote desktop application ports or use social engineering techniques to trick a user into providing them with remote desktop access. It is important that users understand that only authorized support technicians should be granted remote access to systems.

Note

Many organizations disable remote access to computers that they own or administer. For that reason, it may be necessary to request that the user activate it. Other organizations use proprietary or alternative remote desktop applications to mitigate security vulnerabilities that are associated with remote system access.

Remote desktop applications use a client-server model. The remote desktop client is used to connect to the remote system, which acts as a server. Remote access applications can retrieve system data, transfer files to systems, and initiate secure chat sessions with users. Some remote-access applications require the user to be present to authorize access or can access systems without user participation. Other remote-access systems can access the system if it is unattended.

The following are common remote desktop applications:

- Microsoft Remote Desktop
  - Installed on all Windows computers.
  - Permits access from PCs, Android, or iOS devices.
  - Requires a Pro edition of Windows.
- Apple Remote Desktop
  - Available for OS X 10.10.5 or later.

  - Client version 3.6 and higher offer full control.
  - Non-Mac clients must have Virtual Network Computing (VNC) compatible software installed.
- TeamViewer
  - Broad platform access including IoT devices and over 100 mobile devices.
  - Easy to implement and use.
  - Very secure with end-to-end encryption, two-factor authentication, and other security features.
- Zoho Assist
  - Compatible with a wide range of operating systems.
  - Integrates well with third-party applications.
  - Supports up to 2 GB file transfers, voice and video chat, and multi-monitor navigation.

Remote Access with Telnet, SSH, and RDP (37.6.2)

Long before desktop computers with sophisticated graphical interfaces existed, people used text-based systems, which were often just display terminals physically attached to a central computer. After networks became available, people needed a way to remotely access computer systems in the same manner that they did with the directly attached terminals.

The Telnet protocol was developed to meet that need. Telnet dates back to the early 1970s and is among the oldest of the application layer protocols and services in the TCP/IP suite. Telnet provides a standard method of emulating text-based terminal devices over the data network. Both the protocol itself and the client software that implements the protocol are commonly referred to as Telnet. Telnet servers listen for client requests on TCP port 23.

A Telnet connection is called a virtual terminal (vty) session. Rather than using a physical device to connect to the server, Telnet uses software to create a virtual device that provides features of a terminal session with access to the server's command-line interface (CLI).

In Figure 37-39, the client has remotely connected to the server via Telnet. The client is now able to execute commands as if it were locally connected to the command line of the server. Similarly, Telnet can provide access to the CLI, or console, of a networking device so that the device can be configured and monitored.

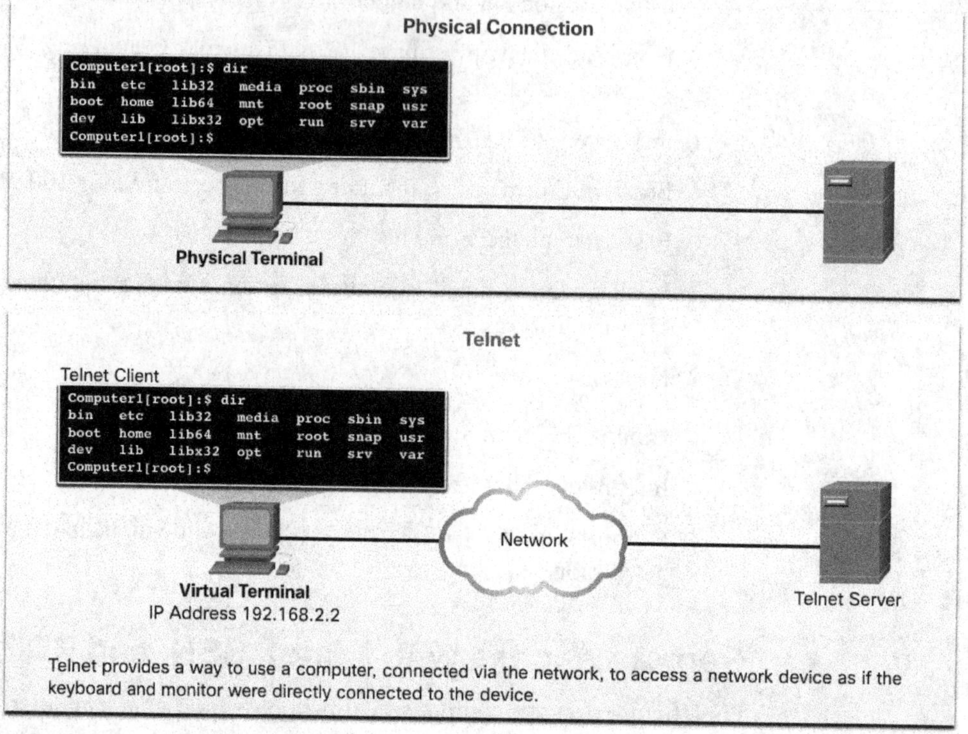

Figure 37-39 Physical Connection and Remote Connection

After a Telnet connection is established, users can perform any authorized function on the server, just as if they were using a command-line session on the server itself. If authorized, they can start and stop processes, configure the device, and even shut down the system.

Although the Telnet protocol can require a user to log in, it does not support transporting encrypted data. All data exchanged during Telnet sessions is transported as plaintext across the network. This means that the data can be easily intercepted and understood. This includes usernames and passwords.

The Secure Shell (SSH) protocol offers an alternate and secure method for server access. SSH provides the structure for secure remote login and other secure network services. It also provides stronger authentication than Telnet and supports transporting session data using encryption. SSH servers listen for client requests on TCP port 22.

As a best practice, network professionals should always use SSH in place of Telnet, if possible.

Figure 37-40 illustrates how SSH is more secure than Telnet. On the left side of the figure, the network technician is using Telnet and logs into the server using the indicated credentials. The threat actor has captured the Telnet traffic and can easily see the credentials used. On the right side of the figure, the technician is using SSH to connect to a different server. The threat actor could still capture the traffic. However, they would not be able to decipher it because SSH encrypts user traffic.

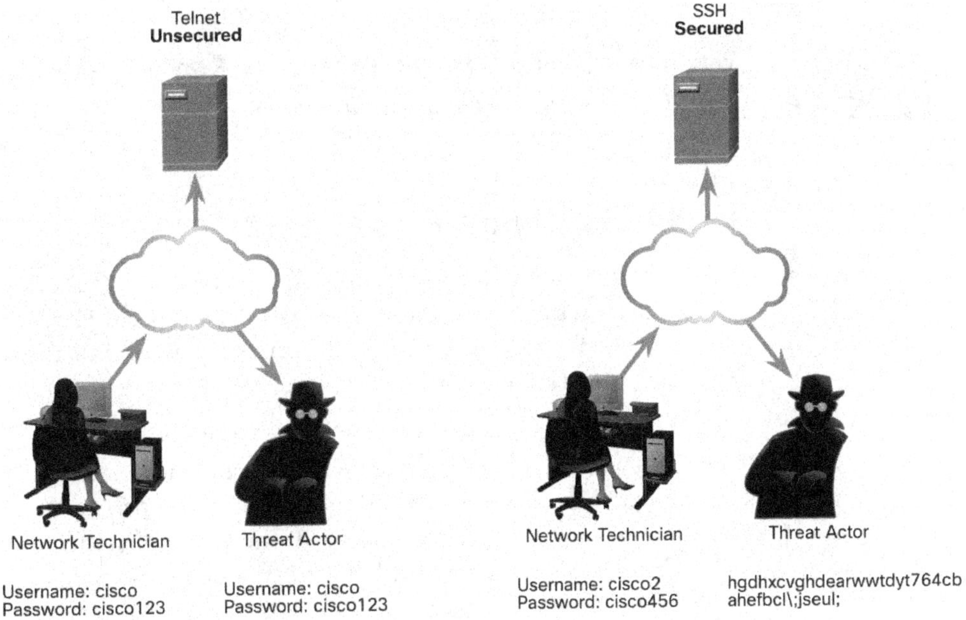

Figure 37-40 Telnet Traffic Is Unsecure and SSH Traffic Is Secure

Connecting to other devices using Telnet or SSH using a terminal window is common in some operating systems. There are also commercial software terminal emulator packages available. PuTTY is a popular free and open-source terminal emulator program. This client application supports SSH, Telnet, and rlogin. Tera Term is another free and open-source terminal emulator that includes a macro scripting language and plugins. PuTTY and Tera Term can both use the SSH protocol for connections. Both assume that an SSH server, such as the one available with OpenSSH, is running on the destination device. OpenSSH is distributed with a wide range of operating systems, including various Linux distributions, Windows, and macOS.

Remote Desktop Protocol (RDP) was created by Microsoft. It uses a client-server model in which the client can connect to an RDP server that is running on a remote system to display the graphical user interface of the remote device. RDP servers and

clients are included with Windows, and are available for OS X, Linux, and Unix via xrdp, which is a free and open-source implementation of the Microsoft RDP server. Other operating systems can also perform these functions. For example, in macOS, remote access functionality is provided by the Screen Sharing feature, which is based on Virtual Network Computing (VNC). Any VNC client can connect to a Screen Sharing server. VNC is a freeware product that is similar in functionality to RDP and works over port 5900.

Video

Video Demonstration—Remote Desktop and Remote Assistance (37.6.3)

Refer to the online course to view this video.

Understanding VPNs (37.6.4)

To securely communicate and share resources over a network that is not secure, such as the Internet, a Virtual Private Network (VPN) is used. The most common types of VPN are used to access a corporate private network either by remote users or by remote corporate sites.

A VPN uses dedicated secure connections, routed through the Internet, from the corporate private network to the remote user. When connected to the corporate private network, remote-access VPN users become part of that network and have access to all services and resources as if they were physically connected to it. VPNs are also used to connect branch offices and other facilities to the corporate network.

VPNs are commonly deployed in one of the following configurations: site-to-site or remote-access.

Site-to-Site VPN

A site-to-site VPN is created when VPN terminating devices, also called VPN gateways, are preconfigured with information to establish a secure tunnel, as shown in Figure 37-41. VPN traffic is only encrypted between these devices. Internal hosts have no knowledge that a VPN is being used.

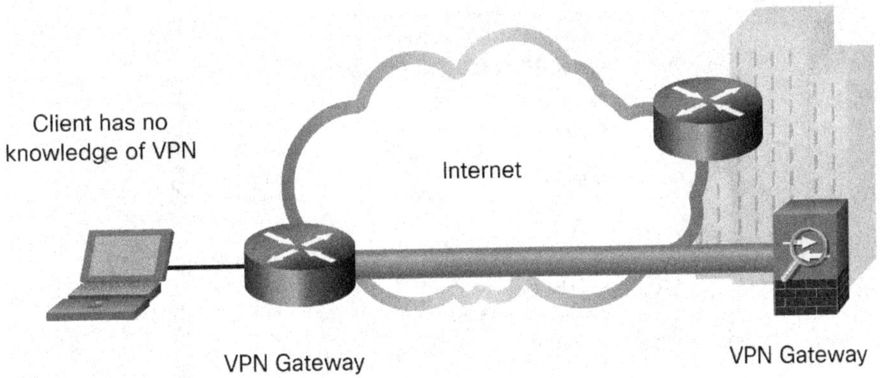

Figure 37-41 An Example of Site-to-Site VPN

Remote-Access VPN

A remote-access VPN is dynamically created to establish a secure connection between a client and a VPN terminating device, as shown in Figure 37-42. For example, a remote-access SSL VPN is used when you check your banking information online.

Figure 37-42 An Example of Remote-Access VPN

Remote-access users must install a VPN client on their computers to form a secure connection with the corporate private network. Special routers can also be used to connect computers to the corporate private network. The VPN software encrypts data before sending it over the Internet to the VPN gateway at the corporate private network. VPN gateways establish, manage, and control VPN connections, also known as VPN tunnels. Windows supports several VPN types; however, for some VPNs, third-party software may be required. The Cisco AnyConnect VPN client is shown in Figure 37-43.

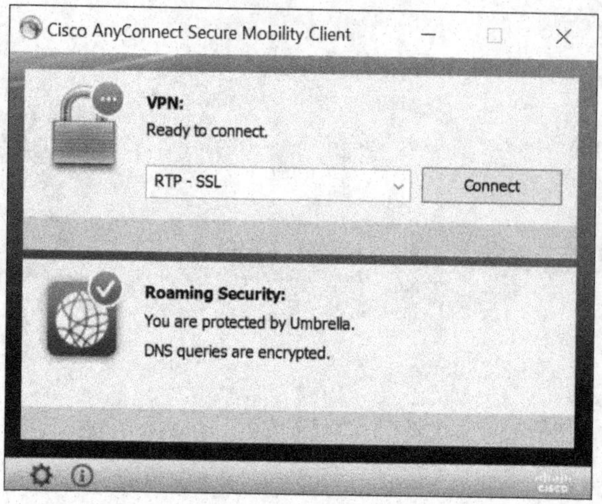

Figure 37-43 Cisco AnyConnect Secure Mobility Client

A VPN in Windows 10 can be set up from Network & Internet settings as shown in Figure 37-44.

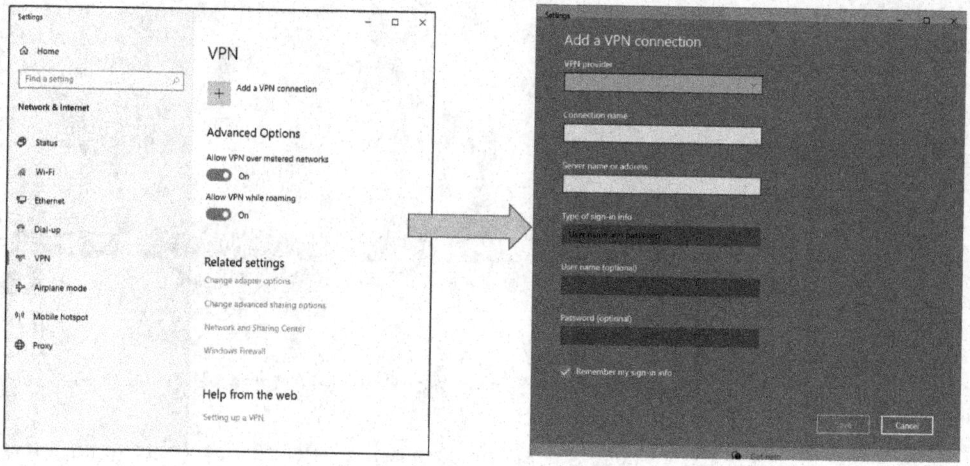

Figure 37-44 Windows 10 VPN Configuration

In addition to securing remote desktop sharing for technical support purposes, users can use remote desktop to remotely access computers within the corporate network in order to carry out their normal work duties. This means that a user can access the desktop of their work computer from their home computer. This permits workers to access work resources from their own devices and access files and programs hosted by their work PC remotely. In addition, computing with cloud-based virtual desktops is becoming popular. Organizations can save money and create efficiencies

by outsourcing management of workstations to the cloud. In this case, user workstations are cloud-hosted virtual machines. This permits users to access their computer resources from virtually any device that supports a compatible remote desktop client.

This can create security challenges, however. Many remote desktop clients are not secure. Using VPNs to access remote and cloud-based virtual computer workstations ensures greater security when this solution is in use. Microsoft Azure and Amazon Web Services provide remote workspace solutions. IT support personnel will be required to help workers access and operate these virtual resources.

Network Management Systems (37.6.5)

Network management refers to two related concepts. First is the process of configuring, monitoring, and managing the performance of a network. Second is the platform that IT and network operations teams use to complete these tasks. Modern network management platforms provide advanced analytics, machine learning, and intelligent automation to continually optimize network performance. As organizations adapt to a more distributed workforce, these network management systems are increasingly deployed in cloud and hosted environments.

Network management systems collect data from connected network devices such as switches, routers, access points, and client devices. They also give network administrators control over how those devices operate and interact with one another. The data captured from these devices is used to proactively identify performance issues, monitor security and segmentation, and accelerate troubleshooting.

Network management systems typically use Simple Network Management Protocol (SNMP) and Remote Network Monitoring (RMON) to gather information from network devices. Host operating systems have management platforms that allow monitoring and configuration of many host computers.

Network management systems are deployed using two operational models, as shown in Table 37-7.

Table 37-7 Cloud-Based and On-Premises Comparison

Cloud-Based	On-Premises
■ Cloud-based systems are designed to provide flexibility and wide-ranging access to networks that are geographically dispersed. ■ These platforms offer easy access and monitoring across highly distributed networks and make provisioning of remote sites simple.	■ On-premises network management systems can be used for large campus networks that require greater performance and scalability. ■ They also provide advanced features such as analytics, assurance, and artificial intelligence (AI) and machine learning (ML).

Cloud-Based	On-Premises
■ They also provide a high level of configurability and customization through open APIs and robust application ecosystems. ■ These platforms also support advanced analytics, automation, and optimization use cases, through large data lakes and the power of cloud computing to support sophisticated machine learning applications.	■ Some organizations must keep close control over their data assets and are prohibited from housing data in dispersed locations. ■ On-premises network management servers avoid such compliance issues because all data can be stored onsite. ■ Because large networks can generate a lot of management data, on-premises systems are usually larger servers that have enough power to process the data so that it can be used to provide the insights IT needs to manage the network. ■ This is one reason an on-premises server is usually located in the core of the network. ■ Although it can be accessed from the Internet, remote access requires a VPN connection.

Cisco Meraki is a leading cloud-based network management platform that provides powerful network management capabilities without consuming user bandwidth. It is secure, flexible, and easy to deploy. With it, networks can be managed from anywhere. It can manage a diverse range of both Meraki and non-Meraki network devices securely. It provides detailed views of large, dispersed, and complex networks down to the individual desktop computer or phone. Figure 37-45 provides a look at one aspect of a Meraki dashboard.

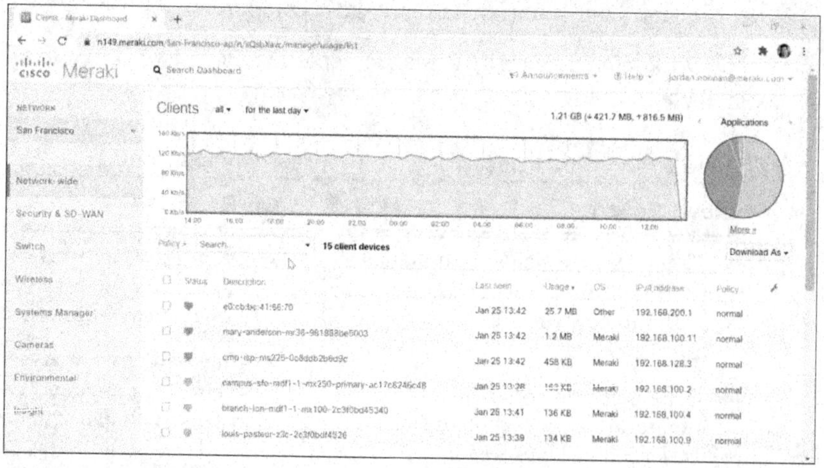

Figure 37-45 Meraki Dashboard

Video

Video—What Is Network Management? (37.6.6)

This video briefly explores network management including cloud network management and Cisco Nexus Dashboard.

Refer to the online course to view this video.

Network Support Summary (37.7)

The following is a summary of each topic in the chapter and some questions for your reflection.

What Did I Learn in This Chapter? (37.7.1)

- **Diagnostics and Troubleshooting Methodologies**—Troubleshooting is a process that should be applied systematically. One approach uses a seven-step process in which the technician defines the problem, gathers relevant information, analyzes the information, eliminates possible causes, proposes a hypothesis about the most likely cause of the problem, and then tests the hypothesis and solves the problem. Another approach is to follow the layers of the OSI model.

  Structured troubleshooting can include the use of seven different methods: bottom-up, top-down, divide-and-conquer, follow-the-path, substitution, comparison, and the educated guess approach.

  The choice of method sometimes depends on the type of issue that is being addressed and the experience of the technician. It is important to always document the issue according to company procedures, including providing information of the eventual resolution of the problem.

- **Network Documentation**—Network documentation is essential to maintaining, securing, and troubleshooting networks. Documentation may consist of physical and logical network diagrams, written documents, and network performance baselines.

  There are nine network topologies that may be documented. These include personal area networks (PANs), local area networks (LANs), virtual LANs (VLANs), wireless LANs (WLANs), wireless mesh networks (WMNs), campus area networks (CANs), metropolitan area networks (MANs), wide area networks (WANs), and virtual private networks (VPNs).

  Physical topology diagrams include the physical locations of devices and documents their connections. Logical topology diagrams include IP addresses and networking device details such as connected ports. Other information such as

cloud services, routing policies, and security and remote-access policies may appear on topology diagrams.

Cloud services can be Software as a Service (SaaS), Platform as a Service (PaaS), or Infrastructure as a Service (IaaS). XaaS means anything/everything as a service, including desktop as a service (DaaS), disaster recovery as a service (DRaaS), communications as a service (CaaS), and monitoring as a service (MaaS).

Wireless standards define the operating characteristics of wireless operations, including signaling specifications, data rates, and power efficiency. Wireless standards form the IEEE 802.11 wireless Ethernet family of standards, such as 802.11b, n, g, and ac. These standards exist in the unlicensed wireless spectrum. Licensed wireless frequencies are controlled by the Federal Communications Commission (FCC) and licenses are granted to radio stations, cellular companies, and television stations.

Device documentation differs depending on the type of devices. It will often include device operating system and software, licensing information, interface status, addressing, routing protocols, etc.

Network baselines are a series of measurements of network performance taken during different types of network usage. The baselines help to understand the parameters of a properly working network so that network performance or security problems can be identified when performance deviates significantly from previous baseline measurements.

Cisco Discovery Protocol (CDP) is a Cisco protocol that runs on Cisco networking devices. It sends CDP advertisements to directly attached neighbor devices. Information sent in these advertisements includes the configured device name, a port identifier, the hardware platform and software versions, and IP addresses. This information is displayed with the IOS commands **show cdp neighbors** and **show cdp neighbors detail**. CDP can be used to reveal information about network topologies.

- **Help Desks**—Security policies specify what employees need to do to ensure that the network is secure. This includes policies regarding user identification and authentication, password length, complexity and refresh interval, acceptable behavior, and remote-access requirements. Standard operating procedures (SOPs) define procedures that must be followed for replacing network devices, installing or removing software applications, new employee onboarding, and employee termination. Guidelines are suggestions for proper procedure that exist when no SOPs are defined.

  A help desk is a specialized team of IT professionals who are the central point of contact for employees and customers who need technical assistance. Help desks use communication tools such as chat, telephone, or email to receive issues from

customers and facilitate the troubleshooting process. A ticketing system is used to manage "trouble tickets" that consist of details of the issues that users report. Users initiate the tickets, and technicians validate the issues, work with users to address the issues, and escalate the tickets if a higher degree of expertise is required to resolve the issues.

A support technician should always be considerate and should empathize with users, who may be under stress and anxious to resolve a problem quickly. Technicians should never belittle, insult, or talk down to users, or accuse users of causing the problem.

The know, relate, and understand skill set is a useful way to relate to customers. To know the customer, call them by their name or ask if there is another name that you can use. To better relate to the customer, attempt to create a one-on-one connection. And to understand the customer, determine their level of technical knowledge as a way to speak to them at an appropriate level. Questioning is important using either open-ended or closed-ended questions. Active listening entails using understanding responses as users talk and summarizing what they tell you to verify your understanding.

When addressing an issue with hosts, gather information about the device, operating system, network environment, and the results of connectivity tests, such as **ping** and **tracert**. Other sources of information are beep codes, Event Viewer logs, Device Manager settings, Task Manager data, and diagnostic tool results.

For Cisco device–related tickets, use IOS commands, packet captures, and device logs to gather information. IOS commands for connectivity testing, such as **ping** and **traceroute**, are useful. Secure Shell (SSH) is the preferred way to connect to the IOS CLI remotely because Telnet is not secure. IOS **show** commands, such as **show ip interface brief**, **show ip route**, and **show protocols**, are useful also.

The next step in the troubleshooting process is to analyze the information that you have gathered and solve the problem. You can consult the ticket system software to locate similar issues, access vendor information resources and FAQs, and search the Internet for relevant information. If you can't solve the problem, then you should escalate it to a higher-level technician for resolution.

- **Troubleshoot Endpoint Connectivity**—To verify the network configuration of a Windows host, check the status of the connections in Network and Sharing Center. You can also use **ipconfig /all** to display this information. Use **ping** and **traceroute** or **tracert** to test connectivity.

  On a Linux host, you can view active connections in the GUI or use the **ifconfig** command in a terminal. In addition to **ping** and **traceroute**, other command-line tools such as **speedtest** and **ncat** (**nc**) are available for network testing.

In macOS, open **Network Preferences > Advanced** to get IP addressing information. The **ifconfig** command can be issued from a terminal as well. Other useful commands are **networksetup -listallnetworkservices** and **networksetup -getinfo** *<network service>*. The Linux commands mentioned above are also available in macOS. The macOS Wireless Diagnostics tool can also help solve connectivity problems.

Apple iOS networking can be verified by accessing the Wi-Fi settings. In Android, information about the device addressing and connections can be accessed from the **About phone > Status** settings. Third-party apps are available that enhance network diagnostics for Android.

- **Troubleshoot a Network**—To gather information to troubleshoot a network problem, Cisco IOS devices have many **show** commands that can provide detailed information. The Cisco IOS software separates management access into two privilege levels: user EXEC mode, which is lower level, and privileged EXEC mode, which has full privileges. Use the **enable** command to enter Cisco privileged EXEC mode. IOS context-sensitive help can be used to locate commands and get information about their usage. Context-sensitive help is available by entering a **?** at an empty prompt or after a command.

  Packet capture and protocol analysis applications enable you to investigate packet content as it flows through the network. The software decodes the protocol layers housed within a packet. Wireshark is an example of a popular open-source packet capture/protocol analysis application.

  Bandwidth and throughput are characteristics of network data flow. Bandwidth is the theoretical amount of data that can be transmitted from one device to another in an amount of time. Bandwidth is typically measured in the number of bits per second. Throughput is the measurement of the actual number of bits per second that are being transmitted across the media. Throughput is always lower than bandwidth because of latency and delay. Online Internet speed test tools and the iPerf Windows tool enable measurement of throughput.

- **Troubleshoot Connectivity Remotely**—When assisting remote users, it may be more efficient to use remote desktop applications. These applications allow a technician to take control of a remote desktop to investigate issues and make configuration changes. Remote desktop applications can create security vulnerabilities and many organizations have desktop sharing disabled on computers. Microsoft Remote Desktop is included in all Pro versions of Windows. Apple Remote Desktop and TeamViewer are examples of other remote desktop software.

  Telnet, SSH, and Remote Desktop Protocol (RDP) are protocols for remote access to systems. Telnet is an old virtual terminal application that is used to access the command line of a remote system. It uses TCP port 23. Telnet has no mechanism for encrypting transmitted data, and so should not be used. SSH, much like

Telnet, enables virtual terminal sessions, but it includes encryption and should be used instead of Telnet. Virtual terminal clients such as PuTTY and Tera Term are available for connection to Telnet and SSH servers.

RDP was created by Microsoft. It also uses a client-server model in which the client accesses an operating system GUI on a remote computer. RDP software is available with Windows, OS X, Linux, and Unix via xrdp. For macOS, remote desktop functionality is provided by Virtual Network Computing (VNC) software.

Virtual private networks (VPNs) enable secure remote network access over unsecured networks like the Internet. A VPN uses dedicated secure connections that encrypt network traffic. Site-to-site VPNs connect entire remote facilities. Remote-access VPNs connect individual users to the corporate network. Remote-access VPN users connect to a corporate network VPN gateway using a software client such as Cisco AnyConnect. Microsoft Windows has its own VPN client.

Network management refers to the process of configuring, monitoring, and managing the performance of a network. Modern network management platforms provide advanced analytics, machine learning, and intelligent automation to continually optimize network performance. Network management systems typically use Simple Network Management Protocol (SNMP) and Remote Network Monitoring (RMON) to gather information. Network management systems can be deployed in cloud-based or on-premises models. Cloud-based deployments are good for distributed environments that are geographically dispersed. On-premises systems require a lot of computing power and storage but are good for situations where compliance with data-sovereignty regulations is required. Cisco Meraki is a leading cloud-based network management platform that provides powerful network management capabilities without consuming user bandwidth.

Network automation is the process of automating the configuring, managing, testing, deploying, and operating of physical and virtual devices within a network. Common labor-intensive tasks can be automated using scripts and network programmability. Python is a popular scripting language for network automation.

Reflection Questions (37.7.2)

Lara did a great job creating a troubleshooting guide for help desk technicians. Sharing her help desk experience will help new technicians quickly become more effective. Was the information practical in this chapter? How are your diagnostic skills? Which troubleshooting approach would work best if a problem is related to cabling? Which troubleshooting approach would work best if the problem is related to an application?

Practice

The following activities provide practice with the topics introduced in this chapter.

Labs

Lab—Verify Address with a Subnet Calculator (37.4.9)

Lab—Install Wireshark (37.5.3)

Lab—Use Wireshark to View Network Traffic (37.5.4)

Packet Tracer Activities

Packet Tracer—Connect a Network Based on a Network Diagram (37.2.7)

Packet Tracer—Use CDP to Map a Network (37.2.12)

Packet Tracer—Troubleshooting Challenge—Document the Network (37.2.13)

Packet Tracer—Troubleshooting Challenge—Use Documentation to Solve Issues (37.5.6)

Check Your Understanding Questions

Complete all the review questions listed here to test your understanding of the topics and concepts in this chapter. Appendix A, "Answers to 'Check Your Understanding' Questions," lists the answers.

1. After a problem is defined, what is the next step in the seven-step troubleshooting process?
   a. Gather information
   b. Analyze information
   c. Propose hypothesis
   d. Eliminate possible causes
2. Which two types of problems are best investigated with a bottom-up troubleshooting method? (Choose two.)
   a. Problems involving an issue not seen before
   b. Problems involving cabling

c. Problems involving software installed on end systems
d. Problems involving routing tables
e. Problems involving subnet addressing

3. Which command will provide information that is useful for mapping a network?

a. **show CDP neighbors**
b. **show ip interfaces brief**
c. **show running-config**
d. **show inventory**

4. Which IEEE WLAN standard supports Wi-Fi 6 and Wi-Fi 6E?

a. 802.11ax
b. 802.11n
c. 802.11ac
d. 802.11g

5. What information could be determined from a network baseline?

a. The areas in the network that are underutilized
b. The layout of the components in the network
c. The operational status of network device interfaces
d. The number of hops between source and destination devices

6. A network technician troubleshoots a user's PC problem and launches the Task Manager to gather more information. What information can the technician gather from the Task Manager output?

a. The processes currently running on the PC
b. The devices configured on the PC
c. The errors that have occurred on the PC
d. The drivers installed on the PC

7. Which Cisco IOS command is used to determine the path of IP packets through the network?

a. **traceroute**
b. **telnet**
c. **show ip route**
d. **ping**

8. A user reports that the computer occasionally loses connectivity to the wireless network. The technician checks the configuration on the user's computer and then replaces the wireless access point with a known good one. What structured troubleshooting method is the technician using to solve the problem?

   a. Comparison
   b. Bottom-up
   c. Divide-and-conquer
   d. Substitution

9. Which question enables the technician to determine the scope of a network issue reported by a user?

   a. Are other users in your area experiencing the same issue?
   b. Are you seeing any error messages when the problem occurs?
   c. Is the problem one that you have experienced before?
   d. Have you added any new applications recently?

10. What is an example of a targeted, closed-ended question?

    a. What operating system is installed on your computer, Windows, Linux, or macOS?
    b. What types of error messages did you see when you experienced the issue?
    c. What steps did you take to attempt to solve the issue before reporting it?
    d. What can you tell me about how you discovered this issue?

11. Which two platforms use the **ifconfig** command to verify interface IP configuration? (Choose two.)

    a. Linux
    b. macOS
    c. Windows
    d. Cisco

12. Which router IOS command displays the equivalent system information as many different **show** commands and is useful for troubleshooting a router?

    a. **show tech-support**
    b. **show version**
    c. **show running-config**
    d. **show cdp neighbors detail**

13. What is the main reason to establish an initial network performance baseline?

   a. To determine normal traffic volume and behavior on the network
   b. To eliminate bottlenecks and congestion affecting performance
   c. To limit the number of devices attached to the network
   d. To reduce the need to monitor traffic after making network changes

14. Which two wireless network standards operate in both the 2.4 and 5 GHz frequency spectrums? (Choose two.)

   a. 802.11a
   b. 802.11g
   c. 802.11n
   d. 802.11ac
   e. 802.11ax

15. Which type of network documentation would a technician use to determine the IP addresses and subnets configured in the network?

   a. Logical topology map
   b. Physical topology map
   c. Three-layer design model diagram
   d. Cloud service architecture diagram

CHAPTER 38

Cybersecurity Threats, Vulnerabilities, and Attacks

Objectives

Upon completion of this chapter, you will be able to answer the following questions:

- What are the threats, vulnerabilities, and attacks that occur in the various domains?
- What are the different deception methods used by attackers to deceive their victims?
- What are common types of network attacks?
- What are common types of wireless and mobile device attacks?
- What are types of application attacks?

Key Terms

This chapter uses the following key terms. You can find the definitions in the Glossary.

Infrastructure as a Service (IaaS) *Page 781*

Platform as a Service (PaaS) *Page 781*

Software as a Service (SaaS) *Page 781*

threat domain *Page 776*

Introduction (38.0)

It's Webster again! The college help desk gets support tickets for a variety of reasons. The troubleshooting guide that Lara created will help the technicians with common computer and network problems. But sometimes, those support tickets result from malware on a user's computer. The web has a lot to offer, but users must be careful because bad actors always want to wreak havoc or profit from you.

Lara did such a great job creating the help desk troubleshooting guide that the college assigned her to work on a cybersecurity awareness campaign. The campaign should educate college users on the threats, vulnerabilities, and common cyber attacks used by threat actors. It should also include information about threat actors who use social engineering techniques to trick users, information about common wireless threats, and an explanation of the threats to applications.

Education is the first line of defense. If users know about the bad stuff that can happen, they can help defend the college against them. So, let's dig deeper and learn more about these threats, vulnerabilities, and cyberattacks.

Common Threats (38.1)

This section examines common internal and external security threats facing organizations.

Threat Domains (38.1.1)

With organizations facing an ever-growing number of cyber threats, it is critical that they have robust security solutions in place. But in order to protect themselves, organizations first need to know what vulnerabilities exist within their threat domains. A *threat domain* is considered to be an area of control, authority, or protection that attackers can exploit to gain access to a system.

There are many ways that attackers can uncover vulnerabilities and exploit systems within a domain.

Attackers can exploit systems within a domain through:

- Direct, physical access to systems and networks
- Wireless networking that extends beyond an organization's boundaries
- Bluetooth or near-field communication (NFC) devices
- Malicious email attachments
- Less secure elements within an organization's supply chain

- An organization's social media accounts
- Removable media such as flash drives
- Cloud-based applications

Types of Cyber Threats (38.1.2)

Cyber threats can be classified into different categories, as shown in Table 38-1. This allows organizations to assess the likelihood of a threat occurring and understand the monetary impact of a threat so that they can prioritize their security efforts.

Table 38-1 Cyber Threat Categories and Examples

Category	Examples
Software attacks	■ A successful denial-of-service (DoS) attack ■ A computer virus
Software errors	■ A software bug ■ An application going offline ■ A cross-site script or illegal file server share
Sabotage	■ An authorized user successfully penetrating and compromising an organization's primary database ■ The defacement of an organization's website
Human error	■ Inadvertent data entry errors ■ A firewall misconfiguration
Theft	■ Laptops or equipment being stolen from an unlocked room
Hardware failures	■ Hard drive crashes
Utility interruption	■ Electrical power outages ■ Water damage resulting from sprinkler failure
Natural disasters	■ Severe storms such as hurricanes or tornados ■ Earthquakes ■ Floods ■ Fires

Internal vs. External Threats (38.1.3)

Threats can originate from both within and outside of an organization, with attackers seeking access to valuable sensitive information such as personnel records, intellectual property, and financial data, as shown in Figure 38-1.

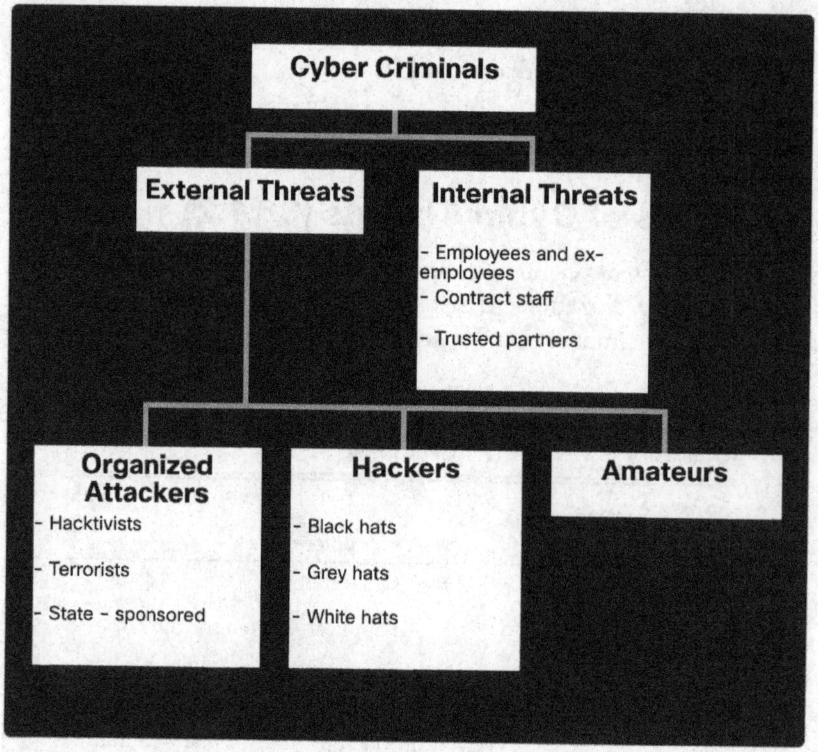

Figure 38-1 External and Internal Threats

Internal threats are usually carried out by current or former employees and other contract partners who accidentally or intentionally mishandle confidential data or threaten the operations of servers or network infrastructure devices by connecting infected media or by accessing malicious emails or websites.

The source of an *external threat* typically stems from amateur or skilled attackers who can exploit vulnerabilities in networked devices or can use social engineering techniques, such as trickery, to gain access to an organization's internal resources.

Interactive Graphic

Practice Item—Threat Origination (38.1.4)

Refer to the online course to complete this activity.

User Threats and Vulnerabilities (38.1.5)

A *user domain* includes anyone with access to an organization's information system, including employees, customers, and contract partners. Users are often considered to

be the weakest link in information security systems, posing a significant threat to the confidentiality, integrity, and availability of an organization's data.

Table 38-2 lists the most common user threats to organizations.

Table 38-2 User Threats to Organizations

User Threat	Description
No awareness of security	Users must be aware of and understand an organization's sensitive data, security policies and procedures, technologies, and countermeasures that are implemented in order to protect information and information systems.
Poorly enforced security policies	All users must be aware of and understand an organization's security policies, as well as the consequences of non-compliance.
Data theft	Data stolen by users can pose a significant financial threat to organizations, both in terms of the resulting damage to their reputation and the legal liability associated with the disclosure of sensitive information.
Unauthorized downloads and media	Many network and device infections and attacks can be traced back to users who have downloaded unauthorized emails, photos, music, games, apps, or videos to their computers, networks, or storage devices. The use of unauthorized media such as external hard disks and USB drives also poses a threat.
Unauthorized virtual private networks (VPNs)	VPNs can hide the theft of unauthorized information because the encryption normally used to protect confidentiality can stop a network administrator from tracking data transmission (unless they have permission to do so).
Unauthorized websites	Accessing unauthorized websites can pose a risk to a user's data and devices, as well as the organization itself. Often, these websites prompt users to download scripts or plugins that contain malicious code or adware. Some of these sites can even take over user devices like cameras and applications.
Destruction of systems, applications, or data	The accidental or deliberate destruction or sabotage of systems, applications, and data poses a serious risk to all organizations. Activists, disgruntled employees, or industry competitors may attempt to delete data and destroy or misconfigure devices to make organizational data and information systems unavailable.

Always keep in mind that there are no technical solutions, controls, or countermeasures that will make information systems any more secure than the behaviors and processes of the people who use these systems.

Threats to Devices (38.1.6)

The following are common threats to devices:

- Any devices left powered on and unattended pose the risk of someone gaining unauthorized access to network resources.
- Downloading files, photos, music, or videos from unreliable sources could lead to the execution of malicious code on devices.
- Cybercriminals often exploit security vulnerabilities within software installed on an organization's devices to launch an attack.
- An organization's information security teams must try to keep up to date with the daily discovery of new viruses, worms, and other malware that pose a threat to their devices.
- Users who insert unauthorized USB drives, CDs, or DVDs run the risk of introducing malware, or compromising data stored on their device.
- Policies are in place to protect an organization's IT infrastructure. A user can face serious consequences for purposefully violating such policies.
- Using outdated hardware or software makes an organization's systems and data more vulnerable to attack.

Threats to the Local Area Network (38.1.7)

The local area network (LAN) is a collection of devices, typically in the same geographic area, connected by cables (wired) or airwaves (wireless).

Because users can access an organization's systems, applications, and data from the *LAN domain*, it is critical that it has strong security and stringent access controls.

Examples of threats to the LAN include:

- Unauthorized access to wiring closets, data centers, and computer rooms
- Unauthorized access to systems, applications, and data
- Network operating system or software vulnerabilities and updates
- Rogue users gaining unauthorized access to wireless networks
- Exploits of data in transit
- Having LAN servers with different hardware or operating systems, which makes managing and troubleshooting them more difficult
- Unauthorized network probing and port scanning
- Misconfigured firewalls

Threats to the Private Cloud (38.1.8)

The *private cloud domain* includes any private servers, resources, and IT infrastructure available to members of a single organization via the Internet. While many organizations feel that their data is safer in a private cloud, this domain still poses significant security threats, including:

- Unauthorized network probing and port scanning
- Unauthorized access to resources
- Router, firewall, or network device operating system or software vulnerabilities
- Router, firewall, or network device configuration errors
- Remote users accessing an organization's infrastructure and downloading sensitive data

Threats to the Public Cloud (38.1.9)

Where a private cloud domain hosts computing resources for a single organization, the *public cloud domain* is the entirety of computing services hosted by a cloud service or Internet provider that is available to the public or shared across organizations.

There are three models of public cloud services that organizations typically choose to use:

- *Software as a Service (SaaS)*—This is a subscription-based model that provides organizations with software that is centrally hosted and accessed by users via a web browser, app, or other software. In other words, this is software that is not stored locally but instead is run from the cloud.
- *Platform as a Service (PaaS)*—This subscription-based model provides a platform that allows an organization to develop, run, and manage its applications on the service's hardware, using tools that the service provides. This platform is accessed via the public cloud.
- *Infrastructure as a Service (IaaS)*—This subscription-based model provides virtual computing resources such as hardware, software, servers, storage, and other infrastructure components over the Internet. An organization will buy access to this infrastructure and use it via the public cloud.

Threats to Applications (38.1.10)

The *application domain* includes all of the critical systems, applications, and data used by an organization to support operations. Increasingly, organizations are

moving applications such as email, security monitoring, and database management to the public cloud.

Common threats to applications include:

- Someone gaining unauthorized access to data centers, computer rooms, wiring closets, or systems
- Server downtime during maintenance periods
- Network operating system software vulnerabilities
- Data loss
- Client-server or web application development vulnerabilities

Interactive Graphic

Practice Item—Threats and Vulnerabilities (38.1.11)

Refer to the online course to complete this activity.

Threat Complexity (38.1.12)

The threat landscape has continued to expand not only in the number of vectors but also in their complexity.

An *advanced persistent threat (APT)* is a continuous attack that uses elaborate espionage tactics involving multiple actors and/or sophisticated malware to gain access to the target's network. Attackers remain undetected for a long period of time, with potentially devastating consequences. APTs typically target governments and high-level organizations and are usually well-orchestrated and well-funded.

As the name suggests, *algorithm attacks* take advantage of algorithms in a piece of legitimate software to generate unintended behaviors. For example, algorithms used to track and report how much energy a computer consumes can be used to select targets or trigger false alerts. They can also disable a computer by forcing it to use up all its RAM or by overworking its central processing unit (CPU).

Backdoors and Rootkits (38.1.13)

Cybercriminals also use many different types of malicious software to carry out their attacks.

Backdoors

Backdoor programs, such as Netbus and Back Orifice, are used by cybercriminals to gain unauthorized access to systems by bypassing the normal authentication procedures.

Cybercriminals typically have authorized users unknowingly run a remote administrative tool (RAT) program on their computer that installs a backdoor. The backdoor gives the criminal administrative control over a target computer. Backdoors grant cybercriminals continued access to a system, even if the organization has fixed the original vulnerability used to attack the system.

Rootkits

This malware is designed to modify the operating system to create a backdoor that attackers can then use to access the computer remotely.

Most rootkits take advantage of software vulnerabilities to gain access to resources that normally shouldn't be accessible (privilege escalation) and modify system files.

Rootkits can also modify system forensics and monitoring tools, making them very hard to detect. In most cases, a computer infected by a rootkit has to be wiped and any required software reinstalled.

Threat Intelligence and Research Sources (38.1.14)

The United States Computer Emergency Readiness Team (US-CERT) and the U.S. Department of Homeland Security sponsor a database of *common vulnerabilities and exposures (CVEs)*. These CVEs have been widely adopted as a way to describe and reference known vulnerabilities.

Each CVE entry contains a standard identifier number, a brief description of the security vulnerability, and any important references to related vulnerability reports. The CVE list is maintained by a not-for-profit, the MITRE Corporation, on its public website.

The following are some other sources of threat intelligence.

The Dark Web

This refers to encrypted web content that is not indexed by conventional search engines and requires specific software, authorization, or configurations to access. Expert researchers monitor the dark web for new threat intelligence.

Indicator of Compromise (IOC)

IOCs such as malware signatures or malicious domain names provide evidence of security breaches and details about them.

Automated Indicator Sharing (AIS)

Automated Indicator Sharing (AIS), a Cybersecurity and Infrastructure Security Agency (CISA) capability, enables the real-time exchange of cybersecurity threat

indicators using a standardized and structured language. Structured Threat Information Expression (STIX) and Trusted Automated Exchange of Intelligence Information (TAXII) are standards used in AIS.

Interactive Graphic

Check Your Understanding—Common Threats (38.1.15)

Refer to the online course to complete this activity.

Deception (38.2)

Deception comes in many forms. This section explores some of the different ways attackers can attempt to deceive a person or organization.

Social Engineering (38.2.1)

Social engineering is a non-technical strategy that attempts to manipulate individuals into performing risky actions or divulging confidential information.

Rather than software or hardware vulnerabilities, social engineering exploits human nature by taking advantage of people's willingness to help or preying on their weaknesses, such as greed or vanity.

The following are some common types of social engineering.

Pretexting

This type of attack occurs when an individual lies to gain access to privileged data. For example, an attacker pretends to need personal or financial data in order to confirm a person's identity.

Something for Something (Quid Pro Quo)

Quid pro quo attacks involve a request for personal information in exchange for something, like a gift. For example, a malicious email could ask you to give your sensitive personal details in exchange for a free vacation.

Identity Fraud

This is the use of a person's stolen identity to obtain goods or services by deception. For example, someone acquires your personal information and attempts to apply for a credit card in your name.

Social Engineering Tactics (38.2.2)

Cybercriminals rely on several social engineering tactics, as shown in Table 38-3, to gain access to sensitive information.

Table 38-3 Social Engineering Tactics

Social Engineering Tactic	Description
Authority	Attackers prey on the fact that people are more likely to comply when instructed by someone they perceive as an authority figure. For example, an executive opens what looks like an official subpoena attachment but is actually an infected PDF.
Intimidation	Cybercriminals will often bully a victim into taking an action that compromises security. For example, a secretary receives a call that their boss is about to give an important presentation but the files are corrupt. The criminal on the phone claims it's the secretary's fault and pressures the secretary to send across the files immediately or risk dismissal.
Consensus	Often called "social proof," consensus attacks work because people tend to act in the same way as other people around them, thinking that something must be right if others are doing it. For example, cybercriminals may publish a social media post about a false business opportunity and get dozens of legitimate or illegitimate accounts to comment on its validity. This encourages unsuspecting victims to make a purchase.
Scarcity	A well-known marketing tactic, scarcity attacks work because attackers know that people tend to act when they think there is a limited quantity of something available. For example, someone receives an email about a luxury item being sold for very little money, but it states that there are only a handful available at this very favorable price. This may spur the unsuspecting victim into impulsively taking action.
Urgency	Similarly, people also tend to act when they think there is a limited time to do so. For example, cybercriminals promote a fake time-limited shipping offer to try and prompt victims to take action quickly.
Familiarity	People are more likely to do what another person asks if they like this person. Therefore, attackers will often try to build a rapport with their victim in order to establish a relationship. In other cases, they may clone the social media profile of a friend of yours, in order to get you to think you are speaking to them.
Trust	Building trust in a relationship with a victim may require more time to establish. For example, a cybercriminal disguised as a security expert calls the unsuspecting victim to offer advice. When helping the victim, the "security expert" discovers a "serious error" that needs immediate attention. The solution provides the cybercriminal with the opportunity to violate the victim's security.

Interactive Graphic

Practice Item—Social Engineering Scenario (38.2.3)

Refer to the online course to complete this activity.

Shoulder Surfing and Dumpster Diving (38.2.4)

Shoulder surfing is a simple attack that involves observing or literally looking over a target's shoulder to gain valuable information such as PINs, access codes, or credit card details. Criminals do not always have to be near their victim to shoulder surf. They can use binoculars or security cameras to obtain this information.

This is one reason why an ATM screen can only be viewed at certain angles. These types of safeguards make shoulder surfing much more difficult.

You might have heard of the phrase, "one man's trash is another man's treasure." Nowhere is this more true than in the world of *dumpster diving*, which is the process of going through a target's trash to see what information has been thrown out.

This is why documents containing sensitive information should be shredded or stored in burn bags until they can be destroyed.

Impersonation and Hoaxes (38.2.5)

Cybercriminals have many other deception techniques to help them succeed.

Impersonation

Impersonation is the act of pretending to be someone else to trick someone into doing something they would not ordinarily do. For example, a cybercriminal posing as an IRS employee recently targeted taxpayers, telling the victims that they owed money that had to be paid immediately via wire transfer—or risk arrest.

Criminals can also use impersonation to attack others. For example, they can pose as their victim online and post on websites or social media pages to undermine the victim's credibility.

Hoaxes

A hoax is an act intended to deceive or trick someone. Hoaxes can cause just as much disruption as an actual security breach.

For example, a message warns of a (nonexistent) virus threat on a device and asks the recipient to share this information with everyone they know. This hoax elicits a user reaction, creating fear and irrational behavior that is propagated through email and social media.

Piggybacking and Tailgating (38.2.6)

Piggybacking or tailgating occurs when a criminal follows an authorized person to gain physical entry into a secure location or a restricted area. Criminals can achieve this by:

- Giving the appearance of being escorted into the facility by an authorized person
- Joining and pretending to be part of a large crowd that enters the facility
- Targeting an authorized person who is careless about the rules of the facility

One way of preventing this is to use two sets of doors. This is sometimes referred to as a mantrap and means individuals enter through an outer door, which must close before they can gain access through an inner door.

Other Methods of Deception (38.2.7)

Be aware that attackers have many more tricks up their sleeve to deceive their victims. Table 38-4 lists some additional methods of deception.

Table 38-4 Other Methods of Deception

Method	**Description**
Invoice scam	Fake invoices are sent with the goal of receiving money from a victim by prompting them to put their credentials into a fake login screen. The fake invoice may also include urgent or threatening language.
Watering hole attack	A watering hole attack describes an exploit in which an attacker observes or guesses what websites an organization uses most often and infects one or more of them with malware.
Typo squatting	This type of attack relies on common mistakes such as typos made by individuals when inputting a website address into their browser. The incorrect URL will bring the individuals to a legitimate-looking website owned by the attacker, whose goal is to gather their personal or financial information.
Prepending	Attackers can remove the "external" email tag used by organizations to warn the recipient that an email has originated from an external source. This tricks individuals into believing that a malicious email was sent from inside their organization.
Influence campaigns	Often used in cyberwarfare, influence campaigns are usually very well coordinated and blend various methods such as fake news, disinformation campaigns, and social media posts.

Interactive Graphic

Check Your Understanding—Social Engineering Attacks (38.2.8)

Refer to the online course to complete this activity.

Defending Against Deception (38.2.9)

Organizations need to promote awareness of social engineering tactics and properly educate employees on prevention measures. Here are some top tips:

- Never disclose confidential information or credentials to unknown parties via email, chat, text messages, or in conversation.
- Resist the urge to click on enticing emails and web links.
- Be wary of uninitiated or automatic downloads.
- Establish and educate employees on key security policies.
- Encourage employees to take ownership of security issues.
- Do not give in to pressure by unknown individuals.

Video

Video—Explore Social Engineering Techniques (38.2.10)

Refer to the online course to view this video.

Lab—Explore Social Engineering Techniques (38.2.11)

In this lab, you will complete the following objectives:

- Part 1: Explore Social Engineering Techniques
- Part 2: Create a Cybersecurity Awareness Poster

Refer to the online course to complete this lab.

Cyber Attacks (38.3)

There are many different types of cyber attacks that can target the end devices or the entire network. This section explores some of the most common cyber attacks.

Malware (38.3.1)

Cybercriminals use many different types of malicious software, or malware, to carry out attacks. Malware is any code that can be used to steal data, bypass access controls, or cause harm to or compromise a system.

Viruses

A virus is a type of computer program that, when executed, replicates and attaches itself to other files, such as legitimate programs, by inserting its own code into the file. Some viruses are harmless yet others can be destructive, such as those that modify or delete data. Most viruses require end-user interaction to initiate activation, and can be written to act on a specific date or time.

Viruses can be spread through removable media such as USB flash drives, Internet downloads, and email attachments. The simple act of opening a file or executing an infected program can trigger a virus. Once a virus is active, it will usually infect other programs on the computer or other computers on the network. Viruses mutate to avoid detection.

For example, the Melissa virus was released in 1999 and spread via email, affecting tens of thousands of users and causing an estimated $1.2 billion in damage.

Worms

A worm is a malicious software program that replicates by independently exploiting vulnerabilities in networks. Unlike a virus, which requires a host program to run, worms can run by themselves. Other than the initial infection of the host, they do not require user participation and can spread very quickly over the network, usually slowing it down.

Worms share similar patterns: they exploit system vulnerabilities, they have a way to propagate themselves, and they all contain malicious code (payload) that causes damage to computer systems or networks.

Worms are responsible for some of the most devastating attacks on the Internet. In 2001, the Code Red worm infected over 300,000 servers in just 19 hours.

Trojan Horse

A Trojan horse is malware that carries out malicious operations by masking its true intent. It might appear legitimate but is, in fact, very dangerous. Trojans exploit the privileges of the user who runs them.

Unlike viruses, Trojans do not self-replicate but often bind themselves to non-executable files, such as image, audio, or video files, that act as a decoy to harm the systems of unsuspecting users.

Logic Bombs (38.3.2)

A logic bomb is a malicious program that waits for a trigger, such as a specified date or database entry, to set off malicious code. Until this trigger event happens, the logic bomb will remain inactive.

Once activated, a logic bomb implements malicious code that causes harm to a computer in various ways. It can sabotage database records, erase files, and attack operating systems or applications.

Cybersecurity specialists have recently discovered logic bombs that attack and destroy the hardware components in a device or server, including cooling fans, central processing units (CPUs), memory, hard drives, and power supplies. The logic bomb overdrives these components until they overheat or fail.

Ransomware (38.3.3)

This malware is designed to hold a computer system or the data it contains captive until a payment is made.

Ransomware usually works by encrypting your data so that you cannot access it. According to ransomware claims, once the ransom is paid via an untraceable payment system, the cybercriminal will supply a program that decrypts the files or sends an unlock code. In reality, many victims do not gain access to their data even after they have paid.

Some versions of ransomware take advantage of specific system vulnerabilities. Ransomware is often spread through phishing emails that encourage you to download a malicious attachment, or through a software vulnerability.

Denial of Service Attacks (38.3.4)

Denial of service (DoS) attacks are a type of network attack that is relatively simple to conduct, even for an unskilled attacker. These attacks are a major risk as they usually result in some sort of interruption to network services, causing a significant loss of time and money. Even operational technologies, which consist of hardware or software that controls physical devices or processes in buildings, factories, or utility providers, are vulnerable to DoS attacks, which can cause system shutdown in extreme circumstances.

The following are two main types of DoS attacks.

Overwhelming Quantity of Traffic

This occurs when a network, host, or application is sent an enormous amount of data at a rate that it cannot handle. This causes a slowdown in transmission or response, or causes the device or service to crash.

Maliciously Formatted Packets

A packet is a collection of data that flows between a source and a destination computer or application over a network, such as the Internet. When a maliciously formatted packet is sent, the receiver will be unable to handle it.

For example, if an attacker forwards packets containing errors or improperly formatted packets that cannot be identified by an application, this will cause the receiving device to run very slowly or crash.

Domain Name System (38.3.5)

There are many essential technical services needed for a network to operate—such as routing, addressing, and domain naming. These are prime targets for attack.

The following are examples of how cybercriminals can take advantage of vulnerabilities in these services.

Domain Reputation

The Domain Name System (DNS) is used by DNS servers to translate a domain name, such as www.cisco.com, into a numerical IP address so that computers can understand it. If a DNS server does not know an IP address, it will ask another DNS server.

An organization needs to monitor its domain reputation, including its IP address, to help protect against malicious external domains. Domain reputation is used to classify emails as spam or potential security threats.

DNS Spoofing

DNS spoofing or DNS cache poisoning is an attack in which false data is introduced into a DNS resolver cache—the temporary database on a computer's operating system that records recent visits to websites and other Internet domains.

These attacks exploit a weakness in the DNS caching software that causes DNS servers to redirect traffic for a legitimate domain to the IP address of an illicit server.

Domain Hijacking

When an attacker wrongfully gains control of a target's DNS information, they can make unauthorized changes to it. This is known as domain hijacking.

The most common way of hijacking a domain name is to change the administrator's contact email address through social engineering or by hacking into the administrator's email account. The administrator's email address can be easily found via the WHOIS record for the domain, which is of public record.

Uniform Resource Locator (URL) Redirection

A uniform resource locator (URL) is a unique identifier for finding a specific resource on the Internet. Redirecting a URL commonly happens for legitimate purposes.

For example, you have logged into an eLearning portal to begin this course. If you log out of the portal and return to it another time, the portal will redirect you back to the login page.

It is this type of functionality that attackers can exploit. Instead of taking you to the eLearning login page, they can redirect you to a malicious site.

Layer 2 Attacks (38.3.6)

Layer 2 refers to the data link layer in the Open Systems Interconnection (OSI) data communication model.

This layer is used to move data across a linked physical network. IP addresses are mapped to each physical device address (also known as media access control [MAC] address) on the network, using a procedure called Address Resolution Protocol (ARP).

In its simplest terms, the MAC address identifies the intended receiver of an IP address sent over the network, and ARP resolves IP addresses to MAC addresses for transmitting data.

Attackers often take advantage of vulnerabilities in Layer 2 security, as the following two attacks demonstrate.

Spoofing

Spoofing, or poisoning, is a type of impersonation attack that takes advantage of a trusted relationship between two systems:

- MAC address spoofing occurs when an attacker disguises their device as a valid one on the network and can therefore bypass the authentication process.
- ARP spoofing sends spoofed ARP messages across a LAN. This links an attacker's MAC address to the IP address of an authorized device on the network.
- IP spoofing sends IP packets from a spoofed source address in order to disguise the packet origin.

MAC Flooding

Devices on a network are connected via a network switch by using packet switching to receive and forward data to the destination device. MAC flooding compromises

the data transmitted to a device. An attacker floods the network with fake MAC addresses, compromising the security of the network switch.

Man-in-the-Middle and Man-in-the-Mobile Attacks (38.3.8)

Attackers can intercept or modify communications between two devices to steal information from or to impersonate one of the devices, as the following describes.

Man-in-the-Middle (MitM)

A MitM attack, also known as an on-path attack, happens when a cybercriminal takes control of an intermediate device without the user's knowledge. With this level of access, an attacker can intercept, manipulate, and relay false information between the sender and the intended destination.

Man-in-the-Mobile (MitMo)

A variation of man-in-the-middle, MitMo is a type of attack used to take control over a user's mobile device. When infected, the mobile device is instructed to exfiltrate user-sensitive information and send it to the attackers.

ZeuS is one example of a malware package with MitMo capabilities. It allows attackers to quietly capture two-step verification SMS messages sent to users.

Zero-Day Attacks (38.3.9)

A zero-day attack, or zero-day threat, exploits software vulnerabilities before they become known or before they are disclosed by the software vendor.

A network is extremely vulnerable to attack between the time an exploit is discovered (zero hour) and the time it takes for the software vendor to develop and release a patch that fixes the vulnerability.

Defending against such fast-moving attacks requires network security professionals to adopt a more sophisticated and holistic view of any network architecture.

Keyboard Logging (38.3.10)

As the name suggests, keyboard logging, or keylogging, refers to recording or logging every key struck on a computer's keyboard.

Cybercriminals log keystrokes via software installed on a computer system or through hardware devices that are physically attached to a computer. The keylogger

software sends the log file to the criminal. Because it has recorded all keystrokes, this log file can reveal usernames, passwords, websites visited, and other sensitive information.

Many anti-spyware suites can detect and remove unauthorized keyloggers.

Interactive Graphic

Practice Item—Confirm Your Details (38.3.11)

Refer to the online course to complete this activity.

Defending Against Attacks (38.3.12)

Organizations can take several steps to defend against various attacks. These include the following:

- Configure firewalls to remove any packets from outside the network that have addresses indicating that they originated from inside the network.
- Ensure patches and upgrades are current.
- Distribute workloads across multiple server systems.
- Network devices use Internet Control Message Protocol (ICMP) packets to send error and control messages, such as whether or not a device can communicate with another on the network. To prevent DoS and DDoS attacks, organizations can block external ICMP packets with their firewalls.

Interactive Graphic

Check Your Understanding—Cyber Attacks (38.3.13)

Refer to the online course to complete this activity.

Wireless and Mobile Device Attacks (38.4)

Protecting wireless and mobile devices presents its own challenges. This section discusses many of these attacks and how to prevent them.

Grayware and SMiShing (38.4.1)

Grayware is any unwanted application that behaves in an annoying or undesirable manner. And while grayware may not carry any recognizable malware, it may still pose a risk to the user by, for example, tracking the user's location or delivering unwanted advertising.

Authors of grayware typically maintain legitimacy by including these "gray" capabilities in the small print of the software license agreement. This factor poses a growing threat to mobile security in particular, as many smartphone users install mobile apps without really considering this small print.

Short message service phishing, or *SMiShing*, is another tactic used by attackers to trick you. Fake text messages prompt you to visit a malicious website or call a fraudulent phone number, which may result in malware being downloaded onto your device or personal information being shared.

Rogue Access Points (38.4.2)

A rogue access point is a wireless access point installed on a secure network without explicit authorization. Although it could potentially be set up by a well-intentioned employee looking for a better wireless connection, it also presents an opportunity for attackers looking to gain access to an organization's network.

An attacker will often use social engineering tactics to gain physical access to an organization's network infrastructure and install the *rogue access point*.

Also known as a criminal's access point, the access point can be set up as a MitM device to capture your login information.

This works by disconnecting the rogue access point, which triggers the network to send a deauthentication frame to disassociate the access point. This process is then exploited by spoofing your MAC address and sending a deauthentication data transmission to the wireless access point.

An *evil twin attack* describes a situation where the attacker's access point is set up to look like a better connection option. Once you connect to the evil access point, the attacker can analyze your network traffic and execute MitM attacks.

Radio Frequency Jamming (38.4.3)

Wireless signals are susceptible to electromagnetic interference (EMI), radio frequency interference (RFI), and even lightning strikes or noise from fluorescent lights.

Attackers can take advantage of this fact by deliberately jamming the transmission of a radio or satellite station to prevent a wireless signal from reaching the receiving station.

To successfully jam the signal, the frequency, modulation, and power of the RF jammer needs to be equal to that of the device that the attacker is seeking to disrupt.

Bluejacking and Bluesnarfing (38.4.4)

Bluetooth is a short-range, low-power protocol that transmits data in a personal area network (PAN) and uses pairing to establish a relationship between devices such as mobiles, laptops, and printers. Cybercriminals have discovered ways to exploit the vulnerabilities between these connections.

Due to the limited range of Bluetooth, an attacker must be within range of their target. Here are some ways that they can exploit a target's device without their knowledge.

Bluejacking

Bluejacking uses wireless Bluetooth technology to send unauthorized messages or shocking images to another Bluetooth device.

Bluesnarfing

Bluesnarfing occurs when an attacker copies information, such as emails and contact lists, from a target's device using a Bluetooth connection.

Attacks Against Wi-Fi Protocols (38.4.5)

Wired Equivalent Privacy (WEP) and *Wi-Fi Protected Access (WPA)* are security protocols that were designed to secure wireless networks.

WEP was developed to provide data transmitted over a wireless local area network (WLAN) with a level of protection comparable to what is usually expected of a traditional wired network. It added security to wireless networks by encrypting the data.

WEP used a key for encryption. The problem, however, was that WEP had no provision for key management and so the number of people sharing the same key continually grew, giving criminals access to a large amount of traffic data. Furthermore, WEP's initialization vector (IV), one of the key components of its encryption key, was too small, readable, and static.

To address this and replace WEP, *WPA* and then *WPA2* were developed as improved security protocols. Unlike with WEP, an attacker cannot recover WPA2's encryption key by observing network traffic. However, they can still use a packet sniffer to analyze the packets going between an access point and a legitimate user.

Wi-Fi and Mobile Defense (38.4.6)

There are several measures that organizations and users need to implement to defend against wireless and mobile device attacks. These include the following:

- Take advantage of basic wireless security features such as authentication and encryption by changing the default configuration settings.
- Restrict access point placement by placing these devices outside the firewall or within a demilitarized zone, which is a perimeter network that protects an organization's LAN from untrusted devices.
- Use WLAN tools such as NetStumbler to detect rogue access points or unauthorized workstations.
- Develop a policy for secure guest access to an organization's Wi-Fi network.
- Employees in an organization should use a remote-access VPN for WLAN access when on public Wi-Fi networks.

Interactive Graphic

Check Your Understanding—Wireless and Mobile Device Attacks (38.4.7)

Refer to the online course to complete this activity.

Application Attacks (38.5)

Applications are also vulnerable to attacks. This section explores some of the more common attacks and how they can best be mitigated.

Cross-Site Scripting (38.5.1)

Attacks carried out through web applications are becoming increasingly common. Threat actors exploit vulnerabilities in the coding of a web-based application to gain access to a database or server.

Cross-site scripting (XSS) is a common threat to many web applications. This is how it works:

1. Cybercriminals exploit the XSS vulnerability by injecting scripts containing malicious code into a web page.
2. The web page is accessed by the victim, and the malicious scripts unknowingly pass to their browser.
3. The malicious scripts can access cookies, session tokens, or other sensitive information about the user, which is sent back to the cybercriminal.
4. Armed with this information, the cybercriminal can impersonate the user.

Code Injection (38.5.2)

Most modern websites use a database, such as a Structured Query Language (SQL) or an Extensible Markup Language (XML) database, to store and manage data. Injection attacks seek to exploit weaknesses in these databases.

The following are common types of injection attacks.

XML Injection Attack

An XML injection attack can corrupt the data on the XML database and threaten the security of the website.

It works by interfering with an application's processing of XML data or query entered by a user.

Cybercriminals can manipulate this query by programming it to suit their needs. This will grant them access to all of the sensitive information stored on the database and allow them to make any number of changes to the website.

SQL Injection Attack

Cybercriminals can carry out an SQL injection attack on websites or any SQL database by inserting a malicious SQL statement in an entry field.

This attack takes advantage of a vulnerability in which the application does not correctly filter the data entered by a user for characters in an SQL statement.

As a result, the cybercriminal can gain unauthorized access to information stored on the database, from which they can spoof an identity, modify existing data, destroy data, or even become an administrator of the database server itself.

DLL Injection Attack

A dynamic link library (DLL) file is a library that contains a set of code and data for carrying out a particular activity in Windows. Applications use this type of file to add functionality that is not built-in, when they need to carry out this activity.

DLL injection allows a cybercriminal to trick an application into calling a malicious DLL file, which executes as part of the target process.

LDAP Injection Attack

The Lightweight Directory Access Protocol (LDAP) is an open protocol for authenticating user access to directory services.

An LDAP injection attack exploits input validation vulnerabilities by injecting and executing queries to LDAP servers, giving cybercriminals an opportunity to extract sensitive information from an organization's LDAP directory.

Buffer Overflow (38.5.3)

Buffers are memory areas allocated to an application. A buffer overflow occurs when data is written beyond the limits of a buffer. By changing data beyond the boundaries of a buffer, the application can access memory allocated to other processes. This can lead to a system crash or data compromise, or provide escalation of privileges.

These memory flaws can also give attackers complete control over a target's device. For example, an attacker can change the instructions of a vulnerable application while the program is loading in memory and, as a result, can install malware and access the internal network from the infected device.

Remote Code Executions (38.5.4)

Remote code execution allows a cybercriminal to take advantage of application vulnerabilities to execute any command with the privileges of the user running the application on the target device.

Privilege escalation exploits a bug, design flaw, or misconfiguration in an operating system or application to gain access to resources that are normally restricted.

The Metasploit Project is a computer security project that provides information about security vulnerabilities and aids in penetration testing. Among the tools they have developed is the Metasploit Framework, which can be used for developing and executing exploit code against a remote target.

Meterpreter, in particular, is a payload within Metasploit that allows users to take control of a target's device by writing their own extensions and uploading these files into a running process on the device. These files are loaded and executed from memory, so they never involve the hard drive. This means that such files fly under the radar of antivirus detection.

Meterpreter also has a module for controlling a remote system's webcam. Once Meterpreter is installed on a target device, the Metasploit user can view and capture images from the target's webcam.

Other Application Attacks (38.5.5)

Every piece of information that an attacker receives about a targeted system or application can be used as a valuable weapon for launching a dangerous attack. Table 38-5 lists some other types of application attacks.

Table 38-5 Other Application Attacks

Application Attack	Description
Cross-site request forgery (CSRF)	CSRF describes the malicious exploit of a website where unauthorized commands are submitted from a user's browser to a trusted web application. A malicious website can transmit such commands through specially crafted image tags, hidden forms, or JavaScript requests, all of which can work without the user's knowledge.
Race condition attack	Also known as a time of check (TOC) or a time of use (TOU) attack, a race condition attack happens when a computing system that is designed to handle tasks in a specific sequence is forced to perform two or more operations simultaneously. For example, operating systems are made up of threads, the smallest sequence of program instructions required to carry out a process. When two or more threads access shared data and try to change it at the exact same time, a race condition attack occurs.
Improper input-handling attack	Data inputted by a user that is not properly validated can affect the data flow of a program and cause critical vulnerabilities in systems and applications that result in buffer overflow or SQL injection attacks.
Error-handling attack	Attackers can use error messages to extract specific information such as the host names of internal systems and directories or files that exist on a given web server, as well as database, table, and field names that can be used to craft SQL injection attacks.
Application programming interface (API) attack	An API delivers a user response to a system and sends the system's response back to the user. An API attack occurs when a cybercriminal abuses an API endpoint.
Replay attack	This describes a situation where a valid data transmission is maliciously or fraudulently repeated or delayed by an attacker, who intercepts, amends, and resubmits the data to get the receiver to do whatever they want.
Directory traversal attack	Directory traversal occurs when an attacker is able to read files on the web server outside of the directory of the website. An attacker can then use this information to download server configuration files containing sensitive information, potentially expose more server vulnerabilities, or even take control of the server!
Resource exhaustion attacks	These attacks are computer security exploits that crash, hang, or otherwise interfere with a targeted program or system. Rather than overwhelming network bandwidth like a DoS attack, resource exhaustion attacks overwhelm the hardware resources available on the target's server instead.

Interactive Graphic

Practice Item—Code and Memory Attacks (38.5.6)

Refer to the online course to complete this activity.

Defending Against Application Attacks (38.5.7)

There are several actions that you can take to defend against an application attack. You will find some of them outlined here.

- The first line of defense against an application attack is to write solid code.
- Prudent programming practice involves treating and validating all input from outside of a function as if it is hostile.
- Use security testing tools to evaluate source code and binary software on an ongoing basis during the software development life cycle.
- Keep all software, including operating systems and applications, up to date and do not ignore update prompts. Remember that not all programs update automatically.

Spam (38.5.8)

Spam, also known as junk mail, is simply unsolicited email. In most cases, it is a method of advertising. However, a lot of spam is sent in bulk by computers infected by viruses or worms—and often contains malicious links, malware, or deceptive content that aims to trick recipients into disclosing sensitive information, such as a social security number or bank account information.

Almost all email providers filter spam, but it still consumes bandwidth. And even if you have security features implemented, some spam might still get through to you. Look out for the following indicators of spam:

- The email has no subject line.
- The email asks you to update your account details.
- The email text contains misspelled words or strange punctuation and characters.
- Links within the email are long and/or cryptic.
- The email looks like correspondence from a legitimate business, but there are tiny differences—or it contains information that does not seem relevant to you.
- The email asks you to open an attachment, often urgently.
- The email originates from an unusual domain or contains links to domains that are not likely to belong to the identified sender.

If you receive an email that contains one or more of these indicators, you should *not* open the email or any attachments. Many organizations have an email policy that requires employees to report receipt of this type of email to their cybersecurity team for further investigation. If in doubt, always report.

Phishing (38.5.9)

Phishing is a form of fraudulent activity often used to steal personal information.

Phishing

Phishing occurs when a user is contacted by email or instant message—or in any other way—by someone masquerading as a legitimate person or organization. The intent is to trick the recipient into installing malware on their device or into sharing confidential information, such as login credentials or financial information.

For example, you receive an email congratulating you for winning a prize. It looks like it was sent from a well-known retail store and asks you to click on a link to claim your prize. This link may in fact redirect you to a fake site that asks you to enter your personal details, or it may even install a virus on your device.

Spear Phishing

A highly targeted attack, spear phishing sends customized emails to a specific person based on information the attacker knows about them—which could be their interests, preferences, activities, or work projects.

For example, a cybercriminal discovers through their research that you are looking to buy a specific model of car. The cybercriminal joins a car discussion forum you are a member of, forges a car sale offering, and sends you an email that contains a link to see pictures of the car. When you click on the link, you unknowingly install malware on your device.

Vishing, Pharming, and Whaling (38.5.10)

Criminals make use of a wide range of techniques to try to gain access to your personal information.

Vishing

Often referred to as voice phishing, this type of attack sees criminals use voice communication technology to encourage users to divulge information, such as their credit card details.

Criminals can spoof phone calls using voice over Internet Protocol (VoIP), or leave recorded messages to give the impression that they are legitimate callers.

Pharming

This type of attack deliberately misdirects users to a fake version of an official website. Tricked into believing that they are connected to a legitimate site, users enter their credentials into the fraudulent website.

Whaling

Whaling is a phishing attack that targets high-profile individuals, such as senior executives within an organization, politicians, and celebrities.

Interactive Graphic

Practice Item—Phishing Attacks (38.5.11)

Refer to the online course to complete this activity.

Defending Against Email and Browser Attacks (38.5.12)

There are many actions that you can take to defend against email and browser attacks. Some of the most important ones are outlined here:

- It is difficult to stop spam, but there are ways to reduce its effects:
  - Most Internet service providers (ISPs) filter spam before it reaches the user's inbox.
  - Many antivirus and email software programs automatically detect and remove dangerous spam from an email inbox.
  - Organizations should educate employees about the dangers of unsolicited emails and make them aware of the dangers of opening attachments.
  - Never assume that email attachments are safe, even when they come from a trusted contact. Always scan attachments before opening them.
- Become a member of the Anti-Phishing Working Group (APWG). It is an international association of companies focused on eliminating identity theft and fraud resulting from phishing and email spoofing.
- All software should be kept up-to-date, with the latest security patches applied to protect against any known security vulnerabilities.

The following are some other common attacks that cybercriminals can launch.

Physical Attacks

Physical attacks are intentional, offensive actions used to destroy, expose, alter, disable, steal, or gain unauthorized access to an organization's infrastructure or hardware.

Examples of physical attacks include

- Loading malware onto a USB flash drive that infects a device when plugged in.
- Fitting cables and plugs such as generic USB cables, mobile device charging cables, and wall or power adapters with advanced technologies, such as a wireless chip, to allow an attacker to control or provide instructions to a device.
- Copying or skimming data from a credit or debit card using a specialized terminal to create a cloned card, which can be used to gain unauthorized access to the victim's accounts.

Adversarial Artificial Intelligence Attacks

Machine learning is a method of automation that allows devices to carry out analysis and perform tasks without specifically being programmed to do so. It powers many of the applications we use today, such as web searching, photo tagging, spam detection, video surveillance, fraud detection, and security automation.

Machine learning uses mathematical models to predict outcomes. However, these models are dependent on the data that is inputted. If the data is tainted, it can have a negative impact on the predicted outcome. Attackers can take advantage of this to perpetrate attacks against machine learning algorithms; for example, using tainted data to trick an autonomous vehicle into misinterpreting street signs.

Supply Chain Attacks

Many organizations interface with a third party for their systems management or to purchase components and software. Organizations may even rely on parts or components from a foreign source.

Attackers often find ways to intercept these supply chains. For example, software can be based on specific support agreements and subject to an end-of-life (EOL) date. Changing this date could mean that an organization is no longer eligible for service and maintenance support.

Cloud-Based Attacks

Rather than developing systems on their own premises, more and more organizations are making the move toward cloud-based computing, as we discussed earlier in this chapter.

The advantage is that the cloud provider will maintain the equipment, but this also opens up an organization to a host of potential threats. Attackers are constantly leveraging ways to exploit sensitive data stored on the cloud, as well as applications, platforms, and infrastructure that are cloud-based, as we saw with SaaS, PaaS, and IaaS.

Interactive Graphic

Check Your Understanding—Application Attacks (38.5.13)

Refer to the online course to complete this activity.

Cybersecurity Threats, Vulnerabilities, and Attacks Summary (38.6)

The following is a summary of each topic in the chapter and some questions for your reflection.

What Did I Learn in This Chapter? (38.6.1)

- Common Threats—A threat domain is an area of control, authority, or protection that attackers can exploit to gain access to a system. Attackers can exploit systems within a threat domain by gaining physical access to systems, breaking into wireless networks, compromising Bluetooth and NFC devices, sending malicious emails, scrutinizing social media accounts, spreading malicious software (malware) through removable media, or exploiting cloud computing environments.

  Attacks can exploit software bugs or human error. Attacks threaten physical systems through sabotage or theft. In addition, equipment failures, utility interruptions, and natural disasters can impact the availability of systems and resources. Internal threats are usually from former or current employees, while external threats come from amateur or skilled attackers.

  The user domain includes anyone with access to an organization's information system, including employees, customers, and contract partners. Users are often considered to be the weakest link in information security systems. User threats come from a lack of security awareness, poorly enforced security policies, data theft, unauthorized downloads and media, visits to unauthorized websites, or intentional destruction of systems, applications, and data.

  Threats to devices include unauthorized access to unattended systems, downloading of malware, and out-of-date software.

  Threats to the LAN include unauthorized access to facilities and equipment, operating system vulnerabilities, rogue access points, interception of data in

transit, and inefficient management practices. Misconfigured security devices, such as firewalls, can also be exploited.

Threats to the private cloud include unauthorized network probing and port scanning, unauthorized access to resources, vulnerabilities in device software, configuration errors, and unauthorized access to internal resources through the cloud.

The application domain includes all critical systems, applications, and data used by an organization to support operations. Threats to the application domain include unauthorized access, server downtime or hardware failure, network operating system vulnerabilities, data loss, and vulnerabilities in web applications or client-server software.

Complex threats take the form of advanced persistent threats (APT) or algorithm attacks. APTs take place over an extended period and use elaborate tactics and malware. Algorithm attacks exploit software processes to generate behaviors that were not intended by the software developers.

Backdoors, such as Netbus or Back Orifice, are used to gain ongoing unauthorized access to systems by bypassing normal authentication procedures. They typically involve the use of remote administrative tools (RATs) to gain access to systems. Rootkits are a type of malware that exploits vulnerabilities to gain unauthorized access (privilege escalation). Rootkits can modify system files and interfere with system forensics and monitoring tools. They are very difficult to detect and remove.

The United States Computer Emergency Readiness Team (US-CERT) and the U.S. Department of Homeland Security sponsor a database of common vulnerabilities and exposures (CVEs). CVE identifiers are a standard way to refer to known security vulnerabilities. The dark web is used by hackers to exchange vulnerability and threat information and stolen data. Security professionals use CVEs and dark web resources to research security threats. Indicators of compromise (IOCs) are the characteristics of attacks that can be used to identify exploits. Automated Indicator Sharing (AIS) provides a standard way for security professionals to exchange exploit information using the Structured Threat Information Expression (STIX) and Trusted Automated Exchange of Intelligence Information (TAXII) standards.

- **Deception**—Social engineering is a non-technical strategy that attempts to manipulate individuals into performing risky actions or divulging confidential information. Pretexting is a social engineering attack in which someone lies to gain access to confidential data. A something-for-something attack uses the offer of a gift for confidential information. Identify fraud is the use of a person's stolen confidential information to acquire goods or services.

Social engineering uses a number of tactics to gain cooperation from victims. Attackers may pretend to be persons of authority or use intimidation to compel people to act in ways that compromise security. They may also use tactics such as consensus, scarcity, urgency, and familiarity. Attackers will even develop a relationship of trust with a victim in order to eventually violate the victim's security.

Shoulder surfing refers to looking over someone's shoulder in order to obtain credentials like passwords, PINs, or credit card numbers. Dumpster diving means literally going through someone's trash to find confidential personal information. Piggybacking and tailgating are ways to gain unauthorized physical access to restricted areas.

Other means of deception are sending fake invoices to get money or credentials, watering hole attacks in which popular websites are infected with malware, typo squatting by creating URLs that look very close to popular websites, prepending by removing email external site warnings, and concerted influence campaigns.

Organizations can defend against deception by teaching employees to never provide confidential information to unknown parties, to detect suspicious emails and resist clicking links, to avoid or terminate uninitiated or automatic downloads, and to resist pressure by unknown individuals.

- **Cyber Attacks**—Malware is software that can steal data, bypass access controls, or cause harm to or compromise a system. Viruses are a type of malware that replicates itself when executed. They can be harmless or destructive. Worms are programs that replicate independently across networks. Trojan horses are malware that masquerade as other software applications or are distributed with legitimate applications. Logic bombs are triggered to act by date and time or other system events. They can damage system hardware and software. Ransomware is a common attack that uses malicious software to encrypt a system hardware drive. Sometimes, but not always, paying a ransom will reverse the damage.

  Denial of service (DoS) attacks are a type of network attack that affects the availability of resources. In one type of DoS attack, a network or application is overwhelmed with an enormous amount of data. This can make systems slow or crash. In another DoS attack, maliciously formatted packets are sent to disrupt system operation.

  The Domain Name System (DNS) is essential to network operations. Attackers can damage the reputation of a domain by creating bogus similar domains or through false news. In domain spoofing, attackers exploit weaknesses in DNS to map legitimate domain names to the IP addresses of malicious websites. If attackers gain access to a target's DNS registration information, they can hijack the domain name by changing the domain name-to-IP address mappings.

Two common types of Layer 2 attacks are spoofing and MAC flooding. MAC address spoofing occurs when an attacker disguises their device as a valid one on the network and can therefore bypass the authentication process. ARP spoofing sends spoofed ARP messages across a LAN to link an attacker's MAC address to the IP address of an authorized device on the network. IP spoofing sends IP packets from a spoofed source address in order to disguise the packet origin. In MAC flooding, an attacker floods the network with fake MAC addresses, compromising the security of the network switch.

Man-in-the-middle (MitM), or on-path, attacks happen when a cybercriminal takes control of an intermediate device in the network, or puts their own device on a path to intercept user data. The attacker can steal information, manipulate data, or relay false information. A man-in-the-mobile (MitMo) attack is a variation of an MitM attack in which a mobile device is infected with malware that steals data from the device.

Zero-day attacks exploit software vulnerabilities before they become widely known to the public. A sophisticated and holistic view of the security infrastructure is required to defend against these attacks.

Keyboard loggers are types of malware that record every keystroke made on a computer. This can reveal confidential information and account credentials.

Several guidelines for defending against attacks are to configure firewalls to filter incoming packets that appear to have originated internally, ensure all software has the most recent updates and patches, distribute workloads between multiple server systems, and block ICMP packets at the network edge.

- **Wireless and Mobile Device Attacks**—Grayware is an unwanted application that behaves in an annoying or undesirable manner. SMiShing is the use of fake SMS messages to lure the user to visit a malicious website or call a fraudulent phone number.

  Rogue access points are installed on networks without authorization. They can masquerade as legitimate access points to trick users into associating with them. They can be used to conduct MitM attacks by deauthenticating users or posing as legitimate access points with more desirable connections in evil twin attacks.

  Wireless signals are susceptible to interference and jamming. Attackers can deny wireless service by jamming Wi-Fi signals. Bluetooth can be used to send unauthorized messages through Bluejacking. Bluesnarfing occurs when an attacker copies information from a mobile device through a malicious Bluetooth connection.

  Wired Equivalent Privacy (WEP) and Wi-Fi Protected Access (WPA) are security protocols that were designed to secure wireless networks. WEP had no provision for key management and so it was vulnerable to attack. To address this and

replace WEP, WPA and then WPA2 were developed as improved wireless security protocols.

To enhance wireless security, it is important to use at least WPA2 encryption. Access points should be placed outside of the network perimeter, if possible. Use tools like NetStumbler to detect rogue access points. Permit only secure Wi-Fi guest access. Finally, employees should always use remote-access VPNs when connecting to the organization's network over public Wi-Fi networks.

- **Application Attacks**—Cross-site scripting (XSS) is a common web application attack in which malicious code is inserted into a legitimate website. The victim's browser executes the malicious code, which downloads malware, redirects to a malicious website, or steals information.

  Injection attacks involve exploiting systems by inserting malformed data or commands in user input fields. They are especially common against databases. XML and SQL injection attacks corrupt databases or cause sensitive information, such as user credentials, to be revealed. Dynamic link libraries (DLLs) are software modules that are used by applications to interact with Windows. Attackers can inject malicious code into DLLs that will then execute when the DLL is used. LDAP injection attacks exploit input validation to execute queries on LDAP servers, potentially giving attackers access to sensitive account information.

  Remote code execution allows a cybercriminal to take advantage of application vulnerabilities to execute commands with the privileges of the user running the application on the target device. Other application attacks are cross-site request forgeries, race condition attacks, improper input-handling attacks, error-handling attacks, and application programming interface (API) attacks. Additional attacks are replay attacks, directory traversal attacks, and resource exhaustion attacks.

  To defend against application attacks, the first line of defense is to write solid code. All user input should be validated. Security testing tools should be used to evaluate code as it is developed and prior to deployment. Finally, all software, including operating systems, should be kept up to date.

  Spam, also known as junk mail, is simply unsolicited email. Spam is usually a nuisance, but it can be malicious. Although spam filters are widely used, it is important that users know how to identify spam.

  Phishing and spear phishing are attacks that appear to come from legitimate sources but want you to download files or submit confidential information. Spear phishing attacks are directly targeted at specific individuals. Vishing uses voice messages to attack. Pharming directs users to fake versions of legitimate websites. Whaling is phishing directed at high-profile users like executives, politicians, or celebrities.

  To defend against email and browser attacks, organizations should use spam filters, deploy antivirus software, and educate users about network security.

Reflection Questions (38.6.2)

Wow, did you know about all these bad things threat actors can do? I didn't, but I'm glad I know more about it now. The awareness campaign should help college users recognize threats. I hope it helped you as well. But remember that threat actors constantly try to find a new way to take advantage of you or your company. So, there's always something new to learn.

Is there something else we should include in the awareness campaign? Will you share some of this information with family members or other users on your network? How can you protect yourself, your computer, and your company from these threats?

Practice

The following lab provides practice with the topics introduced in this chapter.

Labs

Lab—Explore Social Engineering Techniques (38.2.11)

Check Your Understanding Questions

Complete all the review questions listed here to test your understanding of the topics and concepts in this chapter. Appendix A, "Answers to 'Check Your Understanding' Questions," lists the answers.

1. What does a rootkit modify?

   a. Operating system

   b. Programs

   c. Screen savers

   d. Notepad

   e. Microsoft Word

2. An attacker sits in front of a store and wirelessly copies emails and contact lists from nearby unsuspecting user devices. What type of attack is this?

   a. Bluesnarfing

   b. Smishing

   c. RF jamming

   d. Bluejacking

3. What type of attack targets an SQL database using the input field of a user?

   a. XML injection

   b. Cross-site scripting

   c. SQL injection

   d. Buffer overflow

4. What is a nontechnical method that a cybercriminal would use to gather sensitive information from an organization?

   a. Man-in-the-middle

   b. Ransomware

c. Social engineering
d. Pharming

5. An organization adds an "external" tag to incoming emails from outside the domain to warn the internal users that such emails are from outside. Which deception method is used by a cyber attack to trick employees into believing that the organization sent a malicious email by removing the "external" tag?
   a. Watering hole attack
   b. Typo squatting
   c. Prepending
   d. Invoice scam

6. What is the term used when a malicious party sends a fraudulent email disguised as being from a legitimate, trusted source?
   a. Phishing
   b. Vishing
   c. Backdoor
   d. Trojan

7. Users report that a database file on the main server cannot be accessed. A database administrator verifies the issue and notices that the database file is now encrypted. The organization receives a threatening email demanding payment for the decryption of the database file. What type of attack has the organization experienced?
   a. DoS attack
   b. Man-in-the-middle attack
   c. Ransomware
   d. Trojan horse

8. By having narrow viewing angles, an ATM mitigates what kind of attacks?
   a. Dumpster diving
   b. Shoulder surfing
   c. Quid pro quo
   d. Identity fraud

9. Netbus belongs to which malware type?
   a. Backdoor
   b. Logic bomb
   c. Keylogger
   d. Grayware

CHAPTER 39

Network Security

Objectives

Upon completion of this chapter, you will be able to answer the following questions:

- What are foundational security concepts?
- How do you configure access control?
- What are the cybersecurity processes and procedures that protect systems?
- What are the methods of mitigating malware?
- How do firewalls operate to filter traffic and recommend endpoint security measures?
- How do you configure basic wireless security on a home router (WPAx)?

Key Terms

This chapter uses the following key terms. You can find the definitions in the Glossary.

availability *Page 816*

confidentiality *Page 816*

firewall *Page 842*

integrity *Page 816*

malware *Page 836*

Introduction (39.0)

Hello again! The awareness campaign that Lara worked on was a success. Because of this, the college has invited Lara to work on a committee to develop the college's security policy. The security policy is a document that helps college administrators, IT staff, and college users defend the network and endpoints.

Lara will review current security policies on this committee and help develop new ones. These policies inform the IT staff how to keep data confidentiality, ensure data integrity, and ensure the network is available for all users. It also defines how the web can be accessed, which systems and devices will be used to secure it, and how to protect endpoint devices and wireless access. Let's work through this chapter to learn more about what we can do to defend the network and its endpoints.

Security Foundations (39.1)

Security frameworks are used to give us a better understanding of network security.

The Cybersecurity Cube (39.1.1)

Have you heard of the cybersecurity cube? It provides a useful way to think about protecting data. The cube reminds us of what the task of protecting data entails, including the three dimensions of information security.

1. Security Principles

   The first dimension of the cybersecurity cube identifies the goals to protect cyberspace, as shown in Figure 39-1. The foundational principles of confidentiality, integrity, and availability of data provide a focus that enables the cybersecurity expert to prioritize actions when protecting any networked system.

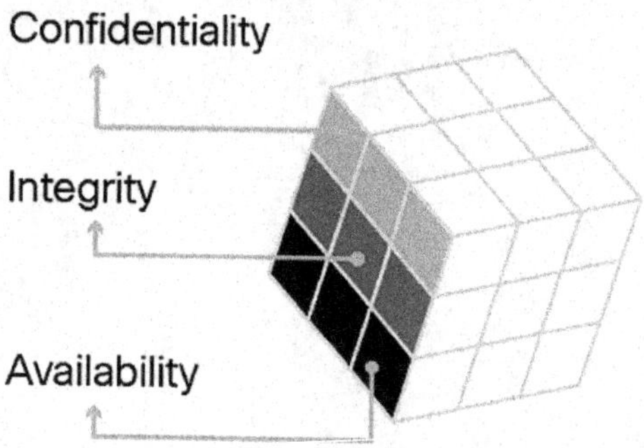

Figure 39-1 Security Principles of the Cybersecurity Cube

- Data *confidentiality* prevents the disclosure of information to unauthorized people, resources, or processes.
- Data *integrity* refers to the accuracy, consistency, and trustworthiness of data.
- Data *availability* ensures that information is accessible by authorized users when needed.

You can use the acronym CIA to remember these three principles.

2. Data States

The cyberspace domain contains a considerable amount of critically important data. But in what state? The second dimension of the cybersecurity cube represents the three possible data states, as shown in Figure 39-2:

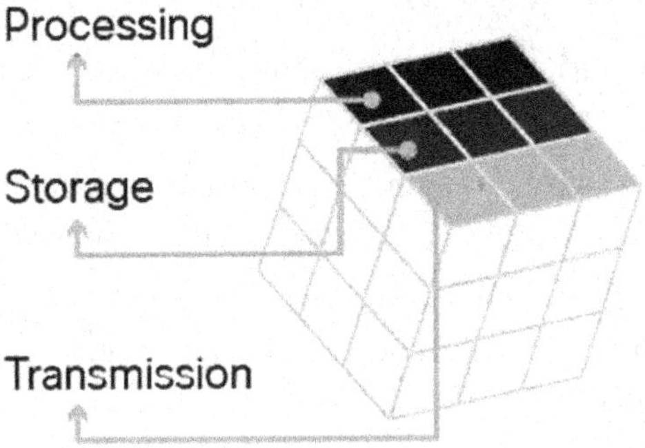

Figure 39-2 Data States of the Cybersecurity Cube

- Data *in transit.*
- Data *at rest* or in storage.
- Data *in process.*

Effective cybersecurity requires the safeguarding of data in all three states. We can't focus only on protecting data that is being processed, nor just on data in storage.

3. Safeguards

The third dimension of the cybersecurity cube defines the pillars on which we need to base our cybersecurity defenses in order to protect data and infrastructure in the digital realm, as shown in Figure 39-3.

These are *technology*, *policy and practices*, and improving education, training, and awareness in *people*.

Cybersecurity professionals must use a range of different skills and disciplines available to them when protecting data and infrastructure in cyberspace.

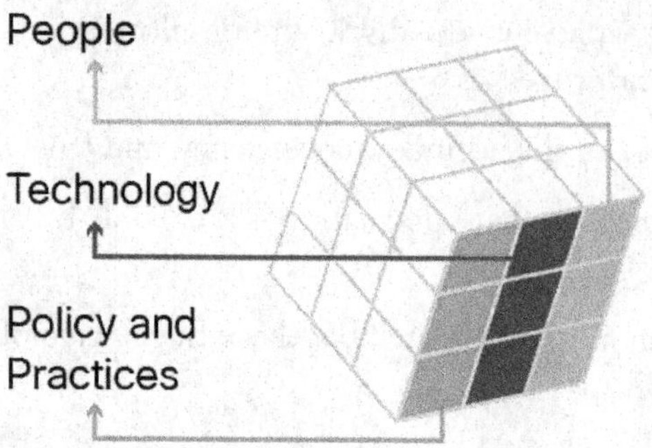

Figure 39-3 Safeguards of the Cybersecurity Cube

Confidentiality, Integrity, and Availability (39.1.2)

It is true that the list of network attack types is long. But there are many best practices that you can use to defend your network, as you will learn in this chapter.

Network security consists of protecting information and information systems from unauthorized access, use, disclosure, disruption, modification, or destruction.

Most organizations follow the CIA information security triad, as shown in Figure 39-4. Since it forms the foundation of cybersecurity practice, it is important that you have a detailed understanding of the three principles:

- *Confidentiality*—Only authorized individuals, entities, or processes can access sensitive information. It may require using cryptographic encryption algorithms such as AES to encrypt and decrypt data.
- *Integrity*—Refers to protecting data from unauthorized alteration. It requires the use of cryptographic hashing algorithms such as SHA.
- *Availability*—Authorized users must have uninterrupted access to important resources and data. It requires implementing redundant services, gateways, and links.

CIA Triad—The Principle of Confidentiality (39.1.3)

To accomplish confidentiality without using encryption, *tokenization* is a substitution technique that can isolate data elements from exposure to other data systems. A random value with no mathematical relationship replaces original data. Outside the system, a token has no value and is meaningless. Tokenization can preserve the data format (its type and data length), which makes it useful for databases and card payment processing.

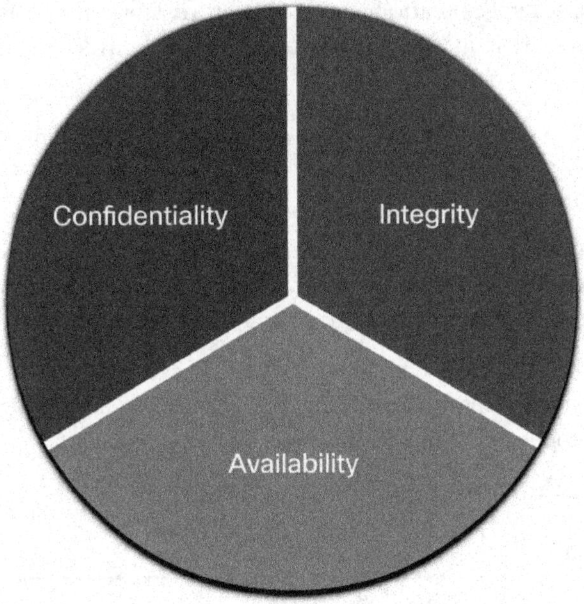

Figure 39-4 The CIA Triad

Rights management covers both *digital rights management (DRM)* and *information rights management (IRM)*. Both protect data from unauthorized access by using encryption.

DRM protects copyrighted material like music, films, or books. When any such content appears in digital form—for instance on CD, mp3, or e-book—it is encrypted, so the media cannot be copied without the decryption key. The decryption key is available only to licensed parties.

IRM is used with email and other files that are relevant to the activities and communications of an organization. When this information is shared with others, IRM allows the document owner, the organization, or one of its members to control and manage access to the document.

Interactive Graphic

Activity—Protecting Data Privacy (39.1.4)

Refer to the online course to complete this activity.

Data Integrity (39.1.5)

Integrity is the accuracy, consistency, and trustworthiness of data across its entire life cycle.

Data undergoes several operations, such as capture, storage, retrieval, update, and transfer. Data must remain unaltered by unauthorized entities during all these operations.

Methods used to ensure data integrity include hashing, data validation checks, data consistency checks, and access controls. Data integrity systems can include one or more of these methods.

Data integrity is a fundamental component of information security. Ensuring data integrity is a constant challenge for most organizations. Loss of data integrity can render entire data resources unreliable or unusable.

However, the importance of data integrity varies based on how an organization uses its data. For example, a bank or financial organization assigns a higher importance to data integrity than a social media channel.

Table 39-1 ranks the levels of data integrity.

Table 39-1 Levels of Data Integrity

Level of Data Integrity	Description
Critical level of need	In a healthcare organization, data integrity might be a matter of life or death. For example, prescription information must be accurate. Therefore, all data is continuously validated, tested, and verified.
High level of need	In an e-commerce or analytics-based organization, transactions and customer accounts must be accurate. All data is validated and verified at frequent intervals.
Mid level of need	Online sales and search engines collect data that has been publicly posted. Little verification is performed, and data is not completely trustworthy.
Low level of need	Blogs, forums, and personal pages on social media are powered by public opinion and open contribution. Data may not be verified at all, and there is a low level of trust in the content.

Interactive Graphic

Activity—Availability (39.1.6)

Availability refers to the need to make data accessible to all authorized users whenever they need it. Cyberattacks and system failures can prevent access to information, systems, and services.

Refer to the online course to complete this activity.

Ensuring Availability (39.1.7)

There are many measures that organizations can implement to ensure the availability of their services and systems, as shown in Table 39-2.

Table 39-2 Examples of Ensuring Availability

Example	Description
Equipment maintenance	Regular equipment maintenance can dramatically improve system uptime. Maintenance includes component replacement, cleaning, and alignment.
Operating systems and software updates and patches	Modern operating systems, applications, and software are continuously updated to correct errors and eliminate vulnerabilities. In every organization, all systems, applications, and software should be updated to a regular schedule. Cybersecurity professionals can subscribe to alerts that announce new update releases.
Backup testing	Backup of organization data, configuration data, and personal data helps ensure availability. Backup systems and backed up data should also be tested to ensure they work properly, and that data can be recovered in the event of data loss.
Disaster planning	Planning for disasters is a critical part of increasing system availability. Employees and customers should know how to respond to a disaster. The cybersecurity team should practice response protocols, test backup systems, and be familiar with procedures for restoring critical systems.
New technology implementations	High availability requires continuous evaluation and testing of new technologies to counter new threats and attacks. Cybercriminals use the latest tools and tricks, so cyber professionals are also required to keep up by using new technologies, products, and devices.
Activity monitoring	Continuous system monitoring increases system availability. Monitoring event logs, system alerts, and access logs provide the cybersecurity professional with real-time system information. Such monitoring can identify attacks within seconds and enable cybersecurity professionals to defend against them when they occur.
Availability testing	All systems should be tested to find vulnerabilities. Testing can include port scans, vulnerability scans, and penetration tests.

Interactive Graphic

Check Your Understanding—Security Foundations (39.1.8)

Refer to the online course to complete this activity.

Access Control (39.2)

An essential goal of network security is controlling access to the network.

Physical Access Controls (39.2.1)

Physical access controls are actual barriers deployed to prevent direct physical contact with systems. The goal is to prevent unauthorized users from gaining physical access to facilities, equipment, and other organizational assets, as shown in Figure 39-5.

Figure 39-5 Examples of Physical Access Controls

For example, physical access control determines *who* can enter (or exit), *where* they can enter (or exit), and *when* they can enter (or exit).

Here are some examples of physical access controls:

- Guards who monitor the facility.
- Fences that protect the perimeter.
- Motion detectors that detect moving objects.
- Laptop locks that prevent theft of portable equipment.

- Locked doors that prevent unauthorized access.
- Swipe cards that allow authorized access to restricted areas.
- Guard dogs that protect the facility.
- Video cameras that monitor a facility by collecting and recording images.
- Mantrap-style entry systems that stagger the flow of people into the secured area and trap any unwanted visitors.
- Alarms that detect intrusion.

Logical Access Controls (39.2.2)

Logical access controls are the hardware and software solutions used to manage access to resources and systems. These technology-based solutions include tools and protocols that computer systems use for identification, authentication, authorization, and accounting.

Logical access control examples include

- Encryption is the process of taking plaintext and creating ciphertext.
- Smart cards have an embedded microchip.
- Passwords are protected strings of characters.
- Biometrics are users' physical characteristics.
- Access control lists (ACLs) define the type of traffic allowed on a network.
- Protocols are sets of rules that govern the exchange of data between devices.
- Firewalls prevent unwanted network traffic.
- Routers connect at least two networks.
- Intrusion detection systems monitor a network for suspicious activities.
- Clipping levels are certain allowed thresholds for errors before triggering a red flag.

Administrative Access Controls (39.2.3)

Administrative access controls are the policies and procedures defined by organizations to implement and enforce all aspects of controlling unauthorized access.

Administrative controls focus on the following personnel and business practices:

- *Policies* are approved ideas or actions that guide behavior.
- *Procedures* are the detailed steps required to perform an activity.

- *Hiring practices* define the steps an organization takes to find qualified employees.
- *Background checks* are a type of employee screening that includes verification of past employment, credit history, and criminal history.
- *Data classification* categorizes data based on its sensitivity.
- *Security training* educates employees about the security policies at an organization.
- *Reviews* evaluate an employee's job performance.

Authentication, Authorization, and Accounting (AAA) (39.2.4)

Let's look into administrative access controls in more detail.

The concept of administrative access controls involves three security services: authentication, authorization, and accounting (AAA).

These services provide the primary framework to control access, preventing unauthorized access to a computer, network, database, or other data resource.

Authentication

The first A in AAA represents authentication. Authentication is the verification of the identity of each user, to prevent unauthorized access. Users prove their identity with a username or ID. In addition, users need to verify their identity by providing one of the following:

- Something they know (such as a password)
- Something they have (such as a token or card)
- Something they are (such as a fingerprint)

In the case of two-factor authentication, which is increasingly becoming the norm, authentication requires a combination of two of the above rather than just one.

Authorization

Authorization services determine which resources users can access, along with the operations that users can perform.

Some systems accomplish this by using an access control list, or an ACL. An ACL determines whether a user has certain access privileges once the user authenticates. Just because you can log onto the corporate network does not mean that you have permission to use the high-speed color printer, for example.

Authorization can also control when a user has access to a specific resource. For example, employees may have access to a sales database during work hours, but the system locks them out after hours.

Accounting

Not related to financial accounting, accounting in AAA keeps track of what users do—including what they access, the amount of time they access it, and any changes they make.

For example, a bank keeps track of each customer account. An audit of that system can reveal the time and amount of all transactions and the employee or system that executed the transactions. Cybersecurity accounting services work the same way. The system tracks each data transaction and provides auditing results. System administrators can set up computer policies to enable system auditing.

The concept of AAA is like using a credit card. The credit card identifies who can use it, how much that user can spend, and accounts for items or services the user purchased.

Cybersecurity accounting tracks and monitors user activities in real time.

What Is Identification? (39.2.5)

Identification enforces the rules established by the authorization policy. Every time access to a resource is requested, the access controls determine whether to grant or deny access.

A unique identifier ensures the proper association between allowed activities and subjects. A username is the most common method used to identify a user. A username can be an alphanumeric combination, a personal identification number (PIN), a smart card, or biometric—such as a fingerprint, retina scan, or voice recognition.

A unique identifier ensures that a system can identify each user individually, therefore allowing an authorized user to perform the appropriate actions on a particular resource.

Federated Identity Management (39.2.6)

Federated identity management (FIM) refers to multiple enterprises that let their users use the same identification credentials to gain access to the networks of all enterprises in the group. While FIM provides convenience to users and administrators, if the system is exploited by hackers, they will have access to many systems instead of just one.

Generally speaking, a federated identity links a subject's electronic identity across separate identity management systems. This could enable access to several websites using the same social login credentials, for example.

The goal of federated identity management is to share identity information automatically across enterprise boundaries. From the individual user's perspective, this means a single sign-on to multiple networks.

It is imperative that organizations scrutinize the identifying information that is shared with partners, even within the same corporate group. The sharing of social security numbers, names, and addresses may allow identity thieves the opportunity to steal this information from a partner with weak security to perpetrate fraud. The most common way to protect federated identity is to tie user identity to authorized devices such as workstations and phones.

Authentication Methods (39.2.7)

As we mentioned earlier, users prove their identity with a username or ID. In addition, users need to verify their identity by providing one of the following.

What You Know

Passwords, passphrases, or PINs are all examples of something that the user knows. Passwords are the most popular method used for authentication.

The terms passphrase, passcode, passkey, and PIN are all generically referred to as password. A password is a string of characters used to prove a user's identity. If this string of characters relates back to a user (for instance, if it is their name, birthdate, or address), it will be easier for cybercriminals to guess this user's password.

Several publications recommend that a password be at least eight characters in length. Users should not create a password that is so long that it is difficult to memorize, or conversely, so short that it becomes vulnerable to password cracking. Password complexity should include a combination of upper- and lowercase letters, numbers, and special characters.

Users need to use different passwords for different systems because if a criminal cracks the user's password once, the criminal will have access to all of the user's accounts. A password manager can help you create and use strong passwords—and makes it unnecessary for you to remember so many complex passwords.

What You Have

Smart cards and security key fobs are both examples of things that users have in their possession that can be used for authentication purposes.

A smart card is a small plastic card, about the size of a credit card, with a small chip embedded in it. The chip is an intelligent data carrier, capable of processing, storing, and safeguarding data. Smart cards contain private information, such as bank account numbers, personal identification, medical records, and digital signatures, using encryption to keep data safe while providing a means to authenticate.

A security key fob is a device that is small enough to attach to a keyring. In most cases, security key fobs are used for two-factor authentication (2FA), which is much more secure than a username and password combination.

For example, let's say you want to access your e-banking, which uses two-factor authentication. First, you enter your username (identification). Then you enter the password, which is your first authentication factor. After that, you need a second means of authentication, because the system uses 2FA. You enter a PIN to your security fob, and it displays a number. This proves that you have physical access to this device, which was issued to you. This number is the second factor. You then enter it to log in to the e-banking account.

Who You Are

Each person has unique physical characteristics, such as a fingerprint, retina pattern, or voice print. These personal biometric characteristics uniquely identify a specific person. Biometric security compares physical characteristics against stored profiles to authenticate users. In this case, a profile is a data file containing known characteristics of an individual. The system grants the user access if their characteristics match the information saved in their profile. A fingerprint reader is a common biometric device.

There are two types of biometric identifiers:

- **Physical characteristics**—Fingerprints, DNA, face, hands, the retina, or ear features
- **Behavioral characteristics**—Patterns of behavior such as gestures, voice, gait, or typing rhythm

Biometrics is becoming increasingly popular in public security systems, consumer electronics, and point-of-sale applications. Implementing biometrics involves a reader or scanning device, software that converts the scanned information into digital form, and a database that has biometric data stored for comparison.

Passwords (39.2.8)

To protect network devices, it is important to use strong passwords. Here are standard guidelines to follow:

- Use a password length of at least 8 characters, preferably 10 or more characters. A longer password is a more secure password.

- Make passwords complex. Include a mix of uppercase and lowercase letters, numbers, symbols, and spaces, if allowed.
- Avoid passwords based on repetition, common dictionary words, letter or number sequences, usernames, relative or pet names, or biographical information such as birthdates, ID numbers, ancestor names, or other easily identifiable pieces of information.
- Deliberately misspell a password. For example, Smith = Smyth = 5mYth or Security = 5ecur1ty.
- Change passwords often. If a password is unknowingly compromised, the window of opportunity for the threat actor to use the password is limited.
- Do not write passwords down and leave them in obvious places such as on the desk or monitor.

Table 39-3 shows examples of weak and strong passwords.

Table 39-3 Examples of Weak and Strong Passwords

Weak Password	Why It Is Weak
secret	Simple dictionary password
smith	Maiden name of mother
Toyota	Make of a car
bob1967	Name and birthday of the user
Blueleaf23	Simple words and numbers
Strong Password	**Why It Is Strong**
b67n42d39c	Combines alphanumeric characters
12^h u4@1p7	Combines alphanumeric characters, symbols, and a space

On Cisco routers, leading spaces are ignored for passwords, but spaces after the first character are not. Therefore, one method to create a strong password is to use the space bar and create a phrase made of many words. This is called a passphrase. A passphrase is often easier to remember than a simple password. It is also longer and harder to guess.

Password Managers

Use a password manager to secure passwords for your online Internet activity. Considered to be the best practice to secure passwords, the password manager automatically generates complex passwords for you and will automatically enter them

when you access those sites. You only have to enter a primary password to enable this feature.

Multi-Factor Authentication

Use multi-factor authentication when available. This means that authentication requires two or more independent means of verification. For example, when you enter a password, you would also have to enter a code that is sent to you through email or text message.

Multi-Factor Authentication (39.2.9)

As we've touched upon earlier, multi-factor authentication uses at least two methods of verification—such as a password and something you have, for example, a security key fob. This can be taken a step further by adding something you are, such as a fingerprint scan.

Multi-factor authentication can reduce the incidence of online identity theft because it means knowing a password will not give cybercriminals access to a user's account.

For example, an online banking website might require a password and a one-off PIN that the user receives on his or her smartphone. In this case, your first factor is your password, and your second factor the temporary PIN, because it proves you have access to what is registered as your phone.

Withdrawing cash from an ATM is another, simple example of multi-factor authentication as the user must have the bank card as well as know the PIN before the ATM will dispense cash.

Note that two-factor authentication (2FA) is a method of multi-factor authentication that entails two factors in particular, but the two terms are often used interchangeably.

Authorization (39.2.10)

Authorization controls what a user can and cannot do on the network after successful authentication. After a user proves their identity, the system checks to see what network resources the user can access and what they can do with the resources.

When to Implement Authorization

Authorization uses a set of attributes that describes the user's access to the network, to answer the question, "What read, copy, edit, create, and delete privileges does this user have with each resource they can access?" It can also specify the day and time that a user can access these resources.

The system compares these attributes to the information contained within the authentication database, determines a set of restrictions for that user, and delivers it to the local device where the user is connected.

Authorization is automatic and does not require users to perform additional steps after authentication. System administrators have set the network up to implement authorization immediately after the user authenticates.

How to Implement Authorization

Defining authorization rules is the first step in controlling access. An authorization policy establishes these rules.

A group membership policy defines authorization based on users' membership in a specific group. All employees of an organization may have a swipe card, for example, which provides access to the premises, but it might not allow access to a server room. It may be that only senior-level employees and IT team members may access the server room with their swipe cards.

An authority-level policy defines access permissions based on an employee's position within the organization.

Accounting (39.2.11)

Accounting traces an action back to a person or process. Accounting then collects this information and reports the usage data. The organization can use this data for such purposes as auditing or billing. The collected data might include the login time for a user, whether the user login was a success or failure, and what network resources the user accessed. This allows an organization to trace actions, errors, and mistakes during an audit or investigation.

Implementing accounting includes technologies, policies, procedures, and education. Log files provide detailed information based on the parameters chosen. For example, an organization may look at the log for login failures and successes. Login failures can indicate that a criminal tried to hack an account, and login successes tell an organization which users are using what resources and when.

The organization's policies and procedures spell out what actions should be recorded and how the log files are generated, reviewed, and stored.

Data retention, media disposal, and compliance requirements all provide accounting. Many laws require the implementation of measures to secure different data types. These laws guide an organization on the right way to handle, store, and dispose of data. User education and awareness of an organization's policies, procedures, and related laws can also contribute to accounting.

Interactive Graphic

Check Your Understanding—Access Control (39.2.12)

Refer to the online course to complete this activity.

Video

Video—Configure Access Control (39.2.13)

Refer to the online course to view this video.

Packet Tracer Activity

Packet Tracer—Configure Access Control (39.2.14)

In the following Packet Tracer activity, you will complete the following objectives:

- Part 1: Configure and Use AAA Authentication Credentials
- Part 2: Configure and Use Email Services
- Part 3: Configure and Use FTP Services

Refer to the online course to complete this Packet Tracer.

Defending Systems and Devices (39.3)

All aspects of the network must be protected for the network to be secure. This includes end devices and intermediary devices, hardware, and software.

Operating System Security (39.3.1)

What does an organization need to do to *harden* an operating system and keep it secure?

A Good Administrator

A good administrator will configure the operating system to protect against outside threats. That means removing any unnecessary programs and services, and making sure that security patches and updates are installed in a timely manner to correct faults and mitigate risks.

A Systematic Approach

It's important to have a systematic approach in place for addressing system updates. An organization should

- Establish procedures for monitoring security-related information.
- Evaluate updates for applicability.
- Plan the installation of application updates and patches.
- Install updates using a documented plan.

A Baseline

Another critical way to secure an operating system is to identify potential vulnerabilities. To do this, establish a baseline to compare how a system is performing against baseline expectations.

Interactive Graphic

Activity—What Do You Know About Antimalware? (39.3.2)

Refer to the online course to complete this activity.

Types of Antimalware (39.3.3)

You've identified types of antimalware that can be used to protect end devices, but there's more to learn. Let's go through some important points to remember about antimalware.

Watch Out for Rogue Antivirus Products

Be cautious of malicious rogue antivirus products that appear while browsing the Internet. Most of these display an ad or popup that looks like an actual Windows warning. They warn that malware is infecting the computer and prompt the user to clean it. But they do not come from legitimate sources, and clicking anywhere inside the window may download and install malware instead.

Fileless Attacks Are Difficult to Detect and Remove

Fileless malware uses legitimate programs to infect a computer. Going straight into memory, this type of malware doesn't rely on files, so it leaves no footprint. A fileless attack ends when the system is rebooted. Fileless viruses use scripting languages such as Windows PowerShell and are hard to detect.

Scripts Can also Be Malware

Scripting languages such as Python, Bash (the command-line language for Apple's macOS and most Linux distributions), or Visual Basic for Applications (or VBA, used in Microsoft macros) can be used to create scripts that are malware.

Always Remove Unapproved Software

Unapproved or non-compliant software may be unintentionally installed on a computer. Users may also intentionally install unauthorized programs. Although unapproved software may not be malicious, it can still violate the security policy and interfere with

the organization's software or network services. Non-compliant software should be removed immediately.

Patch Management (39.3.4)

Cybercriminals work relentlessly to exploit weakness in computer systems. To stay one step ahead, keep systems secure and up to date by regularly installing patches.

What Are Patches?

Patches are code updates that prevent a new virus, worm, or other malware from making a successful attack. Patches and upgrades are often combined into a service pack. Many malware attacks could have been avoided if users had installed the latest service pack.

Operating systems such as Windows routinely check for updates that can protect a computer from the latest security threats. These include security updates, critical updates, and service packs. Windows can be configured to automatically download and install high-priority updates or to notify the user as these become available.

What Do You Need to Do?

As a cybersecurity professional, it's good practice to test a patch before deploying it throughout the organization. A patch management tool can be used to manage patches locally instead of using the vendor's online update service.

An automated patch service provides administrators with more control rather than searching for patches when needed. Let's look at the benefits:

- Administrators can approve or decline updates.
- Administrators can force the update of systems on a specific date.
- Administrators can obtain reports on the update(s) needed by each system.
- There is no need for each computer to connect to the vendor's service to download patches; instead, it gets the verified update from a local server.
- Users cannot disable or circumvent updates.

A Proactive Approach

In addition to securing the operating system, it's important to update third-party applications such as Adobe Acrobat, Java, and Google Chrome to address vulnerabilities that could be exploited. A proactive approach to patch management provides network security while helping to prevent ransomware and other threats.

Endpoint Security (39.3.5)

A host-based security solution is a software application that runs on a local device (or endpoint) to protect it. The software works with the operating system to help prevent attacks.

Host-based solutions include the following.

Host-Based Firewalls

A host-based firewall runs on a device to restrict incoming and outgoing network activity for that device. It can allow or deny traffic between the device and the network. The software firewall inspects and filters data packets to protect the device from becoming infected. Windows Firewall, installed by default during Windows installation, is an example of a software firewall.

You can control the type of data sent to and from the device by opening or blocking ports. Firewalls block incoming and outgoing network connections unless exceptions are defined to permit or deny traffic to or from those ports. You can select "inbound rules" to configure the types of traffic that are allowed to pass through to the system—this will protect the system from unwanted traffic.

Host Intrusion Detection Systems (HIDSs)

HIDS software is installed on a device or server to monitor suspicious activity. It monitors system calls and file system access to detect malicious requests. It can also monitor configuration information about the device that is held in the system registry.

A HIDS stores all log data locally. It is resource-intensive, so it can affect system performance. A HIDS cannot monitor network traffic that does not reach the host system, but it can monitor operating system and critical system processes specific to that host.

Host Intrusion Prevention Systems (HIPSs)

A HIPS is software that monitors a device for known attacks and anomalies (deviations in bandwidth, protocols, and ports), or finds red flags by assessing the actual protocols in packets. If it detects malicious activity, the HIPS tool can send you an alarm, log the malicious activity, reset the connection, and/or drop the packets.

Endpoint Detection and Response (EDR)

EDR is an integrated security solution that continuously monitors and collects data from an endpoint device. It then analyzes the data and responds to any threats it

detects. An antivirus can only block against threats, while EDR can do that and find threats on the device.

Data Loss Prevention (DLP)

DLP tools provide a centralized way to ensure that sensitive data is not lost, misused, or accessed by unauthorized users.

Next-Generation Firewall (NGFW)

NGFW is a network security device that combines a traditional firewall with other network-device-filtering functions. An example is an application firewall using inline deep packet inspection (DPI) on an intrusion protection system (IPS).

Host Encryption (39.3.6)

The Windows Encrypting File System (EFS) feature allows users to encrypt files, folders, or an entire hard drive. Full-disk encryption (FDE) encrypts the entire contents of a drive (including temporary files and memory). Microsoft Windows uses *BitLocker*, shown in Figure 39-6, for FDE.

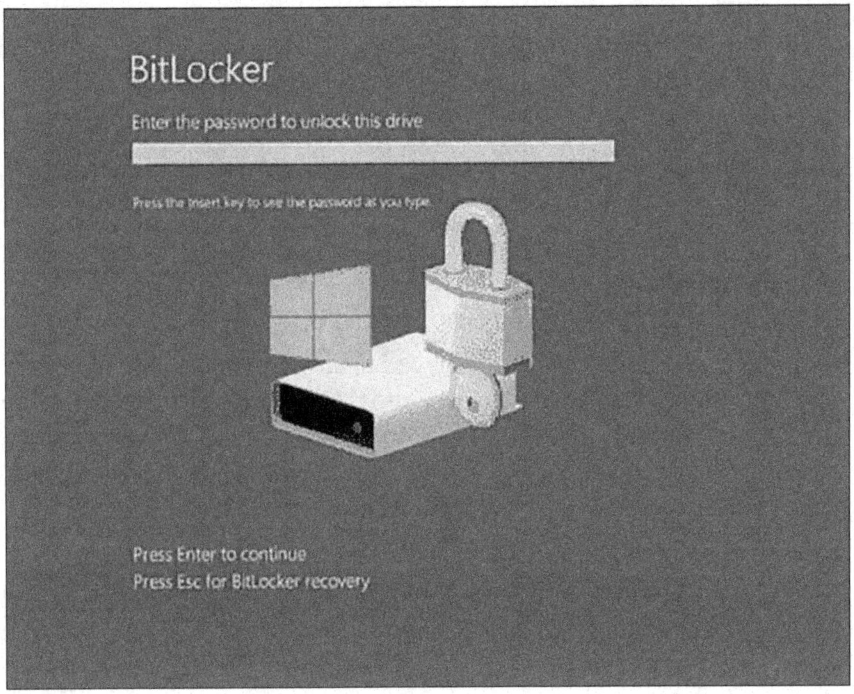

Figure 39-6 BitLocker Unlock Screen

To use BitLocker, the user needs to enable a Trusted Platform Module (TPM) in the BIOS. A TPM is a specialized chip on the motherboard that stores information about the host system, such as encryption keys, digital certificates, and system integrity measurements. When enabled, BitLocker can use the TPM chip.

Similarly, *BitLocker To Go* is a tool that encrypts removable drives. It does not use a TPM chip, but still encrypts the data, requiring a password to decrypt it. Self-encrypting drives (SEDs) automatically encrypt all data in the drive to prevent attackers from accessing the data through their operating system. SED encryption is implemented in the drive hardware by the manufacturer.

Boot Integrity (39.3.7)

Attackers can strike at any moment, even in the short space of time it takes for a system to start up. It is critical to ensure that systems and devices remain secure when booting up.

What Is Boot Integrity?

Boot integrity ensures that the system can be trusted and has not been altered while the operating system loads.

Firmware—software instructions about basic computer functions—is stored on a small memory chip on the motherboard. The basic input/output system (BIOS) is the first program that runs when you turn on the computer.

Unified Extensible Firmware Interface (UEFI), a newer version of BIOS, defines a standard interface between the operating system, firmware, and external devices. A system that uses UEFI is preferred over one that uses BIOS because a UEFI system can run in 64-bit mode.

How Does Secure Boot Work?

Secure Boot is a security standard to ensure that a device boots using trusted software. When a computer system boots, the firmware checks the signature of each piece of boot software, including UEFI firmware drivers, UEFI applications, and the operating system. If the signatures are valid, the system boots, and the firmware gives control to the operating system.

What Is Measured Boot?

Measured Boot provides stronger validation than Secure Boot. Measured Boot measures each component starting with the firmware through to the boot start drivers, and stores the measurements in the TMP chip to create a log. The log can be tested

remotely to verify the boot state of the client. Measured Boot can identify untrusted applications trying to load, and it also allows antimalware to load earlier.

Apple System Security Features (39.3.8)

As we know, Windows and Linux distributions include security features that are designed to protect endpoints. Apple provides system hardware and macOS security features that offer robust endpoint protection as well.

Apple security features are listed in Table 39-4.

Table 39-4 Apple Security Features

Features	Description
Security-focused hardware	The hardware platform has enhanced security features such as a special security processor, boot integrity, and a dedicated AES encryption engine. These features are included in a special system on a chip called the Secure Enclave.
Encrypted storage	Apple Data Protection and FileVault data storage encryption are supported by the hardware-based AES encryption engine. This enables encryption and decryption of files as they are written or read without exposing encryption keys to the main CPU, operating system, or running applications.
Secure boot	The Boot ROM protects low-level hardware and only allows genuine and unaltered Apple OS software to run.
Secure biometric data	Biometric authentication data is processed in the security hardware system. This keeps it segregated from the OS and running application software, including malware.
Find My Mac	Find My Mac helps find lost or stolen macOS devices through its location tracking function. It also enables remote device locking and storage erasing if critical data is at risk.
XProtect	XProtect antimalware technology prevents the execution of malware through signature-based malware detection. It also alerts users to the existence of malware and provides the option to remove detected malware files.
Malware Removal Tool (MRT)	MRT detects and removes existing malware infections when detection rules are automatically updated by Apple. It also monitors for malware infections at system restart and user login.
Gatekeeper	Gatekeeper ensures that only authentic, digitally-signed software that has been created by an Apple-notarized software developer is permitted to be installed.

Physical Protection of Devices (39.3.9)

You have learned a lot about software and hardware threats. But what about the potential physical threats to devices and facilities? The following are some physical security measures you can take to protect equipment.

Computer Equipment

To physically protect computer equipment:

- Use cable locks to secure devices.
- Keep telecommunication rooms locked.
- Use security cages (Faraday cages) around equipment to block electromagnetic fields.

Door Locks

A standard keyed entry lock is the most common type of door lock. They are often easy to force open. A deadbolt lock can be added for extra security. Any lock that requires a key is vulnerable if the keys are lost, stolen, or duplicated.

A cipher lock uses buttons that are pressed in a given sequence to open the door. It can be programmed so that a user's code may only work during certain days or times. It can also keep a record of when the door opened, and the code used to open it.

Radio Frequency Identification (RFID) Systems

RFID uses radio waves to identify and track objects. RFID tags can be attached to any item that an organization wants to track. The tags contain an integrated circuit that connects to an antenna. RFID tags are small and require very little power, so they do not need a battery to exchange information with a reader. RFID can help automate asset tracking, or wirelessly lock, unlock, or configure electronic devices. Contactless credit cards use RFID technology.

Interactive Graphic

Check Your Understanding—Defending Systems and Devices (39.3.10)

Refer to the online course to complete this activity.

Antimalware Protection (39.4)

Malware, is short for "malicious software." *Malware* is any type of software that is specifically designed to damage, disrupt, or gain unauthorized access to end devices

or networks. The intent of malware is to steal sensitive information, compromise system functionality, or perform other harmful actions.

Endpoint Threats (39.4.1)

The term "endpoint" is defined in various ways. For the purpose of this course, we can define endpoints as hosts on the network that can access or be accessed by other hosts on the network. This obviously includes computers and servers, but many other devices can also access the network. With the rapid growth of the Internet of Things (IoT), other types of devices are now endpoints on the network. These include networked security cameras, controllers, and even light bulbs and appliances. Each endpoint is potentially a way for malicious software to gain access to a network. In addition, new technologies, such as cloud, expand the boundaries of enterprise networks to include locations on the Internet for which enterprises are not responsible.

A recent survey of cybersecurity professionals asked the participants what security challenges they are most struggling with. As shown Figure 39-7, the top three are related to endpoint threats. Ransomware (53%) tops the list, following the recent rise in ransomware attacks. The next biggest security challenge is the shift to remote work and the resulting risks (47%), introduced in the wake of the Covid-19 pandemic. Limited visibility into cyber threats (41%) rounds out the top three security challenges experienced by cybersecurity professionals.

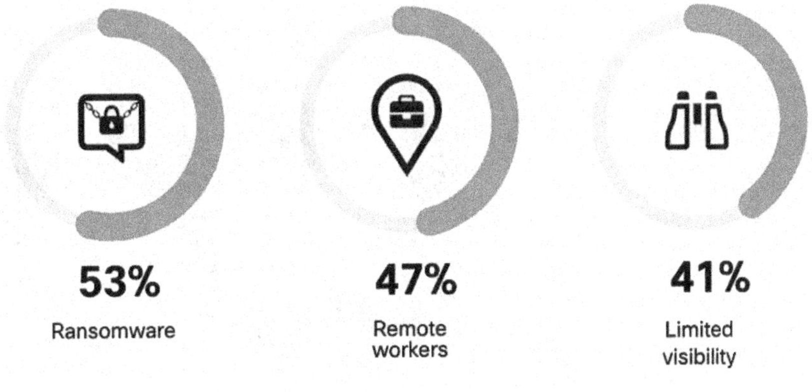

Figure 39-7 Survey—What Are Your Current Security Challenges?

Endpoint Security (39.4.2)

News media commonly cover external network attacks on enterprise networks. These are some examples of such attacks:

- DoS attacks on an organization's network to degrade or even halt public access to it.

- Breach of an organization's web server to deface their web presence.
- Breach of an organization's data servers and hosts to steal confidential information.

Various network security devices are required to protect the network perimeter from outside access. As shown in Figure 39-8, these devices could include a hardened router that is providing VPN services, a next-generation firewall (ASA, in Figure 39-8), an IPS appliance, and an authentication, authorization, and accounting (AAA) services server (AAA Server, in Figure 39-8).

However, many attacks originate from inside the network. Therefore, securing an internal LAN is nearly as important as securing the outside network perimeter. Without a secure LAN, users within an organization are still susceptible to network threats and outages that can directly affect the organization's productivity and profit margin. After an internal host is infiltrated, it can become a starting point for an attacker to gain access to critical system devices, such as servers and sensitive information.

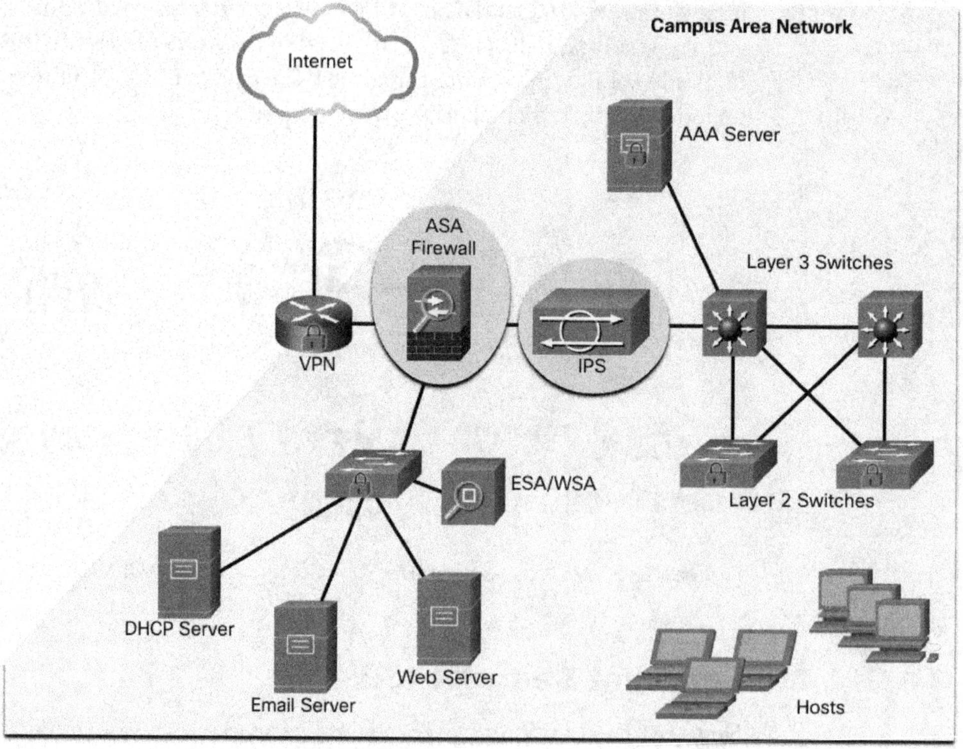

Figure 39-8 Example Topology of Security Devices in a Campus Network

Specifically, there are two internal LAN elements to secure:

- **Endpoints**—Hosts commonly consist of laptops, desktops, printers, servers, and IP phones, all of which are susceptible to malware-related attacks.
- **Network infrastructure**—LAN infrastructure devices interconnect endpoints and typically include switches, wireless devices, and IP telephony devices. Most of these devices are susceptible to LAN-related attacks including MAC address table overflow attacks, spoofing attacks, DHCP-related attacks, LAN storm attacks, STP manipulation attacks, and VLAN attacks.

Host-Based Malware Protection (39.4.3)

The network perimeter is always expanding. People access corporate network resources with mobile devices that use remote-access technologies such as VPN. These same devices are also used on unsecured, or minimally secured, public and home networks. Host-based antimalware/antivirus software and host-based firewalls are used to protect these devices.

Antivirus/Antimalware Software

This is software that is installed on a host to detect and mitigate viruses and malware. Examples are Windows Defender Virus & Threat Protection, Cisco AMP for Endpoints, Norton Security, McAfee, Trend Micro, and others. Antimalware programs may detect viruses using three different approaches:

- **Signature-based**—This approach recognizes various characteristics of known malware files.
- **Heuristics-based**—This approach recognizes general features shared by various types of malware.
- **Behavior-based**—This approach employs analysis of suspicious behavior.

Many antivirus programs are able to provide real-time protection by analyzing data as it is used by the endpoint. These programs also scan for existing malware that may have entered the system prior to it being recognizable in real time.

Host-based antivirus protection is also known as agent-based. Agent-based antivirus runs on every protected machine. Agentless antivirus protection performs scans on hosts from a centralized system. Agentless systems have become popular for virtualized environments in which multiple OS instances are running on a host simultaneously. Agent-based antivirus running in each virtualized system can be a serious drain on system resources. Agentless antivirus for virtual hosts involves the use of a special security virtual appliance that performs optimized scanning tasks on the virtual hosts. An example of this is VMware's vShield.

Host-Based Firewall

This software is installed on a host. It restricts incoming and outgoing connections to connections initiated by that host only. Some firewall software can also prevent a host from becoming infected and stop infected hosts from spreading malware to other hosts. This function is included in some operating systems. For example, Windows includes Windows Defender Firewall with Advanced Security as shown in Figure 39-9.

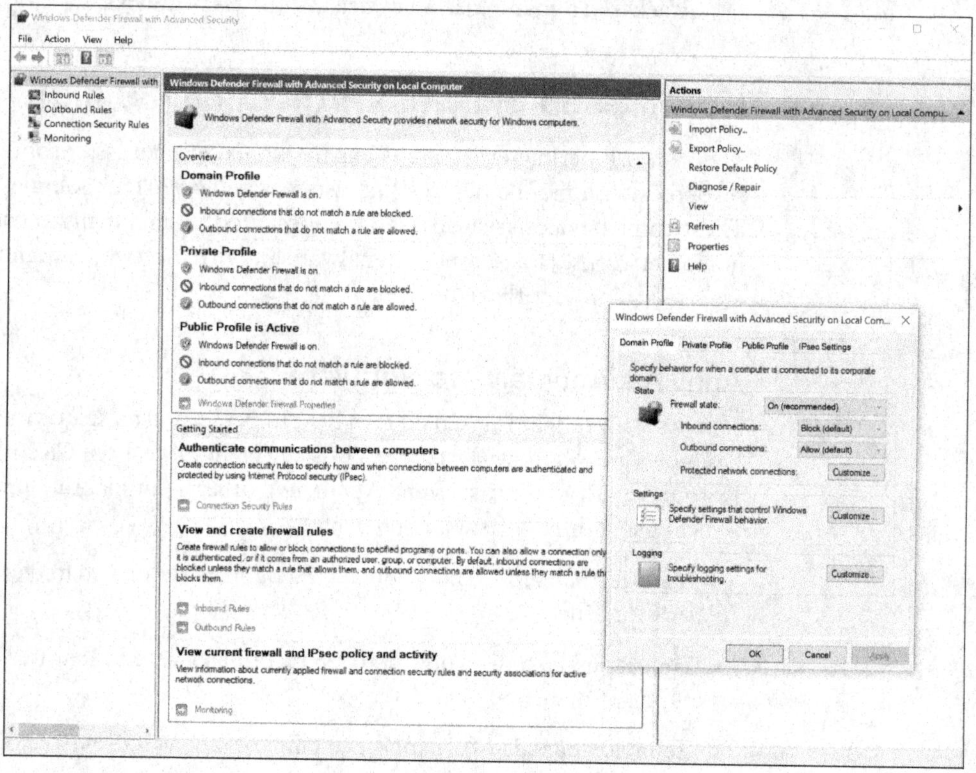

Figure 39-9 Windows Defender Firewall with Advanced Security

Other solutions are produced by other companies or organizations. The Linux iptables and TCP Wrappers tools are examples. Host-based firewalls are discussed in more detail later in the chapter.

Host-Based Security Suites

It is recommended to install a host-based suite of security products on home networks as well as business networks. These host-based security suites include antivirus, anti-phishing, safe browsing, host-based intrusion prevention system, and firewall

capabilities. These various security measures provide a layered defense that will protect against most common threats.

In addition to the protection functionality provided by host-based security products is the telemetry function. Most host-based security software includes robust logging functionality that is essential to cybersecurity operations. Some host-based security programs will submit logs to a central location for analysis.

There are many host-based security programs and suites available to users and enterprises. The independent testing laboratory AV-TEST provides high-quality reviews of host-based protections, as well as information about many other security products.

Search the Internet for the AV-TEST organization to learn more about AV-TEST.

Network-Based Malware Protection (39.4.4)

New security architectures for the borderless network address security challenges by having endpoints use network scanning elements. These devices provide many more layers of scanning than a single endpoint possibly could, as shown in Figure 39-10. Network-based malware prevention devices are also capable of sharing information among themselves to make better-informed decisions.

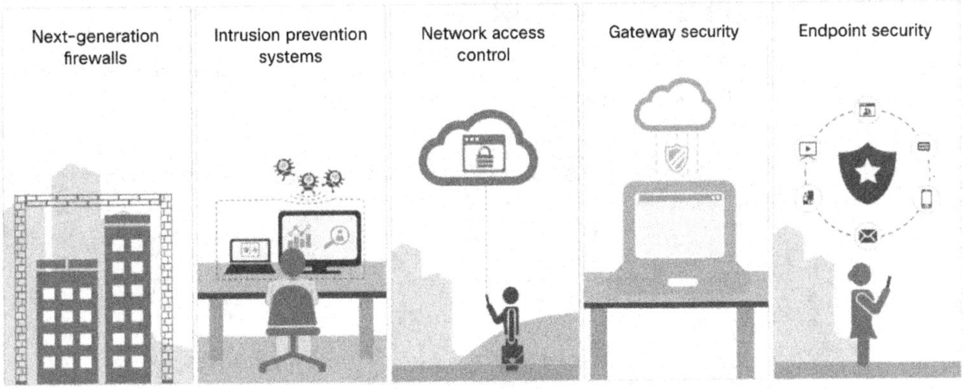

Figure 39-10 Protection for Borderless Networks

Protecting endpoints in a borderless network can be accomplished using network-based as well as host-based techniques, as shown in Figure 39-10. The following are examples of devices and techniques that implement host protections at the network level:

- **Cisco Secure Endpoint**—This provides endpoint protection from viruses and malware.
- **Cisco Secure Email**—This provides filtering of spam and potentially malicious emails before they reach the endpoint. An example is the Cisco ESA.

- **Cisco Umbrella**—This uses DNS requests to provide filtering of websites and blocklisting to prevent hosts from reaching dangerous locations on the web. Cisco Umbrella provides control over how users access the Internet and can enforce acceptable use policies, control access to specific sites and services, and scan for malware.
- **Network Admission Control (NAC)**—This permits only authorized and compliant systems to connect to the network.

Interactive Graphic

Check Your Understanding—Antimalware Protection (39.4.5)

Refer to the online course to complete this activity.

Firewalls and Host-Based Intrusion Prevention (39.5)

Detecting and preventing access data that may be harmful to end devices or the network is a critical part of any security infrastructure.

Firewalls (39.5.1)

A *firewall* is a system, or group of systems, that enforces an access control policy between networks, as shown in Figure 39-11.

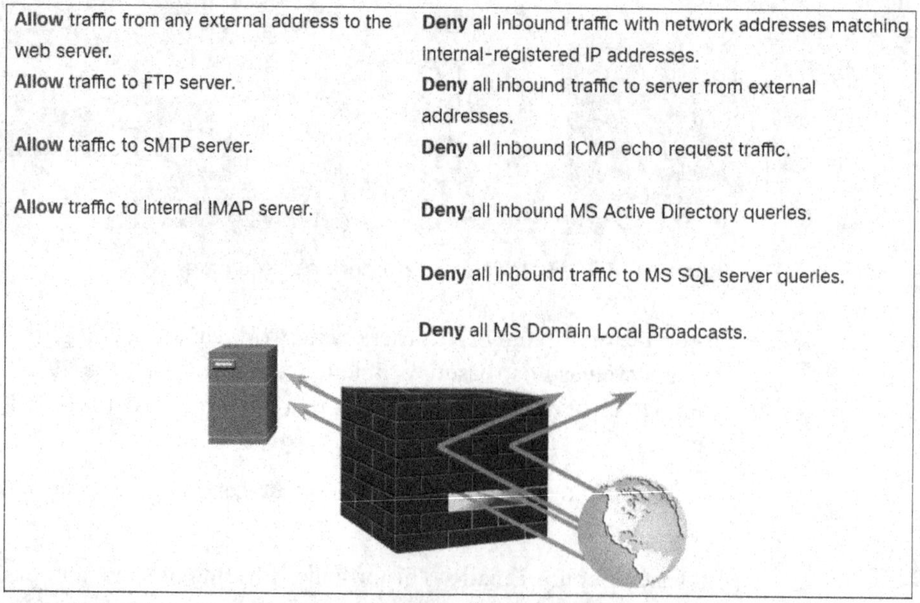

Figure 39-11 Firewalls Enforce Access Control Policies

Common Firewall Properties

All firewalls share some common properties:

- Firewalls are resistant to network attacks.
- Firewalls are the only transit point between internal corporate networks and external networks because all traffic flows through the firewall.
- Firewalls enforce the access control policy.

Firewall Benefits

There are several benefits of using a firewall in a network:

- They prevent the exposure of sensitive hosts, resources, and applications to untrusted users.
- They sanitize protocol flow, which prevents the exploitation of protocol flaws.
- They block malicious data from servers and clients.
- They reduce security management complexity by off-loading most of the network access control to a few firewalls in the network.

Firewall Limitations

Firewalls also have some limitations:

- A misconfigured firewall can have serious consequences for the network, such as becoming a single point of failure.
- The data from many applications cannot be passed over firewalls securely.
- Users might proactively search for ways around the firewall to receive blocked material, which exposes the network to potential attack.
- Network performance can slow down.
- Unauthorized traffic can be tunneled or hidden as legitimate traffic through the firewall.

Types of Firewalls (39.5.2)

It is important to understand the different types of firewalls and their specific capabilities so that the right firewall is used for each situation.

Packet Filtering (Stateless) Firewall

Packet filtering firewalls are usually part of a router firewall, which permits or denies traffic based on Layer 3 and Layer 4 information, as shown in Figure 39-12. They are

stateless firewalls that use a simple policy table lookup that filters traffic based on specific criteria.

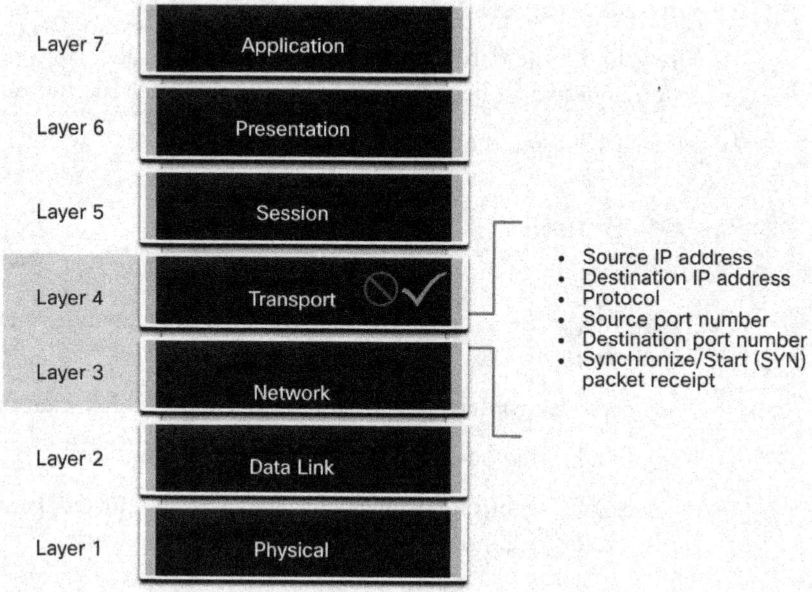

Figure 39-12 Stateless Firewall OSI Layers

For example, SMTP servers listen to port 25 by default. An administrator can configure the packet filtering firewall to block port 25 from a specific workstation to prevent it from broadcasting an email virus.

Stateful Firewall

Stateful firewalls are the most versatile and the most common firewall technologies in use. Stateful firewalls provide stateful packet filtering by using connection information maintained in a state table. Stateful filtering is a firewall architecture that is classified at the network layer. It also analyzes traffic at OSI Layer 4 and Layer 5, as shown in Figure 39-13.

Application Gateway Firewall

An application gateway firewall (proxy firewall), as shown in Figure 39-14, filters information at Layers 3, 4, 5, and 7 of the OSI reference model. Most of the firewall control and filtering is done in software. When a client needs to access a remote server, it connects to a proxy server. The proxy server connects to the remote server on behalf of the client. Therefore, the server only sees a connection from the proxy server.

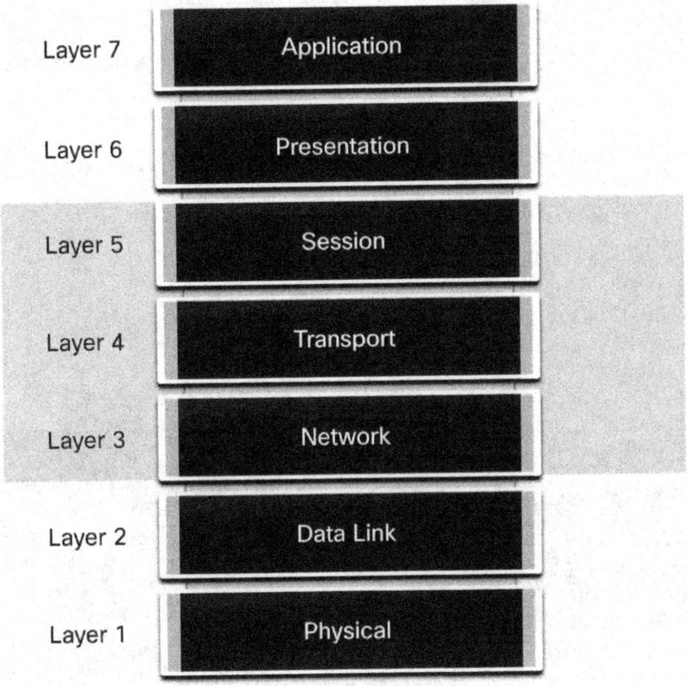

Figure 39-13 Stateful Firewall OSI Layers

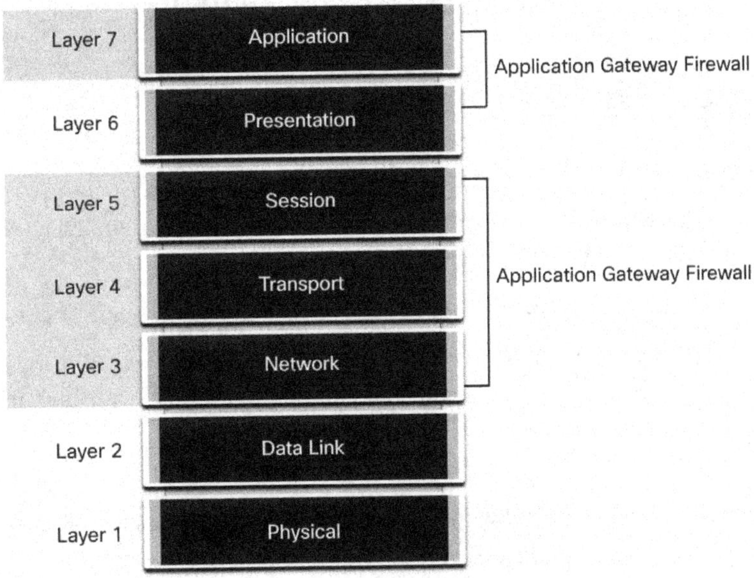

Figure 39-14 Application Gateway Firewall OSI Layers

Next-Generation Firewall

Next-generation firewalls (NGFW) go beyond stateful firewalls by providing:

- Integrated intrusion prevention
- Application awareness and control to see and block risky apps
- Upgrade paths to include future information feeds
- Techniques to address evolving security threats

Figure 39-15 shows the Cisco ASA 5500-X series firewalls.

Figure 39-15 Cisco ASA 5500-X Series Firewalls

Other methods of implementing firewalls include:

- **Host-based (server and personal) firewall**—A PC or server with firewall software running on it.
- **Transparent firewall**—Filters IP traffic between a pair of bridged interfaces.
- **Hybrid firewall**—A combination of the various firewall types. For example, an application inspection firewall combines a stateful firewall with an application gateway firewall.

Interactive Graphic

Check Your Understanding—Identify the Type of Firewall (39.5.3)

Refer to the online course to complete this activity.

Packet Filtering Firewall Benefits and Limitations (39.5.4)

Packet filtering firewalls are usually part of a router firewall, which permits or denies traffic based on Layer 3 and Layer 4 information, as shown in Figure 39-16. They are stateless firewalls that use a simple policy table lookup that filters traffic based on specific criteria, as shown in the figure. For example, SMTP servers listen to port 25 by default. An administrator can configure the packet filtering firewall to block port 25 from a specific workstation to prevent it from broadcasting an email virus.

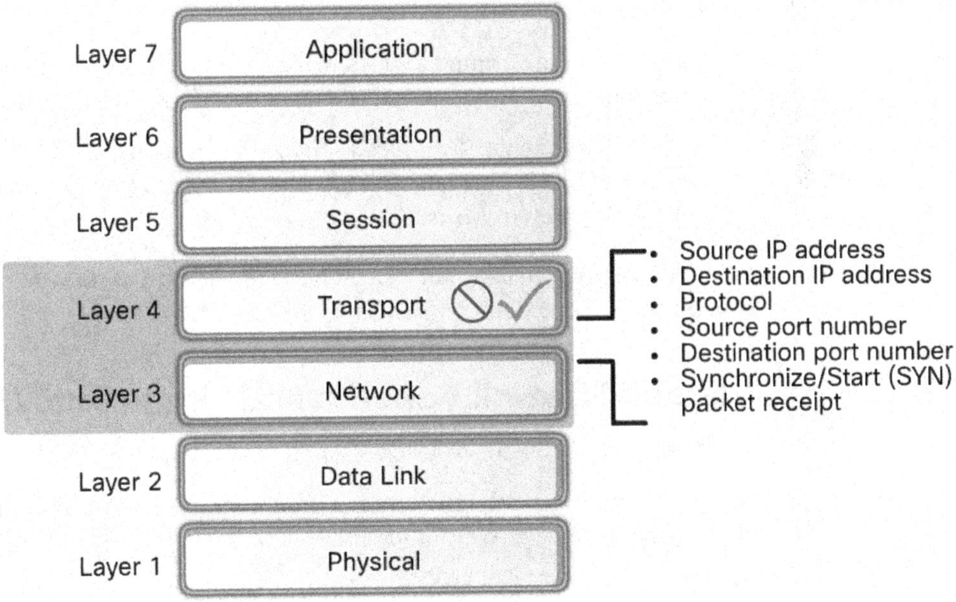

Figure 39-16 Packet Filtering at Layers 3 and 4

There are several advantages of using a packet filtering firewall:

- Packet filters implement simple permit or deny rule sets.
- Packet filters have a low impact on network performance.
- Packet filters are easy to implement and are supported by most routers.
- Packet filters provide an initial degree of security at the network layer.
- Packet filters perform almost all the tasks of a high-end firewall at a much lower cost.

Packet filters do not represent a complete firewall solution, but they are an important element of a firewall security policy. There are several disadvantages of using a packet filtering firewall:

- Packet filters are susceptible to IP spoofing. Threat actors can send arbitrary packets that meet ACL criteria and pass through the filter.
- Packet filters do not reliably filter fragmented packets. Because fragmented IP packets carry the TCP header in the first fragment and packet filters filter on TCP header information, all fragments after the first fragment are passed unconditionally. Decisions to use packet filters assume that the filter of the first fragment accurately enforces the policy.
- Packet filters use complex ACLs, which can be difficult to implement and maintain.
- Packet filters cannot dynamically filter certain services. For example, sessions that use dynamic port negotiations are difficult to filter without opening access to a whole range of ports.

Packet filters are stateless. They examine each packet individually rather than in the context of the state of a connection.

Stateful Firewall Benefits and Limitations (39.5.5)

There are several benefits to using a stateful firewall in a network:

- Stateful firewalls are often used as a primary means of defense by filtering unwanted, unnecessary, or undesirable traffic.
- Stateful firewalls strengthen packet filtering by providing more stringent control over security.
- Stateful firewalls improve performance over packet filters or proxy servers.
- Stateful firewalls defend against spoofing and DoS attacks by determining whether packets belong to an existing connection or are from an unauthorized source.
- Stateful firewalls provide more log information than a packet filtering firewall.

Stateful firewalls also present some limitations:

- Stateful firewalls cannot prevent application layer attacks because they do not examine the actual contents of the HTTP connection.
- Not all protocols are stateful. For example, UDP and ICMP do not generate connection information for a state table and, therefore, do not garner as much support for filtering.

- It is difficult to track connections that use dynamic port negotiation. Some applications open multiple connections. This requires a whole new range of ports that must be opened to allow this second connection.
- Stateful firewalls do not support user authentication.

Table 39-5 summarizes the benefits and limitations of using stateful firewalls.

Table 39-5 Benefits and Limitations of Stateful Firewalls

Benefits	Limitations
Primary means of defense	No application layer inspection
Strong packet filtering	Limited tracking of stateless protocols
Improved performance over packet filters	Difficult to defend against dynamic port negotiation
Defense against spoofing and DoS attacks	No authentication support
Richer data log	

Host-Based Firewalls (39.5.6)

Host-based personal firewalls are standalone software programs that control traffic entering or leaving a computer. Firewall apps are also available for Android phones and tablets.

Host-based firewalls may use a set of predefined policies, or profiles, to control packets entering and leaving a computer. They also may have rules that can be directly modified or created to control access based on addresses, protocols, and ports. Host-based firewall applications can also be configured to issue alerts to users if suspicious behavior is detected. They can then offer the user the ability to allow an offending application to run or to be prevented from running in the future.

Logging varies depending on the firewall application. It typically includes the date and time of the event, whether the connection was allowed or denied, information about the source or destination IP addresses of packets, and the source and destination ports of the encapsulated segments. In addition, common activities such as DNS lookups and other routine events can show up in host-based firewall logs, so filtering and other parsing techniques are useful for inspecting large amounts of log data.

One approach to intrusion prevention is the use of distributed firewalls. Distributed firewalls combine features of host-based firewalls with centralized management.

The management function pushes rules to the hosts and may also accept log files from the hosts.

Whether installed completely on the host or distributed, host-based firewalls are an important layer of network security along with network-based firewalls. Here are some examples of host-based firewalls.

Windows Defender Firewall

First included with Windows XP, Windows Firewall (now Windows Defender Firewall) uses a profile-based approach to firewall functionality. Access to public networks is assigned the restrictive Public firewall profile. The Private profile is for computers that are isolated from the Internet by other security devices, such as a home router with firewall functionality. The Domain profile is the third available profile. It is chosen for connections to a trusted network, such as a business network that is assumed to have an adequate security infrastructure. Windows Firewall has logging functionality and can be centrally managed with customized group security policies from a management server such as System Center 2022.

iptables

This is an application that allows Linux system administrators to configure network access rules that are part of the Linux kernel Netfilter modules.

nftables

The successor to iptables, nftables is a Linux firewall application that uses a simple virtual machine in the Linux kernel. Code is executed within the virtual machine that inspects network packets and implements decision rules regarding packet acceptance and forwarding.

TCP Wrappers

This is a rule-based access control and logging system for Linux. Packet filtering is based on IP addresses and network services.

Antimalware Programs (39.5.7)

Malware includes viruses, worms, Trojan horses, keyloggers, spyware, and adware. These are designed to invade privacy, steal information, damage the computer, or corrupt data. It is important that you protect computers and mobile devices using reputable antimalware software. Table 39-6 summarizes the types of antimalware programs that are available.

Table 39-6 Types of Antimalware Programs

Program	Description
Antivirus protection	This program continuously monitors for viruses. When a virus is detected, the user is warned, and the program attempts to quarantine or delete the virus.
Adware protection	This program continuously looks for programs that display advertising on your computer.
Phishing protection	This program blocks the IP addresses of known phishing websites and warns the user about suspicious sites.
Spyware protection	This program scans for keyloggers and other spyware.
Trusted/untrusted sources	This program warns you about unsafe programs about to be installed or unsafe websites before they are visited.

Windows Defender Firewall (39.5.8)

A firewall selectively denies traffic to a computer or network segment. Firewalls generally work by opening and closing the ports used by various applications. By opening only the required ports on a firewall, you are implementing a restrictive security policy. Any packet not explicitly permitted is denied. In contrast, a permissive security policy permits access through all ports, except those explicitly denied. In the past, software and hardware were shipped with permissive settings. As users neglected to configure their equipment, the default permissive settings left many devices exposed to attackers. Most devices now ship with settings as restrictive as possible, while still allowing easy setup.

To allow program access through the Windows Defender Firewall, search for **Control Panel**, open it, and then locate and click **Windows Defender Firewall** to open it. Click **Allow an app or feature through Windows Defender Firewall**, as shown in Figure 39-17.

If you wish to use a different software firewall, you will need to disable Windows Firewall. To disable the Windows Firewall, click **Turn Windows Firewall on or off**, as shown in Figure 39-18.

Windows Defender Firewall includes many additional features. Click **Advanced settings** to open them, as shown in Figure 39-19.

Here you can create inbound or outbound traffic rules based on different criteria. You can also import and export policies or monitor different aspects of the firewall, as shown in Figure 39-20.

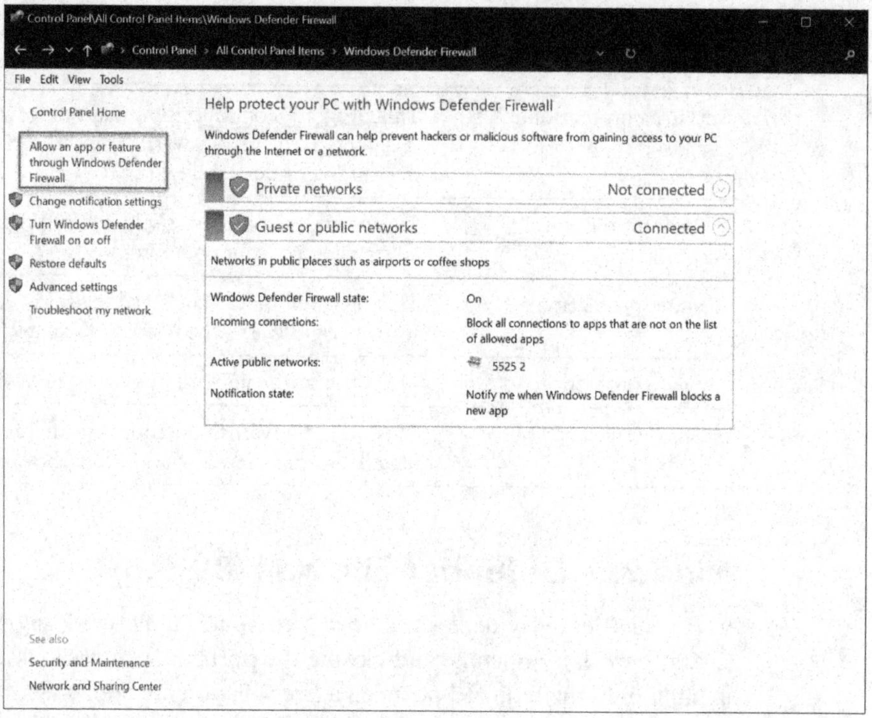

Figure 39-17 Allowing an App Access Through Windows Defender Firewall

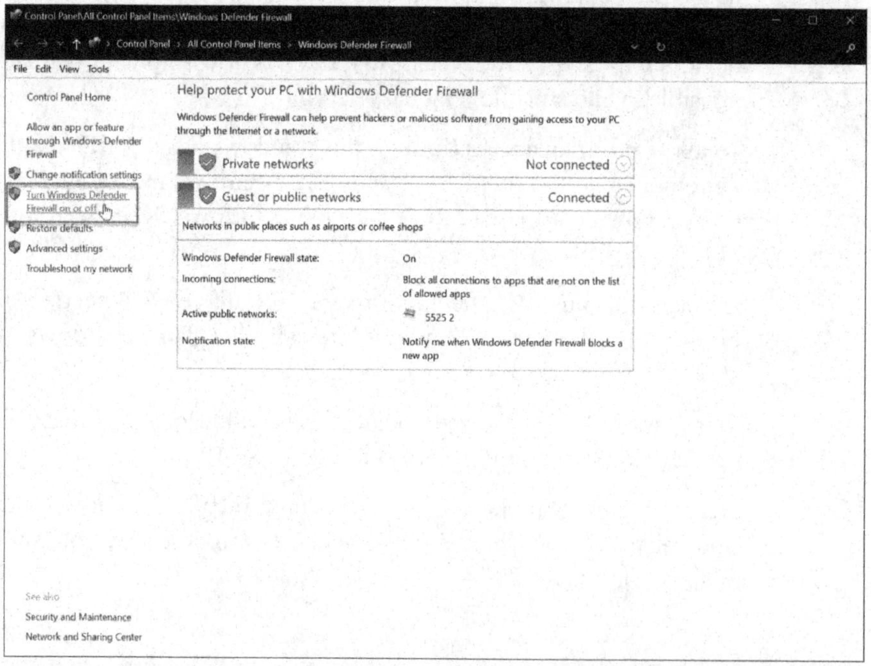

Figure 39-18 Turning Off Windows Defender Firewall

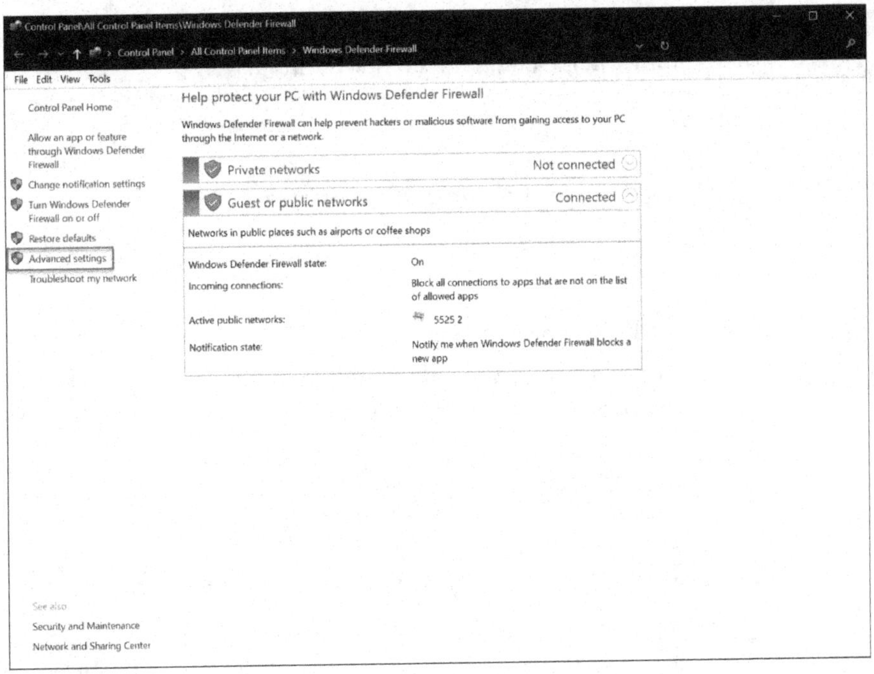

Figure 39-19 Accessing Advance Settings in Windows Defender Firewall

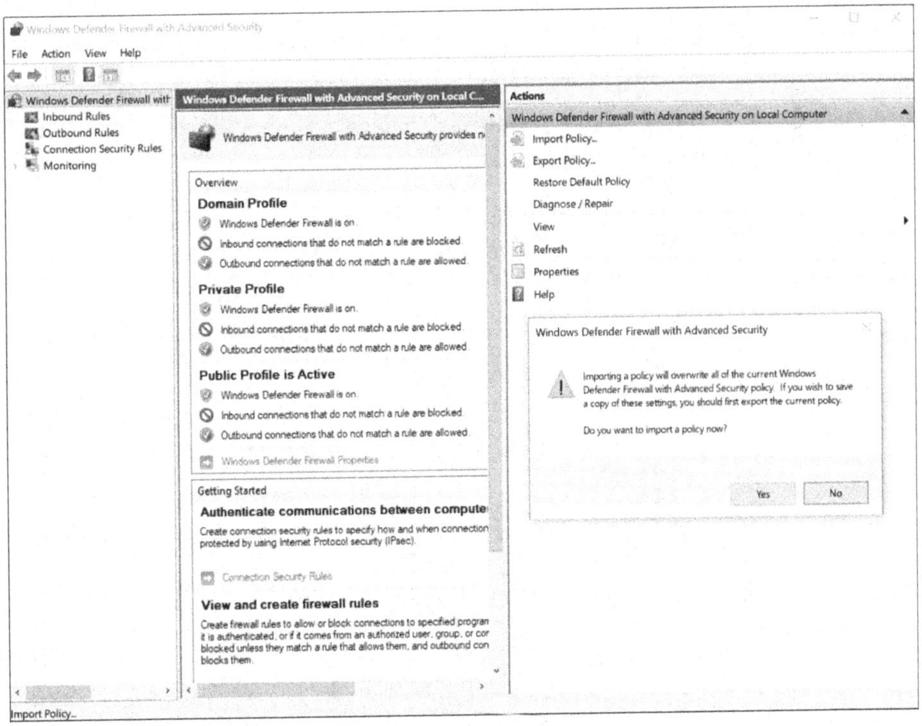

Figure 39-20 Importing a Policy in Windows Defender Firewall

Interactive Graphic

Check Your Understanding—Firewall and Host-Based Intrusion Prevention (39.5.9)

Refer to the online course to complete this activity.

Secure Wireless Access (39.6)

Wireless networks introduce their own unique security concerns.

Video

Video—WLAN Threats (39.6.1)

Wireless networks are growing rapidly. It is important to understand wireless network vulnerabilities, threats, and exploits.

Refer to the online course to view this video.

Wireless Security Overview (39.6.2)

A WLAN is open to anyone within range of a wireless access point (AP) and the appropriate credentials to associate to it. With a wireless NIC and knowledge of cracking techniques, an attacker may not have to physically enter the workplace to gain access to its network over a WLAN.

Attacks can be generated by outsiders, disgruntled employees, and even accidentally. Wireless networks are specifically susceptible to a number of threats, including:

- **Interception of data**—Wireless data should be encrypted to prevent it from being read by eavesdroppers.
- **Wireless intruders**—Unauthorized users attempting to access network resources can be deterred through effective authentication techniques.
- **Denial of service (DoS) attacks**—Access to WLAN services can be compromised either accidentally or maliciously. Various solutions exist depending on the source of the DoS attack.
- **Rogue APs**—Unauthorized APs installed by well-intentioned users, or for malicious purposes, can be detected using wireless network management software.

DoS Attacks (39.6.3)

Wireless DoS attacks can be the result of:

- **Improperly configured devices**—Configuration errors can disable the WLAN. For instance, an administrator could accidently alter a configuration and disable

the network, or an intruder with administrator privileges could intentionally disable a WLAN.

- **A malicious user intentionally interfering with the wireless communication**—Their goal is to disable the wireless network completely or to the point where no legitimate device can access the medium.
- **Accidental interference**—WLANs are prone to interference from other wireless devices including microwave ovens, cordless phones, baby monitors, and more, as shown in Figure 39-21. The 2.4 GHz band is more prone to interference than the 5 GHz band.

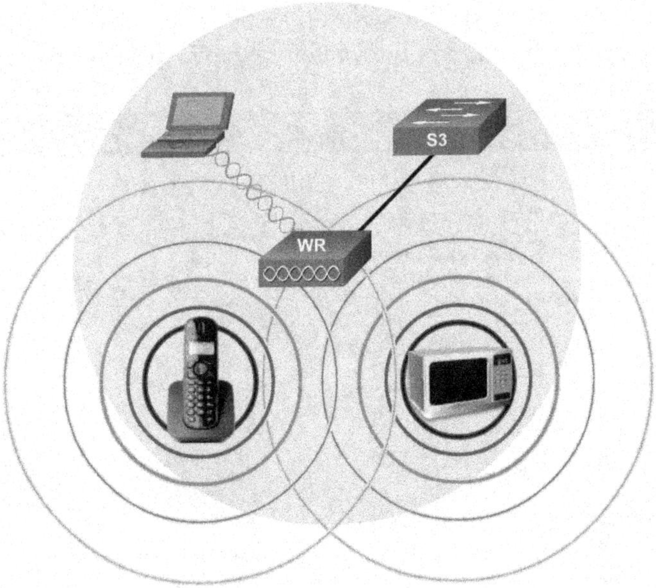

Figure 39-21 Example of Interference on the 5 GHz Band

To minimize the risk of a DoS attack due to improperly configured devices and malicious attacks, harden all devices, keep passwords secure, create backups, and ensure that all configuration changes are incorporated off-hours.

Monitor the WLAN for any accidental interference problems and address them as they appear. Because the 2.4 GHz band is used by other device types, the 5 GHz band should be used in areas prone to interference.

Rogue Access Points (39.6.4)

A rogue AP is an AP or wireless router that has been connected to a corporate network without explicit authorization and against corporate policy. Anyone with

access to the premises can install (maliciously or non-maliciously) an inexpensive wireless router that can potentially allow access to a secure network resource.

Once connected, the rogue AP can be used by an attacker to capture MAC addresses, capture data packets, gain access to network resources, or launch a man-in-the-middle attack.

A personal network hotspot could also be used as a rogue AP. For example, a user with secure network access enables their authorized Windows host to become a Wi-Fi AP. Doing so circumvents the security measures and enables other unauthorized devices to access network resources as a shared device.

To prevent the installation of rogue APs, organizations must configure wireless LAN controllers (WLCs) with rogue AP policies, as shown in Figure 39-22, and use monitoring software to actively monitor the radio spectrum for unauthorized APs.

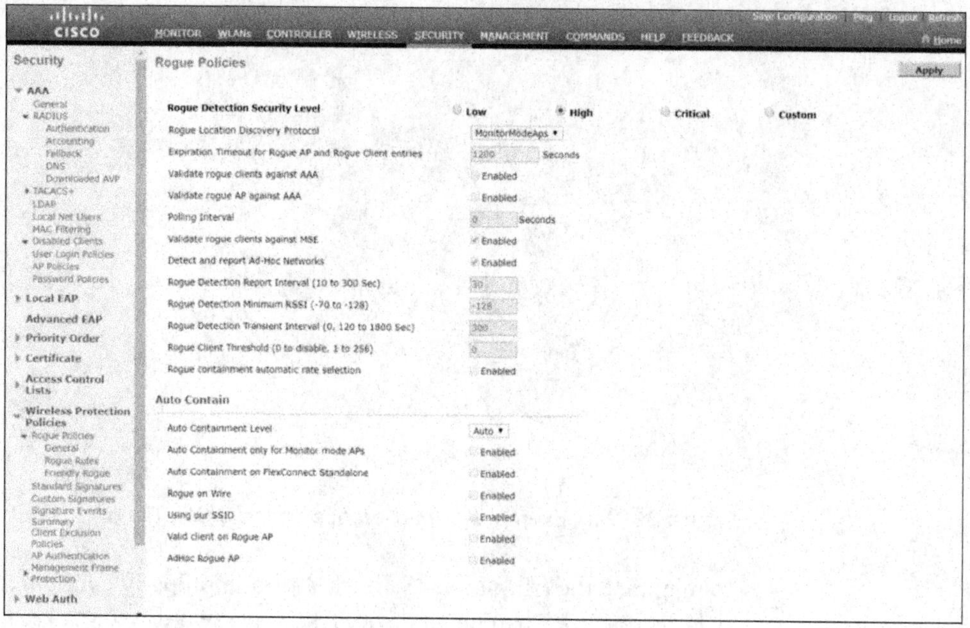

Figure 39-22 Configuring Rogue Policies on a Cisco WLC

Man-in-the-Middle Attack (39.6.5)

In a man-in-the-middle (MITM) attack, also known as an on-path attack, the hacker is positioned in between two legitimate entities in order to read or modify the data that passes between the two parties. There are many ways in which to create an MITM attack.

A popular wireless MITM attack is called the "evil twin AP" attack, where an attacker introduces a rogue AP and configures it with the same SSID as a legitimate AP, as shown in Figure 39-23. Locations offering free Wi-Fi, such as airports, cafes, and restaurants, are particularly popular spots for this type of attack due to the open authentication.

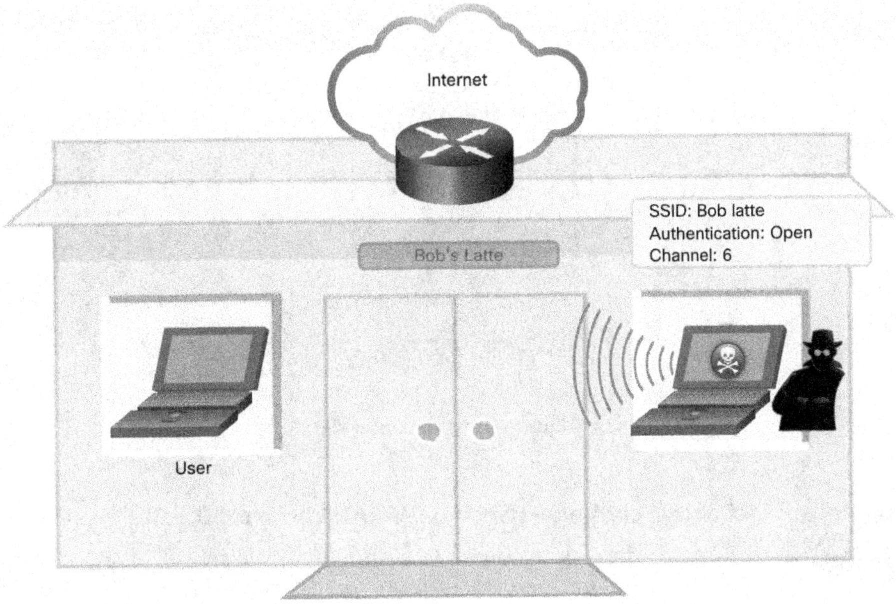

Figure 39-23 Example of an MITM Attack

MITM attacks and their variations are frequently referred to as on-path attacks.

Wireless clients attempting to connect to a WLAN would see two APs with the same SSID offering wireless access. Those near the rogue AP find the stronger signal and most likely associate with it. User traffic is now sent to the rogue AP, which in turn captures the data and forwards it to the legitimate AP, as shown in Figure 39-24. Return traffic from the legitimate AP is sent to the rogue AP, captured, and then forwarded to the unsuspecting user. The attacker can steal the user's passwords and personal information, gain access to their device, and compromise the system.

Defeating an attack like an MITM attack depends on the sophistication of the WLAN infrastructure and the vigilance in monitoring activity on the network. The process begins with identifying legitimate devices on the WLAN. To do this, users must be authenticated. After all of the legitimate devices are known, the network can be monitored for abnormal devices or traffic.

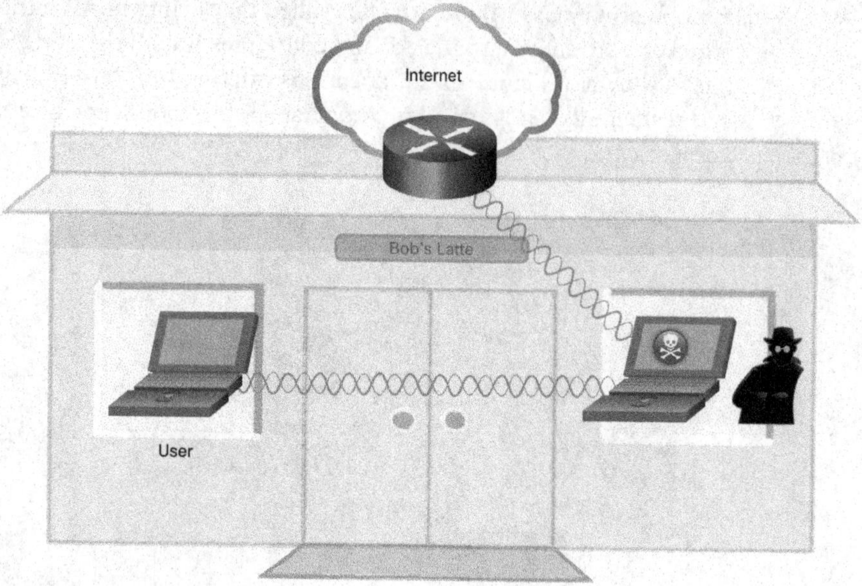

Figure 39-24 Example of a Rogue AP

Interactive Graphic

Check Your Understanding—WLAN Threats (39.6.6)

Refer to the online course to complete this activity.

Video

Video—Secure WLANs (39.6.7)

The previous topic explained the WLAN threats. What can you do to secure the WLAN?

Refer to the online course to view this video.

SSID Cloaking and MAC Address Filtering (39.6.8)

Wireless signals can travel through solid matter, such as ceilings, floors, walls, outside of the home, or office space. Without stringent security measures in place, installing a WLAN can be the equivalent of putting Ethernet ports everywhere, even outside.

To address the threats of keeping wireless intruders out and protecting data, two early security features were used and are still available on most routers and APs: SSID cloaking and MAC address filtering.

SSID Cloaking

APs and some wireless routers allow the SSID beacon frame to be disabled, as shown in Figure 39-25. Wireless clients must manually configure the SSID to connect to the network.

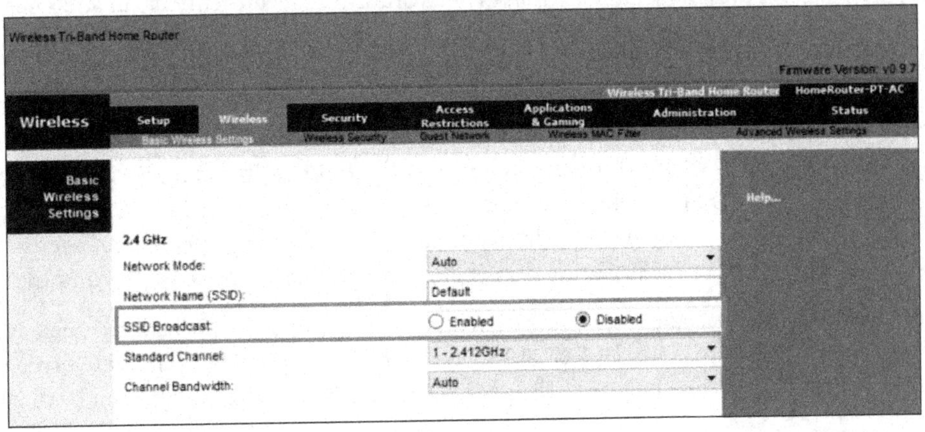

Figure 39-25 Example of Disabled SSID Broadcast

MAC Addresses Filtering

An administrator can manually permit or deny clients wireless access based on their physical MAC hardware address. In Figure 39-26, the router is configured to permit two MAC addresses. Devices with different MAC addresses will not be able to join the 2.4 GHz WLAN.

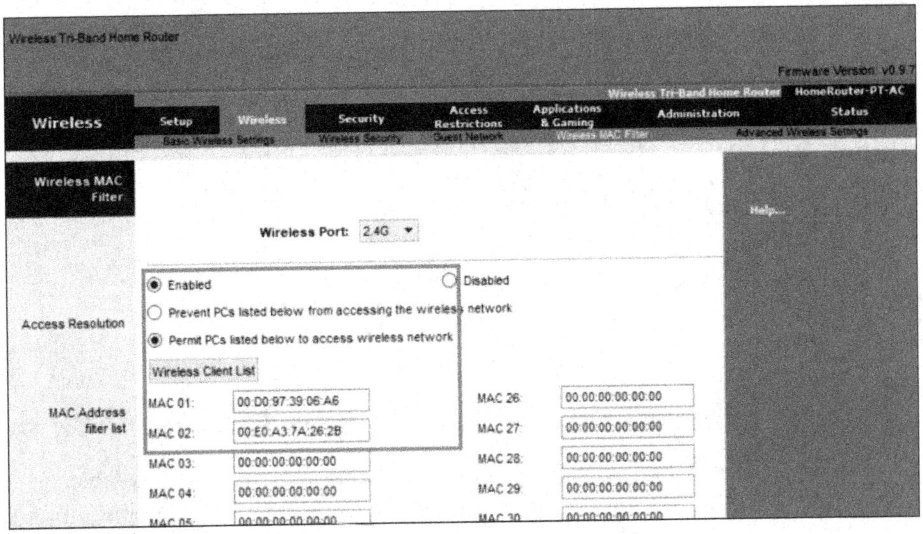

Figure 39-26 Example of Filtering MAC Addresses

802.11 Original Authentication Methods (39.6.9)

Although SSID cloaking and MAC address filtering would deter most users, the reality is that neither feature would deter a crafty intruder. SSIDs are easily discovered even if APs do not broadcast them, and MAC addresses can be spoofed. The best way to secure a wireless network is to use authentication and encryption systems.

Two types of authentication were introduced with the original 802.11 standard:

- **Open system authentication**—Any wireless client will easily be able to connect. Open system authentication should only be used in situations where security is of no concern, such as those providing free Internet access like cafes, hotels, and in remote areas. The wireless client is responsible for providing security, such as by using a virtual private network (VPN) to connect securely. VPNs provide authentication and encryption services. VPNs are beyond the scope of this topic.
- **Shared key authentication**—This provides mechanisms such as WEP, WPA, WPA2, and WPA3 to authenticate and encrypt data between a wireless client and AP. However, the password must be pre-shared between both parties to connect.

The chart in Figure 39-27 summarizes these authentication methods.

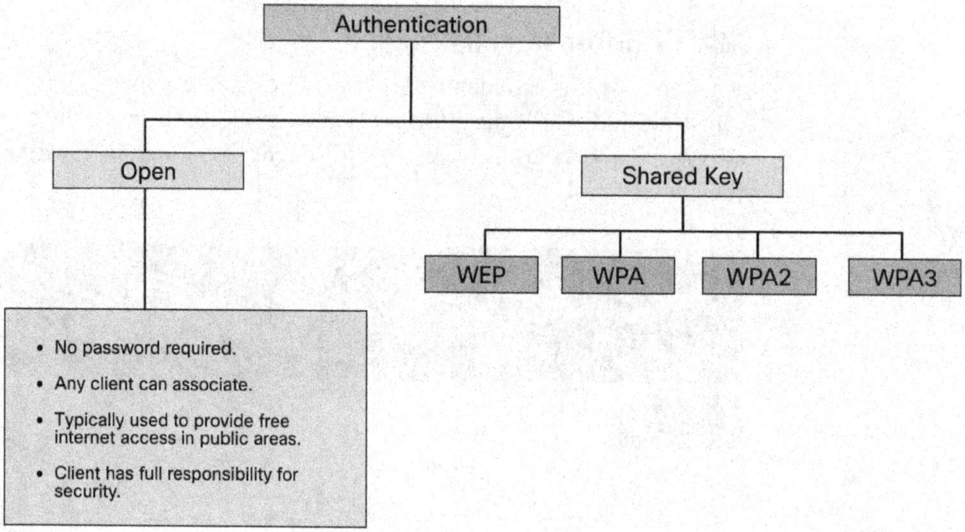

Figure 39-27 802.11 Authentication Methods

Shared Key Authentication Methods (39.6.10)

There are four shared key authentication techniques available, as described in Table 39-7. Until the availability of WPA3 devices becomes ubiquitous, wireless networks should use the WPA2 standard.

Table 39-7 802.11 Shared Key Authentication Techniques

Authentication Method	Description
Wired Equivalent Privacy (WEP)	The original 802.11 specification designed to secure the data using the Rivest Cipher 4 (RC4) encryption method with a static key. However, the key never changes when exchanging packets. This makes it easy to hack. WEP is no longer recommended and should never be used.
Wi-Fi Protected Access (WPA)	A Wi-Fi Alliance standard that uses WEP, but secures the data with the much stronger Temporal Key Integrity Protocol (TKIP) encryption algorithm. TKIP changes the key for each packet, making it much more difficult to hack.
WPA2	WPA2 is the current industry standard for securing wireless networks. It uses the Advanced Encryption Standard (AES) for encryption. AES is currently considered the strongest encryption protocol.
WPA3	This is the next generation of Wi-Fi security. All WPA3-enabled devices use the latest security methods, disallow outdated legacy protocols, and require the use of Protected Management Frames (PMF). However, devices with WPA3 are not yet readily available.

Authenticating a Home User (39.6.11)

Home routers typically have two choices for authentication: WPA and WPA2. WPA2 is the stronger of the two. Figure 39-28 shows the option to select one of two WPA2 authentication methods:

- **Personal**—Intended for home or small office networks, users authenticate using a pre-shared key (PSK). Wireless clients authenticate with the wireless router using a pre-shared password. No special authentication server is required.
- **Enterprise**—Intended for enterprise networks but requires a Remote Authentication Dial-In User Service (RADIUS) authentication server. Although more complicated to set up, it provides additional security. The device must be authenticated by the RADIUS server and then users must authenticate using the 802.1X standard, which uses the Extensible Authentication Protocol (EAP) for authentication.

In Figure 39-28, the administrator is configuring the wireless router with WPA2-Personal authentication on the 2.4 GHz band.

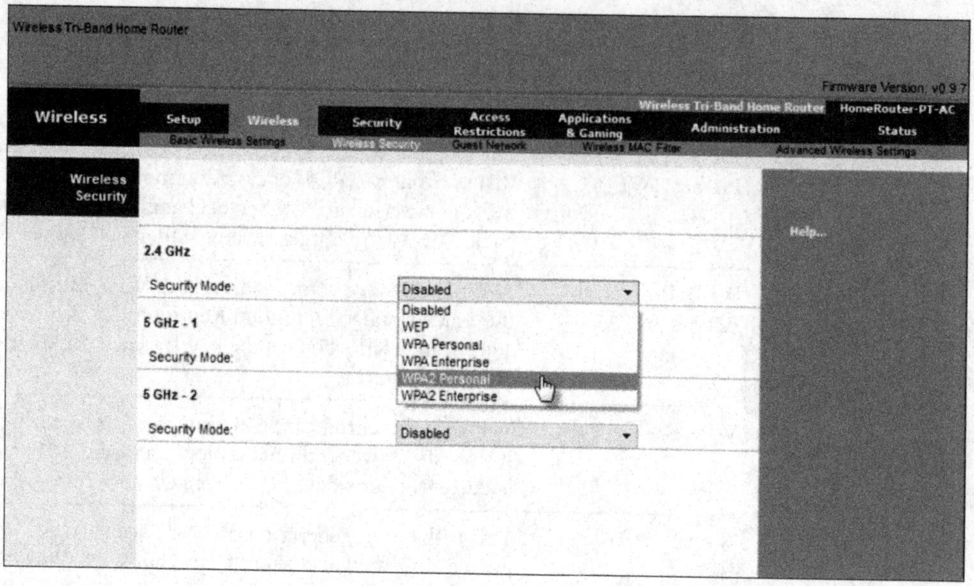

Figure 39-28 Example of Configuring WPA2-Personal Authentication

Encryption Methods (39.6.12)

Encryption is used to protect data. If an intruder has captured encrypted data, they would not be able to decipher it in any reasonable amount of time.

The WPA and WPA2 standards use the following encryption protocols:

- **Temporal Key Integrity Protocol (TKIP)**—TKIP is the encryption method used by WPA. It provides support for legacy WLAN equipment by addressing the original flaws associated with the 802.11 WEP encryption method. It makes use of WEP, but encrypts the Layer 2 payload using TKIP, and carries out a Message Integrity Check (MIC) in the encrypted packet to ensure the message has not been altered.
- **Advanced Encryption Standard (AES)**—AES is the encryption method used by WPA2. It is the preferred method because it is a far stronger method of encryption. It uses the Counter Cipher Mode with Block Chaining Message Authentication Code Protocol (CCMP) that allows destination hosts to recognize if the encrypted and non-encrypted bits have been altered.

In Figure 39-29, the administrator is configuring the wireless router to use WPA2 with AES encryption on the 2.4 GHz band.

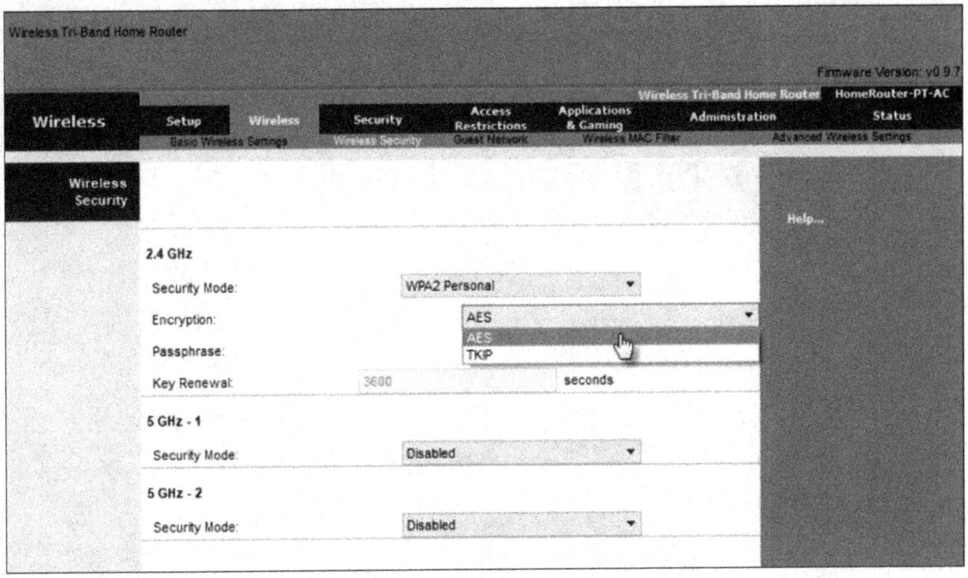

Figure 39-29 Example of Configuring AES Encryption for WPA2

Authentication in the Enterprise (39.6.13)

In networks that have stricter security requirements, an additional authentication or login is required to grant wireless clients such access. The Enterprise security mode choice requires an Authentication, Authorization, and Accounting (AAA) RADIUS server.

- **RADIUS Server IP address**—This is the reachable address of the RADIUS server.
- **UDP port numbers**—Officially assigned UDP ports 1812 for RADIUS Authentication, and 1813 for RADIUS Accounting, but can also operate using UDP ports 1645 and 1646, as shown in Figure 39-30.
- **Shared key**—Used to authenticate the AP with the RADIUS server.

In Figure 39-30, the administrator is configuring the wireless router with WPA2-Enterprise authentication using AES encryption. The RADIUS server IPv4 address is configured as well with a strong password to be used between the wireless router and the RADIUS server.

The shared key is not a parameter that must be configured on a wireless client. It is only required on the AP to authenticate with the RADIUS server. User authentication and authorization are handled by the 802.1X standard, which provides a centralized, server-based authentication of end users.

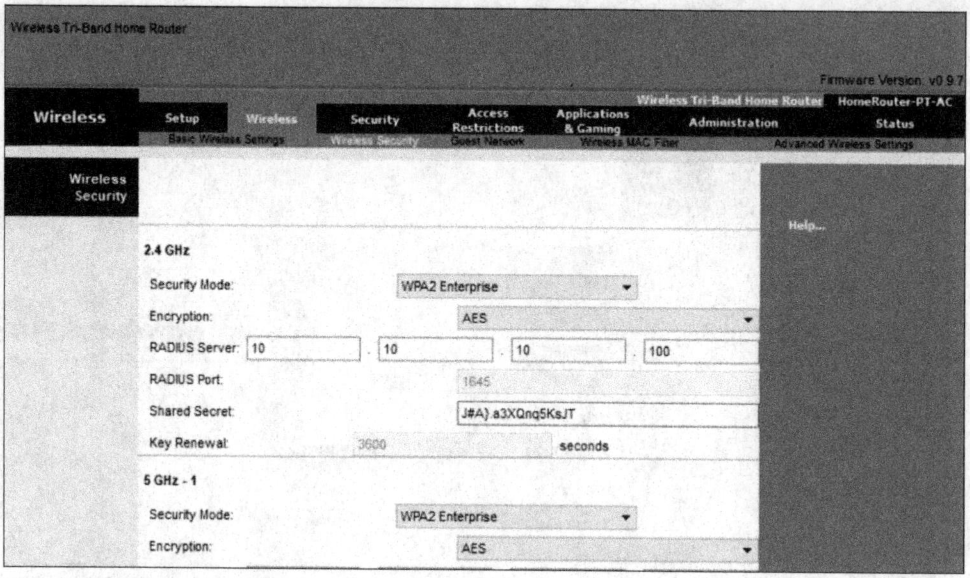

Figure 39-30 Example of Configuring WPA2-Enterprise Authentication

The 802.1X login process uses EAP to communicate with the AP and RADIUS server. EAP is a framework for authenticating network access. It can provide a secure authentication mechanism and negotiate a secure private key, which can then be used for a wireless encryption session using TKIP or AES encryption.

WPA3 (39.6.14)

At the time of this writing, devices that support WPA3 authentication were not readily available. However, WPA2 is no longer considered secure. WPA3, if available, is the recommended 802.11 authentication method. WPA3 includes four applications.

WPA3-Personal

In WPA2-Personal, threat actors can listen in on the "handshake" between a wireless client and the AP and use a brute force attack to try and guess the PSK. WPA3-Personal thwarts this attack by using Simultaneous Authentication of Equals (SAE), a feature specified in IEEE 802.11-2016. The PSK is never exposed, making it impossible for the threat actor to guess.

WPA3-Enterprise

WPA3-Enterprise still uses 802.1X/EAP authentication. However, it requires the use of a 192-bit cryptographic suite and eliminates the mixing of security protocols for previous 802.11 standards. WPA3-Enterprise adheres to the Commercial National

Security Algorithm (CNSA) Suite, which is commonly used in high-security Wi-Fi networks.

Open Networks

Open networks in WPA2 send user traffic in unauthenticated, clear text. In WPA3, open or public Wi-Fi networks still do not use any authentication. However, they do use Opportunistic Wireless Encryption (OWE) to encrypt all wireless traffic.

IoT Onboarding

Although WPA2 included Wi-Fi Protected Setup (WPS) to quickly onboard devices without configuring them first, WPS is vulnerable to a variety of attacks and is not recommended. Furthermore, IoT devices are typically headless, meaning they have no built-in GUI for configuration, and need an easy way to connect to the wireless network. The Device Provisioning Protocol (DPP) was designed to address this need. Each headless device has a hardcoded public key. The key is typically stamped on the outside of the device or its packaging as a Quick Response (QR) code. The network administrator can scan the QR code and quickly onboard the device. Although not strictly part of the WPA3 standard, DPP will replace WPS over time.

Interactive Graphic

Check Your Understanding—Secure WLANs (39.6.15)

Refer to the online course to complete this activity.

Packet Tracer Activity

Packet Tracer—Configure Basic Wireless Security (39.6.16)

In this activity, you will configure wireless security using WPA2-Personal.

Refer to the online course to complete this Packet Tracer.

Network Security Summary (39.7)

The following is a summary of each topic in the chapter and some questions for your reflection.

What Did I Learn in This Chapter? (39.7.1)

- **Security Foundations**—The cybersecurity cube provides a useful way to think about protecting data. The first dimension of the cube identifies the goals of confidentiality, integrity, and availability (CIA). Confidentiality concerns preventing disclosure of information to unauthorized persons. Integrity refers to the

accuracy, consistency, and trustworthiness of data. Data states are in transit, at rest in storage, or in process. The pillars of defense are people, technology, and policies and practices. Confidentiality, integrity, and availability are also referred to as the CIA triad.

Data integrity ensures that data is unaltered by unauthorized entities while it is captured, stored, retrieved, updated, and transferred. Methods used to ensure data integrity include hashing, data validation checks, data consistency checks, and access controls.

Availability refers to the need to make data accessible to all authorized users whenever they need it. Cyberattacks and system failures can disconnect users from the data they need. Availability can be ensured by properly maintaining equipment, keeping software and systems up to date, testing backups and fallbacks, implementing new technologies, monitoring network activity, and analyzing vulnerabilities to detect threats.

- **Access Control**—Physical access controls prevent unauthorized users from physically accessing networks, data, and equipment. Physical access controls determine who, where, and when people can enter or exit a facility. Physical access controls include guards, perimeter fences, motion detectors, device locks, and locked doors that can only be accessed with swipe cards or combinations. Additional physical security measures are guard dogs, video cameras, and alarms.

  Logical access controls are the hardware and software solutions used to manage access to resources and systems. These technology-based solutions include tools and protocols that computer systems use for identification and authentication, authorization, and accounting (AAA). Examples of these controls are encryption, smart cards with embedded chips, passwords, biometrics, access control lists (ACLs), firewalls, and intrusion detection systems.

  Administrative access controls are the policies and procedures defined by organizations to implement and enforce all aspects of controlling unauthorized access. Examples are approved policies, defined procedures, background checks, and data classification.

  Administrative access controls involve three security services: authentication, authorization, and accounting (AAA). Authentication is the verification of the identity of each user, to prevent unauthorized access. Authorization services determine which resources users can access, along with the operations that users can perform, and even when they can perform them. Accounting keeps track of what users do on the network, such as what they access, when they access it, and what they do with it. This information is compiled in logs.

  Identification enforces the rules established by the authorization policy. Unique identifiers are usernames and passwords, personal identification numbers, or biometrics such as fingerprints, retina scans, or voice recognition.

Federated identity management (FIM) refers to multiple enterprises that let their users use the same identification credentials to gain access to the networks of all enterprises in the group. While FIM provides convenience to users and administrators, if the system is exploited by hackers, they will have access to many systems or applications instead of just one.

Password policies help ensure that passwords meet length and complexity requirements. Passwords should be at least 8 to 10 characters. Passwords should include a mix of upper- and lowercase characters, numbers, and symbols.

Combining other means of identity with passwords, such as multi-factor authentication, is increasingly popular.

Accounting traces an action back to a person or process. Accounting then collects this information and reports the usage data. The organization can use this data for such purposes as auditing or billing.

- **Defending Systems and Devices**—An organization needs a good administrator to configure operating systems to protect against outside threats. A systematic approach is required to establish security monitoring procedures, evaluate software updates, and install updates using a documented plan. Baselines help to indicate system compromise when performance deviates significantly from the baseline.

  Fileless malware attacks are difficult to detect and leave no footprint. They can exploit scriptable command shells. Python, Bash, and Visual Basic for Applications (VBA) scripts can be malicious.

  To stay ahead of cybercriminals, software should be proactively patched to eliminate vulnerabilities. Operating systems regularly check for patches, but administrators should evaluate patches before they are installed. Automated patch management systems provide administrators with control over date and time of updates and reporting about the status of systems and patches.

  Host-based endpoint security includes host-based firewalls that can block incoming and outgoing traffic. Host intrusion detection systems (HIDSs) monitor systems and login security and system events. Host intrusion prevention systems (HIPSs) detect malicious activity and can send you an alarm, log the malicious activity, reset the connection, and/or drop the packets. Endpoint detection and response (EDR) is an integrated security solution that continuously monitors and collects data from endpoint devices. Data loss prevention (DLP) tools provide a centralized way to ensure that sensitive data is not lost, misused, or accessed by unauthorized users. Next-generation firewalls (NGFWs) combine traditional firewalls with other network-device-filtering functions.

  Data can be protected through host encryption by Windows Encrypting File System (EFS) that can encrypt files or entire drives (full-disk encryption—FDE)

with BitLocker. BitLocker requires a Trusted Platform Module (TPM) in BIOS. BitLocker To Go is a tool that encrypts removable drives.

Boot integrity ensures that the system can be trusted and has not been altered while the operating system loads. Secure Boot is a security standard to ensure that a device boots using trusted software.

Apple provides system hardware and macOS security features that offer robust endpoint protection. The Mac hardware platform has enhanced security features such as a special security processor, boot integrity, and a dedicated AES encryption engine. Apple Data Protection and FileVault data storage encryption are supported by the hardware-based AES encryption engine. Biometric data is processed in security hardware, isolating it from the operating system. Apple also includes a Find My Device feature, XProtect antimalware technology, a Malware Removal Tool (MRT), and Gatekeeper, which ensures that only authentic, digitally-signed Apple software can be installed.

Physical protection of devices includes controlling access to equipment and facilities, using cable locks, keyed or cipher door locks, and device inventory and tracking with radio frequency identification (RFID) systems.

- **Antimalware Protection**—Various network security devices are required to protect the network perimeter from outside access. These devices could include a hardened router that is providing VPN services, a next-generation firewall, an IPS appliance, and an AAA services server. However, securing an internal LAN is nearly as important as securing the outside network perimeter. Endpoints and the network infrastructure require protection.

  There are three types of antimalware programs: signature-based, heuristics-based, and behavior-based. Host-based antivirus protection is also known as agent-based. Agent-based antivirus runs on every protected machine. Agentless antivirus protection performs scans on hosts from a centralized system. Host-based firewalls restrict incoming and outgoing connections to connections initiated by that host only. Examples are Windows Defender Firewall with Advanced Security and iptables and TCP Wrappers on Linux.

  Protecting endpoints in a borderless network can be accomplished using network-based as well as host-based techniques. Devices and techniques that implement host protections at the network level include Cisco Secure Endpoint, Cisco Secure Email, Cisco Umbrella, and Network Admission Control (NAC) systems. These technologies work together with host-based systems to secure the enterprise.

- **Firewalls and Host-Based Intrusion Prevention**—Firewalls resist network attacks, serve as the only point between internal and external networks, and

enforce access control policies. They protect hosts from exposure, sanitize protocol flow, and block malicious data from servers and clients. Firewalls are ineffective if misconfigured or out of date. They can slow networks and some data cannot be passed over them.

There are various types of firewalls. Packet filtering (stateless) firewalls are usually part of a router firewall. They permit or deny traffic based on Layer 3 and Layer 4 information. Stateful firewalls are the most versatile and the most common firewall technologies in use. Stateful filtering is a firewall architecture that is classified at the network layer. It also analyzes traffic at OSI Layer 4 and Layer 5. An application gateway firewall (proxy firewall) filters information at Layers 3, 4, 5, and 7 of the OSI reference model. Next-generation firewalls (NGFWs) go beyond stateful firewalls. Transparent firewalls filter traffic between two bridged interfaces. Hybrid firewalls combine attributes of the other firewall types.

Packet filtering firewalls are usually part of a router firewall. They use simple permit or deny rules, have low impact on network performance, are easy to implement, and provide initial security at the network layer. They are susceptible to IP spoofing, may not be effective against fragmented packets, and can use complex ACLs that are difficult to use and maintain. Stateful firewalls are often the primary means of defense by filtering unwanted, unnecessary, and undesirable traffic. They are generally more effective than stateless firewalls. However, they cannot prevent application layer attacks, are less effective against stateless protocols, have difficulty tracking dynamic port negotiation, and do not use authentication.

Host-based personal firewalls are standalone software programs that control traffic entering or leaving a computer. Host-based firewalls may use a set of predefined policies, or profiles, to control packets entering and leaving a computer. They also may have rules that can be directly modified or created to control access based on addresses, protocols, and ports. Examples include Windows Defender Firewalls, iptables, nftables, and TCP Wrappers.

Antimalware protection consists of antivirus, adware, phishing, and spyware protection. Some antimalware software combines features of the different types.

- **Secure Wireless Access**—Wireless networks are susceptible to a number of threats, including interception of data, wireless intruders, DoS attacks, and rogue APs. DoS attacks can result from improperly configured devices, malicious user interference, and accidental interference. Rogue APs can be used by an attacker to capture MAC addresses, capture data packets, gain access to network resources, or launch a man-in-the-middle (MitM) attack. In an MitM attack, the hacker is positioned between two legitimate entities in order to read or modify the data that passes between the two parties.

In SSID cloaking, the SSID beacon frame is disabled. For MAC address filtering, an administrator can manually permit or deny clients wireless access based on their physical MAC hardware address.

Open system authentication should only be used in situations where security is of no concern. Shared key authentication provides mechanisms such as WEP, WPA, WPA2, and WPA3 to authenticate and encrypt data between a wireless client and AP. WEP and WPA authentication is outdated and insecure. WPA2 is recommended at a minimum, with WPA3 preferred when it becomes available.

Personal authentication requires configuration of a username and pre-shared password. Enterprise authentication requires the use of a RADIUS authentication server using 802.1x with Extensible Authentication Protocol (EAP).

Encryption protects data by making it unreadable if intercepted. WPA2 uses Temporal Key Integrity Protocol (TKIP) or Advanced Encryption Standard (AES).

WPA3, when available, is the recommended 802.11 authentication method. It includes WPA3-Personal, WPA3-Enterprise, Open Networks, and IoT onboarding. WPA3 open or public Wi-Fi networks still do not use any authentication. However, they do use Opportunistic Wireless Encryption (OWE) to encrypt all wireless traffic. For IoT onboarding, WPA3 uses Device Provisioning Protocol (DPP) to securely onboard IoT devices.

Reflection Questions (39.7.2)

My friend, Lara, has been very busy working at the college. She created a troubleshooting guide for new help desk technicians, then worked on a cybersecurity awareness campaign to educate all college users. Finally, she helped review and develop security policies to secure the college and its users.

As you can see, there are a lot of things that a help desk technician must know. But that is exciting because there is always something new to learn. Can you be a practical help desk technician on a team in an IT department?

Practice

The following Packet Tracer activities provide practice with the topics introduced in this chapter.

Packet Tracer Activity

Packet Tracer Activities

Packet Tracer—Configure Access Control (39.2.14)

Packet Tracer—Configure Basic Wireless Security (39.6.16)

Check Your Understanding Questions

Complete all the review questions listed here to test your understanding of the topics and concepts in this chapter. Appendix A, "Answers to 'Check Your Understanding' Questions," lists the answers.

1. What is the level of need for data integrity in an e-commerce organization?

   a. Low
   b. Mid
   c. High
   d. Critical

2. Which three solutions are examples of logical access control? (Choose three.)

   a. Firewall
   b. Access control list
   c. Biometrics
   d. Fence
   e. Laptop lock
   f. Swipe card

3. What is the purpose of using the Windows BitLocker To Go tool?

   a. To encrypt removable drives
   b. To reformat removable drives
   c. To manage partitions on removable drives
   d. To manage safely inserting and removing removable drives

4. Which Apple macOS security feature prevents the execution of malware through signature-based malware detection?

   a. XProtect
   b. MRT
   c. Gatekeeper
   d. Security-focused hardware

5. Which type of firewall will inspect and filter network traffic based on OSI model Layer 3 and Layer 4 information?

   a. Packet filtering
   b. Stateful firewall
   c. Application gateway firewall
   d. Next-generation firewall

6. Which statement describes a TCP Wrappers host-based firewall?

   a. It is a firewall that uses a profile-based approach to firewall functionality.
   b. It is an application that allows Linux system administrators to configure network access rules that are part of the Linux kernel Netfilter modules.
   c. It is a firewall application that uses a simple virtual machine in the Linux kernel.
   d. It is a rule-based access control and logging system for Linux.

7. Which authentication method uses AES for encryption?

   a. WEP
   b. WPA
   c. WPA2
   d. WPA3-Enterprise

8. Which LAN authentication method is recommended for home or small office networks?

   a. WPA-Personal
   b. WPA-Enterprise
   c. WPA2-Personal
   d. WPA2-Enterprise

9. Which authentication method in WPA3 improves the onboarding process for IoT devices to join wireless networks?

   a. DPP
   b. WPS
   c. CCMP
   d. EAP

10. What statement describes the principle of confidentiality in the CIA information security triad?

    a. Authorized users must have uninterrupted access to important resources and data.
    b. Data must be protected from unauthorized alteration.
    c. Only authorized individuals, entities, or processes can access sensitive information.
    d. Redundant services, gateways, and links must be implemented.

11. What statement describes the principle of integrity in the CIA information security triad?

    a. Authorized users must have uninterrupted access to important resources and data.
    b. Data must be protected from unauthorized alteration.
    c. Only authorized individuals, entities, or processes can access sensitive information.
    d. Redundant services, gateways, and links must be implemented.

APPENDIX A

Answers to the "Check Your Understanding" Questions

Chapter 1

1. B. Availability is the likelihood that the network is available for use when it is required. Scalability indicates how easily the network can accommodate more users and data transmission requirements. Reliability indicates the dependability of the components that make up the network, such as the routers, switches, PCs, and servers, and is often measured as a probability of failure or as the mean time between failures (MTBF). Usability is a software characteristic and not a network characteristic.

2. B. The Internet is an interconnection of networks.

3. B. A binary value has two different values or states, 0 and 1. This is similar to a light switch that has two different states, off and on.

4. A. Media refers to the physical medium on which the signals are transmitted. This can be over a wired or wireless medium.

5. A. An actuator is part of a device that helps create physical movement by converting energy, such as electricity, into mechanical force.

6. A, D, F. Media refers to the physical medium on which the signals are transmitted. Examples of media are copper wire, fiber-optic cable, and electromagnetic waves through the air.

7. D. The Internet is not owned by any individual or group. The Internet is a worldwide collection of interconnected networks (internetwork or Internet for short), cooperating with each other to exchange information using common standards.

8. A. Radio frequency identification (RFID) tags can be placed in or on objects to track them or monitor sensors for many conditions.

9. C. A byte or octet consists of 8 bits.

10. A, B. A bit consists of two values, a 0 and a 1. A bit is used to represent one of two discrete or different states.

11. A. Kbps or Kb/s is used to indicate kilobits or thousands of bits per second.

12. B. To access online shopping or any service connected to the Internet, the home user must also have access to the Internet.

Chapter 2

1. B. In a peer-to-peer (P2P) network, a device can be both a client and a server simultaneously. The device can act as a client in requesting information and at the same time act as a server providing information.

2. A, D. Data is typically originated from an end device, such as a PC or smartphone. The end device is what allows people to connect to the network and the Internet.

3. A. Digital Subscriber Line is used to provide high-speed network connectivity to an ISP using existing telephone lines.

4. C. Many remote areas do not have access to wired Internet services such as DSL or cable. Cellular coverage might also be difficult. Satellite, including low earth orbit satellites, can be a good option for remote areas.
5. C. One of the responsibilities of an Internet service provider is to provide Internet connectivity to end users, including homes and businesses.
6. A. Intermediary devices include all devices between the two end devices exchanging data over the network. This includes firewalls, routers, and switches.
7. C. A peer-to-peer network can have many uses, including sharing an attached printer with other users.
8. C. A server is an end device that is responsible for responding to requests from clients. An example is a web server that provides data to clients that make up the web page.
9. C. A peer-to-peer network can be quickly and easily created.
10. A. P2P applications require that each end device provide a user interface and run a background service. A P2P application allows a device to act as both a client and a server within the same network. A device can be a client, a server, or both.

Chapter 3

1. D. Tethering allows a mobile device to connect to another mobile device or computer by sharing the network connection. Tethering can also be performed with a Wi-Fi connection or a cable connection such as USB.
2. C. Bluetooth technology provides a simple way for mobile devices to connect to each other and to wireless accessories over short distances within 100 meters.
3. B. Bluetooth is an easy and convenient method to allow your cell phone to be used as a hand-free device by connecting to wireless earphones or an external speaker.
4. C. A wireless LAN using a wireless access point would be required for the Wi-Fi capability of the tablet to connect to the Internet.
5. B. Near Field Communication (NFC) is a wireless communication technology that enables data to be exchanged by devices that are in very close proximity to each other, usually less than a few centimeters. For example, NFC can be used to connect a smartphone and a payment system.
6. B. A device can use Bluetooth to communicate with another device that has Internet access. This is known as tethering.
7. A, C. A mobile device typically can use Wi-Fi and cellular for Internet connectivity. Most mobile devices are Wi-Fi enabled, but many mobile devices, such as tablets, may not be enabled for cellular.
8. A. Near Field Communication is a wireless communication technology that enables data to be exchanged by devices that are in very close proximity to each other, usually less than a few centimeters. For example, NFC can be used to connect a smartphone and a payment system.
9. A. The Global Positioning System uses satellites to transmit signals that cover the globe. The smartphone can receive these signals and calculate the phone's location to an accuracy of within 10 meters.

10. B, D. Connecting to a secured wireless network requires knowing both the SSID of the wireless LAN and the password. These are both typically associated with the wireless access point.

11. B. Bluetooth is a low-power, short-range wireless technology that is intended to replace wired connectivity for accessories such as speakers, headphones, and microphones.

Chapter 4

1. A. Wi-Fi is a suite of network protocols based on the group of IEEE 801.11 standards.

2. B. Encryption is required to prohibit users from determining the password used to connect to the wireless LAN from unauthorized users.

3. D. A LAN device such as a desktop computer, laptop, or printer can be connected to the Ethernet switch ports using an Ethernet cable.

4. A. Bluetooth uses the 2.4 GHz band. It is limited to low-speed, short-range communications, but has the advantage of being able to communicate with many peripheral devices at the same time.

5. B. A guest SSID is a special SSID coverage area that allows open access but restricts that access to using the Internet only.

6. D. Wi-Fi can allow mobile devices and devices that cannot be easily connected to a wired Ethernet port to have access to other devices on the network and to the Internet.

7. A. On many home routers with wireless access points, the port that is used to connect to the ISP is labeled as the WAN port.

8. A. An Ethernet category 5e cable consists of four pairs of twisted wires for a total of eight wires.

9. A. SSID broadcast is enabled by default on most wireless routers. This setting automatically advertises the Wi-Fi network to nearby devices.

10. A. The SSID is a case-sensitive, alphanumeric string that contains up to 32 characters.

Chapter 5

1. B. The OSI physical layer is responsible for transmitting the bits as physical signals over the wired or wireless medium.

2. B. Network protocols define the rules that govern the communications between the sender of the information and the final destination.

3. D. A protocol is a set of rules that governs communications. Each layer has protocols that are related to the function and operations of that specific layer of the reference model.

4. D. The transport layer, specifically the TCP and UDP protocols, is responsible for segmenting and reassembling data transmitted over the network.

5. C. Protocols define the rules that govern communications. The rules may include how the data is organized, the timing of the messages, if there are any required responses and timeouts, and the size of the message.

6. A. When a protocol becomes an approved standard by an organization such as IETF or IEEE, the protocol operates the same no matter which vendor is implementing the protocol.
7. D, E, F. The upper three layers of the OSI model (application, presentation, and session, from top down) are the same as the TCP/IP model's single application layer.
8. C. The IETF is responsible for creating and approving protocols for the TCP/IP protocol suite. The document and the process are known as RFC (Request for Comments).
9. A, C. The physical and data link layers of the OSI model are equivalent to the network access layer of the TCP/IP model.

Chapter 6

1. B. Fiber-optic is the best choice when support for high-speed connections over long distances is needed.
2. A, C. Copper cabling and fiber-optic cabling are the most common types of media in networks. UTP is the most common cabling used for connecting end-user devices to the LAN.
3. B. UTP (unshielded twisted-pair) cabling is the most common type of cabling used for connecting end-user devices to the LAN.
4. B, D, E. When choosing any wired or wireless medium, it is import to consider the data transfer rate required, the distance the data needs to travel, and if the medium will be susceptible to any type of interference.
5. D. The photo shows an example of a fiber-optic cable. The type of connector shown in this example is ST or Straight Tip. Two cables are shown. One fiber transmits data in one direction and the other fiber transmits data in the opposite direction.
6. A, C, F. Because fiber-optic cables use light instead of electricity, it is the best choice when needing to support high-speed connections over long distances with no electrical interference.
7. A. Copper media is used for transmitting encoded data as electrical signals. Examples are shielded twisted-pair, unshielded twisted-pair, and coaxial cables.
8. A, C. Copper media is used for transmitting encoded data as electrical signals. Examples are shielded twisted-pair, unshielded twisted-pair, and coaxial cables.
9. C. Fiber-optic cables are used for transmitting encoded data as pulses of light.
10. D. Twisted-pair, typically UTP, is a common choice for connecting end-user devices to the LAN. UTP cables are both inexpensive and easy to install.
11. A. Twisting the pairs of cable helps reduce the possibility of electrical interference.

Chapter 7

1. D. The switch acts similar to a hub and forwards the frame out all ports. The frame is not forwarded back out the incoming port because that would cause duplicate frames.
2. C. Every Ethernet switch maintains a MAC address table, which is a combination of learned source MAC addresses and incoming port numbers.
3. D. An Ethernet switch adds information to its MAC address table based on the source MAC address and incoming port number.

4. D. The FCS (Frame Check Sequence) field is used by switches and end devices to determine if the frame has any errors caused during transmission.

5. D. An Ethernet switch builds its MAC address table based on the source MAC address and incoming port number. It uses this information to forward frames out that port that have a destination MAC address matching the MAC address in the table.

6. E. An Ethernet switch builds its MAC address table based on the source MAC address and incoming port number.

7. C. Encapsulation is the process of prepending additional protocol information.

8. C. The switch examines the destination MAC address of the frame, 12-34-56-78-9A-BE, which entered the switch on port 4. This address does not exist in the switch's MAC address table, so the frame is forwarded out all ports except the incoming port 4.

9. A, D, E. An IEEE 802.3 Ethernet frame consists of a preamble and SFD, a destination MAC (physical) address, a source MAC (physical) address, a Type/Length field, data, and the FCS (Frame Check Sequence).

10. A. When a host receives an Ethernet frame that has a unicast destination MAC address that does not match the MAC address of its own NIC, the NIC will discard the frame.

11. A. An Ethernet switch builds its MAC address table based on the source MAC address and incoming port number. It uses this information to forward frames out that port that have a destination MAC address matching the MAC address in the table.

Chapter 8

1. B. An IPv4 address must be unique within the local network. Originally, IPv4 addresses were to be globally unique, but due to IPv4 address depletion, that could no longer be continued. Private IPv4 addresses and NAT were developed to alleviate this issue.

2. A. An IPv4 address is made up of four 8-bit octets for a total of 32 bits.

3. B, D. An IPv4 address consists of a network portion and a host portion determined by the subnet mask. The number of leftmost 1s bits in the subnet mask indicates the network portion and the remainder of the subnet mask is all 0 bits, which represents the host portion of the address.

4. C. The subnet mask determines the network and host portions of an IPv4 address. The number of leftmost 1s bits in the subnet mask indicate the network portion and the remainder of the subnet mask is all 0 bits, which represents the host portion of the address.

5. A, C, D. Any device with a NIC (network interface card) and connected to an IP network must have an IP address to communicate with other IP devices.

6. B. A physical network can connect devices from different IPv4 logical networks. A router is required for devices on different IPv4 networks to be able to communicate.

7. C. An IPv4 address consists of 32 bits.

8. D. The 255.255.255.0 subnet mask indicates that the first 24 bits (three octets) of the address 172.16.34.10 is the network portion. This means that the network address is 172.16.34.0 255.255.255.0.

9. B, C. An IPv4 address is hierarchical in the sense that it has a network portion and a host portion. A network address has multiple host addresses associated with it. IPv4 is a logical addressing scheme because it is assigned via software and typically changes from one network to another.

10. A, C. The 255.255.255.0 subnet mask indicates that the first 24 bits (three octets) of the address is the network portion, or 192.168.10. Both 192.168.10.2 and 192.168.10.56 have those 24 bits (three octets) in common.

11. A. Routing is required for devices on different IPv4 networks to be able to communicate, whether they are on the same or different physical networks.

Chapter 9

1. C. The 32-bit subnet mask is used with a 32-bit IPv4 address to determine the IPv4 network address of the device. The IPv4 address of the device is logically ANDed, bit by bit, with its subnet mask to determine the network address to which the device is associated.

2. A. Subnetting a network has several purposes, including limiting broadcasts to that subnet. A router is used to connect subnets and by default does not forward broadcasts. Note that the terms *subnet* and *network* are used interchangeably.

3. C. A broadcast message sent to a remote network is known as a directed broadcast. These types of broadcasts are not common. Multicast addresses are typically used to reach multiple devices on a remote network.

4. B. An address beginning with 169.254.x.x is a special IPv4 link-local address. A device typically gives itself an address with these first two octets (bytes) when it does not receive an IPv4 address from a DHCP server. This is known as an Automatic Private IP Addressing (APIPA) address. Note that IPv6 link-local addresses have a specific purpose in IPv6 networks.

5. A, D, E. These three addresses are private IPv4 addresses, defined by RFC 1918. They fall within the following ranges, respectively:
   - 10.0.0.0/8 IP addresses: 10.0.0.0–10.255.255.255
   - 172.16.0.0/12 IP addresses: 172.16.0.0–172.31.255.255
   - 192.168.0.0/16 IP addresses: 192.168.0.0–192.168.255.255

6. - A. 169.254.1.5 is a link-local address.
   - B. 127.0.0.1 is a loopback address.
   - C. 198.133.219.2 is a public address.
   - D. 240.2.6.255 is an experimental address.

7. A. A router is used to separate layer broadcast domains. A router is used to connect networks and by default does not forward Layer 2 (Ethernet) or Layer 3 (IP) broadcasts. Note that the terms *subnet* and *network* are used interchangeably.

8. C. IANA (Internet Assigned Numbers Authority) is responsible for the allocation of IPv4 and IPv6 addresses to RIRs, as well as the overall management of domain names and port numbers.

9. B. 224.0.0.0 through 239.255.255.255 defines the range of IPv4 multicast addresses.

10. C. 192.168.25.10 is a private IPv4 address defined by RFC 1918. Private IPv4 addresses are not routable over the Internet.

11. A. All hosts on the same network will receive broadcasts. A router is used to segment different broadcast domains.

Chapter 10

1. A. IPv6 provides a 128-bit address space of 340 undecillion addresses, compared to a 32-bit IPv4 address space of 4.29 billion addresses. In both cases, these are theoretical maximums. Not all possibilities are available to be assigned to specific devices.

2. B. IPv6 provides a 128-bit address space of 340 undecillion addresses compared to a 32-bit IPv4 address space of 4.29 billion addresses. In the early 1990s it was recognized that we would soon run out of IPv4 addresses. Since then, the combination of private IPv4 addresses and NAT has kept IPv4 going. However, due to many factors, even with these mitigation techniques, IPv4 address depletion is now becoming a bigger issue.

3. A. The letter f is the hexadecimal equivalent of 15 in decimal (or 1111 in binary).

4. A. A device is considered to be dual stacked when it is enabled for both IPv4 and IPv6 addressing. This means that the device can communicate with other devices using either protocol or both.

5. A, B. Leading zeros, and only leading zeros, can be omitted from any hextet (a segment of 16 bits, or four hexadecimal values). Any single continuous string of one or more all-zero hextets can be replaced with a single double colon (::).

6. D. Tunneling refers to encapsulating one IP packet in another IP packet. In this context, it refers to an IPv6 packet encapsulated in an IPv4 packet.

7. A. Any single continuous string of one or more all-zero hextets can be replaced with a single double colon (::).

8. C. An IPv6 address is 128 bits. This includes both the source and destination addresses.

9. A. Network Address Translation 64 (NAT64) allows IPv6-enabled devices to communicate with IPv4-enabled devices using a translation technique similar to NAT for IPv4. An IPv6 packet is translated to an IPv4 packet, and an IPv4 packet is translated to an IPv6 packet.

10. C. The only valid address is 2001:db8:0:1111::200. The addresses in options A and D are invalid because they use the double colon twice, which creates ambiguity in how many all-zero hextets exist in each group. The address in option B is invalid because it contains the letter g, which is not a valid hexadecimal digit. Also, there are currently no uses for IPv6 addresses beginning with the letter a.

11. A, D. IPv6 addresses are 128 bits in length and represented using hexadecimal digits. IPv4 addresses are 32 bits in length and represented using four groups of decimal number separated by dots (periods).

Chapter 11

1.
   - A. DHCPREQUEST
   - B. DHCPACK
   - C. DHCPDISCOVER
   - D. DHCPOFFER

2. A, E. DHCP is helpful in eliminating manual configuration errors. DHCP also reduces the burden of support staff having to manually configure IP address information on all devices.
3. D. After a host receives a DHCPOFFER message, the host replies with a DHCPREQUEST requesting the IP addressing information offered in the DHCPOFFER.
4. C. The DHCPDISCOVER message is sent as a broadcast 255.255.255.255.
5. C. The DHCP server sends a DHCPOFFER message offering IP address information.
6. A. Mobile devices are temporary and these addresses can be returned to the DHCP pool when the device is no longer connected to the network.
7. C. The first address in the DHCP pool is 192.168.0.100 and will be assigned to the first device requesting an IP address.
8. D. The destination IP address of DHCPDISCOVER messages is sent as a broadcast 255.255.255.255.
9. B. A DHCP server provides IP addressing information to hosts.
10. B, D, E. DHCPDISCOVER messages are sent by the client with the destination IP address 255.255.255.255. Broadcasts are received by all devices on the network.
11. D. A DHCPACK message is sent by the DHCP server to inform the client that it is confirming that the IP address offered is now allocated to this client.

Chapter 12

1. B. When two hosts are in the same LAN, this means they both have IP addresses on the same IP network and are connected to the Ethernet switch or series of switches. These hosts can communicate directly.
2. C. Typically, the router that connects the private enterprise network to the Internet is the device that performs NAT.
3. A. The default gateway is the IP address of the local router. The IP address of the default gateway will be on the same IP network as the IP address of the host.
4. D. The default gateway is the local router used to send packets with a destination IP address, which is on a different network than the sending host.
5. B. If a host has the wrong IP address for the default gateway, the host will not be able to communicate with hosts on other networks.
6. A, D, E. RFC 1918 defines the ranges of private addresses as 10.0.0.0 to 10.255.255.255, 172.16.0.0 to 172.31.255.255, and 192.168.0.0 to 192.168.255.255.
7. B. The purpose of NAT is to translate private IP addresses to public IP addresses for Internet-bound packets, and to translate public IP addresses to private IP addresses for packets entering from the Internet.
8. A. NAT allows one or more private IPv4 addresses to share a single public IPv4 address as those packets are forwarded to the ISP.
9. A, B, C. For a device to communicate with devices on its own network, that device must have an IP address and subnet mask. For a device to communicate with devices on other networks and the Internet, that device must also have a default gateway address.
10. A. DHCP servers within a private enterprise network, including a home wireless router, allocate private IP addresses.

11. D. A home wireless router connects the home's private network to the Internet.

Chapter 13

1. C. The Address Resolution Protocol is used when a device needs to get the MAC address associated with a known IPv4 address.

2. C. An ARP requests is sent as a Layer 2 broadcast FFFF.FFFF.FFFF. All devices on the LAN receive and process this frame, including the router. The router does not forward the broadcast out other interfaces.

3. B. An ARP request is sent as a Layer 2 broadcast FFFF.FFFF.FFFF. All devices on the LAN receive and process this frame, including the router. The router does not forward the broadcast out other interfaces.

4. C. An Ethernet switch forwards frames by examining the destination MAC address and searching for a match in its MAC address table.

5. A, E. Ethernet NIC cards have a unique MAC address used to uniquely identify the device on the LAN. Ethernet frames include both a source and destination MAC address to forward the frame from one Ethernet NIC to another Ethernet NIC on the same LAN.

6. A. Because PC1 and PC2 are on the same network, they can communicate directly without one or more routers. PC2 will respond with an ARP reply, providing PC1 with its Ethernet MAC address.

7. A. The ARP protocol is used when a device needs to get the MAC address associated with a known IPv4 address. The MAC address is used as the destination MAC address. The IPv4 address may be the destination IPv4 address if the devices are on the same network. If the destination IPv4 address is on a remote network, the IPv4 address in the ARP request is that of the sender's default gateway.

8. D. Ethernet switches flood broadcasts out all ports except the incoming port. When there are multiple switches on the LAN, all the switches receive and flood the broadcast out all ports. This ensures that all devices on the LAN receive the broadcast.

9. C. Because the destination IPv4 address is on a remote network, the IPv4 address in the ARP request will be that of the sender's default gateway, RTA. RTA will respond with an ARP reply providing its MAC address on that LAN, 00:0D:00:B4:12:F3.

10. A. An Ethernet MAC address is considered the physical address or burned-in-address (bia) because that address is physically embedded on the Ethernet NIC.

11. A, B. An Ethernet MAC address is considered a physical address or burned-in-address (bia) because that address is physically embedded on the Ethernet NIC. Ethernet frames include both a source and destination MAC address to forward the frame from one Ethernet NIC to another Ethernet NIC on the same LAN.

Chapter 14

1. B. A router examines the destination IP address of a packet to search for a match in its IP routing table. The IP routing table is used to determine to which interface to forward the packet.

2. B. If a host has the wrong default gateway, although it will still be able to communicate with hosts on its own network, it will not be

able to communicate with hosts on remote networks.

3. C. A router examines the destination IP address of a packet to search for a match in its IP routing table. The IP routing table is used to determine to which interface to forward the packet.
4. C. The default gateway address is the IPv4 address of a router on the same LAN. This IPv4 address is on the same network as the host.
5. C. Routers are used to forward packets to remote networks. A router examines the destination IP address of a packet to search for a match in its IP routing table. The IP routing table is used to determine to which interface to forward the packet.
6. B. Devices on "remote networks" have IP addresses on different or separate networks. A router is required to forward packets to remote networks.
7. B. Broadcasts are not forwarded by routers. One of the benefits of a router is that it contains broadcasts on that network.
8. A. Because the destination IP address is a broadcast, the router does not forward the packet out any other interfaces.
9. A. The router will process the frame. For example, if the frame is an ARP request, it may match the IP address of the router, and the router will respond with an ARP reply. However, the router will not forward the frame out any other interface.
10. B, C. Routers are used to interconnect networks. One or more routers are typically used to connect networks in geographic locations, even around the world. Routers contain broadcasts to the network they were received.
11. B. Routers are used to forward packets to remote networks. A router examines the destination IP address of a packet to search for a match in its IP routing table. The IP routing table is used to determine to which interface to forward the packet.
12. A. If the router does not have any match between the IP address of the packet and an entry in its routing table, the router drops the packet.

Chapter 15

1. C. HTTP is an application layer protocol used to request and transmit data for web pages. In most cases HTTP has been superseded by HTTPS, which transfers the data securely.
2. D. UDP provides unreliable delivery. There is no three-way handshake to establish the connection. Any segments lost in transmission are not resent and there is no reordering of out-of-order segments. UDP is used for transmission that requires minimal delay such as voice. UDP is also used for transaction-based applications that require only a few messages to be exchanged.
3. C. UDP provides unreliable delivery. There is no three-way handshake to establish the connection. Any segments lost in transmission are not resent and there is no reordering of out-of-order segments. UDP is used for transmission that requires minimal delay such as voice. UDP is also used for transaction-based applications that require only a few messages to be exchanged.
4. B. The transport layer is responsible for the reassembly of messages sent over the network.

5. A. TCP and UDP both operate at the transport layer of the TCP/IP model and the transport layer of the OSI model.

6. A. TCP uses port numbers to identify the target application. The client uses the destination port number to identify the application on the server the data is going to. The server uses a source port number to identify the application the data is coming from.

7. A. IANA uses well-known port numbers 0 through 1023 for widely used network applications.

8. C. The client uses source port numbers to keep track of different conversations on one or more severs.

9. A. UDP requires less overhead than TCP because UDP does not provide reliable delivery. There is no three-way handshake to establish the connection. Any segments lost in transmission are not resent and there is no reordering of out-of-order segments. UDP is used for transmission that requires minimal delay such as voice. UDP is also used for transaction-based applications that require only a few messages to be exchanged.

10. C. UDP provides unreliable delivery. There is no three-way handshake to establish the connection. Any segments lost in transmission are not resent and there is no reordering of out-of-order segments. UDP is used for transmission that requires minimal delay such as voice. UDP is also used for transaction-based applications that require only a few messages to be exchanged.

11. D. Both TCP and UDP use port numbers to identify the applications and keep track of multiple conversations.

Chapter 16

1. C, E. FTP requires two connections: the first is to exchange control traffic and the second is used to transfer the data. A client can download and upload files from the server.

2. B. Network protocols define communication rules including how messages are exchanged between the source and destination.

3. B. HTTP is used by web servers to provide information to display a web page. HTTP has largely been replaced by HTTPS, which provides the same service but does it securely.

4.
   - A. DHCP automatically configures hosts with IP addresses.
   - B. SSH provides remote access to servers.
   - C. DNS resolves Internet names to IP addresses.

5. B, D. IMAP allows users to access their email from any device by reading the information from the email server. SMTP is used by email servers and email transfer agents to send and receive email.

6. A, E. SSH provides secure access to remote servers. Telnet provides the same service but not securely. Telnet should be used only in nonproduction environments.

7. C. SSH provides secure access to remote servers, whereas Telnet provides the same service but not securely. Telnet should be used only in nonproduction environments.

8. A. DNS allows users to use domain names such as www.cisco.com instead of the IP address of the web server. The client just needs to know the IP address of the DNS server, which will respond with the IP address for any domain name.

9. C. HTTP can be used to exchange message between a client's web browser and a remote web server. HTTP has been largely replaced by HTTPS, which performs the same service securely.

10. B, E. HTTP and HTTPS are both used to exchange message between a client's web browser and a remote web server. HTTP has been largely replaced by HTTPS, which performs the same service securely. Many servers now support only HTTPS.

11. - A. Port number 110 is POP3.
    - B. Port number 25 is SMTP.
    - C. Port number 143 is IMAP4.

Chapter 17

1. B. The **ping 10.1.1.1** command tests connectivity to the destination device with this IP address.

2. C. A device will not be able to reach a device on a remote network if it cannot communicate with its own default gateway.

3. A, C, D. The **ipconfig** without the **/all** option displays the IP address and subnet mask of the device, and the address of the default gateway used by the device. The **/all** option will include the IP address of the DHCP server, the IP address of the DNS server, and the MAC address of the device.

4. B. The **ping** command is used to test connectivity to a device on its own network or a remote network. It tests if packets can reach the destination device and if the destination device can reach the source of the ping.

5. B. The **netstat** command is used to display all active network connections to other devices.

6. B. The **ipconfig** command without the **/all** option displays the IP address and subnet mask of the device, and the address of the default gateway used by the device. Adding the **/all** option also displays the IP address of the DHCP server, the IP address of the DNS server, and the MAC address of the device.

7. D. A possible cause is a problem with the DNS server or the client is unable to communicate with the DNS server.

8. D. The technician can use the **ipconfig /renew** command to receive new information from the DHCP server.

9. A. The **ping** command is used to test connectivity to a device on its own network or a remote network. It tests if packets can reach the destination device and if the destination device can reach the source of the ping.

10. - A. **ipconfig** displays IP configuration information.
    - B. **ping** tests connections to other IP hosts.
    - C. **netstat** displays network connections.
    - D. **tracert** displays the route taken to the destination.
    - E. **nslookup** directly queries the name server for information on a destination domain.

Chapter 18

1. A, C. Both a wireless access point and a Layer 2 Ethernet switch make their forwarding decisions based on the destination MAC address. Unlike a Layer

3 router, neither of these devices makes its forwarding decisions based on the destination IP address.

2. B. A scalable network expands quickly to support new users and applications. It does this without degrading the performance of services that are being accessed by existing users.

3. ■ A. Ensuring confidentiality means only the intended recipients can access and read the data.

   ■ B. Maintaining integrity provides the assurance that the information has not been altered during transmission.

   ■ C. Ensuring availability provides the assurance of timely and reliable access to data.

4. D. With quality of service enabled, a router can manage the flow of data and voice traffic, giving priority to voice communications if the network experiences congestion.

5. A. Fault tolerance can minimize or eliminate the impact of a failure on the network. If a path or device fails, fault tolerance can provide an alternate path.

6. A. MAC addresses are embedded on the NIC. Regardless of which network the device is connected to, the MAC address stays the same.

7. A, C, F. The access layer provides a connection point for end-user devices to the network and allows multiple hosts to connect to other hosts through a network device, usually a switch or wireless access point. The distribution layer provides a connection point for separate networks and controls the flow of information between the networks. The core layer is a high-speed backbone layer with redundant (backup) connections. It is responsible for transporting large amounts of data between multiple end networks.

8. A. Fault tolerance can minimize or eliminate the impact of a failure on the network. If a path or device fails, fault tolerance can provide an alternate path. This may have little or no impact on the users.

9. A. With quality of service enabled, a router can manage the flow of data and voice traffic, giving priority to video communications over email communications if the network experiences congestion.

10. A. The distribution layer provides a connection point for separate networks and controls the flow of information between the networks.

11. A. A hierarchical network divides the network into distinct layers, each with it roles. This design provides for fault tolerance, scalability, better security, and better control of traffic flow including quality of service.

12. ■ A. Fault tolerance provides reliability.

    ■ B. Scalability allows the network to grow.

    ■ C. Quality of service prioritizes traffic.

Chapter 19

1. D. Virtualization is the foundation of cloud computing.

2. ■ A. Less power is consumed because consolidating servers lowers the monthly power and cooling costs.

   ■ D. Less equipment is required because virtualization enables server consolidation,

which requires fewer physical devices and lowers maintenance costs.

- E. Improved disaster recovery results because most enterprise server virtualization platforms have software that can help test and automate failover before a disaster happens.

3. D. A Software as a Service (SaaS) cloud provider is responsible for access to applications and services, such as email, communication, and Office 365, that are delivered over the Internet.

4. C. Saving photos to a remote storage location maintained by a cloud provider is an example of cloud computing.

5. D. Cloud-based applications and services offered in a private cloud are intended for a specific organization or entity.

6. B. The company is using Infrastructure as a Service because a DNS server is considered a network application managed by the IT department.

7. A. A hypervisor is a program, firmware, or hardware that adds an abstraction layer on top of the physical hardware. The abstraction layer is used to create virtual machines that have access to all the hardware of the physical machine such as CPUs, memory, disk controllers, and NICs.

8. A. A Type 2 hypervisor is software that creates and runs VM instances. The hypervisor is installed on a host's existing operating system, such as macOS, to support one or more VMs.

9. A. A hypervisor is a program, firmware, or hardware that adds an abstraction layer on top of the physical hardware. The abstraction layer is used to create virtual machines that have access to all the hardware of the physical machine such as CPUs, memory, disk controllers, and NICs.

10. A. A hybrid cloud is made up of two or more cloud types (for example, part private, part public), where each part remains a separate object, but both are connected using a single architecture.

11. A, D. Oracle VirtualBox and VMware Workstation are both examples of Type 2 hypervisor software.

12. A. Cloud-based applications and services offered in a public cloud are made available to the general population. Services may be free or may be offered on a pay-per-use model, such as paying for online storage.

Chapter 20

1. C. 10101101 is converted to decimal 173 with the following calculation:

   $(128 \times 1) + (64 \times 0) + (32 \times 1) + (16 \times 0) + (8 \times 1) + (4 \times 1) + (2 \times 0) + (1 \times 1)$

2. B. A 32-bit IPv4 address is represented using four decimal numbers, each composed of an octet of 8 bits, with periods separating the octets.

3. C. 0x means hexadecimal. Hexadecimal C in decimal is 12. The conversion from hexadecimal to decimal is $(16 \times 12) + (1 \times 9) = 201$.

4. C. Hexadecimal C is 12 in decimal or 1100 in binary. Hexadecimal A is 10 in decimal or 1010 in binary. Combining the two binary values produces 11001010.

5. B. The range of hexadecimal values in a hextet is 0000 to ffff. This comprises every possibility of using four hexadecimal digits.

6. B. Binary 1001 is 9 in decimal or 9 in hexadecimal. Binary 1101 is 13 in decimal or D in hexadecimal. Combining the two hexadecimal values produces 9D.

7. A. An IPv4 address is 32 bits in length.

8. A, B. A binary value consists of 0 or 1. These values represent two discrete states.

9. A. First, determine the number of 16s that can go into 139, which is 8 in decimal and 8 in hexadecimal. This leaves a remainder of 11 in decimal or B in hexadecimal. This gives the converted value of 8B.

10. A. The 16 valid hexadecimal (base 16) values are 0, 1, 2, 3, 4, 5, 6, 7, 8, 9, a, b, c, d, e, and f.

11. A. Decimal 232 is convert to binary 11101000 with the following calculation:

    232 / 128 = 1 with a remainder of 104.

    104 / 64 = 1 with a remainder of 40.

    40 / 32 = 1 with a remainder of 8.

    8 / 16 = 0 (cannot be divided).

    8 / 8 = 1 with a reminder of 0.

    0 / 4 = 0 (cannot be divided).

    0 / 2 = 0 (cannot be divided).

    0 / 1 = 0 (cannot be divided).

    Using the quotient from each results in 11101000.

12. D. The conversion of the binary address to dotted decimal is as follows:

    First octet: 11101100: (128 × 1) + (64 × 1) + (32 × 1) + (16 × 0) + (8 × 1) + (4 × 1) + (2 × 0) + (1 × 0) = 236

    Second octet: 00010001: (128 × 0) + (64 × 0) + (32 × 0) + (16 × 1) + (8 × 0) + (4 × 0) + (2 × 0) + (1 × 1) = 17

    Third octet: 00001100: (128 × 0) + (64 × 0) + (32 × 0) + (16 × 0) + (8 × 1) + (4 × 1) + (2 × 0) + (1 × 0) = 12

    Fourth octet: 00001010: (128 × 0) + (64 × 0) + (32 × 0) + (16 × 0) + (8 × 1) + (4 × 0) + (2 × 1) + (1 × 0) = 10

Chapter 21

1. A. A Layer 3 PDU, such as an IPv4 or IPv6 packet, is typically encapsulated in an Ethernet frame. Other types of messages can also be encapsulated, such as ARP (Address Resolution Protocol), ICMP (Internet Control Message Protocol), or STP (Spanning Tree Protocol).

2. C. With the normal untagged Ethernet frame overhead of 18 bytes (header and trailer), the Ethernet maximum frame size is 1518 bytes. The minimum frame size is 64 bytes, which is a result of the days when Ethernet LANs used half-duplex hubs. Hubs are now considered obsolete.

3. B. The Ethernet MAC address is denoted by the "Physical Address" in the output of the **ipconfig /all** command.

4. B. The Media Access Control (MAC) sublayer is responsible for the processes uses to access the shared Ethernet LAN.

5. D. For every frame that enters the Ethernet switch, the switch examines the incoming port number and the source MAC address. If this information does not exist in the MAC address table, the switch adds it to the table. Next, the switch examines the destination MAC address for a match in the MAC address table. If the address matches one of its entries, the switch forwards the frame out that port. If there is no match or if the frame

is a broadcast, then the switch forwards the frame out all ports except the incoming port.

6. C. For every frame that enters the Ethernet switch, the switch examines the incoming port number and the source MAC address. If this information does not exist in the MAC address table, the switch adds it to the table. Next, the switch examines the destination MAC address for a match in the MAC address table. If the address matches one of its entries, the switch forwards the frame out that port. If there is no match or if the frame is a broadcast, then the switch forwards the frame out all ports except the incoming port.

7. A. Runt frames are discarded, dropped by the switch.

8. C. The 100 refers to the Mbps (Mb/s) of the medium.

9. A, D, E. Although there are some variations, a typical IEEE 802.3 Ethernet frame consists of the following fields: Preamble and Start Frame Delimiter (not always referred to), Destination MAC Address, Source MAC Address, Type/Length, Data, and Frame Check Sequence (FCS).

10.
    - A. BASE means baseband transmission.
    - B. T means twisted-pair cable.
    - C. 100 indicates the speed in Mbps.

11. A, D. IEEE 802.3 is one of the standards that define Ethernet technology. Ethernet is responsible for sending data from one Ethernet NIC to another Ethernet NIC on the same LAN using the Ethernet MAC addresses of the NICs.

12. A. By default, an end device discards any Ethernet frames with a unicast destination MAC address that does not match the MAC address of its own NIC. This behavior can be changed by protocol analysis software such as Wireshark.

Chapter 22

1. D. In IPv4 the TTL (Time-to-Live) field is decremented by 1 by each router. If the TTL is 0, the router drops the packet. In IPv6, this field is called Hop Limit.

2. B. IPv4 has a 32-bit address space, which means addresses can consist of a theoretical range from 32 zero bits to 32 one bits. IPv6 has a 128-bit address space with a theoretical range of 128 zero bits to 128 one bits.

3. C. Network Address Translation, along with RFC 1918 private address space, has slowed down the depletion of IPv4 public addresses and the necessity to transition to IPv6. However, in the last several years the Internet is seeing a significant transition to IPv6.

4. B. Public IPv4 addresses are becoming more scarce and more expensive every year. In the last several years the Internet is seeing a significant transition to IPv6.

5. C. The network layer can encapsulate data of any type, including various upper-layer PDUs.

6. D. The network layer protocols, primarily IPv4 or IPv6, specify the rules used to send data from the original sender (the creator of the data) to its final designation (the intended recipient of the data).

7. B. The network layer is responsible for the logical addressing of packets, either IPv4 or IPv6.

8. B. The application creates the data and includes any protocol information. The

data is encapsulated by the transport layer and becomes a segment. The segment is then encapsulated by the network layer as a packet. The packet is encapsulated by the data link layer as a frame. And finally the frame is transmitted over the physical medium as bits.

9. B. The process of prepending a PDU with control or header information from another PDU is known as encapsulation.

10. D. OSI Layer 3, the network layer, encapsulates other PDUs using an IPv4 or IPv6 header that includes both a source IP address and a destination IP address.

11. C. The MTU is decided by the data link layer depending on the physical medium and the required data link fields. A typical Ethernet frame has an MTU of 1518 bytes with 18 bytes used by Ethernet. This allows for 1500 bytes for the network layer PDU, for example, an encapsulated IP packet.

Chapter 23

1. B. An IPv4 device must have an IPv4 address and a subnet mask. The OS does an AND operation on these to determine the network portion. This tells the device which network it belongs to.

2. C. An IPv4 device must have an IPv4 address and a subnet mask. The OS does an AND operation on both of these to determine the network portion. This tells the device which network it belongs to. The device now knows which IPv4 addresses it can reach directly and that it must communicate with everything else via the default gateway.

3. A. An IPv4 address consists of 32 bits, represented with four octets, each of which is a decimal value representing 8 bits.

4. D. Each decimal value represents 8 bits, 00000000 through 11111111, or 0 through 255 in decimal.

5. A. An IPv4 address uniquely identifies a device on an IP network. Originally, all unicast IPv4 addresses were designed to be globally unique, but with the depletion of IPv4 addresses, now only public IPv4 addresses are globally unique. Private RFC 1918 addresses can be used on any IPv4 network. These addresses can be translated to a public IPv4 address using NAT.

6. C. The subnet mask 255.255.255.224 has 24 1 bits, or /24. In binary, the subnet mask is 11111111.11111111.11111111.11100000.

7. B, D. An IPv4 address consists of a network portion and a host portion as determined by the value of the subnet mask.

8. D. ANDing the bits 11000000.10101000.01 000001.00000011 with 11111111.11111111 .11000000.00000000 results in copying the first 18 bits of the address followed by all 0 bits, 11000000.10101000.01000000.000000 00, or 192.168.64.0.

9. A. Devices on the same IPv4 subnet have the same address for their default gateway.

10. C. A subnet mask of 255.255.252.0 has 10 0 bits indicating the host port of the address. 10 bits allow for 1024 total devices or 1022 assignable IPv4 addresses (subtracting 2 host addresses, one for the network address and one for the broadcast address).

11. A. Performing an AND operation on the IPv4 address and subnet mask results in the network address 10.25.1.64/26. Assignable

host addresses on this network range from 10.25.1.65 through 10.25.1.126, with a broadcast address of 10.25.1.127.

12. B. An IPv4 device must have an IPv4 address and a subnet mask. The OS does an AND operation on both of these to determine the network portion of the address. This indicates to the device which network it belongs to. The rest of the address indicates the host portion of the address.

Chapter 24

1. A. Address Resolution Protocol is used to discover the Ethernet MAC address associated with a known IPv4 address.
2. C. Address Resolution Protocol is used to discover the Ethernet MAC address associated with a known IPv4 address. If the destination IPv4 address of the packet is on the same network as the host, the ARP request will be for the MAC address associated with the known destination IPv4 address of the packet. If the destination IPv4 address of the packet is on a different network than the host, the ARP request will be for the MAC address associated with the known destination IPv4 address of the default gateway.
3. D. Since the ARP request is for the IPv4 address of the default gateway (router), the default gateway responds with an ARP reply containing its MAC address associated with the known default gateway IPv4 address.
4. D. The ARP request is an Ethernet broadcast. If the destination IPv4 address of the packet is on the same network as the host, the ARP request will be for the MAC address associated with the known destination IPv4 address of the packet. If the destination IPv4 address of the packet is on a different network than the host, the ARP request will be for the MAC address associated the known destination IPv4 address of the default gateway.
5. B. An ARP request is sent as an Ethernet broadcast. All devices on the local network receive and process the ARP request. Routers do not forward Ethernet broadcasts out other networks.
6. C. ARP spoofing is typically used by an attacker to respond to ARP requests associated with IPv4 addresses of other devices. This is an attempt by the attacker to create a man-in-the-middle (MITM) attack. There are techniques to mitigate ARP spoofing, such as dynamic ARP inspection.
7. D. The **arp -a** command can be used on a host to determine which MAC address is associated with the IPv4 address of the default gateway.
8. C. A host first searches its ARP table for the MAC address associated with the destination IPv4 address of the packet.
9. C. An ARP request is sent as an Ethernet broadcast, FFFF.FFFF.FFFF. There is no IPv4 header in any ARP message.
10. A. Address Resolution Protocol is used to discover the Ethernet MAC address associated with a known IPv4 address. This includes the IPv4 address of the default gateway.
11. B. PC1's ARP request is for the MAC address of its default gateway, the IPv4 address of R1's G0/0 interface. R1 will send an ARP reply with the MAC address of its G0/0 interface.

Chapter 25

1. A. Dynamic Host Configuration Protocol is used to automatically assign IP addressing information to devices.

2. A, C. A client initially sends a DHCPDISCOVER message. After receiving a DHCPOFFER from the DHCP server, the client responds with a DHCPREQUEST message. The server confirms the assigned address with a DHCPACK. To make it easier to remember the order of the DHCP messages, Discover, Offer, Request, and Ack form the acronym DORA.

3. A. An end device uses the services of its local DNS server, which is the DNS (not DHCP) server whose IP address is configured on the end device. If the local DNS server does not have the answer, it is the responsibility of the local DNS server to contact other DNS servers to get the IP address and provide it to the client.

4. C. Most client devices have DHCP enabled automatically. When a client device boots, it sends a DHCPDISCOVER message to get its IP addressing information, which for IPv4 includes its IPv4 address, subnet mask, address of the default gateway, and address of one or more DNS servers.

5. C. The client sends a DHCPREQUEST message to accept the offer (DHCPOFFER) received from the DHCP server. The DHCP message exchange begins with the client initially sending a DHCPDISCOVER message. After receiving a DHCPOFFER from the DHCP server, the client responds with a DHCPREQUEST message. The server confirms the assigned address with a DHCPACK. To make it easier to remember the order of the DHCP messages, Discover, Offer, Request, and Ack form the acronym DORA.

6. D. Domain Name System is the protocol that enables devices to obtain the IP address for a domain name.

7. C. A DNS mail exchange (MX) record directs email to a mail server. The MX record indicates how email messages should be routed in accordance with the Simple Mail Transfer Protocol (SMTP, the standard protocol for all email).

8. C. Most client devices have DHCP enabled automatically. When the client boots, it sends a DHCPDISCOVER message to get its IP addressing information, which for IPv4 includes its IPv4 address, subnet mask, address of the default gateway, and address of one or more DNS servers.

9. A. If a device can ping the IP address of web server but cannot ping its domain name (www.example.com), the problem most likely has to do with DNS. It could be that the DNS server does not have the information or is malfunctioning. The problem might also be that the client is not able to communicate with the DNS server. The client may have the wrong IP address for the DNS server, or there may be a network problem between the client and the server.

10. A. Domain Name System is the protocol that enables devices to obtain the IP address for a domain name.

11. C. An end device uses the services of its local DNS server, the IP address the end device has for its DNS server. If the local DNS server does not have the answer, it is the responsibility of the local DNS server to contact other DNS servers to get the IP address and provide it to the client. Depending on the DNS cache of the local DNS server, the local DNS server may need to contact the following DNS servers (in

this order): a root name server, a top-level domain server, and/or an authoritative server.

Chapter 26

1. - A. Flow control: TCP
   - B. Application dependent for error correction: UDP
   - C. Reliable delivery: TCP
   - D. Sequence number: TCP
   - E. Fastest delivery: UDP
   - F. Less overhead: UDP

   TCP provides reliability and flow control using several fields including sequence numbers, acknowledgment numbers, and window size. UDP has less overhead, which provides faster delivery; however, the application is required to perform any necessary error detection and correction.
2. D. Both UDP and TCP use source and destination port numbers. From the client device's perspective, the source port number uniquely identifies the application or process on the client. The destination port number identifies the application or service the client is accessing on the server.
3. B, C, E. The UDP header contains a minimal number of fields: Source Port, Destination Port, Length, and Checksum.
4. A. The TCP terminal process can be initiated by the client or the server and consists of sending a FIN and an ACK. 1. Initiator: FIN; 2. Receiver: ACK; 3. Receiver: FIN; 4. Initiator: ACK.
5. B. A server can listen on several ports at the same time. Each port is associated with a different application that the server is actively servicing for clients.
6. A. If the source determines that the TCP segments are either not being acknowledged or not being acknowledged in a timely manner, then it can reduce the number of bytes it sends before receiving an acknowledgment.
7. D. The TCP header includes a group of control bits or flags in the Control Bits field. Two of those bits are the SYN and ACK bits, both of which are used during the three-way handshake: 1. SYN, 2. SYN, ACK, 3. ACK.
8. B, D. TCP provides reliability and flow control, including retransmission of any data not received. This requires more overhead than UDP, which can be used to deliver data quickly when some data loss is tolerable.
9. - A. The maximum segment size (MSS) is the largest amount of data encapsulated in a segment that a device can receive.
   - B. The sequence number is used to identify each segment of data.
   - C. The window size is used to inform the source of the number of bytes it can send before waiting for an acknowledgement: window size.
   - D. An acknowledgment message must be received by a sender before transmitting more segments larger than the window size.
10. - A. Is connection-oriented: TCP
    - B. Is connectionless: UDP
    - C. Uses acknowledgments: TCP
    - D. Has a larger header: TCP
    - E. Is suitable for delay-intolerant applications: UDP
    - F. Best-effort delivery protocol: UDP

11. A. TCP provides reliability and flow control, including retransmission of any data not received. This requires more overhead than UDP, which can be used to deliver data quickly when some data loss is tolerable.

12. D, E. The TCP terminal process can be initiated by the client or the server and consists of sending a FIN and an ACK. 1. Initiator: FIN, 2. Receiver: ACK; 3. Receiver: FIN; 4. Initiator: ACK.

Chapter 27

1. A. Privileged EXEC mode can be identified by the prompt ending with the # symbol.

2. C. The **show version** command is used to display the information regarding memory, including NVRAM, DRAM and flash, along with interfaces and licenses of the device.

3. C. A keyword is a specific parameter defined in the operating system (for example, **address**). An argument is not predefined; it is a value or variable defined by the user (for example, **192.168.1.1**).

4. A. The **exit** command returns the user to the previous level.

5. B. The **Ctrl-Shift-6** key combination is an all-purpose break sequence used to abort DNS lookups, traceroutes, and pings, and to interrupt an IOS process.

6. C. The **configure terminal** command can be entered only from privileged EXEC mode, which will put the administrator into global configuration mode.

7. C. Pressing the **Tab** key completes a partial command or keyword name entry as long as the entered information is a unique match.

8. C. **show** is the command and **running-config** is a keyword.

9. C, E. User EXEC mode display a prompt ending in >. In user EXEC mode, many aspects of the router can be displayed, but configuration changes are not possible. Changes can be made only in privileged EXEC mode.

10. B, E. Since the router has just been booted and no configuration changes have been made, both the running configuration and startup configuration files will be identical, so the administrator can use either command to check the configuration of the router.

Chapter 28

1. D. SSH is the only one of these options that provides encryption.

2. A. By default, all ports (interfaces) on a Cisco switch are part of VLAN 1.

3. A. Since all ports are on VLAN 1, the administrator would configure the IP address belonging to the VLAN 1 interface.

4. C. This command copies the running configuration from RAM to the startup configuration in NRAM.

5. C. Telnet sends all data, including the username and password, in plain text. SSH encrypts all data, including the username and password.

6. C. 172.16.10.100 is a usable and available host on the 172.16.10.0/24 network. 172.16.10.1 is taken by the default gateway, and 172.16.10.255 is the broadcast address for this network. 172.16.1.10 is on a different network.

7. D. This command configures the vty line to use SSH, which means all communication is encrypted.

8. D. The command **enable secret trustknow1** configures trustknow1 as the privileged EXEC password.

9. B. The command **service password-encryption** encrypts all passwords in the running-configuration and startup-configuration files.

Chapter 29

1. D. A successful ping to the loopback address verifies that the TCP/IP stack is functional.

2. D. The **ping** command uses ICMP Echo Request and Echo Reply messages to test connectivity.

3. C. A router decrements the IPv6 Hop Limit field by 1 and drops the packet if the field is 0. This is similar to the IPv4 TTL (Time-to-Live) field in IPv4.

4. D. ICMP provides information and error messaging.

5. C. The ping utility uses ICMP Echo Request and Echo Reply messages.

6. D. The **traceroute** or **tracert** (Windows) command is used to determine where a packet might be dropped or delayed by a router. This command displays the IP addresses of each router in the path that successfully received the packet(s).

7. A. ICMP for both IPv4 and IPv6 provides information and error messaging.

8. A. An IPv6 host can send a Neighbor Solicitation message to see if its IPv6 address is unique before using it. The NS message includes the IPv6 address the device wants to use. If the device does not receive a Neighbor Advertisement message in response, it can assume its IPv6 address is unique. This an optional process, but most operating systems implement it.

9. A. The Windows **tracert (traceroute)** command can be used to determine the last router in the path that successfully received the packets.

10. C. A successful ping to the default gateway indicates that the device can reach the router used to forward packets to other networks.

11. B. The **ping** command only verifies connectivity, whereas the **traceroute** command (Windows **tracert**) verifies connectivity and displays information about the routers in the path.

12. C. The ICMP Time Exceeded message is used by a router when it has decremented an IPv4 TTL or IPv6 Hop Limit field to 0. The source IP address of the ICMP Time Exceeded message sent by the router is used by traceroute to determine the router's IP address.

13. C, D. The **ping** command verifies that the destination IP address is reachable and displays the average round-trip time between the source and destination.

14. D. The traceroute utility identifies the routers in the path to the destination. When a router receives an IP packet from traceroute, it decrements the IPv4 TTL or IPv6 Hop Limit field by 1. If the field results in 0, the router returns an ICMP Time Exceeded message back to the source. The source IP address of the ICMP Time Exceeded message sent by the router is used by traceroute to determine the router's IP address.

Chapter 30

1. B. All bits sent between two devices must be transmitted over the network media, which is the purpose of the physical layer.
2. D. One strand is used for sending and the other strand is used for receiving.
3. B. Crosstalk is a disturbance caused by the electric or magnetic fields of a signal on one wire to the signal in an adjacent wire.
4. B. Cable designers have discovered that they can limit the negative effect of crosstalk by varying the number of twists per wire pair.
5. D. A straight-through cable is used to connect "unlike" devices, such as a PC (computer) and a switch.
6. C. Bandwidth is the amount of data that can be transmitted from one place to another in a specific amount of time, usually measured in bits per second (Kbps, Mbps, or Gbps).
7. D. Encoding is a method of converting a stream of data bits into a predefined "code." This process helps to distinguish data bits from control bits.
8. A. Cancellation occurs when pairing wires in a circuit. When two wires in an electrical circuit are placed close together, their magnetic fields are the exact opposite of each other. Therefore, the two magnetic fields cancel each other and also cancel out any outside EMI and RFI signals.
9. D. Throughput is the measure of the transfer of bits across the media over a given period of time. Throughput is usually lower than the specified bandwidth due to various factors causing latency.
10. D. Fiber-optic cables can transmit signals with less attenuation, which allows the signal to travel farther.
11. C. Signal distortion by the NIC occurs at the physical layer.
12. B. A rollover cable is used to connect a device to a Cisco console port.

Chapter 31

1. D. Logical topologies typically include the devices and types of networks used to transfer data between devices, such as an Ethernet LAN.
2. C. A star topology is when a central device, such as an Ethernet switch, is used to connect all end devices.
3. C. A mesh network or full-mesh network is when all end devices (or nodes) are connected to all other end devices.
4. B. Half-duplex is a type of transmission that is in either direction, but only in one direction at a time.
5. A. CSMA/CD is used by legacy Ethernet hubs. Because today's Ethernet LANs use full-duplex Ethernet switches, CSMA/CD is not required and is not used.
6. C. Wireless networks, IEEE 802.11, use CSMA/CA to manage access to the shared wireless medium.
7. C. CSMA/CD is used to contend for access on a shared, half-duplex media. The use of full-duplex Ethernet switches means that Ethernet NICs can operate in full-duplex and no longer have to contend for access.

Chapter 32

1. B.Routers examine the packet's destination IP address to find the best match in the router's routing table.

2. B. If the destination IP address is on one of the router's directly connected networks, the router will forward the packet directly to the destination host.

3. B. Layer 2 Ethernet frames are removed by the router when the packet is received. The router will encapsulate the packet in a new Ethernet data link frame when forwarding the packet out the appropriate interface.

4. B. 127.0.0.1 is an IPv4 loopback address.

5. C. Routers examine the packet's destination IP address to find the best match in the router's routing table. The information in the routing table determines how to forward the packet.

6. C. The **netstat -r** command will display a routing table on many host operating systems including Windows.

7. A. A static route is manually configured by the network administrator and includes the remote network address and the IP address of the next hop router.

8. B. Dynamic routing protocols such as OSPF can be used to automatically discover remote networks and determine the best path to those networks.

9. C. A default static route will have a source code of S in the IP routing table.

10. C. An end device will have the IPv4 address of the local router interface as its default gateway. The IPv4 address of the end device and of the IPv4 address of the default gateway will be on the same IP network.

Chapter 33

1. E. Pinging a loopback address verifies that the IP is working on the local host. Most host operating systems, including Windows, macOS, Linux, iOS, and Android, have both IPv4 and IPv6 installed by default.

2. B. Leading 0s are omitted and a single contiguous string of all-0 hextets can be replaced with a double colon (::).

3. A. For any device to be enabled for IPv6 requires that the interface only have a link-local address.

4. D. A /64 prefix length indicates that the first 64 bits, 2001:db8::1000, is the network address. This leaves 64 bits for the interface ID, or four hextets, a9cd:47ff:fe57:fe94.

5. A. Leading 0s are omitted and a single contiguous string of all-0 hextets can be replaced with a double colon (::).

6. C. A /64 prefix length indicates that the first 64 bits or first four hextets, 2001:db8:d15:ea, is the network address.

7. B. When a device is enabled for IPv6 on an interface, that interface will automatically assign itself a link-local address. Most host operating systems, including Windows, macOS, Linux, iOS, and Android, have both IPv4 and IPv6 installed by default. This means they will have at minimum an IPv6 link-local address.

8. B. With a /48 global routing prefix and a /64 prefix length, this leaves 16 bits between the global routing prefix and interface ID for the Subnet ID. Subtracting 48 (global routing prefix) from 64 (the prefix length) results in the Subnet ID.

9. D. A /64 prefix length indicates that the first 64 bits or first four hextets, 2001:db8:aa04:b5, is the network address.

10. B. Link-local addresses are only for communications on the local link or network and are not routable off that link.

11. D. IPv6 does not have a broadcast. IPv6 does include an all-IPv6 device multicast address.

Chapter 34

1. B. A Neighbor Solicitation message is a multicast address that begins with ff02::. The "ff" in this destination IPv6 address indicates that this address is a multicast address. The "2" in this destination IPv6 address indicates that this address is of link-local scope.
2. C. A Neighbor Solicitation message is a multicast address that begins with ff02::. The "ff" in this destination IPv6 address indicates that this address is a multicast address. The "2" in this destination IPv6 address indicates that this address is of link-local scope.
3. C. ICMPv6 provides address resolution for IPv6 similar to ARP for IPv4. Specifically, ICMPv6 Neighbor Discovery protocol is used for this purpose.
4. A. A router sends an ICMPv6 Router Advertisement (RA) message to all IPv6 devices on the LAN. The RA message uses the router's link-local address as the source IPv6 address of the messages. End devices on the LAN will then use this source IPv6 address of the RA message for their default gateway address.
5. D. Devices send an ICMPv6 Neighbor Advertisement message to provide the Ethernet MAC address. This is in response to an ICMPv6 Neighbor Solicitation message from a device that knows an IPv6 address but needs the corresponding Ethernet MAC address.
6. C. The destination MAC address of an ICMPv6 Neighbor Solicitation message is a multicast address. There is information contained in this multicast address that can help limit the number of NICs on the network that need to accept the message.
7. C, D. A Neighbor Solicitation message is used when a device knows an IPv6 address but needs the corresponding Ethernet MAC address. An ICMPv6 Neighbor Advertisement message is the device with the IPv6 address responding with its Ethernet MAC address. A Neighbor Solicitation message in IPv6 is the equivalent of an ARP request in IPv4, and a Neighbor Advertisement message in IPv6 is the equivalent of an ARP reply in IPv4.

Chapter 35

1. C. An Ethernet switch is used to connect one or more devices to the same Ethernet LAN.
2. B. Store-and-forward switching is a frame forwarding method that receives the entire frame and computes the CRC. If the CRC is valid, the switch looks up the destination address, which determines the outgoing interface. Then the frame is forwarded out of the correct port. Cut-through switching is a frame forwarding method that forwards the frame before it is entirely received. At a minimum, the destination address of the frame must be read before the frame can be forwarded. There is not frame error checking with cut-through switching.
3. B. An Ethernet switch is used to connect PCs to the LAN. Home routers will typically include a four-port Ethernet switch as part of the router.
4. D. The IOS is copied from NVRAM into RAM where it is executed by the CPU.

5. B. By default, the bootstrap program will first search flash memory for the IOS.
6. C, D. Both Telnet and SSH can be used for in-band management. However, Telnet should only be used in a lab environment because all data, including the password, is sent in clear text.
7. C. A limited IOS is in ROM, typically used for diagnostics when the main IOS is not available.
8. B, E. Ethernet LAN switches provide wired access, and wireless access points provide wireless access to the wired LAN.
9. B. Out-of-band communication requires a computer running terminal emulation software such as PuTTY connected to the console port of the Cisco device using a rollover cable.
10. D. Similar to most computers, the switch will do a POST (power-on self-test) to determine and examine hardware components.
11. D. The NVRAM is considered permanent storage and is used to store the IOS, startup configuration, and any other content.
12. B, D. The console port is the most common, but the AUX port can also be used.
13. B, C. The IOS is loaded from NVRAM into RAM. If there is a startup configuration file in NVRAM, that will also be loaded into RAM.
14. D. The **show startup-config** command displays the contents of the startup configuration file stored in NVRAM.

Chapter 36

1. A. At this point the user needs to contact the cable company that provides their Internet connection.
2. B, D. The **ipconfig /all** command is used to contact the DHCP server to receive IP addressing information. If the client host does not receive this information, there is either an issue with the DHCP server or a network issue communicating with the DHCP server.
3. B. Since the client is able to get IP addressing from the DHCP server, the wireless network is not an issue. DNS is not an issue because the **ping** command is to an IPv4 address. The only other possibility given these options is that the client has received wrong addressing information from the DHCP server.
4. D. Replacing a device such as a cable modem is considered substitution.
5. C. Pinging a device attempts to verify Layer 3 IP connectivity. This is toward the middle of the OSI stack. Depending on the results of the ping, the administrator may try other troubleshooting methods at other layers.
6. C. Traceroute would be used to see at which point the packet is failing to be forwarded.
7. B. The **netstat** command displays all TCP connections and UDP sessions.
8. A, B, C. After solving a problem, it is helpful to document for yourself and others information that can help solve the same or similar problems that might occur in the future.
9. A, C, D. These three questions are related directly to helping the support desk solve the problem.
10. B. A physical layer network connectivity problem would involve either cabling or the NIC.
11. A, C. The output shows that the host can reach the server by pinging its IPv4 address.

However, the host cannot reach the server using its domain name, which typically means this is most likely a DNS issue.

12. A. After solving a problem, it is helpful to document for yourself and others information that can help solve the same or similar problems that might occur in the future.

Chapter 37

1. A. After defining the problem, the next step is to identify any hosts and other devices that need to be investigated. During this step, the technician may gather and document more symptoms, depending on the characteristics that are identified.
2. A, B. The bottom-up approach is typically used when the problem is with the physical layer or the physical components of the network. This can also be useful when the issue is unfamiliar.
3. A. The **show cdp neighbors** command can help provide information about each device and which interfaces are used to connect to neighboring devices.
4. A. The IEEE 802.11ax standard supports both Wi-Fi 6 (2.4 GHz and 5 GHz bands) and Wi-Fi 6E (6 GHz band).
5. A. Establishing a network baseline provides a view of the network under "normal" conditions for a given situation. This can help you determine if areas of the network are being underutilized or overutilized.
6. A. Task Manager displays the applications and background processes that are currently running on a Windows PC.
7. A. The **traceroute** command is used on Cisco IOS to display the path IP packets take to a destination.
8. D. The substitution method is when you physically swap the problematic device or component with a known, working one. If the problem is fixed, then the problem is with the removed item. If the problem remains, then the cause is elsewhere.
9. D. Determining the scope of the problem involves finding out if others are having the same issue and how many are being affected.
10. A. A closed-ended question focuses on obtaining specific information such as the operating system of the device.
11. A, B. The **ifconfig** command can be used on both Linux and macOS. Windows uses the **ipconfig** command. There are various commands that can be used with Cisco IOS including **show ip interface brief** and **show ipv6 interface brief**.
12. A. The **show tech-support** command provides similar information as a variety of **show** commands.
13. A. An initial network performance baseline will give you information for what the network traffic, device CPU usage, and other information typically looks like during that specific day and time.
14. C, E. Both the IEEE 802.11n and 802.11ax Wi-Fi standards operate in both the 2.4 GHz and 5 GHz frequency spectrums.
15. A. A logical topology map provides IP addressing information such as IP addresses and network or subnet addresses.

Chapter 38

1. A. A rootkit is malware that is designed to modify the operating system to create a backdoor that attackers can then use to access the computer remotely. Most rootkits take advantage of software vulnerabilities to gain access to resources that normally shouldn't be accessible (privilege escalation) and modify system files.
2. A. Bluesnarfing occurs when an attacker copies information, such as emails and contact lists, from a target's device using a Bluetooth connection.
3. C. SQL injection is an attack that takes advantage of a vulnerability in which the application does not correctly filter the data entered by a user for characters in an SQL statement.
4. C. Social engineering is a non-technical strategy that attempts to manipulate individuals into performing risky actions or divulging confidential information. Social engineering uses a number of tactics to gain cooperation from victims. Attackers may pretend to be persons of authority or use intimidation to compel people to act in ways that compromise security.
5. C. Prepending is when attackers remove the "external" email tag used by organizations to warn the recipient that an email has originated from an external source. This tricks individuals into believing that a malicious email was sent from inside their organization.
6. A. Phishing occurs when a user is contacted by email or instant message—or in any other way—by someone masquerading as a legitimate person or organization.
7. C. Ransomware is a common attack that uses malicious software to encrypt a system hardware drive.
8. B. Shoulder surfing refers to looking over someone's shoulder in order to obtain credentials like passwords, PINs, or credit card numbers.
9. A. Backdoor programs, such as Netbus and Back Orifice, are used by cybercriminals to gain unauthorized access to systems by bypassing the normal authentication procedures.

Chapter 39

1. C. In an e-commerce or analytics-based organization, transactions and customer accounts must be accurate. All data is validated and verified at frequent intervals and therefore has a high level of data integrity.
2. A, B, C. Logical access controls are the hardware and software solutions used to manage access to resources and systems. These technology-based solutions include tools and protocols that computer systems use for identification, authentication, authorization, and accounting. This includes firewalls, ACLs (access control lists), and biometrics.
3. A. The Windows Encrypting File System (EFS) feature allows users to encrypt files, folders, or an entire hard drive. Full-disk encryption (FDE) encrypts the entire contents of a drive (including temporary files and memory). Microsoft Windows uses BitLocker. BitLocker To Go is a tool that encrypts removable drives.
4. A. XProtect antimalware technology prevents the execution of malware through signature-based malware detection. It also alerts users to the existence of malware and provides the option to remove detected malware files.

5. A. Packet filtering firewalls are usually part of a router firewall, which permits or denies traffic based on Layer 3 and Layer 4 information. They are stateless firewalls that use a simple policy table lookup that filters traffic based on specific criteria.

6. D. TCP Wrappers is a rule-based access control and logging system for Linux. Packet filtering is based on IP addresses and network services.

7. C. WPA2 is the current industry standard for securing wireless networks. It uses the Advanced Encryption Standard (AES) for encryption. AES is currently considered the strongest encryption protocol.

8. C. WPA2-Personal is intended for home or small office networks. Users authenticate using a pre-shared key (PSK). Wireless clients authenticate with the wireless router using a pre-shared password. No special authentication server is required.

9. A. WPA2 included Wi-Fi Protected Setup (WPS) to quickly onboard devices without configuring them first, but WPS is vulnerable to a variety of attacks and is not recommended. Furthermore, IoT devices are typically headless, meaning they have no built-in GUI for configuration, and need an easy way to connect to the wireless network. The Device Provisioning Protocol (DPP) was designed to address this need.

10. C. Confidentiality means that only authorized individuals, entities, or processes can access sensitive information. It may require using cryptographic encryption algorithms such as AES to encrypt and decrypt data.

11. B. Integrity refers to protecting data from unauthorized alteration. It requires the use of cryptographic hashing algorithms such as SHA.

Index

Numerics

A

B

C

D

E

F

G

H

I

J-K

L

M

N

O

P

Q-R

T

U

V

W

X-Y-Z